Parcella '88

Mathematical Research

Parcella '88

edited by
G. Wolf · T. Legendi
U. Schendel

Band 48

48 AKADEMIE-VERLAG BERLIN

In this series original contributions of mathematical research in all fields are contained, such as

— research monographs
— collections of papers to a single topic
— reports on congresses of exceptional interest for mathematical research.

This series is aimed at promoting quick information and communication between mathematicians of the various special branches.

In diese Reihe werden Originalbeiträge zu allen Gebieten der mathematischen Forschung aufgenommen wie

— Forschungsmonographien
— Sammlungen von Arbeiten zu einem speziellen Thema
— Berichte von Tagungen, die für die mathematische Forschung besonders aktuell sind.

Die Reihe soll die schnelle Information und gute Kommunikation zwischen den Mathematikern der verschiedenen Fachgebiete fördern.

Manuscripts
in English and German comprising at least 100 pages and not more than 500 pages can be admitted to this series. With respect to a quick publication the manuscripts are reproduced photomechanically. Authors who are interested in this series please turn directly to the 'Akademie-Verlag'. Here you will get more detailed information about the form of the manuscripts and the modalities of publication.

Manuskripte
in englischer und deutscher Sprache, die mindestens 100 Seiten und nicht mehr als 500 Seiten umfassen, können in diese Reihe aufgenommen werden. Im Interesse einer schnellen Publikation werden die Manuskripte auf fotomechanischem Weg reproduziert. Autoren, die an der Veröffentlichung entsprechender Arbeiten in dieser Reihe interessiert sind, wenden sich bitte direkt an den Akademie-Verlag. Sie erhalten dort genauere Informationen über die Gestaltung der Manuskripte und die Modalitäten der Veröffentlichung.

Parcella '88

Mathematical Research · Mathematische Forschung

Wissenschaftliche Beiträge
herausgegeben von der
Akademie der Wissenschaften der DDR
Karl-Weierstraß-Institut für Mathematik

Band 48

Parcella '88

Parcella '88

Proceedings of the IV. International Workshop on Parallel Processing by Cellular Automata and Arrays held in Berlin (GDR), October 17 – 21, 1988

edited by

Gottfried Wolf

Tamás Legendi

Udo Schendel

Akademie-Verlag Berlin 1988

Herausgeber:

Dr. Gottfried Wolf
Akademie der Wissenschaften der DDR
Zentralinstitut für Kybernetik und Informationsprozesse, Berlin

Dr. Tamás Legendi
Hungarian Academy of Sciences
Research Group on Automata Theory, Szeged

Prof. Dr. Udo Schendel
Freie Universität Berlin
Institut für Mathematik III, Berlin(West)

Die Titel dieser Schriftenreihe werden vom Originalmanuskript der Autoren reproduziert.

ISBN 3-05-500656-9
ISSN 0138-3019

Erschienen im Akademie-Verlag Berlin,DDR-1086 Berlin,Leipziger Str.3-4

Lizenznummer: 202.100/503/88
Printed in the German Democratic Republic
Gesamtherstellung: VEB Kongreß- und Werbedruck, 9273 Oberlungwitz
Lektor: Dr. Reinhard Höppner
LSV 1095
Bestellnummer: 763 961 0 (2182/48)
05000

P R E F A C E

This volume contains the selected papers for the Parcella 88 - The Fourth International Workshop "Parallel Processing by Cellular Automata and Arrays" was held in Berlin, October 17 - 21, 1988.

The profile of Parcella-workshop series is focused on problems of processing by regular structures, i. e. their "flexibilization" or adapting to "irregular" algorithms on the one hand and, closely related to this, on the "regularization" of algorithms for their embedding into regular structures. It seems that these problems will have an increasing priority within the list of central problems in parallelization and will determine the profile of Parcella for the next years.

This workshop - the first of this type in the socialist countries - has gathered, as its predecessors, many scientists engaged and interested in this field. However, the organizers are of the opinion that some steps forward were taken as compared to the foregoing Parcella e.g. the size of the Parcella-community has increased, so that parallel sessions had to be held for the first time in our short Parcella-history, and the volume of the proceedings has increased, too. Nevertheless, the editors had to reject more than 50 % of all papers submitted so that many of them, although of good quality, could be accepted for oral presentation only.

The organizers and promoters of the foregoing Parcella-events, T. Legendi and G. Wolf, has welcomed U. Schendel from Freie Universitaet (Berlin-West) as the third chairman at Parcella 88. They are sure that this decision will support the future development immensely. They will make great efforts to provide a stimulating atmosphere and a fruitful exchange of ideas at this workshop and, by this, help to establish international cooperation in this highly dynamical field of research.

The work to be done by the Chairmen and Editorial Board with T. Legendi (Szeged), U. Schendel (Berlin-West) and G. Wolf (Berlin) was supported by the International Program Committee, consisting of V. Aladyev (Tallinn), A. Albrecht (Berlin), W. Haendler (Erlangen), C. Jesshope (Southampton), A. Jugel (Dresden), N. Kasabov (Sofia), E. Katona (Szeged), V. Kotov (Novosibirsk), S. Levialdi (Rome), I. Miklosko (Bratislava), D. Parkinson (London), A. Rosenfeld (Pittsburgh), I. Toth (Szeged), J.-R. Sack (Ottawa), P. Spirakis (Patras), L. Uhr (Madison), R. Vollmar (Braunschweig), K. Voss (Jena), W. Wilhelmi (Berlin), G. Wunsch (Dresden) and C. K. Yap (New York).

The chairmen would like to express their special thanks to Prof. Haendler and Prof. Vollmar for their kindness and help especially. They are very glad to welcome Prof. Haendler as honory lecturer.

The editors want to thank all contributors for their support to an interesting scientific program of high quality, and thank are also due to all authors who submitted papers for the proceedings even it they could not be accepted.

Finally, the editors are grateful to Prof. Dr. sc. V. Kempe, Director of the supporting institute, the Central Institute for Cybernetics and Information Processes of the Academy of Sciences of the G.D.R., as the scientific adviser, and to Prof. Dr. sc. H. Fuchs, the Deputy Director of this institute, for their untiring efforts in helping to organize the workshop, as well as to Dr. Hoeppner and Ms. Dipl.-Math. Reiher from Akademie-Verlag and Dr. Woessner from Springer-Verlag as the publishing houses providing excellent conditions for the edition of this volume.

The local chairman wants to express his thanks to Dr. Creutzburg as the Head of the International Basic Laboratory "Image Processing and Computergraphics" for giving excellent conditions to prepare the workshop and to Prof. Wilhelmi for his help in preparing the scientific programme.

Furthermore, our thanks are due to Mrs. S. Boettcher, Mrs. I. Schubert and Mrs. M. Stabrey and the whole organizing staff, who did the main organizational work in the background.

Hoping to have provided the best conditions possible for Parcella 88 we look forward to a Parcella 90, as the event to follow.

T. Legendi U. Schendel G. Wolf (local chairman)

T A B L E   O F   C O N T E N T S

INVITED PAPERS

SUBMITTED PAPERS

INVITED PAPERS

MULTIPROCESSOR ARRAYS: TOPOLOGY, EFFICIENCY AND FAULT-TOLERANCE

Prof. em. Dr. Wolfgang Händler[1]

Summary

Starting from categories of the known computer-networks-area like message-handling, bus, protocol etc. may lead to a dead-end with respect to multiprocessor-design. Those terms from the world of networks may persuade computer architects to choose solutions which are not adequate to the requirements of efficient and fault-tolerant operation.

Topological investigations including technological considerations will result in structures which differ contrarily from the traditional monoprocessor as well as from computer networks. The macro-dataflow-concept [11] for instance can ensure in the framework of the usual storage-access a high rate of efficiency. Also, system programming and application programming will not deviate in this case too much from the traditional patterns. Beyond it the approaches for fault-tolerant operation become then simple and effective.

Experiences with multiprocessors, which are accordingly designed are discussed.

Contents:

1. Introduction

A desired topology of a multiprocessor under design can be realized only in the framework of contemporary technology. The respective technology, i.e. buses, interconnection networks (like Omega-Banyan-networks, processor-units and memory-units with their connectors, and multiports), will restrict the potential solutions. In particular universal connections which perhaps will be possible via holographic networks in the future, are not available now (the term <universal> is used here in the sense, that all elements are connected to all other elements like in a crossbar switch).

It seems to be obvious to go back to the bus regarding the repertory of potential technology or for instance to the details of protocols in computer networks. In this sense very often terms like message handling, block transfer etc. are used in the context of multiprocessor design, whereas a more precise requirement engineering should primarily take place. The questions which should be raised are: what is necessary (or indispensible), what is desirable (topology) and what is realizable (technology). Many things which correspond to a well proved experience in the field of computer networks (LAN, WAN) or in the field of the classic universal computer (monoprocessor), have to

---

[1] Institut für Mathematische Maschinen und Datenverarbeitung (Informatik III), Universität Erlangen-Nürnberg, Martensstraße 3, D-8520 Erlangen

be scrutinized in the context of tightly coupled multiprocessors.

Tightly coupled multiprocessors are the subject of this paper. In particular, it is reported on investigations and experiences with respect to existing multiprocessors. It is the opinion of other authors that a common memory must be provided for a multiprocessor which is directly accessible by all processors, or that the communication and synchronization between the processors must be handled via I/O-like-procedures. All this we didn't find useful, efficient or necessary.

2. A Standard-Processor as a starting point

In this paper the question plays a minor role, which computation models (operation principle or operation mode) - deviating from the classic monoprocessor - are possible. Nevertheless we start with an idea of a Standard Processor (STP), which is capable to operate in quite different operation modes (computation models, sometimes called abstract machine models) according to the respective need of runtime. Such an ideal STP can be switched from one operation mode to another - sometimes activating a program counter and sometimes working without it utilizing a cyclic standard-control-program or microprogram.

Possible operation modes are:

a)	General Purpose Processor	(GPP)
b)	Higher-Level-Language-Processor	(HLL)
c)	Reduction Machine	(RED)
d)	Data-Flow-Processor	(FLO)
e)	Associative Parallel-Processor	(APP)
f)	Cellular Processor	(CEL)
g)	Digital Differential Analyser	(DDA),

as it is pointed out in another paper [2]. A Standard-Processor STP, unifying most of these properties would not cost 7 times as much as one GPP (according to the seven computation models), but approximately twice as much instead. This consideration results in a suggestion not to pack merely more processors on one chip in the future but to provide more and flexible logic which connect the register elements internally to one processor. Most of the enumerated computation models (operation modes) are pairwise compatible as it is shown with the operation modes GPP and APP [7]. There are theoretical and experimental results on "Vertical Processing" as it is called. Vertical Processing can be realized in many cases by the utilization of the microprogramming device in industrially available processors.

Whether the proposed Standard-Processor STP is fully hardwired or microprogrammed, would be a separate investigation. Supporter of a pure RISC-philosophy would claim for a code of some fifty instructions and would insist to build up the operations which are typical for the seven above mentioned operation modes from some fifty elementary instructions. This seems to be possible, if one takes into account that many instructions are the same for the 7 operation modes. E.g. the basic instruction "shift" in GPP (and HLL) becomes an instruction in APP, which changes e.g. an index i to $i+1$ (or e.g. i to $i-1$) for all elements of an vector. Or in the case of a DDA summations are performed and the same arithmetic as in GPP can be utilized. Deriving regularly an overflow from the summations one obtains a value of an integral, which may be supplemented by an integration constant. Also other operations correspond with respect to both types, the GPP and DDA.

Nevertheless, it is so far not investigated, whether a RISC-structure with a small number of elementary instructions and longer programs are more favourable or a microprogramming device utilizing a set of microoperations common to all computation models in order to build up an elaborated powerful instruction set. The difficult controversial debate on RISC and CISC-architecture [16] is passed over in this paper in favour of the main point, i.e. the influence of topology of a multiprocessor on efficiency and fault-tolerance.

3. Topology as the key point in multiprocessor design

It is centered in this paper on problems of topological connections between elements of a multiprocessor. Contemporary technology makes it very hard to connect the processors each other completely and directly. The situation may change considerably with the upcoming technology of optical switches. There are nevertheless good examples of multiprocessors with Nearest-Neighbour-connections, as shown in Fig. 1, which is called here a Hoshino-Regenspurg-topology[2] (a) [6].

A most effective topology can be found (Fig. 2), which may be called a Händler-Hofmann-topology (b) [4] in this context.

As easily may be seen, the differences regarding costs are minimal. While (a) demands 32 twoport-memories, (b) demands 16 fiveport-memories. The results for closing the topology to torus-structures do not essentially change the comparison. The effect, nevertheless, is striking.

In order to derive an estimation with respect to the two topologies it is defined a distance d in a processor array as the minimal number of nodes[3], which are overridden by a message or by data starting from a source node (local memory) and being stored at a destination node (again a local memory) (Fig. 3).

---

[2] The names are mentioned with respect to former publications (mainly [6] and [4]).

[3] The place where a communication memory between two processors is located in topology (a), is not a node in this sense.

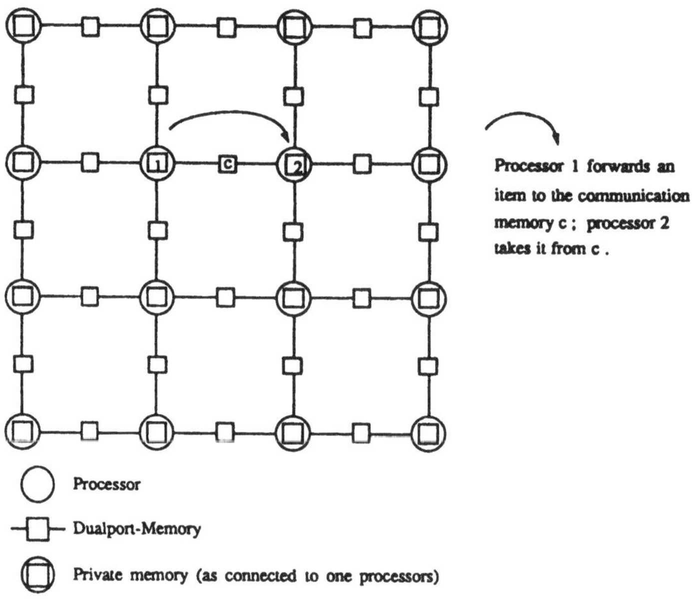

Figure 1: Hoshino-Regenspurg-Topology (PAX-128), (topology (a))
16 Processors
24 2-Port-memories
48 Cables
16 Private memories

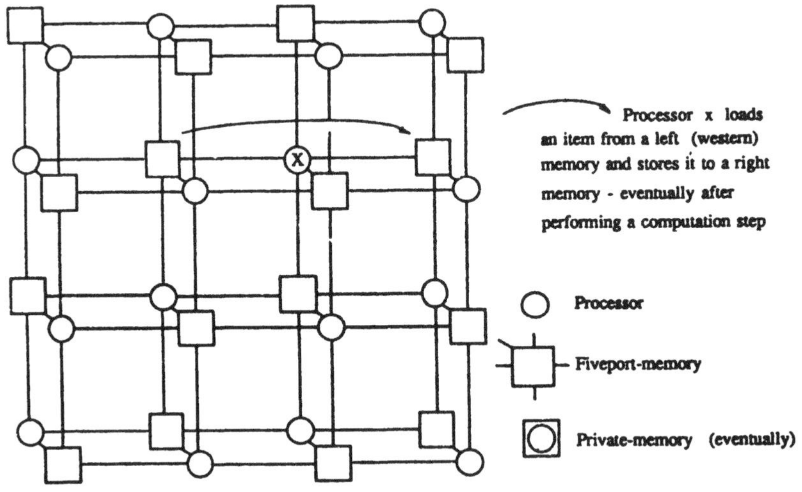

Figure 2: Händler-Hofmann-Topology (EGPA/DIRMU), (topology (b))
16 Processors
16 5-Port-memories
48 Cables

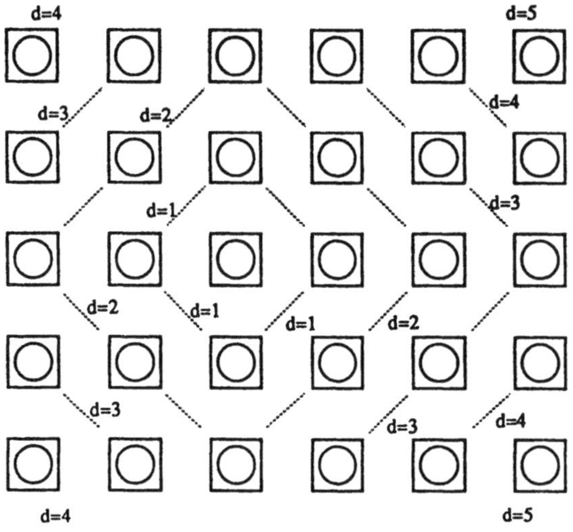

Figure 3: Definition of a distance d in a processor array, not considering a closing to a torus-structure.

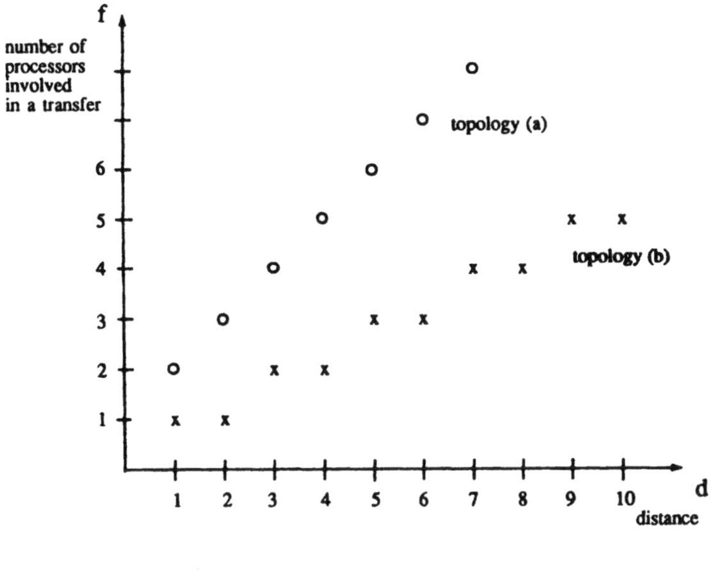

Figure 4: Long distance transfer; number f of processors involved in the process of transfering a message or generally an information over a distance d

Two directly neighboured processors are characterized by d = 1, a transfer skipping one processor by d = 2 etc. This does not necessarily mean that all processors on a shortest path between source and destination are really involved in a transfer. Rather it is possible to state a discrete function of involved processors over the (integral) distance d (Fig. 4) for topologies (a) and (b). In such a way the topology (b) implies a factor of two with respect to the propagation speed. As the same time so far not utilized processors (about half of the whole array) can be utilized either for computing or for another transfers, which makes up in some applications another factor of two.

There are, nevertheless, other considerable differences which result in an substantial advantage of topology (b) (over (a)). Assuming for the present the operation of a conventional GPP, then the flow of program control is characterized by the access of data, combining data to intermediate results, and storing data again into the (primary) memory. Nothing else is done regarding the topology (b): the processor loads a word of data from a location in the neighbourhood, where it was created and stores it, where it will be requested next (after having in general performed one step of processing the data). In such a way a one-address-instruction (of a GPP e.g.) has really two functions: the operation part of the instruction says, which operation has to be performed and the address part says, from what direction a data word has to be accessed or respectively into what direction a data word (or intermediate result) has to be forwarded after an operation (may be: an empty operation).

The address part of an instruction in a GPP (classic von Neumann structure) is utilized in a quite natural way to move data and offers in such a way a processing strategy, which may be called Macro-Data-Flow, Macro-Pipelining [11], or Macro-Systolic, according to the specific form of cooperation, in which the processors are operating.

With this concept of a combined operation-transport separate additional transports (without another useful operation or computation) can be avoided to a large extent. This is a matter of allocating appropriately program code and related data onto the array of processors. One basic concept in this context is to hold tasks on the processors and to make flow the data through the array. In multiprocessor arrays so tasks (code) are for a longer interval resident in a memory local to the specific processor, while these tasks would be objected to a faster traffic between primary and secondary storage in the operation of a conventional monoprocessor. The control of (macro-) data-flow is a very important point. Nowadays mechanisms are under development all over the world, to make the data transfer and herewith the (macro-) data-flow a simple and efficient procedure. Experiences with Erlangen-multiprocessors show that multiport-facilities combined with topology (b) fulfil these conditions optimally.

So far the term `tightly coupled` multiprocessor is not used. In fact, both topologies (a) and (b) are of this class. Nevertheless, topology (b) is even more closely coupled than (a). So the term tightly coupled cannot help in the present discussion.

The direction of a transfer can be maintained by using relative addresses according to the following pattern:

0xxxx location inside a l o c a l memory (xxxx an abritrary address of a defined length).

1xxxx location in the N o r t h e r n (nearest-neighbour) memory.

2xxxx location in the E a s t e r n memory.

3xxxx location in the S o u t h e r n memory.

4xxxx location in the W e s t e r n memory (relative to a considered local memory).

(addresses 5xxxx, 6xxxx, ... may be used for other specific purposes in the case there is a need for).

With respect to topology (b) there is no need for an explicit transfer in the majority of cases, as mentioned above. Nevertheless, there remain some cases where a general transport has to be performed from one processor s to another processor d, not neighboured to s. Such transports may be called <long distance transfers>.

As shown, in particular, in the case of matrix-multiplication a long-distance transfer can be frequently avoided by choosing carefully an appropriate algorithm [8]. Even if this endeavour fails the long distance transfer is quite favourable in memory-coupled (multiport-) configurations of topology (b), since the bandwith of the connections is as mighty as in a conventional primary memory access. Beyond it in some cases only half of all processors are involved in transfers or in broadcasting and it was also shown earlier, that transfer/broadcasting in topology (b) is performed with double speed compared to topology (a).

Some regular structures, for which all the statements mentioned above are valid, are shown in Fig. 5. Structure d) in Fig. 5, in particular, is the so-called EGPA-structure, which is extensively reported on in other papers [4]. The regular structure in it are the rectangular arrays of 4, 16, 64, ... processor/memory-units STP, which are interconnected to a multilevel pyramid configuration. This specific structure diminishes once more the broadcasting and transfer time from $d/2$ to $\log_2 d/2$, where d is counted from node to node in the lowest-level array, the so-called working array (comp. also Fig. 6).

A very important point for rating a multiprocessor is nevertheless its suitability to fault-tolerance (Sect. 5).

Finally, it may be mentioned that the synchronization technology or procedure has a strong influence regarding the efficiency of a multiprocessor (compare Sect. 4). In most

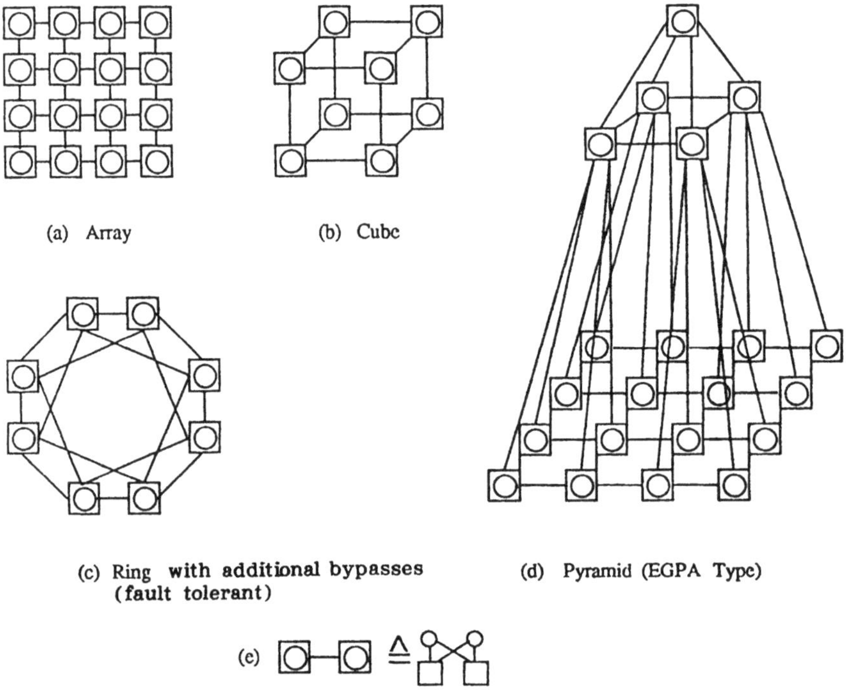

Figure 5: Examples for regular topologies (according to topology (b)). Each 'line' corresponds to a double interconnection (compare (e)).

Topology	Broadcast. time	Local complexity	Memory blocks	Port-Type	Cables	size indep. concept
Simple ring	p/2	2	1	2	2	scalable
Simple ring with DIRMU-connections	p/4	3	1	3	3	scalable
Double connected ring	p/8	5	1	5	5	scalable
Rectangular array acc. to Hoshino	$\sqrt{p}/2$	4	2	2	4	scalable
Rectangular array acc. to Händler/Hofmann	$\sqrt{p}/8$	5	1	5	5	scalable
EGPA-Pyramid	$\log_2\sqrt{p}$	≤9	1	9	≤9	scalable
Hypercube (INTEL-CALT.)	$\log_2 p$	$\log_2 p+1$	1	not relevant	$\log_2 p$	not scalable
Hypercube (DIRMU)	$(\log_2 p)/2$	$\log_2 p+1$	1	$\log_2 p+1$	$\log_2 p+1$	not scalable

Figure 6: Complexity for different topologies related to one processor unit (exept for broadcast-time)

cases bus-connected systems are synchronized by the message-handling. The time for a synchronization (only for the synchronization) then ranges in the order of milliseconds. In memory-coupled systems the pure synchronization shrinks by utilisation of spin-locks down to the order of two memory-access-times (possibly, in the range of some 100 nsec)

Therefore in the case of message-synchronization the long duration of the process must be taken into account: One has to ensure that synchronizations and data transfers appear as seldom as possible. This means, that one is not really free in the choice of algorithms. Rather one has to center on solutions to problems which show an inherent coarse granularity. This can outgrow to a severe restriction, since just such algorithms may be inefficient for other reasons.

The usual buses or rings (e.g. Peirce-rings) connecting several memory-blocks, processors etc. demand always for an extensive use of message handling and don't really compete with multiport-structures (in particular with topology (b)), considering the experience derived from Erlangen-multiprocessors. Therefore in the context of this paper buses and rings[4] are skipped and the encouraging results of multiport-topology (b) are represented as a main point of effort.

[4] In this context are not meant ring topologies, but communication rings like Peirce rings.

4. Practice regarding efficiency

The speedup s of a multiprocessor is usually defined as

$$s = t_1/t_p$$

where t_1 is the time, which is used by one processor (of a considered type) to execute a given program,

t_p is the time, which is used by p processors (of the same type), to execute the given program (which is appropriately modified, to fulfil the requirements of a multiprocessor operation).

One may expect that the speedup s comes close to p, the number of processors, working simultaneously. Efficiency η may be now defined as:

$$\eta = s/p$$

One will expect η to be in the area of $0 < \eta \leq 1$.

Indeed experience shows that s comes close to p in many important applications. There are even some very interesting cases - mainly in the area of combinatorics and graph theory (e.g. travelling salesman) - where s exceeds p and η becomes: $\eta > 1$.

Cases $\eta > 1$ may be characterized as "synergetic effect". Nevertheless the majority of cases is in the area of $\eta < 1$, where also most numeric problems are located.

Losts, which are responsible for η being smaller than 1, are:

1. W o r k l o a d among the processor is not ideal. Dead intervals apppear.

2. C o m m u n i c a t i o n mutually takes place between processors, occupying a time which cannot be utilized for other useful operations.

3. S y n c h r o n i z a t i o n must be controlled by the operating system in order to fulfil requirements of the dependence graph, occupying a time, which cannot be utilized for other useful operation.

4. D a t a t r a n s f e r s have to be executed between the processors, not necessary in the case of a monoprocessor, occupying a certain time, which depends on the parallelized program structure.

Looking at these four points it seems to be incomprehensible that cases $\eta > 1$, or $s > p$, can appear at all.

But there are very simple plausible explanations for this phenomenon. One example is, assuming a problem of Game-Theory, where p procedures (algorithm) have to be investigated with respect to minimal time consumption. If there are p processors available then on each of the processors one of the algorithms is executed. Assuming also that all p algorithms for the solution are programmed objectively, then it is a fair competition. The general problem - "which is the best (shortest) algorithm for a certain problem?" - is solved exactly, when one of the processors[5] finishes and presents an solution.

The time taken by the 1st processor (algorithm) is denoted τ_1, and appropriately the time, taken by the second processor (algorithm) is denoted τ_2 etc. etc., then the following is surely true:

$$p \cdot \min(\tau_1, \tau_2, \tau_3, \ldots \tau_p) \leq \sum_{i=1}^{p} \tau_i$$

with $t_1 = \sum_{i=1}^{p} \tau_i$ and $t_p = \min(\tau_1, \tau_2, \tau_3, \ldots \tau_p)$

and $s = t_1/t_p > p$

and in particular:

$$\eta = s/p > 1$$

This statement is valid in general, if t_p is enlarged by a small amount of time consumed by final synchronization of all processors.

(This consideration is valid for a coarse orientation. Nevertheless an algorithm, which would compute all τ_i explicitely, is inefficient. One had to proceed in the inefficient way, to break off always in a monoprocessor (sequentially) with the following times:

$\min(\tau_1, \tau_2)$, $\min(\tau_1, \tau_2, \tau_3)$, $\min(\tau_1, \tau_2, \tau_3, \tau_4)$ etc.

Then t_1 is accordingly:

$$t_1 = \tau_1 + \min(\tau_1, \tau_2) + \min(\tau_1, \tau_2, \tau_3) + \ldots + \min(\tau_1, \tau_2, \tau_3, \ldots \tau_p)$$

Only for the case that: $\tau_1 = \min(\tau_1, \tau_2, \tau_3, \ldots \tau_p)$ then the former result is not valid.)

Of more practical relevance are the assumptions to partition algorithms always in such a manner that the resulting speedup s comes close to p, or η close to one.

In an earlier paper [13] a table with figures of η which were obtained in practical computations was given. It was shown - also by the means of an appropriate programming environment -, that in a multitude of numerical problems one can achieve a value

[5] Evidently, it is in some cases possible, that two or more processors finish at nearly the same time. Then, possibly, other criteria may be taken for a decision.

$\eta \approx 1$. This mainly depends on the predictability of the data material spread out over the processor array. In all cases, where it is not predictable, how data are distributed throughout an array, the workload cannot be perfect and therefore η is accordingly bad - e.g. minor than .5 . Non-predictable data in this sense are e.g. text passages or images, and data, which are objected to logical (or non-numerical) procedures. It can easily be seen that, for instance, an image may be partitioned regularly onto a processor-array. Then some of the processors are loaded very hard, since there are many details in this part of the image, while other processors become idle because of a lack of detail.

In a similar manner phrases (or text passages) may be distributed to processors. Then some of the processors have to analyse voluminous and complex phrases and others become idle having to analyse only very poor phrases.

The weakly balanced workload - as mentioned above - will diminish the efficiency η beneath the .5-mark. This fact may be improved by providing a multiprogramming of 2nd kind. To bring many programs (may be: quite different problems) at the same time on a multiprocessor may result in a better overall utilization. The strategies to organize and to control such a multiprogramming will remain, nevertheless, for a long time a hard research and development problem. Another opportunity to improve η is the "Neighbourhood's help"-concept: Idle processors are looking around to help busy neighbours [17].

Evidently control procedures for multiprogramming (in the forementioned sense) should not take an essential portion of the whole operation time in an multiprocessor. Rather one has to search for a mixed hard-and software-solution for it, as e.g. it was pragmatically designed in the multiprocessor HEP [14].

Amdahl's Law may show in some cases the limits of parallelism. Nevertheless, it is wrongly considered a fundamental obstacle or a dreadful vision regarding multiprocessors. It says, if f is the portion of code, which cannot be parallelized ($0 \leq f \leq 1$), that speedup s is:

$$s \leq \frac{1}{f + (1 - f) / p}$$

where p is again the number of processors.

Assuming $f = .1$ (i.e. a tenth of the program cannot be parallelized), then the speedup can never exceed $s = 10$. The number of processors p does'nt play any role in this context. Assuming $f = .5$ (i.e. half of the program cannot be parallelized), then the speedup is maximally $s = 2$. This sounds horrible, since cost is rather proportional to p at least with respect to the array of processors.

Nevertheless, two remarks should be made on the range of validity of Amdahl's Law:

First: in the past the consideration was made with some evidence regarding vector-processors[6] (Amdahl, Cray, Fujitsu etc.). f then has to be rated accordingly to the portion of v e c t o r i z a b l e code. Indeed it was then observed that the decrease is as bad as expected from Amdahl's Law. In the meantime a lot of tricks are known for vectorization. The result remains nevertheless quite poor. Users of vector-processors are content with a comparable poor speedup.

Another situation arises if f is taken for p a r a l l e l i z a b l e portions of a given code. In many cases, where a vectorization is not possible at all, a parallelization of code can very often take place most efficiently. So it is quite understandable that Cray Ass. are going into the field of what they are calling "multitasking" For this reason the new computers contain up to eight separate vector-processors, achieving much better results for η .

Second: the parallelization in most realistic cases results in a shrinking value of f (or: $f/(1-f) \rightarrow 0$). This comes from the fact, that parallelizable code has a growing portion (1-f) if the dynamic running (or duration) of the problem becomes bigger, which is a realistic assumption just in cases, where an application of a monoprocessor doesn't seem to be realistic with respect to computing time. In order to say it in other words: in many standard problems the time for organizational provisions remains constant, while the time for useful operation (e.g. for proper matrix operation) is increasing the more the assumptions are realistic.

The number of processors p may go into some hundreds and the speedup will accordingly increase nearly linearly (or: efficiency η will nearly stay constant). This statement makes Amdahl's Law less important for practical applications, and scalable multiprocessors (compare Sect. 6 and Fig. 6).

5. Fault-tolerance as a boundary condition

According to requirements, which exist in critical areas like the operation of nuclear plants or in air traffic control there is not only a demand for reliable VLSI-elements but also for fault-tolerant operation in multiprocessor ensembles.

In this paper predominately is investigated, what can be done with respect to the overall design, in order to make the best regarding efficiency and fault-tolerance. For the present may be disregarded, what - beyond it - can be done by VLSI-design for reliable switching.

---

[6] The classic vector-processor has no more than one processor (in the sense of program interpretation), but one or more arithmetic pipelines.

A possible concept for ensuring efficiency and fault-tolerance at the same time, is the following (comp. [10]): A cylinder-shaped multi-chip-carrier [9] is covered by an rectangular array of processors according to the topology (b), as introduced in sec. 2. The rectangular array is not only closed to the form of a cylinder (Fig. 7), but also utilizing the inner surface of the cylinder-shaped carrier, in order to configure a torus topologically (the global topology).

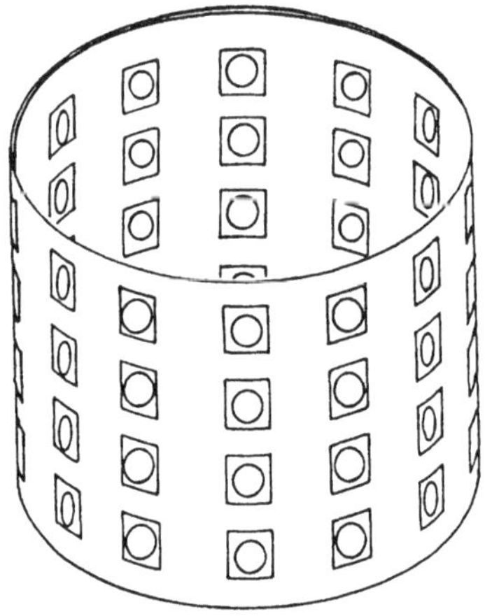

Figure 7: Topology taken into geometry: A cylinder - possibly designed as a Multi-Chip-Carrier (MCC) [9] from ceramic material - incorporates processors and memories (of the multiprocessor). Elements are directly bonded configuring a torus (covering the surface of the cylinder inside and out).

Programming a multiprocessor on a torus then concentrates on the following activities:

1. A given problem (algorithm) is partitioned into tasks, which - each one - can be executed on a single processor.

2. The tasks are programmed (or coded) and a requirement graph R is developed (data dependance graph) according to the necessary data transfer between the tasks.

3. Assuming the multiprocessor with its interconnenctions between the processors (existing hardware) is represented by a configuration graph C, then an ideal solution is a homomorphic embedding $R \simeq C$ of a graph R into the graph C.[7]

4. According to the requirement of fault-tolerance eventually must be ensured, that for the graph R there are many possible homomorphic embeddings $R \simeq C'$, which

[7] In the context of this paper it is abandoned a more rigorous representation of homomorphisms, isomorphisms etc. (comp [15]).

can take place in the case, that C must be reduced to C' as a consequence of a possible defect of the hardware C.

Evidently a great flexibility regarding a possible manifold of homomorphic embeddings can be achieved by choosing regular configurations for the basis C. In the case of the cylinder- or torus-configuration the subgraphs are to be searched from the surface of the torus. In the case of defects always a subgraph C' with a healthy structure in the sense of a requirement graph R may be found. Essentially, this is the concept of fault-tolerance. Apparently C, the available hardware, has to be mighty enough to fulfil the requirements of a reasonable substitution process, taking embeddings

$R \simeq C$

$R \simeq C'$

$R \simeq C''$ etc. etc.

as a basis.

In the case $C \setminus R$, the primarily idle part of the structure is sufficiently big enough, it can be utilized to perform a preventive maintenance. In periods, where there are no defects, one can proceed accordingly to a maintenance schedule, changing - say - every two hours the area $C \setminus R$, in order to make the availability of the multiprocessor very high [11]. In periods, where there are defects, diagnozed e.g. by an appropriate periodically running program, the strategy may be changed accordingly.

In general, centrally symmetric structures like rings, cylinders, spheres etc. offer as sketched the opportunity to fulfil the requirements of performance and at the same time the requirements of a prescribed degree of fault-tolerance.

Since e.g. the EGPA-structure [4] has a rectangular working area (working array), which is closed to a torus, the same statements are valid for this topology.

6. Outlooks

Nearest-neighbour-topologies, as they are developed in Sect. 3 to 5, mainly the topology (b), as it was characterized, have outstanding properties. A series of known topologies is summarized in a table (Fig. 6).

Data in this table represent the relative time for a broadcasting process (I/O-complexity) which corresponds at the same time to the maximal time foı a transfer. Evidently the average time for a long distance transfer is smaller compared to the maximal time. More then this, in the great majority of cases there is no explicit transfer, but a direct access to a neighbour takes places instead (comp. Sect. 3).

Coprocessors and private memory blocks are ignored in this paper. Remarks on this point would be valid essentially for all topologies.

As principles for the design of multiprocessors one may summarize the following points now:

1. Simple topology and at the same time homogeneous simple hardware are the characteristic features of good computer-architecture and, in particular, of good multiprocessor-architecture.[8] Complex hardware may inhibit satisfying efficiency and may also be a severe obstacle to a fault-tolerant operation.

2. Scalability, resp. expandability, is indicated with respect to the size of the multiprocessor-array. It is required, that it is of no concern what specific configuration or size is demanded: the hardware nodes (processors), memory blocks and interconnections must be always combined in the same way.[9]

3. Scalability with respect to appliations must be ensured. The designer has to endeavour, that for sufficiently big problems the number of points n, n-1, n-2, ... n+1, n+2 ... etc., or of elements, rows and similar play a minor role for the computations, and in particular for the efficiency of the computation.

4. Rotation-symmetric configurations like cylinders, torus, rings etc. are suggestive with respect to efficient and fault-tolerant operation of a multiprocessor. The possibility of preventive maintenance must be offered.

5. Aided by an appropriate programming environment an efficiency value of approximately "one" ($\eta \approx 1$) can be achieved mostly in numerical applications. The efficiency η will diminish to a distinctly lower value only in cases, where - as a consequence of lacking a load prediction - a fair balance of workload cannot be reached.

6. A Standard-Processor (STP) - eventually complemented by a co-processor for vector operations - may be created as a node processor to fulfil the requirement for an individualization in runtime. The individuali-

---

[8] Any criticism: "This and that is too simple" shows a lack of understanding. The hardware must be most transparent with respect to all levels of operation - operating system, compiler systems and, in particular, application programming. Simple, transparent architecture should be the trademark of good research, development and design.

[9] It is unacceptable, that one multiprocesssor configuration for the order of ten nodes, another configuration for the order of hundreds of nodes, and e.g. a configuration for the order of thousands of nodes each follow another principle of interconnection or clustering.

the requirement for an individualization in runtime. The i n d i v i d u a l i z a t i o n in the direction to an operation mode (or: operation principle) may be achieved mainly by microprogramming and should include data-structures, resp. object-structures.

Acknowledgment

Members of the staff of IMMD, University Erlangen-Nürnberg, gave several suggestions regarding paper. I am obliged in particular to Prof. Dr. A. Bode (now with Technical University of Munich) and Dr. J. Volkert.

References

[1] Enslow, Philip H. edit.: Multiprocessors & Parallel Processing; John Wiley & Sons, New York, London etc. 1974

[2] Händler, W.: Dynamic Computer Structures for Manifold Utilization; Parallel Computing 2 (1985), 15 - 32

[3] Händler, W.: Bericht über eine Dienstreise nach Japan in der Zeit vom 31. Mai bis 15. Juni 1986; Interner Bericht, hektographiert Erlangen 1986

[4] Händler, W.; F. Hofmann and H. J. Schneider: A general purpose array with a broad spectrum of applications, Proc. Workshop on Computer Architecture IFB (Springer, Berlin, 1975) 311 - 335 (und zahlreiche andere Veröffentlichungen zum Projekt EGPA)

z. B. auch: Händler, W.; U. Herzog, F. Hofmann and H. J. Schneider: Multiprozessoren für breite Anwendungsbereiche - Erlangen general purpose array, Conf. Proc. 8. GI-NTG Fachtagung 'Architektur und Betrieb von Rechensystemen' (Springer, Berlin, 1984) 195 - 208

[5] Händler, W.; H. Rohrer: Gedanken zu einem Rechner-Baukastensystem; Elektronische Rechenanlagen, 22 (1980), 3 - 13 (sowie weitere Veröffentlichungen zum Projekt DIRMU)
z. B. auch:
Händler, W.; E. Maehle and K. Wirl: The DIRMU Testbed for High-Performance Multiprocessor Configurations; Proc. of the First International Conference on Supercomputing Systems (Dec. 16 - 20, 1985, St. Petersburg, FL.) 468 - 475

[6] Hoshino, T.: An Invitation to the World of PAX (using contemporary LSI and simple architecture, we can construct a multiple-purpose machine PAX with a 1 Gflops speed. Our Goal for the 1990's: a 1 Tflops PAX); Computer, May 1986, 68 - 79
oder:
Momoi, S.; S. Shinada, M. Kobayashi and T. Ishikawa: Hierarchical Array Processor System (HAP); Proceeding CONPAR '86 Conference on Algorithms and Hardware for Parallel Processing Aachen, September 1986, Händler et al. (edit.), vol. 237, Lecture Notes in Computer Science, Springer-Verlag Berlin, Heidelberg, New York etc. 1986

[7] Albert B.; A. Bode, W. Händler: A case study in vertical migration: The implementation of a dedicated associative instruction set; in: Microprocessing and Mikroprogramming 8 /1981, 257 - 262
(Schriftum siehe auch [2]).

[8] Henning, W.; J. Volkert: Programming EGPA-Systems; Proc. 5th Intern. Conf. on Distributed Computing Systems, Denver 1985, 552 - 558

[9] MCC: Multi-Chip-Carrier - compare sources of IBM. A Ceramic-carrier allows to combine a multitude of chips on a minimal space. The chips are mutually connected by a direct bonding.

[10] Händler, W.: Multiprozessoren: Effizienz und Fehlertoleranz; NTG Fachberichte 92, VDE-Verlag GmbH 1986

[11] Händler, W.: The concept of Macro-Pipelining with high availability. In: Eletronische Rechenanlagen 6, 1973, 269 - 274

[12] Galil, Z.; W. Paul: Effizienz paralleler Rechner. In: IFB 33, 10. GI-Jahrestagung, Springer-Verlag Berlin, Heidelberg, New York 1980

[13] Händler, W.; G. Fritsch, J. Volkert: Applications implemented on the Erlangen General Purpose Array. (main lecture) 12 - 31. In: Parcella '84, Proceedings of the II. Intern. Workshop on Parallel Processing by Cellular Automate and Arrays (Berlin, Sept. 25 - 27, 1984)

[14] Smith, B.J.: A pipelined shared resource MIMD computer. In: Proceedings of the 1978 Intern. Conference on Parallel Processing, 6 - 8, IEEE, New York

[15] Maehle, E.; K. Moritzen and K. Wirl: A Graph Model and its Application to a Fault-Tolerant Multiprocessor System. Proc. 16th Intern. Symp. on Fault-Tolerant Computing 'FTCS-16', Wien 1986, 292 - 297
or:
Maehle, E.; H. Joseph: Selbstdiagnose in fehlertoleranten DIRMU-Multi-Mikroprozessorkonfigurationen. In: Fehlertolerante Rechensysteme, Informatik-Fachberichte Vol. 55 1982

[16] Patterson, D. A.; C. H. Sequin: A VLSI RISC. IEEE Computer 15 (1982) No. 9 (Sept.) 8 - 21
or e.g.:
Horster, P.; D. Manstetten, H. Pelzer: RISC, Reduced Instruction Set Computer. Konzepte und Realisierungen, Hüthig-Verlag, Heidelberg 1987

[17] Fritsch, G.: Memory-Coupled Arrays for a Broad Spectrum of Applications. Proc. WOPPLOT 83, Parallel Processing: Logic, Organization and Technology, Springer-Verlag Berlin, Heidelberg, New York, Tokyo 1984, 158 - 177

UNSOLVED THEORETICAL PROBLEMS IN HOMOGENEOUS STRUCTURES

VICTOR ALADYEV [1], AIDA KRASNOPROSHINA [2]
and VLADIMIR KRYSCHANOVSKII [2]

1. INTRODUCTION

The homogeneous structure(HS) is an information parallel processing system consisting of intercommunicating identical finite automata. We can interpret HS as theoretical framework of artificial parallel information processing systems and a formal model of parallel computations. From the logical point of view the HS is a infinite automaton with characteristic internal structure. The HS theory can be considered to be the structural and dynamic theory of the infinite automata. At present, this theory forms original part of the modern cybernetics[7].

During the recent years there has been considerable interest in the HS theory about which many interesting results have been obtained. Much of this work has been motivated by the growing interest in computer science and mathematical modelling [1-15].

The modern point of view to the HS theory has been formed under the influence of works of E.F. Moore, H. Yamada, A. Burks, A.R. Smith, H. Nishio, R. Vollmar, G. Wolf, T. Legendi, T. Toffoli, E. Katona and others. The applied aspects of the HS theory in respect to perspective computers very intensively worked out by scientific schools of T. Legendi in Hungary, R. Vollmar in FRG, G. Wolf in GDR and T. Toffoli at the MIT Laboratory for Computer Science(USA).

In our previous works [1-9] we investigated the different aspects of the HS theory and their applications in computer science and mathematical modelling. Results in this directions contributed much that is new to the HS theory and its applications. Systematic survey of our results in this topic can be found in work [11] and in the citized literature in it. However, there exist a number of open problems and areas for the further investigations in this direction. The answers to these problems will help, in our opinion, to clear the essence and possibilities of cellular-like dynamical parallel systems, in more detail.

The present work is organized so as to discuss on the profound level the most general open problems in the HS theory and their applications. It is rather unfortunate that we have no space here to discuss in detail the whole rich problems in this area. Choice of the conside-

1) Tallinn-35 Paldiski mnt 171-26 SKB MPSM ESSR

2) Kiev-56 Kiev Polytechnical Institute

red problems reflect only own taste and the present interest and do not embrace the whole of class of open problems, which can be discussed within the framework of the HS theory and their numerous applications. On the other hand, we present problems, which are believed to constitute a representative sample of the HS theory.

However, for all that the presented here problems allow to outline ways of the further interesting investigations in this topic.

The all general definitions, concepts and designations can be found in works [1-15], in item 2 or are well-known. All the others are introduced as the necessity arises.

2. GENERAL DEFINITIONS AND CONCEPTS

The classical d-dimensional HS(d-HS) is an ordered quadruple $HS=(Z^d, A, \tau^{(n)}, X)$, where:

(1) Z^d is a d-dimensional regular array

(2) $A=\{0,1,2, \dots, a-1\}$ is the alphabet of the d-HS

(3) $\tau^{(n)}$ is the global transition function of the d-HS

(4) X is the neighbourhood index of the d-HS

(5) n is the number of neighbouring machines in the d-HS

The state of the entire array Z^d is called a configuration(CF) of the array and is simply the complete set of current states of each of the individual machines. A CF is any mapping CF: $Z^d \rightarrow A$. C_A denotes the set of all CFs with respect to Z^d and A, i.e., $C_A= \{CF | CF: Z^d \rightarrow A\}$. Let c(z) be the current state of the machine located at cell $z \in Z^d$. The support of a CF c is the set of all cells z such that $c(z) \neq 0$, i.e., the support is the nonquiescent part of CF c. CFs with finite support are of considerable interest; the set of all such CFs is denoted by $\overline{C}_A$.

The operation of the d-HS is specified by a local function $\sigma^{(n)}$ which produces the next state of an individual machine z in terms of the states of the machines which are directly connected to z. For the rest, a local function is any mapping $\sigma^{(n)}: A^n \rightarrow A$. The simultaneous application of a local function to the neighbourhood of every cell-machine of the array Z^d defines a global function $\tau^{(n)}$ of the current CF c into the next CF $c\tau^{(n)}$. The operation of a d-HS is particularly simple. If $c=c_o$ is an initial CF of the array Z^d at time t=0, then the CF at time t=m is $c_o \tau^{(n)m}$, the result of applying function $\tau^{(n)}$ to the array m times. Let now $\langle c_o \rangle [\tau^{(n)}]$ denote the CF-sequence generated by function $\tau^{(n)}$ from the CF $c_o \in C_A$. The investigation of CF-sequence dynamics play the general role in the HS theory. In the present work we shall be concerned with a local functions $\sigma^{(n)}$ which are defined to be a mapping from A^n to A such that $\sigma^{(n)}(0^n)=0$. With this provision, symbol $0 \in A$ is called the quescent symbol of A.

Such formal d-HS models have been applied in the different areas and present enough interesting independent objects of investigation as well[7]. Thus, 1-HS can be considered as a formal model of parallel computations, just as well as the Turing machine is considered as a formal model of the sequential computations.

3. THE UNSOLVED PROBLEMS

Now we shall discuss a number of the most general open problems in the HS theory and their applications, the solutions of which play, in our opinion, a very important role for the further development of this topic.

PROBLEM 1. Great cognitive and gnosiological interest present the study of hierarchical properties of the classical d-HS with respect to general parametres: d, A, n and X. This question was studied[1-4,14] as to some features of d-HS such as: nonconstructibility, some problems of solvability and others. The detailed investigation of the question is absent up to this point.

PROBLEM 2. The study of the constructive possibilities and limitations is one of the most general problems of the HS theory and their applications. E.F. Moore and J. Myhill were the first to look at these problems and gave the first incitement to intensive investigations on the problems in the d-HS. The nonconstructibility problem in the classical d-HS (including the polygenic ones) is studied in detail enough. The modern state of the problem can be found in works[1-6,11-15]. Thus, with the purpose of to embrace all possibilities in the problem, we introduced and investigated three types of nonconstructibility in the d-HS(NCF, NCF-1 and NCF-2). Enough complete and comprehensive investigation of the nonconstructibility problem is presented in[1-6,14]. The received in this direction results give arguments in favour of the essential difference between types of nonconstructibility NCF and NCF-1, in the one hand, and NCF-2, on the other hand. Thus, at present, we have criteria of the existence of NCF or/and NCF-1, whilst there is a criterion of the existence of NCF-2 without NCF in the d-HS, only. It is desirable to receive a criterion of the existence of NCF-2 in the d-HS in the common case.

Particular interest present the algorithmical aspect of the nonconstructibility problem. It is proved[6,14] that the problem of the existence of an arbitrary set of NCF, NCF-1 and NCF-2 in 1-HS is decidable. Furthermore, the problems of the existence of NCF-1 and NCF-2 in d-HS without NCF are decidable, also. However, no one has been able, as yet, to solve the decidability problem in the common case. With point of view of the modelling in the d-HS it is desirable to have constructive methods for solution of the problem (if it possibly, of course).

The concept of nonconstructibility with respect to the given set of configurations in the d-HS has a number of interesting interpretations. It is said that CF $c \in \overline{C}_A$ is nonconstructible with respect to the set $B \subset C_A$, if there exists no CF $c' \in B$ such that $c' \tau^{(n)} = c$. In this direction we have a number of enough simple results [2,4,14], in the meantime the detailed investigation of the problem is absent.

Practically, no one has been able, as yet, to establish relations between of classes of local transition functions and form of NCF, NCF-1 or NCF-2 in the d-HS.

Broadly speaking, it is required to connect either investigated property of the d-HS with structure(type) of the local transition function, bearing in mind the constructive aspect of the HS theory.

The results in the nonconstructibility problem allowed to form enough effective methods for investigation of the d-HS dynamics [1-7,11]. In this connection the solution of the above questions it is extremely desirable.

PROBLEM 3. In contrast with the nonconstructibility the study of the common properties, which reflect the maximal constructive possibilities of the d-HS, present the great interest. One of them can to serve so-called universal reproductability, when each finite CF in d-HS is self-reproducing in Moore's sense [2,4]. The class of d-HS with universal reproductability is enough interesting in many respects. Results in this direction allowed to discover a number of interesting correlations between the nonconstructibility and the universal reproductability in d-HS, and to solve a number of the mathematical problems, also [4,6,14]. It is necessary to note that the d-HS of such type is only one out of many known at present time. Are there any other d-HS of such a type? Is there a class of such d-HS and can it be characterized?

PROBLEM 4. The problem of modelling of one d-HS by another one with suppressing of either property of the modelled structure plays a very important role in the HS theory itself and its applications. Thus, T. Toffoli showed that any d-HS can be modeled by reversible (d+1)-HS (i.e., HS without NCF) [10]. Roughly speaking, a reversible d-HS can never forget its state: for any CF $c \in \overline{C}_A$ at moment t can be recovered the unique CF-sequence which contains the all predecessors of the CF c. The problem is closely connected with reversibility of computations in the (d-HS)-like models. However, the Toffoli's result was achieved at the high price by means of dimensionality. In consequence of which two questions present undoubted interest:

- Whether an arbitrary d-HS can be modeled by a reversible one of the same dimensionality?
- Whether at all there are computation- and construction-universal reversible 1-HS?

With respect to NCF-1 similar problems has enough simple solution [2]: Each d-HS can be modeled by a d-HS without NCF-1. Similar result we have for case of NCF-2, also. Namely, let d-HS be an arbitrary structure with local function $\sigma^{(n)}$ in alphabet A. Define a d-HS with alphabet

$A'=A\cup\{p\}(p\notin A)$ and local transition function $\sigma_1^{(n)}$ as follows:

$$\sigma_1^{(n)}(y_1,\ldots,y_n) = \begin{cases} 0 & , \text{ if } y_i=p \quad (i=\overline{1,n}) \\ \sigma^{(n)}(\overline{y}_1,\ldots,\overline{y}_n) & , \text{ otherwise} \end{cases}$$

$\overline{y}_i=y_i \pmod p$)

Using now the NCF-2 definition[5], the following result can be easily established: Each d-HS can be modeled by a d-HS without the NCF-2.

Furthermore, we are inclined to believe that both above problems have negative solution. Indeed, on the basis of the introduced concepts (WM- and W-modelling), which embrace a wide class of methods of modelling, we corroborated this conclusion[4]. The conclusion appear to hold, further work on this problems is, however, badly needed.

Broadly speaking, the problem of modelling of one d-HS by another with certain properties is a rather wide theme of investigations and present considerable theoretical and applied interest.

PROBLEM 5. A series of scientists have dealt with the many-aspect problem of modelling in the d-HS, but it is necessary to note that neither the neighbourhood nor the state-set reduction techniques are necessarily optimum. In this context we made an attempt to obtain the optimum technique along these lines[2,4]. Thus, we proved that for an arbitrary d-HS there exists a binary d-HS, which 1-models it and whose template size is

$$L=\left[(p_1+1)(\log_2 a+E+p_1)\right]xp_2xp_3x \ldots xp_d ,$$

where $p_1xp_2x \ldots xp_d$ is template size of the modeled d-HS, E=4 for $a<2^{19}$ and E=5 otherwise. To our knowledge this result is the best of its kind. We leave as an intriguing open question whether there exists an optimal technique which will use another idea, but which will allows better results. This problem presents a special interest from the point of view of investigation of the d-HS as a formal model of computers of parallel action.

PROBLEM 6. In connection with universal computability in the d-HS a question arises about minimum complexity of such structures. For an estimation of the complexity, the product axnxd can be introduced, where a is the number of elements in alphabet A, n is the template size, and d is dimensionality of the d-HS. Then a very interesting and important question arises: What is the minimum product axnxd for computation-universal d-HS(d-CUHS)? Establishing the minimum product axnxd is a problem which, in our opinion, as difficult as finding the minimum product sxq for the universal Turing machine(UTM(s,q)) with s symbols on tape and q internal states.

A.R. Smith has found the 1CUHS with: axn=2x40, 3x18, 6x7, 8x5,9x4, 12x3 and 14x2=28, i.e., the minimum product axn for the 1-CUHS is founded by the same value as the product sxq for the UTM(s,q). The best result for product axnxd in 2-CUHS was given by E. Banks, who showed that axnx2=3x5x2=30. The particular interest present the binary 1-CUHS. In this direction we showed[4] that there exists the binary 1-CUHS with template size n=17, i.e., axn=2x17. To our knowledge this result is the best of its kind. However, we have no example of the d-CUHS with the least possible product axnxd. The problem presents undoubted both theoretical and applied interest.

PROBLEM 7. Formal grammar theory(FGT) is a part of automata theory. Therefore, the study of the d-HS dynamics from the point of view of the FGT present undoubted interest. The introduced by us in 1974 so-called $L(\tau_n)$-languages can be defined as the set of all finite CFs generated by global function $\tau^{(n)}$ from the initial CF(axiom) $c_o \in \overline{C_A}$, i.e., $L(\tau_n)=\langle c_o\rangle[\tau^{(n)}]$. In this case d-HS can be considered as a formal parallel grammar(τ_n-grammar). We investigated τ_n-gtammars in conformity with traditions of the FGT. The systematic exposition of the τ_n-grammar theory is presented in works[2-6]. Many results in τ_n-grammars were spread on the case of non-deterministic T_n-grammars[14]. In our opinion, grammars are powerful means of the mathematical semantics both for microprogramming languages of parallel microprogrammed computation structures and for description of all kinds of cellular systems. At present, τ_n-grammar theory is limited, in general, by 1-dimensional case. In this context, it would be extremely perspective to spread these investigations on the case of higher dimensionality of d-HS(d>1).

Along with the d-dimensional(d>1) τ_n- and T_n-grammars, it would be of interest to determine and investigate other generalizations[1-4] of these parallel grammars and concrete interpretations can be given for them.

PROBLEM 8. The general decomposition problem(GDP) of global functions in the d-HS immediatly adjoins the question of constructive complexity of d-HS, which plays a very important role both in concrete realizations of parallel computers on the basis of the (d-HS)-models, and for modelling in d-HS[2-8,14]. The GDP can be presented as follows: Can any global function $\tau^{(n)}$ of d-HS be presented in the form of the composition

$$\tau^{(n)} = \tau_1^{(n_1)} \tau_2^{(n_2)} \ldots \tau_k^{(n_k)} \quad (n_i < n;\ i=\overline{1,k}) \quad (1)$$

It is shown[2] that the GDP has negative solution, broadly speaking. The systematic exposition of results in the problem is presented in work[6]. On a level with well-known GDP was investigated the so-called global decomposition problem(GLDP) of the global functions of the d-HS. The GLDP is the question whether or not any global function $\tau^{(n)}$ of d-HS will possess the representation of type (1) on condition that we may use arbitrary global functions as functions $\tau_i^{(n_i)}$ $(i=\overline{1,k})$ in (1). The GDP and the GLDP are not equivalent, generally. Both problems are studied in detail enough[2-7,14], however, in spite of the received results in this direction. the further investigation on the GDP/GLDP would be extremely desirable, taking into consideration its practical significance[4,7,15].

Thus, the common problems of decidability of the GDP/GLDP for arbitrary global function $\tau^{(n)}$ in the d-HS are open, so far, in spite of the decidability of these problems in the case of alphabet $A=\{0,1,\ldots,a-1\}$ (a-prime)[6]. Taking into consideration the practical significance of the GDP/GLDP, it is extremely desirable to obtain the constructive criteria of decidability in the general case.

The optimization problem is directly linked with the GDP or GLDP. The problem has two aspects: (1) - decomposition of global functions into the simplest possible functions, and (2) - decomposition on minimal number of more simple functions[4]. The detailed investigation of the problem is absent up to this point.

We finally mention two problems which play essential role for further development of the GDP/GLDP. In the former case it is interesting to investigate the partial decomposition problems linked with special classes of global functions or special types of decomposition. In the latter case can be investigated finite basic sets TF(d,a) from which by decomposition we can to obtain enough wide classes of global functions in the same alphabet.

PROBLEM 9. The complexity is one of the most intriguing and vague concepts of the modern science. Investigations in this direction would be extremely desirable. To this effect we introduced and investigated a concept of complexity of the finite CFs in d-HS[2-7,11,14,15]. At present, we know three approaches to the definition of complexity of the finite objects: combinatorical, probabilistic and algorithmical. For the last case N.Kolmogorov defined the relative complexity of some object G (comparatively of object S) by the minimum length of Turing machine's program of deriving of G from S. Our approach can be also called algorithmical but it differ from Kolmogorov's one. The essence of our concept of complexity A(X) consists in the estimation of minimum strategy of generating of arbitrary finite d-dimensional CFs from some primitive CF $c_p \in \overline{C}_A$ by means of the finite number of d-dimensional global functions from some basic finite set TF(d,a). The complexity A(X) was studied, in detail, and on this basis we received a series of interesting results in the HS theory[2-7,11,14,15]. Thus, the results allow to clarify some deep distinctions between parallel and sequential processing models. Along with that, these results are directly linked with the complexity of modelling in d-HS, the GDP/GLDP, and some others, and the further investigations in this direction are badly needed. The urgent task in this direction consists in the following. Our concept of complexity A(X) is based on two fundamental results:

(1) For any alphabet A there exist no the finite sets of d-dimensional CFs $c_i \in \overline{C}_A$ and global functions $\tau^{(n_i)}$ of d-HS such that $\bigcup_i \langle c_i \rangle [\tau^{(n_i)}] = \overline{C}_A \ (i=\overline{1,k})$

(2) For any alphabet A there exist the finite set TF(d,a) of global

functions $\tau^{(n_i)}$ of d-HS such that any d-dimensional CF $c \in \overline{C}_A$ can be generated from some primitive CF $c_p \in \overline{C}_A$, i.e., $c=c_p \tau_1^{(n_1)} \ldots \tau_k^{(n_k)}$; $\tau_i^{(n_i)} \in TF(d,a)$ $(i=\overline{1,k})$

Obviously, the properties of the set TF(d,a) are important for the more deep understanding of the essence of above complexity concept. We received a number of common results in this direction[6,14]. However, this problem is open, as a whole so far. It is desirable to receive a minimal basic sets TF(d,a) and to investigate the global functions from them.

Relative to the above problem it is of interest to investigate the finite sets of CFs $c_i \in \overline{C}_A$ and global functions $\tau^{(n_i)}$ of d-HS such that the set $\underset{i}{U}\langle c_i\rangle[\tau^{(n_i)}]$ would be maximally near to the set $\overline{C}_A (i=\overline{1,k})$. Is it possible to state some hierarchy with respect to degree of nearness to the set $\overline{C}_A$?

Are there other types of complexity comparisions which take parallel action of d-HS into consideration? This investigation is likely to appear very useful for comparisions among closely related parallel cellular dynamic systems.

PROBLEM 10. Working out the HS theory, we up to this point gave small attention to quantitative aspects. However, the theme presents considerable interest for both the theoretic and applied investigations in the d-HS. Thus, on the basis of the results in minimal sizes of NCF, mutually erasable(MECF), passive(PCF) and vanishing(VCF) CFs we received a number of interesting results in 1-HS theory[1-4]. In particular, the decidability of the existence of CFs of the above types in the 1-HS was stated. In the light of these facts, it is extremely desirable to investigate the questions linked with the quantitative estimations of the minimal sizes of NCF, NCF-1, NCF-2, MEC, VCF and PCF in d-HS$(d>1)$.

PROBLEM 11. It is important to observe that we know not enough about the connection between form of local function $\sigma^{(n)}$ of the d-HS and the structure of sets of NCF, NCF-1, NCF-2, PCF, MECF and so on, whereas similar questions play a very essential role for constructive properties of the d-HS and their dynamics. The beginning of this work was laid in [1-4], but ibid a number of partial results was obtained, only. Broadly speaking, it is required to connect either investigated property of the d-HS with structure of the local function, bearing in mind the constructive questions of modelling in the d-HS.

PROBLEM 12. In recent years a new trend has developed with respect to parallel algorithms and parallel computations in the d-HS. A number of authors(T. Legendi, R. Vollmar, G. Wolf, V. Aladyev, T. Toffoli and others[1-20]) considered some related questions, however, more detailed investigations of parallel algorithms defined by d-HS and embedded in d-HS would be extremely desirable. One difficulty in dealing with the parallel algorithms in d-HS is that we need a satisfactory measure for complexity of such class of algorithms. Can a class of algorithms, which are most effectively realized by means of d-HS, be more precisely characterized and described?

PROBLEM 13. In the process of investigation of the GDP by the group methods, we proved[4] that a semigroup L(a,d) of all d-dimensional maps $\tau^{(n)}: C_A \rightarrow C_A$ can be presented in the form of union of subsemigroups L_i $\{(\forall i)(\forall j)(i \neq j \rightarrow L_i \cap L_j = \emptyset)$; $(i,j=\overline{1,4})$, which has no finite systems of generators and a maximum group G(d). The further investigations[14] shown that for 1-dimensional case a maximum group G(1) is union of subgroup SG of all identical maps $\tau_0^{(n)}$ $(n>2)$ and symmetrical subgroup P(a) of periodical maps(global functions) $\tau^{(n)}$ $(n>1)$ with finite system P(a,2) of generators and correlation $\tau^{(n)(a-1)!} = \tau_0^{(2)}$, and, possibly, subgroup of one-one maps, which differ from the above ones. Thus, the question with group G(d) is open to a certain extent up to this point. The further work in this direction is badly needed. It is desirable to present the semigroup L(a,d) with the most detalization.

PROBLEM 14. The problem of finding d-HS with definite properties which generate the given sequences of the finite configurations can be called as realization problem. The problem was shown[1-4,8,9,14,15] to be constructively decidable for the many interesting cases, while the decidability has not been proven even for a few important CF-sequences. This problem appears to be quite difficult, except enough simple cases, but plays extremely important both theoretical and applied role.

PROBLEM 15. During the recent years there has been considerable interest in the new interdisciplinary direction of the modern science - Synergetics[16] , which investigate the role of collective and cooperative effects in self-organizing processes, systems and devices. It is hardly too much to say, that the dynamics of d-HS answers the synergetics problems, at all points. Similar to synergetics, one of general problems of the d-HS dynamics is the question of the existence of general principles directed by rise of self-organizing finite configurations and(or) local transition functions. The modern synergetics is based on three general concepts: unstability, subordination principle and parametres of oder. The concepts have enough simple interpretation, but employment of its to any real system(for example, d-HS) demand essential efforts. In this context, it would be extremely perspective to investigate the general principles of self-organization in (d-HS)-like systems. From more practical point of view, it would be desirable to carry out parallel processing in d-HS computation models on the basis of self-organization of elementary automata(or block of automata) without employment of central parallelized devices. Similar problems can be formulated for many other parallel models embedded in d-HS, for which self-organization approach can to play very essential role.

The following problems, as distinct from the above ones, have the more applied nature. However, solution of these problems will allow, in our opinion, to clarify a number of the important properties of parallel algorithms defined by d-HS, the questions of self-recovery in cellular systems and so on. Furthermore, the progress in the problems allow to build kind of bridges betweeen the developmental biology and computer science[2,3,7,13,15].

PROBLEM 16. The classical concept of d-HS is very bulky for modelling of complex processes and phenomena, in a number of cases. The modelling itself in such d-HS become complex, boundless and lose sometimes any sense. In consequence of which, we introduced and investigated a class of d-HS(d-HS'), which to a certain extent is similar to nervous tissue[2-4]. Each automaton in such d-HS' can directly receive information from its immediate neighbours and each automaton can synchronously change its state and outcome impulses at discrete time steps as a function of its state and income impulses. The d-HS', by definition, is a four-tuple (Z^d, A, I, F), where Z^d and A are defined as for d-HS, I is a set of impulses and F is a functional algorithm(FA) of d-HS'. Such d-HS' are very suitable for describing and modelling of many discrete processes, and allow to obtain extremely lucid picture of information streams which operate by functioning of realized in d-HS' algorithms and concrete models.

We, in particular, investigated the interconnection between d-HS' and d-HS. Namely, a number of the sufficient conditions for embedding of $HS'=(Z^d, A', I, F)$ into $HS=(Z^d, A, \tau^{(3)}, X)$ were received, where $A'=A\cup I$ and X is Moore's neighbourhood index. We denoted the class of d-HS', which answer that condition, by SG. Proceeding from the importance of the classical d-HS, we shall find it extremely interesting to consider the sufficient and the necessary conditions of belonging of any d-HS' to class SG(membership problem for d-HS' respect to class SG, in the long time).

Now, within the framework of d-HS', we shall discuss the so-called limited growth problem(LGP). The LGP has great cognitive value since it allows us to a certain extent to estimate that quantity of information which is required for growing of complex multicellular systems. We shall formulate the LGP relative to 1-HS', without infringement of community. Given is a finite CF c_o of length l. The LGP is to find the FA F of the 1-HS' which allow to grow the CF c of the form $c=\bar{0}SSS \ldots S\bar{0}$ of maximum length from initial CF c_o. It is shown[2] that for $HS'=(Z^1, A, I, F)$ with $\#(A)=12$ and $\#(I)=4m+17$, where m is the minimum speed of impulses and $\#(W)$ is cardinality of a set W, there exist FA F which allow to grow the automata chain of states S of length L from initial CF c_o of length l, where L is defined as follows:

$$L=l(2m+1)\uparrow\Big(\sum_{i=0}^{u} w_i^2 + 2(u+1)\Big), \quad w_o=2\uparrow 4lm(m+1), \quad u=2\Uparrow l,$$

$$w_i=2(L_i-1), \quad L_1=l(2m+1)\Uparrow(w_o^2+2), \quad L_i=L_{i-1}(2m+1)\Uparrow 2\uparrow(2L_{i-1})+2,$$

where $a\uparrow b=a^b$. For growing of automata chain of such famtastic length

$T=(3/2+1/2m)L$ steps of 1-HS' are needed.

Obviously, that theoretical time of growing of automata chain of length L in 1-HS' is equal $T=L/2$. A modification of above FA F allows to grow the automata chain for $T\sim(1/2+1/2m)L$ steps, and length of such chain is equal

$$L=l((2m+1)\uparrow(u+2)-2m) \qquad u=4\uparrow(l+1)+1$$

We leave as an intriguing open question whether there exist an FA which will use another idea, but which will allow to receive the better results. It is desirable to spread the LGP on the d-HS'.

PROBLEM 17. As a formal model for the study of the processes of auto-organization in systems of cellular nature we introduced so-called d-HS with refractority(d-HSR)[1]. HS with refractority can be defined as follows. Let $HSR=(Z^d, A, \tau^{(n)}, X)$, where $A=\{0,1\}\cup\{w_1,w_2, \dots ,w_l\}$; global function $\tau^{(n)}$ is defined by local function $\sigma^{(n)}$ such that

$$\begin{cases} \sigma^{(n)}(0,0, \dots ,0)=0 & \\ \sigma^{(n)}(0,x_1,x_2, \dots ,x_n)=1 & \text{iff the number of 1's in} \\ \sigma^{(n)}(w_g,x_2, \dots ,x_n)=w_{g+1} & \langle x_1,x_2, \dots ,x_m\rangle \geqslant P \\ & \text{P is threshold of excitation in structure} \\ \sigma^{(n)}(w_l,x_2, \dots ,x_n)=0 & \\ \sigma^{(n)}(1,x_2, \dots ,x_n)=w_1 & x_i\in A;\ i=\overline{2,n};\ g=\overline{1,l-1} \end{cases}$$

We shall denote such HS with refractority by d-HSR(l,P). As regards the states of the automaton in d-HSR(l,P) the most general states are chosen: rest (0), excitation (1) and refractority of l-depth ($w_1,w_2,\dots,w_l$). According to the neighbourhood index X, there is the possibility of various structural interrelations between the automata in such HS. The general objec in d-HSR(l,P) is investigation of the dynamic distribution of automata in states "1" in conformity with the initial CF c_o, the neighbourhood index and the depth of refractority.

We investigated d-HSR(l,P) by means of both theoretical and computer modelling approaches. In particular, theoretical approaches allowed to investigate in d-HSR(l,P) a number of interesting questions such as: types of nonconstructible CFs, the decomposition problem and so on[1,4]. Whereas computer modelling allowed to obtain a number of important results of dynamics of spreading of excitements in d-HSR(l,P) for different conditions[8,17]. However, it is necessary to note that the detailed characterization of d-HSR(l,P) is absent, so far. Consequently, the d-HSR(l,P) is a rather wide theme of investigations and present considerable both theoretical and applied interest. For example, d-HSR(L,P) assume a number of interesting modifications on a deterministic and stochastic plane, and present a good basis for modelling of excitable tissue. The further work in this direction is badly needed.

PROBLEM 18. During the recent years there has been considerable interest in the new generation of parallel computer systems. A number of interesting workings in this direction used d-HS as the direct formal model for parallel computations and processing. Among these workings the most famous are Legendi's cellular processors(so-called L-processors) [20] and Toffoli's cellular automata machines(so-called CAM-6) [10]. On the other hand, the classical d-HS is very bulky for adequate modelling of complex parallel devices and processes linked with parallel processing. In consequence of which, we introduced a class of d-HS with memory(d-HSM), which to a certain extent is similar to parallel computation devices with memory [15].

Each automaton in such d-HSM has finite memory of deep P and can directly receive information from its neighbours in conformity with neighbourhood index X. Memory of elementary automaton presents itself P-digit register, the states of each digit of which are elements of alphabet $M=\{m_1, m_2, \ldots, m_k\}$. Each automaton in d-HSM can synchronously change its state and contents of memory at discrete time steps as functions of its state and contents of its memory at the previous step (functions F and R accordingly). The d-HSM, by definition, is a six-tuple (Z^d, A, M, X, F, R), where Z^d, A and X are defined as for classical d-HS, M is memory alphabet, F and R are above-mentioned discrete functions. The functioning of the d-HSM is defined by the following discrete equations:

$$\begin{cases} c(z,t+1) = F(c_z^x(t), S(z,t)) \\ S(z,t+1) = R(c_z^x(t), S(z,t)), \end{cases}$$

where $z \in Z^d$ is an arbitrary automaton in d-HSM, $c(z,t) \in A$ is state of z-automaton at time t, $c_z^x(t)$ is a CF of z-automaton template at time t, and $S(z,t) \in M$ is contents of z-automaton memory at time t.

In our opinion, d-HSM can serve as the basis for modelling of many discrete processes linked with parallel computations and processing and they present enough interesting independent objects of investigation as well. Nowadays, we have not enough developed theory of d-HSM. Consequently, the work in this direction must be done.

PROBLEM 19. Development should, obviously, be considered as a part of the subject matter of cybernetics, since developing systems are complex control ones which depend on large number of interconnected processes. From the cybernetic point of view the problem of understanding of development may be approached by construction and investigation of formal models, which simulate some, or all, of the phenomena of developing biological systems which have just been indicated. Enough detailed survey of such investigations on this basis of automata theory can be found in works [1-3,7,11,13,15]. We to this effect enough wide used both the classical d-HS and d-HS of other types. The most interesting phenomena of developmental biological systems with cell interactions such as: self-reproduction, growth, differentiation, regeneration and regulation, and a number of biology motivated aspects were investigated [1,2,13]. However, in spite of a series of the received interesting results in this direction, we for a number of reasons left out of account some important aspects. Thus, the d-HS models dealt with general phenomena of development taken separately.

Furthermore, having enough large group of biological models in d-HS, we in a number of clases have not satisfactory biological interpretations [1,2,13]. It is therefore important to investigate the problem of adequacy of the embedded in d-HS biological models with their originals.

Investigations of a series of the applied problems on the basis of d-HS has an essential nuance. The essence of d-HS itself exercise influence on the modelled processes and phenomena. The estimation of a degree of such influence in each concrete case(or for general classes of the modelled objects, at most) would be extremely desirable. It is a rather difficult problem, in the main. However, without similar estimations we shall find ourselves in a rather awkward predicament when we shall give biological or other interpretations to obtain results. Consequently, the work in this direction must be done.

It would be extremely desirable to have a developmental system in d-HS which would satisfy general developmental phenomena, as a whole. Such abstract model must be to address the question: How can a complex, multicellular organism, possessed to a certain extent the above phenomena as a whole, grow and develop from a single cell assumming that each cell behaved like an elementary automaton of d-HS and executed a finite program of development?

One general problem of development is the question of efficiency, that is, the question of how to produce a given complex multicellular organism using the smallest number of instructions possible. This question is important from both the point of view of understanding of development in living systems and for parallel algorithms embedded in d-HS.

The most fundamental problem of the development is to understand how a system can make itself more complex, and how it can do it to the degree that one supposes is involved in higher organisms. One difficulty in dealing with this problem is that we need a satisfactory measure for complexity, which will reflect the essence of the modeled in d-HS developing complex multicellular systems.

PROBLEM 20. It is well known that theoretical investigation of the dynamic properties of d-HS is very difficult. Therefore, we shall find it interesting to use the computer modelling for investigation of d-HS dynamics. As far as our knowledge goes, a number of scientists(A. Burks, R. Vollmar, T. Toffoli, V. Aladyev and others) used to an either extent the approach for investigation of some dynamic properties of the d-HS. However, the employment of the approach was episodical nature, so far. Therefore, using our previous experience in the HS theory and computer science we worked out an interactive program system(IPS) [8,9,17] for the many-sided experimental investigation of the theoretical and applied aspects of d-HS. The IPS presents oneself the integrated interactive package A-SVEGAL for the personal computer ISKRA 226 in BASIC-language, which is compatible with well-known programming language BASIC WANG 2200 MVP. The detailed description of the package can be found in our work [17]. The IPS allows(in the present realization) enough effectively to carry out the diverse experiments with d-HS of the more interesting types, and to demonstrate in display form many interesting phenomena of the d-HS dynamics, and to obtain essential premises for the further investigations in this direction. At the same time, the software of the package is open with respect to extending of cycle of the investigated phenomena in the d-HS as well as with respect to replenishing it with new types of the d-HS, too. The attempted investigations of diverse aspects of the HS theory and its applications by means of package A-SVEGAL show that there is good reasons to believe that the following versions of the IPS can be a very powerful instrument for the studying of the d-HS. It is hardly too much to say that the IPS is in the making, and the further work on this theme is badly needed. Furthermore, the further development and exploitation of the package will allow, in our opinion, to clarify a series of important questions linked with modelling of parallel dynamic system(including d-HS) on computers of the sequential action, as well as to considere a number of problems of working out of parallel software.

PROBLEM 21. Nowadays, a very contradictory situation turn up in the HS theory and its applications. On the one hand we have enough well-developed HS theory which is based on a series of the fundamental results, whilst on the other hand these results have not an influence on its applied aspects. That is to say, the theoretical and applied aspects of the d-HS are developed as isolated branches of the united whole, generally speaking. This can be explained provide that, as is reasonable, the theoretical and applied aspects deal with infinite and finite d-HS, accordingly. The vital increase of number of elementary automata in the d-HS models, may therefore be assumed, will contribute the greater applicability of the fundamental theoretical results in applied aspects of the HS theory. The question now is what correlations, if any, there are between the size of the finite d-HS and degree of applicability of the general fundamental results of the HS theory. The problem presents undoubted both theoretical and applied interest. We attempted to carry out an investigation [14] in this direction. The further work on this problem is, however, badly needed.

PROBLEM 22. The following problem is one of the basic questions in the HS theory and takes the particular place. It therefore seems appropriate to indicate the possibilities for continued work along these lines. The question resolves itself into necessity of the very wide popularization of the HS theory and their possibilities in the modern modelling for the purpose of attracting the largest number of researchers of the different areas to investigations on the HS theory and its applications as a new environment of modelling. It is important direction for the further development of this area, also. We expect to see new investigators of the different areas become interested in the above problems that the modern state of the HS theory have made urgent.

4. CONCLUDING REMARKS

The main purpose of this work has been to formulate the more interesting, in our opinion, open problems and the perspective directions of the further investigations in the HS theory and their applications. From the numerous investigations in this province it follows that at present there are good reasons for the further development of the HS theory. The presented above open problems will allow to outline some important ways of the further investigations in this topic.

Thus, many aspects of the HS theory demand active participation of scientists of the different areas: pure and applied mathematics, physics, theoretical and mathematical biology, cybernetics, computer science and a number of others. On the other hand, the HS theory can exercise considerable influence on a number of areas. The appearance of great many new problems in the HS theory is waited for employment of the d-HS for modelling in a new areas.

It is hardly too much to say that the HS theory is in the making, and the further work in this direction is badly needed.

LITERATURE

[1] Aladyev, V.Z.: To Theory of Homogeneous Structures. Estonian Academic Press, Tallinn 1972.

[2] Aladyev, V.Z.: Mathematical Theory of Homogeneous Structures and Their Applications. Valgus Press, Tallinn 1980.

[3] Parallel Processing and Parallel Algorithms (Ed. by V.Z. Aladyev). Valgus Press, Tallinn 1981.

[4] Parallel Processing Systems (Ed. by V.Z. Aladyev). Valgus Press. Tallinn 1983.

[5] Aladyev, V.Z.: New results in the theory of homogeneous structures. Informatik-Scripten 8(1984), Braunschweig, 3-15.

[6] Aladyev, V.Z.: Recent results in the theory of homogeneous structures. PARCELLA-86. Akademie-Verlag, Berlin 1986, 30-48.

[7] Aladyev, V.Z.: Homogeneous structures in mathematical modelling. Sixth Intern. Conf. on Mathem. Modelling. Book of Abstracts. Washington University, St.-Louis 1987, 326.

[8] Aladyev, V.Z. et al.: Personal Computer ISKRA 226. Software and Hardware Architecture. Ukrainian Soviet Encyclopedia Press, Kiev 1988.

[9] Aladyev, V.Z. et al.: Software Designing for Personal Computer ISKRA 226. Technika Press, Kiev 1988.

[10] Toffoli, T., Margolus, N.: Cellular Automata Machines. MIT Press, Massachusetts 1987.
[11] Aladyev, V.Z.: The behavioural properties of homogeneous structures. The First Intern. Symp. on USAL, Tokyo 1975, 12-22.
[12] Aladyev, V.Z., Osipov, O.B.: Introduction into Hardware Architecture of EC-computers. Valgus Press, Tallinn 1976.
[13] Aladyev, V.Z. et al.: Mathematical Developmental Biology. Nauka Press, Moscow 1982.
[14] Aladyev, V.Z.: Solutions of a Number of Problems in the Theory of Homogeneous Structures. TR-040684. P/A "Silikaat", Tallinn 1985.
[15] Aladyev, V.Z.: Theoretical and Applied Aspects of Homogeneous Structures, in: Analogous and Discrete Computers. Valgus Press, Tallinn 1988.
[16] Haken, H.: Advanced Synergetics. Instability Hierarchies of Self-organizing Systems and Devices. Springer Verlag, Berlin 1983.
[17] Aladyev, V.Z. et al.: Computer investigation of homogeneous structures (submitted for IMYCS'88), Bratislava 1988.
[18] Aladyev, V.Z., Sirodscha, I.B.: Instrumental Programming for Personal Computer ISKRA 226. Harkov Aviation Institute Press, Harkov 1988.
[19] Vollmar, R.: Algorithmen in Zellularautomaten. B.G. Teubner, Stuttgart 1979.
[20] Vollmar, R., Legendi, T.(Eds): Beiträge zur Theorie der Poluautomaten, no. 2, Braunschweig 1982.

FURTHER LITERATURE

Seidel, S.: Language recognition and the synchronization of cellular automata. Tech. Rep. Department of Computer Science. Uinversity of Iowa (1979).

Willson, S.: Cellular automata can generate fractals. Dis. Appl. Math. 8 (1984), 91-99.

Choffrut, C. and Culik II K.: On real-time cellular automata and trellis automata. Acta Inform. 21 (1984), 393-409.

Umeo, H., Morita, K. and Sugata K.: Deterministic one-way simulation of two-way real-time cellular automata and its related problems. Inform. Process. Lett. 14 (1982), 159-161.

Zinkevich, T.G.: Homogeneous Structures. Tech. Rep. 1285.06/1985. P/A "Silikaat". Tallinn 1985.

Vollmar, R. and Legendi, T.(Eds): Cellprocessors and Cellalgorithms II. Rep. on a common research project. Informatik-Scripten 13(1985) T. U. Braunschweig.

Legendi, T.: Cellware implementation. Proc. of the 3-rd Intern. Workshop on Parallel Processing by Cellular Automata and Arrays. Berlin 1986, 61-65.

Harao, M. and Nogushi S.: Fault Tolerant Cellulat Automata. J.Comp. Syst. Sci. 11 (1975), 171-185.

Burks, A.: Essays on Cellular Automata. Univ. Ill. Press. Illinois 1970.
Codd, E.F.: Cellular Automata. Academic Press 1968.
Farmer, D., Toffoli T., and Wolfram S.: Cellular Automata, North-Holland 1984.
Fredkin, E., Toffoli T.: Conservative Logic. Int. J. Theor. Phys. 21 (1982), 219-253.
Hayes, B.; The cellular automaton offers a model of the world and a world unto itself. Scientific American 250 (1984) 3, 12-21.
Hedlund, G.A.: Endomorphism and Automorphism of the Shift Dynamical System. Math. Syst. Theory 3 (1966), 218-230.
Maruoka, A., Kimura M.: Injectivity and Surjectivity of Parallel Maps for Cellular Automata. J. Comp. Syst. Sci. 18 (1979), 47-64.
Packard, N., Wolfram, S.: Two-dimensional cellular automata. J. Stat. Phys. 38 (1985), 901-946.
Preston, K., Duff, M.: Modern Cellular Automata. Theory and Applications. Plenum Press 1984.
Smith, A.: Cellular Automata Theory. Tech. Rep. 2, Stanford Electronic Lab., Stanford Univ. (1969).
Tucker, J.: Cellular automata machine: the ultimate parallel computer. High Technology 4 (1984) 6, 85-87.
Vichniac, G.: Simulating physics with cellular automata. Physica 10D (1984), 96-115.
Zuse, K.: Calculating Space. Tech. Transl. AZT-70-164-GEMIT. MIT Project MAC (1970).
Wolfram, S.: Computation Theory of Cellular Automata. Adv. Applied Math. 7 (1986), 123-169.
Legendi, T., Parkinson, D., Vollmar, R. and Wolf, G.(Eds): Parallel Processing by Cellular Automata and Arrays. Akademie-Verlag, Berlin 1987.
Martin, O., Odlyzko, A. and Wolfram, S.: Algebraic properties of cellular automata. Comm. Math. Phys. 93 (1984), 219-259.
Jen, E.: Invariant strings and pattern-recognizing capabilities of one-dimensional cellular automata. J. Stat. Phys. 43 (1986), 243
Boghosian, B.: The simulation of partial differential equations with cellular automata. Book of Abstracts. Sixth Int. Conf. on Math. Modelling. Institute for Applied Sciences. St.-Louis 1987.
Takahashi, S.: Limiting behaviour of liniar cellular automata. Proc. Japan Acad. 63 (1987), 182-185.
Kobuchi, Y.: A note on symmetrical cellular spaces. Information Processing Letters 25 (1987), 413-415.
Szwerinski, H.: Symmetrical one-dimensional cellular spaces. Inf. and Contr. 67 (1985), 163-172.
Dyer, C.: One-way bounded cellular automata. Inf. and Contr. 44 (1980), 54-69.

ON SIMULTANEOUS REALIZATIONS OF BOOLEAN FUNCTIONS, WITH APPLICATIONS

Andreas Albrecht 1)

Abstract

Simultaneous realizations are defined as the evaluation of a boolean function on several input tuples at the same time. For the corresponding Shannon functions one can show that a relatively large number of simultaneous inputs is compatible with a small enhancement of size and depth. These realizations can be applied to various computational tasks, e.g. to the design of fault-tolerant systems, the point-inclusion problem of binary images, and the simultaneous memory access.

1. Introduction

The design and analysis of computer algorithms is mainly concerned with the behaviour of algorithmic solutions on single input instances. However, the design of algorithms is of interest only for problems with a sufficiently large set of possible inputs. Moreover, there are many computational problems being used as subroutines of global tasks, where it is necessary to solve these problems on different inputs with certain constraints on time and hardware (e.g. problems from image analysis, arithmetical problems etc.). Commonly, in the literature only two approaches are discussed in order to settle this problem: pipelining and the independent use of hardware for each input instance.

To our knowledge there exist only few papers in which the problem of simultaneous computations is discussed under the assumption that the enhancement of hardware is not necessarily proportional to the number of simultaneous inputs, see [4],[8] and [9]. These papers are related to the realization of boolean functions on disjoint sets of variables. In our paper the same problem is discussed, where we try to combine an extremely large number of independent inputs with a moderate hardware growth.

Unfortunately, we are able to present only realizations which are of theoretical interest because of the considerable influence of constant factors on the complexity estimations. But we think that for small

1) Humboldt University, Dept. of Mathematics, P.O.Box 1297, Berlin, 1086 GDR

values of simultaneous inputs there exist applications in various fields of hardware design.

2. Basic definitions and previous work

We consider the gate-complexity of boolean circuits, i.e. let $B:=\{0,1\}$, $B_n := \{f \mid f: \times_n B \longrightarrow B\}$ and

$X_n := \{x_i \mid i = 1,\ldots,n\}$. OP_2 is our set of basic operations, $OP_2 \subset B_2$, where OP_2 is a complete set in the sense of the algebra of boolean functions.

A circuit C (for the computation of $f \in B_n$ over the operations in OP_2) is a directed, acyclic graph such that

(1) each node has indegree 0,1 or 2; the nodes ν with indegree 0 are entries and are labelled with a variable from X_n;

(2) each non-entry ν is labelled by an $op(\nu) \in OP_2$.

With each node ν of C we associate a function $res_C(\nu)$ which is obtained by applying $op(\nu)$ to the result of the two nodes that precede ν.

The corresponding Shannon functions for size and depth are denoted by

$$s(f) := \min \text{card} \{\text{non-entries in } C \mid C \text{ computes } f\},$$

$$s(n) := \max_{f \in B_n} s(f) \text{ , and}$$

$$d(n) := \max_{f \in B_n} \min_{C \text{ comp. } f} d(C) \text{ ,}$$

where d(C) is the length of the longest path from entries to the node computing f.

It is well-known from Lupanov's theorem [7] that

$$s(n) \sim 2^n/n \quad \text{and}$$

$$d(n) \sim n \text{ ,}$$

where for almost all $f \in B_n$ the behaviour of s(f) and d(f) is asymptotically equivalent to s(n) and d(n)[1].

In our definition of boolean circuits it is possible to declare several nodes (not necessarily with outdegree 0) as outputs of the circuit, i.e. the circuit realizes boolean vector functions.

For $f \in B_n$ we consider vector functions F_f^m of the special kind

$$F_f^m = [f(x_1^1,\ldots,x_n^1),\ f(x_1^2,\ldots,x_n^2),\ldots,f(x_1^m,\ldots,x_n^m)].$$

1) $a(n) \sim b(n)$ means $\lim_{n\to\infty} a(n)/b(n) = 1$.

Let C^m denote circuits with $m \geq 2$ output-gates where the entries are labelled with variables from $X_{m \cdot n} := \{x_i^j \mid 1 \leq i \leq n,\ 1 \leq j \leq m\}$.
Furthermore, let

$$s^m(f) := \min \operatorname{card} \{\text{non-entries in } C^m \mid C^m \text{ computes } F_f^m\},$$

$$d^m(f) := \min_{C^m \text{ comp. } F_f^m} d(C^m) \quad \text{and}$$

$s^m(n)$, $d^m(n)$ denote the corresponding Shannon functions.

In [9] D. Uhlig described an encoding of boolean functions that ensures for $m \leq \exp(\underline{o}(n/\log_2 n))$ the surprising result that

$$s^m(n) \sim s(n) \text{ and } d^m(n) \sim d(n).$$

Independently of [9] W. Paul proved in [8] that for any $\varepsilon > 0$ there are functions $F: \times_n B \rightarrow \times_n B$ such that

$$s^2(F) \leq (1+\varepsilon)\, s(F).$$

The situation changes if we restrict the circuits to the monotone case ($OP_2^{mon} = \{et(x,y),\ vel(x,y)\}$) : Fischer/Galbiati showed in [4] that

$$s_{mon}^2([f,g]) = s_{mon}(f) + s_{mon}(g).$$

3. Simultaneous realizations with polynomial size enhancement

The result proved by D. Uhlig [9] shows that for a hyperpolynomial number of inputs the complexity of simultaneous realizations is asymptotically equal to the single input case. Unfortunately, up to now methods for proving trade-offs concerning the relation of m (the number of simultaneous inputs) and $S^m(n)$ have not been known. Thus we are forced to combine a large number of simultaneous inputs with an enhancement of circuit size which should be as small as possible.

Theorem 1

For each $f \in B_n$ and $m \leq 2^n$ there exists a circuit C_f^m such that

$$s(C_f^m) = O(2^n n^2) \text{ and}$$

$$d(C_f^m) = O(n \cdot \log_2 n).$$

Sketch of Proof: The realization is described in terms of sequential circuits. As the basic structure we use a sorting network. The entries are built by simple processors where each processor has a fixed number of registers, e.g. for the input value $\tilde{a}$, the input number $\tilde{b}$, the value $f(\tilde{a})$ and auxiliary values, $l(\tilde{a}) + l(\tilde{b}) = 2 \cdot n$.

The sorting network has $m + 2^n$ inputs of length $O(n)$. The first 2^n inputs (from the left) are the tuples $(0,\dots,0),\dots,(1,\dots,1)$ together with the corresponding values of the boolean function f.

The processors of the entries can directly communicate with their neighbours. Additionally, the outputs of the sorting network are connected with a binary tree network where each node represents a simple processor for arithmetical and logical operations on binary strings of length $O(n)$.

The m inputs of length n together with the input numbers and the first 2^n inputs are sorted in $O(n)$ steps.
Each comparison step is realized by simple logical operations concerning the first component - the input tuples and the addresses of the values of the function f. Therefore, each comparison step can be realized by a circuit of the depth at most $O(\log n)$.

The size and depth of the sorting network do not exceed

$O(2^n \cdot n^2)$ and

$O(n \cdot \log_2 n)$,

see [1].

In our definition of simultaneous realizations it is allowed that several (or all) inputs are of the same value; therefore, we have to distribute the values $f(\tilde{a}_r)$ to the processors storing information about inputs $\tilde{a}$ and numbers of inputs (these processors are neighbouring after sorting). Here we use a special procedure working on the binary tree network which is associated with the outputs of the sorting network.

Using once again the sorting network we can establish the initial position of the input information together with the needed values of $f(\tilde{a}_r)$. qed

Compared with the lower bounds we obtain for almost all n-ary functions an enhancement of size and depth which is upper bounded by $O(n^3)$ and $O(\log_2 n)$, respectively.

It is easily to see that the construction described above is in fact the realization of a memory structure for 2^n single bit information with simultaneous access. The same realization can be used for simultaneous writing into the memory (with some additional procedure for conflict resolution if more than one input tries to write into the same memory location).

The point-inclusion problem is one of the basic tasks in computational geometry [3] . For binary images this problem has a natural interpretation in terms of boolean functions. We consider binary images defined by a square matrix with 2^n elements, $n = 2 \cdot l$. The regions formed by the value One will be characterized by the number k of corner elements (defined in a natural way). We do not require that the regions are connected.

The binary matrices will be encoded as described by I. Haverlik in [5]. This (rather complicated) encoding reduces, for almost all functions, the number of essential variables to $\lceil \log_2 k \rceil + \underline{o}(\log_2 k)$. Thus one can show

Theorem 2

For all binary images $I: \{0,1\}^n \longrightarrow \{0,1\}$,
$n = 2\,l$, defined by k corner elements,
$n \leq k < 2^n$,
there exists a circuit C_I^m deciding simultaneously the point inclusion problem for

$m \leq k$ points, where

$s(C_I^m) = O(n \cdot k \cdot \log_2 k)$ and

$d(C_I^m) = O(\log_2^2 k)$.

4. Concluding remarks

We have discussed simultaneous realizations for extremely large numbers m of independent inputs. As already mentioned in section 3 we think that the presented method is too complicated to be relevant for practical purposes.

But we believe that for smaller values of m - perhaps, even for the encoding introduced by D. Uhlig - there exist applications e.g. for the design of fault-tolerant PLA's or the synthesis of memories with simultaneous access.

It would be interesting to know more about the complexity of simultaneous computations for problems where "good" parallel solutions probably do not exist (e.g. log-space-complete problems for the complexity class P).

5. Literature

[1] Ajtai, M., J. Komlos, and E. Szemeredi: Sorting in c·log(n) Parallel Steps. Combinatorica 3(1983)1, 1-19.

[2] Albrecht, A.: On Hardware Algorithms for Geometrical Computation Problems. - In: Proc. 10th IFIP Computer Congress, Dublin 1986, 989-994.

[3] Edelsbrunner, H.: On Key Problems and Key Methods in Computational Geometry. Proc. STACS, Paris 1984.

[4] Fischer, M.J., and F. Galbiati: On the Complexity of 2-output Boolean Networks. Theor. Comp. Science (1981), 177-185.

[5] Haverlik, I.: On the Synthesis of Circuits for Matrices with a Defined Number of Corner Elements. Banach Centre Publ. 7(1982), 177-195 (in Russian).

[6] Leighton, F.T.: New Lower Bound Techniques for VLSI. - In: Proc. 22nd FOCS, 1981, 1-9.

[7] Lupanov, O.B.: On the Synthesis of some Classes of Control Systems. Probl. of Cybernetics 10(1963), 63-97 (in Russian).

[8] Paul, W.: Realizing Boolean Functions on Disjoint Sets of Variables. Theor. Comp. Science (1976), 383-396.

[9] Uhlig, D.: On the Synthesis of Self-Correcting Circuits with a Small Number of Reliable Elements. Mathem. Notes 15(1974)6, 937-944 (in Russian).

PARALLEL MICROPROGRAMMING AS A TOOL FOR MULTI-MICROPROCESSOR SYSTEMS

O.L. Bandman, S.V. Piskunov[1)]

1. INTRODUCTION

Since microprocessors are cheap and easy to reach, the idea is exciting of introducing them into high-performance systems designed to solve complicated computation tasks. Here belong signal processing, image processing, process simulation in media, etc. These tasks usually incorporate subtasks related to computing on data arrays such as matrices, vectors, sequences, etc. As the subtasks have many similar operations and constitute a good proportion of computation, it is reasonable to consider them as independent operators to be implemented in homogeneous structures of the cell type. Parallel-sequential or parallel-pipeline composition of these operators matches best the natural parallelism of a task.

When designing special-purpose processors from serial microprocessors, much labour is required to design architecture. The purpose of architecture design is to produce the structural scheme of a computing system, i.e. a set of processor elements with microprogram sets assigned to them and connections between them.

A range of tools for architecture design are referred to as the architecture compiler. The basis for the architecture compiler is provided by the ways in which problem solution algorithms are represented in the parallel form. They should meet the following requirements:

a) make the system architecture as similar as possible to computation processes and

b) make automation and the use of the experience gained (architecture libraries) possible.

Here we suggest a new approach to systematic design of multi-microprocessor systems. Its underlying postulates are as follows.

1) Computing and control algorithms are represented in the form of parallel microprograms [1]. Parallel microprogram notation as well as the simulation language and structural synthesis techniques are based on the fundamental algorithmic system - the parallel substitution algorithm [2]. This algorithmic system is, on the one hand, a parallel version of the Markov algorithm and, on the other hand, the cellular automaton generalization.

2) Asynchronous composition of algorithmic descriptions of operators over arrays and parallel microprograms is based on the model called the Petri net [3]. The well-developed tool for Petri net analysis allows an automated test for parallel algorithm correctness, a formalized synthesis of control over interactions between microprocessors and assessment of hardware performance.

---

1) Computing Center, Siberian Division, the USSR Academy of Sciences, Novosibirsk, 630090, USSR.

3) The design is carried out in the interactive mode with the use of the extendable library of architecture solutions already made to implement basic algorithms. Interactivity implies that all important decisions such as the choice of an original architecture hypothesis, synchronization techniques, composition and control are the designer's responsibility, mapping them into parallel microprograms texts. All other manipulations with microprogram description such as validity test and structural scheme plotting are computer-aided.

The process of architecture design has three stages. The first one, which is preliminary and non-formalized is to determine basic operators of array processing and make a general algorithmic schedule. The second stage includes the construction of parallel microprogram operators and the control microprogrogram and combining them into a complete microprogram description of a special-purpose processor. The third stage incorporates formal computer-aided procedures converting parallel microprograms into structural schemes, mapping of these schemes into microprocessor net and their microprogramming.

The paper has three main sections. Section 1 dwells on theoretical substantiation of the approach in question. It introduces fundamental concepts of parallel programming and offers the techniques for compiling parallel microprograms. In Section 2, we describe the composition of operators and the synthesis of the control microprogram based on Petri net simulating asynchronous interactions among operators. In Section 3, we present a formal way of transfer from microprogram description to a structural scheme.

2. PARALLEL MICROPROGRAM

Methods of the structure synthesis of a special-purpose processor rely on microprogram representation of parallel algorithms implemented by it.

The major distinction between a parallel microprogram and an ordinary (sequential) one is that the order of microinstructions in a parallel microprogram is not defined. Instead, each microinstruction includes the condition of its execution in the form of data values list with the indication of their coordinates in the array processed. At every step, all the microinstructions are executed either simultaneously or in an arbitrary order for which execution conditions are satisfied.

The parallel microprogram class is a subclass of parallel substitution algorithms [2]. Formally, parallel substitution algorithms are defined as follows.

Let A be a finite alphabet, M - a set of names whose cardinality is but enumerable. The pair (a,m) belonging to A x M is called a <u>cell</u>, a is the state of a cell, and m is the name of a cell. In a parallel substitution algorithm, the object for convertion is the <u>cellular array W</u>, a finite set of cells having not a single pair of cells with the same names. The set of all W is denoted by $K(A,M)$.

Let W_1, W_2, W_3 be cellular arrays at least one of arrays W_1, W_2 being not empty, and $W_1 \cup W_2$ be a cellular array, then $\theta^9 : W_1 * W_2 \to W_3$ is called a substitution, $W_1 * W_2$ is the left-hand side of the substitution, W_1 is the base, W_2 is the context, W_3 is the right-hand side of the <u>substitution.</u> Substitution θ^9 bears a relation to a certain transformation W which can be written as follows: if $W_1 \cup W_2 \subseteq W$, then θ^9 is applicable to W and the result of its application denoted by $\theta^9(W)$ equals to $(W \setminus W_1) \cup W_3$; if $W_1 \cup W_2 \not\subseteq W$, the substitution is not applicable and $\theta^9(W) = W$. Such an operation of substituting is called an <u>elementary operation.</u>

Example 1. Application of the elementary operation $\theta^9 : \{(a_1,1)(a_2,2)\} * \{(a_3,0)\} \to \{(a_3,1)(a_3,2)\}$ ($A = \{a_1,a_2,a_3\}$, $M = \{0,1,2\}$) to the array $W = \{(a_3,0)(a_1,1)(a_2,2)\}$ will change the state of the cell named $m = 1$ and $m = 2$ so that the result will be $\theta^9(W) = \{(a_3,0)(a_3,1)(a_1,2)\}$.

Let us introduce the concept of configuration. <u>Configuration</u> $S(m)$ is an expression of the form $\{(a_1,\varphi_1(m)) \dots (a_k,\varphi_k(m))\}$. Pair $(a_i,\varphi_i(m))$ is called the i-th component of configuration, $a_i \in A$ is a character of the alphabet, $\varphi_i : M \xrightarrow{in} M$ is a function (partial in the general case). Functions φ_i, $i = 1,\dots, k$ are called <u>naming.</u> They are selected so that for any i_1 and i_2 configuration $S(m)$ components and for any $m \in M$ holds the following: if functions $\varphi_{i_1}(m)$ and $\varphi_{i_2}(m)$ are defined, then $\varphi_{i_1}(m) \neq \varphi_{i_2}(m)$. Such a choice of naming functions results in the cellular array $W_l = \{(a_1, \varphi_1(m_l)) \dots (a_k, \varphi_k(m_l))\}$ if configuration of a certain $m_l \in M$ is substituted into all $\varphi_i(m)$ and all $\varphi_i(m_l)$ are defined. Note that even if one function is not defined, W_l is not constructed (is considered empty). W_l is called a configuration element. We may say that $S(m)$ specifies a one-type set of cellular array elements of configuration S.

Example 2. A cellular array is evidently a single-element configuration. In this configuration all the naming functions are constants.

The next example is a configuration having an infinite number of elements.

But before considering the example, we shall make some comments. Hereafter we shall normally make use of the following notations. An alphabet character which is the Cartesian product of certain original alphabets $A_1,\dots, A_d$, will be written as $\langle a_1,a_2,\dots,a_d \rangle$. A name which is an element of the Cartesian product of the set of names $M_1,\dots,M_g$ will be written as $[m_1,\dots,m_g]$. In case when a set of positive integers N (or its subset) is selected as M, an arbitrary name will be denoted by x. If $M \subseteq N \times N$, an arbitrary name will be written as $[x,y]$. The naming functions of the form $\varphi : x \to x + a$ ($\varphi : [x,y] \to [x + a, y + b]$), where a,b are integers, will be written as $x + a$($[x + a, y + b]$).

Example 3. Let $A = \{0,1\}$, $M = N \times N$. When names are substituted from M, configuration $S = \{(1,[x - 1,y])(0,[x,y - 1])(1,[x,y])\}$ specifies the infinite set of cellular arrays:

$\{(1, [1,2])(0, [2,1])(1, [2,2])\}$,
$\{(1, [1,3])(0, [2,2])(1, [2,3])\}$,
$\{(1, [1,4])(0, [2,3])(1, [2,4])\}$,
...

If names from M are interpreted as integral coordinates of cells into which the plane is divided, cellular sets may be graphically presented as a set on cells on the plane, into which characters from alphabet $\{0,1\}$ are written. The configuration element for $x = 3$, $y = 4$ is depicted in Figure 1.

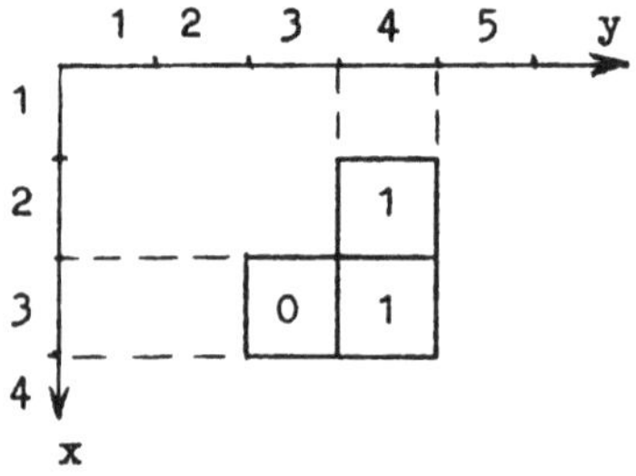

Figure 1.

Let two configurations be given $S_1 = \{(a_1, \varphi_1(m)) \ldots (a_{n_1}, \varphi_{n_1}(m))\}$ and $S_2 = \{(b_1, \psi_1(m)) \ldots (b_{n_2}, \psi_{n_2}(m))\}$ such that for any m^1 M^1 and any i,j, $i = 1,\ldots,n_1$, $j = 1,\ldots,n_2$ if $\varphi_i(m)$ and $\psi_j(m)$ are defined, $\varphi_i(m) \neq \psi_j(m)$.

The product of configurations S_1 and S_2 denoted by $S_1 * S_2$ is called the configuration of the form $\{(a_1, \varphi_1(m)) \ldots (a_{n_1}, \varphi_{n_1}(m))(b_1, \psi_1(m)) \ldots (b_{n_2}, \psi_{n_2}(m))\}$.

Note. To write the product of an arbitrary configuration $S(m)$ and a certain one-component configuration $\{(a, \varphi(m))\}$, we shall make use of the expression $\{(S(m))(a, \varphi(m))\}$.

Now we can introduce the key concept of a parallel substitution. Expression of the form $\theta : S_1 * S_2 \rightarrow S_3$, where S_1, S_2, S_3 are configurations, is called a parallel substitution. Any of the configurations may be left out, but at least one of the configurations S_1 or S_2 must be present. By analogy with the elementary operation: $S_1 * S_2$ is called the left-hand side of a parallel substitution, S_1 is the base, S_2 is the context, S_3 is the right-hand side.

Let there be given an arbitrary cellular array W. A parallel substitution operation is that each cell is associated with a certain procedure denoted by f which from a cell name and the text of parallel substitution configuration constructs the corresponding elementary operation (if it exists) and executes it if it is applicable. Application of procedure

f to all the cells W is as follows. Let $M' = m_1,\ldots,m_p$ be a subset of names for which $S_1(m_l)$, $S_2(m_l)$, $S_3(m_l) \neq \emptyset$ and $S_1(m_l) \cup S_2(m_l) \subseteq W$, $l = 1,2,\ldots,p$. If $M' \neq \emptyset$, θ is applicable to W. The result of its application is

$\theta(W) = \left\{ W \setminus \bigcup_{l=1}^{p} S_1(m_l) \right\} \cup \left\{ \bigcup_{l=1}^{p} S_3(m_l) \right\}$. If $M' = \emptyset$, it is not applicable to W.

Note. The effective construction of M' is normally provided by including the left-hand side θ of the identical function $\varphi(m) = m$ into the naming functions' set.

In [4], the concept of configuration is usefully extended, which allows a more flexible way of specifying its elements. The point is that in the text of configuration components, the first element of the pair may be specified not only by a particular character from A but also by a variable assuming the values from A or by a certain function with the areas of determination and values belonging to A. In this case, to perform parallel substitution is to execute all elementary operations for which application conditions are satisfied at certain values of variables. As it takes place, the states of cells of base configurations adopt values of the functions indicated for these celles in the right-hand side of the parallel substitution. Such a substitution is called functional. Greek letters, as a rule, β, γ, δ, may be with indices, will stand for the variables. An arbitrary character from A alphabet will be denoted by $\otimes$.

Example 4. The parallel substitution

$$\theta : \{(\beta,x)(1+\beta,\ x+1)\} * \rightarrow \{(2\beta,x)(\beta,x+1)\}$$

is applicable to the array $W = \{(-1,1)(0,2)(0,3)(0,4)\}$ only if $x = 1$. The result of its execution is $\theta(W) = \{(-2,1)(-1,2)(0,3)(0,4)\}$.

The finite set of substitutions $\Phi : \{\theta_i : S_{i1} * S_{i2} \rightarrow S_{i3},\ i = 1,\ldots,\nu$, written in an arbitrary order is called the <u>parallel substitution system.</u> Application of Φ to $W \in K(A,M)$ is set by an iterative procedure. Let a cell array W^i be the result of the i-th step. If no substitution is applicable to W^i, W^i is called the result of applying Φ to W. If the subset $\theta^i = \{\theta_1^i,\ldots,\theta_r^i\}$, $r \leq \nu$, of substitutions applicable to W^i is not empty, i.e. to each $\theta_j^i \in \theta^i$ corresponds $M_j^i = \{m_1^i,\ldots,m_{p_j}^i\}$, then, applying Φ to W^i, we get

$$W^{i+1} = \left\{ W^i \setminus \bigcup_{j=1}^{r} \bigcup_{l=1}^{p_j} S_{j1}^i(m_l^i) \right\} \cup \left\{ \bigcup_{j=1}^{r} \bigcup_{l=1}^{p_j} S_{j3}(m_l^i) \right\} .$$

System Φ together with the above stated iteration procedure is called the <u>parallel substitution algorithm.</u>

Substitution $\theta : S_1 * S_2 \rightarrow S_3$ is <u>called stationary</u> if for any $m \in M$ the set of cell names in $S_1(m)$ coincides with the set of cell names in $S_3(m)$. The algorithm of parallel stationary substitutions is referred to as a <u>parallel microprogram</u>. A stationary substitution is referred to as a <u>microinstruction</u>. Elementary operations built according to a stationary substitution are called <u>microoperations</u>.

Note. When determining both parallel substitution algorithms and parallel microprograms, consistent substitution systems [1,2] are considered such that for any original $W \in K(A,M)$ at each i-th iteration step, W^i is a cell array.

Example 5. Microprogram

$$\Phi = \begin{cases} \theta_1: \{(\beta,x)(1+\beta,x+1)\} * \to \{(2\beta,x)(\beta,x+1)\}; \\ \theta_2: \{(0,x)\} * \{(0,x-1)\} \to \{(1,x)\}; \end{cases}$$

for the original $W = \{(-1,1)(0,2)(0,3)(0,4)\}$ in two steps will yield the result $W^2 = \{(-4,1)(-2,2)(1,3)(1,4)\}$.

Example 6. A parallel microprogram for adding many binary numbers. $A = \{0,1\}$, $M = N \times N$, the cell array W is a two-dimensional rectangular table whose squares are indexed according to the left coordinate system (x is abscissa and y is ordinate). Binary integers to be added are on the table lines, the lower line being zero. Less significant digits of integers are listed in column at $x = 1$. The microprogram includes microinstructions:

$$\theta_1: \{(1,[x,y])(1,[x,y+1])(0,[x+1,y])\} * \{(0,[x+1,y-1])(0,[x,y-1])\} \to \{(0,[x,y])(0,[x,y+1])(1,[x+1,y])\};$$

$$\theta_2: \{(1,[x,y])(0,[x,y+1])\} * \{(0,[x,y-1])\} \to \to \{(0,[x,y])(1,[x,y+1])\}.$$

θ_1 and θ_2 microoperations are depicted in Figure 2,a. The steps of transforming the original cell array in which the integers 9, 15, 5 are stored are shown in Figure 2,b.

As is known [1,2], parallel program Φ is interpreted by an automata net, the cell name set corresponding to the automata name set. We will assume the name set finite and denote it by M'. Hereafter we will refer to such a net as a <u>block</u>, and the automata constituting it - as <u>cells</u>. Let us assume that each this automaton is a microprogrammed one.

To each cell with the name $m' \in M'$, a set of microoperations (denoted by $F_{m'}$) is assigned in a certain way containing the cell name m' in the basic parts and obtained from the microprogram Φ text. Set $F_{m'}$ defines the contents of microprogram memory cell m', and various names used in microoperations text are the names of the cells - neighbours of m' cell with respect to inputs and outputs. There are many ways in which a set of microoperations may be assigned to a cell. Watch each microoperation to be assigned to at least one cell of the block. Here is an example to illustrate the ways of assigning a set of microoperations to a

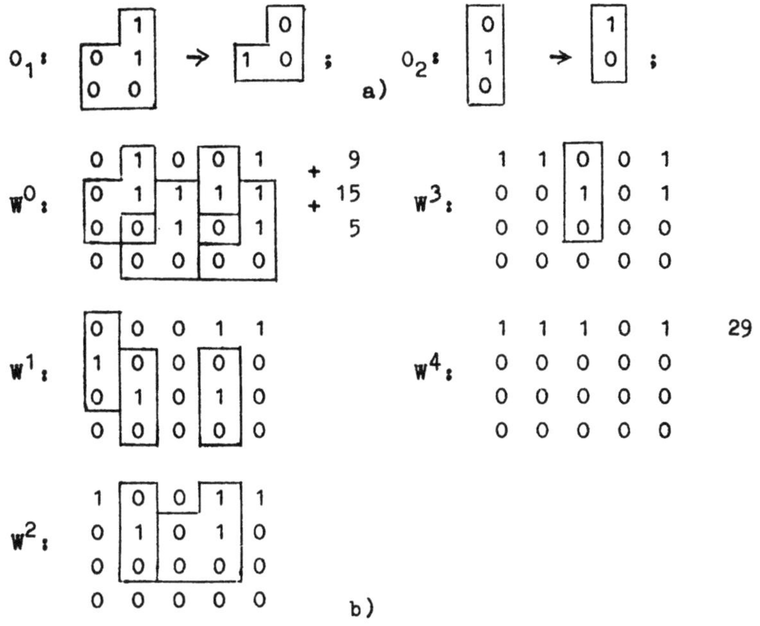

Figure 2 .

cell and building a block.

Example 7. Given $A = \{a_0, a_1\}$, $M' = \{1,2,\ldots, n\}$, where n is a certain fixed integer, and Φ containing one microinstruction

$$\{(a_1, x-1)(a_0, x)(a_1, x+1)\} * \{(a_1, x+2)\} \to \{(a_0, x-1)(a_0, x+1)\}.$$

The block structure need be defined.

The set of microoperations is of the form:

1. $\{(a_1,1)(a_0,2)(a_1,3)\} * \{(a_1,4)\} \to \{(a_0,1)(a_1,2)(a_0,3)\}$;

2. $\{(a_1,2)(a_0,3)(a_1,4)\} * \{(a_1,5)\} \to \{(a_0,2)(a_1,3)(a_0,4)\}$;

. . .

n - 2. $\{(a_1, n-3)(a_0, n-2)(a_1, n-1)\} * \{(a_1, n)\} \to$

$\{(a_0, n-3)(a_1, n-2)(a_0, n-1)\}$.

Two variants are possible.

1) Each cell is assigned one microoperation: the cell named 2 - the first microoperation, the cell named 3 - the second one, etc. A block fragment containing all the cell named 4 links is depicted in Figure 3. Figure 4 shows the block-diagram of a cell with the filled microprogram memory consisting of the two parts: part I into which the left part of

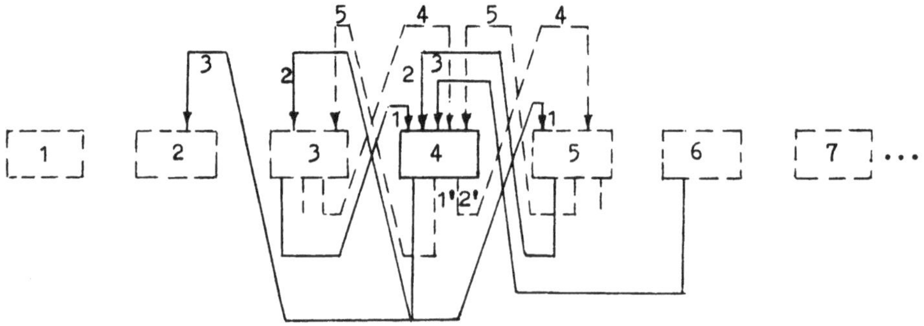

Figure 3.

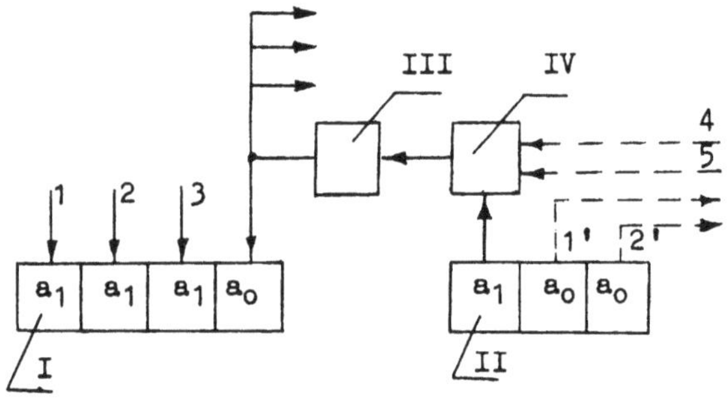

Figure 4.

the microoperation is stored and part II into which the right part of the microoperation is stored, state memory III, join gate IV. Inputs and outputs in Figures 3, 4 are indexed similarly. A cell has two types of outputs: those shown by the solid line are connected with part I of microprogram memory (comparison inputs), and those shown by the dashed line are connected with the join gate entrances (writing inputs). Cell operation is as follows. If characters at comparison inputs coincide with the corresponding characters of a line of part I of microprogram memory, the characters of the line with the same index from part II of this memory are written via join gate into memory elements of respective cells. 2) To the cell named 3, microoperations 1,2,3 are assigned; to the cell with name 6 - microoperations 4,5,6; etc. In this case, cells named 3,6,... are microprogrammed automata analogous to those obtained in the first part of the example, while cells 1,2,4,5,... are memory cells. If a microprogram contains but this type of microinstructions (with specific characters of alphabet A in first elements of pairs) like in Example 7, a cell may be regarded as a microprogram automaton with associative access to a microoperation from microoperation memory. Things get more complicated when some microinstructions of the microprogram are functional. It is necessary then, using the input vector formed by the characters at comparison inputs, to compute the first characters of the pairs in left and right sides of all these microoperations extracted from functional microinstructions, and then just to access the next microoperation. Between the two extreme cases, i.e. the completely parallel execution of all preliminary computation and the fully sequential one, is a wide range of intermediate cases. This allows compromising variants when constructing block cells from the elements of microprocessor sets, varying such parameters as the complexity of a cell implementation and the time of the next microoperation selection.

The set of cells may be divided into those computing and storing by using space-time transformations of parallel microprograms [5]. These transformations are in substituting the k-dimensional cellular array with (k-1)-dimensional array by deleting the k-th coordinate from microinstructions and inserting the microinstructions of data shift along the k-th coordinate. The parallel microprogram converted requires less hardware, making the computation process longer, which makes the optimal cost-performance ratio for the system under design easy to achieve.

3. ASYNCHRONOUS COMPOSITION OF PARALLEL MICROPROGRAMS

Asynchronous composition of parallel programs is created with the help of the language of parallel flow-chart of algorithms (hereafter flow-charts). Unlike the flow-charts algorithm language widely applied in microprogramming technology, the parallel flow-chart language includes the means of mapping the parallel processes.

A flow-chart maps the cause and effect relationship among parallel programs which are parts of the composition. It is an oriented graph having vertices of the two types: 1) operator ones further divided into functional (Φ_i), initial (B) and final (E), and 2) control subdivided into parallelizing vertices (fork and join) and branch on condition vertices (Ω, Δ) (Figure 5). Every functional vertex Φ_i has a matching parallel microprogram Φ_i executed by a block. All the other vertices and arcs define interblock links with respect to both data (information links) and control (control microprogram).

There exists information among the units executing Φ_i and Φ_j microprograms if in the flow-chart, there is a path from nodes Φ_i to node Φ_j, and name sets in Φ_i and Φ_j microprograms have a non-empty intersection, $M_i \cap M_j \neq \emptyset$. It means that computation result Φ_i is employed by microprogram Φ_j. Hence there is an information channel between blocks Φ_i and Φ_j.

A control microprogram is specified by the flow-chart structure. It is compiled as a substituting description of the Petri net simulating the development of the computing process and is called the control Petri net [6]. This net is created by replacing the nodes of a graph-scheme by the corresponding Petri net fragments (Figure 5).

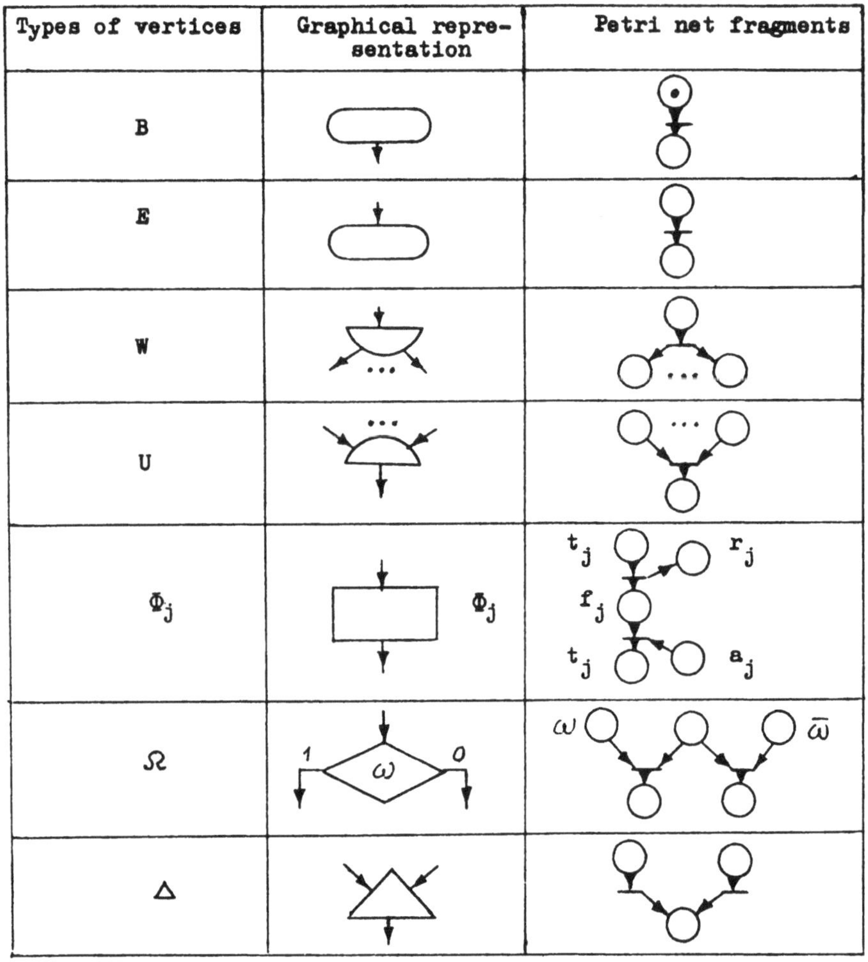

Figure 5.

Control Petri net is an oriented biohromatic graph $\langle P, T, ^{\bullet} \rangle$. Here $P = \{p_1, \ldots, p_m\}$ is a set of vertices called places and depicted by circles; $T = \{t_1, \ldots, t_n\}$ is a set of vertices called transitions and depicted by segments. The Point $^{\bullet}$ means that the incidence relation is such that $^{\bullet}t(t^{\bullet})$ is the input (output) place set to transition t, $^{\bullet}p(p^{\bullet})$ is the set of input (output) transitions to place p. The marking function is defined over set P $Q : P \rightarrow N^0$ $(N^0 = N \cup \{0\})$. If $Q(p) = 1$, they say that the place p has one marker, if $Q(p) = 0$, the place is not marked. The set $\{(Q(p_i), p_i) : i = 1, \ldots, m\}$ is called the state of the Petri net. State changes are mapped by moving marks which is governed by the following rule. If all the input places to transition t have at least one mark, the transition is enabled and can fire. In doing so, it subtracts one mark from each input place and adds one mark to each output place. Firing of transition t is defined by the microoperation of the form:

$$\theta_t: \{(\alpha_{i_1}, p_{i_1}) \cdots (\alpha_{i_k}, p_{i_k})(\alpha_{j_1}, p_{j_1}) \cdots (\alpha_{j_l}, p_{j_l})\} * \rightarrow$$

$$\{(\alpha_{i_1} - 1, p_{i_1}) \cdots (\alpha_{i_k} - 1, p_{i_k})(\alpha_{j_1} + 1, p_{j_1}) \cdots (\alpha_{j_l} + 1, p_{j_l})\},$$

where

$$\alpha_{i_g} \geqslant 1, \quad \alpha_{i_g} = Q(p_{i_g}), \quad g = 1, \ldots, k, \quad k = |{}^{\bullet}t| \ ;$$

$$\alpha_{j_h} = Q(p_{j_h}), \quad h = 1, \ldots, l, \quad l = |t^{\bullet}|.$$

The Petri net generated by substituting the fragments from Figure 5 for the flow-chart vertices satisfies the persistency conditions [7]. It means that its functioning at each step is determined, and therefore, the set of microoperations $Q(t)$ for all $t \in T$ is the parallel microprogram $\Phi_c = \{\theta_t : t \in T\}$ referred to as a control microprogram. Alphabet for Φ_c is $\{0,1\}$, and the name set is the place set P. The net state $Q = \{(Q(p), p) : p \in P\}$ is the cellular array, the initial state $Q^0 = \{(1, p_0)(0, p_i) : p_i \in P \setminus p_0\}$.

Another reason for representing the control algorithm in the form of Petri nets is that it allows the flow-chart validity test to be reduced to the Petri net analysis for safeness and liveness.

Example 8. Figures 6,7 show flow-chart of two parallel microprograms Φ_1 and Φ_2 composition and control Petri net. Microoperations corresponding to transitions t_1, t_2, t_2' appear as:

$$\theta_{t_1}: \{(1, p_1)(0, p_4)(0, p_2)\} * \rightarrow \{(0, p_1)(1, p_4)(1, p_2)\} \ ;$$

$$\theta_{t_2}: \{(1, p_2)(0, r_2)(0, f_2)\} * \rightarrow \{(0, p_2)(1, r_2)(1, f_2)\} \ ;$$

$$\theta_{t_2'}: \{(1, f_2)(1, a_2)(0, p_3)\} * \rightarrow \{(0, f_2)(0, a_2)(1, p_3)\} \ .$$

Parallel microprograms constituting the composition should be able to receive signals on computation start permitted ("start" signal) and give a signal on the result obtained ("completion" signal). It means that the cellular array of parallel microprogram Φ included into the composition should have two cells named r and a corresponding to the operator fragment places of control Petri net and therefore, belonging also to the cellular array of control microprogram Φ_c.

Let these cells in the initial cellular array W of microprogram are in the states $a = 0$, $r = 0$, i.e. $\{(0,r)(0,a)\} \subset W \cap Q^0$. When started, Φ_c microprogram replaces the cell $(0,r)$ by $(1,r)$ which is included in the contexts of all microinstructions $\theta \in \Phi$. The result of execution obtained, the cell (1,r) becomes again (0,r) and the cell (0,a) is replaced by (1,a), reporting the end of computations to the control microprogram.

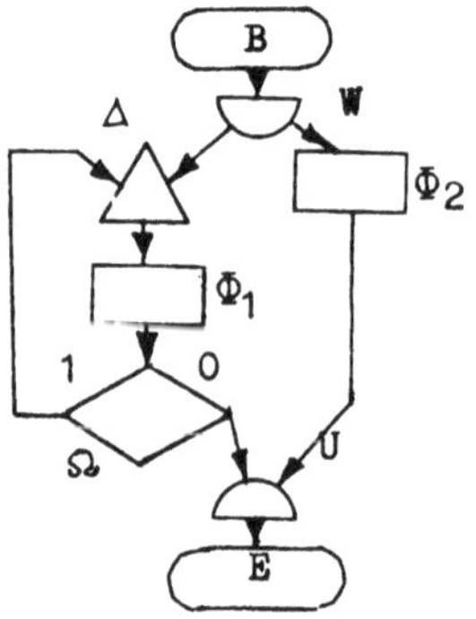

Figure 6

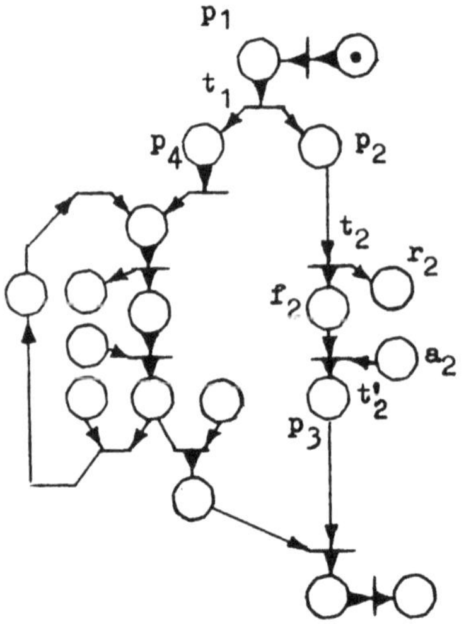

Figure 7

If cellular array W contains no cells identifiable with r and a cells from Q^0, they should be input in W together with the microinstructions signalling "completion" using any sign of the result available. Such a modification Φ is called compositional extension and the resulting microprogram is an extended one.

A common technique for generating a compositional extension of Φ microprogram is to supplement cellular array W with the subset $\{(0,r)(0,a)(0,m')(0,m'')\}$.

Each microinstruction $\theta_j \in \Phi$ of the form $S_{1j}(m) * S_{2j}(m) \rightarrow S_{3j}(m)$ is replaced by θ_j':

$$\theta_j': \{(S_{ij}(m))(0,m')\} * \{(S_{2j}(m))(1,r)\} \rightarrow \{(S_{3j}(M))(1,m')\},$$

$$j = 1,2,\dots,\nu,$$

and the three microinstructions are added

$$\theta_{\nu+1}: \{(0,m'')\} * \{(1,r)\} \rightarrow \{(1,m'')\};$$

$$\theta_{\nu+2}: \{(1,m')(1,m'')\} * \{(1,r)\} \rightarrow \{(0,m')(0,m'')\};$$

$$\theta_{\nu+3}: \{(1,m'')(0,a)(1,r)\} * \{(0,m')\} \rightarrow \{(0,m'')(1,a)(1,r)\}.$$

These three microinstructions signal completion when none of Θ_j', $j = 1,\dots,\nu$, is applicable. When $\Phi' = \{\Theta_1',\dots,\Theta_\nu',\Theta_{\nu+1},\Theta_{\nu+2},\Theta_{\nu+3}\}$ is in operation, computing microinstructions Θ_j' and the control microprogram $\Theta_{\nu+2}$ are executed alternatingly. Computation time doubles. This is due to the test performed at each step as to whether at least one microinstruction is applied. If not, $\Theta_{\nu+3}$ generates the signal (1,a).

Generating completion signal at the cost of greater time - consuming is not the best way out. Therefore, if the algorithm allows us to find another completion sign, it should be used instead of applicability test of all the microinstructions. In practice, such a possibility occurs rather often. Here are some typical cases.

1) The number of cycles necessary to obtain the result is known in advance. Then to the cellular array a cell-counter is added. The counter cell state specified is the completion sign.

2) A parallel microprogram includes the substitutions executing transfers of a data subset and is completed wheh the transfer is over. In this case, the data array transferred is supplemented by a control character not belonging to the main alphabet. If this character appears in a cell of the name specified, computation is completed.

Example 9. A known algorithm for sorting by exchanges(even-odd rearrangement [8]) is applied to the sequence $D = (d_1,d_2,\dots,d_n)$ and is executed concurrently in a linear structure incorporating n processors (Figure 8). Each processor contains d_j in its initial state. The j-th processor contents is hereafter denoted by β_j. The following transformations are performed. At each odd cycle, pairs of numbers β_{2x-1} and β_{2x} ($x = 1,\dots,[n/2]$) are compared. If $\beta_{2x-1} > \beta_{2x}$, the processors named $j = 2x - 1$ and $j = 2x$ exchange numbers. A parallel microprogram describing this computation makes the use of $M = \{1,2,\dots,n\}$ as a set of names and $A = A_0 \times A_1$ as an alphabet where $A_0 = \{\beta, \gamma, \delta\}$ is a set of characters denoting variables whose domain are integers of the bit capacity given. $A_1 = \{0,1\}$ is a control alphabet necessary to organize alternations of even and odd cycles. The following functions are used in the microprogram:

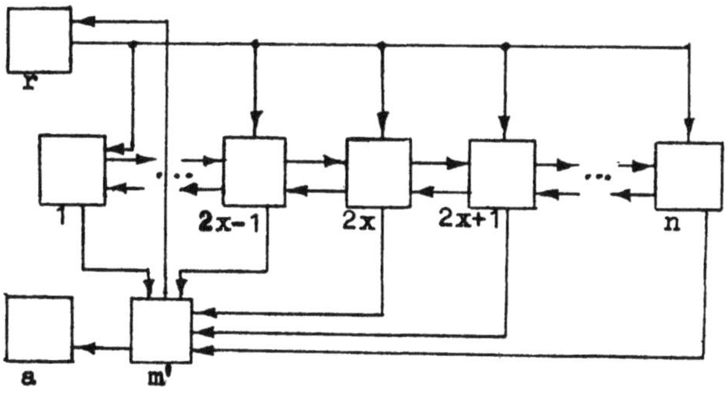

Figure 8

$$\beta \underset{1}{\sim} \gamma = \begin{cases} \gamma, & \text{if } \beta > \gamma, \\ \beta, & \text{if } \beta \leq \gamma, \end{cases} \qquad \beta \underset{2}{\sim} \gamma = \begin{cases} \beta, & \text{if } \beta > \gamma, \\ \gamma, & \text{if } \beta \leq \gamma. \end{cases}$$

The initial cellular array is

$$W = \{(\langle \beta_x, 1\rangle, x) : x = 1, \dots, n\}.$$

The parallel microprogram $\Phi = \{\theta_1, \theta_2\}$ is of the form:

$$\theta_1 : \{(\langle \beta, 1\rangle, 2x - 1)(\langle \gamma, 1\rangle, 2x\} * \rightarrow (\langle \beta \underset{1}{\sim} \gamma, 0\rangle, 2x - 1)$$
$$(\langle \beta \underset{2}{\sim} \gamma, 0\rangle, 2x)\} ;$$

$$\theta_2 : \{(\langle \beta, 0\rangle, 2x)(\langle \gamma, 0\rangle, 2x + 1)\} * \rightarrow \{(\langle \beta \underset{1}{\sim} \gamma, 1\rangle, 2x)$$
$$(\langle \beta \underset{2}{\sim} \gamma, 1\rangle, 2x + 1)\} .$$

Φ' extension of Φ parallel microprogram may be obtained in two ways.

1) Completion signal is generated following n cycles after the beginning since n cycles are sufficient to sort any number sequence of length n. Cycles are counted by the counting cell named c. The set of names M is supplemented with names of control cells and that of the counting cell $M' = M \cup \{a, r, c\}$; $A' = A \cup A_1$; $\Phi' = \{\theta_1', \theta_2', \theta_3\}$; $W' = W \cup \{(1, r)(0, a)(0, c)\}$.

$$\theta_1' : \{(\langle \beta, 1\rangle, 2x - 1)(\langle \gamma, 1\rangle, 2x)(\delta, c)\} * \{(1, r)\} \rightarrow \{(\langle \beta \underset{1}{\sim} \gamma, 0\rangle,$$
$$2x - 1)(\langle \beta \underset{2}{\sim} \gamma, 0\rangle, 2x)(\delta + 1, c)\} ;$$

$$\theta_2' : \{(\langle \beta, 0\rangle, 2x)(\langle \gamma, 0\rangle, 2x + 1)(\delta, c)\} * \{(1, r)\} \rightarrow \{(\langle \beta \underset{1}{\sim} \gamma, 1\rangle, 2x)$$
$$(\langle \beta \underset{2}{\sim} \gamma, 1\rangle, 2x + 1)(\delta + 1, c)\} ;$$

$$\theta_3 : \{(n, c)(0, a)(1, r)\} * \rightarrow \{(0, c)(1, a)(0, r)\} .$$

2) Completion signal is generated according to non-applicability as soon as exchanges are over. The function $\sigma(\beta, \gamma)$ is introduced which indicates whether exchange of numbers takes place or not:

$$\sigma(\beta, \gamma) = \begin{cases} 1, & \text{if } \beta > \gamma, \\ 0, & \text{if } \beta \leq \gamma. \end{cases}$$

The set of names is supplemented with the names of the three cells: $M' = M \cup \{a,r,m'\}$. $A' = (A \times A_1 \times A_1) \cup A_1$ is chosen as an alphabet, and the array $W' = \{(\langle \beta_1,0,1\rangle,1) \ldots (\langle \beta_n,0,1\rangle,n)(1,r)(0,a)(0,m')\}$ as the initial cellular array. In order to obtain microprogram Φ', we change microinstructions θ_1 and θ_2 from Φ and add three microinstructions θ_3, θ_4, θ_5. θ_3 and θ_4 microinstructions register the exchange. Microinstruction θ_3 increases the number stored in the cell named m' at every even cycle. Microinstruction θ_4 returns m' cell to the state 0, if at two prior cycles there was at least one exchange (in a processor $\delta(\beta,\gamma) = 1$). If there was no exchange, the cell $(2,m')$ will appear, which provides applicability of θ_5, to generate the completion signal. Φ' microprogram reads:

$$\theta_1': \{(\langle\beta,\otimes,1\rangle,2x-1)(\langle\gamma,\otimes,1\rangle,2x)\} * \{(1,r)\} \rightarrow$$

$$\rightarrow \{(\langle\beta \tilde{_1} \gamma, \delta(\beta,\gamma),0\rangle,2x-1)(\langle\beta \tilde{_2} \gamma, \delta(\beta,\gamma),0\rangle,2x)\} \;;$$

$$\theta_2': \{(\langle\beta,\otimes,0\rangle,2x)(\langle\gamma,\otimes,0\rangle,2x+1)\} * \{(1,r)\} \rightarrow$$

$$\rightarrow (\langle\beta \tilde{_1} \gamma, \delta(\beta,\gamma),1\rangle,2x)(\langle\beta \tilde{_2} \gamma, \delta(\beta,\gamma),1\rangle,2x+1)\} \;;$$

$$\theta_3: \{(\gamma,m')\} * \{(1,r)(\langle\beta,\otimes,0\rangle,1)\} \rightarrow \{(\gamma+1,m')\} \;;$$

$$\theta_4: \{(1,m')\} * \{(1,r)(\langle\beta,1,1\rangle,x)\} \rightarrow \{(0,m')\} \;;$$

$$\theta_5: \{(2,m')(0,a)(1,r)\} * \rightarrow \{(0,m')(1,a)(0,r)\} \,.$$

The structural scheme implementing Φ' is shown in Figure 8.

The set of extended microprograms $\{\Phi_1', \ldots, \Phi_q'\}$ together with the control Φ_c forms a complete microprogram description which is initial for computer-aided construction of the complete structural scheme of the system under design. The scheme is constructed in two stages. Stage 1 - structural schemes of blocks are determined; Stage 2 - information and control links between them are established. Dividing the complete microprogram into blocks depends on the control technique chosen, which is either concentrated or distributed.

Under concentrated control, the control microprogram Φ_c is implemented on a separate block. This unit is connected with all the functional blocks $\Phi_1', \ldots, \Phi_q'$ by the control links connecting the cells of the same names in Φ_c and in Φ_j'.

Under the distributed control no separate control block is available in the structural scheme. The set of instructions $\Phi_c = \{\theta_i\}$ is partitioned into q subsets: $\Phi_c = \{\Phi_c^1, \ldots, \Phi_c^q\}$ thus $\bigcup_1^q \Phi_c^j = \Phi_c$. Partitioning is performed so that the microinstructions $\theta_{t_j'}$ and $\theta_{t_j''}$ belong to Φ_c^j. Each subset Φ_c^j is assigned to Φ_j' microprogram.

As it takes place, cells corresponding to places f_j, are deleted from the microinstructions $\Theta_{t'_j}$ and $\Theta_{t''_j}$ since they duplicate the states of r_j and a_j cells in this very microprogram. Then for every $\Phi''_j = \Phi'_j \cup \Phi^j_c$ $(j = 1,\dots,q)$ a structural scheme corresponding to the block is created. Inter-block links are established according to the rules applied to inter-cell links in a block.

Conclusion

The proposed architecture design methods for problem-oriented microprocessor systems are based on the parallel type algorithmic system parallel substitution algorithms. Algorithm representation in the form of a parallel substitution system has allowed the creation of a series of formal procedures and software tools for architecture design of complicated multimicroprocessor systems. A distinguishing feature of the approach outlined is that the distributed algorithm implemented in the system is of primary importance for the system structure. Thus, design starts from the creation and debugging of an algorithmic description (parallel microprogram) and following that logical and engineering design is carried out. To implement the structural scheme both custom VLSI chips and serial microprocessor set chips may be used.

References

[1] Anishev, P.A., S.M. Achasova, O.L. Bandman, S.V. Piskunov. S.N. Sergeev (ed.by O.L. Bandman): Metody parallelnogo mikrorpogrammirovania. Novosibirsk, Nauka, 1981,180 s.

[2] Kornev,Y.N., S.V. Piskunov, S.N. Sergeev: Algoritmy obobscennyh podstanovok i ih interpretacia setiami avtomatov i odnorodnymi mashinami. Izvestia AN SSSR. Tehnicheskaia kibernetika 6 (1971), 131-142.

[3] Peterson, J.L. Petri net theory and the modeling of systems. Englewood Cliffs (N.J.): Prentice-Hall, 1981, 290 p.

[4] Sergeev, S.N.:Implementing parallel substitution algorithms in microprocessor systems. Voprosy teorii i postroenia vychislitelnyh sistem. Novosibirsk, 1978. Vypusk 73: Vychislitelnye sistemy. 25-39.

[5] Bandman, O.L.: Space and time transformations of parallel microprograms. Avtomatika i telemehanika (1988) 3.

[6] Bandman, O.L., S.V. Piskunov, S.N. Sergeev: Synthesis of parallel microprogram structures. Kibernetiks (1981) 5, 48-54.

[7] Landweber, L.H., E.L. Robertson: Properties of conflict-free and persistent Petri nets. Journal of Association for Computing Machinery. 25 (1978) 3, 352-364.

[8] Lorin, H.: Sorting and sort systems. Addison-Wesley Publishing Company, 1975, 384 p.

A Survey of Parallel Computational Geometry Algorithms[1]

by

Frank Dehne and **Jörg-Rüdiger Sack**
School of Computer Science
Carleton University
Ottawa, Ontario
Canada K1S 5B6

Abstract

We survey computational geometry algorithms developed for various models of parallel computation including the PRAM, hypercube, mesh-of-processors, linear processor array, mesh of trees, and pyramid.

1. Introduction

In this paper we survey a number of results in a recent and fast growing field of research: the design of parallel algorithms for computational geometry problems.
During recent years, computational geometry has emerged as a field of its own and generated a large number of results dealing with the computational complexity of geometric problems. Its recent offspring, parallel computational geometry, is concerned with the computational complexity of geometric problems under parallel models of computation.

There are mainly two reasons why parallel algorithms for geometric problems have become of special interest:

A steadily increasing number of parallel machines has become commercially available.

Geometric algorithms are mainly used for on-line applications where short response times are a necessity. However, these geometric applications often require large amounts of data to be processed which makes it hard to obtain reasonable response times on standard sequential computers, even if optimal algorithms can be applied.

In contrast to sequential computational geometry, there exists a variety of models which are considered for designing parallel geometry algorithms. The following are some of the most commonly used architectures which will be used throughout this paper:

(a) The parallel random access machine, PRAM (of size n): a set of n processors which are all connected to a global shared memory (Figure 1a). In the CREW PRAM model, processors are allowed to read concurrently from one memory location but may not write concurrently into it; in the CRCW PRAM model, both operations can be executed concurrently.

(b) The hypercube (of size $n = 2^d$): a set of n processors $P_0,...,P_{n-1}$ with O(1) memory space, each,

---

[1] Research supported by the Natural Sciences and Engineering Research Council of Canada.

where processors P_i and P_j are connected by a communication link if the binary representations of i and j differ in exactly one bit (Figure 1b).

(c) The mesh-of-processors (of size $n = m^2$): a set of n processors, with O(1) memory space, each, arranged in a square grid where each processor is connected to its direct neighbors (Figure 1c).

(d) The linear processor array (of size n): a set of n processors, with O(1) memory space, each, arranged in linear order where each processor is connected to its (at most two) direct neighbors (Figure 1d).

(e) The mesh of trees (of size n): a mesh-of-processors of size n and in addition, for every row and column, a tree of processor whose leaves are the processors of that row or column, respectively.

(f) the pyramid (of size n): a sequence of $k=\log_4 n$ meshes-of-processors $M_1,\ldots,M_k$ of size n, $\frac{n}{4}$, $\frac{n}{16}$, ..., 1 where every processor in M_{i+1} is connected to a quadruple of processors in M_i (Figure 1f).

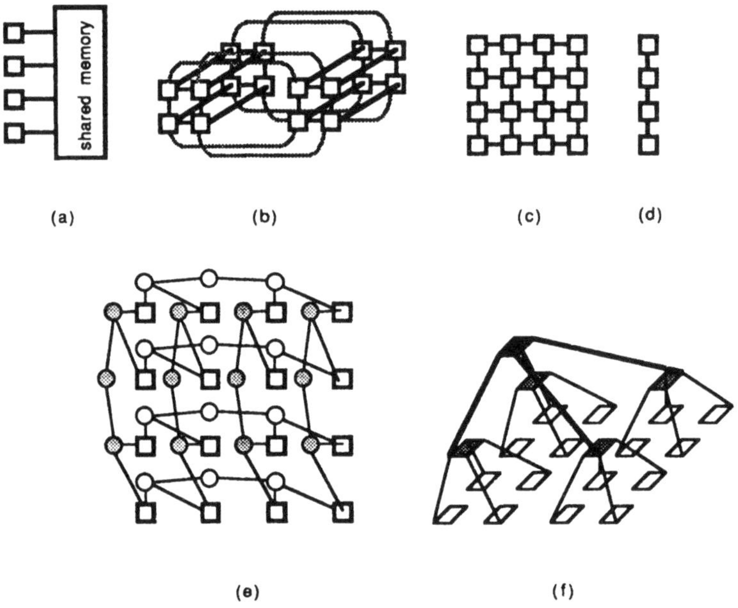

Figure 1: (a) PRAM, (b) Hypercube, (c) Mesh-of-Processors
(d) Linear Processor Array, (e) Mesh of Trees, (f) Pyramid

Since the parallel complexity of a geometric problem is best studied using the PRAM model, a large number of geometric algorithms has been designed for this model. In fact, Yap [Y87] has shown by that "most" computational geometry problems are in NC*; this result is derived by a reduction to the cell decomposition problem which is known to be in NC [KY85]. Although this theoretical result is very important, in practice it is still necessary to design parallel PRAM algorithms for the individual problem because, in general, the reduction technique does not yield optimal solutions. A number of these results will be presented in the forthcoming sections.

The major disadvantage of PRAM algorithms is, however, that even a CREW PRAM can not actually be built because it requires each individual memory cell and any combination of them to be concurrently accessible by an unbounded number of processors in constant time. In practice, a multi-processor must either be a set of processors connected by a bus system (which limits the number of processors which may be connected to the bus without degenerating performance), or a bounded degree network of processors connected by point to point communication links, or a combination of both.

This motivated the studies of parallel algorithms for other parallel models: the hypercube (this is not a bounded degree network but it can be efficiently simulated on one [PV79]), mesh-of-processors, linear processor array, mesh of trees, and the pyramid. These model resemble architectures which have actually been built, at least as a prototype. As it turns out, algorithm design on these models is more complicated than on the PRAM because a variety of data routing problems have to be solved which do not occur in the PRAM. Because of its global shared memory, the PRAM allows e.g. instant communication between any pair of processors.

Since the major reason for studying parallel architectures is a decrease of the execution time, the obvious question is, how much of a speed-up can we expect.

Clearly, a lower bound of T(n) for the sequential time complexity of a particular problem implies that, on any parallel machine with p processors, an $O(\frac{T(n)}{p})$ time algorithm is optimal. In general, poly-logarithmic time algorithms are considered efficient for parallel machines with a linear number of processors [Y87]. For processor networks, however, the lower bound for the majority of problems is the diameter D of the network. For comparing two data items stored in two processors, D time steps may be necessary to route the data from one processor to the other.

Hence, for most problems $O(\sqrt{n})$ and O(n) time solutions are optimal for the mesh-of-processors and linear processor array, respectively, and O(log n) time algorithms are optimal for the hypercube, mesh of trees, and pyramid. In this sense, the latter ones appear to be superior to the former ones. However, the mesh-of-processors and linear processor array have the major advantages that they are easy to scale and that the length of all communication links is the same and constant. For the hypercube, mesh of trees, and pyramid this is not the case; in fact, whatever geometric layout is used for building these networks, the maximum wire length increases with the number of processors. In the above computational models, however, communication time is considered to be constant between any two adjacent processors. In this sense, these models are not realistic and one can also consider other complexity models which take wire length into account [CM81], [MC80]. However, the majority of authors considers communication between adjacent processors a constant time operation which will also be done for the remainder of this paper.

In the following we will survey parallel algorithms for geometric problems which have been proposed for the parallel models listed above. The paper is sorted by geometric problems which are grouped similar to [LP84]. For each group of geometric problems, a survey of parallel algorithms is given. Section 2 surveys convex hull and related problems, Section 3 intersection problems, Section 4 proximity and geometric searching problems, Section 5 visibility problems, and Section 6 decomposition problems. It is, however, in the nature of such a survey that it is not complete. An omission of a paper is not meant to imply a judgement on the part of the authors.

2. Convex Hull

Among all problems studied in computational geometry, the determination of the convex hull has probably received the most attention in the sequential or parallel model of computation. This is due to the variety of applications this problem arises in (e.g., in robotics to approximate complex objects), as well as due to its occurrence as intermediate step when solving other computational geometry problems (e.g., in the calculation of the diameter of a set of points).

Convex hull problems have been studied for sets of points, polygons, and polyhedra, in the plane, 3-space and d-dimensional space. Variants of the problem are:

Identify Convex Hull

determine the vertices of the convex hull

Determine Convex Hull Polygon

compute the convex hull polygon for a set of points, or for a polygon, in the plane (the output is an ordered list of the convex hull vertices),

Determine Convex Hull Polyhedron

compute the convex polyhedron for a set of points, or for a polyhedron, in space.

A related problem is that of finding the *maxima* of a set in 2 (or 3) dimensions where a point p is a maximum if there is no other point in the set which has larger x, y (and z) coordinate than p. For a digitized object the set of maxima (sorted by x-coordinate) is called the 1st *contour*. The kth contour of an object S is defined recursively as:

1st contour(S) := sorted maxima of S

$k+1$ contour(S) := 1st contour(S - (1st contour(S) $\cup \dots \cup$ k^{th} contour(S)),

where the operator "-" between sets denotes the set difference.

Digitized objects are frequently described by rectilinear (orthogonal) polygons. For these objects, the notion of rectilinear convexity has been studied. A polygon is *rectilinearly convex* if any horizontal or vertical line intersects the polygon in at most one connected region. The rectilinear hull of a rectilinear polygon P is the smallest rectilinearly convex polygon containing P. We define the kth rectilinear hull analogously to contours. The following problems have been studied:

Determine Rectilinear Hull

Determine the rectilinear hull for a given object

Determine All k^{th} Rectilinear Hulls

Determine all k^{th} rectilinear hulls for a given object

On the 1-dimensional array of processors, Chazelle [C84] gives simple O(n) algorithms for both, Identify Convex Hull and Determine Convex Hull Polygon problem for sets of points in the plane. Each processor containing a point p can determine whether it is a convex hull vertex or not by computing the maximal wedge centered at p with respect to all other points. If this wedge is convex and contains all other points of the set then p is a convex hull vertex; otherwise, p is interior to the convex hull. This operation is done by propagating the point p through the array, thereby visiting each other element of the point set once and updating the wedge, if necessary, at each processor visited. All points can perform this task in parallel by a "fold-over" operation defined by Chazelle which can be seen as a row-rotation. This yields the O(n) solution to the Identify Convex Hull problem. Having solved the Identify Convex Hull problem, the Determine Convex Hull Polygon problem can be solved by sorting each of the convex hull points by polar angle around any interior point. Since sorting on a 1-dimensional array is performed in O(n) time, an O(n) solution to the Determine Convex Hull Polygon problem is derived. (For the latter problem, Chazelle describes a different approach.)

A variant of the 1-dimensional processor array, allowing cyclic shift operations among the array elements, has been introduced in [CCL87]; the convex hull algorithms derived for this model are similar to ones just discussed.

For the mesh-of-processor of size n, Miller and Stout [MS86] give $O(\sqrt{n})$ time algorithms for the convex hull problems in two dimensions. Their approach is based on the divide and conquer paradigm. They first partition the data into four roughly equal parts by sorting the points by x-coordinates and, recursively, solve the problems in each of the four regions. The remaining problem consists of merging the four hulls. To merge two disjoint convex hulls, two bridges connecting the hulls need be found. A bridge has the property that its endpoints belong to different convex hulls and that all other points of both hulls lie on the same side of the line defined by the bridge. By using a binary search on the sorted sub-list of vertices defining the two convex hulls a bridge can be found in O(log n) steps. Each step reduces the number of points to be considered by a constant factor. By using data compression after each step, the total time complexity of the algorithm becomes $O(\sqrt{n})$. An alternate $O(\sqrt{n})$ convex hull algorithm was presented in [S87].

For the mesh-of-processor architecture Dehne, Sack and Stojmenović have shown that the 3-dimensional convex hull of a set of n points in 3-space can be found in $O(\sqrt{n}\ \log(n))$ time [DSS88]. Their approach is using in addition to a divide and conquer and data compression, an efficient techniques for finding supporting planes in 3 dimensions due to [DK87].

They also noted a space/time trade-off by showing that an $O(\sqrt{n})$ algorithm can be designed for a mesh in which each processor has O(log n) extra local memory. It is open whether an $O(\sqrt{n})$ algorithm can be found for the usual mesh-of-processor architecture (i.e., each processor has only O(1) memory).

For digitized pictures, convexity is defined as follows: a digitized point set is convex iff the corresponding set of integer lattice points is convex. The following results have been obtained [MS84, KE86, DSS87].

The convex hull of a digitized point set is determined in $O(\sqrt{n})$ time on a mesh-of-processors of size n. Since for certain applications the input point set may belong to differently labeled sets, the convex hull points for each of these sets may have to be computed. This problem can also be solved in $O(\sqrt{n})$ time using a variation of the above algorithm [MS84].

Kumar and Eshaghian studied computational geometry algorithms on a mesh-of-trees os size n [KE86]. They showed that in O(log n) time the convex hull vertices of a digitized picture can be identified and enumerated. For several figures stored simultaneously on the mesh-of-trees, the convex hulls of all figures can be determined in $O(\log^4 n)$ time.

Dehne, Sack, Santoro [DSS87] have given optimal algorithms for the following problems related to convex hulls: determine all k^{th} contours and all rectilinear k-hulls of a digitized set of points. Furthermore, their results yield a parallel solution to the problem of finding all longest common subsequences of two strings. The latter result improves on the algorithm by [RT85] in that it computes all such subsequences and all processing elements are of the same type.

For the hypercube architecture few results are known, as yet:
On the Intel iPSC Miller and Miller discuss design and implementation issues for a convex hull algorithm based on the gift-wrapping principle [MM87].
In [S87] Stojmenović showed that the 2-dimensional convex hull can be determined in $O(\log^2 n)$ time by adapting the PRAM algorithm due to [AG85]. The trivial lower bound is O(log n), thus this result is not optimal. However, solving the convex hull problem takes at least as long as sorting n numbers which currently requires $O(\log^2 n)$ time. Thus, better convex hull algorithms can not be found before a better sorting algorithm has been discovered.

Many results have been obtained on the PRAM model(s). We commence our discussion with an argument due to Akl [A82] who remarked that if one allows the number of processors to be polynomial in the number of input points then a constant time algorithm can be designed to identify the convex hull vertices. The reader will probably see that $O(n^4)$ processors suffice to obtain a constant time algorithm. This is using the simple geometric argument that a point is not a convex hull vertex if it is enclosed in a triangle formed by three other points in the set. Akl reduces this bound to $O(n^3)$ [A82]. Akl also presented an optimal algorithm for computing the convex hull of n points in $O(n^{\varepsilon} \log h)$ using $O(n^{1-\varepsilon})$ processors, where h denotes the number of edges on the convex hull [A84].

It is easy to see that, using n processors, an $O(\log^2 n)$ time PRAM-algorithm can be designed by implementing the sequential divide-and-conquer algorithm in parallel (see [C80 , NMB81]).
Atallah and Goodrich presented an optimal O(log n) divide-and-conquer algorithm for determining the convex hull (polygon) of n points in the plane for the CREW-PRAM of size n [AG85]. A similar strategy was employed by [ACGDY85]. The idea is to split the point-set into $\sqrt{n}$ equal-sized subproblems and subsequently solve the subproblems recursively in parallel. The merging step consist of creating the bridges and is done by a reduction to sorting. Wagener independently solved the problem in the same time using also the divide-and-conquer paradigm [W85]; his approach is to half the problem rather than splitting it into $\sqrt{n}$ subproblems.

Wang and Tsin presented another optimal algorithm for finding the convex hull of a set of n points in 2 dimensions [WT87]. They give an algorithm for triangulating the set of points which explicitly builds the (upper) convex hull of the set. Their strategy is to partition the problem into $\sqrt{n}$ subproblems of size $\sqrt{n}$ and solve the resulting problems recursively. Each of the subproblems is triangulated and its (upper) convex hull is found. The bridges for each pair of adjacent subproblems is computed via a binary search. Each polygon formed by a bridge edge and its two chains is of a simple nature (one concave, one convex chain) which is easily triangulated.

Recently, using O(n/log n) processors, Goodrich presented an (optimal) O(log n) algorithm for determining the convex hull of n points which are sorted along some axis [G87].
In 3 dimensions, the convex hull of a set of points can be determined in $O(\log^3 n)$ time as was demonstrated in [C80, ACGDY85]. Furthermore, all 3-dimensional maxima can be determined in O(log n loglog n) time [AG86a]. The latter problem can be solved with high probability in time O(log n) [RS87]; i.e., the probability that the time is O(log n) approaches 1, for n approaching infinity.

As in the sequential model of computation several problems can be solved efficiently in parallel once the convex hull is available. Such problems include: deciding whether a point set is convex, testing whether two sets are linearly separable, finding the smallest enclosing box for a set of points, determining the diameter, supporting etc. We refer the reader to the literature discussed above.

3. Intersection Problems

Another class of geometric problems which has been thoroughly studied under the sequential model of computation deals with intersection problems for geometric objects (e.g., points, lines, rectangles, polygons). There exist two major classes of intersection problems: *intersection detection problems* are concerned with detecting whether there exists an intersection between any two elements of a given set of objects (yes/no answer), *intersection determination problems* consist of computing the intersection (e.g., reporting all intersection points between any two of several polygons).

For parallel models of computation, nearly all of the proposed algorithms solve intersection detection problems only; the major obstacle to solving intersection determination problems on parallel computers is the potential size of the output which may cause bottlenecks in storing and/or reporting the result. (Thus current parallel algorithms for intersection determination problems typically report only the size of the result.)

The intersection problems studied for parallel machine models are the following:

Line Segment Intersection Detection

detect whether any two of n given line segments intersect

Polygon Intersection Detection

detect whether two polygons (with a total of n edges) intersect

Area of Intersection for Iso-oriented Rectangles

determine the area of intersection of n iso-oriented rectangles

Iso-oriented Line Segments Intersection Counting

count the number of intersections between n horizontal or vertical line segments

For the mesh-of-processor architecture, independently, Miller and Stout [MS86], [MS87], and Jeong and Lee [JL87a], [JL87b] studied the problem of detecting whether any two of n given line segments (in the plane) intersect. The solutions are quite similar and obtain an optimal (for the mesh) $O(\sqrt{n})$ time complexity (using n processors). To achieve this bound, the set of line segments is split, by vertical lines, into a constant number of subsets of equal size for which the problem is recursively solved in parallel. The problem arising is that portions of line segments may be contained in several subsets which may increase the problem size during the recursive calls (exponentially, in the worst case). To solve this, they observe that the portions of these line segments contained in one subset can be ordered (i.e., sorted by y-coordinate). Detecting intersection among these as well as with the remaining line segments, is then easily achieved; in case no intersection occurs, these line segments are eliminated from any further consideration.

Atallah and Goodrich [AG86a] studied the line segment intersection detection problem for the PRAM model. Their solutions are based on a parallel implementation of the well known (sequential) plane sweep technique [LP84]. For this intersection problem, they obtain $O(\log^2 n)$ and $O(\log n \log \log n)$ time algorithms for the CREW (of size n) and CRCW PRAM (of size n log n), respectively.

The above algorithms lead to a variety of algorithms of the same time complexity, in particular for detecting whether any of several given polygons with a total number of n edges intersect. They also solve the problem of counting the number of intersections between n horizontal or vertical line segments in

O(log n loglog n) time [AG86a]. Other problems solved using this technique are discussed in the respective sections.

The line intersection detection problem was also studied by Chazelle [C84] for the 1-dimensional array of processors. His algorithm has a time complexity of O(n) for n processors and is based on the same "fold-over" strategy used for convex hull determination (see Section 2).

Lu, Varman [LV86] studied the problem of determining the area of intersection of n iso-oriented rectangles. For the mesh-of-processors of size n they obtain an $O(\sqrt{n})$ time solution which is based on splitting the set of rectangles into vertical slabs such that each slab contains one vertical edge of a rectangle. Within each slab the problem is solved directly (in parallel) and then the results are merged.

4 Proximity and Geometric Searching Problems

Proximity problems arise in a wide field of application such as spatial data analysis, image processing, CAD, etc. Let $S=\{s_1, ..., s_n\}$ be a set of n objects and let $d(s_i,s_j)$ denote a distance metric between objects s_i and s_j. Some typical distance-related problems which have been extensively studied for the sequential model of computation are:

Nearest Neighbor Problem for a given object s (not necessarily contained in S) find its nearest neighbor in S,

All Nearest Neighbor Problem for each $s_i \varepsilon S$ find its closest neighbor $s_j \varepsilon S-\{s_i\}$, and

Closest Pair Problem find the pair $(s_i,s_j) \varepsilon S$ which minimizes $d(s_i,s_j)$ over all index pairs i,j

Another related problem, referred to as the *minimum distance problem*, is to find for two given sets S_1 and S_2 of objects (e.g., arbitrary or convex point sets) the pair $(s_i,s_j) \varepsilon S_1 x S_2$ which minimizes $d(s_i,s_j)$.

In [MS84] and [MS86], Miller and Stout study the all nearest neighbor problem for sets of n points in the plane and derive an $O(\sqrt{n})$ upper bound for the mesh-of-processors. The main technique applied in this solution is to split the problem by four vertical lines into five subsets of equal size and recursively solve each subproblem in parallel. Then the same procedure is again executed, this time, however, using four horizontal lines. Now, every point has assigned to it the nearest neighbor with respect to its region in the 5x5 rectangular grid determined by the horizontal and vertical lines. It is easy to prove that for every region there are at most 8 points whose nearest neighbor is outside the regions and that these points are closer to one of the corner points of the region than to the nearest neighbor determined so far. These at most 25*8 points are then simply broadcast to all points.

For the 1-dimensional array of processors, Chazelle [C84] described an O(n) time algorithm for computing all nearest neighbors; it is based on the same "fold-over" strategy used for convex hull determination (see Section 2) and, essentially, compares all pairs of points.

Atallah and Goodrich [AG85] study the closest pair problem for the PRAM. They split the point set into $\sqrt{n}$ sets, of size $\sqrt{n}$, each, using vertical cut lines. For each set, the closest pair is recursively computed in parallel. Let D denote the distance between the closest of these $\sqrt{n}$ pairs. The problem is to reduce the number of vertical cut lines with distance closer than D. For this, adjacent slabs which are too small are merged first, using a similar divide-and-conquer technique (this time using horizontal cut-lines). Subsequently, these solutions are combined. The total time complexity of their algorithm, using a PRAM of size O(n), is O(log n log log n).

For the related minimum distance problem for two convex sets whose boundaries are convex polygons (the sequential time complexity of this problem is O(log n)), Atallah and Goodrich described an $O(k^{1+\varepsilon})$ time algorithm for a PRAM with $O(n^{1/k})$ processors (with arbitrary, selectable, k and arbitrarily small ε). For k=1, this yields a constant time algorithm on a linear size PRAM.
In [S87b], Stojmenovic' describes an O(log n) time hypercube solution for the same problem.

An interesting generalization of the above problems was considered by Boxer and Miller [BM87] who studied dynamic versions, where n points are moving in Euclidean space. Each coordinate of a moving point is given by a time-dependent polynomial, say of degree at most k. For such a system of moving points, they solve the dynamic one-to-all nearest neighbor problem; i.e., they compute for the time interval from zero to infinity the sequence of nearest neighbors of one of the points. The time complexity of their solution is $O(\log^2 n)$ on a PRAM consisting of $\lambda(n-1,2k)$ processors where $\lambda(n,k)$ is the number of pieces of the minimum of n polynomials of degree k (lower envelop); $\lambda(n,k)=\Omega(n)$ and $\lambda(n,k)=O(n \log^* n)$. The algorithm is based on an $O(\log^2 n)$ time parallel algorithm to compute the description of the minimum of n polynomials of degree k (i.e., the pieces of the minimum in sorted order).

The closest pair and minimum distance problems have also been studied for pixels of a digitized image of size $\sqrt{n}x\sqrt{n}$. The mesh-of-processor architecture of size n is optimally suited to such image processing tasks. For this model Miller and Stout [MS85] presented $O(\sqrt{n})$ time algorithms for (a) computing the minimum distance between sets of black pixels and (b) the maximum distance between two black pixels in each set. For the pyramid computer $O(\sqrt{n})$ and O(log n) time solutions to the closest pair problem for the set of black pixels have been developed by [D80] and [S87], respectively. [KE] presents O(log n) time mesh-of-tree algorithms for the all nearest neighbor and minimum distance problem.

Under the sequential model of computation, the nearest neighbor problem for sets of points in the plane can be solved in time O(log n) per query (with O(n log n) time preprocessing). Hence, interesting parallel solutions are hard to obtain; they should have a time complexity close to O(1).
Therefore, the computationally more expensive problem of finding for m query points their nearest neighbors among a set of n given sites has been considered; this problem will be referred to as the *multi-*

point nearest neighbor problem. For the remainder of this paper, we will assume, for simplicity, that m=n.

As in the sequential case, this problem has been solved via construction of the Voronoi diagram [LP84] for the set of sites. For the PRAM of size n, Aggarwal et al. [ACGDY85] have presented an $O(\log^2 n)$ time Voronoi diagram construction algorithm; for the mesh-of-processors an $O(\sqrt{n})$ time algorithm is described in [JL87a] and [JL87b]. Both algorithms resemble the well known sequential divide-and-conquer algorithm [SH75]. First, the point set is divided into two linearly separable subsets and, recursively, the two Voronoi diagrams are constructed for these sets. The main step is to construct the "line" at which the two Voronoi diagrams are merged. Either algorithm identifies, in parallel, those edges in the Voronoi diagrams which are intersecting the merge line; subsequently, this merge line is actually computed.

Besides its application to the nearest neighbor problem, the Voronoi diagram is an interesting structure of its own, has a lot of other applications, and generalizes to other metrics, higher orders, higher dimensions and for types of objects other than points (see e.g. [LP84]).

Assume that the Voronoi diagram has been computed as described. To solve the multi-point nearest neighbor problem, for each query point q, the Voronoi polygon containing q is to be located. This problem is a particular instance of the more general multi-point location problem: Given a planar straight-line graph defining a subdivision of the plane, determine for each query point q from a given set the region of the subdivision q falls into.
For the mesh-of-processors, the multi-point location problem (and, hence, the multi-point nearest neighbor problem) can be solved in time $O(\sqrt{n})$ [JL87a], [JL87b]. For the PRAM, Dadoun and Kirkpatrick [DK87] present a very interesting solution. They compute for any given planar subdivision, on a PRAM of size n, the well known subdivision hierarchy [Ki83] in time $O(\log n \log^* n)$ (or $O(\log n)$ expected time). The general structure of the algorithm and the final result is the same as in the sequential case [Ki83]. Once the subdivision hierarchy has been constructed, every processor can locate one point in $O(\log n)$ sequential time; hence, their methods results in a $O(\log n \log^* n)$ (or $O(\log n)$ expected) time solution to the multi-point location and multi-point nearest neighbor problem.

5. Visibility Problems

Problems dealing with the visibility of objects have been studied extensively in computer graphics, robotics and computational geometry. Different aspects of visibility problems have been considered.
Let P be a set of segments or polygonal region possibly containing holes. Two points p and q are mutually visible if the line-segment connecting them does not intersect any edges of P or of the holes (if present).

Compute Visibility Of Segments

For a set of line-segments in the plane or in 3-space, determine which (portions of) segments are visible from a given point.

Compute Visibility Between Segments

For a given set of line-segments compute all pairs of segments which are mutually visible, where two segments see each other if there exists a pair of mutually visible points, located on different segments.

This problem arises e.g. in VLSI-design for the particular instance of orthogonal line-segments.

Compute Visibility Polygon

For a polygon with or without holes determine the portion of the polygon that is visible from a given view-point p. This visibility problem arises in computer graphics as well as in robotics (e.g., in planning a shortest path for a polygonal object among polygonal obstacles). A view-point may be located either inside or outside of the polygonal region. Both of these problems are referred to as *perspective visibility problems*. The *parallel visibility problem* arises if the view-point is located at infinity. An alternate way of seeing this problem is to determine which regions of the polygonal region(s) are illuminated by a light-source located at infinity. Notice that the two models are equivalent; i.e., one can transform one problem instance into the other by applying a simple geometric transformation.

The Compute Visibility Of Segments problem for n vertical line-segments can be solved in O(log n) time on a mesh-of-trees architecture, as shown by Lodi and Pagli [LP86]. Their paper gives a detailed low-level implementation as well as an area-time (AT^2) lower bound of $\Omega(n^2 \log^2 n)$ for the visibility problem.

For the linear processor array Asano and Umeo [AU87] gave an O(n) algorithm to compute the visibility polygon from a point (or from infinity) for a polygonal region possibly containing holes. They classify each vertex v to be of one of four types, using the turns between the viewpoint, v, and the vertices adjacent to v (in the polygonal order). Based on this, a 2-stage algorithm was designed, where the first stage consists of loading the array with the vertices and determining their type, while the second stage transmits the edges checking whether there exist edges which intersect the rays from the view-point. By combining vertex-type and intersection information the visibility problem is then solved.

On the mesh-of-processors work has been done, both, in image space (i.e., for digitized objects) as well as in object space.

For a digitized set of objects stored on a mesh-of-processors of size n, the visibility polygon in the parallel model can be determined in $O(\sqrt{n})$ time [DHSS87]. They split the image into strips parallel to the direction of visibility. Through each strip, in parallel, a hole is is sent in the direction of visibility which represents the portion of the strip that is still visible from the light source. It must be ensured that at any time both (1) the size of messages sent by each processor, as well as (2) the number of messages sent or received by a processing element are bounded by a constant.

Using message passing by layers starting at the point of visibility and updating visibility wedges instead of strips, the perspective model of visibility has been solved in $O(\sqrt{n})$ time in [H88].

For polygons, possibly with holes, in object representation (i.e., each edge of the polygon or a hole is stored in one arbitrary processor) $O(\sqrt{n})$ time algorithms for both models of visibility have been presented in [D88]. For the point visibility problem (and similarly for parallel visibility), the polygon is split by rays, emanating from the view point, into sectors of equal number of vertices. For each sector the problem is solved recursively in parallel, and then the results (i.e., the portions of the visibility polygon in each sector) are merged. The merge step is obvious; however, the split step creates problems since edges that intersect a split ray have to be duplicated (one part for each adjacent sector). This may create O(n) new edges in each recursion step which would result in an over-flow of the mesh. The solution consists of several steps after each split phase which delete edges or parts of edges which are found to be invisible and, if this is not sufficient, determine a better split ray that intersects fewer edges.

As mentioned earlier, Atallah and Goodrich implemented the plane sweep technique in parallel [AG86a]. One of the applications of this technique is an O(log n log log n) algorithm for the problem Compute Visibility Of Segments on an n processor PRAM architecture.

Very recently, Dehne and Pham [DP88] presented, for the hypercube architecture, $O(\log^2 n)$ time algorithms for solving the visibility problems, in image space, in the parallel and perspective model of computation by reducing it to a generalized partial sum operation and a tree partial sum operation, respectively.

6. Decomposition Problems

Decomposition problems have been studied in pattern recognition, image analysis and robotics. The problem is to decompose an object into simpler often more meaningful components. A common task is to decompose an object into convex parts. Decompositions are obtained by adding segments inside the object. Several types of decompositions arise: *partitionings*, i.e., decompositions where no two components may overlap, and *coverings* where components may overlap. A decomposition may introduce new vertices, called *Steiner-points*, or may consist entirely of segments, called diagonals, which join only existing vertices. An example of the former category is the *trapezoidal partitioning*, where an object given as a simple polygon is to be partitioned into trapezoids such that each newly inserted segment is horizontal and incident to a vertex of the polygon. An example of a decomposition without additional vertices is the *triangulation*; i.e., the task of partitioning a simple polygon into triangles by inserting only diagonals. A triangulation of a set of points is a graph whose vertices are the points and whose edges are a maximal number of diagonals making each bounded face a triangle.

For a survey of sequential decomposition techniques the reader is referred to [KS85]. This reference deals in particular with decompositions in which some criterion is to be minimized; e.g., finding a minimum weight triangulation (where the weight is the total length of all diagonals added), or minimizing the number of convex polygons resulting from a partitioning of a simple polygon into convex pieces, etc.

The following problems have been studied in the parallel models of computation.

Trapezoidal Partitioning

Find a partitioning of the input polygon into trapezoids

Triangulate Line Segments

Find a triangulation of the input line segments which are typically assumed to intersect at most at their endpoints to include as a special case the triangulation of a polygon

Triangulate Point Set

Find a triangulation of the input point set in 2 or higher dimension

For the linear processor array, trapezoidal partitioning and triangulation of polygonal regions [AU77] and triangulation of sets of points [C84] can be performed in linear time. Trapezoidal decomposition on a mesh-of-processors of size n can be performed in $O(\sqrt{n})$ time as shown by Jeong and Lee [JL87]. Their algorithm is based on the $O(\sqrt{n})$ solution to the multi-point location problem discussed in Section 4.

As mentioned above, Atallah and Goodrich developed a parallel implementation of the sequential plane-sweep technique for the PRAM. They showed that, based on this parallel plane sweep, the problems Trapezoidal Partitioning of Polygon and Triangulate Line Segments can be solved in O(log n loglogn) time using O(n) processors and O(n log n) space. If space is restricted to O(n) then the time bound is $O(\log^2 n)$ [AG86a]. According to Yap [Y87] the O(log n loglog n) bound has been improved to O(log n) by Atallah, Cole and Goodrich. Optimal, randomized O(log n) time, parallel algorithms for triangulation and trapezoidal partitioning were given in [RS87].

An optimal PRAM algorithm for triangulating a set of points in the plane was presented by Merks [M86]. The algorithm is optimal in that it takes O(log n) time using n processors. Again, the divide and conquer paradigm of splitting the point set into $\sqrt{n}$ subproblems is applied. They first show how to reduce the problem into the simpler one of triangulating a set of points located in a triangle. Then they show how to solve this simpler problem instance. The final merge is to connect these subsolutions.

More recently, Wang and Tsin gave another algorithm for this problem [WT87]. Their approach was discussed in the section on convex hull problems and we refer the reader to that section.

ElGindy gave an $O(f(d) \log^2 n)$ time PRAM algorithm for triangulating points in d-dimensional space, where $f(d) = d^4 \log(4^d/(4^d-1))$. The number of processors used by the algorithm is O(n/log n). The algorithm is an efficient parallel implementation of the sequential algorithm proposed in [AE86]. For fixed dimensions the speed-up (product of time and number of processors) is optimal. It remains open whether optimal speed-up can be achieved using O(n) processors for dimensions d>2.

References

[ACGDY85] Aggarwal, A., B. Chazelle, L. Guibas, C. O. Dunlaing, and C. Yap, "Parallel computational geometry", *Proc. IEEE Symp. on Found. of Computer Science*, Portland, Oregon, Oct. 1985, pp. 468-477

[A82] Akl, S., "A constant-time parallel algorithm for computing convex hulls", *BIT* 22, 1982, pp. 130-134

[A84] Akl, S., "Optimal parallel algorithms for computing convex hulls and for sorting", *Computing* 33,1 11, 1984, pp. 1-11

[AG85] Atallah, M. J. and M. T. Goodrich, "Efficient parallel solutions to geometric problems" , *Proc. 1985 Int'l Conference on Parallel Processing*, Aug. 20-23, 1985, pp. 411-417

[AG86a] Atallah, M. J. and M. T. Goodrich, "Efficient plane sweeping in parallel (Preliminary Version)", *Proc. Second ACM SIGGRAPH Symposium on Computational Geometry*, Yorktown Heights, NY, June 2-4, 1986, pp. 216-225

[AG86b] Atallah, M. J. and M. T. Goodrich, "Parallel algorithms for some functions of two convex polygons", *Proc. 24th Allerton Conference on Comm., Control and Comput.*, Monticello, Ill., Oct. 1-3, 1986, pp.758-767

[AU87] Asano, T. and H. Umeo, "Systolic algorithms for computing the visibility polygon and triangulation of a polygonal region", *Proc. Int'l Workshop on Parallel Algorithms and Architectures*, Suhl, GDR, May 25-30, 1987, pp.77-85

[AE86] Avis, D. and H. ElGindy, "Triangulating simplicial points set in space: extended abstract", *Proc. ACM Symp. on Computational Geometry*, York Town Heights, 1986, pp. 133-142

[BM87] Boxer, L., R. Miller, "Parallel dynamic computational geometry", Tech. Rep. 87-11, Dept. of Computer Science, SUNY at Buffalo, Buffalo, NY, Aug. 1987

[C84] Chazelle, B. M., "Computational geometry on a systolic chip", *IEEE Trans. on Computers*, Vol. C-33, No. 9, Sept. 1984, pp.774-785

[CCL87] Chen, G.H., M.-S. Chern, and R.C.T. Lee, "A new systolic architecture for convex hull and half-plane intersection problems", *BIT* 27, 1987, pp. 141-147

[C81] Chow, A., "Parallel algorithms for geometric problems", PhD. thesis, Dept. of Computer Science, Univ. of Illinois, Urbana-Champaign, 1980

[CM81] Chazelle, B. M., L. M. Monier, "A model of computation for VLSI with related complexity results", *Proc. 13th ACM Symp. on Theory of Comp.*, 1981

[DK87] Dadoun, N., D. G. Kirkpatrick, "Parallel processing for efficient subdivision search", *Proc. Third ACM SIGGRAPH Symposium on Computational Geometry, Waterloo*, 1987, pp. 205-214

[D85b] Dehne, F., "Solving geometric problems on mesh-connected and one-dimensional processor arrays", *Proc. 11th Int'l Workshop on Graph-theoretic Concepts in Computer Science (WG'85)*, June 18-21, 1985, Schloß Schwanberg, Würzburg, W.-Germany, Trauner Verlag 1985, pp. 43-59

[D85c] Dehne, F., "A one dimensional systolic array for the largest empty rectangle problem", *Proc. 23rd Annual Allerton Conference on Comm., Control and Comput.*, Monticello, Ill., Oct. 2-4, 1985, pp. 518-524

[D86b] Dehne, F., "O(n1/2) Algorithms for the maximal elements and ECDF searching problem on a mesh-connected parallel computer", *Info. Proc. Let.* 22 , 1986, pp. 303-306, May 1986

[D87a] Dehne, F., "Computational geometry and VLSI", *1987 CompEuro Conference*, Hamburg, FRG, May 11-15, 1987, pp. 870-875

[DHSS87] Dehne, F., A.-L. Hassenclover, J.-R. Sack, and N. Santoro, "Parallel visibility on a mesh-connected parallel computer", *Int. Conference on Parallel Processing and Applications*, L'Aquila, Italy, September 23-25, 1987, pp. 173-180

[DS87c] Dehne, F. and I. Stojmenovic, "An optimal parallel solution to the ECDF searching problem for higher dimensions on a mesh-of-processors", *Proc. 25th Annual Allerton Conference on Comm., Control and Comput.*, Monticello, Ill., Sept.30-Oct.2, 1987, pp. 660-661

[DP88] Dehne, F. and Q. T. Pham, "Visibility algorithms for binary images on the hypercube and perfect-shuffle computer", to appear in *Proc. IFIP Working Conference on Parallel Processing*, Pisa, Italy, April 25-27, 1988

[DSS87] Dehne, F., J.-R. Sack, and N. Santoro, "Computing on a systolic screen: hulls, contours and applications", *Conference on Parallel Architectures and Languages Europe*, Eindhoven, The Netherlands, June 15-19, 1987

[D80] Dyer, C. R., "A fast parallel algorithm for the closest pair problem", *Info. Proc. Let.* 11:1, 1980, pp. 49-52

[E86] ElGindy, H., "A parallel algorithm for triangulating simplicial point sets in space with optimal speed-up", *Proc. 24th Annual Allerton Conference on Comm., Control and Comput.*, Monticello, Ill., Oct. 1-3, 1986

[G87] Goodrich, M., "Finding the convex hull of a sorted point set in parallel", *Info. Proc. Let.* 26 , 1987/88, pp. 173-179

[H88] Hassenklover, A.-L. "Visibility for binary images on a mesh-connected computer", Master's thesis, School of Computer Science, Carleton University, April 1988

[Ki83] Kirkpatrick, D. G., "Optimal search in planar subdivisions", *SIAM Journal of Computing* 12:1,1983, pp. 28-35

[JL87a] Jeong, C. S. and D. T. Lee, "Parallel geometric algorithms on mesh-connected computers", *Proc. IEEE Fall Joint Computer Conference*, 1987

[JL87b] Jeong, C. S. and D. T. Lee, "Parallel geometric algorithms on mesh-connected computers", Tech. Rep. 87-02-FC-01 (Revised), Technological Inst., Northwestern Univ., Evanston, Ill, 1987

[KS85] Keil, J. M. and J.-R. Sack, "Minimum decomposition of polygonal objects", in Computational Geometry, ed. G.T. Toussaint, North Holland, Amsterdam, The Netherlands, 1985

[KE86] Kumar, V. and M. Eshaghian, "Parallel geometric algorithms for digitized pictures on mesh of trees", *Proc. 1986 Int'l Conference on Parallel Processing*, St. Charles, Ill., Aug. 19-22, 1986, pp. 270-273

[KY85] Kozen, D. and C.K. Yap, "Algebraic cell decomposition in NC", *Proc. IEEE Symp. on Found. of Computer Science*, Portland, Oregon, Oct. 1985, pp. 515-521

[LP84] Lee, D.T. and F. P. Preparata, "Computational geometry - a survey", *IEEE Trans. on Computers*, Vol. C-33, No. 12, Dec. 1984, pp. 1072-1101

[LP86] Lodi, E. and L. Pagli, "A VLSI solution to the vertical segment visibility problem", *IEEE Trans. on Computers*, Vol. C-35, No. 10, Oct. 1986, pp. 923-928.

[Lu86] Lu, M. "Constructing the Voronoi diagram on a mesh-connected computer", *Proc. 1986 Int'l Conference on Parallel Processing*, St. Charles, Ill., Aug. 19-22, 1986, pp. 806-811

[LV85] Lu, M. and P. Varman, "Solving geometric proximity problems on mesh-connected computers", *Proc. 1985 IEEE Computer Society Workshop on Computer Architecture for Pattern Analysis and Image Database Management*, pp.249-255, Nov. 1985

[LV86] Lu, M. and P. Varman, "Mesh-connected computer algorithms for rectangle intersection problems", *Proc. 1986 Int'l Conference on Parallel Processing*, St. Charles, Ill., Aug. 19-22, 1986, pp. 301-307

[M86] Merks, E., "An optimal parallel algorithm for triangulating a set of points in the plane", *Int'l Journal on Parallel Programming*, Vol. 15, No. 5, 1986, pp. 399-411

[MC80] Mead, C. A. and L. A. Conway, "Introduction to VLSI Systems", Addison-Wesley, Reading, MA, 1980

[MM87] Miller, R. and S. E. Miller, "Using the hypercube to determine geometric properties of digitized pictures", *Proc. Int'l Conf. Parallel Processing*, 1987, pp. 638-640

[MS84] Miller, R. and Q. F. Stout, "Computational geometry on a mesh-connected computer", *Proc. Int.l Conf. on Parallel Processing*, 1984, pp. 66-73

[MS85] Miller, R. and Q. F. Stout, "Geometric algorithms for digitized pictures on a mesh-connected computer", *IEEE Trans. on Pattern Analysis and Machine Intelligence*, Vol. PAMI-7, No. 2, March 1985, pp 216-228

[MS86] Miller, R. and Q. F. Stout, "Mesh computer algorithms for computational geometry", Tech. Rept. 86-18, Department of Computer Science, Univ. of Buffalo, 1986

[MS87] Miller, R. and Q. F. Stout, "Mesh computer algorithms for line segments and simple polygons", *Proc. Int.l Conf. on Parallel Processing*, Aug. 1987, pp. 282-285

[NMB81] Nath, D., S. N. Maheshwari, and P.C. P. Bhatt, "Parallel algorithms for convex hull determination in two dimensions", *Conf. Analysis Problem Classes and Programming for Parallel Computing*, 1981, pp. 358-372

[PS85] Preparata, F. P. and M. I. Shamos, "Computational Geometry, An Introduction", Springer Verlag Berlin, Heidelberg, New York, Tokyo1985

[PV79] Preparata, F. P. and J. E. Vuillemin, "The cube-connected cycles: a versatile network for parallel computation", *Proc. 20th IEEE Symp. on Found. of Comp. Sci.*, 1979, pp.140-147

[RS87] Reif, J. and S. Sen, "Optimal randomized parallel algorithms for computational geometry", *Proc. Int'l Conf. Parallel Processing*, 1987, pp. 270-277

[SH75] Shamos, M. I., D. Hoey, "Closest point problems", *Proc. 16th Symp. on Foundations of Computer Science*, 1975, pp. 152-162

[St85] Stout, Q. F., "Pyramid computer solutions for the closest pair problem", *J. Algorithms*, No. 6, 1985, pp. 200-212

[S87b] Stojmenović, I. "Parallel computational geometry", Tech. Rept. CS-87-176, Computer Science, Washington State University, 1987

[TK77] Thompson, C. D. and H. T. Kung, "Sorting on a mesh-connected parallel computer", *C. ACM*, Vol. 20, No. 4, April 1977, pp. 263-271

[UL84] Ullman, J. D., "Computational Aspects of VLSI", Principles of Computer Science Series, Computer Science Press, 1984

[W85] Wagener, H., "Parallel computational geometry using polygonal order", PhD. thesis Technical University of Berlin, FRG, 1985

[WT87] Wang, C. A. and Y. H. Tsin, "An O(log n) time parallel algorithm for triangulating a set of points in the plane, *IPL* 25, 1987, pp. 55-60

[Y87] Yap, C.K., "What can be parallelized in computational geometry", *Proc. International Workshop on Parallel Algorithms and Architectures*, Suhl, GDR, May 25-30, 1987, pp. 184-195

PARALLEL MEMORIES FOR STRAIGHT LINE AND RECTANGLE ACCESS

M. Gössel [1], V. V. Kaversnev [2], B. Rebel [1]

[1] Academy of Sciences
Central Institute for Cybernetics
and Information Processes
Kurstr. 33, P.O.Box 1298
DDR - 1086 Berlin
G. D. R.

[2] Leningrad Electrotechnical
Institute "V. I. Uljanov"
Prof. Popov str. 5
SU - 197022 Leningrad
Soviet Union

Abstract. This paper deals with parallel memories for generalized straight lines and rectangles, which are useful in computer graphics and vector processing. Classical results concerning the existence of module assignment functions which are conflict-free with respect a set of generalized straight lines and rectangles are described. The problem how to determine cost-effective parallel memories for $N = 2^n$ memory modules is investigated in detail. To simplify the address computations conflict-free access for some access formats is only demanded for non-overlapping and covering placement sets.

As a surprising result it is shown that a special dyadic module assignment function (derived by a simple permutation of the bits of the module assignment function of the well-known STARAN-computer) is conflict-free with respect to rectangles (with restricted placement sets) and to horizontal and vertical straight lines, respectively.

A systematic description of all till now proposed address functions is given.

1. Introduction

In this chapter, simple examples of parallel memories are described. The basic components and notions of parallel memories are introduced at an informal level.

Figure 1a shows a picture in a two-dimensional scanning field and Figure 1b shows a parallel memory. The parallel memory consists of 4 memory modules S_0, S_1, S_2, S_3, four address computing circuits A_0, A_1, A_2, A_3 and a permutation network π.

The binary picture of Figure 1a consists of black (hatched) and white (not hatched) pixels in a (8 x 4)-scanning field R. Every pixel $(i,j) \in R$ of the scanning field is labeled with a grey value $v(i,j)$, 1 for black and 0 for white. The picture of Figure 1a is stored in the parallel memory of Figure 1b. The number $S(i,j) \in \{0,1,2,3\}$, under which the grey value $v(i,j)$ is stored within the memory module $S(i,j)$, is assigned to every scanning point $(i,j) \in R$. In this example we have

$$S(i,j) = i + 2j \mod 4, \tag{1}$$

$$a(i,j) = i/4 + 2j. \tag{2}$$

The function $S: R \longrightarrow \{0,1,2,3\}$ is called the <u>module assignment function</u>, and $a: R \longrightarrow \{0,1,\dots,7\}$ is called the <u>address function</u>. Every scanning point (i,j) in Figure 1a is marked with the values of $S(i,j)$ above $a(i,j)$. Every memory module S_0, S_1, S_2 and S_3 in Figure 1b has 8 address locations 0, 1, ..., 7. Since $v(1,1) = 1$, $S(1,1) = 3$ and $a(1,1) = 2$, the value 1 is stored in the memory module S_3 under the address location 2, labelled in Figure 1b with ∇.

Parallel memories are designed to access data in parallel in a special form, the so-called access format or window, and in a special order, determined by the access format.

The pixels (3,1), (4,1), (3,2), (4,2) represented by thick lines are an example of a quadratic access format or window $R_{2,2}(3,1)$ with the emphasized point (3,1). The pixels (6,0), (6,1), (6,2), (6,3) marked by " x " form the vertical straight line $G_v^4(6,0)$ with the emphasized point (6,0). The emphasized point is labelled with " • " .

Let us consider now the parallel access to $R_{2,2}(3,1)$. The pixels (3,1), (4,1), (3,2) and (4,2) are stored according to (1) and (2) in the memory modules $S(3,1) = 1$, $S(4,1) = 2$, $S(3,2) = 3$ and $S(4,2) = 0$ and under the address locations $a(3,1) = 2$, $a(4,1) = 3$, $a(3,2) = 4$, and the circuits A_0, A_1, A_2, A_3 have to compute the addresses 5, 2, 3 and 4, respectively. The output of the memory modules S_0, S_1, S_2, S_3 is 0, 1, 1, 0, respectively. Since the outputs of the parallel memory have to be in the order $v(3,1)$, $v(4,1)$, $v(3,2)$, $v(4,2)$ as determined by the geometric form of $R_{2,2}$, the permutation network has to execute the permutation

$$\pi((3,1),\ R_{2,2}) = \begin{pmatrix} 1 & 2 & 3 & 0 \\ 0 & 1 & 2 & 3 \end{pmatrix} . \qquad (3)$$

Parallel access to $G_v^4(6,0)$ is impossible, since $S(6,0) = S(6,2) = 2$ and $S(6,1) = S(6,3) = 0$, and $v(6,0)$ and $v(6,2)$ are both stored in memory module 2, and $v(6,1)$ and $v(6,3)$ are both stored in the memory module 0. Since only one address location of every memory module can be accessed at a time, a conflictfree access to $G_v^4(6,0)$ is impossible.

Figure 2 shows the module assignment function

$S(i,j) = (i_1 i_0) \oplus (j_0 j_1)$

for a (4 x 4)-scanning field, where $\oplus$ denotes the componentwise addition modulo 2. The access format $R_{2,2}$ can be placed without conflict at the pixels marked by x, which are called the maximal placement set $P(S,R_{2,2})_{max}$ of $R_{2,2}$.

In this example we have

$P(S,R_{2,2})_{max} = \{(0,0),(0,1),(0,2),(1,0),(1,2),(2,0),(2,1),(2,2)\}$.

The placement set

$P(S,R_{2,2}) = \{(0,0),(0,2),(2,0),(2,2)\} \subset P(S,R_{2,2})_{max}$

is a covering placement set of R, since for every $r \in R$ there exists a vector $r' \in P(S,R_{2,2})$ for $r \in R_{2,2}(r')$.

The pixel (1,1) can not be a member of any placement set.

2. Definitions and notations

In this chapter, the basic definitions, notations and concepts of parallel memories are introduced at a more formal level.

A parallel memory consists of N memory modules S_0, S_1, ..., S_{N-1}, a permutation network π and N address computing circuits A_0, A_1, ..., A_{N-1}.

If the grey values $v(r)$ of a scanning field R are stored in a parallel memory for every pixel $r \in R$, the memory module $S(r)$ and the address $a(r)$ within $S(r)$, where $v(r)$ is stored, have to be determined. Formally, the module assignment function

$$S: R \longrightarrow \{0, 1, \ldots, N-1\} \quad (4)$$

and the address function

$$a: R \longrightarrow \{0, 1, \ldots, a_{max}\} \quad (5)$$

are to be determined. The condition

$$r \neq r' \text{ implies } (S(r),a(r)) \neq (S(r'),a(r')) \quad (6)$$

has to be fulfilled. Condition (6) guarantees that different pixels of the scanning field are not stored in the same memory module under the same address.

The data are accessed in parallel in a special form, which is determined by the access format or window F. A window F is an ordered set of M vectors e^i, $i = 1, \ldots, M$ with $M \leq N$,

$$F = (e^1, e^2, \ldots, e^M), \quad e^1 = (0, \ldots, 0), \quad e^k = (e^k{}_1, \ldots, e^k{}_n) \quad (6a)$$

where $e^k{}_l$, $(l = 1, \ldots, n)$, are integers and n is the dimension of the scanning field.

For simplicity of presentation we suppose $n = 2$.

A window $F(r)$ at the scanning point r is the ordered set of pixels

$$F(r) = (r+e^1, r+e^2, \ldots, r+e^M). \quad (7)$$

The pixel $r \in R$ is called the emphasized point of $F(r)$.

In this paper we are interested in the special windows

- straight lines,
- generalized straight lines,
- rectangles parallel to the axis' of coordinates.

A window $F = (e^1, e^2, \ldots, e^M)$ is called a generalized straight line, if we have for $k = 1,2,\ldots,M$

$$e^k = (k-1)e \quad \text{for} \quad k = 1, 2, \ldots, M. \quad (8)$$

The vector e is called the defining vector of the generalized straight line. Thus, a generalized straight line consists of M pixels with constant displacements e between successive pixels. A generalized straight line is called a straight line if the coordinates e_l, $(l = 1, \ldots, n)$ of the defining vector are 1, 0 or −1. A straight line has no holes between successive pixels. A generalized straight line consisting of M pixels with the defining vector e is denoted by $G(e)^M$. If the emphasized point is r, we write $G(e)^M(r)$. Since horizontal and vertical straight lines are of special interest, we use the special notations $G_h{}^M$ and $G_v{}^M$ for these straight lines.

A rectangle parallel to the axis' of coordinates with lenghts u and v, respectively, we denote by $R_{u,v}$.

Figure 3 shows different straight lines, generalized straight lines and rectangles.

A window F(r) describes a set of data, which is needed in parallel. To access a window in parallel all the elements of the accessed window have to be stored in different memory modules.

<u>Definition 1.</u> A module assignment function $S: R \longrightarrow \{0,1,\ldots,N-1\}$ is called <u>conflict-free with respect to F(r)</u> if, for $r' \neq r''$,

$$r', r'' \in F(r) \text{ implies } S(r') \neq S(r''). \qquad (9)$$

The set of pixels where a window can be placed without conflict is called the placement set of the considered window.

<u>Definition 2</u>. Let $S: R \longrightarrow \{0, \ldots, N-1\}$ be a module assignment function and $F = (e^1, \ldots, e^M)$ a window. A set $P(S,F) \subseteq R$ for which we have

$$r \in P(S,F) \text{ implies that } F(r) \text{ is conflict-free}$$

is called a <u>placement set</u> of F with respect to S. If $P(S,F) \subseteq R$ is such a placement set of F that for all

$$r' \in R \setminus P(S,F) \text{ the set } P(S,F) \cup \{r'\}$$

is not a placement set of F, i.e. F(r') is not conflict-free for all $r' \in R \setminus P(S,F)$, then P(S,F) is called a <u>maximal placement set</u> $P(S,F)_{max}$ of F. If P(S,F) is a placement set of F such that for all $r' \in R$ there exists a pixel $r \in P(S,F)$ with $r' \in F(r)$, then P(S,F) is called a covering placement set of F.

If $r_1, r_2 \in P(S,F)$, $r_1 \neq r_2$ implies $F(r_1) \cap F(r_2) = \emptyset$ then $P(S,F)$ is called non-overlapping placement set of F.

Conclusion 1. A module assignment function S is called conflict-free with respect to F if $P(S,F)_{max} = R$.

Definition 3. A module assignment function is called conflict-free with respect to a set $\underline{F} = \{F_1, F_2, \ldots, F_L\}$ of windows, if it is conflict-free with respect to every $F_i \in \underline{F}$.

For the address function $a: R \longrightarrow \{0, 1, \ldots, a_{max}\}$ condition (6) has to be valid. For a given module assignment function a lot of different address functions are possible, but all published address functions are of a special type, which we call $\underline{F}$-regular.

Definition 4. Let $S: R \longrightarrow \{0, 1, \ldots, N-1\}$ be a module assignment function, $F = (e^1, e^2, \ldots, e^M)$, $(M \leq N)$ a window and $P(S,F)$ a covering and non-overlapping placement set of F. Then an address function $a: R \longrightarrow \{0, 1, \ldots, a_{max}\}$ is called F-regular, if

$$r_1, r_2 \in F(r) \text{ and } r \in P(S,F) \text{ implies } a(r_1) = a(r_2), \qquad (10)$$

and

$$a(r) \neq a(r') \text{ for } r, r' \in P(S,F) \text{ and } r \neq r'. \qquad (11)$$

Examples.

a. For the scanning field $R = \{(i,j) \mid 0 \leq i,j < 1024\}$ and the module assignment function $S(i,j) = i + 4j \bmod 16$, the address functions

$$a_1(i,j) = i/16 + 64j \quad \text{and} \quad a_2(i,j) = i/4 + 256\,(j/4)$$

are F_1- and F_2-regular, respectively, with

$$F_1 = G_h^{16}, \quad P_1(S,F_1) = \{(i,j) \in R \text{ with } i \bmod 16 = 0\},$$

$$F_2 = R_{4,4}, \quad P_2(S,F_2) = \{(i,j) \in R \text{ with } i \bmod 4 = 0,\ j \bmod 4 = 0\}.$$

b. For the scanning field $R = \{(i,j),\ 0 \leq i,j < 10\}$ and the module assignment function $S(i,j) = i + 3j \bmod 5$ the address functions

$$a_3(i,j) = i/4 + 3j \quad \text{and} \quad a_4(i,j) = (i+10j) \bmod 20$$

are F_3- and F_4-regular, respectively, with

$$F_3 = G_h^{\,4}, \qquad P_3(S,F_3) = \{(i,j) \in R \text{ with } i \bmod 4 = 0\},$$

$$F_4 = G(0,2)^5, \; P_4(S,F_4) = \{(i,j) \in R \text{ with } 0 < j < 1\}.$$

In the case of a_3 some address space of every memory module is wasted. The window F_4 is a generalized straight line and the address function a_4 and the module assignment function S are both linear functions.

For a given window $F = (e^1,\dots,e^M)$ with $M = N$ the permutation network $\pi(N)$ of a parallel memory has to execute the set π of permutations

$$\pi = \left\{ \begin{pmatrix} S(r) & S(r+e^2) & \dots & S(r+e^N) \\ 0 & 1 & \dots & N-1 \end{pmatrix} , \; r \in R \right\}. \tag{12}$$

If we have $M < N$, the permutations are partially determined. The permutation network guarantees that the output of data is in an order determined by position within the accessed window, which is independent on the position of the emphasized scanning point.

The architecture of a parallel memory is mainly influenced by the choice of the module assignment function and the address function from special classes of functions.

The most important classes of module assignment functions are linear, dyadic, isotropic and periodic functions. Address functions are F-regular for some simple window F in all known applications.

At the end of this chapter a short explanation of different classes of functions is given. We suppose the module assignment function S to be $S\colon\; R \longrightarrow \{0,\; 1,\; \dots,\; N-1\}$ and $R = \{(i,j);\; 0 \leq i < L_i,\; 0 \leq j < L_j\}$. L_i and L_j are the lengths of the scanning field axis', respectively.

<u>a.) Linear functions.</u> S is called linear if we have

$$S(i,j) = ai + bj \bmod N, \tag{13}$$

used for example in [1-3].

<u>b.) Dyadic functions.</u> S is called a simple dyadic function if we have

$$S(i,j) = (i \bmod N) \oplus p(j \bmod N), \qquad (14)$$

where $\oplus$ denotes the componentwise addition modulo 2 of the binary representations of $(i \bmod N)$ and $p(j \bmod N)$, and

$$p(j \bmod N) = j_{p(n-1)} \cdots j_{p(0)}$$

is a permutation of the bits of $(j \bmod N)$. Such type of functions is used e.g. in [4-6,29,30].

c.) Isotropic functions. S is called isotropic [7,8] if we have

$$S(i,j) = S(i',j') \text{ implies } S(i \pm 1,j) = S(i' \pm 1,j') \text{ and } S(i,j \pm 1) = S(i',j' \pm 1). \qquad (15)$$

d.) Periodic functions. S is called (n_1,n_2)-periodic if we have

$$S(i,j) = S(i+m_1 n_1,\ j+m_2 n_2) \qquad (16)$$

for all $(i,j) \in R$, where m_1 and m_2 are arbitrary integers. For a more general definition see e.g. [9,10].

3. Results.

In this chapter we present results concerning the possibilities of conflict-free access to sets of generalized straight lines and rectangles and discuss the feasibilities for address computations and permutations. The conditions under which a module assignment function S, which is conflict-free with respect to a set of generalized straight lines exists, are essentially contained in [2,3].

We describe these results in the following Theorems.

Theorem 1. There exists an (N,N)-periodic module assignment function $S: R \longrightarrow \{0, \ldots, N-1\}$ which is conflict-free with respect to a set $\underline{F} = \{G_1, G_2, \ldots, G_k\}$ of generalized straight lines, each of them consisting of N pixels, if and only if there exists a linear module assignment function which is conflict-free with respect to F.

For the proof see [2].

Lemma 2. Let $S: R \longrightarrow \{0, \ldots, N-1\}$ be conflict-free with respect to $G_h{}^N$. Then we have

$S(i+N,j) = S(i,j)$ for $(i,j) \in R$. (18)

Proof. Since S is conflict-free with respect to $G_h^N \in (i,j)$, all the values $S(i,j)$, $S(i+1,j)$, ..., $S(i+N-1,j)$ are mutually different. Since S is also conflict-free with respect to $G_h^N \in (i+1,j)$, the values $S(i+1,j)$, $S(i+2,j)$, ..., $S(i+N,j)$, too, have to be mutually different and we conclude $S(i+N,j) = S(i,j)$.

Lemma 3. Let $S: R \text{ ---> } \{0, \ldots, N-1\}$ be conflict-free with respect to $F = \{G_h^N, G_v^N\}$. Then S is (N,N)-periodic.

Theorem 4. There exists a module assignment function $S: R \text{ ---> } \{0, 1, \ldots, N-1)\}$ which is conflict-free with respect to $\underline{F} = \{G_h^N, G_v^N, G_1, \ldots, G_k\}$ if and only if there exists a linear module assignment function which is conflict-free with respect to F.

Proof. Theorem 4 immediately follows from Theorem 1 and Lemma 3. Since linear module assignment functions can be characterized by two (or n) parameters (for n dimensional scanning fields) it is relatively simple to determine for a given set F of straight lines whether there is a linear module assignment function that is conflict-free with respect to $\underline{F}$, or not. Some papers are concerned with this problem. We mention here [1,2,11].

For a linear module assignment function conflict-free access to generalized straight lines is determined by elementary number theory. As a typical example of such results we present here

Theorem 5. Let $S(i,j) = ai + bj \bmod N$ and let $G(e)^N$ with $e = (e_1,e_2)$ a generalized straight line. Then S is conflict-free with respect to N, iff $S(e) = ae_1 + be_2 \bmod N$ and N have no common factor $\neq 1$.

Proof. The values $S(r)$, $S(r+e) = S(r) + S(e) \bmod N$, ..., $S(r+(N-1)e) = S(r) + (N-1)e \bmod N$ are mutually different, iff $S(e)$ and N have no common factor $\neq 1$.

From a theoretical point of view it seems to be reasonable to choose N as a prime.

Now we discuss the address computation for parallel memories which are conflict-free with respect to generalized straight lines.

Let S be linear and conflict-free with respect to $G(e)^N$.

Defining $r_P \in R$ by $r_P \in G(e)^N(r)$ and

$$S(r_P) = P, \tag{19}$$

we conclude with

$$r_P = r + m_P e, \tag{20}$$

that $\quad P = S(r) + m_P S(e) \bmod N$

and with $S(e)S(e)^{-1} \bmod N = 1$

that

$$m_P = (P-S)\, S(e)^{-1} \bmod N. \tag{21}$$

If we access $G(e)^N(r)$, the pixel r_P of this generalized straight line stored in the memory module P is determined by (20) and (21). Therefore the address computer A_P of Figure 1b has to compute

$$a(r_P) = a(r + (P - S(r))\, S(e)^{-1}) \bmod N) \tag{22}$$

and the permutation network π has to execute the permutation

$$\pi\,(r, G(e)^N) = \begin{pmatrix} S(r) & S(r)+S(e) & \dots & S(r)+(N-1)S(e) \\ 0 & 1 & \dots & N-1 \end{pmatrix}, \tag{23}$$

where the additions and multiplications in (23-25) are taken modulo N. With $S(e) = d$ and $S(r) = S$ the permutation (23) can be decomposed into $\tau_d \cdot \sigma_s$ where

$$\tau_d = \begin{pmatrix} 0 & d & 2d & \dots & (N-1)d \\ 0 & 1 & 2 & \dots & N-1 \end{pmatrix} \tag{24}$$

and

$$\sigma_s = \begin{pmatrix} S & S+1 & \dots & S+N-1 \\ 0 & 1 & \dots & N-1 \end{pmatrix}. \tag{25}$$

The analytical representation of (24) and (25) is

$$\mathcal{T}_d(v) = v\ d^{-1} \bmod N \qquad (26)$$

and

$$\sigma_s(u) = u - S \bmod N, \qquad (27)$$

respectively.

$\sigma_s(u)$ describes a cyclic shifting. According to (26) the value v is multiplied by d^{-1}. For N prime, the multiplication modulo N is isomorph to the addition modulo N-1. Therefore, even (24) can be realized as a cyclical shifting modulo N-1 and an additional line for the input 0, which is directly connected to the output 0.

Since barrel-shifters are now commercially available up to 16 inputs and 16 outputs [12] and since it is possible to realize barrel shifters with a desired number of inputs and outputs by use of available barrel shifters, the design of the needed permutation networks is now a real possibility.

As we have seen, there are good theoretic reasons to choose N as a prime number. But the modulo N operation in (22) is relatively expensive and time consuming if N is a prime number.

The papers [13-17] are concerned with the problem of designing prime memory systems. Some number-theoretical results for $N = 2^n \pm 1$ as described e.g. in [18] can be used, but the corresponding implementations are relatively costly.

The most simple modulo N operation we have for $N = 2^n$, but the possibilities for conflict-free access are very restricted. So it is easy to show that there is no conflict-free access to G_h^N, G_v^N and the diagonals $G(1,1)^N$ or $G(-1,1)^N$, respectively.

For N = 2, in [19] the nonlinear module assignment function

$$S(i,j) = (i + L_i j + a(i + L_i j)/N + b((i + L_i j)/N)/N \bmod N, \qquad (28)$$

where L_i is the length of the scanning field in i-direction, is proposed in [19]. The divisions and modulo operations are simple since N is a power of two. But the lengths of the straight lines and generalized straight lines which can be accessed without conflict are less than N and they are of variable size, depending on the direction and the emphasized point of the accessed line.

In [19] the number of memory modules is much greater than the number of processors: Instead of a permutation network, a routing network is used. The processors request a desired memory module and an address within the requested memory module.

The next simple exampe is of theoretical interest.

For $N = 4$ the Figure 4 shows a periodic nonlinear module assignment function which is conflict-free with respect to G_h^N and G_v^N and which has the maximal placement sets

$$P(S,G(1,1)^4) = \{(i,j) \in R \text{ with } (i+j) \bmod 2 = 0\} \quad (29)$$

$$P(S,G(-1,1)^4) = \{(i,j) \in R \text{ with } (i+j) \bmod 2 = 1\} \quad (30)$$

for the diagonals $G(1,1)^4$ and $G(-1,1)^4$, respectively.

It is easy to show that there is no linear module assignment function $S(i,j) = ai + bj \bmod 4$ which is conflict-free with respect to G_h^4, G_v^4 and which has the placement sets (28) and (29) for $G(1,1)^4$ and $G(-1,1)^4$, respectively. This example, described in [20] shows that there is no corresponding theorem to Theorem 1 if $P(S,G)_{max} \neq R$ for some generalized straight line G. But this example is no "counter-example" to Theorem 1 as claimed in [20].

An ingenious solution for word- and bit-access to N words of N bits where $N = 2^n$ is given in [4] and known as the memory of the STARAN-computer.

Bit i of the word j is stored in memory module

$$S(i,j) = i \oplus j \quad (31)$$

under the address

$$a(i,j) = i \quad \text{with } 0 \leq i,j < 2^n. \quad (32)$$

The operation $\oplus$ denotes the componentwise addition modulo 2 of the binary representations of i and j. We interprete this memory as a two-dimensional memory for a scanning field. The placement sets for word-

access G_h^N and bit-access G_v^N
are

$$P(S,G_h^N) = \{(0,j) \mid j = 0, \ldots, 2^n - 1\} \tag{33}$$

and

$$P(S,G_v^N) = \{(i,0) \mid i = 0, \ldots, 2^n - 1\}, \tag{34}$$

respectively.

If we access $G_h^N(0,j)$ (word access), then we have for the pixel $r_P \in G_h^N(0,j)$, which is stored in the memory module $S(r_P) = P$,

$$r_P = (i_P, j)$$

$$P = S(r_P) = i_P \oplus j$$

and, therefore,

$$i_P = P \oplus j. \tag{35}$$

Since the address of (i_P,j) is determined by (32), the address of the memory module P for word-access $G_h^N(0,j)$ is

$$a(i_P,j) = P \oplus j, \tag{36}$$

and the address computation (36) is without any carry bit. If we access $G_v^N(i,0)$ (bit access), the address for every memory module is i. For details and other possible access formats see [4,21,30].

Now we discuss the possibilities to access rectangles together with horizontal and vertical straight lines. This problem is of interest for raster graphics and image processing.

The following results are obvious.

For $N = pq$ the module assignment function

$$S(i,j) = i + pj \bmod N \tag{37}$$

is conflict-free with respect to G_h^N and $R_{p,q}$.

For $M = pq + 1$ the module assignment function

$$S(i,j) = i + pj \bmod M \tag{38}$$

is conflict-free with respect to G_h^M, G_v^M and $R_{p,q}$ (p and M have no common factor $\neq 1$). Corresponding parallel memories are described in [22-24].

For $M = pq + 1$ the address computation is relatively expensive. For practical applications the case $N = 2^n$ is essential. However, the following theorem shows that in this case conflict-free access to G_h^N, G_v^N and $R_{p,q}$, $N = pq$, is impossible.

Theorem 6. Let $N = pq$, then there does not exist a module assignment function $S: R \longrightarrow \{0, 1, \ldots, N-1\}$ which is conflict-free with respect to G_h^N, G_v^N and $R_{p,q}$.

Proof. For simplicity we prove Theorem 6 for $p = q = 4$. The idea of the proof is illustrated in Figure 5. We suppose that S is conflict-free with respect to G_h^N, G_v^N and $R_{p,q}$. Let $S(0,0) = 0$. Since S is conflict-free with respect to $G_h^N(0,0)$ and $G_v^N(0,0)$, we have $S(4,0) \neq 0$ and $S(0,4) \neq 0$. Since S is conflict-free with respect to $R_{4,4}(1,0)$ and $R_{4,4}(0,1)$, we conclude

$$(a = 0) \vee (b = 0) \vee (c = 0)$$

and

$$(d = 0) \vee (e = 0) \vee (f = 0),$$

and S is not conflict-free with respect to $R_{4,4}(1,1)$.

Different attempts have been made to overcome this difficulty by restricting the placement set $P(S, R_{p,q})$ of $R_{p,q}$.

As a very surprising result we consider the dyadic solution for $p = q = 2$, $N = 2^{2n}$ in [5].

Denoting

$$I = i \bmod N = i_{2n-1} \ldots i_0,$$

$$J = j \bmod N = j_{2n-1} \ldots j_0,$$

$$SWAP(J) = j_{n-1} \ldots j_0 \, j_{2n-1} \ldots j_n, \tag{39}$$

the module assignment function S is

$$S(i,j) = SWAP(J) \oplus I. \tag{40}$$

For the different windows G_h^N, G_v^N and $R_{m,n}$ with $m = 2^n$ we consider the non-overlapping and covering placement sets

$$P(S, G_h^N) = \{(i,j) \in R \text{ with } I = 0\},$$

$P(S,G_v^N) = \{(i,j) \in R \text{ with } J = 0\}$,

$P(S,R_{m,m}) = \{(i,j) \in R \text{ with } i \bmod 2^n = 0 \text{ and } j \bmod 2^n = 0\}$. (41)

It is easy to show that $S(i,j)$ as defined in (40) is conflict-free with respect to $F(r)$, $r \in P(S,F)$ for $F = G_h^N$, G_v^N, $R_{m,m}$, respectively. If the address function $a(i,j)$ is defined by

$$a(i,j) = i/2^n + (j/2^n)(L_i/2^n) \quad (42)$$

where L_i is the dimension of the scanning field in the i-direction then $a(i,j)$ is $R_{m,m}$-regular. If we access $R_{m,m}(i,j)$ with $(i,j) \in P(S,R_{m,m})$ the address for every memory module is $a(i,j)$.

If we access $G_h^N(i,j)$, $(i,j) \in P(S,G_h^N)$ we have $I = 0$.

For the pixel $r_P \in G_h^N(i,j)$ stored in the memory module P we conclude

$$r_P = (i,j) \oplus (i_P,0),$$
$$P = S(r_P) = i_P \oplus \mathrm{SWAP}(J), \quad (43)$$
$$i_P = P \oplus \mathrm{SWAP}(J).$$

Because of $I = 0$ we have

$$a(r_P) = a(i,j) + (P \oplus \mathrm{SWAP}(J)) / 2^n. \quad (44)$$

If we access $G_v^N(i,j)$, $(i,j) \in P(S,G_v^N)$, we have $J = 0$.

In this case we conclude for the pixel $r_P \in G_v^N(i,j)$ stored in the memory module P

$$r_P = (i,j) + (0,j_P),$$
$$P = S(r_P) = i \oplus \mathrm{SWAP}(j_P), \quad (45)$$
$$j_P = \mathrm{SWAP}(P \oplus i)$$

and, finally,

$$a(r_P) = a(i,j) + (L_i/2^n)\, \mathrm{SWAP}(P \oplus i). \quad (46)$$

The additions in (44) and (46) are without carry bits. Hence, the implementation of the address computing circuits is almost as simple as in the case of the STARAN-computer.

For $n = 2$, i.e. for $N = 16$, the module assignment function S defined by (40) is shown in Figure 6. Conflict-free access to different regular lattices is also possible. The permutation network is simple. However, it is impossible to place $R_{m,m}$ or even $R_{m-1,m-1}$ at arbitrary places. So we have $S(7,8) = S(8,7) = 5$ for $n = 2$. For details see [6,21]. Some further investigations in this field are of interest, too. For $N = 2^m$ conflict-free access to G_h^N, G_v^N and $R_{r,s}$ with $r = 2^{m-p}$, $s = 2^p$ and $P(S,R_{r,s}) = \{(i,j) \in R \text{ with } i \bmod r = 0\}$ by use of so-called special diamond schemes is investigated in [25]. For $N = 2^{2n}$ the module assignment functions

$$S_1(i,j) = (\mathrm{SWAP}(J) + 2^n \mathrm{MSB}(J) + I) \bmod N, \tag{47}$$

and S_2 with

$$\left.\begin{aligned} \mathrm{MSB}(S_2(i,j)) &= \mathrm{LSB}(J) + \mathrm{MSB}(I) \bmod 2^n, \\ \mathrm{LSB}(S_2(i,j)) &= \mathrm{LSB}(I) - \mathrm{MSB}(J) \bmod 2^n \end{aligned}\right. \tag{48}$$

and

$$\mathrm{LSB}(J) = J \bmod 2^n, \quad \mathrm{MSB}(J) = J/2^n$$

are investigated in [26]. MSB and LSB are the n most significant bits and the n least significant bits, respectively. These module assignment functions are conflict-free with respect to G_h^N, G_v^N, $R_{m-1,m-1}$ and to $R_{m,m}$, respectively, with the placement set

$$P(S,R_{m,m}) = \begin{cases} \{(i,j) \in R \text{ with } i \bmod 2^n = 0\} & \text{for } S_1, \\ \{(i,j) \in R \text{ with } (i \bmod 2^n = 0) \vee (j \bmod 2^n = 0)\} & \text{for } S_2. \end{cases}$$

Finally, we mention the theoretically interesting results of [27], which are based on the ideas of [28], where the possibilities of conflict-free access to all rectangles consisting of less than M pixels and to G_h^N and G_v^N are studied with the result that N has to be approximately $\sqrt{5} \cdot M$. Since $\sqrt{5}$ is relatively large these results are of theoretical interest only.

We thank R. Creutzburg for stimulating discussions and for the assistence during the preparation of this paper.

References.

[1] Budnik, P., and D. J. Kuck: The organization and use of parallel memories. IEEE Trans. Comp. C-20, 1566-1569, (1971)

[2] Shapiro, D. H.: Theoretical limitations on the use of parallel memories. Ph. D. Thesis, Dept. Comput. Sience, Univ. Illinois Urbana-Champain, Report No. UIUCDCS-R-75-776, (1975)

[3] Shapiro, D. H.: Theoretical limitations on the efficient use of parallel memories, MEE Trans. Computers C-27, 421-428, (1978)

[4] Batcher, K. E.: Multidimensional access solid state memory. US Patent 3 800 289, G 06 F 9/20, (1972, 1974)

[5] Kaversnev, V. V., and E. A. Metzlitzky: Memory with different access formats. SU Patent 10 437 747, G 11 C 11/34, (1981,1983)

[6] Kaversnev, V. V.: Design and investigation of memories with parallel access to different access formats (in russ.). Ph. D. Thesis, LETI Leningrad, (1985)

[7] Rebel, B., and M. Gössel: Ein paralleler Speicher. Report, ZKI Berlin, 1982

[8] Gössel, M., and B. Rebel: Flexible processor array with parallel memory, Proc. PARCELLA'84, (Berlin), (in: Mathematical Research 25, Eds.: Händler, Legendi and Wolf), 33-43, (1985)

[9] Gössel, M., B. Rebel, and R. Creutzburg. Speicherarchitektur und Parallelzugriff, Berlin, 1989.

[10] Wijshoff, H. A. G., and J. van Leeuwen: The structure of periodic storage for parallel memories. IEEE Trans. Comp. C-34, 501-505, (1985)

[11] Wijshoff, H. A. G., and J. van Leeuwen: On linear skewing schemes and d-ordered vectors. IEEE Trans. Comp. C-36, 233-239, (1987)

[12] Schräder, K.: Schnellste Daten-Bit-Multiplikationen mit Barrel-Shiftern. Elektronik 6, 65-71 (1986)

[13] Lawrie, D. H., and C. R. Vora: Multidimensional parallel access computer memory system. US Patent 4 051 551, G 06 F 15/16 (1976, 1977)

[14] Lawrie, D. H.: Access and alignment of data in an array processor. IEEE Trans. Computers C-24, 1145-1155, (1975)

[15] Lawrie, D. H., and C. R. Vora: The prime memory for array access, IEEE Trans. Computers C-31, 435-442, (1982)

[16] Ranade, A. G.: Interconnection networks and parallel memory organizations for array processing. Proc.. 1985 Int. Conf. Parallel Processing, 41-47

[17] Gössel, M., and B. Rebel: Parallel memory with recursive address computation. Proc. Parallel Computing'83, (Ed.: Feilmeier, Elsevier: Amsterdam 1984), 515-520

[18] McClellan, J. H., and C. M. Rader: Number Theory in Digital Signal Processing. Prentice Hall: Hempstead (NJ), 1979

[19] Tomlinson, C. J.: Parallel access computer memory system employing a power of-two memory modules. US Patent 4 400 768, G 06 F 15/16 (1980, 1983)

[20] Deb, A.: Conflict-free access of arrays - a counter-example. Inf. Proc. Letters 10, 20, (1980)

[21] Kaversnev, V. V., and E. A. Metlitzky: Parallel memories (in russ.) Leningrad 1989 (in print)

[22] Morrin, T. H., and D. C. Voorhis: Method and apparatus for accessing horizontal sequences and rectangular subarrays from an array stored in modified word organized random access memory system. US Patent 3 938 102, G 06 F 15/20, (1974,1976)

[23] Voorhis, D. C., and T. H. Morrin: Memory systems for image processing. IEEE Trans. Comp. C-27, 113-125, (1978)

[24] Park, J. W.: An efficient memory system for image processing. IEEE Trans. Comp. C-35, 669-674 (1986)

[25] Jalby, W., J. Frailong and J. Lenfant: Diamond Schemes - An organization of parallel memories for efficient array processing. Rapports de Recherche, No. 342, INRIA, Centre de Rocquencourt (France), 1984
[26] Pöschel, R., M. Gössel and D. Powollik: Organization of a high resolution raster graphics memory with $N = 2^{2n}$ memory modules. Journal New Generation Computer Systems 1, 145-156 (1988)
[27] Chor, B., C. E. Leiserson, R. L. Rivest and J. B. Shearer: An application of number theory to the organization of raster graphics memory. Journal ACM 33, 86-104 (1986)
[28] Gupta, S.: Architectures and algorithms for parallel updates of raster scan displays. Ph. D. Thesis. Carnegie-Mellon Univ. 1981
[29] Shirakawa, H. and T. Kumagai: An organization of a three-dimensional access memory. Proc. 1980 Int. Conf. Parallel Processing, 137-138
[30] Shirakawa, H. and T. Kumagai: Structure of a three-dimensional access memory system. Memoirs Res. Inst. Science Engineering, Ritsumeikan Univ. Kyoto 41, 27-50 (1983)

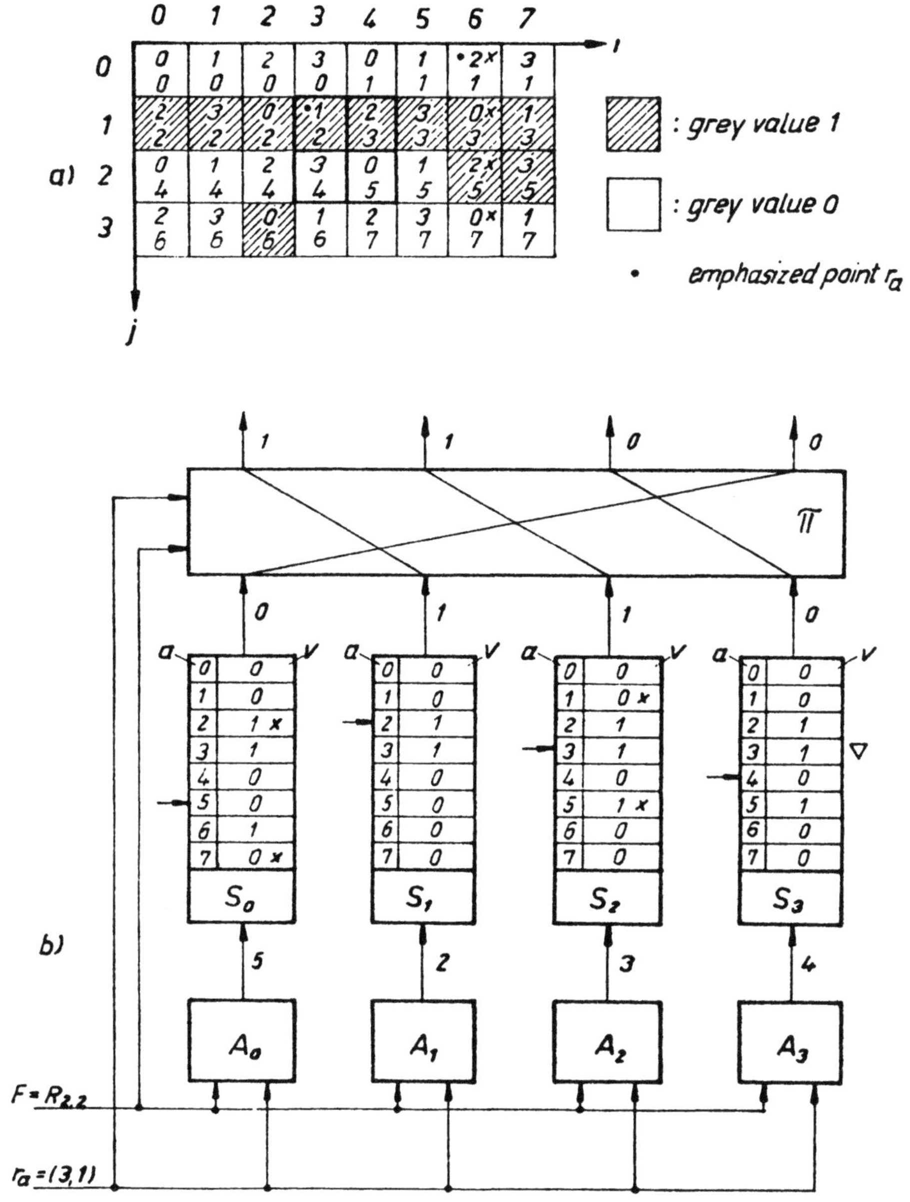
a)
: grey value 1
: grey value 0
emphasized point r_a
b)
Π
S_0
S_1
S_2
S_3
A_0
A_1
A_2
A_3
F = R_2,2
r_a = (3,1)

Fig. 1

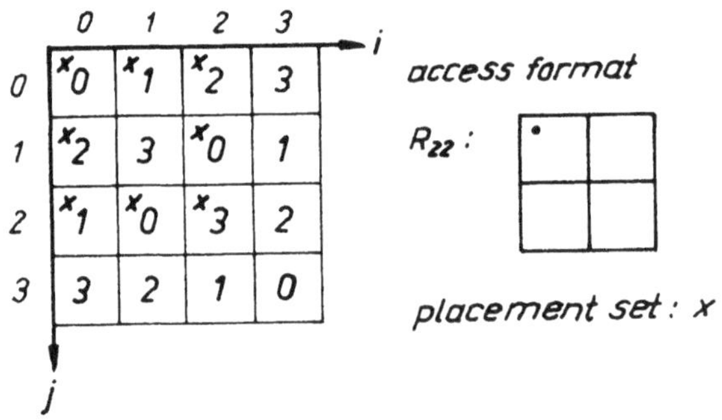

Fig. 2

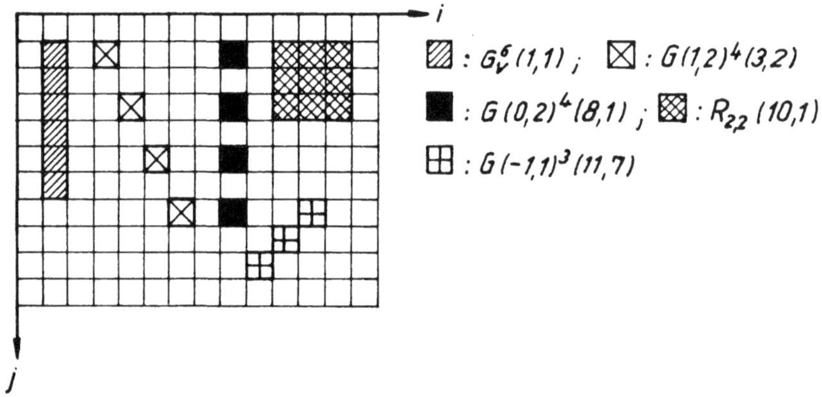

Fig. 3

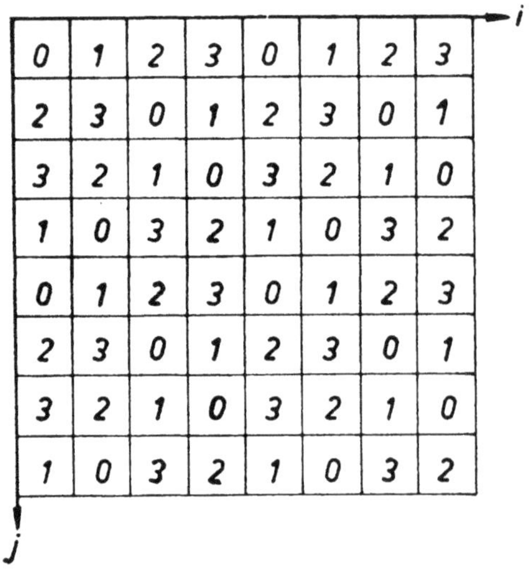

Fig. 4

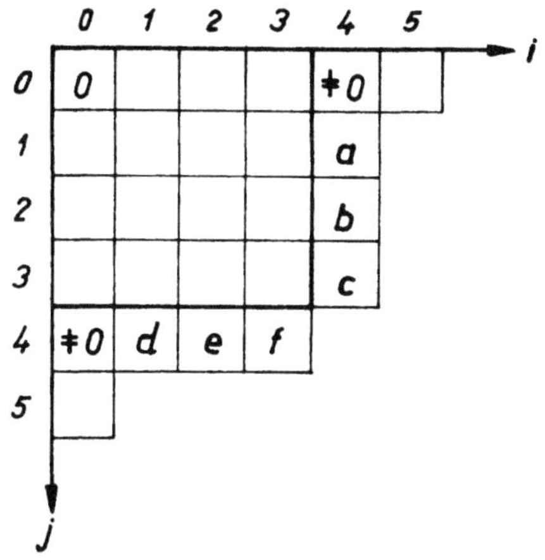
0 1 2 3 4 5
i
0 0 ≠0
1 a
2 b
3 c
4 ≠0 d e f
5
j

Fig. 5

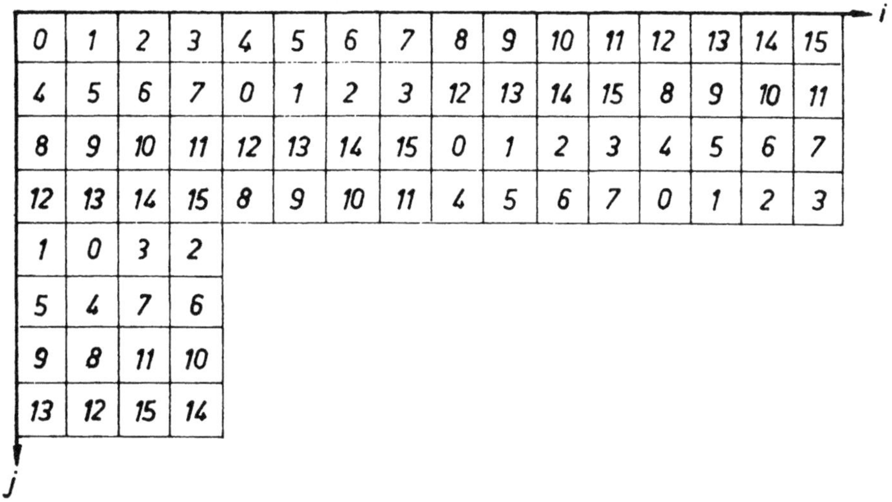
i
0 1 2 3 4 5 6 7 8 9 10 11 12 13 14 15
4 5 6 7 0 1 2 3 12 13 14 15 8 9 10 11
8 9 10 11 12 13 14 15 0 1 2 3 4 5 6 7
12 13 14 15 8 9 10 11 4 5 6 7 0 1 2 3
1 0 3 2
5 4 7 6
9 8 11 10
13 12 15 14
j

Fig. 6

PROGRAMMING WITH ACTIVE DATA

Chris Jesshope, Philip Miller and Jelio Yantchev[1]

1. INTRODUCTION

It has become clear over the last decade, that parallelism in the form of replication has been able to provide cost-effective improvements in computer performance. Replication is cost effective, because it allows relatively slow but dense technologies such as MOS to compete with intrinsically faster technologies such as ECL. The technique of replication is most successful if the replication factor is high, and the unit of replication is simple. Recent developments in both SIMD and MIMD computer systems give evidence of this.

One example of the exploitation of replication is the the AMT DAP, which is one of many second-generation, grid array-processors that have followed ICL's pioneering work in this field[1]. The AMT DAPs use CMOS chips containing 64 very simple (1 bit) processors; a 1024 processor system uses 4 boards each containing 8 (4 master + 4 slave) of these chips, plus additional interface and memory components. This is a very economical implementation compared with the first generation ICL DAPs, which used 4 chips per PE. Indeed it is quite probable that more than 64 of these simple processing elements could be accommodated on a state of the art CMOS VLSI chip. This however would lead to severe problems in providing the required number of I/O pins.

A second and quite different example of the use of replication can be found in the implementation of transputer systems [2]. With this VLSI chip there is considerably more investment in the design, but even so, the design still embodies the concept of simplicity. The T414 and T800 devices are complete computers on single CMOS VLSI chips; the latter includes a floating-point co-processor. These devices have significant support for replication in their design, including communications channels, timers and schedulers. This additional support has been made possible through the use of the RISC principles in the processor design. Many computer manufacturers are now using the transputer as a component in parallel computer systems.

The problems experienced by the user in exploiting the concurreny found in both of these approaches to replication, is in the lack of any general software which makes programming these computers an abstract and portable task. The AMT DAP, like its predecessors, are programmed in a dialect of FORTRAN now called FORTRAN +, which can manipulate concurrent array structures, providing that they conform to the size of the underlying DAP array. For example arrays may be declared with their first two subscripts elide, which implicitly declares an array of size 32x32 for the 1024 PE DAP. For a given sized problem, the portability of such code, even between different generations of

---

[1]Department of Electronics and Computer Science,
The University, Southampton, SO9 5NH, England

DAPs, is obviously limited.

The transputer is little better, even though the occam implementation on transputers does provide some abstraction in the target system, the code is still at a low level and parallel occam processes must be assigned statically to transputers in the hardware configuration. The language was designed for, and is well suited to the implementation of embedded systems. In such systems only two target hardware configurations would be typical, namely a single transputer for development and the final implementation, which would be speed optimised using the performance of a multiple transputer network.

The occam language and its implementation do not lend themselves well to general scientific or symbolic computation, where it is often more convenient to program using the abstraction of data concurrency. This style of programming is difficult to describe in the occam language, because it requires the manipulation of whole data structures, including those operations which contain implicit communications between data mapped on different processors. In occam, the data structure must be mapped onto the hardware resources by embedding substructures within parallel processes mapped onto those resources. Now the appropriate communication structure must be provided at a very low level, using elemental or block I/O statements over named channels. The naming of channels and blocking of communications provides severe restrictions to portable programming; it is not impossible, just tedious.

One can generalise the major problem in both of the above language approaches, although their style and implementation are widely separated; neither language provides an abstraction for the transparent mapping of the problem domain, onto the machine domain. This paper considers this problem, by proposing a virtual systems architecture (VSA), onto which data structures may be mapped, for the benefit of compilers and compiler writers. By providing this abstract layer between the compiler and the various target architectures, compiler and user code development becomes far simpler, and is not restricted to a single target machine configuration. Compilers for the VSA may be ported to new target architectures by the simple expedient of implementing the abstract systems architecture on the new target machine. The virtual systems architecture that is being defined, is based on concurrent operations over whole data structures, or subsets of those data structures. These are known as ***active data structures***, or simply ***active data*** and proposals for implementation are given in [3].

2. ABSTRACTION AND EFFICIENCY

In implementing any form of abstraction, a software layer will normally be introduced between the abstraction and the object over which it is abstracted .(which itself may be an abstraction). This use of one or more layers of interpretation or transformation will invariably give a loss of efficiency. It is imperative then that due consideration be given efficient implementation when gaining the additional expressiveness of the abstraction.

The advantages of abstraction are well known, and include programmer efficiency, portability and maintainability. Moreover, there are secondary benefits in some circumstances which can actually improve the efficiency of a computation. These occur when the abstraction provides additional information or flexibility which may be exploited in implementation. In our model of data concurrency, this can occur in a number of areas, as detailed below.

Load-balancing: A mapping of a data structure onto the underlying replicated hardware can be made *a priori* for a static structure with a static set of resources. This mapping can be made so that most of the resources are being used for most of the time (providing of course that there are sufficient data structure elements to cover the available resources). However, when selective computation is performed over a structure, or when a structure is dynamically evolving, it may not be possible to maintain this high utilisation of resources. Given a set of abstract resources, with compilation onto the abstract rather than the real resources, it is possible to defer this mapping until run-time, should this be necessary, and thus gain efficiency through improved resource allocation.

This run time allocation of resources will impose quite stringent requirements on the communications structure of the implementation of the abstraction. For example in its most general application, where data structure elements are being dynamically created and destroyed, it is desirable to have a general virtual network as an abstraction for the communication, in which each virtual processor may define a virtual channel to any other virtual processor in existence. This can lead to non-deterministic communication strategies and data flow control strategies.

Simulation: Another area that can benefit from abstraction is that of the simulation of one machine model with another. For example, the model of data concurrency embodied within active data is naively one of SIMD or synchronous computation. However most computers, including SIMD computers such as the AMT DAP, embody some aspect of asynchronous operation. It is desirable therefore to include some form of asynchronous concurrency within the model, which will enable the hardware concurrency to be exploited. However, the introduction of this concurrency should not be limited in this model by the implementation dependant components found in a given target system. It must be included in a more general manner, but this leads to a requirement to simulate a general MIMD code structure over a SIMD machine. (Memory restrictions excepted, the converse is trivial).

Such a model may be provided by allowing the concurrent data structure abstraction to be extended over a process type. For example given a data structure S, whose elements s_i (i in {o...n}) are data, and a data structure P, whose elements p_i (i in {0...n}) are processes, then the application of P to S, will apply the process p_i to s_i, for all i in {0...n}. In general not all of the p_i will be unique, for example if the p_i belong to the set of active processes $P = p_i$ i in {0...m} and m<n, then one or more of the processes will be a concurrent data operation and we have a general model of concurrency. Obviously this further abstraction may be efficiently implemented on a MIMD model of hardware, for example a transputer array, but on a SIMD array we would expect inefficiencies. In fact provided that each of the process types is associated with a sufficiently large set of data (virtual processors), when compared with the set of physical resources, then an efficient implementation may be provided by time-slicing a SIMD processor. In such an implementation, because the processing elements do not have control units themselves, the process structure may be represented by a set of m+1 tags,

which may be selected by association from a broadcast instruction stream, and used to activate the appropriate virtual processors associated with a given active process. Activation by association, which must occur prior to a process being broadcast from the single control unit, is a common technique in data concurrency. Thus the active data abstraction may be used to provide the description and simulation of a MIMD model over SIMD hardware. The efficient simulation relies on effective load balancing, and the constraint given above, concerning the data covering each active process.

3.THE DEFINITION OF AN ABSTRACT MACHINE

A collaborative Alvey project (ARCH/001) is currently attempting to define an abstract compiler target language for concurrent data operations. It should be noted that the proposals below do not represent a definition of this Virtual Systems Architecture (VSA), as it has not yet been defined for the purposes of that collaboration. They do however represent the personal views of the authors, and as such will provide Southampton University's input to the discussions defining the VSA.

The Virtual Systems Architecture (VSA) is esentially an abstract definition of a concurrent machine, in which operations are defined across whole data structures or subsets of data structures, and where the individual elements updated by an operation are deemed to be updated as if in parallel. The view we have adopted is one of an object based environment, in which the whole data structures are represented as objects. Within this context, an object comprises a set of resources or Processor-Memory units (P-M units), a set of methods, and sets of activated data. An implementation of the VSA would require an object memory management unit, because the mapping of the data structure elements onto the physical processor-memory space must come below the VSA definition and hence within the domain of the implementation of the VSA.

Two reference mechanisms are provided within a VSA object: the object variables, which provide a mapping onto the values that define the resources associated with that object, and also a mapping onto the set of values which comprise the elements of the data-structure object; and activation sets, which provide a reference mechanism to the individual elements of a data structure. The concept of Virtual Processors and single Memory cells (VP-M units), where the size of the cell is dependant on the type of the data structure element, is used as the referencing mechanism to the values of the data structure. This provides a useful abstraction which avoids the details of the mapping and storage of the data on a set of real resources (P-Ms), and allows compiler generated code to be concerned only with the virtual resources of the system(VP-Ms). Many of the normal addressing and control concepts of sequential language semantics are provided by the second referencing mechanism, that of activation sets. An activation set is a simply a set of Virtual Processors (VP-Ms), which is bound to a class of object. Operationally they define the active virtual processors required to update the elements of a data structure for a given operation.

Given these definitions, it is possible to define the VSA, as follows:

- A VSA operation requires a method, which is a process providing one or more operations between corresponding elements of the same class of objects; and an object to which the results are assigned. The specification of this result object requires an object name and an activation set (this latter may default to the universe set).

- o The effect of a VSA operation is that the elements of the result object that are referenced by the activation set are updated by the corresponding values generated in the method.
- o VSA operations may be combined by sequential and concurrent threads of control (constructed with SEQ and PAR constructors, as in occam [4]), without restriction.
- o A VSA operation is indivisible, i.e synchronisation between concurrent threads of control is only possible at the start and finish of a VSA operation.
- o A data structure element, for a given class of data structure, may be referenced by a mapping from a set of values, which are the VP-M indices to a set of values, which are the data structure elements. This structure is invariant for a given class of VSA object.
- o The primitive VSA object classes are defined by their superclass, type, extent, and by the methods available to them.
- o The type of the elements of a VSA object is implementation dependant, but would require at least *Binary, Byte* and *Integer* types.
- o The VSA objects belong to one of the following superclases.
  - i) The most general superclass of data structure is effectively the Xector defined by Hillis [5]. It provides a mapping from VP-M id onto a value (which may be of a composite type). It can be used to implement arbitrary data structures by interpreting the data value as a further VP-M id or pointer.
  - ii) Arrays are a more specific superclass, defined by an index set $(i_1,\ldots,i_n)$, whose values $(v_1,\ldots,v_n)$ are in the range $(0..r_1,\ldots,0..r_n)$. This index set defines a mapping onto the VP-M set for that object, whose range is:
    $(0,\ldots, \prod_{i=1}^{n} (r_i+1))$,
    such that element $v_1,\ldots,v_n$ is associated with the VP-M whose id is given by:
    $\sum_{i=1}^{n} v_i \prod_{k=i}^{n} (r_k+1);$
  - iii) The final superclass of VSA object is the activation set, which is a mapping from a VP-M id onto a boolean value. An activation set is always bound to class of VSA objects.
- o The extent of a VSA object in its most general form, i.e. in i) above, is determined by the range of VP-M values onto which it is mapped. The range of the class of array objects is determined by the extent of each value in its index set, such that two arrays that map onto the same range of VP-M values may themselves belong to different classes.

There are obviously higher level abstractions and constraints that would aid the compilation process, for example a dataflow or graph representation of a program. These definitions however, represent a level of abstraction which is very close to the machine domain, and below which we feel it is undesirable to descend when implementing languages and their data structures.

4. DATA MAPPING STRATEGIES

The model of computation described above is not sufficient for general computation, unless the processes performed on VSA object allow the migration of values between VP-Ms. The data manipulation processes required will depend on the type of object and the the algorithms being implemented.

The most common manipulations used on array objects can be described by translations and rotations of the values within the n-space defined by the array's index set. Less common but equally important is the class of data remapping defined a pair of index sets which map onto the same range of VP-M ids. For example the fast Fourier transform algorithm can be described as the repeated application of a constant process (including translations) over a 2-space array object, which for a length l transform can initially be defined by the index set (l,1), and which at each stage is remapped using the following transformation between index sets:

(i,j) ==> (i/2,2*j),

until the object has the index set (1,j).

All of the above classes of data manipulations can be implemented deterministically using only translations over a k-ary n-cubes, or more specifically over 2-dimensional grid processors[6], with the restriction that the array object is mapped within a bounding n-space in which each dimension is an integral power of two and greater than the corresponding index of the array. Obviously this mapping of the array may lead to inefficient operation, and we may bound the efficiency below by:

$e > 2^{-n}$.

However, it should be noted that only the remapping operations require this mapping, all other elemental operations can be performed with an efficiency bounded below by:

$e > 0.5$,

by remapping the data between 1-space and n-space representations.

The most common remapping in more general data structures can be defined by a pair of VSA xectors, and this interprets the values associated with the first as further VP-M ids or addresses and transfers the values associated with the second xector to the corresponding addresses from the first xector. The values stored in the first xector must be bound above by the extent of the xector which results. Where there is convergence of data, this mapping is non-deterministic and there must be some constructor function or reduction operation associated with the remapping to define the semantics of the operation. The most general constructor is to generate a VSA object whose base type is a set.

It is this abstraction, that when applied to the real resources (P-M units) can provide the dataflow semantics of active-data implementation, by providing queues of data to be consumed by processes at each P-M unit, with one queue for each concurrent VSA operation.

This data general manipulation is however, not efficiently implemented on grid-connected SIMD arrays[3], and we use the remainder of this paper to present recent research which we believe will achieve an efficient implementation of this class of data movements on synchronous and asynchronous array systems.

5. NON-DETERMINISTIC DATA TRANSPORT

In order to provide a fully dynamic arbitrary connectivity in a fixed valence network of processors, transport mechanisms must be implemented, which provide the propagation of data from processor to processor, based on addresses contained within a packet of data. In such a network each processor might wish to send a message to any other. An algorithm for this must satisfy a number of requirements depending on the particular application. Among the most demanding ones are:

- the routing protocol must be deadlock free;
- no packet is infinitely delayed in the network;
- a packet always takes the shortest route to its destination;
- the routing mechanism must adapt to traffic conditions and exploit the full available communications bandwidth (no restriction on the routing must be imposed);
- a node must not refuse the input of a message from its user for ever;
- the highest possible throughput must be achieved;
- the lowest possible latency must be achieved.

In this section we show how to design a routing protocol which meets all these requirements and provides for a great deal of design freedom to make compromises in order to achieve a desired cost/performance ratio. This protocol can be applied to arbitrary networks. However we will restrict our attention to 2-D toroidal arrays, with a note that the techniques are easily extended to k-ary n-cubes, or indeed arbitrary networks.

Deadlock freedom: The requirement for deadlock freedom determines to a great extent the whole design. A method is outlined here for designing deadlock free packet routing systems, which is described in more detail in [7]

Deadlock arises in packet routing networks from the combination of two effects: firstly, we must have local convergence of data, where more than one packet arriving at a node competes for the same output; we must also have the existence of cycles in the directed communication graph, which occurs if each node must accept and forward messages in any direction. The first can always lead to the filling up of the available buffer space and the second (given the first) leads to cycles of ungranted requests, and thus to local and possibly global deadlock. The occurrence of a deadlock cannot be detected locally, so deadlock recovery algorithms must be global, and therefore difficult to detect rapidly. An approach which guarantees deadlock freedom by design is therefore desirable if buffering is to be tightly bounded. First we establish two theorems on deadlock.

Theorem 1 [8] If V is a busy, triple disjoint and strong conflict free network, then any deadlock state contains a cycle of ungranted requests (a cycle of at least three processes, each of which is blocked by the next). #

Theorem 2 [7] Suppose $V = \{P_i \mid 1 \leq i \leq n\}$ is a triple disjoint, busy, strong conflict free network. Suppose further that there is a partial order on the elements of the network, such that every pair of nodes is comparable, and the communications pattern of each process is such that it either offers communications to *all* its neighbours less than itself (as components of a general choice (ALT) say) or communicates with one or more of its neighbours greater than itself in an arbitrary manner. Then the network is deadlock free. #

Proof Suppose the network can deadlock. Each cycle of ungranted requests generated by Theorem 1 must include a maximal element. Suppose P_i is the maximal element of such a cycle and its predecessor and successor in the cycle are P_j and P_k. Since $j,k<i$ then if P_i offers a communication to P_k it must also be willing to communicate with P_j which contradicts the fact that P_j has an ungranted request to P_i. Hence no cycle of ungranted requests can ever appear thus proving the network deadlock free. #

Suppose the communications of each process with all its neighbours less than itself are inputs. Then this theorem proves deadlock free the class of networks which have no directed cycles in their communication graphs, and whose component processes always offer inputs as components of a general choice (ALT) to all their neighbours connected to them via input channels. Since a multiple-input, multiple-output bounded buffer process is exactly such a process, then all directed-cycle free networks composed of buffer processes are deadlock free. Indeed, the multiple-input, multiple-output bounded buffer process if not full always offers communications on all its input channels, and if not empty always tries to output a message along an output channel. The input and the output of messages can be considered atomic events as far as the communications pattern of the buffer is concerned.

Now, if we can split our physical network into a set of independent virtual networks satisfying the conditions of Theorem 2 then the whole network will be deadlock free. In the 2-D array, although each node of the physical grid must route messages in all four directions, this provides for a large amount of unnecessary connectivity,when considering a particular packet and we can divide all packets into four classes according to the directions they need to be routed:

Class I (+X,+Y)
Class II (-X,+Y)
Class III (-X,-Y)
Class IV (+X,-Y)

Four independent virtual networks, each routing messages in one of the four quadrants, can provide for the necessary routing paths provided each packet is initially injected into the proper network. These virtual networks represent four systolic arrays, as shown in fig. 1. Each node is a buffer process as described above. A possible partial order is given in the figure. These systolic arrays all satisfy the conditions of Theorem 2 and the whole network is therefore deadlock free by design. Provided that appropriate flow control is exercised, corresponding nodes of the virtual networks may be mapped onto the same physical nodes of a real network.

If minimum storage space is required or the number of virtual channels needs to be reduced, then another arrangement is possible. This only needs two systolic arrays routing in mutually exclusive directions (say (+X,+Y) on plane A and (-X,-Y) on plane B). They cannot now be fully independent, since none of them can route messages in the other two quadrants ((-X,+Y) and (+X,-Y)). If we allow for messages to be routed from plane A to plane B but not vice versa, then messages can be routed in all quadrants if all messages from classes II and IV are first injected into plane A routed properly in the +X or +Y dimension and then transferred to plane B for routing in the -X or -Y dimension. The price to pay for the reduction in the necessary storage space at each

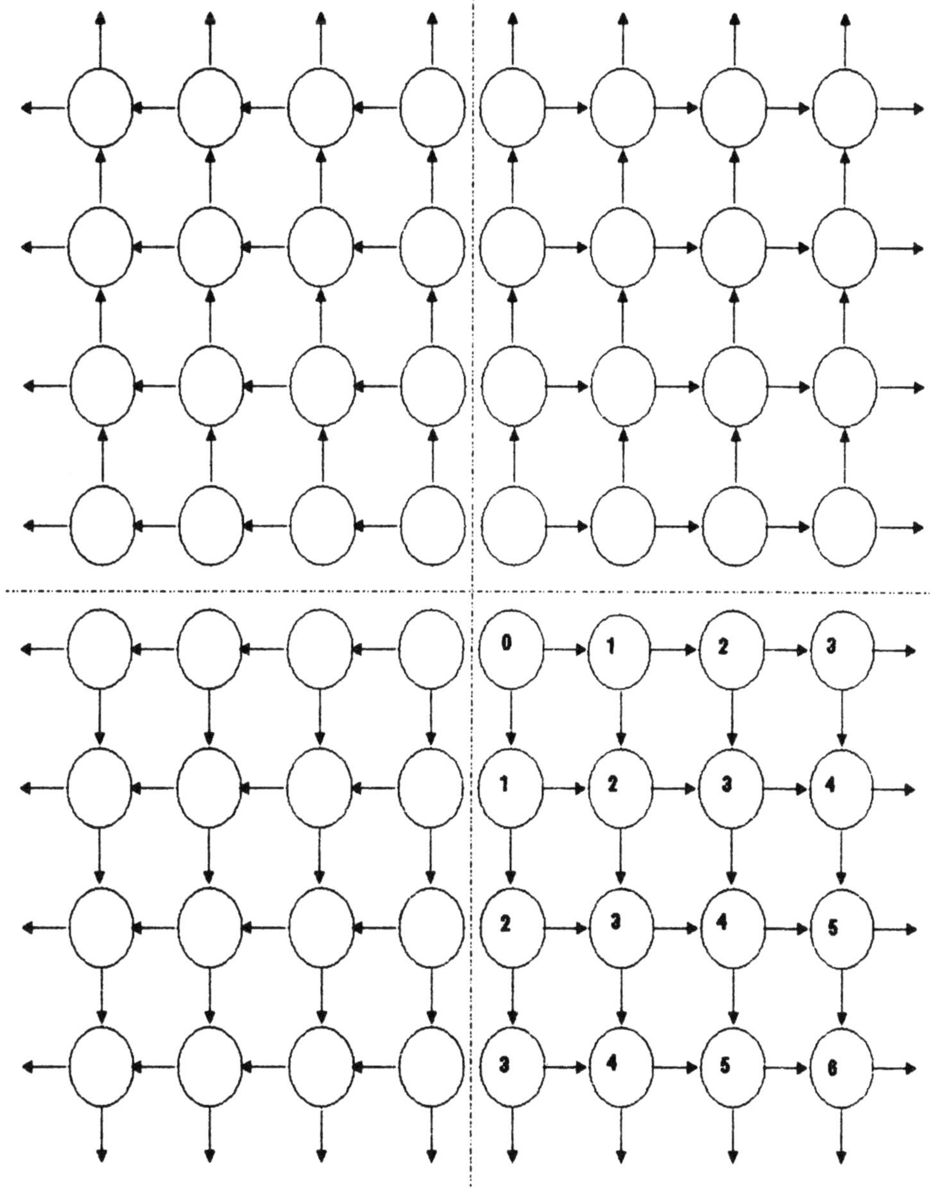

FIG. 1. Four cycle free systolic arrays implementing a two dimensional regular network, e.g. +X+Y, −X+Y,−X−Y,+X−Y.

physical node is the restriction of a unique routing paths for a message moving in the two quadrants not fully covered by the two systolic arrays.

Another advantage of the above arrangement is that it maps nicely onto the available physical links in a 2-D array, as there is no need for multiplexing. This 2-plane scheme works for n-dimensions as well. In general, each node is connected to its 2n neighbours and the A-plane is used for increasing coordinates and the B-plane for decreasing; again there is again no need for multiplexing.

For a toroidal network, at a first glance, it seems impossible to close a mesh in such a way so as to allow for communications between opposite ends of the mesh, without introducing any directed cycles in the communication graph. However, by stating the problem in a convenient form, a simple solution which provides the connectivity of a torus among the physical nodes, preserving the deadlock freedom of the whole network is possible[7]. This creates two classes from each of those described above. the division of messages into these classes is determined by the shortest route to the message destination, which in a toroid may be in increasing or decreasing node order.

An advantage of this method of avoiding deadlock is the design freedom it offers. The designer can always make a trade-off between storage space, speed, number of possible paths, etc.. For example, a packet routing protocol for a 4-D cube can be designed in at least two different ways. Firstly, the 4-D cube can be split into sixteen 4-D systolic cubes, thus utilizing all possible paths the physical network provides. Alternatively, the 4-D cube can be split into two cascaded 2-D subnetworks each in turn split into four systolic arrays. Each packet is then routed in the first two dimensions and then in the next two. The first network strips off the first two addresses of each packet before passing them to the second subnetwork, which then treats the next two symbols as addresses in the next two dimensions and routes packets accordingly. This reduces the number of possible paths to some extent, but still allows for adaptive routing.

Routing strategy: Among our top requirements were those for adaptive routing, high throughput and low latency. It is easy to see that the method proposed above provides for a fully adaptive routing strategy. Also, the processing of packets can be fully distributed and thus all available channel bandwidth may be exploited. We therefore propose a routing strategy which, with the same channel bandwidth, reduces the latency of routing packets by more than one order of magnitude in comparison to the other known present time routing strategies, such as store and forward, wormhole routing and virtual cut through [9,10]. We call this strategy the 'mad postman'.

We define latency here, as elsewhere [9], as the delay in delivering a single message in isolation. In the treatment below we will assume bit-serial internode communication. We first start with a comparison of the present known routing strategies in order to provide comparison with the mad postman. We first define:

L is the packet length in words;

W is the word length;

T is the time to transmit one bit;

D is the number of channels traversed;

then, i) store-forward routing, latency = LWTD;

ii) wormhole routing, latency = WTD + LWT;

iii) virtual cut-through, latency = WTD + LWT.

Virtual cut-through provides for the same latency as wormhole but eliminates the deteriorating effect of blocked messages. Obviously, for minimum latency one must route along the dimension of the leading address digit. Latency will be further reduced if when each packet has been fully routed in a particular dimension then the associated address digit is stripped off. This will also increase the efficiency of transmitting packets. If a packet cannot be routed in the first dimension then it can either be routed in some other dimension or wait till the necessary channel is available.

To summarise, if virtual cut-through routing with all features mentioned above is implemented then the minimal achievable latency would be WTD + LWT, and accordingly the delay per node would be WT seconds. For example, in case of asynchronous communication with eight data bits, one start bit, one stop bit and T=50 nsec., it means a delay per node of at least 500 nsec. This delay is necessary to accumulate enough information (a full address digit) for a routing decision to be made.

One important consideration is, as always, in the efficiency of the utilisation of the available hardware resources. If dedicated routing hardware is available, then there is nothing inherently wrong in using it for any purpose, if it would otherwise stay idle. Furthermore, there is nothing wrong if some (even all) of the additional work turns out to be useless, if this helps us achieve latency far less than the minimum latency achievable otherwise. This is the strategy adopted in mad postman routing, and if wish to reduce latency without changing any of the terms L,W,D,T, then the only choice we are left with is to output every packet along the same dimension that it arrived, as soon as its first bit arrives. This delays the routing decisions and the latency becomes:

iv) Mad postman routing, latency = kTD + LWT

where k is a coefficient between 0 and 1 and is implementation dependent. In case of synchronous communication k is most likely to be 1, and in case of asynchronous communication kT will be the time to restore the pulse waveform. When the whole leading address digit has been examined, one of the following will be true:

i) the leading address digit indicates that the packet, indeed, had to be forwarded further along the same dimension. Then simply continue transmitting the packet, thus achieving minimum latency.

ii) the leading address digit indicates that the packet has been fully routed in this dimension, and has to be routed in the next dimension or it has arrived at its destination. In this case one must stop the transmission on the first dimension, strip off the first address digit and start transmitting the second digit along the next routing dimension. The second address digit need not be delayed for more than kT time and again minimum latency is achieved! The penalty is that a 'dead' address digit has been transmitted along the first routing dimension.

Using the figures quoted above, the mad postman will result in a delay per node of less than 50 nsec. which represents an improvement of ten times achieved without any change in the available channel bandwidth. This is indeed a big leap towards reducing the communications cost in a highly parallel computer.

What then, if any, are the costs of this reduction in latency? The mad postman only works for the class of directed cycle-free networks described above. However, as shown in [7], any network can be split into a set of virtual directed cycle free networks

networks which can then be multiplexed onto the physical network. The only additional requirement to obtain this low latency is that the reverse acknowledge signals introducing discipline in the processing of packets be implemented in hardware.

The mad postman works properly in any traffic conditions and can be made to adapt to traffic density. Of course, in conditions of increased traffic some blocking is inevitable due to the inevitable contentions for output channels. If, due to blocking at some intermediate node, a packet cannot be routed in the dimension of the leading address digit then it can either wait for the corresponding output channel to be freed or be routed along some other dimension by swapping the first address digit with any other depending on the traffic conditions (i.e. adapting to traffic density). If swapping of address digits is implemented then it may be necessary to tag them suitably and to explicitly code which one is the last. Note that no dead address digit is generated when a packet changes its dimension of routing due to traffic conditions.

In general, in an empty network the maximum number of generated dead address digits will equal the degree of the network. However, they will never reduce the performance beyond that of virtual cut-through or wormhole routing. By comparing it with the local address, a dead address digit can always be recognised as such and ignored by the intermediate nodes on its way. It will either quickly reach the boundary of the associated virtual network or will be blocked at some intermediate node. In both cases it will be immediately discarded from the network. Of course, a dead address digit may affect some other packet if there is a contention for the output channel of the associated routing dimension. However, the delay will never be greater than the duration of one address digit and this is precisely the minimum delay introduced at each node by virtual cut-through or wormhole routing. By the time the first address digit has been accumulated the blocking dead address digit will have left the node and the packet may be routed properly. Since normally a whole packet is much greater than an address digit then the probability of a 'good' packet blocking a dead address digit (which will result in discarding the dead digit from the network) is much greater than the probability of a dead address digit blocking a 'good' packet.

As traffic density increases, the number of blocked packets will also increase and correspondingly, the number of dead address digits per packet will decrease and the dead address digits will disappear quicker from the network. In the extreme case of a maximum traffic density no dead address digits will be generated and packets will propagate in virtual cut-through or wormhole fashion. However, it seems likely, that due to the much lower latency of the mad postman and hence better relaxation properties of the routing network, it will allow for higher throughput as well.

6. CELLULAR AUTOMATA FOR NON-DETERMINISTIC DATA-TRANSPORT

In this section we present some preliminary designs for a synchronous routing engine, based on the above theory. The routing strategy introduced by the mad postman represents a departure from the conventional SIMD concept, in that the communication nodes are no longer functioning in lockstep when considering the execution of instructions. The engine is in fact data-driven, with the heads of addressed packets causing activation, and the tails deactivation, of a cellular automata of independent finite-state machines.

In the development of an initial design for such a network, the approach taken has been to consider simply the requirements of a 2-dimensional mesh without wraparound, as depicted in one of the virtual networks shown in fig. 1. The theory above has shown how networks may be decomposed safely into this unit. Furthermore the designs considered do not include an adaptive routing strategy. This however, does not imply that it would be impossible to incorporate redirection of packets upon blockage; it has simply been omitted for the sake of simplicity. A brief discussion of this is considered later, in relation to the buffering requirements.

The format of data in the network is such that every eight-bit byte has a preceeding 'validity' bit, which indicates whether the following byte is part of the packet or not. Any non-valid data must be all-zero for the network to function correctly. Therefore, the trail of information at a point in the network would typically resemble that shown in fig.2. The provision of the **first_dimension** bit within the address byte allows flexibility in routing. The packet can be routed first in X and then in Y, or vice-versa, or solely in X or Y by suitable arrangement of the addresses and the first_dimension bit. Furthermore, this scheme provides uniformity in the nature of packets. Whether information is being routed solely in X, say, or whether it has previously been routed in Y and is now in the X dimension is not recognised by the incident node. All information is treated in a consistent manner.

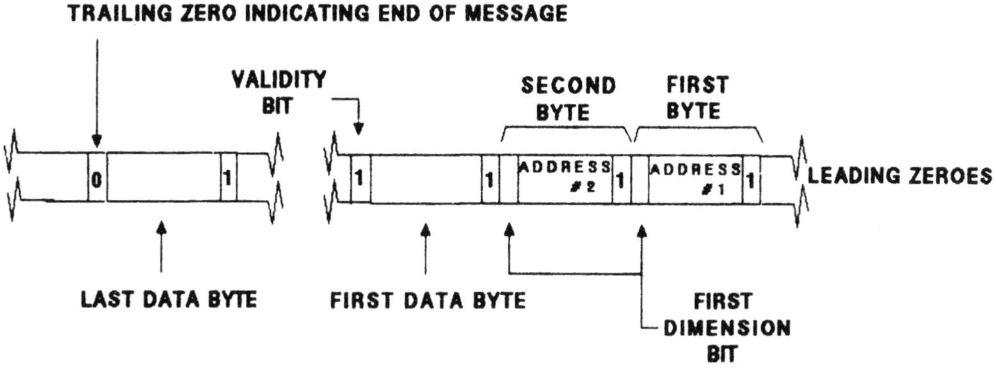

FIG 2: PACKET FORMAT OF MESSAGES IN THE NETWORK

Before considering the finite-state machine mechanism that constitutes the network, let us consider the nature of travelling messages and the various conditions that may arise. If we assume that at each node there is an X dimension machine and a Y dimension machine, and that if necessary data incident upon X can be subsequently redirected into Y upon an address match in the first dimension (more concisely referred to as a ***Junction***), then the following possibilities arise:

- o A message can be directly routed in both or, if required, just one dimension, without intermediate buffering.
- o The head of a message, in either dimension, is incident upon a busy machine

and therefore requires temporary buffering.

- o A message has arrived in the first dimension, but the complementary machine at that node is busy. A junction cannot be formed and so the message requires temporary buffering.
- o A message has arrived in the second dimension and therefore requires buffering as an arrival.

Handshaking: It is clear from the range of possibilities that each finite-state machine must generate two busy signals. One for the previous node in the same dimension, and the other for its complemetary machine serving the other dimension but located at the same physical node. Let these be referred to as **busy_back** and **this_busy** respectively.

This_busy presents no problem when one considers a hardware implementation, as the provision of a dedicated line, on-chip, is insignificant. However, the converse is true of the **busy_back** line since it will regularly be crossing chip boundaries. With pin-count becoming a limiting factor in VLSI implementations on silicon, it would be desirable to limit the number of connections to one per node-pair. This constraint requires a single-line handshake mechanism employed either universally or just on chip boundaries, where data travels in one direction, and the busy signal in the other. Notice that the exclusivity of the two signals permits a single line to be shared as if the next node is busy then data is not required on the line.

A circuit diagram of an implementation of this handshaking mechanism is given in fig.3. Assuming that the shift registers are clocked on the negative edge, then data is only valid on the line when the clock is high. Conversely, when the clock is low the 'next_busy' signal to the FSM is valid. **Busy_back** is only asserted when the FSM is

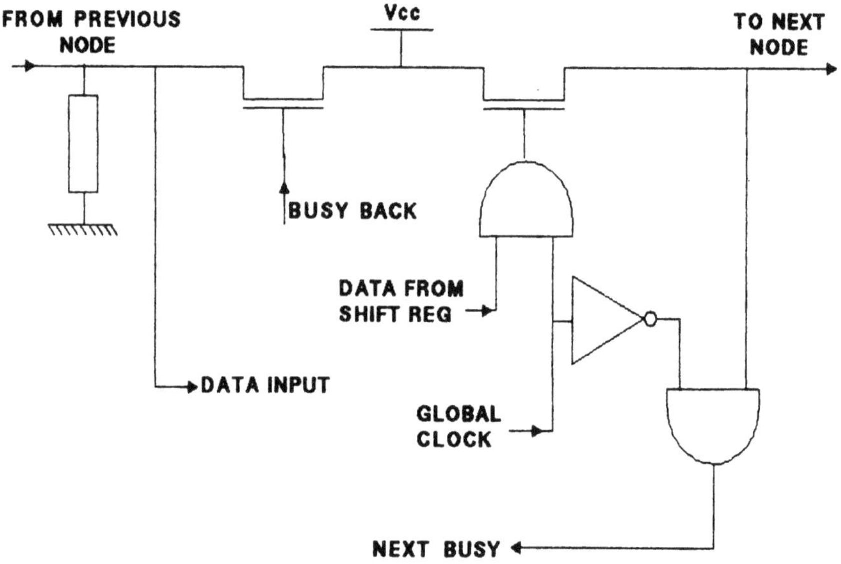

FIG 3: HARDWARE SOLUTION TO SINGLE LINE HANDSHAKE

sourcing data, or if it is the first node in the second dimension of a junctioned message. The **this_busy** signal to the other FSM at that node is asserted whenever valid data is present. Figure 4 illustrates these principles. Notice the way in which the message generates a busy field around itself, like a protective barrier.

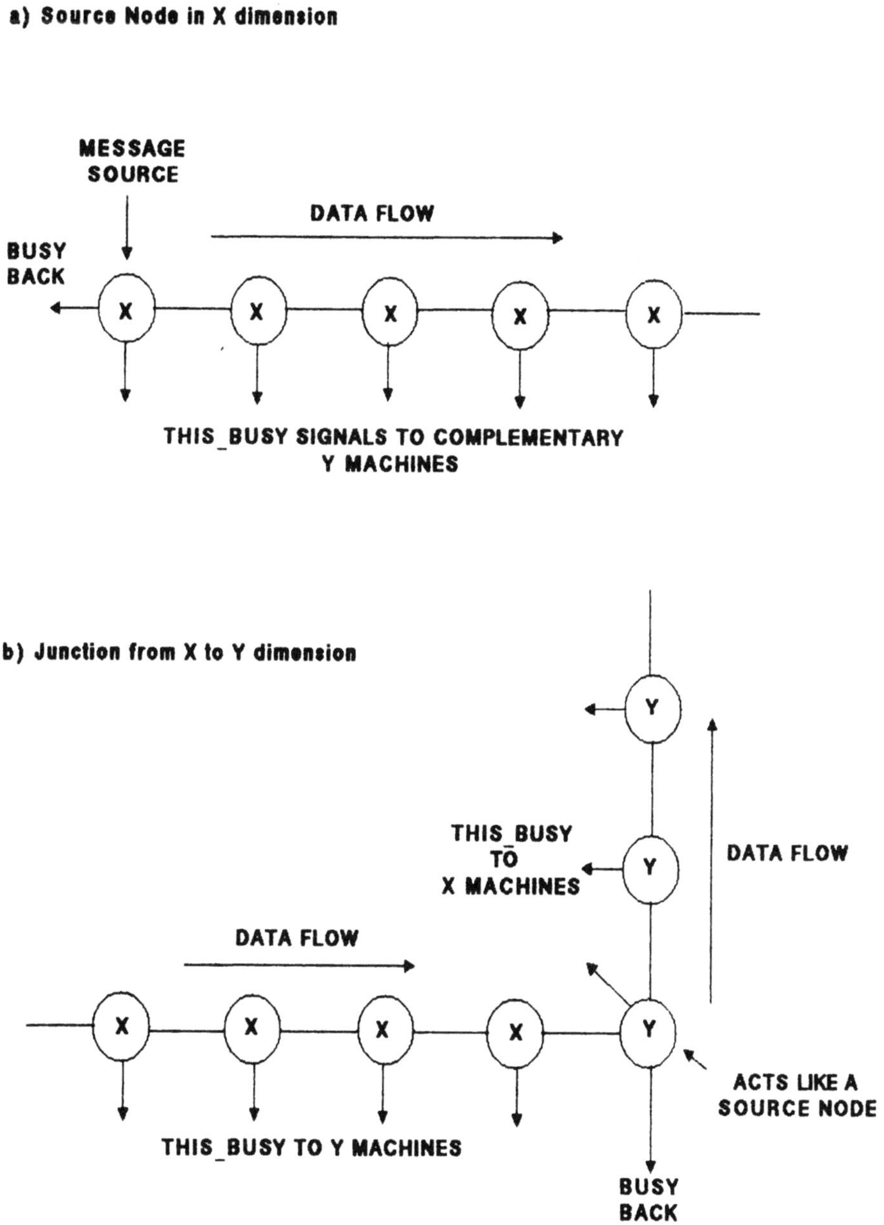

FIG 4: EXAMPLES OF THE BUSY MECHANISM

Another interesting point to note here is the simplicity **and symmetry** of the handshake mechanism. With the addition of very little extra selection hardware the sense of the data-flow/busy handshake can be reversed. The implications of this are that the same 2-degree hardware network can be used sequentially to emulate the full 4-degree mesh network. Put another way, it introduces a linear trade-off between cost and performance.

The Finite-State Machine: At each node there are two identical finite-state machines, one for each dimension. Until a message is incident upon a machine, or that machine wishes to source data, it remains in what we shall call its **latent** mode.

The leading '1' of a packet sets the machine into its active mode, and nine-cycles later, when the first address byte is resident and address comparisons can be made, a further state change is made dependent on the comparison result, the dimension, and the two busy lines **next_busy** and **other_busy**. There are five actions that can be taken at this point:

- o Put incident message into the arrival buffer.....BUFF_ARRIVE
- o Put incident message into this temporary buffer..BUFF_TMP_HERE
- o Put incident message into other temporay buffer..BUFF_TMP_OTHER
- o Create a junction into the other dimension.......JUNCTION
- o Reset the finite-state machine..................KILL

Any of the first four actions will apply to the whole message. Therefore they can take the form of flags, set by the result of the decision on the first address byte of the packet, and reset by the end of the message.

The KILL state will effect a complete reset of the state-machine into its **latent** mode. It is generated by an address comparison yielding 'greater-than'. The only time this will occur is when a junction was formed at the previous node in that dimension and the first address byte is lost. However, by the time the byte is KILLed in this FSM it will be resident in the next machine, and so on. This lost byte will continue along the dimension until it meets a **busy back** signal, whereupon it will be lost or until it falls of the end of the machine.

Figure 5 shows a diagrammatic representation of the state-machine. Note that the transition from the **message present** state leaves that flag set until the end of message or kill assertions. Source request is a signal applied whenever the temporary buffer is not empty. However, as the diagram shows, it only initiates the setting of the source flag from one of two states. If the FSM is latent then it can become a source, but also if it is a junction node. Now the states have been identified the two busy signals can be generated:

this_busy = message_present + source

busy_back = (source.junction) + other_junction

Notice that if the machine becomes a source whilst junctioned, then no busy_back signal should be generated since the junctioned packet will still be on the incoming data line. As soon as the other machine is reset, by the tail of the message, the busy_back will be asserted. It should be noted that the transitions a,b,c,d or e will only occur on the ninth-cycle of the packet.

Now that the FSM is understood the data channel itself can be explained. Figure 6 shows the configuration for uni-directional transport, where if the source state is

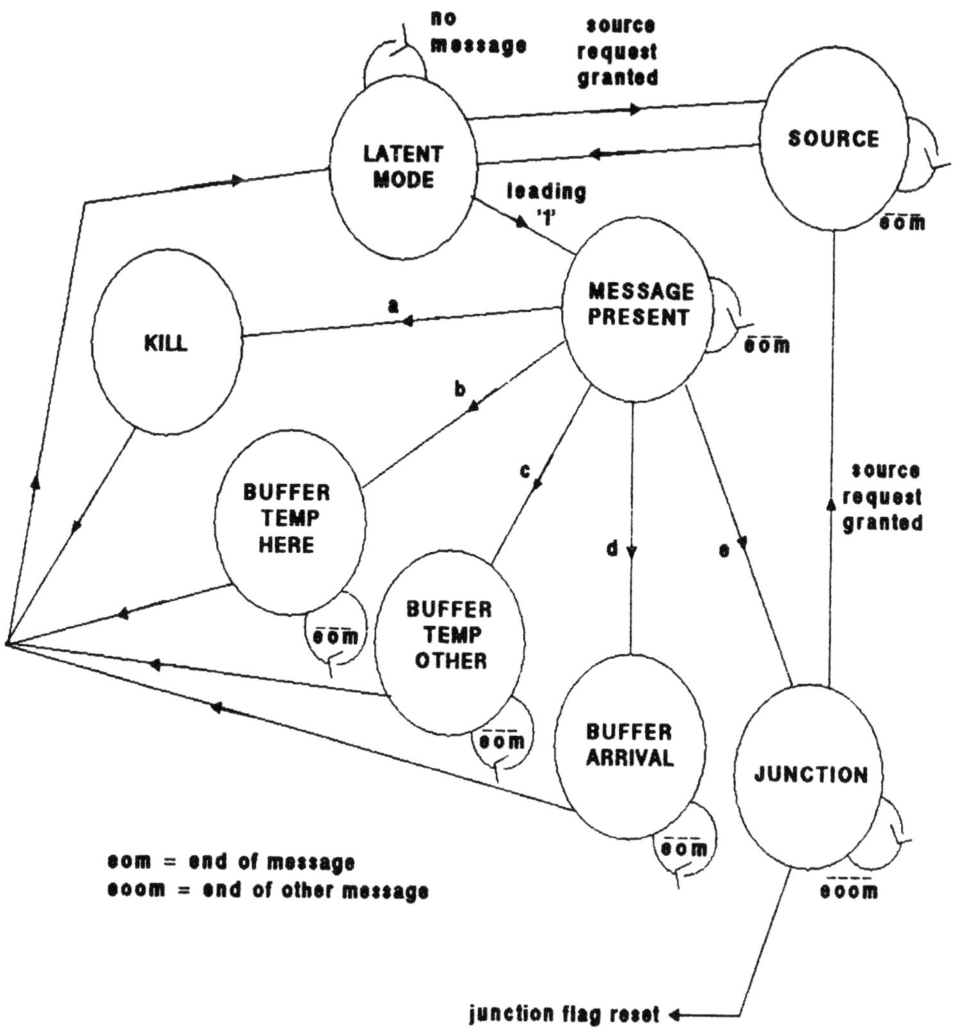

FIG 5: THE FINITE-STATE MACHINE

entered then the message to be output is parallel loaded into the 9-bit shift register, 8-bits at a time, with the validity bit being consequently set. The output multiplexer is controlled by the source state flag. Input data selection is also achieved by the use of a multiplexer, this time controlled by the junction flag of the complementary machine. The output of the input multiplexer is always zero if the junction flag of this machine is set. This prevents invalid data entering the register. Every ninth-cycle the resident data is either copied to, or read from, an 8-bit buffer register. This allows the full nine cycles to either load or save data.

Buffering: High level simulation of the communication strategy has not yet been

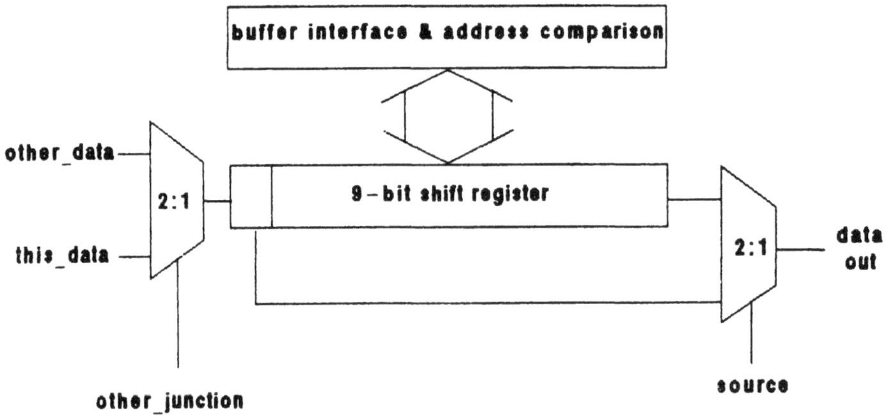

FIG 6: DATAPATH CONFIGURATION

performed, so consequently the buffering requirements of the network are not known in detail. However, it is envisaged that the arrival and temporary buffers will be separate, with the latter employed as a FIFO.

In the ideal buffer arrangement, we have a temporary buffer, of the required size, for each of the FSM's at a node, and each has one output pointer and two input pointers. Messages to be sent from this node are resident in the buffer. The output pointer is utilised when the machine is in its source state, and the two input pointers are necessary to cope with incident data from both dimensions. If data from the other dimension requires a JUNCTION but is blocked because this dimension is busy then, with the exception of the first byte, we want to buffer the packet in the dimension that it now wishes to travel. By incrementing the input pointers LENGTH times, and adding LENGTH upon completion of storage, and by initialising the pointers to be LENGTH bytes apart, a buffer of this nature can be realised. However, although ideal, it is of course expensive in hardware.

Research is currently in progress to find a suitable buffering strategy. The provision of hardware to effect an interchange of the first two address bytes and inversion of the first_dimension bits will provide adaptive routing. Therefore, a message in the first dimension, upon blockage, will redirect into the other dimension. A delay of nine cycles will of course be incurred but, when compared to the delay of complete message buffering, the advantages are obvious. Simulation results will give more indication of the requirements. Due to the bit-level functionality of the system, there is really no convenient abstract model for the purposes of simulation. As such it has been necessary to design the logic-level implementation prior to commencing the simulation. The circuitry has been described using the hardware description language ELLA and is currently undergoing verification and iterative correction. Once complete, simulation will be performed using an AMT DAP.

7. CONCLUSIONS

In this paper we have defined a virtual systems architecture (VSA), which combines both data parallel and process parallel models of computation. Data manipulations strategies for the efficient implementation of the VSA have been considered for various data types and algorithms, which show that a packet based virtual array implementation is required. We introduce a packet routing scheme *the mad postman* that is shown to have considerably better latency properties than previously published results and considered synchronous cellula automata to implement this scheme. In general, the mad postman is most advantageous to use in lower dimension networks, for example 2-D meshes, where latency is usually higher due to higher network diameter. In such networks the efficiency of the mad postman routing will be higher due to the smaller number of dead address digits generated per each packet. Such networks match form to function, and in current implementation technologies (i.e VLSI chips and PCBs), they will therefore provide cheaper hardware, thus allowing for a higher cost/perfomance ratio to be achieved.

8. ACKNOWLEDGEMENTS

We would like to acknowledge the Alvey directorate for support under the project ARCH/001, and the SERC for the support of Mr Miller by a Research Studentship.

9. REFERENCES

[1] Reddaway, S. F.: DAP - a distributed array processor, *First Ann. Symp. on Computer Architecture*, Gainsville, (1973), 61-65.

[2] INMOS Ltd,: *The transputer family 1987*, INMOS Ltd, 1987.

[3] Jesshope, C. R.: Implementations of load balanced active-data models of parallel computation. *Concurrent Computations: Algorithms, Architectures and Technology* (Eds. S. K. Tewksbury, B. W. Dickinson and S. C. Schwartz) Plenum press, New York.

[4] INMOS Ltd.: *The Ooccam 2 reference manual*, Prentice Hall, Hemel Hempstead 1988.

[5] Hillis, W. D.: *The connection machine*, MIT Press, Massacvhusetts, 1985.

[6] Cruz, A. J. O.: *The design of a control unit and parallel algorithms for a SIMD computer*, Ph.D. Thesis, Southampton University, Dept. of Electronics and Comp. Sci., 1988.

[7] Yantchev J. and C. R. Jesshope: Deadlock free packet routing with bounded buffering for asynchronous regular arrays of processors, Preprint submitted to IEE Proc E.

[8] Roscoe, A.W. and Dathi, N.,: The Pursuit of Deadlock Freedom, Oxford University Computing Laboratory technical monograph PRG-57.

[9] Dally, William J.: *A VLSI Architecture for Concurrent Data Structures*, Kluwer Academic Publishers, Boston, 1987.

[10] Kermani, P. and L. Kleinrock: Virtual Cut-Through: A New Computer Communication Switching Technique, *Computer Networks*, 3, (1979), 267-286.

PROLOG IMPLEMENTATIONS FOR CELLULAR ARCHITECTURES

Peter Kacsuk

Computer Research and
Innovation Center (SZKI)
H-1015 Budapest,
Donati u. 35-45.
Hungary

ABSTRACT

In this paper three research projects are overwied. The first intended to explore the possibilities of implementing logic programs on MIMD, non-shared memory type, massively parallel computers, where the processor elements are identical and connected in a regular, neighbourhood oriented network. The second project investigates the possibility of implementing Prolog on a tipical SIMD machine, called Distributed Array Processor (DAP). The third project focusses on systolic arrays and proposes a special wavefront array for parallel unification in logic programming languages.

INTRODUCTION

Recent advances in micro-electronics, particularly in the area of VLSI fabrication has made experimentation with massively parallel computers a reality. Parallelism is seen in AI as absolutely necessary to reach intelligence and consequently a lot of researchers are now focussing on the development of these new architectures and the development of radically new computational paradigms to utilize the massive parallelism inherent in the problems to be solved and available in the architecture level.

The main motivation of the researches described in this paper is derived from the "semantic gap" between the logic programming languages and the architecture of the massively parallel computers. On the one hand there is a widely accepted, popular programming language for solving AI problems and on the other hand there are available massively parallel computers. The main question raised by the semantic gap is how to implement logic programming languages on parallel computers in an effective way capable of exploiting the inherent parallelism of logic programs and utilising the parallel architecture offered by the massively parallel computers.

The majority of proposals has been aimed at implementing logic programs on shared memory multiprocessors where the number of processors are strongly limited by the access mechanizm of the shared memory. Another large group of researchers has been delt with the question how to implement logic programs on computer networks

Relatively small number of proposals has been regarded the massively parallel computers as the target architecture for logic programs and there was no attempt at all for exploiting SIMD architectures for this purpose.

In this paper three research projects are overwied. The first intended to explore the possibilities of implementing logic programs on MIMD, non-shared memory type, massively parallel computers, where the processor elements are identical and connected in a regular, neighbourhood oriented network. The second project investigates the possibility of implementing Prolog on a tipical SIMD machine, called Distributed Array Processor (DAP). The third project focusses on systolic arrays and proposes a special wavefront array for parallel unification in logic programming languages.

1. PARALLEL PROLOG ABSTRACT MACHINE

In [Kacs84] the so-called Extended Cellular-Dataflow Model (ECDAM) was introduced for parallel execution of logic programs in cellular architectures. ECDAM merges two computational paradigms in the following way:

1. Dataflow graphs are mapped into the cellular space in such a way that each operator of the graph belongs to one cell and arcs of the graphs are realized by data paths connecting the cells.
2. Operators have inner states like in the cellular model.
3. Operators work asynchronously based on the so-called Extended Transition Function (ETF) that involves the dataflow firing rule.

Based on ECDAM, implementation of logic programs in cellular architectures can be obtained through the following steps:

1. Creating the AND-OR tree of the Prolog program
2. Transforming the AND-OR tree into the so-called Dataflow Search Tree (DST).
3. Mapping the DST into the homogeneous processor space
4. Loading the DST
5. Parallel program execution in the processor space based on the ETF

In order to realize the Prolog interpreter by means of the ECDAM model five operator types were introduced:

UNIFY: for executing unification on clause heads and entering binding results into clause bodies
UNIT: for executing unification on unit clause heads or realizing built-in procedures
AND: for connecting body goals
OR: for connecting alternative inference routes for a goal
BUILTIN: for executing built-in predicates

The graphical notation of operators can be seen in Fig. 1.1. By means of these operators the corresponding dataflow graph can be constructed for each part of a logic program.

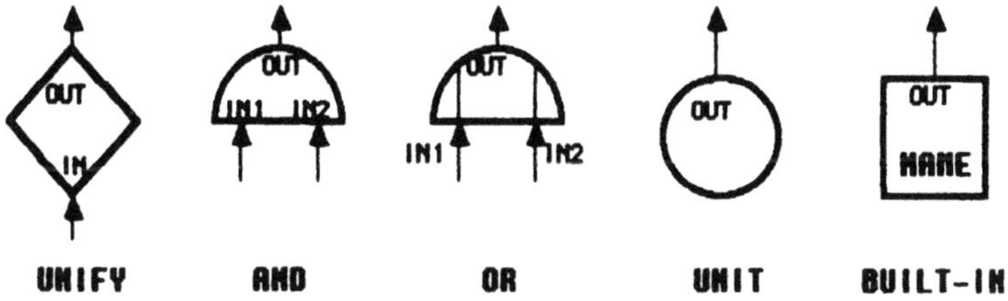

Figure 1.1. Graphical notation of operators

Like Warren proposed an abstract machine for sequential execution of Prolog [Warr83], based on the ECDAM we can define an abstract machine targetted for parallel implementation of logic programs on cellular architectures. The abstract machine will be called PPAM (Parallel Prolog Abstract Machine). The instruction set of PPAM can be partitioned into 2 classes:

1. Instructions corresponding to the operator types of ECDAM:

UNIFY <stored_arg_list>, <send_arg_list>
UNIT <stored_arg_list>
BUILTIN <function_id>
AND <send_arg_list>
OR

2. Instructions supporting the mapping of DST into the cellular architecture:

DEF <name>
CALL <name>

The order of PPAM instructions generated from a Prolog program supports the mapping algorithm. The possible schemes of the compiled definitions are the followings:

a/ definition consisting of a single unit-clause:

DEF <name>
UNIT <stored_arg_list>

b/ definition consisting of N unit-clauses:

DEF <name>
<OR-chain>

The structure of the OR-chain is as follows:

```
OR
UNIT    <stored_arg_list>        ; 1st clause
OR
UNIT    <stored_arg_list>        ; 2nd clause
```

```
OR
UNIT     <stored_arg_list>                 ; (N-1)th clause
UNIT     <stored_arg_list>                 ; Nth clause
```

c/ Whenever a rule is used instead of a unit-clause, then the corresponding UNIT instruction is substituted with a <UNIFY_block>. The structure of a <UNIFY_block> is as follows:

```
UNIFY    <stored_arg_list>, <send_arg_list>
<AND_chain>
```

where the structure of the <AND_chain> is the following if the body of the rule contains N subgoals:

```
AND      <send_arg_list>
CALL     <name>                            ; 1st subgoal
AND      <send_arg_list>
CALL     <name>                            ; 2nd subgoal
.
:
AND      <send_arg_list>
CALL     <name>                            ; Nth subgoal
BUILTIN  true
```

The BNF description of the PPAM code generated by the compiler is as follows:

```
<definition>:==<def_id><def_name><def_body>
<def_body>:==<unit_op>|
             <unify_block>|
             <or_chain>
<unit_op>:==<unit_id><stored_arg_list>
<or_chain>:--{<or_op><unit_op>|
              <or_op><unify_block>}[<unit_op>|<unify_block>]
<unify_block>:==<unify_op><and_chain>
<unify_op>:==<unify_id><stored_arg_list>,<send_arg_list>
<and_chain>:=={<and_op><proc_call>}<true_op>
<proc_call>:==<definition_call>|
              <built_in_call>
<or_op>:--<or_id>
<and_op>:--<and_id><send_arg_list>
<true_op>:==<built_in_id>true
<definition_call>:==<call_id><def_name>
<built_in_call>:==<built_in_id><function_id>
<def_id>:==DEF
<unit_id>:==UNIT
<unify_id>:==UNIFY
<or_id>:--OR
<and_id>:--AND
<call_id>:==CALL
<built_in_id>:==BUILTIN
```

Example

To illustrate the PPAM code generation, consider the following simple Prolog program:

```
affordable(F,C):-price(F,P), P<50,product(C,F).

price(apple,40).
price(lemon,60).
price(plum,55).

product(hungary,apple).
product(spain,lemon).
product(italy,plum).

?affordable(F,C).
```

The PPAM code of the example Prolog program is as follows:

```
DEF  affordable
      UNIFY             ([v1,v2],[v1,v2,v3])
        AND             [v1,v3]
          CALL          price
        AND             [v3,c-50]
          BUILTIN       less
        AND             [v2,v1]
          CALL          product
          BUILTIN       true

DEF  price
   OR
          UNIT          [c-plum,c-55]
   OR
          UNIT          [c-lemon,c-60]
          UNIT          [c-apple,c-40]
DEF  product
   OR
          UNIT          [c-hungary,c-apple]
   OR
          UNIT          [c-spain,c-lemon]
          UNIT          [c-italy,c-plum]
```

For the query a special definition is created with the name "query". The DO token generated for the query is placed on the output arc of the first AND operator in the goal chain. The initial DO token contains the variables of the query. In the case of our example Prolog program the generated code for the

```
     ?affordable(F,C).
```

query is the following:

```
DEF  query
        AND             [v1,v2]
```

```
CALL        affordable
BUILTIN     true
```

The DST of the example Prolog program can be seen in Fig. 1.2. Notice that the PPAM code of a Prolog program is the exact description of its DST.

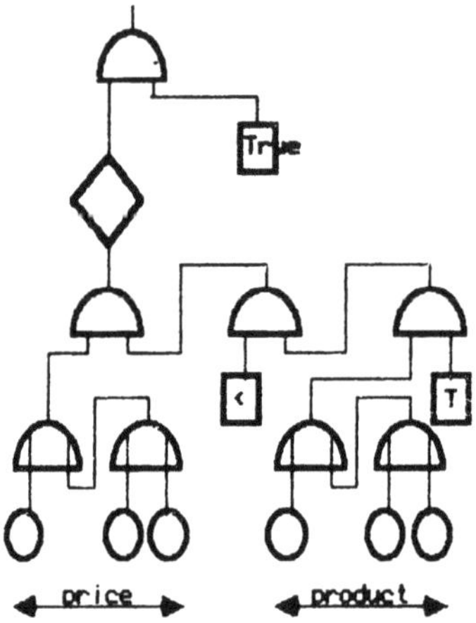

Figure 1.2. DST of the example Prolog program

By modifying the ETF of operators different types of parallelism can be achieved by the model:

- Lazy OR-parallelism [Kacs84]
- Eager OR-parallelism [Kacs85]
- Restricted AND-parallelism [Kacs84]

The PPAM code has been implemented on two parallel computers:

- iPSC (Intel's Personal SuperComputer) [KaSE86]
- DAP (Distributed Array Processor) [Kacs88]

Both implementations justified the functional correctness of the model and motivated further investigations. The model was realized in OCCAM too [KaES86] and in [Kacs86] it was shown how to map the DST on a Transputer array.

2. THE DAP IMPLEMENTATION OF PPAM

We implemented the OR-parallel PPAM interpreter and its compiler on AMT's DAP in the Queen Mary College of the University of London. Over the DAP's square next-neighbour interconnection network a binary tree network and four "pseudo-shift" instructions working on it was realized on the DAP:

- shift_up_to_left (shul)
- shift_up_to_right (shur)
- shift_down_to_left (shdl)

- shift_down_to_right (shdr)

For illustrating the principle of the mapping of the binary tree on the DAP consider an 8*8 DAP configuration which has room for a six level binary tree (2**6 = 64). The elements of each level of the tree are distributed as illustrated by Fig. 2.1.b. The mapping of DST of Fig. 1.2 (without the query part) based on this tree distribution technique is shown in Fig. 2.1.a. (The last two UNIT operators of the DST are missing due to the choosen size of the space).

					And1		
	And3		And2		Or2		Or1
True	Or4	Or3		Unit3		Unit2	
		Unit4	"<"		Unify		Unit1

(a)

5	6	5	6	5	6	5	6
6	4	6	3	6	4	6	3
5	6	5	6	5	6	5	6
6		6	4	6	2	6	4
5	6	5	6	5	6	5	6
6	4	6	3	6	4	6	3
5	6	5	6	5	6	5	6
6	2	6	4	6	1	6	4

(b)

Figure 2.1. Mapping of DST into the DAP

2.1. Representation of PPAM code in the DAP

Since the DAP is designed for effective handling of homogeneous data structures we had to choose data structures suited to the SIMD nature of the DAP. According to this requirement all data structures of the PPAM code are matrices. For each operator type we introduced a logical plane defining the positions of the corresponding operators in the DST.

```
logical unify_op(,)
logical unit_op(,)
logical or_op(,)
logical and_op(,)
logical built_op(,)
```

If the value in a position is .true. than the corresponding operator is placed in that position. In each position only one operator is allowed. The <function_id> parameters of the BUILTIN instructions are represented by the following matrix:

```
integer function_id(,)
```

Three matrices serve for describing the <stored_arg_list> parameter of the UNIFY and UNIT instructions:

integer stored_arg_num(,)
integer stored_arg_value(,,MAX_ARG_NUM)
logical stored_arg_type(,,MAX_ARG_NUM)

Each argument is described by a two-field record:

stored_arg	stored_arg_type	stored_arg_value
variable	VAR (FALSE)	id_number
number	ATOM (TRUE)	number
symbol	ATOM (TRUE)	symbol pointer

In this demonstration version of implementation compound terms are not used therefore the logical type of DAP FORTRAN was enough to define the type of Prolog simple terms. The following matrices serve for describing the <send_arg_list> parameter of the UNIFY and AND instructions:

integer send_arg_num(,)
integer send_arg_value(,,MAX_ARG_NUM)
logical send_arg_type(,,MAX_ARG_NUM)

The DAP planes representing the PPAM code are shown in Fig. 2.1.1.

2.2. The Dynamic Behaviour of the PPAM Interpreter

In an SIMD machine like the DAP the asynchronous firing of operators should be simulated. For this purpose a mask technique is used indicating which operators are active in a given moment. Similarly the asynchronous consumption and production of tokens should be simulated on the DAP. For this purpose the matrices representing the inner state of operators and the token configuration should be duplicated.

The operator states are described by an integer matrix called state:

integer state(,,2)

The tokens are described by six planes:

1. INPUT TOKEN PLANE
2. OUTPUT TOKEN PLANE
3. SHDL TOKEN PLANE
3. SHDR TOKEN PLANE
5. SHUL TOKEN PLANE
6. SHUR TOKEN PLANE

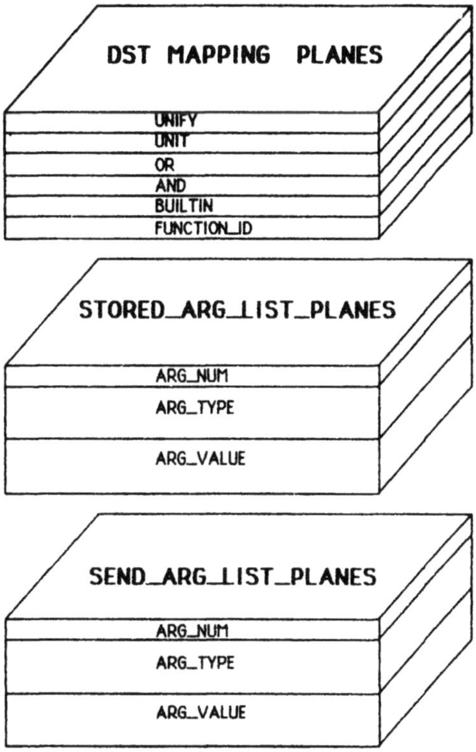

Figure 2.1.1. DAP planes representing the PPAM code

The INPUT and OUTPUT TOKEN PLANEs are represented by 5 matrices:

```
logical token_pos(,,2)
integer token_type(,,2)
integer token_arg_num(,,2)
integer token_arg_value(,,MAX_ARG_NUM,2)
logical token_arg_type(,,MAX_ARG_NUM,2)
```

Where token_pos=.true. there is a token. The representation of the SHDL TOKEN PLANE:

```
logical shdl_pos(,)
integer shdl_type(,)
integer shdl_arg_num(,)
integer shdl_arg_value(,,MAX_ARG_NUM)
logical shdl_arg_type(,,MAX_ARG_NUM)
```

The structure of the SHDR/SHUL/SHUR TOKEN PLANEs is the same. Whenever a token is consumed by an operator the corresponding token_pos should be written into FALSE in the INPUT TOKEN PLANE. The result token should be written into the OUTPUT TOKEN PLANE, or into one of the SHDL/SHDR/SHUL/SHUR TOKEN PLANEs depending on the target position.

A clock is introduced into the execution mechanism. For each clock step every operators that are able to fire, consume the input tokens, modify the inner state and produce output tokens.

When all operators consumed their inputs from the INPUT TOKEN PLANE, the corresponding shift is performed on the SHDL/SHDR/SHUL/SHUR TOKEN PLANEs and they are copied to the OUTPUT TOKEN PLANE. After this action a new clock cycle starts where the OUTPUT TOKEN PLANE is used as INPUT TOKEN PLANE and the INPUT TOKEN PLANE plays the role of the OUTPUT TOKEN PLANE.

Similarly in each clock step one of the state planes represents the current state while the other represents the new cell states generated in the current clock step. In the next clock step the state planes change role.

The DAP implementation is supplied with a graphical output generating two kinds of view of DST:

- mesh (or DAP-like) view as shown in Fig. 2.1.a.
- tree view

The user can change the view by simple commands. Similarly the user can select one of the two modes of token moving:

- step mode
- auto mode

In step mode the user can initiate the firing of operators and special trace commands are available to examine the state of operators and their tokens. In auto mode the operator firing is controled by an inner scheduler and the graphical output assures a movie-like view what happens during the interpretation of Prolog programs.

3. SET-ORIENTED INTERPRETATION OF LOGIC PROGRAMS

A SIMD machine is able to operate on large data sets in a naturally associative fashion. Therefore an interpretation method was designed to use this associative power by considering sets of facts (unit clauses) as unitary objects, enabling data base oriented Prolog programs to execute very effectively with little rewriting. The method is called set-oriented interpretation and it was realized first on the miniDAP [KaBa87].

In the DAP-Prolog Set mode, a set-oriented interpreter adopts a mixed depth first/breadth first search strategy in which the multiple fact branches of a conventional Prolog search tree are considered as generating binding sets rather than single binding values:

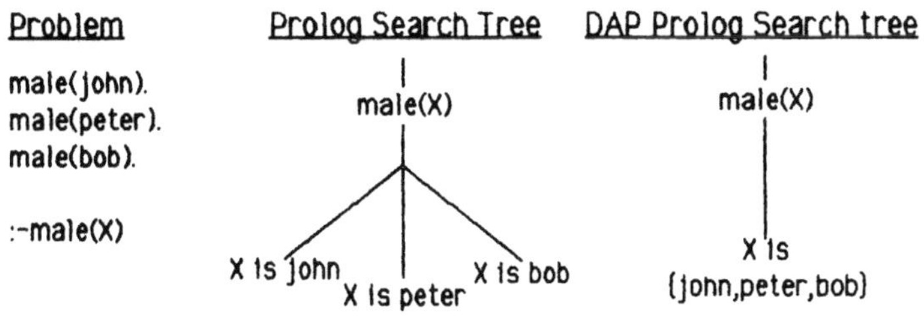

The semantics of this fit well with predicate logic: given the set

male={john,peter,bob}

the solution of

X:X Œ male

is exactly the set {john,peter,bob} returned by DAP Prolog (and returned in a sequential fashion by Prolog). Of course, multiple <u>rule</u> branches are still preserved as true choice points by the interpreter:

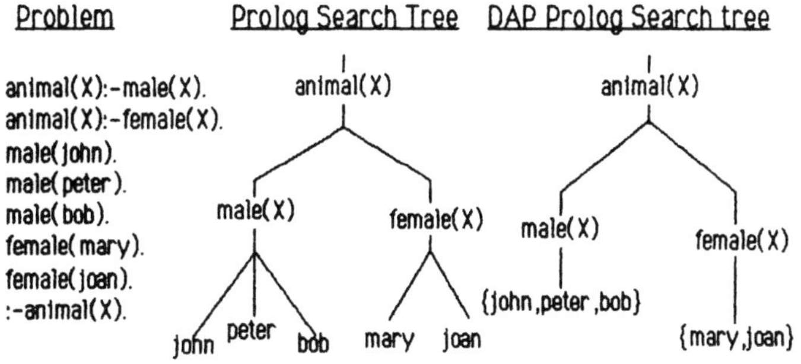

so that the "true" set solution is the union of the solutions returned by DAP Prolog.

There are several advantages to this set oriented approach:

Speed-up
The interpreter can handle the breadth first stage in a single step (on a SIMD machine) eliminating a significant amount of back-tracking when there are a large number of clauses in a set.

Semantics
In the above query ":-male(X)" the semantics are that X should be bound to the full set of solutions. There is no semantic ordering in the above program. A conventional Prolog interpreter will return with the answer "X=john", however, and must be forced to backtrack to generate any further solutions.

The theoretical speed-up (TS) obtainable by the set-oriented interpreter is:

$$TS = \frac{\text{Number of arcs in sequential Search tree}}{\text{Number of arcs in Set-oriented Search tree}}$$

TS is, of course, an upper limit on actual speed-up, which was about 450 in the best cases on the miniDAP.

4. WAVEFRONT METHOD FOR PARALLEL UNIFICATION

The success of systolic arrays is owing to the fact that they aim only at executing numerical subproblems but with extremely high speed due to the great degree of parallelism they can achieve. Similarly we suggest a systolic like array called Proputer-array for implementing only the unification of Prolog but with high performance.

For implementing the unification of Prolog we introduce a special wavefront array, in which each element plays the same Prolog-oriented role, so they will be called Proputers. Each Proputer has two input arcs and two output arcs directed to East and to South respectively as it is shown in Fig. 4.1.

The Proputer-array (PA) is connected to a host machine via an input interface unit and output interface unit. The host machine realizes the whole Prolog interpreter except for the unification.

The unification is executed by the PA. Since there is no other other task of PA it is sufficient to map the clause heads into the PA. The ith clause of a definition is distributed in the ith line of the array. The jth argument of a clause head is stored in the jth Proputer of the corresponding line. For example consider the following simple Prolog program:

```
s(L,[],L):- !.                          /* s stands for "subtract" */
s([H|T],L,U):- m(H,L), !, s(T,L,U).
s([H|T],L,[H|U]):- !, s(T,L,U).
s(_,_,[]).

m(H,[H|_]).                             /* m stands for "member" */
m(I,[_|T]):- m(I,T).

i([H|T],L,[H|U]):- m(H,L), i(T,L,U).    /* i stands for "intersect" */
i([_|T],L,U):- i(T,L,U).
i(_,_,[]).
```

The mapping of clause heads of this program into a 3*4 PA is shown in Fig. 4.1. It can be seen that the different clause definitions can share the same lines of the PA. It is obvious that the minimal width of a PA is determined by the definitions with the highest arity, while the minimal length of the PA is determined by the clause definition containing the largest number of clauses.

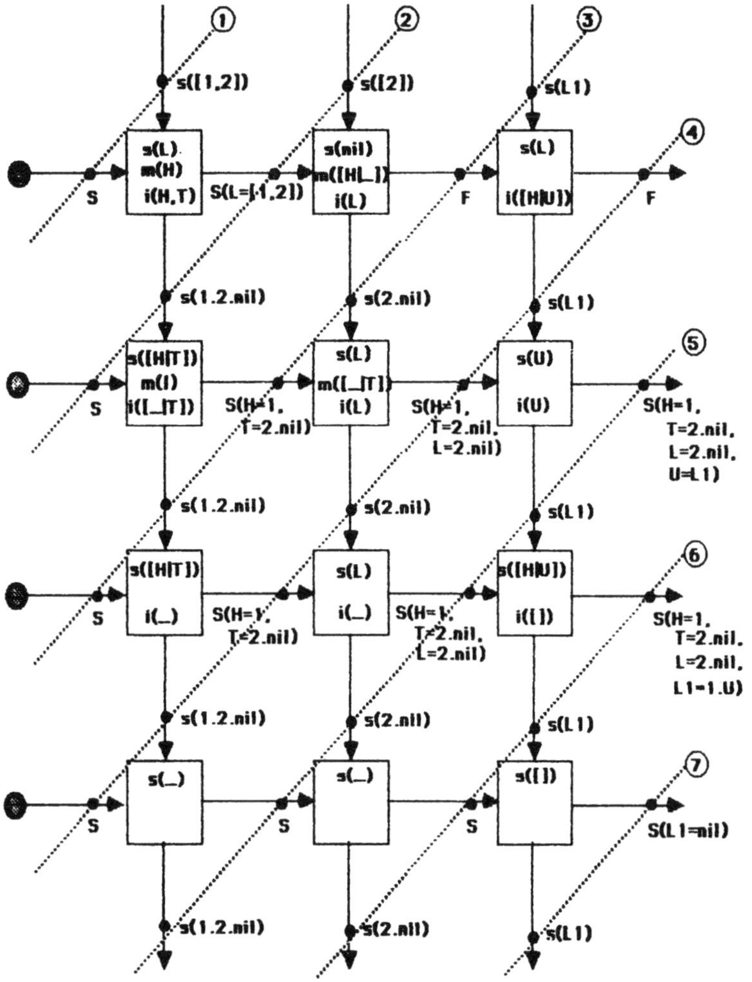

Figure 4.1. Parallel unification in Proputer-array

The execution of unification in the PA is as follows: Each Proputer is constructed to unify one of the locally stored arguments with a goal argument arriving on its N (Northern) input arc. The result of the unification will be packed into a binding list token. Binding list tokens have two types:

FAIL: indicating failed unification
SUCC: indicating successful unification

SUCC tokens contain in their data field the binding values of variables. FAIL tokens have no data field. (In figures SUCC tokens are denoted by S and FAIL tokens by F). The binding token is sent to the right-hand neighbour on the E (Eastern) output arc while the original goal argument of the N input arc is passed to the Southern neighbour on the S output arc. The binding list arriving on the W input arc is also used for eliminating the consistency checking problem deriving from the common variables of a clause head. Those variables of the locally stored arguments which have a binding value in the token are substituted by their binding value before the unification.

To start the work of the Proputer-array the host machine has to send the arguments of the current goal to the input interface unit which passes the arguments to different columns, i.e. the ith argument is sent to the ith Proputer of the first line. The PA has a special Western edge assuring that Proputers in the first column always receive an empty SUCC token. Fig. 4.1 shows the propagation of wavefronts (denoted by dashed lines) in the Proputer-array during the unification of the following goal for the example program:

? s(1.2.nil,2.nil,L1)

Numbers in cicles next to wavefronts represent the step when the wavefront was created. Processors before the same wavefront work in parallel. The figure well illustrates that goal arguments are moving in vertical direction without any changes meanwhile partial results of unifications propagate in horizontal. The final result of unification between a goal and a clause appears in the Eastern edge of the PA.

The real advantage of a wavefront array appears when it is used in a pipeline manner, i.e. without waiting for the exit of a wavefront, a new wavefront is created. This way many wavefronts can move at the same time in the wavefront array.

In the Proputer-array each wavefront corresponds to a goal unification. The pipeline use of the PA means that several goals are unified in parallel. In a sequential Prolog interpreter only one goal can be selected for unification. Therefore if we want to exploit the full advantage of the PA we should use one of the following two methods:

1. Using an OR- or AND-parallel Prolog interpreter on the host machine
2. Using a set-oriented Prolog interpreter on the host machine

In the first case the host machine should be a multiprocessor system. Fig. 4.2 shows an example where three processors running a parallel Prolog interpreter uses a shared PA in pipeline. The current goals of the processors are as follows:

processor #1:	?m(2,1.2.nil).
processor #2:	?s(1.2.nil,2.nil,L1).
processor #3:	?i(3.nil,4.3.nil,3.nil).

The figure illustrates that three wavefronts corresponding to the three goals are propagating in the PA. (Responses for the second (s) goal are not shown in Fig. 4.2 because they are identical with the ones shown in Fig. 4.1.) A further characteristics of PA can be observed in Fig. 4.2. If the Proputer contains no arguments of the clause definition identified by the argument token then the Proputer will be transparent for the input tokens and copies them on the output arcs without any changes. As a consequence the "empty" linesgenerate on their output an empty SUCC token. However this is not confusing since the system knows where the empty lines are starting for different definitions.

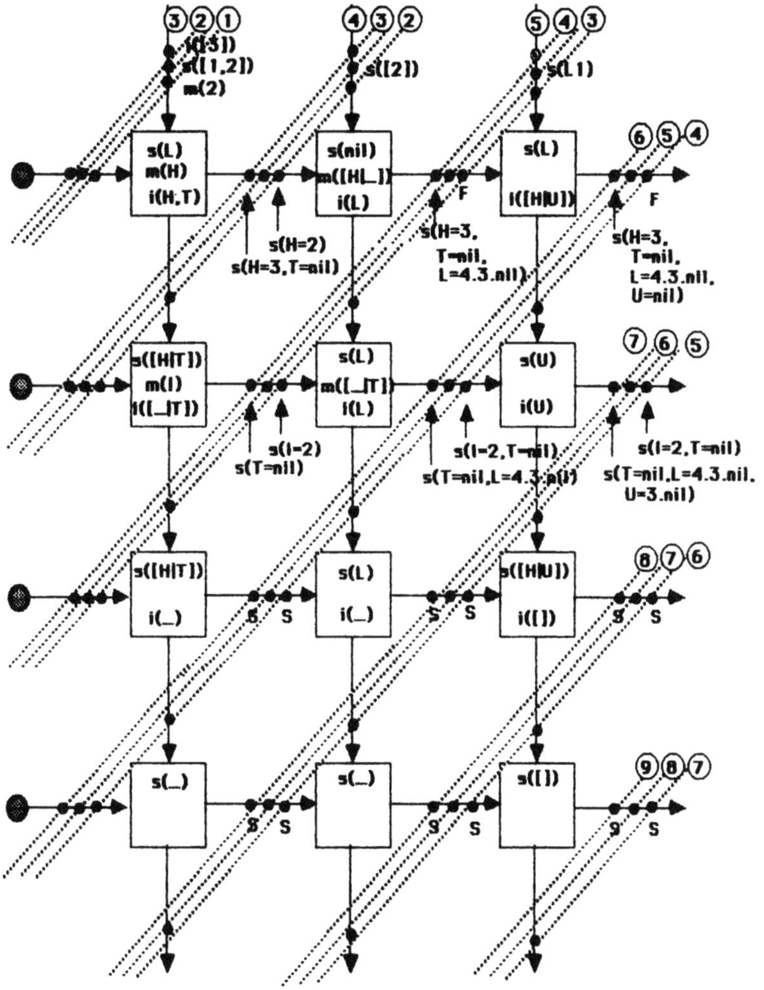

Figure 3.2. Pipeline use of the Proputer-array

In case of a set-oriented interpreter the host machine can be even a uniprocessor computer The PA is able to generate a binding set for a goal and this set can be used in pipeline in the consecutive unification.

The maximal throughput of a MxN PA can be achieved when it is connected to a multiprocessor host computer running set-oriented interpreters. In each step M unification results are produced at the output of the PA and N new arguments enter into the PA. If the average number of clauses in the definitions is K (K<M) we can suppose that in each step K unification result is created. If the time of a step in the PA is L-times less than the average time of the unification for one argument in the host computer than the speed-up of the PA will be:

$$S = N \times L \times K$$

CONCLUSION

The research projects described in this paper prove that logic programs can be implemented on cellular architectures. However the implementation experiences showed that only the inherently parallel subparts of logic programs are worth implementing on parallel way. The granularism of parallelism in the architecture and in the program should carefully be suited to each other for achieving a desirable speed-up.

ACKNOWLEDGEMENT

The research presented in this dissertation was done in the Theoretical Laboratory of the Computer Research Institute and Innovation Center (SZKI) led by Bálint Dömölki and in the DAP Support Unit (DAPSU) of the Queen Mary College of the University of London led by Dennis Parkinson. I owe a special debt to Bálint Dömölki who has always been supported my research. I am greatful to Dennis Parkinson who invited me into the Queen Mary College and ensured all the conditions needed for a fruitful research work. Special thanks are due to Andrew Bale who assisted me in the implementation of DAP Prolog on the DAP

REFERENCES

[KaBa87] Kacsuk,P. and Bale,A. *DAP Prolog: A Set-Oriented Approach tc Prolog*, The Computer Journal, vol. 30, no. 5, 1987, 393-403

[Kacs84] Kacsuk,P. *A Highly Parallel Prolog Interpreter Based on the Generalized Data Flow Model*, Proc. of the 2nd Int. Logic Prog. Conf., Uppsala, 1984, 195-205

[Kacs85] Kacsuk,P. *Eager Evaluation of Prolog Programs in Homogenous Processor Space*, Proc. of Parallel Computing 85, West-Berlin, 1985.

[Kacs86] Kacsuk,P. *Some Approaches to Parallel Implementations of Prolog*, Proc. of IFIP'86 Congress, 1986, 803-809

[KaES86] Kacsuk,P. Errington,L. and Sary,A. *Parallel Implementation of Logic Programs in OCCAM*, University of Waterloo, 1986

[KaSE86] Kacsuk,P. Sary,A. and Errington,L. *Parallel Implementation of Logic Programs on iPSC*, University of Waterloo, 1986

[Warr83] Warren,D.H.D. *An Abstract Prolog Instruction Set*, Technical Note 309, SRI International, 1983

MODULAR HIGHLY-PARALLEL COMPUTATION AND ARCHITECTURES

(Extended abstract)

V.E.Kotov

Most of the highly-parallel architectures support more or less special applications. We are advocating and developing a modular approach to designing parallel computers with larger number of communicating processors. These computers with flexible, open architecture should make easier the adaptation of various application tasks to efficient parallel processing. The approach may be considered as an extension of the transputer design methodology towards more flexibility and generality.

1. INTRODUCTION

The times of extensive inventing of new parallel architectures based on inspiration, common sense and semi-formal schemas, seem to be approaching an end. For some years afforts have been made to define more precisely and formally naive concepts and models of concurrent computation. These researches are going in two main directions:

1) elaboration of formal models of concurrent computation and structures (process algebras, process logics, the net theory, etc.);

2) architectural experiments with the design of highly-parallel multiprocessors which are close as much as possible to real applications.

These two directions merge in most advanced developments. The convinsing example was given by the INMOS chain: the CSP model [1] -- the Occam language [2] -- the transputer architecture [3].

The greater part of the highly-parallel architectures was recently related to the fine-grain parallelism, i.e. the parallelism expressed at the level of operations and instructions rather than at the level of (user-defined) processes. It is quite natural, because the technological restrictions did not allow to provide sufficient computational resourses for many processors and because the properties of simple parallel operations are more transparent and predictable, the involved data

---

1) Computing Center, 630090 Novosibirsk, USSR

structures are, as a rule, regular, communications between parallel processes are restricted.

Also, the parallel computational methods for these computers do not present major departure from the sequential methods. This is valid, for example, for the SIMD-machines and systolic architectures. The computers of this type are usually more or less specialized and gain their peak performance in some narrow domains of computation. So, the next problem arises: is it possible to design the highly-parallel computers that maintain basic advantages of general-purpose computers, for example, mobility of application programs?

We look for a solution of this problem investigating the MIMD-structures composed of general-purpose processors. There are now quite a number of examples of multimicroprocessor systems built of standard commercial microprocessors. Their main weak points are lack of convincing computational models behind the design and bottlenecks in the input-output abilities of the microprocessors. The transputer design philosophy was a major breakthrough in this area. However, some features of the transputer and the model it supports still keep, as we suspect, the multitransputer systems in the domain of specialized parallel computers. We know that the problem of generality is practically solved for multiprocessor computers consisting of a relatively small number of processors. What changes should be introduced in the architecture of a basic processing element of such a multiprocessor, in distributed operating systems, in programming languages, etc., if the number of processors is increasing up to 100, 1000, 10 000, ...? Which of many possible schemas of the interprocessor communication are efficient for the solution of a broader scope of numerical and non-numerical computation?

To answer this questions, we have directed our work toward the experimental design of a modular, open multiprocessor architecture as an alternative to rigid parallel structures and processes. According to this design methodology, a multiprocessor computer represents a (statically) reconfigurable structure of the tightly-coupled processing modules which form a basis for the construction of different virtual multiprocessor machines. This architecture gives us the possibility to achieve two goals. At the first stage of our research, we are constructing a test-bed to make experiments with different concurrent structures, communication methods and mechanisms and to study relationship between computer structures and algorithms. Later on, we will be able to propose a set of final configurations for the efficient solution of different end-user problems. We hope this modular approach helps to smooth over the contrariness between the efficiency of special- and general-purpose machines, the contrariness which grows when the number of processors is increasing.

2. MODEL

Data-flow is a popular computational model for MIMD-computers that proposes a number of advantages for the effective exploiting of parallelism [4]: unlimited number of processors can be combined into extensible multiprocessor structures; scheduling and synchronization of concurrent activities may be built in at the hardware level; the number of processors can be changed without changing application code. However, the data-flow programming technics differ radically from those used in the conventional programming practice. Their efficient implementation requires 'unproductive' system activities and additional hardware. (This situation is quite typical for 'pure' and radical architectural philosofies.) Instead, we take as a basis a more traditional control-flow parallel model and augment it with some data-flow principles. The goal is to express and implement both fine-grain and coarse-grain parallelisms in an effective way (concurrent processes can vary from instructions or operations to tasks). The resulting architecture is expected to be less dependent on the parallelism granularity and, therefore, on specific features of applications.

We choose the CSP model as a starting point for development of modular concurrent models. Our primary reason for choosing this model that it is simple, well-studied and is implemented in the parallel programming language Occam. We would remind that process is the main concept of Occam. An Occam program is a process, a composite process may represent a collection of parallel subprocesses. Parallel processes communicate by input and output over so-called channels. An output process sends a value over a channel, an input process receives a value from the channel. Each of these communication actions waits for the other, so that an output is not completed until the corresponding input happens, and vice versa. Also, Occam requires that each channel has a unique input-process and a unique output-process.

We extend this communication model toward more asynchronism and modularity in the following way.

(1) Processes may exchange by arbitrary structured data through channels.

(2) A channel is a FIFO-buffer. After an input process sends data to a channel, it does not wait for the completion of the exchange procedure and continues to execute its subsequent actions. This communication schema is more asynchronous and it is supported by the special hardware component called asynchronous channel [5].

(3) Processes are created dynamically, the recursive creation is allowed.

Such a model is implemented in the parallel programming language Polar developed in the Novosibirsk Computing Center [6]. This language of functional programming style is used now for the design of the CAD systems, which actively use dynamic and recursive data structures (arrays, sets, records, lists, etc.).

3. IMPLEMENTATION

For the experimental examination of the worked-out models we are constructing prototypes of multiprocessor computers which use, as a basic processor, the 32-bit processor Kronos designed at the Novosibirsk Computing Center [7]. From the architectural point of view, it is a RISC-machine with the instruction set derived from the Lilith computer [8] and supporting the Modula-2 language. (There is no conventional assembler language, Modula-2 has proved to be efficient system implementation language, so the operating system is written in this language). The processor has the wide addressable memory space, the hardware mechanisms for creating and synchronization of processes. The evaluation stack is used to evaluate expressions and to hold parameters for procedure calls. The domains of memory for code, data and for global links between modules are fully separated. Special instructions simplify implementation of control primitives (loop, case, procedure calls) and array processing. Most of the executed instructions are encoded in a single byte, so the object code for Kronos is typically 4 times more compact than the code for the PDP computers.

The Kronos processor, memory block and asynchronous channels form a minimal processing module. The module may contain several processors and may be augmented by additional memory blocks, by an arithmetic coprocessor for 64-bit floating-point operations and by other specialized coprocessors. The processing modules are combined into multiprocessor configurations in different ways. They may form regular distributed networks (like, hipercubes) or more complex specialized connections. They may be combined into hierarchical clusters of different or identical structures. One of such more general configurations is organized as follows: several modules, communicating via asynchonous channels and by access to common shared memory, form a macro-module; the latters are combined in the same way to form super-modules, etc. The internal and external interfaces of processing modules are designed in such a way that they must provide easy assembling of multiprocessor configurations for architectural experiments and for final tayloring problem-oriented virtual machines.

Concurrent processes can be created dynamically and run concurrently at an arbitrary number of processing modules (allowing time-sharing processes at one processor). The main communication mechanism is based upon asynchronous channels. A logical (software) channels represents a queue together with synchronization primitives. A process can work with a channel if it is idle, i.e. it is ready to accept or send data. At the hardware level, each processing module contains only input or output 'half' of a channel. Two 'halves' are merged physically when a configuration is assembled. Each channel has a pointer which is set to the nil state or indicates some process waiting for an access to the channel. If the channel is idle and the pointer is set to a process identifier, then the pointer is set to nil and the channel number is put into a queue of active channels. When the processor executes a communication instruction, a data exchange between its stack and the channel memory occurs. If the required channel is not ready for such an exchange, then the pointer to the correspondent process is placed into the table of delayed processes at the location which is associated with this channel. This is aquainted in the channel pointer. If the waiting list is not empty, then the processor picks up the first element and starts the execution of the process which waits for the channel with the appropriate number. If the queue of the idle channels is empty, then an interruption occurs.

To make communication between processes more efficient in different virtual parallel machines, the following additional features are supported:

(1) Priority of processes accessing channels is introduced. The priority of a process is known when the process is created. There are different queues of ready channels for each priority level. Low priority processes will have access to a channel only when the higher priority processes do not require this channel.

(2) The time which a processor waits for a channel is limited. The time-out is stored in a control register of a channel, This allows, in particular, to recover the system after communication failures.

(3) The channels are protected from non-authorized accesses.

A processing module is seen from outside as a set of hardware and software asynchronous channels. The allocation of processes among processors and the relationship between hard and soft channels may be arranged automatically by the special modules of the operating system or it may be left to an user for choosing his own strategy. The important consequense of the proposed communication mechanism is that processes are logically independent. The complex and low-effective synchronization of the type "process-to-process" is replaced by the "data-to-process" synchronization.

The extensive facilities implemented in the proposed processing module to support concurrency allow to split any task into lousely- or tightly-coupled processes of various size and to minimize overhead losses for the interprocess communication. This gives us a hope that the overall performance of parallel computers built of such modules will be proportional to the number of modules for a wider class of problems.

The considered model and its architectural implementation allow to simulate computers built of transputers. The main design objective was to make the transputer methodology more flexible, to provide more evolutionary transition from the conventional programming practice to highly-parallel computation. The main differencies between the transputer and Kronos architecture may be summarized as follows:

(1) the transputer architecture is defined at the level of the Occam language, whereas the Kronos architecture is defined at the level of the interpreters from more convential languages, like Modula-2 and Ada;

(2) bufferized channels;

(3) "data-to-process" instead of "process-to-process" synchronization.

4. OPERATING SYSTEM

The modular architecture does not match traditional structures of 'monolithic' operating systems. Instead, the operating system is split into a relatively small core and a collection of basic programming systems (virtual operating systems). The core should support the openness and flexibility of the architecture and the efficiency of the interprocess communication. Thus, it represents a set of software modules with well-defined interfaces. The modules may form a hierarchical structure. Each module makes higher the abstraction level of the operations executed by hardware components or by the lower-level software modules.

Though the core is extensible, some permanent set of interfaces, called the interface layer, is established. The interface layer is used in basic programming systems to create their system environment. The further extentsion of the functional abilities of the core of the operating system is provided by the composition of operations of the interface layer or by addition of new basic modules to the core.

The main classes of the core modules are:

(1) Resourse management modules, which supply the interface layer with the declaration of the system resources and definition of operations over resources: seize, release, transfer, etc.

(2) Process management modules, which define several notion of processes, starting from simplest ones, like a processor, to such complex

notions, like Ada tasks. The main classes of operations over processes are creation, initiation, partial or total termination, history of a process. The set of synchronization primitives may include both simple operations, like communication between coroutines, and much more complex mechanisms, like rendez-vous, conditional critical sections, monitors, etc. The presense of these operations does not exclude the access to low-level primitives, like interruptions, handling real-time events. A programming system may deal with the interruprions which occur in its processes by means of the standard core operations or using own disciplines.

5. ALGORITHMS AND APPLICATIONS

As it was emphasized above, we aim at highly-parallel architecture which can be made efficient in a broad scope of applications. The open architecture principle and software and hardware modularity are considered to be basic approaches to solution of this problem. The first step consists in the design of the basic hardware and software modules which give the possibility to configurate virtual parallel machines for particular applications. At the second step, virtual parallel machines are designed as a result of the thorough analysis of different classes of algorithms and special requirements of different applications. The third step is development of problem-oriented sotware environments for these applications.

This process of the step-by-step construction of a final 'layered architecture' starting from the basic modular structure of 'building blocks' may be of iterative character. It is quite natural, that the first versions of the modular multiprocessor computers will be used for distributed computation with regular and easy parallelized algorithms, which do not reguire the cardinal revision of the traditional computational methods . The transition to new algorithms for MIMD-computers is a fundamental problem. In particular, the artificial intelligence is an area which may provide new opportunities for the concurrent computation supplying it with non-traditional algorithms and methodology. To test the maximal scope of potential applications for modular multiprocessor computers, we have chosen the evolutionary strategy. We have started the small series of the 32-bit monoprocessor work stations to validate the basic processor design and the basic software. Then we have built multiprocessor system MARS-T with up to 16 processor to extend our experiments with the basic processor and operating system at the concurrent programming context. The main experiments with the modular highly-parallel architecture will begin the next year when all components of the basic processing module (64-bit coprocessor, asynchronous channel, local bus) be completed in the on-chip versions.

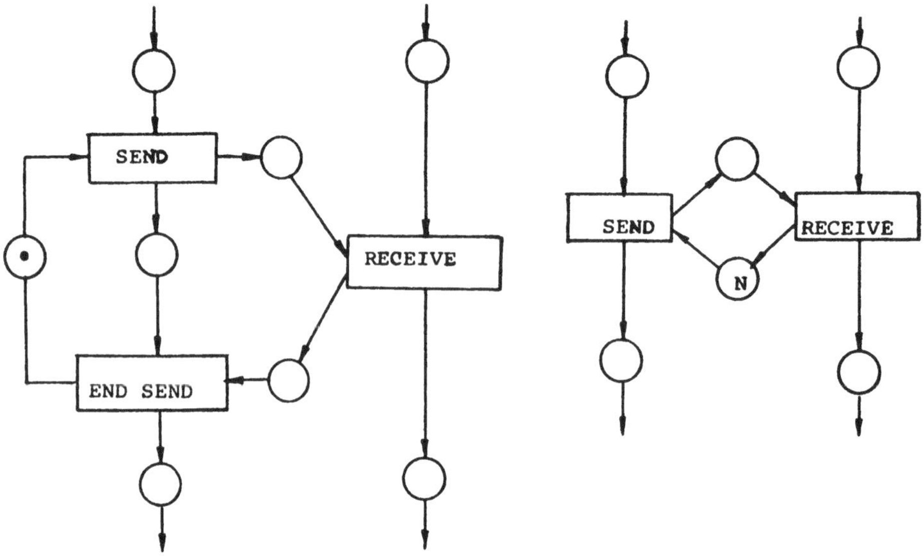

a/ Transputer link synchronization

b/ Asynchronous channel synchronization /N is the channel capacity/

Figure 1. The difference between link and asynchronous channel synchronizations /in terms of Petri nets/.

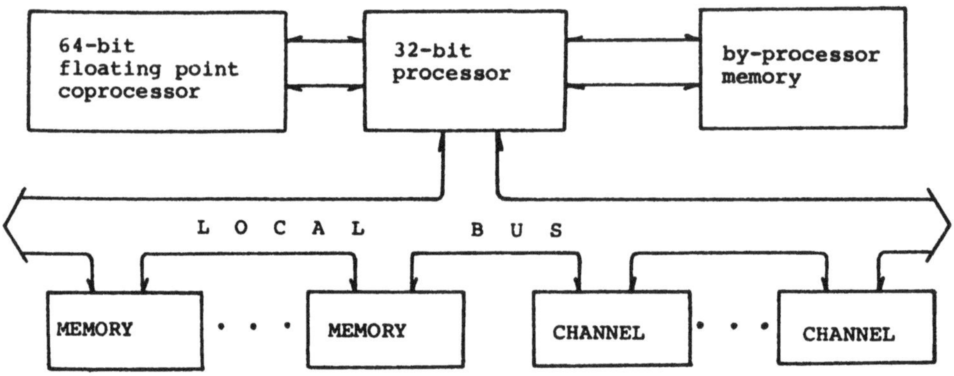

Figure 2. The basic processing module.

REFERENCES:

[1] Hoare C.A.R. Communicating sequential processes. CASM. Vol. 21, No 6, 1978.

[2] May D., Taylor R. OCCAM - an overview. Micro- processors and microsystems. Vol. 2, No 2, 1984.

[3] Barron I.M. The transputer and Occam. Proceedings of the I FIP-86 Congress. North Holl. Co., 1986.

[4] Gurd J., Kirkham Ch. Dataflow: Achievments and prospects. Proceedings of the IFIP-86 Congress. North Holl. Co., 1986.

[5] Kotov V.E., Marchuk A.G. The architecture of the MARS prototype. - In: Computer system and software. Novosibirsk, 1986 (in Russian).

[6] Marchuk A.G., Lelchuk T.I. The programming language Polar. Nauka, Novosibirsk, 1989 (in Russian).

[7] Kuznetsov D.N., Nedorya A.E., Osipov A.V., Tarasov E.V. The processor Kronos in a multiprocessor system. - In: Computer systems and software. Novosibirsk, 1986 (in Russian).

[8] Wirth N. The personal computer Lilith. Report No.40, Swiss Federal Institute of Technology, Zurich,1981.

PARALLEL COMPUTATION AND SUPERCOMPUTERS AND APPLICATIONS

by

U. Schendel

Institut für Mathematik III
Freie Universität Berlin

Report of the Research-Project "Parallele Numerik"
Sponsored by the DFG-Germany

1. INTRODUCTIONAL REMARKS

The development of high-speed-computers makes it necessary to reconfigurate well-known methods for solving large and complex systems or to develop new algorithms which are efficient.
The structure of these algorithms and their software are deeply dependent on the architecture of the used computer system and vice versa.
The following figure gives an idea of the importance to respect the adaption of the methods and the architecture of the computer system to the given problem.

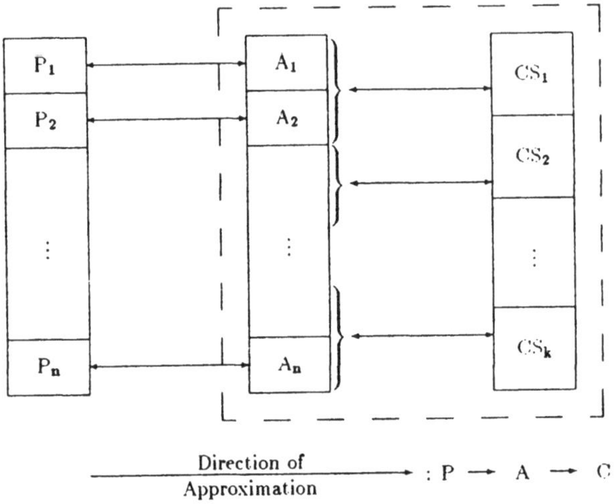

P : problem
P_i : subproblems
A_i : subalgorithms
CS_k : computer systems

$A := [A_1, A_2, \ldots, A_n]$

$C := [CS_1, \ldots, CS_k]$

Some significant applications are:

curve fitting; weather forecast; spin model; simplex optimization; physical field evaluation; evaluation of P/N transitions; solution of linear systems of equations; structure analysis; image processing and others.

2. CHARACTERIZATION OF PARALLEL COMPUTER ARCHITECTURES

A coarse and famous classification of computer systems is the classification of Flynn.

(i) SISD-Machine: Single-Instruction-Single-Data-Stream-Machine
(ii) SIMD-Machine: Single-Instruction-Multiple-Data-Stream-Machine
(iii) MISD-Machine: Multiple-Instruction-Single-Data-Stream-Machine
(iv) MIMD-Machine: Multiple-Instruction-Multiple-Data-Stream-Machine

Development of new computer architectures with different levels of parallelism requires a detailed classification which is essentially to the comparisons of computers.
A more detailed classification is introduced by D. Kuck.

Modern Computers are:
- CYBER 203/205 (SEA-Computer respectively SIMD-Machine)
- CRAY - 1 S (MEA-Machines)
- CRAY - X-MP
- CRAY - 2
- HEP-Denelcor (MEA-Machine respectively MIMD-Machine)
- Hitachi S9/IAP (Integrated Array Processor) (SIMD-Machine)
- Alliant
- FPS (Floating Point System)
  an others

The different levels of parallelism in parallel computation are shown in the following figure.

Levels of Parallelism

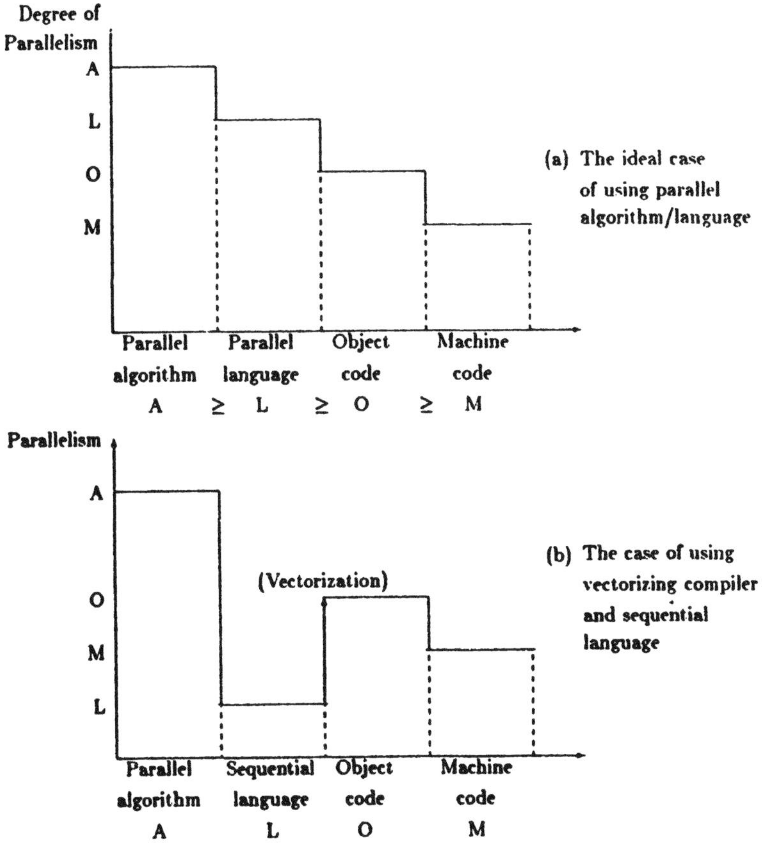

In sequential languages like Fortran, Pascal, and Algol, we still have $L = 1$. The natural parallelism in a machine is determined by the hardware. For example, the Cray 1 had $O = M = 64$ or 32. In the ideal situation with well-developed parallel-constructed user languages, we should expect $A \geq L \geq O \geq M$, as illustrated in Fig. (a).

At present, the parallelism in an algorithm is lost when it is expressed in a sequential high-level language. To promote parallel processing in machine hardware, an intelligent compiler is needed for the regeneration of parallelism lost in using serial codes. This regeneration process is called vectorization, as illustrated by Fig. (b).
In the terms of Mflops (1 Mflop = 1 million floating point operations per second) supercomputers are often defined by performing more than 100 Mflops

Both pipelined and array supercomputers are designed mainly for vector processing of large arrays of data. Presently, most of the commercially available vector supercomputers are pipelined machines owing to their cost-effectiveness. Besides using multiple pipelines in uniprocessor systems, supercomputer manufacturers are also challenging multitasking through the use of multiple processors.

The speedup of using an n-processor system over a uniprocessor system has been theoretically estimated to be within the range $(\log_2 n, n/\ln n)$. For an example, the speedup range is less than 6.9 for $n = 16$. Most of today's commercial multiprocessors have only 2 to 4 processors in a system.

The development of supercomputers is shown in the figure of the <u>space of supercomputers</u>:

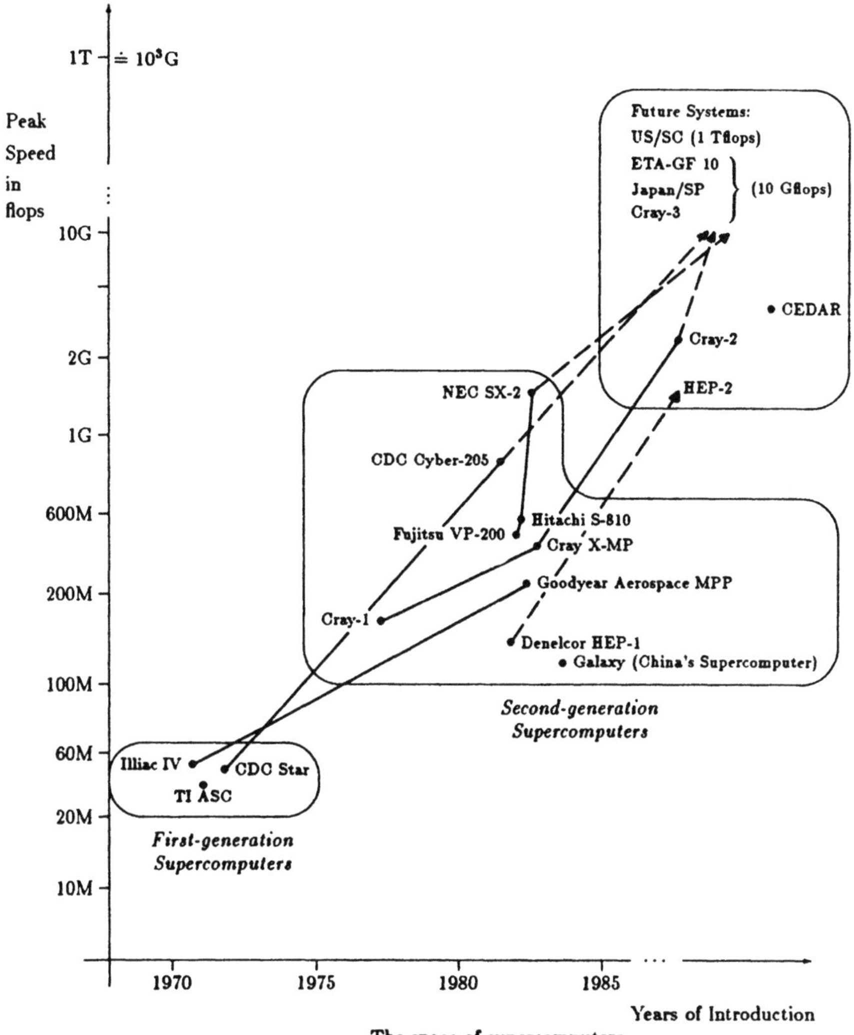

The space of supercomputers

At the highest level MIMD computers are classified; they are defined to be control-flow computers capable of processing more than one stream of instructions. The different instruction streams may be processed by seperate instruction processing units as in a multi-microprocessor design or they may timeshare a single instruction processing unit.
Because of the high importance we look a little bit more in detail what physical units make up the MIMD computer and how they are interconnected.

The following figures illustrate the <u>structural taxonomy of MIMD-computer systems</u>

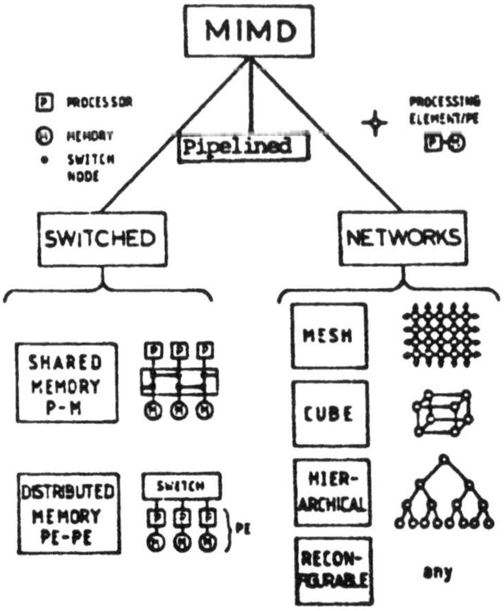

A structural taxonomy of MIMD computer systems.

<u>Subdivisions within the Switched class of MIMD computer systems.</u>

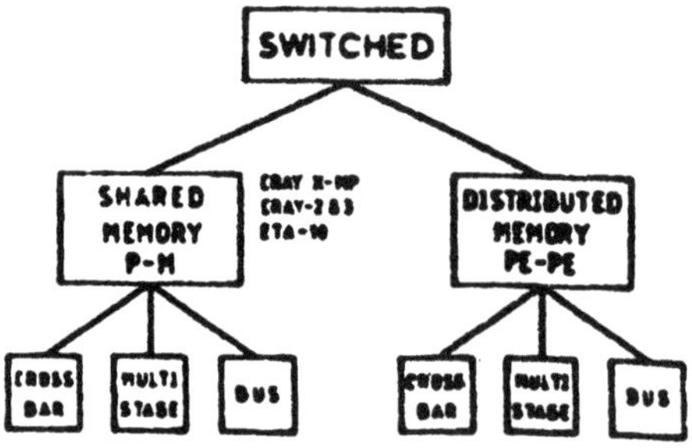

Subdivision within the Network class in MIMD computer systems

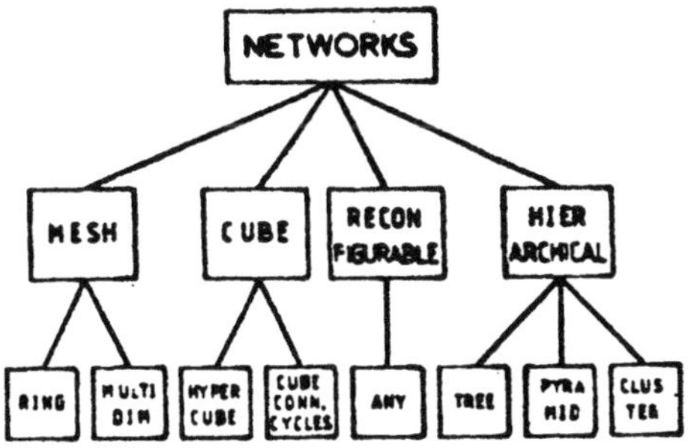

3. SOME BASIC CONCEPTS FOR THE DEVELOPMENT OF PARALLEL NUMERICAL ALGORITHMS

Structure of parallel algorithms

In a parallel algorithm, because more than one task module can be executed at a time, concurrency control is needed to ensure the correctness of the concurrent execution. The concurrency control enforces desired interactions among task modules so that the overall execution of the parallel algorithm will be correct. The following figure represents the space of concurrency controls that can be used in parallel algorithms:

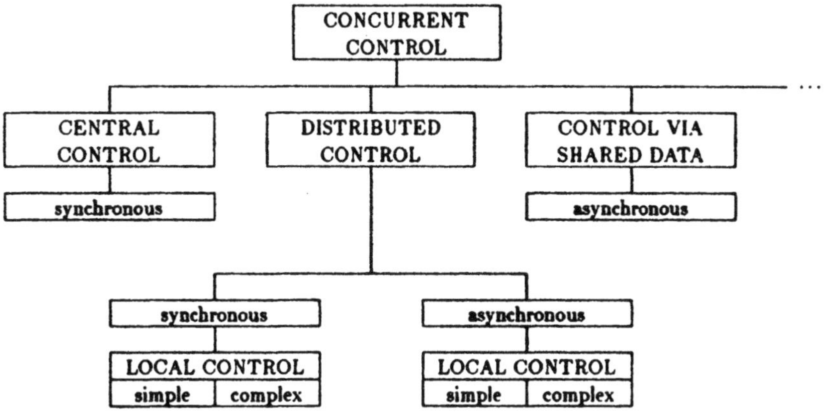

The leafes of the tree represent various types of concurrency controls. Concurrent control has a great influence on the structure of algorithm.

Characterization of the algorithms

Type	Concurrent Control	Remarks
SIMD-algorithm	central control unit -SIMD-	SIMD machines correspond to synchronous algorithms that require central controls
MIMD-algorithms	asynchronous, Shared memory -MIMD-	MIMD machines correspond to asynchronous algorithms with relatively large granularities
Systolic-algorithms	distributed control achieved by simple local control	LSI and VLSI machines for special algorithms.

Remarks:

(i) Systolic algorithms are designed for direct hardware implementations.

(ii) MIMD algorithms are designed for executions on general purpose multiprocessors.

(iii) SIMD algorithms are lying between the two other types.

Some remarks on the development of parallel algorithms

The previous considerations show, that the "kind" of parallelism of the computer (SIMD- or MIMD-machine) has an essential influence on the algorithms. Moreover, the arrangement and dynamic sorting of data in memory, on which the algorithm wants to have parallel access is of importance.

Numerical methods are based on the evaluation of arithmetic expressions. The exploitation on such expressions can be represented by graphs (trees). Application of the laws of the real numbers often leads to "tree-hight-reduction" whose possible utilization is dependent on the considered type of computer; that is that an algorithm A is a composition of arithmetic expressions E_k :

$$A = E_1 \circ E_2 \circ \ldots \circ E_n$$

One idea, how arithmetic expressions could be parallelized, is supplied by the simple expression

$$A := a_4 + (a_3 + (a_2 + a_1)), a_i \in \mathbb{R}$$

which by utilization of the associativity of addition can be transformed into

$$\tilde{A} = (a_4 + a_3) + (a_2 + a_1)$$

which means that two additions can be done in parallel. Given an arbitrary expression A_0 one tries to split this into two smaller expressions A_1 and A_2, which can be calculated simultaneously, each by one processor. For execution on a SIMD-machine the following conditions must be valid:

1. There exist a function f with $A_0 = f(A_1, A_2)$.

2. A_1 and A_2 are computed independent of each other and are of the same complexity.

3. A_1 and A_2 requires the same series of computation.

Further splitting of A_1 and A_2 according to 1. - 3. leads to A_0 by recursive doubling.

Example 1: Recursive doubling [Kogge]

Given

$$S := \{a_1, a_2, \ldots, a_N \mid N = 2^k, k \in \mathbb{N}\} \subset \mathbb{R}$$

and an associative operation op $\in M := \{+, *, \max, \ldots\}$ in S.

$$A := a_1 \text{ op } a_2 \text{ op } \ldots \text{ op } a_N$$

shall be calculated.

Example: There are two trees G and $\tilde{G}$ for the expressions

$$A := a_1 + a_2 + a_3 + a_4$$

and

$$\tilde{A} := (a_1 + a_2) + (a_3 + a_4)$$

respectively

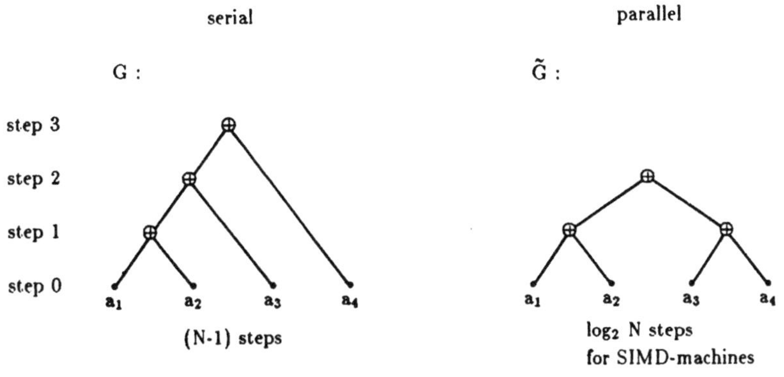

With $N = 2^k$ elements the recursive doubling requires $\log_2 N$ steps on a SIMD-computer.

Example 2: Mixed expressions

Given

$$A := a_1 + a_2 * a_3 + a_4$$

By associativity no tree-hight-reduction is achieved. The tree G for serial exploitation of A is not unique. Communication law for addition transforms A into

$$A := (a_1 + a_4) + a_2 * a_3$$

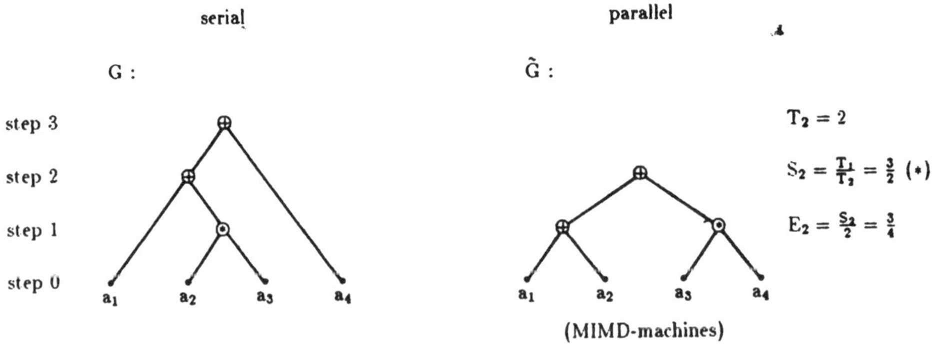

Tree-hight-reduction on a MIMD-computer is possible.
Among others the following questions arise (s.[Beatty], [Baer], [Bovet], [Kuck], [Murocoka]):

1. How many tree-hight-reductions can be performed for an arithmetic expression A ?
2. Do exist algorithms for tree-hight-reduction ?
3. How many processors are necessary ?

<u>Recurrent relations</u>

Recurrent relations are qualified for the solution of problems which are solved by a sequence $x_1, x_2, \ldots, x_n$, $x_i \in \mathbb{R}$ and where each $x_i, i = 1, \ldots, n$ could be dependent on other components $x_j (j < i)$.

A common example of recurrent relations is a time-varying linear system where the state of the system x_t at time t is a linear function with initial condition x_1

(*) Note: T_p is the number of time unit steps required by a parallel algorithm designed to utilize $p \geq 1$ processors. T_1 is the time for the corresponding serial algorithm.
$S_p := \frac{T_1}{T_p}$ is called <u>speed-up</u> and $E_p := \frac{S_p}{p}$ is called <u>efficiency</u> .

$$x_1 := c_1 \qquad \text{initial condition}$$

$$x_2 := a_2 x_1 + c_2$$

$$\vdots$$

$$x_t := a_t x_{t-1} + c_t \qquad \text{recurrent equation}$$

$$\vdots$$

$$x_n := a_n x_{n-1} + c_n$$

On the surface only a sequential evaluation seems to be possible.

Definition

An m-th order linear recurrent system of n equations R <n,m> is defined for $m \leq n-1$ by

$$R\langle n,m\rangle := x_n := \begin{cases} 0 & , k \leq 0 \\ c_k + \sum_{j=k-m}^{k-1} a_{kj}\, x_j, & 1 \leq k \leq n \end{cases}$$

If m = n-1 the system is called an ordinary linear recurrent system R<n>. Now we can consider recurrent relations in general.

Definition

A general m-th order recurrent system R<n,m> is defined by

$$R\langle n,m\rangle := x_k := H[\bar{a}_k;\, x_{k-1}, x_{k-2}, \ldots, x_{k-m}],\ 1 \leq k \leq n$$

with m initial values $x_{-m+1}, \ldots, x_0$.

H is called the recurrence funktion and $\bar{a}_k$ is a vector of parameters independent of any of the x_i .

These systems are qualified for SIMD-machines.

Example:

For a first order recurrent systems we get

$$x_1 := c_1 \qquad \text{initial value}$$

$$x_k := a_k x_{k-1} + c_k,\ 2 \leq k \leq n$$

$$= H[\bar{a}_k; x_{k-1}]$$

with

$$\bar{a}_k := [a_k, c_k];$$

H is defined by addition and multiplication.

Example

Linear recurrent relations of first order

$$
\begin{aligned}
x_1 &= b_1 \\
x_2 &= -a_2 x_1 + b_2 \\
&\vdots \\
x_k &= -a_k x_{k-1} + b_k \\
&\vdots \\
x_n &= -a_n x_{n-1} + b_n
\end{aligned}
$$

finally $Lx = b$

with
$$
\left.\begin{aligned}
l_{ii} &= 1, \quad i = 1,\dots,n \\
l_{i,i-1} &= a_i, \quad i = 2,\dots,n \\
l_{ik} &= 0 \quad \text{else}
\end{aligned}\right\} \quad L = \begin{bmatrix} 1 & & & 0 \\ a_2 & 1 & & \\ & a_3 & & \\ & 0 & a_n & 1 \end{bmatrix}
$$

solution: $x = L^{-1}b = L_n^{-1} L_{n-1}^{-1} \dots L_3^{-1} L_2^{-1} b$

$$
L_i^{-1} = \begin{bmatrix} E_{i-2} & & 0 \\ & 1 & \\ & -a_i \quad 1 & \\ 0 & & E_{n-i} \end{bmatrix} \longleftarrow \text{row } i
$$

↑ column i-1

serial:

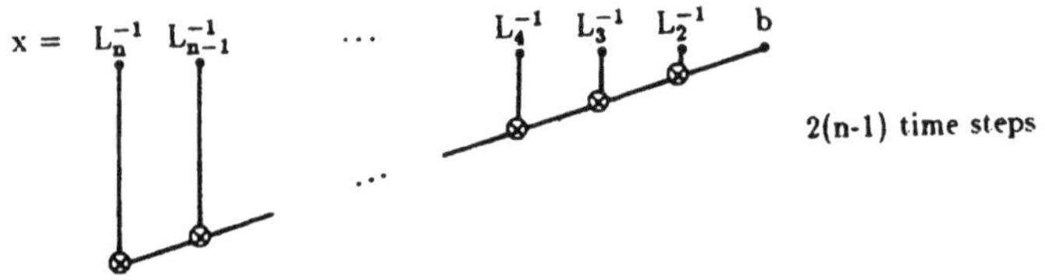

Parallel factorization: $n=2^N$

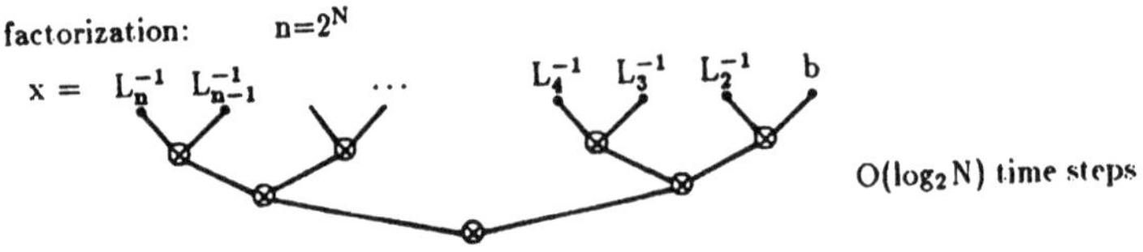

Note:

The parallel solution of linear recurrent relations of order (n-1) with $O(n^3)$ processors requires

$$\frac{1}{2}(\log_2 n)^2 + O(\log_2 n)$$

time steps with $O(n^3)$ operations.
For a parallel solution of these systems the associativity of the recurrence function H must be required.
If the given H-function is not associative, there often exist so called companion functions G with associative properties.

Definition

A function G is called companion function of the recurrence function H if for all x and for all parameter vectors $\bar{a},\bar{b} \in \mathbb{R}^p$

$$H[\bar{a};H[\bar{b};x]] = H[G(\bar{a},\bar{b});x]$$

with $\qquad G : \mathbb{R}^p \times \mathbb{R}^p \to \mathbb{R}^p$

All companion functions have the following property:

Theorem

Each companion function G is associative with respect to its recurrent function H; that means: for all x and for all parameter vectors $\bar{a},\bar{b},\bar{c} \in \mathbb{R}^p$

$$H[G(\bar{a},G(\bar{b},\bar{c}));x] = H[G(G(\bar{a},\bar{b}),\bar{c});x]$$

Conclusion

The existence of G allows the construction of a parallel algorithm by the log-sum-algorithm.

Example for companion-functions in recurrent relations

$x_k := H[\bar{a}_k;x_{k-1}]; \ \bar{a}_k \in \mathbb{R}^p \ ; \ x_o$ initial value

$$\begin{aligned}
x_2 &= H[\bar{a}_2;x_1] \\
&= H(\bar{a}_2;H(\bar{a}_1;x_o)) = H(G(\bar{a}_2,\bar{a}_1);x_o); \text{ G companion-function} \\
x_4 &= H[\bar{a}_4;x_3] \\
&= H(\bar{a}_4;H(\bar{a}_3;x_2)) = H(G(\bar{a}_4,\bar{a}_3);x_2) \\
&= H(G(\bar{a}_4,\bar{a}_3);H(G(\bar{a}_2,\bar{a}_1);x_o)) \\
&= H(G(G(\bar{a}_4,\bar{a}_3),G(\bar{a}_2,\bar{a}_1));x_o) \\
x_8 &= H[\bar{a}_8;x_7] \\
&= H(\bar{a}_8;H(\bar{a}_7;H(\bar{a}_6;H(\bar{a}_5;x_4)))) \\
&= H(G(\bar{a}_8,\bar{a}_7);H(G(\bar{a}_6,\bar{a}_5);x_4)) \\
&= H(G(\bar{a}_8,\bar{a}_7);H(G(\bar{a}_6,\bar{a}_5);H(G(G(\bar{a}_4,\bar{a}_3),G(\bar{a}_2,\bar{a}_1);x_o)))) \\
&= H(G(G(\bar{a}_8,\bar{a}_7),G(\bar{a}_6,\bar{a}_5));H(G(G(\bar{a}_4,\bar{a}_3),G(\bar{a}_2,\bar{a}_1);x_o))) \\
&= H(G(\underbrace{G(\underbrace{G(\bar{a}_8,\bar{a}_7)}\underbrace{,G(\bar{a}_6,\bar{a}_5)}),G(\underbrace{G(\bar{a}_4,\bar{a}_3)}\underbrace{,G(\bar{a}_2,\bar{a}_1)})}));x_o)
\end{aligned}$$

Graph for x_{2^k}

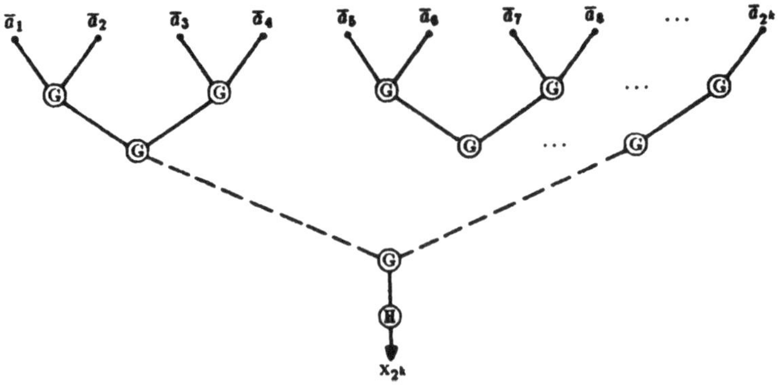

4. INTRODUCTIONAL REMARKS ON HYPERCUBE-SYSTEMS

The Hypercube or n-cube or cosmic cube is an example of a distributed-memory, message-passing multiprocessor-system ($64 \leq N \leq 1024$ or more processors) with a large-scale parallel architecture.
The processors have private local memory and their activities are coordinated by sending messages among themselves through an interconnection network.

Definition

An n-cube consists of 2^n nodes that are numbered by n-bit binary numbers i with $0 \leq i \leq 2^n-1$ and interconnected so that there is a link between 2 processors if their binary representation differs by one and only one bit.

Processors-called nodes- are usually identical.
The master-controller-processor is called host.

Jobs of the host

- initiate a computation
- collect results upon completion
- serve as link to the outside world

Because of local memory a distributed operating system is necessary.
A hypercube is a true MIMD-computersystem (s.a.)

n=1: 1-cube with 2 nodes

n=2: 2-cube with 4 nodes

n=3: 3-cube with 8 nodes

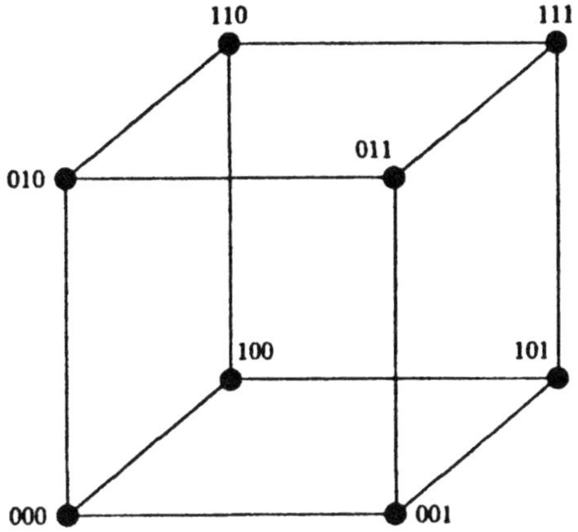

In a hypercube, each processor is connected to all other processors whose binary tags differ from its own by exactly one bit. Topologically, this arrangement places the processors at the vertices (corners) of an N-dimensional cube.

n=1:

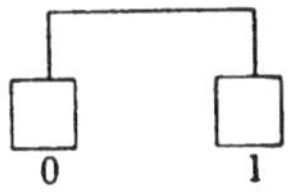

n=2:

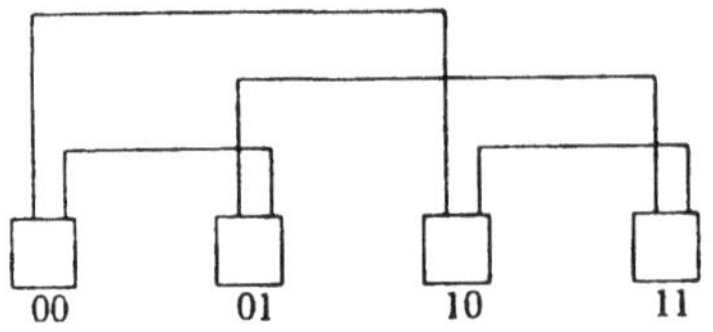

n=3:

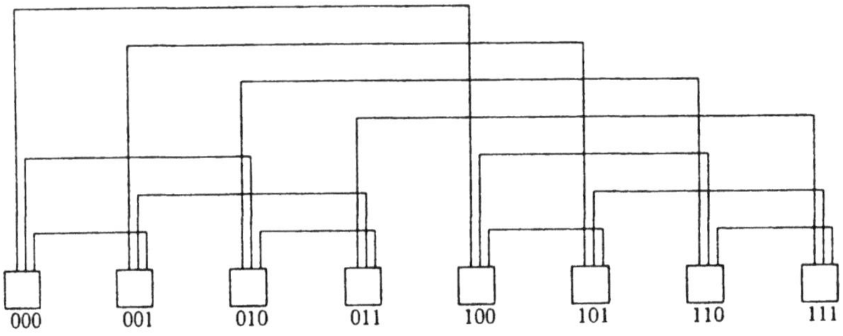

Hypercubes of arbitrary dimension can be made by using a linear arrangement with connecting wires.
High-level programming language on a link-based hypercubesystem is LINDA (AT&T Bell Labs)

Special Hypercube:

- NCUBE/ten is a VLSI Parallel Supercomputer with cost-performance figures beyond other systems
- Computational and I/O performance in the supercomputer range
- $500 \cdot 10^6$ floating-point-operations/sec (500 M flops)
- 8 I/O channels with 180 million bytes/sec bandwidth
- AXIS-operating system in a UNIX-style (extended UNIX)

  AXIS is a virtual memory, multitasking multiuser system on the host
- VERTEX is a nucleus of an operating system which runs on each of the nodes

  AXIS & VERTEX support an efficient programming style.

Classical example

Matrix Computation in a hypercube -as a Distributed Memory Message Passing machine -DMMP-machine-

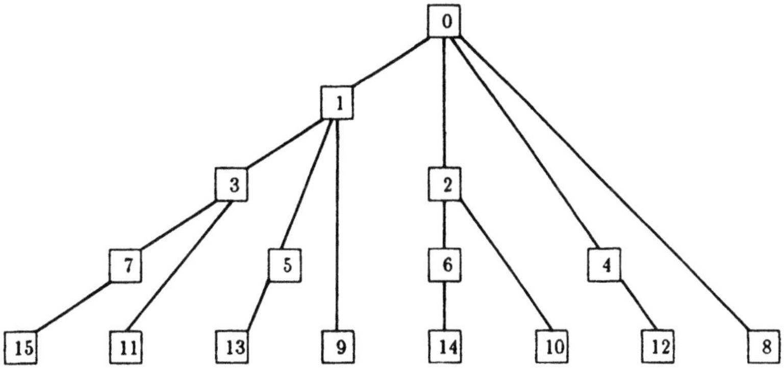

Note: Global Operations: Global send := send a vector from one processor to all other processor (= gsend)

Global sum := form the vector sum of p vectors, one from each processor (= gsum)

"Use of spanning trees" for calculation of $y := \sum_{k=o}^{p-1} y_k$.

Each processor k has a vector quantity y_k .

Important applications

- Gaussian elimination for large symmetric banded linear systems is important when solving elliptic PDE's.

- Multigrid methods

  Multigrid methods use a hierarchy of coarser grids (in addition to the one on which the solution is sought) in order to improve the rate of convergence to the solution process.

  This hierarchy presents a challenge when attempting to minimize the communication overhead in a parallel implementation.

  The grid points x_i will be mapped to special nodes of the hypercube.

5. APPLICATION

Domain Decomposition Techniques

Another class of techniques that received much attention recently is the class of domain decomposition techniques in which the physical domain is divided into separate subdomains each handled by a different processor.

Let us consider the numerical solution of the partial differential equation

$$\frac{\partial u}{\partial t} = F(x,u,t,D_x u,D_x^2 u,\ldots)$$

where $x \in \Omega \in \mathbb{R}^n$, $0 \le t \le \tau$ and $u(x,t) \in \mathbb{R}^m$ satisfies given boundary and initial conditions. Then at t*,

$$\Omega = \bigcup_{j=1}^{k(t^*)} \Omega_j(t^*)$$

and on each Ω_j

$$\frac{\partial u}{\partial t} = F_j(x,u), \; j = 1,2,\ldots,k(t^*)$$

is defined. Each processor P_j solves one of these partial differential equations over a prespecified time interval.

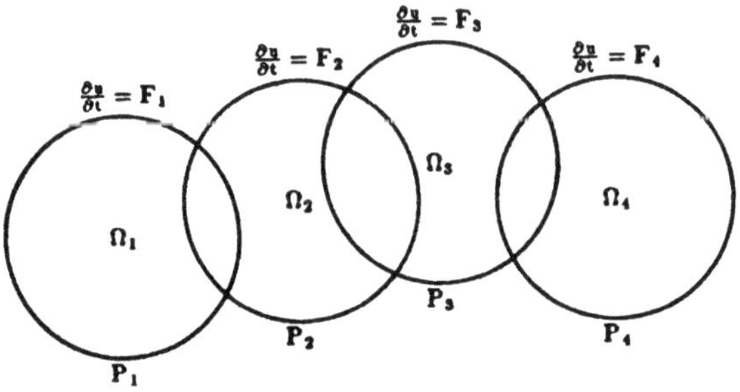

Discretization of the PDE by finite differences or finite elements gives the linear system:

$$L^h\bar{u} = \begin{bmatrix} A_1 & B_1 & & \\ B_1^T & A_2 & B_2 & \\ & & & B_{n-1} \\ & B_{n-1}^T & & A_n \end{bmatrix} \begin{bmatrix} \bar{u}(1) \\ \bar{u}(2) \\ \vdots \\ \bar{u}(n) \end{bmatrix} = \begin{bmatrix} \bar{b}(1) \\ \bar{b}(2) \\ \vdots \\ \bar{b}(n) \end{bmatrix} = \bar{b}$$

$\bar{u}(i)$ is the numerical approximation to $\bar{u}$ on the points (x_i,y_j), for $j = 1,2,\ldots n$

A_i, B_i are (n,n)-tridiagonal matrices with $A_i = A_i^T$

A solution can be obtained by an iterative process, e.g.

- SOR-method
- preconditioned cg method
- multigrid method
- Schwarz algorithm

6. TRENDS AND PROBLEMS

Only some interesting projects will be mentioned:

- Different projects on parallel software and parallel algorithms at LLNL and ANL, U.S.A.
- CEDAR-project at the University of Illinois at Urbana-Champaign
- Other projects in the U.S.A.

- Japanese Supercomputer-Project
  "BIG SIX": Fujitsu, Hitachi, NEC, Mitsubishi, Oki, Toshiba .
  Production of a supersystem > 10 Gflops and main memory of 10^9 bytes (~ 1990) including high-speed-components and the fifth-generation-project (~ 1993)
- European Project ESPRIT
- SUPRENUM-Project (GMD-Germany)
  - Development of a high-performance computer for large scale problems in numerical simulation and scientific computing.
  - Some characteristics
  - highly parallel computing (MIMD multiprocessor system)
  - Solving a very large class of numerical grid problems
  - supporting the multilevel principle
  - algorithmic speed-up
  - multiprocessor speed-up

One root of the SUPRENUM-development is the continually increasing need of computing power in a variety of disciplines in natural and engineering sciences; e.g. problems in fluid dynamics, metereology, nuclear physics, plasma physics, geology, micro electronics and others.
For this purpose highly complex mathematical models are provided which describe the corresponding real world phenomena.

References

[1] Feilmeier,M., Joubert, G. & Schendel, U., eds.,
Parallel Computing 83,
North-Holland, Amsterdam (1984)

[2] Feilmeier, M., Joubert, G. & Schendel, U., eds.,
Parallel Computing 85,
North-Holland, Amsterdam (1986)

[3] Flynn, M.J., Very high speed computing systems,
Proc. IEEE, 14, 1901-1909(1966)

[4] Giloi, W.K., Rechnerarchitektur,
Springer-Verlag, Berlin, Heidelberg, New York (1981)

[5] Golm, K. & Schendel, U.,
On Special Parallel Algorithms for Parabolic Differential
Equations, Parallel Computing 85, North-Holland, Amsterdam (1986)

[6] Hockney, R.W. & Jesshope, C.R.,
Parallel Computers, Adam Hilger Limited (1981)

[7] Hwang, K., Tutorial Supercomputers: Design and Applications,
IEEE Computer Society Press, Silver Spring, MD (1984)

[8] Kowalik, J.S., ed.,
Parallel MIMD computation: HEP Supercomputer and Its Applications,
The MIT Press, Cambridge, Massachusetts (1985)

[9] Metropolis, N., Sharp, D.H., Worlton, W.J. & Ames, K.R., eds.,
Frontiers of Supercomputing, University of California Press,
Berkeley (1986)

[10] Moto-oka, T., ed.,
Fifth Generation Computer Systems,
North-Holland, Amsterdam (1982)

[11] Müller-Wichards, D. & Gentzsch, W.,
Performance comparisons among several parallel and vector computers
on a set of fluid flow problems,
DVFLR, Report No. IB262-82R01, Göttingen (1982)

[12] Schendel, U.,
Introduction to Numerical Methods for Parallel Computers,
John Wiley & Sons, New York (1984)

[13] Schendel, U., On Basic Concepts in Parallel Numerical Mathematics,
CONPAR 81, Springer-Verlag, Berlin, Heidelberg, New York (1981)

[14] Schendel, U. & Brandenburger, J.,
Algorithmen zur Lösung Rekurrenter Relationen,
Preprint No. 101/79, Freie Universität Berlin (1979)

[15] Schendel, U. & Westphal, K.-P.,
MIMD-Rechner und Anwendungen,
Preprint No. 203/85, Freie Universität Berlin (1985)

[16] Wouk, A., ed.,
New Computing Environments: Parallel, Vector and Systolic,
SIAM, Philadelphia (1986)

Fast Parallel Algorithms and the Complexity of Parallelism
(Basic issues and recent advances)

Paul G. Spirakis

Computer Technology Institute, PO BOX 1122,
26110, Patras, Greece
and
Courant Institute of Math. Science, NYU, USA

Abstract

The paper classifies the problems solvable very fast in parallel with a feasible number of processors and contrasts them with problems hard to parallelize. The notions of NC^1-reducibilities, RNC^1-reducibilities, log-space reducibilities are presented and problems complete (or randomly complete) for P are defined and discussed. The notion of optimal parallel time-number of processors tradeoff is highlighted and several techniques to achieve optimal tradeoff are presented. Several results about fast parallel approximations to P-complete problems are described. Finally, certain milestones in the design of efficient parallel algorithms are noted and their impact is discussed.

1. Introduction

Interest in parallel architectures and parallel algorithms has grown steadily in the past few years. Commercial parallel processors have become a reality and large-scale multiprocessors are being built. The main challenge now is whether these machines can be programmed to make efficient use of their increased computing power. Hence, the issue of feasible parallel computation is now a challenge for computer scientists. Today it is known that a lot of problems can be solved very rapidly in parallel (say, in time polynomial in logn, n being the problem size) by a parallel computer with a feasible (say, polynomial) number of processors. This class of problems was first identified and characterized by Pippenger [Pippenger, 1979] and people call it NC (for "Nick's class" eg see [Cook, 1981], [Ruzzo, 1981], [Dymond, Cook, 1980], [Cook, 1985]). It has been also found, however that certain limits exist (or quite possibly exist) in the speed-up given by the parallelism. There seem to be two reasons for the existence of such limits. Firts, parallelism is restricted by the need for an intensive interprocessor communication and a simultaneous memory access. Large information flow between the processing elements is necessary in certain cases, but it cannot be supported efficiently by the parallel architectures that we know of. One can imagine a device which has no communication and memory access restrictions. But, even in this case, there exist lower bounds to the computational time, which are due to the intrinsic parallel complexity of problems. In very general terms, parallelism is restricted because some intermediate results must be known before other parts of the computation can start.

A big number of formal parallel computer models have appeared in the literature (see [Cook, 1981], [Vishkin, 1983] for surveys). Most frequently used is a parallel variant of a random access machine with weak restrictions to a simultaneous memory access. This PRAM (Parallel Random Access Machine) (see [Fortune, Wyllie, 1978]) assumes the possible use of arbitrarily many identical processors working synchronously in the processing mode SIMD (single instruction, multiple data) and using a common memory (shared, global) which is unlimited. Processors can store integers into the memory, load them in their own registers and perform logical and arithmetic operations. The memory read/write cycle is assumed to take one time unit. Let us assume that each step of a parallel RAM consists of three parts: first each processor may read one cell of the common memory, then do its internal computation, and finally try to write into one cell. Let E stand for "exclusive", C for "concurrent", R for "read" and W for "write". The EREW PRAM (or PRAC, as in [Lev, Pippenger, Valiant, 1981]) may not perform any simultaneous access, while the PRAM (or CREW PRAM, [Fortune, Wyllie, 1978]) may perform simultaneous reads. If one allows also simultaneous writes (CREW PRAM or WRAM) then several conventions are possible for the resolution of write conflicts. For example, in the SIMDAG model [Goldschlager, 82], the lowest numbered processor succeds in the case of a write conflict. (This model is also called priority-conflict resolution rule PRAM). The WRAM (of [Shiloah, Vishkin, 81] is another version of CRCW PRAM where some processor succeeds in case of a write conflict but we don't care which. Other conventions that appeared in the literature are (a) the weak-conflict resolution rule PRAM in which simultaneous writing is allowed only to selected memory locations containing the numbers 0 or 1 only and all processors writing simultaneously into the same memory location must store the value 1. Also, (b) the "Equality conflict resolution rule-PRAM" where simultaneous writing into the same memory location is allowed provided that all processors involved store the same value. It has been shown ([Kucera, 82]) that the computational power of all those versions of CRCW PRAM is equal in a certain sense, namely that if a version of a CRCW PRAM solves a problem in time f(n) then for any particular other version of CRCW PRAM there is a constant β such that the same problem can be solved in time $\beta f(n)$ in that model.

As [Cook, 85] remarks, a reason for favoring the CRCW PRAMs (especially the priority one) is that the circuitry needed to implement them seems not to be substantially more complicated than that needed to implement a machine which disallows read and write conflicts. A better reason

is that the complexity classes defined by the SIMDAG or other CRCW-PRAMs have nice characterizations in terms of the alternation depth required on circuits (see [Chardra, Stockmeyer, Vishkin, 1982]) or alternating Turing Machines(see [Ruzzo, Tompa, 1982]).

Although the various PRAMs seem a good way to go, the possible variations of their detailed definition make them unappealing to some researchers (eg [Cook, 85]). The model of uniform Boolean circuits (see [Borodin, 1977]) is more fundamental than the others considered since it seems that all real computers can be built from circuits. Finally, in this not ending model story, one of the earliest models used is that of the parallel computation tree. There one does not care how interprocessor communication is realized. A processor can use all the results computed by its colleagues at previous steps. There is a very recent interest to a restricted form of this model (processors can exchange values only along the lines of a certain dag with them as nodes), because one can model interprocessor communication by a pure delay parameter when values are exchanged among different processors (see [Papadimitriou, Yannakakis, 1988]).

Fortunately, the parallel class NC remains the same whether uniform circuits or shared memory computers of any kind are used to define it (although its subclasses NC^k may be different).

One criticism raised by various researchers about the general theory of parallel complexity is that real computers must exist in 3-dimensional space and, therefore, the communication time for just one parallel step must be $\Omega(n^{1/3})$. Thus it is meaningless to say that a problem is solved in time $O(\log^k n)$. Of course, one can immediately answer that, by the same argument, sequential memories ough't to have access times $\Omega(n^{1/3})$ and yet in Computer Science it is assumed that the access time in sequential machines is $O(1)$ or $O(\log n)$ and this assumption led to may useful results.

2. Related Complexity Classes

The complexity of any parallel algorithm can be characterized by its processor bound $P(n)$ and its time bound $T(n)$. (We ignore the space bound $S(n)$ in parallel algorithms for simplicity and because it is often close to the processor bound, i.e. space is less valuable than processors). In terms of PRAM complexity measures, the class NC is the class of problems solvable in $T(n)=O(\log^{O(1)} n)$ and $P(n)=O(n^{O(1)})$. Of course, if $T_{seq}(n)$ is the best known asymptotic sequential time for a problem, we say that a solution of the problem in a PRAM has optimal time-processor tradeoff if $P(n).T(n)=O(T_{seq}(n))$. A "precise" definition of NC in terms of Boolean circuits is the following: (See [Cook, 1985]).

DEFINITION: Let NC^k be the set of all problems solvable by a uniform Boolean circuit formily F_n, with number of gates $c(F_n)=n^{0(1)}$ and with length of the longest path from some input to some output of F_n (depth, $d(F_n)$) being $d(F_n)=0(\log^k n)$.

DEFINITION: $NC=\bigcup_k NC^k$

DEFINITION: Let AC^k be the class of all functions computable by CRCW PRAM in $0(\log^k n)$ time with $n^{0(1)}$ processors. Then, $NC=\bigcup_k AC^k$ and also $AC^k \subset NC^{k+1}$ (see [Cook, 1985], [Ruzzo, 1981]. In fact, AC^k consists of those problems solvable by uniform unbounded fan-in circuits in $0(\log^k n)$ depth and polynomial number of gates, [Cook, Ruzzo, 1983].

There is a very interesting relation between parallel time and sequential space. As shown in [Fortune, Wyllie, 1978], if L is a language accepted by a deterministic T(n) time-bounded PRAM then L is accepted by a T(n) space-bounded deterministic Turing Machine. This result can be produced by first constructing a nondeterministic Turing Machine simulation of the PRAM computation and then by doing a Savitch-type simulation of the nondeterminism without increasing the space bound. The inverse of this result is also very intriguing:

Lemma [Fortune, Wyllie, 1978] if L is accepted by a deterministic T(n)-space bounded deterministic Turing Machine with $T(n) \geq \log n$, then L is accepted by a (deterministic) cT(n)-time bounded PRAM P for some constant c, and the number of processors of P is at most $2^{dT(n)}$, for some constant d, depending on the machine.

An interesting corollary of the above is that the class DSPACE (logn) of all problems solved by a deterministic Turing Machine in space 0(logn) is a subset of the class AC^1.

By adding to the PRAMs (or to the Boolean circuits) the ability to do random choices between alternatives, one can arrive to the definition of a class similar to the class BPP ([Gill, 1977]) of all sets recognizable in polynomial time by a probabilistic Turing Machine with error probability at most (say) 1/4. This class is called RNC (Random NC) and contains all problems solvable by probabilistic PRAMs in parallel polylog time and by using a polynomial number of processors, with error probability at most 1/4 (or any number bounded away and smaller than 1/2). RNC can also be defined in terms of probabilistic Boolean circuits. Here a probabilistic circuit is a Boolean circuit with ordinary inputs x and "coin-tossing" inputs Y. NC is contained in RNC almost by definition, but it is not known whether RNC is a subclass of NC, or even of P (the class of all problems solvable in deterministic polynomial time). It seems unlikely that P⊆RNC (it also seems unlikely that P=NC). A number of problems in RNC have been found, and they are considered to be "practically" efficiently parallelizable. One of the most famous problems known to be in RNC but not known to be in NC is the problem of constructing a perfect matching in graphs (see [Karp, Upfal, Wigderson, 1985]). RNC^k can be defined in a similar way with NC^k (or with AC^k) and [Borodin et al, 1982], [Von zur Gathen, 1983] present problems which are in RNC^2. In most cases, to show that a problem is in RNC creates big hopes that the problem is in NC. For example, this happened with the (also famous) problem of two-processor scheduling, shown initially to be in RNC by [Vazirani, Vazirani, 1985] and later shown to be in NC by [Helmbold, Mayr, 1986].

3. Log space Reductions and problems complete in P

In the study of sequential time complexity, polynomial time reducibility has become standard (see eg. [Garey and Johnson, 1979]). In the study of space complexity, log-space reducibility is used (see [Jones and Laaser, 1977], usually in its "many to one" or "Karp" form. [Cook, 1985] argued that NC^1 reducibility is the appropriate one for parallel computation. Many authors used log-space reducibilities instead (since DSPACE (logn) is a subset of AC^1).

DEFINITION Let L and L' be languages over an alphabet Σ. We say L' is log-space reducible to L iff there exists a function f such that
(a) for each $w \in \Sigma^*$, $w \in L'$ iff $f(w) \in L$;
(b) f is computable in log-space by a determinstic Turing Machine.

One gets AC^1 reducibility from the above by replacing "log-space" with "logarithmic parallel time" and "deterministic Turing Machine" by "CRCW PRAM" with a polynomial number of processors. The precise definition of NC^1 reducibility follows: (see [Cook, 85]).

DEFINITION A problem R is NC^1-reducible to S if there is a uniform family F_n of circuits for solving R, with $d(F_n)=O(\log n)$, and F_n is allowed to have oracle nodes for S. An oracle node for S is a node with some sequence of input edges $\langle y_1,\dots,y_r\rangle$ and a sequence $\langle z_1,\dots,z_s\rangle$ of output edges, whose values satisfy $S(y_1,\dots,y_r, z_1,\dots,z_s)$. The oracle node counts as depth $\lfloor \log(str) \rfloor$.

All the above kinds of reductions are closed under composition. One of the ways to use reductions is to discover "hard" problems in P, i.e. problems which are probably not in NC (not efficiently parallelizable). The way this works, is similar to the way for NP-complete problems. Let P be the class of problems solved in deterministic polynomial time.

DEFINITION: A language L is complete in P under log-space (or NC^1 or AC^1) reductions (P-complete) if

(a) L $\in$ P and

(b) for each L'$\in$ P, L' is log-space (NC^1, AC^1 correspondingly) reducible to L.

Indeed, if R is complete in P and R is in NC, then P=NC, an unlikely event. Examples of problems complete for P are the circuit value problem [Ladner, 75] and its variations (monotone, planar [Goldschlager, 77]), linear programming [Khanchian, 1979], [Dopkin, Lipton, Reiss, 1979], the maximum network flow (with exponentially large capacities - given in binary) (see [Goldschlager, Shaw, Staples, 82], also the deadlock detection problem for multinuit resources [Spirakis, 87]. A list of several such problems is in [Hoover, Ruzzo, 84].

For the problems complete in P, we can be less ambitions and try to find fast (i.e. in NC) parallel algorithms that give <u>approximate</u> solutions. It seems that such approximations of P-complete problems do not fall in NC for all values of the approximation <u>absolute performance ratio</u> R (see [Garey, Johnson, 79]). R is a number in $[1,\infty]$ whose closeness to 1 indicates how close to the optimal value (solution) is the value produced by the approximation. We know of one P-complete problem (the High degree subgraph problem [Anderson, Mayr, 86]), which cannot be approximated by an $R<2$ unless P=NC. This problem is stated as follows: Given a graph G(V,E) and an integer k, does G contain an induced subgraph with minimum degree at least k? It is complete in P for $k\geq 3$. Also, we know that the circuit value problem cannot have an approximation in NC with $R<\infty$ unless P=NC (see [Kyrousis, Spirakis, 88]). Here the approximation to the circuit value problem is the depth at which the ones arrive in the circuit. An interesting open problem is the investigation of the <u>threshold</u> for R, such that the approximation is parallelizable for all values above the threshold. A similar question can be raised for polynomial time approximations of NP-complete problems.

If, in the definition of AC^1-reductions one replaces the PRAM by a probabilistic PRAM and requests a bounded away from zero error probability, one gets another, new, interesting kind of reductions.

<u>DEFINITION</u> (see [Kyrousis, Spirakis, 88])

A language A is reducible to B through RNC^1-reductions iff these exists a random function f computable by a probabilistic PRAM in logarithmic time and with polynomial number of processors, and a number $\delta\in(0,1]$ such that:

(1) for every x, $x\in A \Rightarrow$ all $f(x)\in B$

(2) for every x, $x\notin A \Rightarrow$ prob $\{f(x)\notin B\}\geq\delta$

□

Clearly, the RNC^1-reductions are closed under composition (see [Kyrousis, Spirakis, 88]). A problem A∈P is called randomly complete for P if there exists a problem B which is complete in P under AC^1 reductions and if B reduces (RNC^1 way) to A. Clearly, if A is randomly complete for P and A∈RNC then P⊆RNC, another unlikely event. We believe that randomly complete for P problems are hand to parallelize. Indeed, there are problems in P which are not known to be P-complete but can be shown to be randomly complete for P. (See [Kyrousis, Spirakis, 88]).

4. Some problems that are easy to parallelize

4a. Some interesting complexity classes

Let NL be the class of sets accepted by a nondeterministic Turing Machine in space O(logn). Examples of sets complete for NL are the dag accessibility problem, directed k-connectivity, and unsatisfiability of 2-CNF boolean formulas ([Jones, Lien and Laaser, 1976]). Let NL^* be the closure of NL (as a class of 0-1 functions) under NC^1-reducibilities.

LEMMA (see [Cook, 85]) $NL^* \subseteq AC^1$

Some interesting examples of problems in NL^* are the transitive closure of a Boolean matrix, the shortest path problem for graphs with positive edge weights in unary and the problem of finding a minimum spanning forest for an n-node undirected graph with n-bit positive integer weights. The proof of this last result about the spanning forest is a parallel version of the sequential greedy algorithm (see e.g. [Papadimitriou. Steiglitz, 1982]).

Let LOGCFL be the class of all sets log space reducible to the class CFL of context free languages. Let CFL^* be the closure of CFL under NC^1 reductions.

PROPOSITION (see [Cook, 85]) LOGCFL $\subseteq CFL^* \subseteq AC^1$

Another interesting parallelizable class of problems in the class DET which is the set of all problems NC^1-reducible to the problem of computing the determinant of an nxn matrix A of n-bit integers.

PROPOSITION $NL^* \subseteq DET \subseteq NC^2$

4b Computational Geometry

In Computational geometry it seems that we have a language to express most problems of interest. This is Tarski's language of elementary algebra and geometry i.e. the first order language with variables ranging over the real numbers R, constants of 0,1 the equality and inequality relation and the functions of +,- and x. Most geometrical problems actually require the weak second order version of this language (i.e. the ability to have variables for finite sets or tuples, e.g. polygons). Geometric objects can be expressed as subsets of $\mathbb{R}^d$ whose points satisfy polynomial equations or inequalities with rational coefficients and some more special structure (geometric complexes). Many problems of computational geometry amount to the construction of geometric complexes together with their adjacency relations. Such constructions were shown to be in NC by [Kozen, Yap, 85].

Indeed, most of the problems of Computational Geometry were found to be in NC^+ (NC with real number arithmetic). The cell decomposition result of [Kozen, Yap, 85], however, leads to solutions which, although in NC, are far from optimal in terms of time-number of processors tradeoff, and special techniques have been already developed for many such problems. For example, the convex hull problem was solved by [Aggarwal et al, 85] in the CREW PRAM model with T(n)=O(logn), P(n)=O(n).

The problem of Triangulating a set of disjoint line segments was recently shown by [Attalah, Cole, Goodrich, 87] to have a P(n)=O(n), T(n)=O(logn) solution. [Goodrich, 84] shows that the all-nearest neighbor problem for a convex polygon can be solved with optimal speedup i.e. O(p, n/p+logn) (standing for O(P(n), T(n)). [Aggarwal et al, 85] also considered the problem of computing the smallest triangle enclosing a convex polygon and gave an O(n, logn) answer. The computation of a closest pair of points among n planar points was done by [Goodrich, Attalah, 85] in O(n, logn log logn).

Many of these problems require sorting as a basic step. Since the breakthrough of [Ajtai, Komlos, Szemeredi, 83], it is known how to sort n numbers by a uniform circuit F_n of $c(F_n)=O(n)$ and $d(F_n)=O(\log n)$. If we are willing to work with PRAMs, the best (practical) algorithm up to now is due to [Cole, 87], in a CREW PRAM model with T(n)=O(logn) and P(n)=O(n) and very small constants.

4c Special Techniques

In the pursuit of optimality, [Cole, Vishkin, 86] discovered some fundamental techniques for exploiting the idle time of processors in a PRAM computation. They observed that many of the problems solved by parallel algorithms obey the following framework: Given an input of size n, the parallel algorithm employs a reducing procedure to produce a smaller instance of the same problem (say, of size $\leq n/2$). The smaller problem is solved recursively until this brings us below some threshold for the size of the problem. An alternative procedure is then used to complete the parallel algorithm (technique of accelerating cascades). Typically, one needs to reschedule the processors in order to apply the reducing procedure efficiently to the smaller size problem. Cole and Vishkin managed to provide an algorithm for performing approximate rescheduling (work is only approximately evenly partitioned among processors), deterministically in O(1) time. This involves the use of expander graphs for redistribution of work to the PRAM processors and lead to the following important result:

PROPOSITION [Cole, Vishkin, 86]

n tasks are given, each of length between 1 and elogn where e is a constant. The total length of the tasks is bounded by cn, c a constant. A task can be thought of as a program. We don't know in advance the lengths of the individual tasks. They way vary, depending on the order of execution of the tasks. there is a way to schedule the n tasks in an EREW PRAM of n/logn processors so that the tasks are completed in O(logn) time.

Alternatively, one can achieve a good redistribution of work of the processors by randomized allocation schemes. Such techniques can use dynamic properties of the problem input (e.g. sparseness) in an effective way. For example, [Spirakis, 88] provides a randomized technique for parallel addition which computes the result in O(logm) parallel time in a CRCW PRAM model, where m is the count of nonzero entries among the n numbers to be added. Such techniques, which are sensitive to run-time properties of the input may beat the known lower bounds for the general case of the corresponding problems.

Randomization, as a technique to be used for efficient parallel algorithms, justified itself many times already. Local random decisions done by each processor reduce the (time-consuming) interprocessor communication which (even in the PRAMs) is done (through shared memory) anyway. Also, due to laws of large numbers and limit theorems, certain statistical properties of a large number of random independent drawings can be predicted with high probability. The result of [Karp, Upfal, Wigderson, 85] about constructing a perfect matching in a graph through an RNC algorithm is the best (up to now) justification of those techniques. (This problem is not known to be in NC). They first reduce the problem of finding a perfect matching to the problem of identifying a large set of redundant edges in a graph that has a perfect matching and is not very sparse. (A set of edges is redundant if the removal of those edges results in a graph that still has a perfect matching). A large set of redundant edges is constructed through an RNC technique which calls as a subroutine an RNC procedure to compute a certain integer-valued function (the "rank") defined over all subsets of edges of the graph. In fact, for a subset S of edges, rank (S) is the maximum number of edges of S that occur together in a perfect matching in the graph. The rank function relates to the degree of a multivariate polynomial defined by the graph and S. To find the degree of a multivariate polynomial (wrt to a certain variable) one has to find which coefficients (which are also polynomials with many indeterminates) are identically zero. A well known probabilistic method of [Schwartz, 80] does that, and is directly parallelizable.

References

[Aleliunas, Karp, Lipton, Lovasz, Rackoff, 79] "Random Walks, Universal Traversal Sequences and the Complexity of Maze problems", 20th IEEE FOCS Symposium, Oct. 1979, pp. 218-223.

[Anderson, Mayr, 86] "Approximating P-complete problems" by Anderson R. and Mayr E., Tech. Report, Stanford University.

[Adleman, L., 1978] "Two theorems on random polynomial time", in Proc. 19th IEEE Found. Comput. Sci., pp. 75-83.

[Aho, Horcroft, Ullman, 1974] "The Design and Analysis of Computer Algorithms", Addison-Wesley, Reading, Mass.

[Awerbuch, Shiloach, 1983] "New connectivity and MSF algorithm for ultracomputer and PRAM", preprint, IBM-Israel Scientific Center, technion, Haifa.

[Aggarwal et al, 1985] "Parallel computational geometry", A. Aggarwal, B. Chacelle, L. Guibas, C. O'Dunlaing, C. Yap, IEEE Foundations of Computes Science, pp. 468-477, 1985.

[Ajtai, Kamlcs, Szemeredi, 1983] "Sorting in clogn parallel steps", Canbinatorica 3:1-19, 1983.

[Borodin, Von zur Gathen, Hopcroft, 82] "Fast parallel matrix and GCD computations" by Borodin A., Von zur Gathen J. and Hopcroft J., Inform. and Control 52, 241-256.

[Berkowitz, 1984] "On computing the determinant in small parallel time using a small number of processors, Inform. Process, Lett. 18, 147-150.

[Borodin, 1977] "On relating time and space to size and depth." SIAM J. Comput. 6, 733-744.

[Borodin 1982] Structured vs. general models in computational complexity, in "Logic and Algorithmic", Enseign. Math. (no. 30) pp. 47-65, Univ. Geneva, Geneva.

[Beame, Cook, Hoover, 1984] "Log depth circuits for division and related problems", in Proc. 17th IEEE Found. Comput. Sci.

[Borodin, Cook, Pippenger, 1983] "Parallel computation for well-endowed rings and space-bounded probabilistic machines", Inform. and Control 58, 113-136.

[Borodin, Von zur Gathen, Hopcroft, 1982] "Fast parallel matrix and GCD computations", Inform. and Control 52, 241-256.

[Cole, 87] "Parallel Merge Sort" R. Cole, 27th IEEE FOCS.

[Cole, Vishkin, 86] "Approximate and Exact Parallel Scheduling with Applications to List, Tree and Graph problems", R. Cole, U. Vishkin, 27th IEEE Symposium on Foundations of Computer Science, 1986.

[Chandra, Kozen, Stockmeyer, 1981] Alternion, J. Assoc. Comput. Mach. 28, No. 1, 114-113.

[Chandra, Stockmeyer, Vishkin, 1982] "Complexity theory for unbounded fan-in parallelism", in Proc. 23rd IEEE Found. Comput. Sci., pp. 1-13.

[Cook, 1981] "Towards a complexity theory of synchronous parallel computation, Enseign. Math. 27, 99-124.

[Cook, 1983] "The classification of problems which have fast parallel algorithms", in Proc. 1983 International FCT Conference, Lecture notes in Computer Science Vol. 158, pp. 78-93, Springer-Verlag, Berlin/New York.

[Cook, Ruzzo, 1983] unpublished theorem.

[Csanky, 1976] Fast parallel matrix inversion algorithms, SIAM J. Comput. 5, 618-623.

[Dymond, Cook, 1980] "Hardware complexity and parallel computation", in Proc. 21st IEEE Found. Comput. Sci., 360-372.

[Doakin, Lipton, Reiss, 1979] "Linear programming is log-space hard for P, Inform. Process. Lett. 8, 96-97.

[Dekel, Nassimi, Sahni, 1981] "Parallel matrix and graph algorithms, SIAM J. Comput. 10, 657-675.

[Feather, 1984] M.Sc. thesis, Department of Computer Science, University of Toronto.

[Furst, Saxe, Sipser, 1981] "Parity, circuits, and the polynomial-time hierarchy", in Proc. 22nd IEEE Found. Comput. Sci., pp. 260-270.

[Garey, Johnson, 1979] "Computers and Intractability: A Guide to the Theory of NP-Completeness", Freeman, San Francisco.

[Von zur Gathen, 1983] "Parallel algorithms for algebraic problems", in Proc. 15th ACM Sympos. Theory of Comput., pp. 17-23.

[Gill, 1977] "Computational Complexity of probabilistic Turing Machine", SIAM J. Comput. 6, 675-695.

[Goldschlager, 1977;1978;1982] "Synchronous Parallel Computation", Ph.D. thesis, University of Toronto; in Proc. ACM Sympos. Theory of Comput., pp. 89-94, Assoc. Comput. Mach. 29, No. 4, 1073-1086.

[Goldschlager, 1977] "The monotone and planar circuit value problems are log space complete for P. SIGACT News 9, No. 2, 25-29.

[Greibach, 1973] "The hardest context-free language", SIAM J. Comput. 2, 304-310.

[Goldschlager, Shaw, Staples, 1982] "The maximum flow problem is log space complete for P. Theoret. Comput. Sci. 21, 105-111.

[Gupta, 1985] M.Sc. thesis, Dept. of Computer Science, University of Toronto.

[Hoover, Ruzzo, 1984] "A compendium of problems complete for P", by H. Hoover and W.L. Ruzzo, unpublished manuscript, 1984.

[Hong, 1980] "On some space complexity problems about the set of assignments satisfying a boolean cormula", in Proc. 12th ACM Sympos. Theory of Comput., pp. 310-317.

[Hoover, 1979] "Some Topics in Circuit Complexity", M.Sc. thesis, University of Toronto, Department of Computer Science, Department of Computer Science Technical Report, 139/80.

[Ibarra, Mcran, Rosier, 1980] "A note on the parallel compexity of computing the rank of order n matrices", Inform. Process. Lett. 11, 162.

[Ja'Ja'J, Simon, 1982] "Parallel algorithms in graph theory Planarity testing", SIAM J. Comput. 11, 314-328.

[Jones, Laaser, 1977] "Complete problems for deterministic polynomial time, Theoretical Computer Science 3, 105-117.

[Jones, Lien, Laaser, 1976] "New problems complete for nondeterministic log space", Math. Systems Theory 10, 1-17.

[Kyrousis, Spirakis, 1988] "Probabilistic log-space reductions and problems probabilistically hard for P", L. Kyrousis and P. Spirakis, "Scandinaviocn Workshop on Algorithm Theory (SWAT 88)", July 5-8, 1988, Proceedings.

[Kozen, Yap, 1985] "Algebraic cell decomposition in NC", D. Kozen & C. Yap, IEEE Foundations of Computer Science Proceedings, pp. 515-521, 1985.

[Karp, Upfal, Wigderson, 1985] "Constructing a perfect matching is in Random NC", 1985, ACM STOC, pp. 22-33.

[Khachlan, 1979] "A polynomial time algorithm for linear programming", Dokl. Akad. Nauk. SSSR 144, No. 5, 1093-96; transl. in Soviet Math. Dokl. 20, 191-194.

[Karp, Upfal, Wigderson, 1985] "Constructing a perfect matching is in random NC", in Proc. 17th ACM Sympos. Theory of Comput., pp. 22-32.

[Karp, Wigderson, 1984] "A fast parallel algorithm for the maximal independent set problem", in Proc. 16th ACM Sympos. Theory of Comput., pp. 266-272.

[Ladner, 1975] "The circuit value problem is log space complete for P", SIGACT News 7, No. 1, 18-20.

[Lev., 1978] "Size-Bounds and Parallel Algorithms for Network", Doctoral thesis, Report CST-8-80, Dept. of Computer Science, University of Edimburgh.

[Lynch, 1977] "Log space recognition and translation of parenthesis languages, J. Assoc. Comput. Math. 24, No. 4, 583-590.

[Lipton, Snyder, Zalcstein, 1976] "The complexity of the Word and Isomorphism Problems for Finite Groups", Tech. Rep. 91/76, Yale University.

[McKenzie, 1984] "Parallel Complexity and Permutation Groups", Ph.D. thesis, University of Toronto, Department of Computer Science.

[Miller, 1978] "On the $n^{\log n}$ isomorphism technique", in Proc. 10th Sympos. Theory of Comput., pp. 51-58.

[McKenzie, Cook, 1983] "The parallel complexity of the Abelian permutation group membership problem", in Proc. 24th IEEE Found of Comput. Sci., pp. 154-161.

[McKenzie, Cook, 1985] "The parallel complexity of Abelian Permutation group problems, University of Toronto, Dept. of Computer Science, Technical Report No. 181/85.

[Muller, Preparata, 1975] "Bounds to complexities of networks for sorting and switching", J. Assoc. Comput. Mach. 22, No. 2, 195-201.

[Pippenger, 1979] "On simultaneous resource bounds (preliminary version)", in Proc. 20th IEEE Found. of Comput. Sci., pp. 307-311.

[Papadimitriou, Steiglitz, 1982] "Combinatorial Optimization: Algorithms and Complexity", Prentice-Hall, Englewood Cliffs, N.J.

[Pratt, Stockmeyer, 1976] "A characterization of the power of vector machines", J. Comput. System Sci. 12, 198-221.

[Reif, 1982] "Symmetric complementation", in Proc. 14th ACM Sympos. Theory of Comput. pp. 201-214.

[Reif, 1983] "Logarithmic depth circuits for algebraic functions", in 24th IEEE Found. of Comput. Sci., pp. 138-145, revised version, Preprint, 1984.

[Ruzzo, 1980a] unpublished list of problems in NC^2.

Ruzzo, 1980b "Tree-size bounded alternation", J. Comput. System Sci. 21, No. 2, 218-235.

[Ruzzo, 1981] "On uniform circuit complexity", J. Comput. System Sci. 22, No. 3, 365-383.

[Ruzzo, 1984] private communication

[Ruzzo, Tompa, 1982] unpublished result. See Stockmeyer, L. and Vishkin L., "Simulation of Parallel Random Access Machines by Circuits", Report RC-9362. IBM Research. Yorktown Heights. N.Y.

[Savage, 1976] "The Complexity of Computing", Wiley, New York.

[Skyum, Vallant, 1981] "A complexity theory based on Boolean algebra", in Proc. 22nd IEEE Found. of Comput. Sci., pp. 244-253.

[Schwartz, 1980a] "Ultracomputers", ACM Trans. Program, Lang. Systems 2, No. 4, 484-521.

[Schwartz, 1980b] "Probabilistic algorithms for verification of polynomial identities", J. Assoc. Comput. Mach. 27, No. 4, 701-717.

[Shannon, 1949] "The synthesis of two terminal switching circuits", BSTJ 28, 55-98.

[Subsgrough, 1978] "On the tape complexity of deterministic context-free languages", J. Assoc. Comput. Mach. 25, No. 3, 405-414.

[Spirakis, 1987] "The parallel complexity of deadlock detection", P. Spirakis, Theoretical Computer Science, 52, 1987, 155-163.

[Spirakis, 1988] "Optimal Parallel Randomized Algorithms for Sparse Addition and Identification", P. Spirakis, Information and Computation Journal, Academic Press, New York, Vol. 76, No. 1, Jan. 1988, pp. 1-12.

[Schwartz, 1980] "Fast probabilistic algorithms for verification of polynomial identities", JACM 27, 4, 1980, pp. 701-717.

Tompa, 1984 private communication.

[Vallant, 1979] "Completeness classes in algebra", in Proc. 11th ACM Sympos. Theory of Comput., pp. 249-261.

[Vallant, Skyum, Berkowitz, Rackoff, 1983] "Fast parallel computation of polynomials using few processors", SIAM J. Comput. 12, No. 4, 641-644.

[Vishkin, 1983] "Synchronous parallel computation - A survey, preprint Courant Institute, New York University.

[Wilson, 1983] "Relativised circuit complexity", in Proc. 24th IEEE Found. of Comput. Sci., pp. 329-342.

[Warmuth, 1987] "Parallel Approximation Algorithms for One-Dimensional Bin Packing", by M. Warmuth, tech. report, Univ. of California Santa Cruz, 1987.

[Yap, 1987] "What can be parallelized in computational geometry?" C.K. Yap, Parallel Algorithms and Architectures, Academic-Verlag, Berlin, May 25-30, 1987.

PROCESS-STRUCTURED ARCHITECTURES TO TRANSFORM INFORMATION FLOWING THROUGH

Leonard Uhr[1]

Abstract

It is rapidly becoming possible to build networks of many millions of processors. These massively parallel networks should be capable of perceiving, remembering, and reasoning in real time, even approaching the brain's speed and power - IF we knew how to build them. This paper proposes and explores a promising but largely ignored information-flow approach.

For maximum speed and efficiency, massively parallel networks should be structured so that processes can, brain-like, transform information flowing through them with minimal delay. And all should be embedded in appropriate structures of processors. Therefore hardware, software, and information structures should all be designed to work together. This paper examines the set of issues involved in developing such systems, and describes several designs for structures that process information flowing through.

These information-flow structures are brain-like in that processes continually execute: integrate, differentiate, compare, decide, resolve, and compute a general-purpose repertoire of useful functions. The structures of processors that carry out these processes are all built from neuron-like micro-modular primitive structures. They must work without any global or local controllers, and without any operating system (of today's traditional sort) that synchronizes, handles communication, and avoids contention. These issues must be handled instead by the system's structure and the types of processes executed.

Introduction: Micro-Electronics; Information-Transforming Structures; Appropriate Processes

First, brain-like processes are contrasted with today's serial computers and parallel networks, and the possibilities offered by micro-electronics are described. These make clear what is feasible, and what near-future technologies will make possible - and also the constraints imposed if these technologies are used in conventional designs.

Then we will briefly examine already-developed structures of processes that can be used to transform information flowing through them, when embedded into structures of (ideally isomorphic) physical processors. Data-flow computers that embody Petri nets are a first step toward this goal; but the actual hardware topologies built today to handle what are called data-flow systems only simulate true data-flow processes, with major delays because at the hardware level the actual data-flow topology is destroyed and even more memory is needed that in conventional computers. When used appropriately, pipelines, arrays, and pyramids actually come closer; However these (at least as designed to date) appear to be chiefly usable for specialized purposes.

Next, several designs for possible future information-transforming structures will be described and assessed. These depend heavily upon the use of appropriate processes, ones that can repeatedly iterate, combining and contrasting information moving toward solutions. Several key, brain-like, examples of such massively parallel processes will be given, along with more global structures into which they can be combined.

---

1. Computer Sciences Dept., University of Wisconsin, Madison Wis. USA 53706

The Living Mind/Brain As Our Most Suggestive Approximate Model

The living brain/mind is probably our prime example of an information-transforming structure: It is certainly tremendously successful; it is capable of far more powerful processing than anything we have achieved with computers. It appears to be more like a massively parallel finite-state automaton (that is, a structure of processors that execute processes embedded in them), and to synchronize computations because of the very nature of the processes it executes.

In contrast to today's computers, it neither has a single global controller that executes the same instruction everywhere, in "Single instruction multiple data-stream" "SIMD" fashion; nor is each processor coupled to its own independent controller, in "Multiple instruction multiple data-stream" "MIMD" fashion.

Rather, the transformations the brain carries out appear to be of a kind that can self-coordinate, as processors interact, e.g., to integrate information, discriminate differences, choose among alternatives, and impose and relax constraints. Continuous cycling through these processes appears to approach and lock into solutions and resolutions.

This suggests the following conjecture: the brain uses a repertoire of operations that are appropriate for a data-flow, information-transforming system. These processes themselves serve to coordinate and synchronize as needed.

This further suggests that the particular operations such a system uses must also be chosen with great care, to fit and work with the overall processor/process/information structures.

The brain is an enormously powerful perceiver and reasoner. But it is not clear how efficient the brain actually is (judged by standards used for computers). Indeed, if the brain is as inefficient as it might well be (e.g., we consciously think and attend to only one thing at a time - is the rest of the brain therefore relatively idle?), that may throw some light on the bounds of efficiency in practical situations - that is, when we use massively parallel multi-computers to handle really large and difficult problems.

Technological Possibilities, Both Today and Into the Near Future

Computers are rapidly growing faster and more powerful, roughly doubling in power every 12-20 months. The continuing development of micro-electronic chips, on which increasingly large numbers of components are etched, underlies this rapid and phenomenal increase in computer power.

The Traditional General-Purpose Stored-Program Serial Computer of Today

A traditional serial computer is, basically:

* One single processor (including a controller),
* Plus memory (where data and program are stored),
* Plus necessary input and output devices (to communicate with the external world).

This is typically called a "single-CPU serial stored-program computer." It operates as follows (note how carefully everything must be handled and coordinated):

Information, including the program to be executed, is input to memory

The "CPU" ("central processing unit") contains a general-purpose processor (that is, a processor capable of executing - possibly with a long sequence of instructions - any possible process) plus a controller that decodes instructions and tells the processor what to do next.

The CPU fetches the next instruction from memory; decodes it; fetches whatever data that instruction needs; executes that instruction; follows that instructions' orders in terms of storing results; and continues in this manner, fetching, decoding and executing instructions. Thus such systems are "serial," since one instruction or piece of information is fetched at a time, from memory to processor, and then processed. They are "stored program" since instructions are stored in memory, fetched and decoded.

The memory simply contains all the information that the CPU works with. Each cell in main memory has a location associated with it, so that information can be pointed to and fetched from or stored to it in one instruction cycle.

Usually many auxilliary, successively slower, memories are also used. Information is swapped into the main memory as needed. It is crucial to have whatever information the processor needs available as fast as possible. This often means that the system has additional memories that are even faster than the main memory - a few very high-speed registers and a cache memory into which information is loaded that clever algorithms anticipate the CPU will need in the future.

This kind of computer can be represented as a 1-node graph: ->O-> with input in and output out. At a somewhat more detailed level, the Processor, Memory, and additional registers and slower memories can be represented each by a different node, with links put where there are actually data paths. But so long as such a system has only a single CPU, it is still a serial computer.

The Enormous Range of Possibilities for Parallel Computers

A parallel computer has more than one processor - anything from 2 to a potentially infinite number. The traditional 1-CPU serial computer is a 1-node graph. Parallel computers are the class of all possible N-node graphs (N>1). In addition, processors, input-output devices, memories, and different types of memories, can all be distributed in whatever manner seems most desirable.

Thus the traditional computer is the simplest (by far), and the set of all parallel computers is overwhelmingly large. We will return to look at some of the most promising topologies. But first it is important to see how large such a system can be made.

Building with Chips (Modular Packages), Transistors (Processors), and Pins (Input-Output)

The 1880s was the era during which chip densities rose from a few thousand to a few million transistors. This startling increase has been accomplished basically by making each component successively smaller.

To do that, an intertwined set of technologies had to be developed, including the following:

* Light microscopes, and now X-ray microscopes, are needed to make the chip's layout plan small enough to fit.
* Appropriate materials (e.g., silicon and gallium arsenide wafers each containing several hundred chips, and the metals and plastics to be placed on and injected into these chips) must be developed.
* Materials must be pure enough so that imperfections do not ruin things.
* Immaculate clean rooms are needed to keep microscopic dust from similarly ruining things.
* Precise, fast, stepping-motor-based machines are needed to control the actual fabrication.
* Precisely controlled ovens are needed to cure and finish the wafer.
* The wafer must be perfectly diced into hundreds of individual chips.
* Each chip must be thoroughly tested, to be discarded if faulty.
* A complex range of good software is needed to help design, simulate, and test out new chips.

* Sturdy, compact packaging is needed to provide input-output for each chip, and to build the appropriate larger structures that combine many chips.

Each individual chip is a roughly 4-6 mm square or rectangle (roughly the size of a fingernail). A wafer is about 6-15 cm in diameter, each typically containing several hundred identical chips. The wafer is diced, and each chip tested and packaged in a plastic carrier with several dozen to several hundred pins that link to the outside world. This carrier is put into a socket, and, along with a number of other chips, embedded into a board. A number of boards are put into the computer's chassis.

The total computer might contain several chassis, that contain in total from one to several hundred thousand chips (plus power supply, memory devices like tape and disk drives, and input and output devices). A small computer might have 1-10 chips, a micro-computer 100-1000, a mini-computer 1000-10,000, a relatively large "mainframe" 10,000-100,000, a "super-computer" several hundred thousand.

But each individual chip will have thousands or millions of transistors! Hence most of the power results from the individual chip's enormous power.

The number of transistors on each chip has doubled roughly every 12-20 months for the past 20-30 years, and this startling steady increase will almost certainly continue for the next 10-20 years, and probably much longer.

Putting millions of transistors on a single 4mm by 4mm chip, all linked as and where needed by tiny buses (wires), is probably the most complex design problem that human beings have ever faced. Today a combination of design art, science of how to embed graphs into the plane, and computer-based tools for graphical displays and design tests, makes such enormous enterprises possible. But only barely, and they are extremely expensive multi-million dollar ventures. Fortunately, the needed art, science, methodology, and technology are all sufficient - and in their infancy, so that we can expect continuing major improvements.

Essentially, one must embed non-planar graphs as compactly as possible onto the 2-dimensional planar surface of a chip. It is possible, and often necessary, to burrow into the chip to make paths where wires must cross; but that's expensive and must be minimized. The more regular the design, the nearer the devices that must communicate, the fewer the needed wire crossings, the more compact and efficient will be the design.

The Size of Component Processors and Memories

What kinds of systems are built with such chips today, and what kinds might be built tomorrow?

Today a traditional relatively powerful CPU (one that executes 1-50 million instructions per second) can be put on a single chip, although more typically 2-10 or so chips are used. Up to several million bits of memory can similarly be put on a single chip. But traditional computers need as much memory as possible, hence many memory chips, so that the CPU is not stopped for want of the information it needs. Roughly 4-40 million bytes (each byte built from 8-10 bits, including several for error-checking and) is usually considered desirable. So a total computer might have 1-10 chips in its CPU, plus 40-400 chips in its main memory.

That is not a large number of chips, and can easily be handled. The cost of the chips will be less than the cost of their packaging into boards and chassis; and the total cost of that will usually be substantially less than the cost of display monitors, additional slower memories, and printers and other output and input devices.

In fact the cost of the chips - which are the actual computer's heart - is small enough so that one is tempted to be lavish, for example, adding still more memory, specialized co-processors (e.g., for floating-point arithmetic or vector processing), additional high-speed register and cache memories, and processors to handle input from and output to disks and other slower memories.

To Achieve Many Processors in Massively Parallel Structures, Each Must Be Efficient

But in sharp contrast, parallel computers demand the simplest, most efficient possible, designs. We can lavish extras on one single serial processor; but when we have hundreds, thousands, or many millions, the costs multiply out of bounds.

The whole thrust in parallelizing is to speed up processing. One must parallelize the algorithms used as much as possible, and build appropriate parallel architectures and operating systems that execute these parallel algorithms as fast as possible.

It is often true that unless at least 50-100 parallel processors are used, the speed-ups will hardly be worth bothering with. This is because at best N processors give N-fold speed-ups, but in actuality they will often be used with far less efficiency. (What is known as Minsky's conjecture suggests that N processors will give only logN speed-up; but that is clearly not true when appropriate algorithms are run on appropriate hardware.) Today's parallel computers give 2-4 orders of magnitude degradations, and it seems likely that we may always have to live with 2-10-fold slowdowns. That is, to process 100 times as fast (or to process 100 times more information), rather than 100 processors, we may well need 1000, or more.

We don't know today how many problems can be handled with algorithms that can be sufficiently parallelized, and in ways that lend themselves to running on appropriate multi-computers that can make sufficiently effective use of those parallelizations.

* Will we need a different special-purpose multi-computer for each algorithm?
* Or will several different specialized designs be efficient enough, each handling the sub-set of algorithms for which it is appropriate? But will we be able to combine such diverse resources into a single efficient system?
* Or will we succeed in developing a single generally usable parallel architecture, one that can execute any problem with adequate efficiency and speed - or, the ultimate goal, with optimal efficiency and speed?

A Summary Look at the Resources Available, and Needed

Today's chip can easily have 10-50,000 transistors. With especially careful design and packing it can have 100,000 to 2,000,000. In 5 or 10 years these numbers will grow ten-fold, or more.

To store 1 bit of information, 1-10 or more transistors are needed (the more the faster).

The simplest general-purpose 1-bit processor needs 50-500 transistors. A 4-, 8-, 16-, or 32-bit processor needs roughly 4, 8, 16, or 32 times as many.

An even simpler special-purpose processor (e.g., to integrate, differentiate, compare, or choose) might need even fewer transistors, say 10-20.

The Total Computer's Resources Must Be Divided Among As Many Processors as Possible

We can assume that, roughly, the total cost of the computer will be a function of the total number of chips (e.g., 10 times the cost of the chips). And packaging and power problems will set an upper bound to what is feasible. Today "feasible" appears to be roughly $10,000,000-20,000,000 and 100,000-500,000 chips. More reasonably, a "mini" might cost $100,000-500,000 and use 1,000-50,000 chips, a "micro" $1,000-50,000 and use several hundred chips, a "personal" computer $200-900 and use a dozen or so.

Processors come in greatly varying levels of complexity. A traditional CPU needs 50,000-500,000 transistors. But a smaller, slower processor needs substantially less. The most striking examples are the 1-bit general-purpose processors used in the massively parallel arrays like Clip, DAP, MPP, and Connection machine. These are built with only 50-500 transistors for each entire processor!

Roughly, a 32-bit processor will need 32 times as many transistors as a 1-bit processor. The 1-bit processor will be (at least) 32 times as slow, since it must process information 1 bit at a time, rather than in 32-bit chunks (note that actually the traditional 32-bit word is a form of parallelization).

Thus a powerful processor will need a large percent of one entire chip, plus many other chips for the memory that contains all the information it needs to keep it busy. In striking contrast, hundreds of thousands of small and simple processors (but they are still general-purpose) can be put on a single chip - but only if two very important things are done. A. The topology over the processors must be embeddable into the chip with reasonable efficiency. B. Memory must be handled in radically different ways.

True Information-Flow multi-computers will not need traditional large memories. They should be built so that information flows through processors, and processors are judiciously placed so that each is right next to the processor to which it should pass its results. If everything were perfectly designed, the only memories needed would be the registers that hold the information the processor is to work on next; and that information would be put there by up-stream processors just before it is needed.

It is unreasonable to expect things to work out that perfectly. The design of systems that approach these goals will be a major research enterprise. It is not at all clear whether to be efficient these will be specialized, or whether generally usable information-flow systems can be achieved (brains appear to be generally usable and powerful; but are they efficient?). However, the crucial point for now is that memory becomes a relatively small part of the system, rather than by far the largest part.

The Major Multi-Computer Topologies Designed and Built To Date

A multi-computer might be given any possible graph topology. This is such an embarrasment of riches that it is hard to know where to start.

Yet almost all the computers built or even designed to date have had one of the following relatively simple topologies:

* pipeline (1-dimensional array),
* mesh (2-dimensional array),
* tree (graph without cycles whose root links to many leaves via internal nodes),
* pyramid (a logarithmic stack of each logarithmically smaller tree-linked arrays),
* hyper-cube (N-dimensional array with processors only at corners),
* NlogN network (logN banks of N switches that shuffles N pieces of information in logN steps).

Only the first four can be built with many processors on a single chip, short wires, few crossings, and compact designs that use chip area efficiently. But long pipelines are hard to keep full and busy; meshes are slow passing information great distances or executing global operations; trees and pyramids can bottleneck moving toward the apex; and trees are awkward for local operations (for which arrays and pyramids are superb).

There are many other possible topologies (some simpler, some far more complex) that, according to the criteria usually proposed for evaluating topologies, may well be substantially better than these. These include optimally or nearly optimally dense graphs, De Bruijn networks, and graphs built using a variety of compounding operations. And there are almost certainly many other still undiscovered topologies that are better yet.

Packing Information-Flow Multi-Computers Into Chips

The particular topology makes little difference in terms of building multi-computers with their traditional processors and their very large memories. Since each processor needs several chips, a large network can have only a few thousand processors at most, and processors will be linked off-chip. It is only when several, or many, processors are put on the same chip that we must try to get an efficiently embeddable topology across processors. Small processors, minimal memory, and short links are needed to multiply these numbers. So information-flow structures seem ideal. Since pipelines, arrays, trees, and pyramids can be used in this way, let's look at them first.

Arrays pack most efficiently onto a 2-dimensional chip. Each processor is linked to its 2 (if a pipeline), 4 or 8 nearest neighbors. So wires are short. If each processor is also small and simple, arrays are densely packable.

Each processor can be given its own memory, of whatever size desired. These memories are today relatively small (1K-16K 1-bit words is typical). Small is appropriate: the total memory is very large, and each processor usually needs direct access to only a very small fraction of the total information involved. The only crucial necessary memory is the set of registers used to pass information from processor to processor. So if true information-flow processing is achieved memory might be made substantially smaller, e.g. 256, or even 64, 32, or 8 1-bit registers. Thus instead of memory using almost all the transistors (as in conventional computers), each 50-500 transistor processor might have only roughly 8-500 transistors in its directly accessible memory.

Trees cannot be packed as densely as arrays, but they are a close second. If a tree is packed with its apex at one corner, so that it grows its children nodes moving toward the opposite apex, and nodes are folded into empty spaces (so that the tree becomes irregular) all the chip area can be filled.

Other topologies, and in particular the today very popular hypercube (that is, an N-dimensional cube, where N is usually between 8 and 20 with nodes at vertices only) and NlogN network (that is, logN banks of N switches linking N processors) embed quite poorly on planar chips. So they either use a lot of chip area, or are linked off the chips (but that simply means much larger, more expensive linking hardware must be used).

Toward Good Information-Flow Topologies

Good information-flow structures should pack very large numbers of very simple processors so that information flows among them with minimal need for memories. They will therefore be radically different from networks of traditional computers. Each should be designed to mirror as closely as possible the structure of processes to be executed. This might be a specialized design for a single important problem, or it might be a more general design (e.g., an array, tree, or pyramid) that is reasonably appropriate for a whole range of problems. Or it might be an as-yet-unknown truly general-purpose design (e.g., a network that judiciously links several more specialized sub-networks, with sufficient switches interspersed to reconfigure everything as appropriate). But it is important to note that developing a massively parallel information-flow algorithm when this is carried out within the constraints of chip technology at the same time designs the hardware structure of processors.

Let's assume that in the near future 10^6-10^8 transistors can be fabricated on a single chip, and that 10^2-10^6 chips can be combined into a single multi-computer.

Each 1-bit-worth of general-purpose or special-purpose processor needs 10-500 transistors.

Consider the following two types of chip, either of which can be used in data-flow fashion:

A. An R-by-C array of processors (R=rows; C=columns).

B. A tree of N processors.

Possibly the simplest use is to treat a 2-dimensional R-by-C array as a 1-dimensional 1-by-RC pipeline. Information will flow into and through the top row, then back through the next row, continuing to snake left-to-right, then right-to-left through the entire R rows. This would be used as are today's vector and image processing pipelines.

But the pipeline would almost certainly be far too big for programmers to be able to fill it effectively. The following appear to be more usable and more promising designs.

The array can input R pieces of information into its first column, and flow that information through to the opposite side. Or it can, via its lateral links, spread and diverge, or converge and combine, information, cycle it back, and effect whatever type of flow is desired (and handleable).

The tree can input information to its leaves (or, if a folded tree is used, to those leaves that are linked to the off-chip world). then this information can be combined, converged, and passed upward to the root. Or information can be input to (or passed to or computed by) the root and broadcast out to all, or to any, of the tree's other nodes. Or information can be flowed upward and also downward, in whatever pattern desired.

In such a system, not every pattern of simultaneously cycling information can be handled. It is up to the programmer/architect to design an appropriate system, and then use it in appropriate ways. And the actual operations executed by each processor become a crucial factor that impacts on the total system.

The following appear to be systems with interesting properties that are worth exploring.

Bundles of Pipelining Arrays

Each array chip can efficiently handle the flow of a 1-by-R set of information. If these pieces of information are related (as they are when the problem is to recognize objects in 2-dimensional images), then local structures of information can be examined, transformed, and combined as this information flows through. If pieces are unrelated (e.g., when separate strings are being processed), each line of processors can work separately, in traditional pipeline fashion.

There can be a certain amount of looping back, e.g., for feedback or constraint relaxation on the chip itself. But this is probably best handled by off-chip wiring that links chips to chips, and also links chips to themselves (e.g., one edge to the opposite edge).

One such chip will execute C processes on a 1-by-R slice of information. N such chips would handle N-by-R arrays of information. But they would be somewhat awkward, since the only place where adjacent slices could interact is off the chip.

Much preferable would be a 3-dimensional technology, where there could be interaction from slice to slice as well as within each slice. Bundles of polymers, or even of genetically engineered DNA or protein molecules, would appear to be most suitable for this. But they are in the farther-off future of promising ideas, rather than proved, relatively mature, technologies.

Design Constraints Imposed by Micro-Electronic Chip Technologies

Let's assume the following design constraints:

Each chip can contain 10^6 transistors for today's designs, and 10^8 for tomorrow's designs (that is, for 5-20 years into the future).

Assuming that simple processors with minimal memory are used, each processor plus its memory will need from 10 to 1,000 transistors for each bit of information that it processes.

Today's chips must be near-planar, although there is a real possibility of 3-dimensional chips or other technologies in the future.

To use the chip effectively, simple, regular processors and memory banks appear to be preferable, since they minimize wasted space. Similarly, wire crossings should be minimized, since they need more space.

Processors should be as close as possible to those processors they communicate with - that is, to which they send, and from which they receive, information.

Pins from each chip to the outside world (over which all communication, including controlling signals, must take place) are severely limited. The limit today is only several hundred, and it appears that this will grow only slowly. Roughly, the number of pins is $O(T^{1/2})$ (T=transistors).

Several Potentially Promising Designs for Information-Transforming Structures

A. Since 2-dimensional arrays are among the most compact and best designs, packing compactly into 2-dimensional chips, they form an attractive basis. They should be usable when desirable as banks of 1-dimensional arrays through which information is pipelined, the processors transforming it along the way. The lateral array links are quite appropriate for assessing and combining information from near-neighbors.

Additional links to more distant neighbors, and also feedback loops, would sometimes also be desirable. But since these would not be as efficiently fabricated on the chip, it might be best to use off-chip wires for these purposes.

Therefore the following range of possibilities should be investigated:

Put an N-by-N array on each chip, with input to one side and output from the opposite side. This has the problem that distant neighbors can interact only via the array topology, and backward flow of information can similarly take place only through the array topology. That means that these processes are slow, since distances through the array are great, and when they are executed they interrupt and stop the ordinary forward flow of information.

B. Put an N-by-M array on each chip (N much larger than M). Now the off-chip links can play a far larger role in providing channels for communication between more distant neighbors, and for feedback. But the limits on pins will probably keep N from growing to more than a few hundred or so.

C. Additional links can be put on each chip, to handle more distant interactions and feedback loops. These might be of any sort, but they all will use a good deal of space, and they should be chosen and designed with great care. Probably a tree-, pyramid- or multi-pyramid-based design would be the best, since they convert distances from linear to logarithmic. Alternately, an NlogN network might be used, but it is appreciably more expensive in chip area.

D. The pipelines might be linked to adjacent pipelines not only in the 2d dimension (that is, from row to row on the chip), but also in the 3d dimension. This would be very useful for processing 2-dimensional information, such as images. But it would be relatively expensive in terms of extra links, crossings and chip area.

E. Rather than use an array or pipeline that at each stage applies the same amount of processing power, the system should be able to converge, or/and diverge, information as appropriate. Processes usually output smaller structures of information than they input, since most processes organize, abstract, make succinct - so outputs should be converged, giving a cone/pyramid structure. Sometimes the volume of information remains constant; occasionally there is a need to expand (e.g., broadcasting to many processors working on different aspects of the problem). This suggests an overall converging-diverging multi-apex tree-linked structure that can expand and narrow as needed. We might try to design large structures of processors from which such information-transforming structures can be carved out as needed.

F. Most important, the particular structure needed for a particular problem, or class of problems, should be built when indicated and efficiently realizable.

G. Several different types of chip could be used to achieve the total design. Routing chips might contain NlogN networks, crossbars, or other appropriate linking topologies. Different types of processors might be put on special chips. Prime candidates are powerful 32-bit processors with their own controllers, arrays, trees, pyramids, and special-purpose processors of various sorts (e.g., to convolve, multiply).

The Feasible Types of Operations for Such Information-Flow Structures

It is crucial that this kind of information-transforming system, to work with speed and efficiency, be given an appropriate repertoire of operations. It must work effectively even though it has neither one global nor many local controllers. Processors cannot afford to wait and do nothing until the appropriate information arrives. As many processors as possible should work as much as possible, productively. Processors will not longer have an external controller to handle contention, synchronize, and in general tell them what to do.

There appear to be a number of feasible operations that fill these requirements, and ones that are highly appropriate at that. This is not surprising, since the brain does all the things we want such a system to do, and these are chiefly brain-like operations.

Integration of Information (to Combine)

Possibly the most basic operation is simply one that integrates. A neuron-like processor that receives many inputs combines them, e.g., by adding. This summation of incoming impulses might take place over time as well as over space. It might be modulated, e.g., decaying over time or space, or scaling down large changes. Thus the brain appears to modulate incoming impulses using Gaussian bell-shaped weights. This very naturally gives a detector a smaller voice the more distant it is.

This is especially appropriate when a processor receives redundant inputs from several nearby processors. For example, all might be identical detectors of the same feature, but at slightly different locations, or different detectors of the same feature, only some of which can be expected to succeed. And since each processor repeatedly, redundantly, sends its message that the feature was detected, these messages are best integrated, and also scaled down, as appropriate.

Integration can also serve to average, smooth, and eliminate random anomalies, as in noisy images.

More generally, integration gives a linear combination of the several components combined. This can be useful for many purposes - but only up to a certain point: where non-linear combinations are needed (as for spatially oriented structures), more complex compounding functions must be used, as described below.

It is important to note that in all these cases processors do useful work simply by repeatedly integrating, since repetition combines information over time. Most important, when this is part of a network where other processors are attempting to converge toward some solution, goal, or desired state, repeated integrations give a running summary of the current state of affairs.

Differentiation of Information (to Contrast)

Differentiation is the natural companion to integration - again, both in space and in time. Parallel integrations build up local summary pictures; differentiation assesses whether they contrast.

Brains routinely integrate nearby impulses, and at the same time differentiate. Neuron-like units can handle this by adding to integrate, and subtracting to differentiate.

Thresholding or in Other Ways Deciding Whether to Fire Out

The simplest kind of processor would simply fire out its integrated result (if it were a differentiator this would be a function of negative as well as positive values).

It is often useful to set a threshold below which the processor does not fire. Now there are several alternative possibilities when the threshold is exceeded: 1. The output is simply the input, or some function of the input; 2. The output is some independent value that the processor stores or computes; 3. The output is some function of both 1. its inputs and 2. its independent values.

A type 1 operator whose threshold is 0 acts like a basic integrate-differentiate operator, since it simply fires out what was input to it. A type 2 operator can effect any desired conversion to symbolic information.

Once again, the threshold function is intimately related to integrate-differentiate, and the system can usefully continue to combine, contrast, and threshold.

Compounding (Non-Linear Combining)

Rather than simply integrate, several inputs can be combined in a non-linear manner. This is crucial for image-processing systems, in determining objects' shape and other structural information. For example, depending upon how a vertical and horizontal bar are positioned the result might be any of 4 angles, or a T, +, or still other shapes.

Once again, it is often useful to do this repeatedly, to get a firmer estimate, and to continually evaluate what might be there as a function of attempts to iteratively converge.

Comparing Two or More Values

Another useful operation makes comparisons - again, in space, in time, or in both. This serves a variety of purposes, from noticing simple changes to leading toward decisions.

These Kinds of Information-Flow Operations Build Into Useful Larger Structures

Each individual operation of this sort can be usefully repeated if it is an appropriate part of a larger structure of operations. For example, outputs from functions of this sort are usefully integrated over time, then these results differentiated and thresholded to find peaks, as when an object is resolved.

Choosing (Winner-Take-All)

Comparing indicates which is "more"; but then a whole structure of comparisons can choose a winner. This can conveniently be handled by flowing the alternatives up through a tree each of whose nodes makes a local comparison and passes along the better. The apex of the tree's choice will be the grand choice, the winner over all the alternatives.

Alternately, a node representing each alternative can fire negatively into all other nodes, so that after iterations only the most highly activated node still fires.

Building Larger, More Complex, More Abstract, More General Structures

Trees and Pyramids that successively build larger compounds, using structures of operations of the sort suggested above, appear to be among the most promising relatively general examples of systems that can hierarchically compute complex functions of the sort needed for intelligent perception and cognition.

At least these are the most widely used to date. They reflect the basic requirements: that complex processes be decomposed (divided-and-conquered) into suitably simple processes - from which the tree/pyramid structure follows - and information be flowed upward until the processors toward the apex complete the global process.

Almost certainly, better structures can be found for a particular problem, for the structure of the total system should, ideally, reflect the structure of processes needed to solve the specific problem being handled. For these to be of the efficient information-flow type they would best be built to handle processes that can usefully be repeated, moving toward solutions.

It is too early to know whether it will be possible to achieve structures of this sort that are both general-purpose and also powerful and efficient.

Constraining-Relaxing, To Reduce Possibilities and Settle into Conclusions

The differencing and compounding operations can impose constraints. Successively combining, differencing, and choosing, then noticing how results of choosing change (by applying this same structure of operations) can effect resolutions of the various influences, and relax to what are judged good, or stable, or sufficient, states.

Reinforcing a Continuing Sequence of Converging Decisions

In general, a network that repeatedly integrates, differences, compounds, compares, and chooses - then attempts to monitor (by integrating, differencing, etc.) its success at choosing, can move successively toward better and better results, yet as appropriate decide to stop, judging no more can be done.

The Possibility of Still Other Structures of Usefully Repeated Information-Flow Operations

The operations described above are only examples of what information-flow systems can usefully do. They were mentioned because they are brain-like, and using them much can be done. But they also appear to be sufficient for much of perceptual recognition and cognitive reasoning.

An important goal to work toward is a general-purpose, and also efficient and powerful, set of such operations, ones that need little synchronization and are usefully repeated. These should be of the sort that can be embedded efficiently into an appropriate network of processors.

The crucial point is that processors, processes, and information should all be structured together, so that information is transformed as it flows through structures of processes appropriately embedded into structures of processors.

Acknowledgements and References

This paper grows out of research conducted over the years under a number of grants from the National Science Foundation, developing parallel-hierarchical brain-like systems for perception and cognition, and investigating appropriate parallel hardware architecture.

The following following books contain a number of references to this research, and to related work by others.

General References

[1] Uhr, L., *Algorithm-Structured Computer Arrays and Networks: Architectures and Processes for Images, Percepts, Models, Information.* New York: Academic Press, 1984.

[2] Uhr, L. (Ed.), *Parallel Computer Vision,* Boston: Academic Press, 1987.

Uhr, L., *[3] Multi-Computer Architectures for Artificial Intelligence: Toward Fast, Robust, Parallel Systems.* New York: Wiley, 1987.

[4] Uhr, L., Preston, K., Levialdi, S. and Duff, M.J.B. (Eds.), *Evaluation of Multi-Computers for Image Processing.* New York: Academic Press, 1986.

BASIC RESEARCH FOR CELLULAR PROCESSING

- A Short Survey of Some Results on Cellular and Systolic Systems -

Roland Vollmar¶

0. Introduction

In this article cellular processing is understood as a processing by (almost) homogeneous systems with fine granularity for which cellular automata and their modifications and systolic automata are appropriate models.

During the last years an increased interest has been devoted to these topics, on the one hand because the limitations of tuning computers by usual methods became clearer, on the other hand because the VLSI technology offered possibilities for the realization of massively parallel systems.

Since the space for this article is limited it is tried to describe the relations between the different models only under the aspect of the recognition capability for formal languages. Even then (and under this point of view) a selection has to be made which has nothing to do with an assessment. For example it was not possible to treat the closure properties of the classes of languages defined by automata which will be considered; moreover only 1-dimensional (resp. $1^1/_2$-dimensional) systems have been included. Also such a topic as "fault tolerance" which is highly important for massively parallel systems has not been treated, and at all problems of hardware realization, e.g. by transputers, have not been discussed.

Neural computers have been excluded because the homogeneity condition is not fulfilled: The connections between neurons are inhomogeneous and even time-variability would be highly desirable. In this connection in [Ko88] it is suggested that for the development of artificial sensory systems "...one should not apply heuristically derived operations at all, but first [...] create an extremely adaptive network that then finds its own structures and parameters automatically...". For such systems it seems at least extremely difficult to apply the classical complexity measures.

¶ Institut für Theoretische Informatik, Technische Universität Braunschweig, Postfach 3329, D-3300 Braunschweig

1. Notions and basic properties

Almost all concepts will be introduced informally.
The systems considered in this article may be understood as polyautomata in the sense of A.R. Smith III [Sm76], namely as "a multitude of interconnected automata operating in parallel to form a larger automaton".
The first basic system is the cellular automaton which in the following will be specialized.

A cellular automaton (A, d, N, F) may be considered as a finite part of a d-dimensional space where at the points with integer valued coordinates finite deterministic Moore automata (of the same type) with the state set A are fixed. These automata are connected according to a certain scheme N, called the neighbourhood template. The global behaviour is controlled by the global transition function F : a central clock stimulates transitions of each single automaton dependent on the states of the neighboured automata (according to N) where the automaton itself may or may not be included. It should be emphasized that homogeneity holds in the whole (finite part of the) space as well for the "static assignments" as for the neighbourhood structure.
For any $\underline{i} \in \mathbf{Z}^d$ ($\mathbf{Z}$ the set of integers) it is defined: $| \underline{i} | := \sum_{\nu=1}^{d} | i_\nu |$. Then the so-called von Neumann neighbourhood is given by $H_k := \{ \underline{i} \,/\, | \underline{i} | \leq k \}$ for $k \in \mathbf{N}_0$.
Especially the one-dimensional case is of interest: H_1 denotes the neighbourhood which contains an automaton and its two neighbours (in the usual sense); furthermore $\bar{H}_1$ equals H_1 without the left neighbour and $-\bar{H}_1$ equals H_1 without the right neighbour.

Cellular automata (CA) are well suited to solve some pattern recognition problems, whereby the appropriateness is given by a higher recognition speed compared with sequential devices.
In the following different types of cellular automata will be compared with each other and with systolic systems on the basis of this ability. To this end it is important to distinguish between the modes of input and the definitions of recognition. In the one-dimensional case - the only one which will be discussed in this article - "patterns" are reduced to words of (formal) languages.
There are some reasons to study the properties of systems with the help of formal languages:

- Formal languages are intensively investigated and their relations are well understood.
- Formal languages are not only relevant for the understanding of e.g. programming languages or pattern recognition, but there are also connections to numerics as has been stated in [CuY84]: "It should be pointed out that the techniques used in systolic programs for language recognition or string manipulation are not much different from

those used in numerical systolic algorithms. For example, a systolic system recognizing the language $\{ww \,/\, w \in \Sigma^+\}$ can be converted into a system which computes the scalar product of two vectors simply by reinterpreting the basic operations (* and + as comparison and `and`)."

The notion "cellular system" is used as a category for cellular automata and their modifications.

Under "systolic systems" two specific types, namely systolic tree and systolic trellis automata will be understood. These systems emerged in connection with the progress of VLSI technology. Quoting Kung ([Ku82]) a "systolic system consists of a set of interconnected cells, each capable of performing some simple operation... Information in a systolic system flows between cells in a pipelined fashion, and communication with the outside world occurs only at the `boundary cells`." As the word "systolic" expresses, the emphasis is put on the data flow through the system.

The following descriptions are rather informal, too. Moreover only restricted classes will be introduced. Details, a lot of results, and generalizations may be found in the survey article [Gr84].

A systolic tree automaton is characterized by an infinite rooted binary (balanced) tree (see Fig. 1).

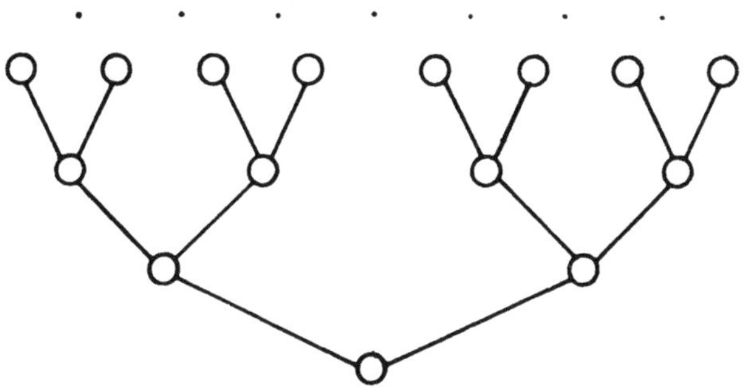

Fig.1 : Systolic (binary) tree automaton

The nodes of the tree are labeled by letters from an alphabet in such a way that it contains only finitely many different infinite subtrees. The labels denote the types of processors fixed in the corresponding nodes. The nodes with a distance $k \geq 0$ from the root node form the k-th level. The processors of the k-th level receive information from the

connected processors of level k+1 and give transformed values (according to a certain function) to the connected processors of the level k-1.
The transformation process does not need any time; but to transport the information along an edge one time unit is used. These processes are synchronized.
Systolic trellis automata have a neighbourhood structure as sketched in Fig.2 and are defined in analogy to tree automata.

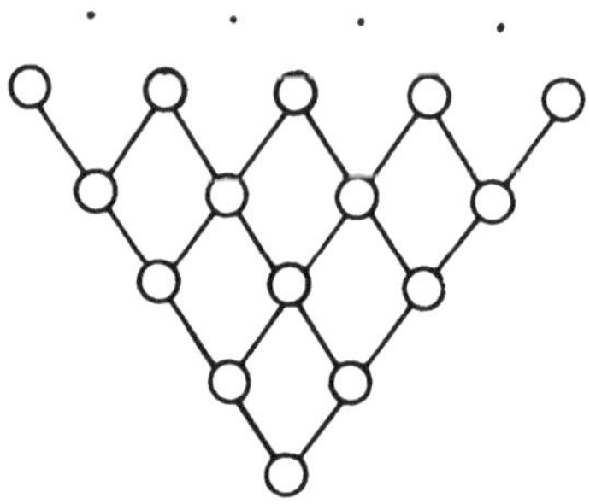

Fig. 2 : Systolic trellis automata

Here only triangulary shaped systolic trellis automata will be considered. Automata with a generalized shape sometimes are also called systolic trellis automata (e.g. in [IKM85]).

The main differences between cellular systems and systolic systems are characterized by the input mode and the flow of data. Normally in cellular automata only the behaviour under the input of a single word is considered; in a systolic system at each time step a new word is input, and this is possible because the data flow in one direction through the system. (It should be remarked that other input modes -not only the iterative one, discussed below- are considered; see e.g. [Gr84]).
It should be pointed out that this distinction on the basis of the input behaviour -and not of the structure- is quite uncommon, but it accentuates the advantage of systolic sytems as models for "fast" parallel processing. At the end of paragraph 3 it will be seen that there are some problems to demarcate the systems unambiguously.

The notion "systolic system" is used in a narrower sense than in the literature about VLSI systems. In [FoW87] the behaviour of a processor is described in the following manner: "The basic operation performed in each cycle by each processing element in the various systolic arrays can range from a simple bit-wise operation, to word-level multiplication and addition, and even to execution of a complete program." Although there may be no formal contradiction, in systolic systems at least the execution of a program by a processor in one step is not intended.

Another concept should be introduced: In cellular automata it is a laborious task to transmit information from one end to the other end. To save time it is obvious to install far reaching lines between the automata -although this contradicts the postulates of an only local behaviour. Such broadcasting capabilities have been introduced for different systems. To avoid confusion it is important to distinguish between some modes (the following is not a complete specification and only a rough description):

- Broadcasting (see e.g. [St82]): A cellular automaton of length n is modified in that sense that each single automaton is augmented by a storage of size $O(\log n)$, and each automaton "knows" n and its relative position. Information can be broadcasted on a (global) bus to all automata attached to this bus in one time unit. At one time at most one information can be sent on the bus.
- Direct central control (see e.g. [Se77]): From a distinct automaton (in iterative systems the automaton where the input is fed) information is sent to all other automata with a constant delay or without delay.
- Global control (see e.g. [IPK85b]): Also from a distinct automaton information is sent, but not on a bus, rather from automaton to automaton without any delay, but every automaton has the possibility to modify the transmitted information.

2. Cellular systems

2.1. Cellular systems without time restrictions

First one-dimensional cellular systems with H_1 template, i.e. with bidirectional data flow will be considered. As mentioned above the systems should be classified according to the input mode and the definition of recognition.

As for Turing machines there are two main types of input modes:

- At the beginning the word to be analyzed is contained in the cellular automaton. In more detail: A word w (unequal to the empty word), for which it is to be decided whether it belongs to a (formal) language L or not, is coded symbol by symbol as a chain of states in subsequent automata. These automata form a so-called retina which is bounded at either end by an automaton in a special state, the border state. These border automata do not change their states. One of the end automata of the retina, say the leftmost one, called the accepting automaton, shows the result of the recognition process: two disjoint subsets A' and A'' of the state set A are specified. The accepting automaton assumes a state from A' (A'') if and only if $w \in L$ (or $w \notin L$ resp.) (see Fig. 3). In the following this type of cellular automata is referred to as "CA".
- At each time step one symbol of a word is input to a special single automaton, usually the first one in the chain of automata. At this automaton also the result is observed. To emphasize the inhomogeneity of this type of cellular systems the notion

(linear) iterative automata (abbreviated by IA) is used (see Fig. 4). In contrast to cellular automata where the retina is determined by the length of the word, in iterative automata the number of automata involved in the recognition process is not bounded.

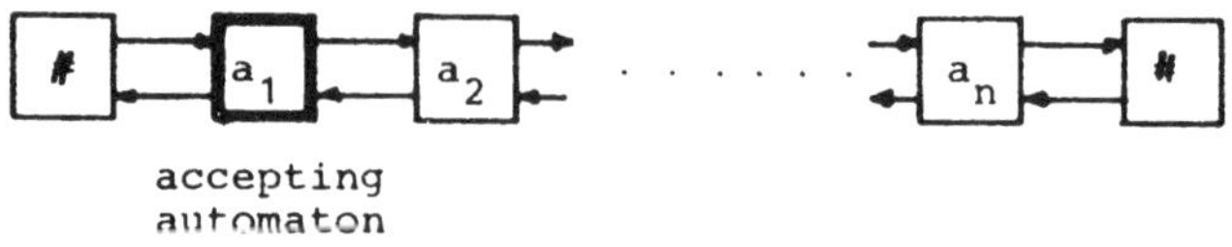

Fig.3 : Cellular automaton with bidirectional data flow (CA)

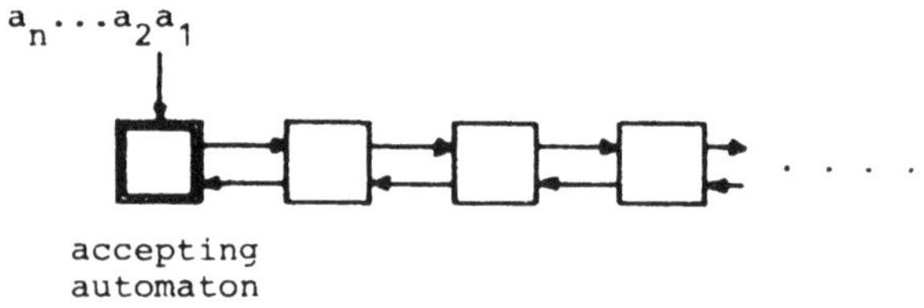

Fig. 4 : Iterative automaton with bidirectional data flow (IA)

With the last remark in mind it is clear that cellular automata have the recognition power of deterministic linear bounded automata and iterative automata that one of Turing machines.

As a first specialization cellular automata with unidirectional information flow (also called one-way cellular automata and abbreviated OCA) will be considered. If (as e.g. in [Dy80]) a $-\bar{H}_1$ neighbourhood is used, it is meaningful to define the rightmost automaton in the retina as the accepting automaton (see Fig. 5). In [Dy80] it has been shown that the class of the corresponding nondeterministic variant has the same accepting power as the class of nondeterministic cellular automata (with bidirectional information flow).
Whether the class of languages accepted by deterministic one-way cellular automata forms a proper subclass of the class of languages accepted by two-way cellular automata is an open problem -provided there are no time restrictions.

Fig. 5 : Cellular automata with unidirectional data flow (OCA)

2.2. Cellular systems with restrictions

By definition CA are restricted in space. The best investigated class of cellular systems is that one of one-dimensional cellular automata with a real-time behaviour. For these CA it is required that the result of the analysis of a word is delivered (in the accepting automaton) at latest at a time which is equal to the length of this word. This is a reasonable requirement because there exist simple languages for which a decision for a word about the membership can only be made after the knowledge of the last symbol. And with an H_1- (or a smaller) neighbourhood the information about the content of the rightmost automaton in the retina is available to the accepting automaton after $|w|-1$ steps[1]. Generally it is said that a word of length n is accepted within time $T(n)$ if the accepting condition is fulfilled within $T(n)$ steps. The notions linear time, quadratic time,... are used correspondingly.
In addition to space and time restrictions other requirements can be made to get a better understanding of the classes of CA. E.g. in [Vo81] the number of proper state changes is proposed as an additional measure for real-time CA. There and in [Vo82] some results about a finer classification are contained.

Besides some algorithms for picture processing in [St82] it has been shown that in CA with broadcasting the sum of n numbers which are stored one per automaton can be obtained in $O(n^{1/2})$ time steps; and this time is optimal.
In [St86] a systematic approach has been made to find "good" layouts for bus systems. There it is also allowed to have many buses where each of them can be used only on a part of the cellular system. Some interesting results have been obtained.

Now there can be made some propositions about the relation of OCA and CA: From [UMS82] it can be seen that to any real-time CA an OCA may be constructed which simulates[2] the CA in twice real-time. It should be explicitly remarked that the proof is made under the assumption that the accepting automata in the CA and in the OCA are on different ends of the retina.
Real-time CA are more powerful than real-time OCA: In [Se79] it has been proved that languages over a one-letter alphabet recognized by real-time OCA are regular. But e.g. the (nonregular) language $\{ a^{2^k} / k \in \mathbf{N} \}$ is recognizable by a real-time CA. It is also recognizable by a linear-time OCA.
In effect, in [ChC84] it has been shown that real-time CA and twice real-time OCA are equivalent (where again the accepting automata are at different ends of the retina).

1 $|w|$ denotes the length of the word w. Only words unequal to the empty word are considered.

2 The notion "simulation" is used here in a straightforward way, meaning that the same recognition power is available.

One of the results in [IPK85b] is that OCA with global control (the direct connections are opposite to them of Fig.5 and the distinct automaton is the accepting automaton which at the beginning contains a_1) are strictly more powerful than "normal" OCA and even than OCA with direct central control.

Now some modifications of cellular automata with respect to the definition of the acceptance will be reported: To reduce the minimal recognition time in CA (i.e. real-time) in [SoW83] an acceptance is reached if at some time all automata in the retina assume accepting states. Then it is possible to recognize some nontrivial languages, e.g. $\{(ab)^k / k \in \mathbf{N}\}$, in constant time. In [IPK85a] it has been shown that there exists a non-contextfree language, namely
$\{ b_n\$b_{n-1}\$ ....\$b_2\$b_1 / b_i$ is the binary representation of i with no leading zeroes, $1 \leq i \leq n \}$, which can be accepted by such a cellular automaton in time O(log n). The proof is by use of an equivalent sequential model - a principle which will be discussed later on in some detail. The same authors proved that languages which are accepted by this type of cellular automata in time o(logn) are regular.

There are some very interesting results concerning the relations between different types of iterative automata:
In [Co66] it is proved that it does not exist a real-time iterative automaton which recognizes the language

$$\{ uv / u, v \in X^* , |v| \geq 3, v=mi(v) \}$$ [3] ;

but there exists a real-time CA for this language ([Sm72]).

A generalization of (linear) iterative automata, called iterative tree automata (ITA), has been considered in [CuY84] and in [CuY86]. An ITA is a tree automaton as sketched above, but the input word is given sequentially to the root automaton and to increase its power compared with an IA in [CuY84] it is stated (without proof) that it is necessary to have different transition functions for left and right sons. Moreover an ITA cannot be understood as a systolic system because for ITA a two-directional information flow is important. (The IA are ITA with a degenerate tree.)
Using the equivalence relation defined in [Co66] in [CuY84] it has been shown that the language

$$\{x_1\%x_2\% ...\%x_n¢y¢^t / n>0, x_1,...,x_n,y \in \{0,1\}^+ , t=2|y|+1, y=x_i \text{ for some } 1 \leq i \leq n\}$$

is not accepted by any d-dimensional real-time IA. Since there exists a real-time ITA which accepts this language, as a consequence it follows that the class of real-time (linear) IA languages is a proper subclass of the real-time ITA languages.

---

3 mi(w) denotes the mirror image of the word w .

As a further generalization ITA with k-ary trees as underlying structures (called k-ary ITA) have been considered. For a k-ary ITA k+1 transition functions are used -correspondingly to the definition of the binary ITA. For this model a hierarchy has been established: The family of k-ary ITA languages is properly contained in the family of (k+1)-ary ITA languages.

Another concept has been introduced in [CuY86]: the pseudo real-time computation. A k-ary ITA is called to work in pseudo real-time if only at every c-th step (c>1) a symbol of the input word is fed and if c-1 steps after reaching its last symbol the result is given.

A surprising result is the following ([CuY86]): The families of real-time, pseudo real-time, and linear-time ITA languages coincide, if all the ITA of positive integer arities are considered.

In [CuY86] ITA with direct central control have been considered (more exactly also with global control, but without utilizing all the capabilities) and it has been shown (among others) that languages which are acceptable by such modified k-ary ITA in real-time are also accepted by k^2-ary ITA in real-time.

In [IPK85b] among other results it has been proved that IA, IA with direct central control and IA with global control are equivalent and use the same amount of time.

Whereas for the types of automata discussed until now it was quite obvious which automaton should work as an accepting automaton, this is not so in the case of one-way iterative automata (OIA) (see Fig. 6), because it is not clear immediately the use of how much space should be allowed. In [CIV86] it is remarked that e.g. $\{0^n1^n / n \in \mathbf{N}\}$ can be accepted by an OIA with O(log n) automata, but in contrast $\{ w\$mi(w) / w \in \{o,1\}^* \}$ cannot be accepted by an OIA with a sublinear number of automata.

However this is possible if the input mechanism is changed: The same authors propose to apply cyclically the input word to the first automaton. With such a model the above mentioned mirror language can be accepted by only O(log n) automata. The lower bound for accepting non-regular languages is loglog n automata, and this bound is tight.

In the following OIA of length |w| will be considered.

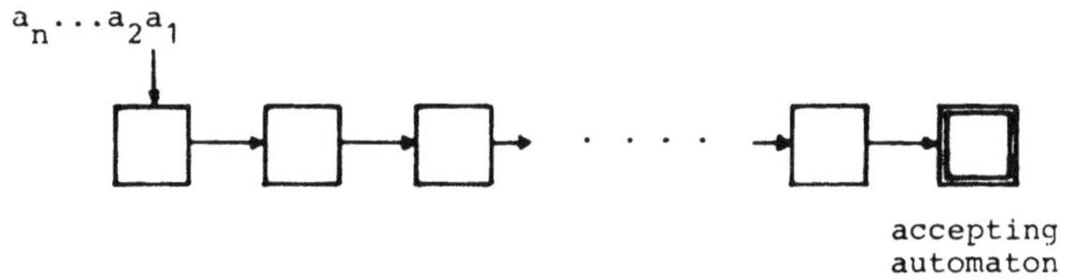

Fig. 6 . Iterative automata with unidirectional data flow (OIA)

In [IbJ87] a very surprising result about the relations of OCA and OIA has been proved: OCA and OIA have the same accepting power.

While one direction of the proof, the simulation of an OCA by an OIA, is easy -also under the aspect of available information-, for the other the difficulty results from the fact that in an OIA every automaton "sees" the whole word whereas in an OCA every automaton - with the exception of the accepting one- receives only information from a subword.

This part of the proof will be sketched, not only under the aspect of the assertion but also because a proof technique ("serialization") has been applied which is very useful for similar problems and was developed by Ibarra and coauthors.

It can be shown that the following modified Turing machine, called SMI, is equivalent to an OIA: An SMI is a Turing machine with one semi-infinite worktape bounded at the left. At the beginning it contains only a special symbol ¢. The finite state control receives input words $a_1a_2....a_n$, at the end of the word a special symbol $ is added. The (read-write) head makes left-to-right sweeps of the worktape starting at the left boundary symbol ¢ in start state q_0. In the i-th sweep $(1 \leq i \leq n)$ the input symbol a_i is read and the head moves right rewriting (and possibly changing) non-blank symbols and assuming only states different from q_0 until a blank symbol is reached. It is rewritten and the head is set back to the left boundary symbol ¢ and the control unit assumes state q_0. (This prevents the transfer of information to the left.) At the sweep n+1 -distinguishable by the $ as input- the SMI behaves as before but at the end a blank symbol is rewritten by this special symbol $ which will never be changed such that the length of the working tape area is fixed for the rest of the process. Then during the following sweeps only changes of symbols on the tape and of states take place. A word $a_1a_2....a_n$ is accepted by an SMI if (after at least n+1 sweeps) the finite control assumes an accepting state when the head reaches the right boundary marker.

The sweep complexity S(n) of an SMI with input $a_1a_2...a_n$ is the smallest number of sweeps which is necessary to accept this word.

A similar model is given by an SMC with a semi-infinite tape which is bounded at the right. It makes also left-to-right sweeps but starts at the rightmost blank symbol in the state q_0. In other respects it is analogous to an SMI.

In [IbJ87] it has been shown that a language is accepted by an OCA in time S(n)-1, provided $S(n) \geq n+1$, if and only if its reverse can be accepted by an SMC with sweep complexity S(n).

With these results for the proof mentioned above it is "only" necessary to show that to each SMI there exists an SMC which simulates it.

First the word is read. Dependent on the length of the word equal-sized regions on the tape are created. The main idea is to generate systematically all strings (over the alphabet) of this length, to simulate for each such string the behaviour of the SMI and to check whether an accepting state is reached and whether the processed string is equal

to the input word. This systematic generation and the count of the different possible configurations can be done in the available space.
The advantages of the sequentialization become clear by the consideration of details of the proof; e.g. the shifting of markers is much easier to handle than directly in a parallel working system.

Generalizations of OCA and OIA by extending the number of involved automata are depicted in Fig.7 and Fig.8.

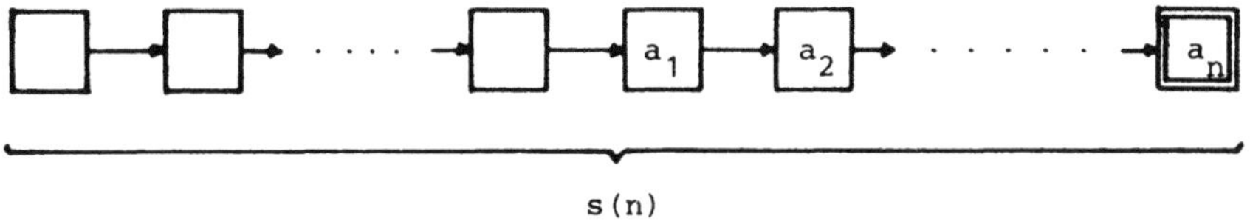

a) s(n) - OCA_1

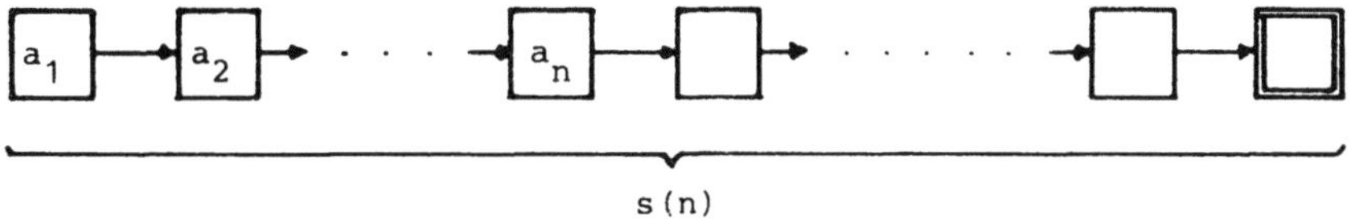

b) s(n) - OCA_2

Fig. 7 : Two types of OCA with extended space

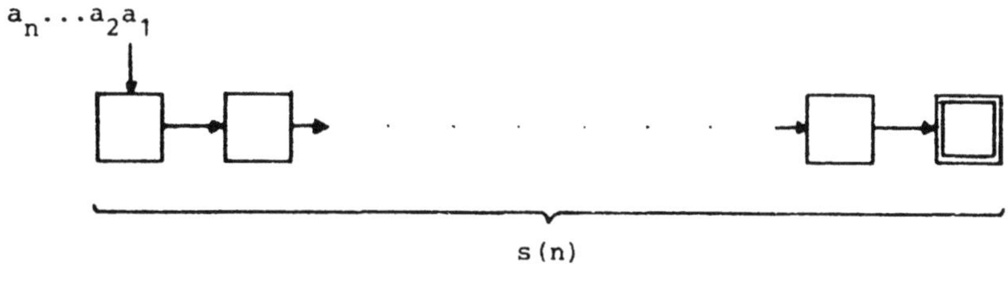

Fig. 8 : OIA with extended space (s(n) - OIA)

In [IbJ87] it is proved that for $s(n) \geq n$ $s(n)$-OCA_1, $s(n)$-OCA_2 and $s(n)$-OIA accept the same class of languages. (For s(n)-OIA the input words are padded by special symbols.) In the same article it has been also shown that linear-time OCA have the same power as OIA working in time 2n which is for OIA the minimal time accepting nontrivial languages. In this connection it should be pointed out that in [BuC84] it has been proved that (constructible) linear-time OCA can be simulated by OCA which need 2n time steps.

Some results quoted in this section are depicted in the following scheme:

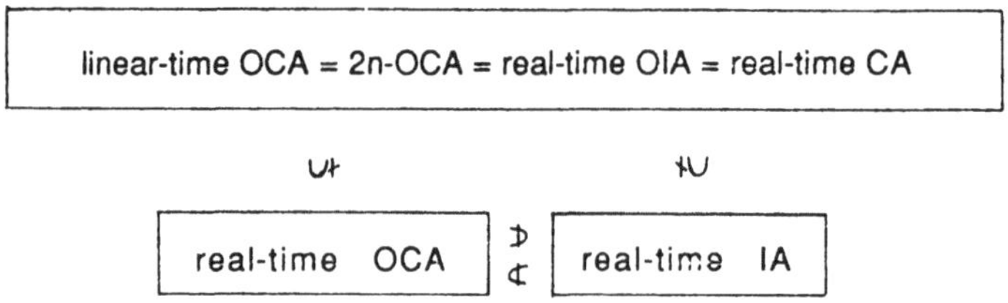

It should be remarked that real-time OIA work in 2n steps; they are also called pseudo-real-time OIA (e.g. in [IbJ87]).
The sequentialization method shortly described above is not only used for the simulation of different types of cellular systems, but sometimes it makes easier to understand the behaviour of an accepting system, too. For instance in [CIV86] it has been shown by the construction of an SMI that the set of true quantified Boolean formulas, i.e. a PSPACE-complete language, can be accepted by OIA.

3. Systolic systems

First systolic tree automata will be considered.
As for cellular systems in principle two types of input behaviour have to be distinguished: A parallel input of a word at a "fitting" level (see among others [CGS83], [CSW84] for a more general model as reported here and [Sa85] for a formal definition of this type) and a sequential input to the root of the tree (see among others [CuY84], [CuY86]). But because here -as mentioned above- cellular and systolic systems are distinguished by its input behaviour and not by the structure the second type has been treated in the paragraph before.
For the first input type the processing of a word w over an alphabet is done in the following way: Let m be the smallest integer such that there are $\geq |w|$ nodes at the m-th level of the tree. If the number of nodes exceeds $|w|$, to w a corresponding number of special symbols is added. To each type of processor two functions are assigned, an input

function which maps an input symbol into a symbol of an operating alphabet and an output function which maps pairs of symbols of the operating alphabet into a symbol of the operating alphabet.
Each symbol of the word (possibly padded by special symbols) is fed into one processor, processed by the input function of the corresponding node (without any time delay) and transmitted to the connected node of the level m-1. For this transmission one time unit is needed. This process continues until the root node outputs a symbol (according to its output function). If this symbol belongs to a specified set, the input word (without the possibly added symbols) is accepted, otherwise it is rejected.

It should be noted that the recognition time is in the order of the logarithm of the word length.
An example for the behaviour of a systolic tree automaton is the following (after [Gr84]):
A binary tree consists of processors of only one type. a is the input symbol and \$ the special symbol to extend the input words. The operating alphabet is {A,R}, and {A} is the "accepting set". The (only) input function f is defined by f(a)=A, f(\$)=R and the (only) output function g is defined by g(A,A)=A and g(A,R)=g(R,A)=g(R,R)=R. Obviously, the set of words accepted by this automaton equals $\{a^{2^n} / n \in \mathbf{N}\}$.
(To avoid special considerations the empty word remains excluded.)
It is sufficient to consider only such simple systolic tree automata (with only one proces - sor type), because they have the same accepting power as general ones (see e.g. [Sa85]).
All the regular languages are acceptable by systolic tree automata ([CSW84]) and there exist nonregular contextfree languages (see e.g. [Pa82]) and non-contextfree context - sensitive languages (see e.g. the example above) which are acceptable.
On the other side e.g. the languages $\{a^n b^n / n \in \mathbf{N}\}$ and $\{a^{3^n} / n \in \mathbf{N}\}$ can not be accepted by systolic tree automata ([CSW84]).
In [IbK84a] a characterization of systolic tree automata by sequential machines, so-called "deterministic binary counter synchronized Turing machines" has been presented.

In connection with systolic systems two important concepts have been introduced: stability and superstability ([CGS83]). Above it was required that an input word has to be fed to the processors of the smallest possible level. This is quite unnatural because then first the level has to be determined and moreover for a device it is advantageous to have only one level which is connected to the external world.
A systolic tree automaton is called stable if the accepted language remains the same independent of the level the words are fed; the padding (with a special symbol) must be done on the right end. If this last requirement is dropped, i.e. the symbols of the input word may be scattered (but not permuted), and the accepted language remains invariant, the systolic tree automaton is termed superstable.

In [CGS83] it has been proved that to each systolic tree automaton an equivalent stable one can be effectively constructed. There is also shown that in general superstability for these automata cannot be reached: This follows from the proposition that every language accepted by a superstable systolic tree automaton is regular.

A second type of systolic system is the systolic trellis automaton which has been investigared in more detail. Since here only to a few results will be referred, again it should be hinted to [Gr84], especially about different input modes.
First it should be observed that - in contrast to tree automata - for every length of a word there exists a fitting level. Another difference lies in the fact that "a trellis-like structure of processors has the property that data can move from one processor to another along different paths, i.e., different contexts may be used" (from [CGS84a]).

Here only two types of systolic trellis automata will be considered, semihomogeneous ones and homogeneous ones. Semihomogeneous systolic trellis automata are defined as sketched above, i.e. there exists only a finite number of different labeled subtrellises. And they are called homogeneous systolic trellis automata if all nodes are labeled by the same symbol. The acceptance of a word is defined in an obvious way: The root processor has to assume a marked state.
Under the aspect of language acceptance semihomogeneous and homogeneous systolic trellis automata have the same power ([CGS84a]). Therefore only some results concerning the last ones will be quoted.
Real-time OCA and (real-time) systolic trellis automata are equivalent ([ChC84]). This can be seen immediately considering the time-space-diagram of the recognition process of a word in an OCA and the bent underlying trellis.

Since it is easy to construct a systolic trellis automaton for the language $\{a^n b^n \mid n \in \mathbf{N}\}$ from the remarks above it follows that the classes acceptable by systolic tree automata and by systolic trellis automata are incomparable.

As for systolic tree automata to each systolic trellis automaton an equivalent stable one can be constructed but moreover -in contrast to systolic tree automata- also an equivalent superstable systolic trellis automaton can be obtained ([CGS86]).

Concerning the "sequential complexity" in [IbK84b] it has been proved -using the serialization method sketched above- that every language which is acceptable by a systolic trellis automaton can be accepted by a deterministic (one-tape) Turing machine in time $O(n^2)$ and space $O(n)$. Since e.g. $\{w\$mi(w) \mid w \in \{a,b\}^+\}$ is acceptable by a systolic trellis automaton, it follows that the time bound is tight.

As pointed out above, the notion "systolic system" was used to emphasize the pipelined input behaviour, i.e. -varying a proposal from [JMKN86] where such questions are treated in more detail, especially under architectural aspects- if the intervals between the inputs of different words are independent of the lengths of these words. At a first glance it does not seem possible to attain such an input behaviour for CA; but in [Vo87] real-time CA with a "skewed input" have been investigated: If an input word has the length n , at a time t the n-th symbol of the input word is fed to the last automaton of the retina, at time t+1 the (n-1)st symbol to the second automaton from the right, and so on. It has been shown ([Wo87]) that only for regular languages a constant pipeline period can be obtained; for these languages and the skewed input mode CA can be seen as systolic systems. But there exist languages which cannot be recognized with a pipeline period of $O(|w|^{1/2})$.

Acknowledgement: The author is grateful to Hiroshi Umeo and to Thomas Worsch for some hints to the literature and for many helpful discussions.

Literature

In the following list only the articles labeled by [...] *have been explicitly referred to; but the other ones are closely related to the topics covered in this article.*

Bleck, B., Kröger, H.: Palindrome Recognition by Stepwise Activated Cellular Algorithms.
Techn. Rep. 8712, Univ. Kiel, 1987, 52 pp.

Bleck, B., Kröger, H.: Time-Distorted Cellular Algorithms.
Techn. Rep. 8715, Univ. Kiel, 1987, 27 pp.

Bokhari, S.H.: Finding maximum on an array processor with a global bus.
IEEE Trans. on Comp. C-33 (1984), 133-139

[BuC84] *Bucher, W., Culik II, K.*: On real time and linear time cellular automata.
R.A.I.R.O. Inf. théor. 18 (1984), 307-325

Cerny, A., Gruska, J.: Modular real-time trellis automata.
Fundamenta Informaticae IX (1986), 253-282

Chang, J.H., Ibarra, O.H., Palis, M.A.: Parallel parsing on a one-way array of finite-state machines.
IEEE Trans. on Comp. C-36 (1987), 64-75

[CIV86] *Chang, J.H., Ibarra, O.H., Vergis, A.*: On The Power of One-Way Communication.
Techn. Rep. TR 86-11,Univ. of Minnesota, Minneapolis, Minn., 1986, 35 pp.
(also in FOCS 1986, 455-464)

[ChC84] *Choffrut, C., Culik II, K.*: On real-time cellular automata and trellis automata. Acta Informatica 21 (1984), 393-407

[Co66] *Cole, S.N.*: Real-time computation by n-dimensional iterative arrays of finite-state machines. IEEE Conf. Rec. of Seventh Ann. Symp. on Switching and Automata Theory, 1966, 53-77

Culik II, K., Fris, I.: Topological transformations as a tool in the design of systolic networks. Theoretical Computer Science 37 (1985), 183-216

[CGS83] *Culik II, K., Gruska, J., Salomaa, A.*: Systolic automata for VLSI on balanced trees. Acta Informatica 18 (1983), 335-344

[CGS84a] *Culik II, K., Gruska, J., Salomaa, A.*: Systolic trellis automata. Part I. Intern. J. Computer Math. 15 (1984), 195-212

[CGS84b] *Culik II, K., Gruska, J., Salomaa, A.*: Systolic trellis automata. Intern. J. Computer Math. 16 (1984), 3-22

[CGS86] *Culik II, K., Gruska, J., Salomaa, A.*: Systolic trellis automata: Stability, decidability and complexity. Inf. and Contr. 71 (1986), 218-230

[CSW84] *Culik II, K., Salomaa, A., Wood, D.*: Systolic tree acceptors. R.A.I.R.O. Inf. théor. 18 (1984), 53-69

Culik II, K., Yu, S.: Fault-tolerant schemes for some systolic systems. Intern. J. Computer Math. 22 (1987), 13-42

[CuY84] *Culik II, K., Yu, S.*: Iterative tree automata. Theoretical Computer Science 32 (1984), 227-247

[CuY86] *Culik II, K., Yu, S.*: Real-time, pseudo real-time, and linear-time ITA. Theoretical Computer Science 47 (1986), 15-26

[Dy80] *Dyer, C.R.*: One-way bounded cellular automata. Inf. and Contr. 44 (1980), 261-281

[FoW87] *Fortes, J.A.B., Wah, B.W.*: Systolic arrays - From concept to implementation. Computer 20 (1987), 12-17

[Gr84] *Gruska, J.*: Systolic automata - Power, characterizations, nonhomogeneity. In: *Chytil, M.P., Koubek, V.* (Eds.) : Mathematical Foundations of Computer Science, Berlin, 1984, 32-49

Ibarra, O.H.: Systolic arrays: Characterization and complexity. Proc. of MFCS ´86, Berlin, 1986, 140-153

[IbJ87] *Ibarra, O.H., Jiang, T.*: On one-way cellular arrays. SIAM J. Comput. 16 (1987), 1135-1154

[IbK84a] *Ibarra, O.H., Kim, S.M.*: A characterization of systolic binary tree automata and applications. Acta Informatica 21 (1984), 193-207

[IbK84b] *Ibarra, O.H., Kim, S.M.*: Characterizations and computational complexity of systolic trellis automata.
Theoretical Computer Science 29 (1984), 123-153

[IKM85] *Ibarra, O.H., Kim, S.M., Moran, S.*: Sequential machine characterizations of trellis and cellular automata and applications.
SIAM J. Comput. 14 (1985), 426-447

Ibarra, O.H., Kim, S.M., Palis, M.A.: Designing systolic algorithms using sequential machines.
IEEE Trans. on Comp. C-35 (1986), 531-542

Ibarra, O.H., Palis, M.A.: On efficient simulations of systolic arrays by random-access machines.
SIAM J. on Comp. 16 (1987), 367-377

Ibarra, O.H., Palis, M.A.: Two-Dimensional Iterative Arrays:Characterizations and Applications.
Techn. Rep. 85-1, Dptm of Computer Science, Univ. of Minnesota, Minneapolis, Minn., 1985, 59 pp.

Ibarra, O.H., Palis, M.A.: VLSI algorithms for solving recurrence equations and applications.
IEEE Trans. on Acoustics, Speech, and Signal Processing ASSP-35 (1987), 1046-1064

[IPK85a] *Ibarra, O.H., Palis, M.A., Kim, S.M.*: Fast parallel language recognition by cellular automata.
Theoretical Computer Science 41 (1985), 231-246

[IPK85b] *Ibarra, O.H., Palis, M.A., Kim, S.M.*: Some results concerning linear iterative (systolic) arrays.
J. of Parallel and Distributed Computing 2 (1985), 182-218

[JMKN86] *Jagadish, H.V., Mathews, R.G., Kailath, T., Newkirk, J.A.*: A study of pipelining in computing arrays.
IEEE Trans. on Comp. C-35 (1986), 431-440

[Ko88] *Kohonen, T.* : The role of adaptive and associative circuits in future computer designs.
In: *Eckmiller, R., v.d. Malsburg, C.* (Eds.): Neural Computers.
Berlin, 1988, XIII+566 pp., 1-8

Kosaraju, S.R., Atallah, M.J.: Optimal simulations between mesh-connected arrays of processors.
STOC 1986, 264-272

[Ku82] *Kung, H.T.*: Why systolic architectures?
Computer 15 (1982), 37-46

[Pa82] *Paterson, M.*: Solution to P8, Number 17, June 1982.
EATCS Bull. 18 (1982), 29

Prasanna Kumar, V.K., Raghavendra, C.S.: Array processor with multiple broadcasting.
J. of Parallel and Distributed Computing 4 (1987), 173-190

[Sa85] *Salomaa, A.*: Computation and Automata.
Cambridge, 1985, XIII+282 pp.

[Se79] *Seidel, S.R.*: Language Recognition and the Synchronization of Cellular Automata.
Ph.D. Diss., Univ. of Iowa, Iowa City, 1979, XIV+329 pp.

[Se77] *Seiferas, J.I.*: Iterative arrays with direct central control.
Acta Informatica 8 (1977), 177-192

[SoW83] *Sommerhalder, R., van Westrhenen, S.*: Parallel language recognition in constant time by cellular automata.
Acta Informatica 19 (1983), 397-407

[Sm76] *Smith III, A.R.*: Introduction to and survey of polyautomata theory.
In: *Lindenmayer, A., Rozenberg, G.* (Eds.): Automata, Languages, Development. Amsterdam, 1976, 405-422

[Sm72] *Smith III, A.R.*: Real-time language recognition by one-dimensional cellular automata.
JCSS 6 (1972), 233-253

[St82] *Stout, Q.F.*: Broadcasting in mesh-connected computers.
Proc. 1982 Conf. on Inform. Sciences and Systems, Princeton, NJ, 1982, 85-90

Stout, Q.F.: Mesh-connected computers with broadcasting.
IEEE Trans. on Comp. C-32 (1983), 826-830
FOCS 1986, 264-273

Umeo, H.: A class of SIMD machines simulated by systolic arrays.
J. of Parallel and Distributed Computing 2 (1985), 391-403

[UMS82] *Umeo, H., Morita, K., Sugata, K.*: Deterministic one-way simulation of two-way real-time cellular automata and its related problems.
Information Processing Letters 14 (1982), 158-161

[Vo81] *Vollmar, R.*: On cellular automata with a finite number of state changes.
Computing, Suppl. 3 (1981), 181-191

[Vo82] *Vollmar, R.*: Some remarks about the "efficiency" of polyautomata.
Int. J. of Theor. Physics 21 (1982), 1007-1015

[Vo87] *Vollmar, R.* : Some remarks on pipeline processing by cellular automata.
Computers and Artificial Intelligence 6 (1987), 263-278

[Wo87] *Worsch, T.* : Personal communication.

PARALLEL ALGORITHMS IN IMAGE PROCESSING

Wolfgang Wilhelmi[1)]

Abstract

Many methods of image restoration, geometric rectification, and image pattern recognition can be described by local operators. Processor arrays with centralized control accomplishing SIMD processing are considered as effective means for these tasks. The paper explains the main ideas and the theoretical background of representants of the before mentioned methods.

1. Introduction

It is broadly accepted that image processing needs parallelization with fine granularity. The aim of this paper is to show that there are many unexpected sources of parallelization if the tasks are investigated without prejudice and the models are selected as local ones /1/. The examples concern a MAP restoration technique, geometric dewarping, and iterative digital curve analysis.
The presented approach is based on the SIMD concept. According to Evans /2/ a SIMD machine has a control unit (CU) which commands a number of identical processing elements (PE) working in a step-lock fashion. The CU broadcasts identical instructions to the PE`s. These are connected by a communication network including local and global memories. The SIMD principle avoids access conflicts and excessive communication overhead. We will observe that a global ready signal should be provided additionally to overcome data dependencies of processes in different PE`s. Existing technologies restrict the number of interprocessor channels to about 4. If the number of PE`s is not greater than the number of image columns then a 2-neighborhood is sufficient for the implementation of any local operator. The following investigations suppose a virtual 4-connected array with as many PE`s as image pixels. The algorithms can be easily deparallelized to any real 2- or 4-connected array configuration.

2. Image restoration by stochastic relaxation

Linear restoration methods like Wiener filtering have not been approved in image processing /3/. A better approach is the estimation according to the maximum a posteriori probability (MAP). Let us consider the figure 1.

---

1) Akademie der Wissenschaften der DDR, Zentralinstitut für Kybernetik und Informationsprozesse, Kurstraße 33 , DDR Berlin 1086

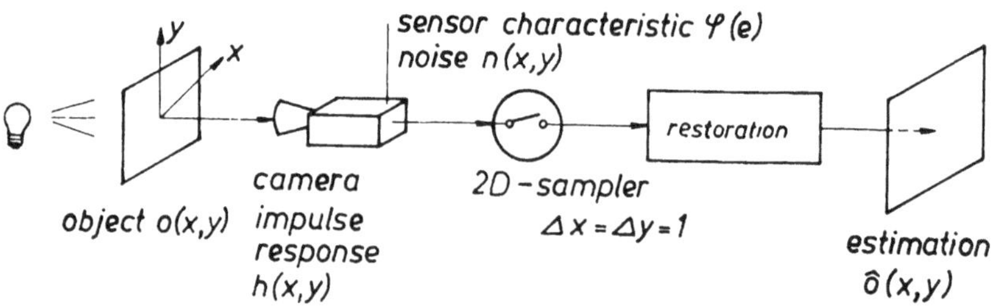

Fig. 1 Imaging and restoration

2.1 Object model

The object is assumed to be binary, i.e. it is either transparent (O(x,y)=1) or opaque (O(x,y)=0) at the point x,y. The region boundaries are straight line segments approximately parallel to the axes. The contour vertices are not closer together then the sampling step (width 1). Two real values $0 \leq p(i,j) \leq 4$, $0 \leq q(1,j) \leq 1$ are assigned to every sampling square (i,i+1;j,j+1). They have the following meanings (Fig.2):

(a) p(i,j) is the point on the perimeter of the sampling interval where the contour intrudes. The object is assumed to be on the right hand side of the contour.
(b) q(i,j) is the area of the sampling interval occupied by the object.

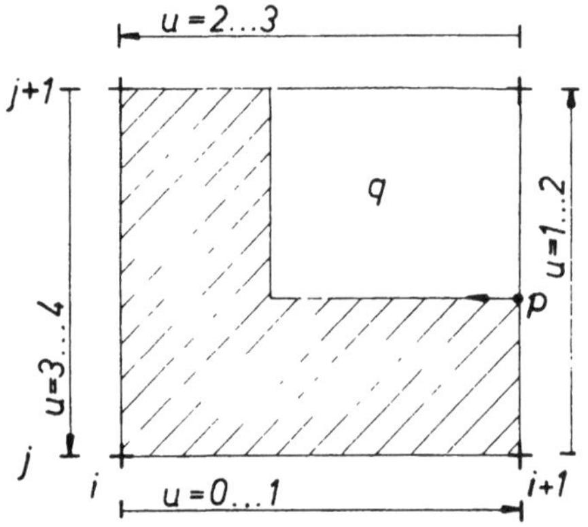

Fig. 2 Definition of pixel attributes p and q

The sampled image contains M=m.n samples and 2M pixel attibutes p,q. An ensemble of images should be described by a Gibbs probability density function.

$$\rho(p,q) = Z^{-1}\exp(-E/T_0) \tag{1}$$

E is a positive function of the pixe' ~s. Z and To are respectively a normalizing factor and the distributions n analogy to statistical mechanics /3/ $\mathcal{S}$(p,q) means the relative number of s. images) having states (attribute configurations) p,q in the 2M-dimensional parallelepiped

$$p_1,\ p_2,\ \ldots,\ p_M,\ q_1,\ q_2,\ \ldots,\ q_M$$

and

$$p_1+dp_1,\ p_2+dp_2,\ \ldots,\ p_M+dp_M,\ q_1+dq_2,\ q_2+dq_2,\ \ldots,\ q_M+dq_M\ .$$

Eq. (1) describes a system in a stationary thermodynamical equilibrium with the total energy E. The energy is usually a sum of terms each depending only on the contribution of one particle to the system state (potential and kinetic energy) and the interaction with a small number of neigboring ones (coupling energy).

$$E=\sum_{i=0}^{m}\sum_{j=0}^{m}\left[V_o(p(i,j),q(i,j)) + \sum_{c\in C} V_c(p,q)\right] \tag{2}$$

In eq. (2) C is a set of pairs, triplets etc. of state variables from the neighborhood of the current particle (pixel). We will not touch the problem of finding experimentally the potential $V_{o,c}(.)$. Instead a continuity constraint helps us to design the model. Let us look at Fig. 3.

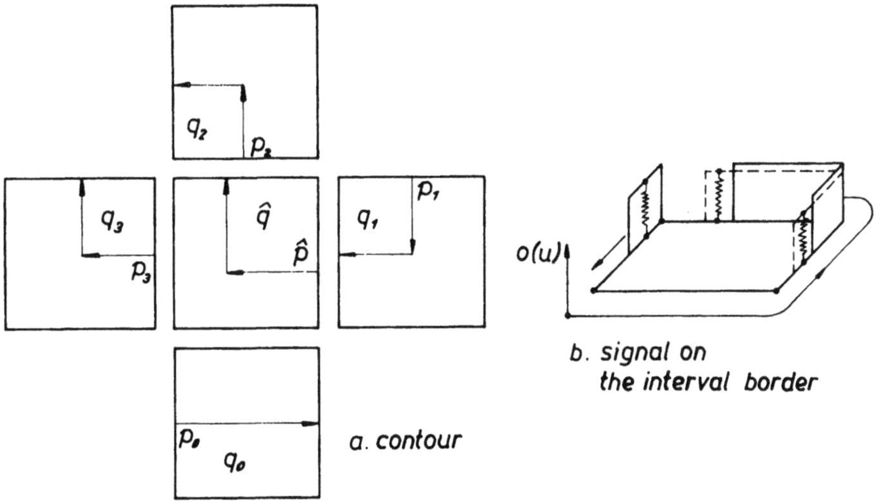

Fig. 3 Interaction on the edges of a the sampling interval

The 4 neighbors of the considered sampling square generate a certain signal distribution O(u) along its outer perimeter. On the other hand the state $\hat{p},\hat{q}$ corresponds to another distribution $\hat{O}(u)$. The coupling energy is modeled by the stress load between the profiles O(u) and $\hat{O}(u)$ which is outlined in fig. 3 by springs. This workload is given by the following functional

$$V_c(p,q) = V_f(0,0) = (c/2)\int_1^4 (O(u)-\hat{O}(u))^2 du \qquad (3)$$

with the spring constant c. Small values of V_c mean that the contours match well. The local energy V_o could be defined as

$$V_o(p,q) = G^2(p) + H^2(q-w) \; . \qquad (4)$$

G(p) defines the probability of the contour's crossing point, i.e. the expected orientation, and H(q-w) the variance of the difference between the observed covering and the expected value w. Both may be estimated easily by experiments or theoretical considerations. G(.) and H(.) may depend on the coordinates i,j too without violating the following derivations.

2.2 Optical imaging and recording

The image arises from the object by convolution with the impulse response (IR) h(x,y).

$$b(x,y) = \iint_{-\infty}^{\infty} O(x+\xi, y+\eta)\, h(\xi,\eta)\, d\xi d\eta \qquad (5)$$

The signal samples can be computed by discrete summation of integrals taken over the sampling intervals as follow:

$$b(i,j) = \sum_{k=-\infty} \sum_{l=-\infty} \int_{\Box} O(k+i+\xi, l+j+\eta)\, h(k+\xi, l+\eta)\, d\xi d\eta \qquad (6)$$

We assume that the object contour is rectilinear. For a given IR the integrals are nonlinear functions of p and q. Further the IR can be neglected outside a certain distance from the origin which results in

$$b(i,j) = \sum_{l=-K}^{K} \sum_{k=-K}^{K} f_{kl}\left[p(i+k,j+l), q(i+k,j+l)\right] . \qquad (7)$$

If the boundaries are not rectilinear then eq. (7) has to be corrected by an error term. Although it is not correct we include this term into the noise n(i,j) which is assumed to be statistically independent from the uncorrupted signal. We will regard additionally a nonlinear but invertible characteristic $\varphi(.)$ of the recording medium.

$$g(i,j) = \varphi(b(i,j)) \blacksquare n(i,j) \tag{8}$$

$\blacksquare$ symbolizes the before mentioned invertible operation (e.g.addition, multiplication). due to this feature we can estimate n from the observed g and known b.

$$n(i,j) = g(i,j) \blacksquare^{-1} (b(i,j)) \tag{9}$$

Let the noise be Gaussian and white with zero expected value. The M-dimensional probability density is

$$\mathcal{P}(n) = (g \mid p,q)$$

$$= (2\pi\sigma^2)^{-M/2}\exp((-1/2\sigma^2)\sum_i\sum_j\left[g(i,j) \blacksquare^{-1} \varphi(b(i,j))\right]^2 \tag{10}$$

$\mathcal{P}(n)$ is the conditional probability density for an observation for a given configuration p,q. The exponent in eq. (10) may be interpeted as an energy term like that in eq. (3). It is obvious that the coupling terms contains values from a $(2K+1)^2$-neighborhood and the observations g(i,j) act as external potentials.

$$V_g = \left\{g(i,j) \blacksquare^{-1}\varphi\left[\sum_{k=-K}^{K}\sum_{l=-K}^{K} f_{kl}(p(i+k,j+l),p(i+k,j+l))\right]\right\}^2 \tag{11}$$

2.3 MAP estimation

The best estimation P, Q for a permissible configuration p,q is that one with

$$\mathcal{P}(P,Q \mid g) = \max_{p,q} \mathcal{P}(p,q \mid g) \tag{12}$$

Applying the Bayes identity and eqs. (2),(10) yields

$$\mathcal{P}(p,q \mid g) = \frac{\mathcal{P}(g \mid p,q)\ \mathcal{P}(p,q)}{\mathcal{P}(g)} = B\exp(-W(p,q)) \tag{13}$$

with

$$W(p,q)=(1/T_0)\sum_i\sum_j(V_0+(T_0/2\sigma^2)V_g+\sum_{c\in C}V_c) \tag{14}$$

The quantity B depends on g and is a constant for a given observation. The maximization of eq. (13) or the minimization of eq. (14) corresponds to the determination of the system state with the greatest likelihood. If it is possible to generate an ensemble of systems with $V_0(.)$, $V_c(.)$, $V_g(.)$ then most of them have states near the optimal P,Q. We take one of them as an approximative solution. This is the main idea of the thermodynamically motivated stochastic relaxation. The generation of a new configuration is done by replacement of an old configuration in such a manner that the probability density function converges to eq. (13). Geman & Geman /5/ have proposed the Gibbs sampler. It utilizes the observation that the conditional probability density of the local p(i,j), q(i,j) for fixed configuration outside is a function depending only on a neighborhood defined by V_c and V_g.

$$\wp(p(i,j)\mid p(k,l);\ (k,l)\neq(i,j))$$

$$=\frac{\wp(p,q)}{\int\wp(p,q)dp(i,j)}=\frac{\exp(-W(p,q))}{\int\exp(-W(p,q))dp(i,j)} \tag{15}$$

and similar for q.

This Markov property is due to the additive form of W which allows the truncation of terms contained in nominater and denominator of eq. (15).

2.4 Parallel implementation

The implementation by means of any SIMD array is straightforward. Each PE gets the pixel attributes from its neighborhood as defined by the function W. If direct data pathes are not available some intermediate routing steps are necessary. An example is shown in Fig. 4 , where a 4-connected array has to accomplish reading of a 8-neighborhood.

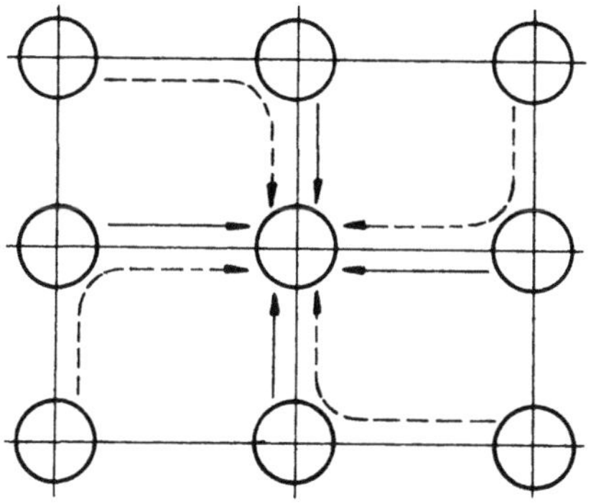

Fig. 4 Routing in a 4-connected array
_________ direct with 1 step
- - - - - indirect with 2 steps

The read attributes allow the computation of the conditional probability for a new p,q in the current pixel which can be implemented with a random generator and some static functions. This computation is done in parallel and under central control if one ensures that no neighboring data are read which are updated in the same time slice. This condition will be fulfilled by an appropriate tesselation of the array. A rectangular field of influence with the dimension (2r+1)(2s+1) is especially important and easy to investigate (Fig. 5). The selected tesselation results in an updating of one pixel every (r+1)(s+1) time slices without any forbidden interaction. The degree of parallelism cannot exceed $m^2/(r+1)(s+1)$.
Other not rectangular neighborhoods allow yet better tesselation as Murray et al. /6/ have shown for the 4-connected case.

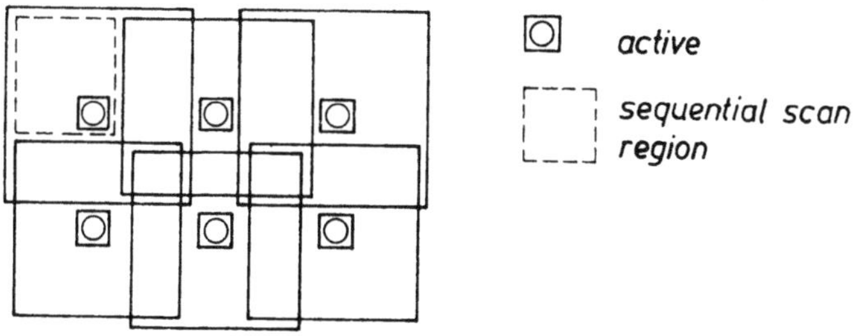

Fig. 5 Overlapping but not interacting regions

An especially simple approach for iterative computation of the pixel attributes is the Metropolis algorithm /7/. A new vector p, q is drawn from an uniform distribution. The resulting energy increment ΔW controls the acceptance of the new vector p,q with the probability

$$P(\Delta W) = \begin{cases} 1 & \text{for } \Delta W \leq 0 \\ \exp(-\ W) & \text{for } \Delta W > 0 \end{cases} \qquad (16)$$

In this case a local computation is sufficient too, because changes of p(i,j), q(i,j) influence only some terms of W.
Finally it should be noted, that instead of exp(-W) usually exp(-(To/T)W) will be maximized. A scheduled decrease of T during the relaxation ensures that the state converges to the global extremum. This approach is known as simulated annealing.

3. Image warping

Geometric rectification is an essential preprocessing step for multiimages. The mapping includes usually an interpolation of the signal for preservation of edges and textures. Let us start with a continuous mapping of the source image coordinates x, y to the destination coordinates u, v.

$$u=f(x,y);\ v=g(x,y);\quad 0 < x,y < m-1 \qquad (17)$$

There are only few proposals to solve this problem on SIMD machines /8/-/11/. The presented solution is based on /12/.

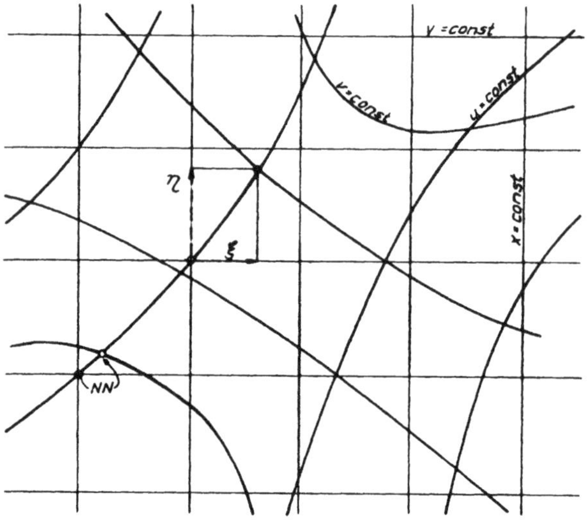

Fig. 6 Continuous mapping

3.1 Interpolation of the coordinates

Usually eq. (17) is defined by a set of reference points

$$f(x_i,y_i), \quad g(x_i,y_i) \quad i = 1,\dots,K.$$

A parallel implementation is accomplished best by the following equation

$$f(x,y) = \sum_{i=1}^{K} f(x_i,y_i)\, h_i(x-x_i,y-y_i) \tag{18}$$

Let the reference points be equidistately distributed and the functions h_i be independent on i. This situation can be achieved approximately by solving eq. (18) for a set of arbitrarily distributed left hand terms and given h(x,y). Our experience have proved as good interpolators:

(a) The Ideal Resampler

$$h(x,y) = \text{sinc}\,(\pi x/\Delta x)\ \text{sinc}\,(\pi y/\Delta y) \tag{19}$$

(b) The Bilinar Interpolator

$$h(x,y) = (1-|x|/\Delta x)\ (1-|y|/\Delta y) \text{ for } |x|<\Delta x \text{ and } |y|<\Delta y \tag{20}$$

(c) The Fourier Interpolator

$$h(x,y) = \frac{\sin(\pi x/\Delta x)}{(m/\Delta x)\ \sin(\pi x/m)} \cdot \frac{\sin(\pi y/\Delta y)}{(m/\Delta y)\ \sin(\pi y/m)} \tag{21}$$

The parallel implementation of eq. (18) proceeds as follow. The CU broadcasts to every PE the 2K reference coordinates. Every PE computes the function values $h(x-x_i,\ y-y_i)$. Due to the separability of eqs. (19) - (21) 2 table lookups and 1 multiplication are required for every reference coordinate. The weighted summation (18) needs 2K multiplications and 2(K-1) additions.

Generally the destination coordinates do not correspond to the discrete lattice. We consider the mapping of a sampling interval according to figure 7. With the vector $r=(u,v)^T$ and X as the outer product operator a bilinear approximation yields destinations for subpixel source locations corresponding to integer destinations.

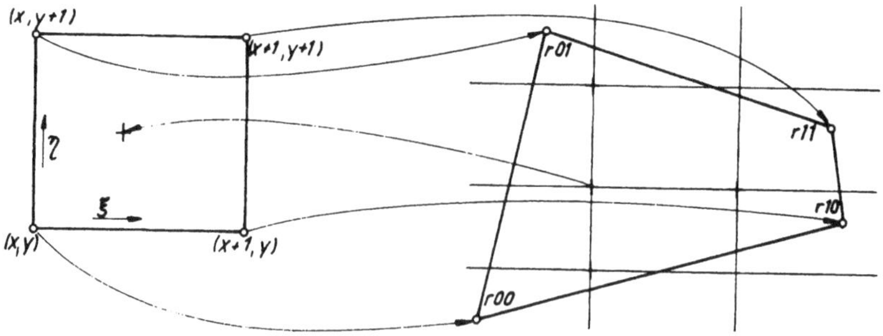

Fig. 7 Mapping of a source image interval

$$\xi = S + \left(1+ \frac{(r_{11}-r_{01})X(r \;\; -r_{10})}{(r_{01}-r_{10})X(r_{11}-r_{10})}\right)*\left(1+ \frac{(r_{00}-r_{01})X(r \;\; -r_{10})}{(r_{01}-r_{10})X(r_{00}-r_{10})}\right) \tag{22}$$

$$\eta = S + \left(1+ \frac{(r_{11}-r_{10})X(r \;\; -r_{01})}{(r_{10}-r_{01})X(r_{11}-r_{01})}\right)*\left(1+ \frac{(r_{00}-r_{10})X(r \;\; -r_{01})}{(r_{10}-r_{01})X(r_{00}-r_{01})}\right) \tag{23}$$

$$S = \left(1+ \frac{(r_{01}-r_{00})X(r \;\; -r_{11})}{(r_{00}-r_{11})X(r_{01}-r_{11})}\right)*\left(1+ \frac{(r_{10}-r_{00})X(r \;\; -r_{11})}{(r_{00}-r_{11})X(r_{10}-r_{11})}\right) \tag{24}$$

By inserting integer valued r_{pq} in eqs. (22) - (24) a set of ξ, η from $[0,1)$ is estimated. If a local magnification exists then one source interval is accompanied by serveral quadrupels u, v, ξ, η. They should be stacked in arbitrary order in the PE corresponding to the source location p,q. The parallel implementation of eqs. (22) - (24) after the routing of 3 neigboring vectors $(u,v)^T$ is straightforward. Here a strong data dependency can occur which must be sychronized by the before mentioned global ready signal.

3.2 Signal interpolation

The subpixel vector $(\xi, \eta)^T$ is an argument of the signal approximation. The image is assumed to be a Fourier finite function which is represented according to the sampling theorem as follows.

$$b(x,y) = \sum_{i=-\infty}^{\infty} \sum_{j=-\infty}^{\infty} b(i,j) \operatorname{sinc} \pi (x-i) * \operatorname{sinc} \pi (y-j) \tag{25}$$

This sum is replaced by the help of a piecewise Tshebyshev approximation of $\mathrm{sinc}(\pi x)$. With $x=i+\xi$, $y=j+\eta$ one gets

$$\begin{aligned} b(x,y) &\approx s(i,j,\xi,\eta) \\ &= (1-\xi)(1-\eta)b(i,j)+(1-\xi)\eta b(i,j+1)+\xi(1-\eta)b(i+1,j)+\xi\eta b(i+1,j+1) \\ &+ \sin\pi\xi \sin\pi\eta \sum_{k=-K}^{K} c_k \sum_{l=-K}^{K} c_l\, b(i+k,j+l) \end{aligned} \tag{26}$$

The coefficients are shown in the following table.

i	c_i	Error
0	.14319	.051330
1	-.21974	.026830
2	.12889	.009291
3	-.09151	.004690
4	.07100	.002827
5	-.05802	.001887
6	.04906	.001350
7	-.04250	.001012
8	.03749	.000789

Fig. 8 gives a comprehensive interpretation of eq. (26) as the superposition of a bilinear term with a highpass filter output weighted by a function of subpixel coordinates.

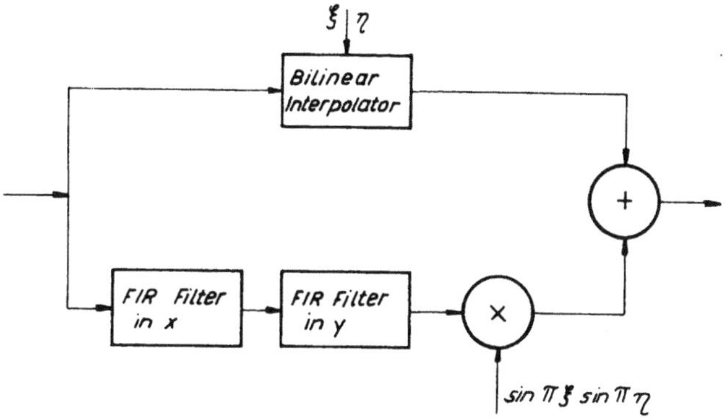

Fig. 8 Signal interpolation scheme

The desribed procedure is well suited for SIMD processing. It includes the routing of K data from the upper and lower neighbors, and K data from the left and right sides. After signal interpolation the values ξ, η are not necessary and will be replaced by the signal sample s. Fig. 9 shows the resulting data structure in one PE.

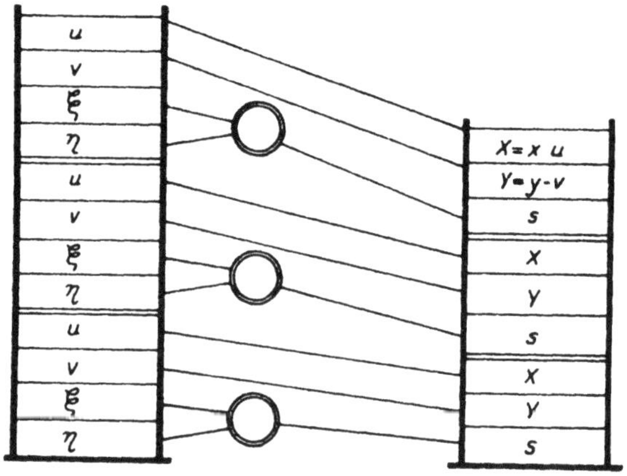

Fig. 9 Local data structure

The processor array is now covered by tripels u, v, s. The grey value s has to shifted to the PE which corresponds to the destination u, v. We propose a version of an odd-even-transposition algorithm which is well known in the context of parallel sorting /13/. Further instead of u, v the shift vector $(X=u-x,Y=v-y)^T$ is considered. The algorithm proceeds as follow.

(a) All data items with X=Y=0 have been arrived at their destination. The correspnding s is stored in the location reserved for it. Then a new tripel X,Y,s is popped from the stack. An empty stack results in labeling the PE as empty with the reserved word e (X=Y="e"). If all PE are labeled, the algorithm stops.

(b) Shift the data items along the colums with the goal to make to zero as many Y as possible. We consider all disjoint pairs of neigboring PEs (i),(i+1). An exchange between the members of every pair occurs if and only if
 - both are not empty and Y(i)>Y(i+1)+1
 - (i+1) is empty and Y(i)>0
 - (i) is empty and Y(i+1)<0.

 An exchange means that the data items X,Y,s change their place and the Y are decremented or incremented depending on their relocation. This comparison exchange is done in parallel. Then new pairs of neighboring elements used to be in different pairs are utilized in an additional parallel comparison exchange step. This process is repeated until no exchange occurs.

(c) Save all pixels as in (a). Our first experiments have been carried through with saving pixels immediately during the exchange comparison process. Paradoxically there were drawbacks both in respect to computational effort and to the total number of iterations. An explanation could be that one can avoid redundant exchanges by retaining already arrived pixels as "walls". This conjecture is supported by the fact that continuous transformations produce a certain preordering of shift vectors.

(d) Apply the odd-even transposition scheme along the rows. An exchange between the members of every pair occurs if and only if
   - both are on their destination row and X(i)>X(i+1)+1
   - only (i+1) is on the destination row and X(i)>0
   - only (i) is on the destination row and X(i+1)<0
   - both are not on their destination row and X(i)>X(i+1)+1

   - only (i) is empty and X(i)>0
   - only (i+1) is empty and X(i+1)<0.

   The exchange is accompanied by an updating of the X values. The process is repeated with new pairings until a stable state has been reached. Then goto (a).

3.4 Analysis

A general investigation of the described algorithm seems difficult. It stops after a finite number of iterations with all pixels arriving at their final destinations. It follows an outline of the proof. Firstly there is at least one stable configuration which do not satisfy any of the exchange conditions. Secondly it is known that an arbitrary permutation of a m-sequence may be achieved in not more than m iterations of an odd-even transposition scheme /13/. If a stable configuration exists where some pixels have not been arrived then any of the exchange conditions is positive which contradicts the assumption.
Let (17) be an one to one mapping (e.g. a rotation by 90°). Then we have a sorting problem, because the exchange conditions corresponds to comparison exchange steps of the ordinary sort. The proposed algorithm performs better than an odd-even-transposition algorithm for a snakelike arrangement of rows to a m^2-sequence. It needs not more than m^2 iterations in the worst case /13/. Thompson et al. /14/ have proposed an sorting algorithm in a 4-connected processor array requiring O(m) iterations. This cannot achieved by our proposal. Simulations with centered rotations have shown that the iteration number Z is approximately given by

$$Z_{45} \approx 2.283\ m^{1.190}$$
$$Z_{90} \approx 2.476\ m^{1.347} \qquad (27)$$

4. Digital curve evaluation

Line images are usually the result of extensive preprocessing. Lines may be the closed contours of regions or their middle axes (sceletons). Based on results of Pavlidis /15/ it was shown that derivation and postprocessing of sceletons can be done efficiently by SIMD machines /16,17/. The key operation is the recieving of the 8 neighbors and the labeling of this local configuration by an appropriate table lookup. The analysis of digital curve segments relies broadly on the evaluation of a running average. Usually it is assumed that such tasks must be carried through with a line following strategy. The author gratefully acknowledges the help of J.Saedler for showing a possibility to implement such tasks on a SIMD array.

4.1 Problem

Let a digital curve segment be represented by a sequence of l contiguous pixels r_i.

$$L_l = r_1, r_2, \ldots, r_l \qquad (28)$$

Special cases are the isolated pixel ($L_1 = r_1$) and the closed curve ($r_l = r_1$). An attribut $G(r_i) \neq 0$ is assigned to every r_i. Background pixels r_B have $G(r_B) = 0$. In analogy to the continuous curve integral

$$g(s,\Delta s) = \int_{s-\Delta s}^{s+\Delta s} G(r)dr \qquad ; \; dr - \text{arc element} \qquad (29)$$

for any n > 1 the running sum

$$g(r_j,n) = \sum_{i=-n}^{n} G(r_{j+i}) \qquad (30)$$

has to be computed. The average is obtained after division by 2n+1. The addition is possibly done modulo 2.
Some examples should illustrate the importance of eq. (30):

(a) G(.) is the distance of sceleton points to the region s contour. The running average results in a perfectly smoothed contour after reconstruction.
(b) G(.) = 1. Eq. (30) indicates the checkerboard distance of the pixel r_j to the next endpoint of the line segments if the distance is smaller than n.
(c) G(.) corresponds to the directional code of the curve´s chord in a 3 x 3 local neighborhood around the current pixel. This code is easily available after a lookup of the 8 neighbors /18,19/. The summation is implemented as a modular one and generates the direction of the chord between 2 points located 2n+1 pixels apart on the curve.
(d) G(.) is the difference between the direction code as explained in (c) in 2 adjacent pixels. The running average gives a smoothed approximation of the curvature in analogy to the continuous case $\varkappa = d\varphi/ds \approx \Delta\varphi/\Delta s$.
(e) G(.) is the difference chain code. By accumulating it we can recognize critical points of the curve /20 /. They are candidates for vertices of a polygonal approximation.

4.2 Difference equation

Eq. (30) is solved by an iterative procedure with n steps regarding a 3x3-neighborhood only. It utilizes the fact that in such surrounding of a curve point reside only 1 or 2 pixels of the same segment but no point of any other segment. Therefor any 3x3-operator do not touch more than one curve segment and has not more than 3 input operands. It is easy to show by induction that the following difference equation has the required solution.

$$g(r_j,0)=G(r_j);\; g(r_j,1)=G(r_{j+1}) + G(r_{j-1}) + G(r_j) \qquad (31)$$

$$g(r_1,k-2) = g(r_1,k-2) = 0;\; k\geq 2 \qquad (32)$$

$$g(r_j,k) = g(r_{j+1},k-1) + g(r_{j-1},k-1) - g(r_j,k-2);\; k\geq 2 \qquad (33)$$

Fig. 10 illustrates the iterative solution of the system (31)-(33). It is easy to implement for SIMD machines by maintaining in every PE the locations $a:=g(r_j,k-1)$ and $b:=g(r_j,k-2)$ according to eq. (33) after routing and selection from the 3x3-neighborhood. b is cleared according to (32) at all end points if any. PE which are assigned to background pixels have not to be busy of course.

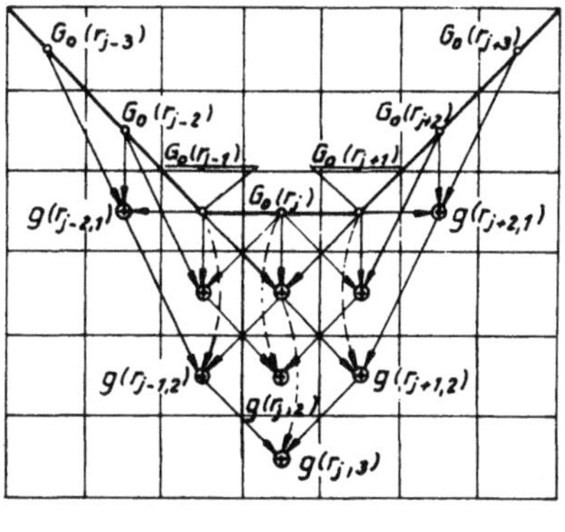

Fig. 10 Iterative computation of $g(r_j,3)$
- - - - - - - multiply with -1

5. References

/1/ Quinn, M.J.: Designing Efficient Algorithms for Parallel Computers. McGraw-Hill 1987.

/2/ Evans, D.J.(Ed.) Parallel Processing Systems. Cambridge University Press, Cambridge 1982.

/3/ Freundt, S.: Angepaßte Filterung von speckleverrauschten Bildern durch Anwendung des Wiener-Filters. Technical Report ZKI Juli 1987.

/4/Wassmuth, A.: Grundlagen und Anwendungen der statistischen Mechanik. Friedr. Vieweg & Sohn, Braunschweig 1915.
/5/Geman, St.; Geman, D.: Stochastic Relaxation, Gibbs Distributions, and the Bayesian Restoration of Images. IEEE-Trans. on Pattern Analysis and Machine Intelligence, Vol. PAMI-6 (1984). No. 6. (November), pp. 721-741.
/6/ Murray, D. W.; Kashko, A.; Buxton, H.: A parallel approach to the picture restoration algorithm of Geman and Geman on a SIMD Machine. Image and Vision Computing vol. 4 (1986) No. 3 (August), pp. 133-142.
/7/ Metropolis, N.; Rosenbluth, A. W.; Rosenbluth, M. N.; Teller, A.H.; Teller, E.: Equation of State Calculations by Fast Computing Machines. J. Chem. Phys. Vol.21 (1953), pp.1087 -1091
/8/ Kempe. V.; Rebel, B.; Wilhelmi, W.: The Interactive Image Processing Console A 6471. Proc. 6 ICPR München Okt. 1982, pp. 607-609.
/9/ Colletti, N.B.: Image Processing on MPP-like Arrays. Rep. No. UIUCDCS-R-83-1132. Univ. of Illinois Urbana 1982.
/10/Arabnia, H.R.; Oliver, M.A.: Arbitrary Rotation of Raster Images with SIMD Machine Architectures. Computer Graphics Forum 6 (1987) pp. 3-12.
/11/ Luth, N.: Affine Transformations on Images Represented by a List Data Structure. Proc. CAIP 87 Wismar Sept. 1987, pp. 95-100.
/12/Wilhelmi, W.: Geometric Transformations of Raster Images on SIMD Processors. Proc. IV. International Conference on Image Analysis and Proc. Cefalu Sept. 1987.
/13/ Baudet, G.; Stevenson, D.: Optimal Sorting Algorithms for Parallel Computers. IEEE-Trans on Computers C-27 (1978), No. 1, pp. 84-87.
/14/ Thompson, C.D.; Kung, H.T.: Sorting on a Mesh-Connected Parallel Computer. Comm. of the ACM Vol. 20 (1977), No. 4, pp. 263-271.
/15/Pavlidis, T.: Algorithms for Graphics and Image Processing. Computer Science Press Inc. 1982, Rockville (USA).
/16/ Saedler, J.: Anwendungsbeispiel Verdünnung. ZKI-Information 2/84: Programmierwerkzeuge und Anwendungsprogramme des Bildverarbeitungssystems A6470, pp. 9-30...9-39.
/17/ Saedler, J.; Wilhelmi, W.; Kovalevski, W.; Eichhorn, N.: Implementierte Algorithmen auf dem Displayprozessor K2027. Bild und Ton 39(1986), Nr. 5, pp. 140-145 und Nr. 6, pp. 165-173.
/18/Saedler, J.; Gössel, M.: Patent WP G06K2978102 - Verfahren zur schnellen Verarbeitung von Linienbildern Dez.1986.
/19/ Saedler, J.; Gössel, M.: Parallele Berechnung von Linienkodierungen mit einem Displayprozessorsystem und seine Anwendungen zur Krümmungsberechnung (to be published).
/20/ Hung, S.H.Y.; Kasvand, T.: Linear Approximation of Quantized Thin Lines. In R. H. Haralick (Ed.): Pictorial Data Analysis, Springer Verlag 1983, pp. 15-28.

SUBMITTED PAPERS

VLSI ARRAYS IMPLEMENTING PARALLEL LINE-DRAWING ALGORITHMS

Valeriu Beiu [1)]

Abstract: After a short description of the problems encountered in graphic systems concerning the image memory, the first part of this paper describes several algorithms which are easily parallelizable. The second part shows possible VLSI arrays implementing the above mentioned algorithms and area and time estimations.

Index terms: Graphics, line-drawing algorithms, parallel algorithms, VLSI arrays, VLSI-based architecture, area-time complexity.

1. INTRODUCTION

1.1. Basic ideas

Most graphics systems being produced today employ an image memory in which one or more bits are associated with each pixel on a raster-scan CRT. These memories, which are usually called "frame buffers" or "bit-mapped displays" are popular because [8]: they are economical, the update rate is independent of the refresh rate and they allow very high-quality characters. Also they look so attractive they do have a shortcoming: performance; typical random update rates are less then 0.5 microseconds per pixel, thus leading to about half a second for an entire image change (for a 1024*1024 display).

On the other hand are high-performance applications which use random-deflection CRT because of their faster line-drawing rate, but require costly power supplies to deflect the electron beam and also special character-generation hardware, not mentionning their inadequance to produce shaded polygonal areas.

In these conditions the aim is clear: to design an image memory for a scan-conversion CRT which is able of ultra fast line rendering and so approaching random-deflection CRT for line-drawing performance, and capable of high-quality characters like any raster-scan CRT.

1.2. The image memory

Focusing our attention on the image memory we find that it implies limitations concerning the time required to do the arithmetic of scan-conversion (i.e. determining which pixel to alter) and because of their limited bandwith. Because image memories are usually constructed from nMOS RAM chips, the update rate is ultimately governed by the cycle time of these chips. In [8] it is described a high-performance organization that will, under the best circumstance, scan-convert a suitable set of geometric primitives and access the image memory at the maximum rate atteinable. The image memory system described scan-converts polygons,

---

1) Department of Control and Computer Science, Polytechnical Institute of Bucharest, Splaiul Independentei Nr. 313, sector 6, Bucharest 77206, Romania

lines and characters using a custom nMOS Image Memory Processor (IMP) formed of two completely self-timed asynchronous processors. The system uses a two-level hierarchical busing structure with interleaved processor along each bus. All data passes through a Parent Processor which is not a custom chip but a microprogammed processor with the primary purpose to prepare the geometric primitives for scan conversion.

Another solution is that of [13] which uses the fact that the image data is arranged in rows and that the processing algorithms frequently require accesss to pixel's neighborhs; this has suggested the idea that a processor which allows the pixels to be moved through it in a locally parallel manner would be a more efficient configuration than the standard mode general-purpose computer. The locally parallel processor is a machine that analyzes a section of a window of an image using hardware wired in parallel. A previous example is the Coulter diff3 [11].

Finally another design approach would be to have one processing unit for each pixel so that all the pixels in an image would be processed at one time. An example is the CLIP4 (cellular logic image processor) of University Colledge, London [10].

1.3.A classical line-drawing algorithm

A raster display consists of a rectangular array of n*n pixels. For each pixel location, associated memory maintains a value and the monitor displays light relative to this value. A line-drawing algorithm plots a set of points which best approximate a line. Many algorithms have been proposed but all of them generate the points in an iterative fashion. As an example [9] presents an algorithm first developed by Bresenham [6] concluding that it is simple to implement in VLSI.

```
/*Line-drawing from (0,0) to (x,y), in the first octant (y<x)*/
     xt:=0
     yt:=0
     setpixel (xt,yt)
     slope:=2*y-x
     error:=slope
     inc1:=2*(y-x)
     inc2:=2*y
     for xt:=1 to x do
          if error>0
               then
                    yt:=yt+1
                    error:=error+inc1
               else
                    error:=error+inc2
          endif
          setpixel (xt,yt)
     endfor
```

The comparison, the alternative adds and the incrementing by one would be done in parallel, but the solution is still iterative.

2.PARALLEL SOLUTIONS

2.1.Parallel algorithms

In the following we shall suppose [3] that the line being drawn is defined by: starting point I(Xs,Ys) and finishing point F(Xf,Yf). We define a point P(Xp,Yp) and dX = Xf-Xs, dY = Yf-Ys.

The first algorithm we propose is naive: a structure where each pixel in the memory can answer the question: " Do I belong to the line which is currently being drawn ?". The mathematical solution to this question leads to computing the following expresion [3]:

$$D^2(I,P)=D^2(Xs,Ys,Xp,Yp)=A*(Xp-Xs)^2+B*(Yp-Ys)^2+C*(Xp-Xs)*(Yp-Ys) \quad (1)$$

where:

$$A = dY^2/(dX^2+ dY^2) \quad (2)$$

$$B = dX^2/(dX^2+ dY^2) \quad (3)$$

$$C = 2*dX*dY*(dX^2- dY^2)/(dX^2+ dY^2) \quad (4)$$

So we can write the first algorithm:

```
/*Naive line-drawing algorithm = Algorithm A*/
     compute A,B,C
     brodcast A,B,C to any (i,j) processor (1≤i≤n, 1≤j≤n)
     for each 1≤i≤n parallel do
          for each 1≤j≤n parallel do
                                2
               compute D (Xs,Ys,i,j)
                  2                    2
                if D (Xs,Ys,i,j)<line_width
                     then setpixel(i,j)
          endfor
     endfor
```

This algorithm has time complexity O(1) but needs n*n very complicated processors.

The second algorithm is based on two types of processors: the first one solves the intersection of the given line with a vertical (or horizontal) line, while the second one activates the pixel only if it recognizes its "address". The algorithm (which is also O(1) and needs n*n very simple processors and 2*n more complicated processors) can be written:

```
/*Parallel line-drawing = Algorithm B (for dY<dX)*/
     for each 1≤i≤n parallel do
          compute Yi:=dX/dY*(Xi-Xs)+Ys
          brodcast Yi
     endfor
     for each 1≤i≤n parallel do
          for each 1≤j≤n parallel do
               if j==round(Yi)
                    then setpixel (i,j)
          endfor
     endfor
```

Two observations have to be made: the algorithm gives only one intersection point Yi for one Xi (if the line has dY>dX than we have to generate intersections with horizontal lines) and the algorithm can set only one pixel on a vertical (or horizontal) line, so the intensity of the line will not match the real one.

The third algorithm is derived from a recursive procedure:

```
/*Sequential recursive line-drawing procedure (for dY<dX)*/
/*based  on the divide-and-conquer technique*/
     procedure draw (Xs,Ys,Xf,Yf)
          ddx:=(Xf-Xs)/2
          ddy:=(Yf-Ys)/2
          if (ddx==⌊ddx⌋  and  ddy==⌊ddy⌋ )
               then
                    setpixel (Xs+ddx,Ys+ddy)
               else
                    setpixel (Xs+⌊ddx⌋,Ys+⌊ddy⌋)
                    setpixel (Xs+⌈ddx⌉,Ys+⌈ddy⌉)
          endif
          call draw (Xs,Ys,Xs+⌊ddx⌋,Ys+⌊ddy⌋)
          call draw (Xs+⌈ddx⌉,Ys+⌈ddy⌉,Xf,Yf)
     end
```

This third solution is O(log(max{dx,dy})) and needs n*n very simple processors (identical to the second type utilized previously formed by memory cells and comparators) and 2*n more complicated processors. This algorithm generates the line with more pixels set on a vertical (or horizontal) line, so the intensity is closer to the real one (it is a small step twards antialiasing [2],[4]).

2.2.VLSI arrays for parallel line-drawing

VLSI computation involves the simultaneous use of a great number of very simple processors [7]. More recently WSI extends the idea of interconnection by using the full surface of the wafer. In these conditions the implementation of an algorithm in a dedicated structure is possible.

For algorithm A the complexity of the computation is clear so what we shall do is to split the problem in two: (i) we construct a specialised chip capable to compute A, B, C, which shall be brodcast to all the cells of the memory, (ii) we design a cell capable to compute D(I,P). The resulting structure is presented in figure 1.

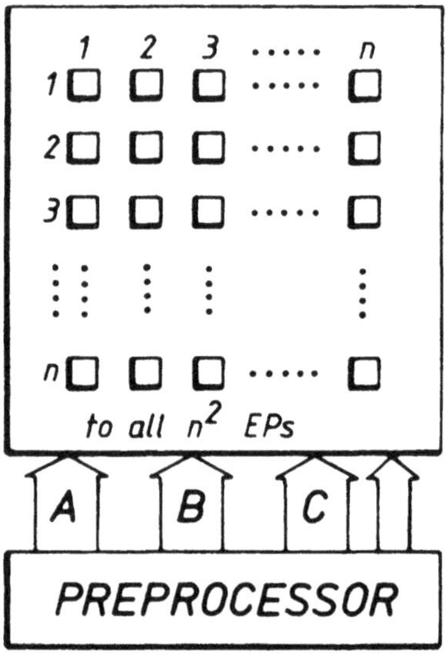

Fig.1. Processor array implementing the first algorithm

If the first part of the problem is not impossible, the second one is not a viable one because of the floating-point representation which seems obvious, and because of the complex operation needed to be implemented in each cell (which is of the form S=a*b*c+d).

Let us first consider the floating-point representation. Is it relly necessary? The answer is NO as by a proper scaling we can use only integers. Unfortunately this scaling factor is very large and a bit-serial multiplication scheme [1], [2], [4] still occupies too much area.

Facing the second problem we propose a simple method, not to eliminate it but to simplify it: the area on the screen which is fully parallel processed will be much smaller so that the scaling factor will be small and a bit-serial multiplication is feasible taking into account the reduced number of bits. This structure will be replicated to occupy the whole screen and will be controled by a similar chip working at the second level of a tree and generating all the data needed by the low level chips. In this way a very powerful line-drawing unit can be constructed with only two building chips; the resulting architecture is similar to that of the EGPA-pyramid [12].

In a bit-based model the optimal time and area to perform a d-digit multiplication are [14]:

$$A'T'^2 = 0(d^2)$$

for all values of T' in the range: $(\log d) \leqslant T' \leqslant 0(\sqrt{d})$.

If we suppose that m bits are used for the intensity than the area of the array can be computed:

$$A \approx n^2 * (\log n + m)$$

where logn is the area needed for multiplication, as logn bits are used. The time will be 0(logn) as we need to propagate serially all the bits of the result (2*logn). Thus the first algorithm is:

$$AT_A^2 = 0(n^2 \log^3 n)$$

We have neglected m as compared with logn not because m is small but as logn is only the proportionality factor.

For algorithm B the structure is depicted in figure 2. Each square processor (SP) contains: the intensity of the pixel to which it is

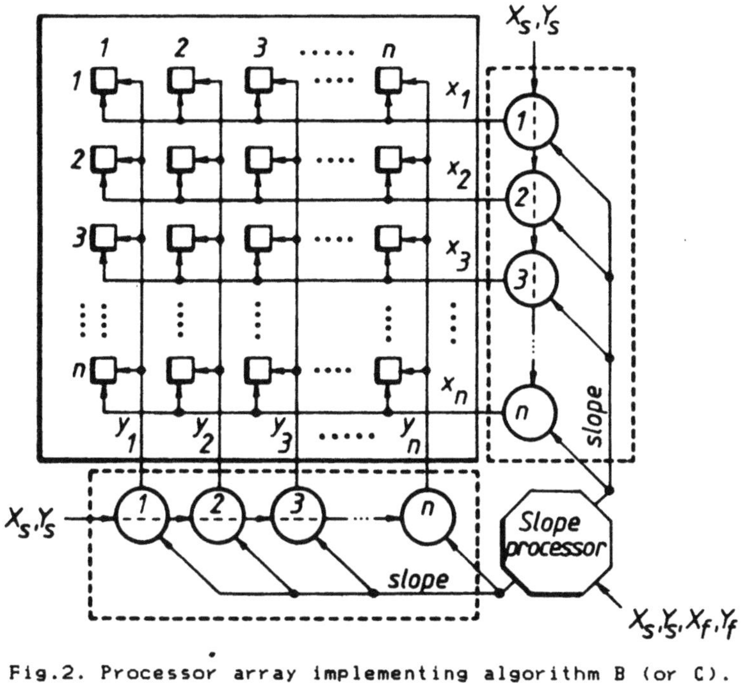

Fig.2. Processor array implementing algorithm B (or C).

associated, its address and a serial comparator. Each round processor (RP) solves the intersection of the given line with a vertical (or horizontal line).

The octogonal processor (OP), which may be viewed as a preprocessor, is the most complicated: it computes the slope of the line dX/dY, but it can be implemented as a ROM or a PLA or as a divide processor based on semi on-line algorithms [5]. It has also another function: after comparing the current slope with 1 it decides which RPs will be activated: the row or the column (if dY/dX>1 than the line is not in the first octant so the column RPs should be activated and if dY/dX<1 than the line is in the first octant so the row RPs should be activated).

It may be seen that the area ocupied by this array is:

$$A \approx n^2 * (m+1) + 2n*\log n$$

where m represents the bits of the intensity, 1 is for the serial comparator and logn for the inner-product.

The time complexity is also O(logn), so we obtain:

$$AT^2_B = O(n^2 * \log^2 n)$$

For algorithm C the structure of the array implementing it is the same with that for algorithm B (see figure 2.) but the RP and OP are a little different (only the SPs are identical). The OP now computes only the sign of the slope (so it is much more simpler) and decides to activate the row or the column of RPs. The RP is not an inner-product; each RP implements the algorithm presented in appendix A.

The area occupied by this array will be the same as that of algorithm B, but because the pixels which belong to the line are activated in a tree-like sequence the time to draw a line will be log(max{dX,dY})*t, where "t" is the time to set a pixel. In the worst-case the algorithm takes logn because an RP needs a time proportoinal to logn to make the comparisons. The area-time complexity is:

$$AT^2_C = O(n^2 * \log^4 n)$$

3.CONCLUSIONS

The presented algorithms are highly parallel. The VLSI arrays implementing them are relizable with present day technologies. WSI offers a good solution for the implementation of one array on a wafer.

Comparing the presented solutions we can see that the first one is far from optimal; algorithm B is the best but algorithm C is also good. It may be possible that algorithm C be much better than algorithm B in reality, because the estimations are for great values of n. Further work should be done in this direction.

REFERENCES

[1] ATRUBIN,I.,"An Iterative One-Dimensional Real Time Multiplier", IEEE Trans.on Comp.,EC-14, 1965, 3, pp.394-399.

[2] BEIU,V.,"Self-testable and Self-repairable Antialiasing Unit",Proc. of MICROELECTRONICS'86, Plovdiv, 23-25 Oct. 1986, pp.183-195.

[3] BEIU,V.,"Parallel Processing in a Line-Drawing Image Memory Array", (in roumanian), presented at the Conference on Microprocessors, Microcomputers & Applications, Bucharest, 28-30 Novembre 1986.

[4] BEIU,V.,C.CONSTANTINESCU,"Fault-Tolerant Systolic Arrays for Antialiasing", Proc.of COMPEURO'87: "VLSI and Computers", Hamburg, 11-15 May 1987, pp.720-723.

[5] BEIU,V.,M.IONESCU,E.PASOL,L.ZUZU, "Adaptive Multiplexing Algorithm and Its Possible VLSI Implementation",34th ISMM Conf:MIMI,Lugano, 29 June - 1 July, 1987.

[6] BRESENHAM,J.,"Algorithm for Computer Control of a Digital Plotter", IBM System J., 4, 1965, 1, pp.25-30.
[7] CHAZELLE, B.,"Computational Geometry on a Systolic Chip",IEEE Trans. on Comp.,C-33, 1984, 9, pp.774-785.
[8] CLARK,J.H.,M.R. HANNAH,"Distributed Processing in a High-Performance Smart Image Memory", LAMBDA, Fourth Quarter, 1980,pp.40-45.
[9] DOBKIN,D.P.,"VLSI Algorithms and Graphics",in Foundation of Computer Science IV,Distributed System 1: Algorithms and Complexity,J.W. DE BAKKER and J. VAN LEEUWEN (eds.), Mathematisch Centrum, Amsterdam, 1983.
[10] FOUNTAIN,T.J.,"CLIP4: A Progress Report",in Languages and Architectures for Image Processing, M.J.B. DUFF and S. LEVIALDI (eds.), London:Academic, 1981.
[11] GRAHAM,M.D.,P.E. NORGEN,"The Diff3 Analyzer: A Parallel/Serial Golay Image Processor",in "Real-Time Medical Image Processing",M. ONOE, K. PRESTON,A. ROSENFELD (eds.), NY:Plenum, 1980.
[12] HANDLER, W., G.FRITSCH, J.VOLKERT, "Applications Implemented on the Erlangen General Purpose Array",in PARCELLA'84, W. HANDLER, T. LEGENDI, G. WOLF (eds.), Akademie-Verlag, Berlin 1985.
[13] HERRON,J.M.,J. FARLEY,K. PRESTON,H. SELLNER,"A General Purpose High-Speed Logical Transform Image Processor",IEEE Trans.on Comp.,C-31 1982, 8 ,pp.795-800.
[14] MEHLHORN, K.,"AT^2-Optimal VLSI integer division and square rooting", Integr. the VLSI J., 2., 1984, pp.163-167.

APPENDIX A

```
/*The algorithm of row RP i  for mod(dX)>mod(dY)*/
if Xi==Xs
   then
      brodcast Ys
   else
      if Xi==Xf
         then
            brodcast Yf
         else
            if Xi>min{Xs,Xf} and Xi<max{Xs,Xf}
               then
                  ddX:=dX/2
                  ddY:=dY/2
                  activated:="NO"
                  while not activated repeat
                     if (Xi==Xs+⌊ddX⌋ or Xi==Xs+⌈ddX⌉)
                        then
                           activated:="YES"
                           if ddY==⌊ddY⌋
                              then
                                 brodcast Ys+ddY
                              else
                                 if ddX==⌊ddX⌋
                                    then
                                       brodcast Ys+⌊ddY⌋
                                       brodcast Ys+⌈ddY⌉
                                    else
                                       if sgnslope<0
                                          then
                                             if Xi=Xs+⌊ddX⌋
                                                then
                                                   brodcast Ys+⌈ddY⌉
                                                else
                                                   brodcast Ys+⌊ddY⌋
                                             endif
                                          else
                                             if Xi=Xs+ ⌊ddX⌋
                                                then
                                                   brodcast Ys+⌊ddY⌋
                                                else
                                                   brodcast Ys+⌈ddY⌉
                                             endif
                                       endif
                                 endif
                           endif
                        else
                           if Xs<Xi<Xs+ ddX
                              then
                                 Xf:=Xs+⌊ddX⌋
                              else
                                 Xs:=Xs+⌈ddX⌉
                           endif
                     endif
                     ddX:=ddX/2
                     ddY:=ddY/2
                  endwhile
            endif
      endif
endif
```

PARALLEL CONFLICT-FREE OPTIMAL ACCESS TO COMPLETE EXTENDED Q-ARY TREES

Reiner Creutzburg

Academy of Sciences of the G.D.R.
Central Institute of Cybernetics
and Information Processes
International Basic Laboratory for
Image Processing and Computer Graphics
Kurstrasse 33, P.O.Box 1298
DDR - 1086 Berlin

Abstract.
In this paper we investigate the parallel conflict-free access to complete extended q-ary subtrees of complete q-ary trees. Thereby the memory module assignment function S is supposed to be recursively linear and nonlinear. Known results for extended binary subtree access are generalized to the case of extended q-ary subtrees. Furthermore optimal solutions for isotropic nonlinear extended q-ary subtree access are given.

1. INTRODUCTION

Much research work has been done in designing parallel memories to access arrays and array-like data structures [2,6,7,9,10,13-17,19,20]. Trees are another important data structure in computer science [11,12]. It is an interesting problem to design parallel memories to access trees or tree-like data structures [3-5,7-10,18,20].

In recent papers [3,4,7,8] we have investigated the parallel access to complete subtrees of trees.

The aim of this paper is to investigate the parallel isotropic conflict-free access to complete extended binary and nonbinary subtrees of trees. The complete extended binary tree [12] is the fundamental data structure in modern logic programming languages, like LISP [1] and PROLOG. Therefore the results of this paper are assumed to be of significant interest for the design of specialized hardware structures for future parallel artificial intelligence machines.

Also the known results for complete extended binary subtree access [5] are generalized to the case of q-ary subtrees ($q \geq 2$) and optimal solutions for isotropic extended subtree access are given.

We use the terminology given in [11] to describe trees. Consider a labelled q-ary tree such that the immediate successors of the node x are qx+1, qx+2, ..., qx+q and the label of the root is 0. The level of a node is defined by initially letting the root be at level 1. The level of every node is one more than the level of its immediate predecessor. The height t of a tree is defined as the maximum level of any node in the tree.

Parallel access to complete extended q-ary trees means the conflict-free access to all the q(t-1)+1 nodes of a complete extended q-ary subtree of height t with an arbitrary node x as root, as shown in Figure 1.

By definition a q-ary tree is called a complete extended q-ary tree if it contains exactly q nodes in each level, exactly q-1 of them are leafs (except of the root level which contains no leaf and the last level which contains q leafs). We consider complete left-, right-, and general-extended q-ary subtrees:

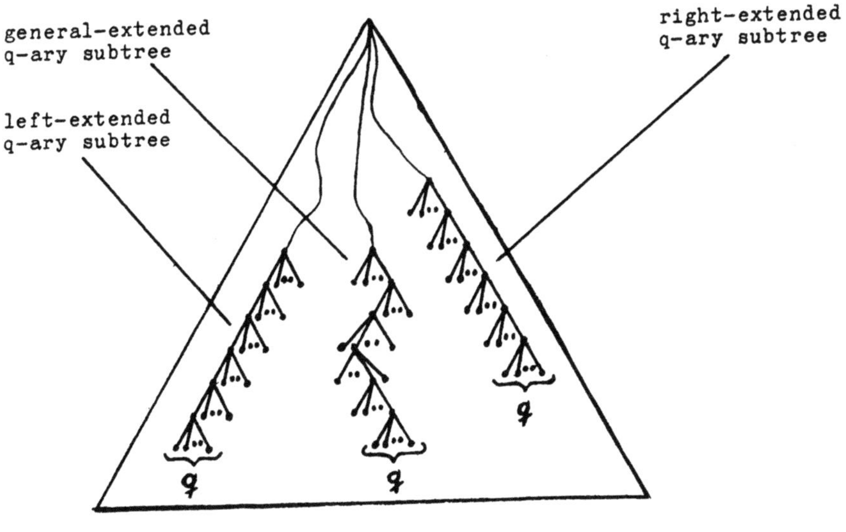

Fig.1 Labelled complete extended q-ary subtrees of height 7 with 6q+1 nodes in a complete q-ary tree.

2. RECURSIVELY LINEAR MODULE ASSIGNMENT FUNCTIONS

A memory module assignment function S is a mapping from the set of the labels of an extended binary tree to the N memory modules. We denote the set of indices of memory modules by

$$E_N = \{0,1,\dots,N-1\}.$$

Theorem 1. A parallel conflict-free access to all the $q(t-1)+1$ nodes of an arbitrary complete left-extended q-ary subtree of height t of a complete binary tree is possible with $N = q(t-1)+1$ memory modules using the recursively linear module assignment function S

$$\left.\begin{aligned} S(0) &\equiv 0 \\ S(qx+1) &\equiv S(x) + 1 \\ S(qx+2) &\equiv S(x) + t \\ S(qx+3) &\equiv S(x) + 2t-1 \\ \dots &\quad \dots \\ S(qx+q) &\equiv S(x) + (q-1)t-(q-2). \end{aligned}\right\} \mod q(t-1)+1. \qquad (1)$$

The proof is illustrated by the following figure. The module assignment function (1) yields the following conflict-free structure of the complete left-extended q-ary subtree:

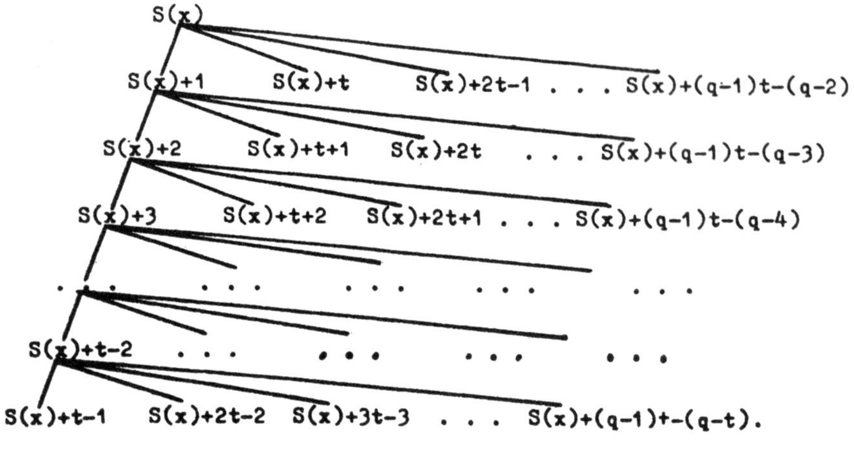

Corollary 2. A parallel conflict-free access to all the $q(t-1)+1$ nodes of an arbitrary complete right-extended q-ary subtree of height t of a complete binary tree is possible with $N = q(t-1)+1$ memory modules using the recursively linear module assignment function S

$$\left.\begin{array}{ll} S(0) & \equiv 0 \\ S(qx+1) & \equiv S(x) + (q-1)t-q-2 \\ \quad\dots & \quad\dots \\ S(qx+q-2) & \equiv S(x) + 2t-1 \\ S(qx+q-1) & \equiv S(x) + t \\ S(qx+q) & \equiv S(x) + 1 \end{array}\right\} \mod q(t-1)+1.$$

The proof follows simply from Theorem 1 by exchanging the successor function parts in (1).

Theorem 3. A parallel conflict-free access to all the $q(t-1)+1$ nodes of an arbitrary complete left- or right-extended binary subtree of height t $(t > 3)$ of a complete binary tree is possible with

$$N = qt \tag{2}$$

memory modules using the recursively linear module assignment function S

$$\left.\begin{array}{ll} S(0) & \equiv 0 \\ S(qx+1) & \equiv S(x) + 1 \\ S(qx+2) & \equiv S(x) + t \\ S(qx+3) & \equiv S(x) + 2t-1 \\ \quad\dots & \quad\dots \\ S(qx+q) & \equiv S(x) + (q-1)t-(q-2) \end{array}\right\} \mod qt. \tag{3}$$

The proof is given in an extended version of this paper.

3. RECURSIVELY NONLINEAR MODULE ASSIGNMENT FUNCTIONS

Although the recursively linear module assignment function S according to (3)

- is easy to implement in hardware,
- needs only $q - 1$ more memory modules than accessed nodes,
- and allows the conflict-free linear access to complete left- or right-

extended q-ary subtrees,

it does not allow the conflict-free access to general-extended q-ary subtrees, in general.

In this chapter we show how the number of memory modules can be further reduced and isotropic complete general-extended q-ary subtree access is possible by use of a nonlinear module assignment function.

Remark. Isotropic subtree access [4,7-9] means that a given node has always the same successors in the memory function (independent of its level in the tree). Clearly, the recursively linear module assignment functions in Theorems 1 - 3 are isotropic.

Theorem 4. A parallel isotropic conflict-free access to all the $q(t-1)+1$ nodes of an arbitrary complete left-, right- or general-extended q-ary subtree of height t $(t > 2)$ of a complete q-ary tree is possible with

$$N = qt \tag{4}$$

memory modules using the recursively (nonlinear) module assignment function S given by

$$S(0) = 0 \bmod N$$

and the table form

S(x)	0	1;2;...;q	q+1;q+2;...;2q	2q+1;2q+2;...;3q	...
S(qx+1)	1	q+1	2q+1	3q+1	
S(qx+2)	2	q+2	2q+2	3q+2	
...	...	...	...	...	...
S(qx+q-1)	q-1	2q-1	3q-1	4q-1	
S(qx+q)	q	2q	3q	4q	...

S(x)	q(t-3)+1;q(t-3)+2;...;q(t-2)	q(t-2)+1;q(t-2)+2;...;q(t-1)
S(qx+1)	q(t-2)+1	q(t-1)+1
S(qx+2)	q(t-2)+2	q(t-1)+2
...	...	...
S(qx+q-1)	q(t-1)-1	qt-1
S(qx+q)	q(t-1)	0 .

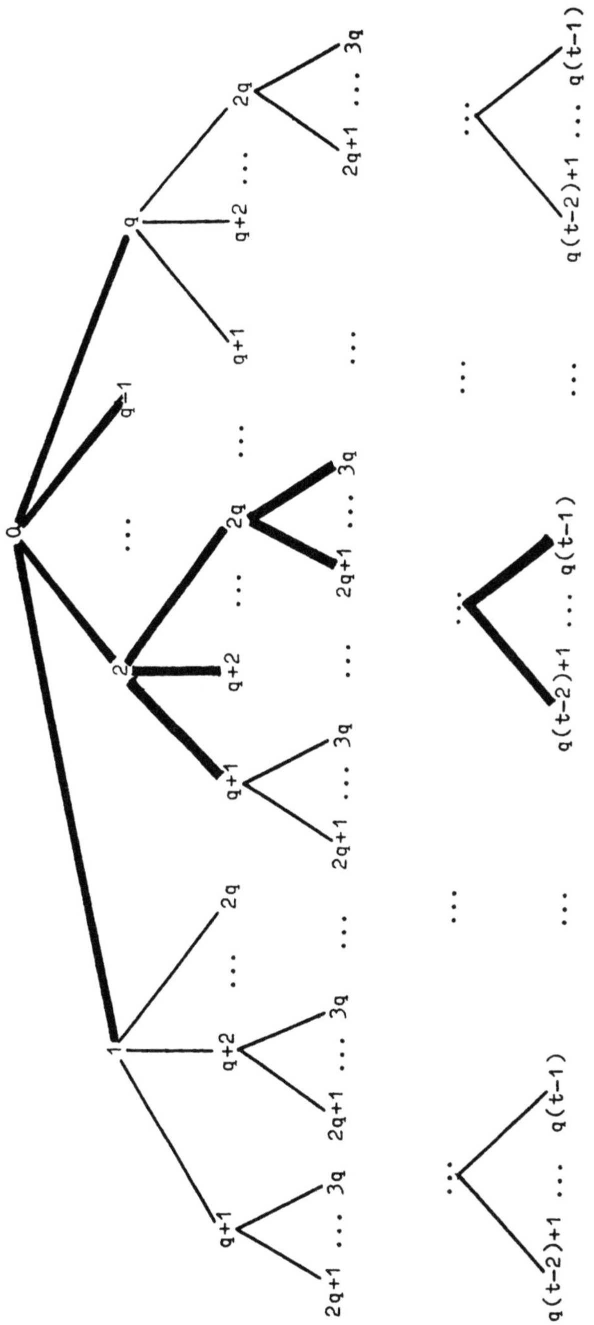

Fig. 2

The **proof** is illustrated using the next figure. Starting with $S(0) = 0 \mod qt$ we obtain the structure of a complete q-ary tree shown in Fig. 2. Obviously every complete general-extended q-ary subtree of height t can be accessed conflict-free and isotropic. (An example is marked with bold lines.)

To obtain the minimal number N of memory modules for isotropic complete q-ary extended subtree access we consider the successors of the nodes that are stored in the memory modules $q(t-2)+1$, ..., $q(t-1)$, respectively. If one of these successor nodes is stored in the memory modules 1, ..., $q(t-1)$, respectively, then we have conflict in the complete extended q-ary subtree access with roots 1, 2, ..., or $q(t-1)$, respectively. So we take the memory modules 0 and $q(t-1)+1$, $q(t-1)+2$, ..., $qt-1$ as successors in the next level (see Fig. 2.). In this way we obtain the minimal value of

$$N = q(t-1)+1 + q-1 = qt$$

memory modules and the isotropic table function of Theorem 4.

REFERENCES

[1] Allen, J. R.: Anatomy of LISP. McGraw-Hill: New York 1978

[2] Budnik,P., and D.J.Kuck: The organization and use of parallel memories. IEEE Trans. Comput. C-20 (1971), pp. 1566-1569

[3] Creutzburg, R.: Parallel optimal subtree access with recursively linear memory function. Proc. PARCELLA'86 Berlin, (Eds.: T. Legendi, D. Parkinson, R. Vollmar, G. Wolf) Akademie-Verlag: Berlin 1986, pp. 203-209

[4] Creutzburg, R.: Parallel linear conflict-free subtree access. Proc. Internat. Workshop Parallel Algorithms Architectures (Suhl 1987), (Eds.: A. Albrecht, H. Jung, K. Mehlhorn) Akademie-Verlag: Berlin 1987, pp. 89-96

[5] Creutzburg, R.: Parallel conflict-free access to extended binary trees. (submitted for publication)

[6] Gössel,M., and B.Rebel: Parallel memory with recursive address computation. Proc. Int. Conf. Parallel Computing'83 Berlin, (Ed.: M. Feilmeier) Elsevier: Amsterdam 1984, pp. 515-520

[7] Gössel, M., and B. Rebel: Data structures and parallel memories. Proc. PARCELLA'86 Berlin, (Eds.: T.Legendi, D. Parkinson, R. Vollmar, G. Wolf) Akademie-Verlag, pp. 49-60

[8] Gössel, M., and B. Rebel: Memories for parallel subtree access. Proc. Internat. Workshop Parallel Algorithms Architectures (Suhl 1987), (Eds.: A. Albrecht, H. Jung, K. Mehlhorn) Akademie-Verlag: Berlin 1987, pp. 122-130

[9] Gössel, M., B. Rebel, and R. Creutzburg: Memory Architecture and Parallel Access. (in German). Akademie-Verlag: Berlin (in print)

[10] Hockney, R. W., and C. R. Jesshope: Parallel Computers. Hilger: Bristol 1981

[11] Horowitz, E., and S. Sahni: Fundamentals of Data Structures. Computer Science Press. Woodland Hills (Ca.) 1976

[12] Knuth, D. E.: The Art of Computer Programming, Fundamental Algorithms. Addison-Wesley: Reading (MA) 1968

[13] Kuck, D. J., and R. A. Stokes: The Burroughs scientific processor. IEEE Trans. Comput. C-31 (1982), pp. 363-376

[14] Lawrie, D. H.: Access and alignment in an array processor. IEEE Trans. Comput. C-24 (1975), pp. 1145-1155

[15] Lawrie, D. H., and Ch. R. Vora: The prime memory system for array access. IEEE Trans. Comput. C-31 (1982), pp. 435-442

[16] Rebel, B., and M. Gössel: Ein paralleler Speicher. Report ZKI der AdW, Berlin, Nov. 1982

[17] Shapiro, H. D.: Theoretical limitations on the use of parallel memories. Univ. Illinois, Dept. Comp. Sci., Rep. No. 75-776, Dec. 1975

[18] Shirakawa, H.: On a parallel memory to access trees. Unpublished manuscript. (Ritsumeikan Univ., Kyoto, Japan, 1984)

[19] Wijshoff, H. A. G., and J. van Leeuwen: The structure of periodic storage schemes for parallel memories. IEEE Trans. Comput. C-34 (1985), pp. 501-505

[20] Wijshoff, H. A. G.: Data organization in parallel computers. Ph.D. Diss. (Rijksuniv. Utrecht, Netherlands) 1987

SYSTOLIC PRECONDITIONING ALGORITHMS FOR THE JACOBI ITERATIVE SOLUTION OF SPARSE LINEAR SYSTEMS

D.J. Evans and G.M. Megson*
Department of Computer Studies
Loughborough University of Technology
Loughborough, Leicestershire,
U.K.

ABSTRACT

Systolic algorithms for preconditioned iterative procedures are described and discussed in relation to existing systolic arrays for iterative methods applied to the systems of linear equations arising from the solution of partial differential equations. In boundary value problems it is shown that if the cost of the preconditioned systolic arrays in terms of hardware is related to the (standard) iterative methods, then savings in the number of array cells can be made when the system involved is large and sparse (narrow bandwidth) with a significant improvement in convergence rate.

1.0 INTRODUCTION

This paper is concerned with the application of preconditioning methods for the solution of n linear equations of the form,

$$Au = d \ , \tag{1.1}$$

where A is positive definite, non-singular, banded and often of large order. Such problems arise from the application of finite difference techniques to the solution of partial differential equations. The solution of (1.1) by using the standard iterative procedures such as the Gauss-Seidel (including overrelaxation) and Jacobi schemes is by no means new, and has been discussed by Berzins, Buckley, and Dew for sparse systems in [1], while the authors have extended the methods to the Quadrant Interlocking (QI) iterative schemes in [2]. However the development of so-called preconditioned methods which are primarily aimed at increasing the convergence rate of the original system (1.1) by premultiplication and/or postmultiplication with a suitable additional matrix offer new possibilities in the reduction of computation and hardware costs of systolic arrays. The use of preconditioning increases the arithmetic work in the solution process, which must be offset against the greatly improved convergence rates of the algorithm in order to produce a faster solution.

1.1 Preconditioning

Consider the solution of (1.1) which if A was easily invertable would be given by,

$$u = A^{-1}d \ ,$$

and can be easily found. However it is often the case that difficulties arise with the inversion of A, especially when A results from the approximation of certain partial differential equations. The concept of preconditioning is to select some non-singular matrix R, where R^{-1} approximates the inverse of A, but whose construction is much simpler than forming A^{-1}. (1.1) is then preconditioned by a premultiplication by

*Oriel College, Oxford

R^{-1} to give,

$$R^{-1}Au = R^{-1}d \ , \tag{1.2}$$

where R is called the conditioning matrix. In order to achieve a good convergence rate, the condition matrix must approach A^{-1} so that the spectral condition number of $R^{-1}A$ is much less than the corresponding value of A.

Definition: The spectral condition number of a non-singular matrix Q is given by,

$$\kappa(Q) = ||Q||.||Q||^{-1} \ .$$

From (1.2) we can easily form a general iterative procedure,

$$u^{(i+1)} = u^{(i)} + \omega R^{-1}(d-Au^{(i)}) \ , \tag{1.3}$$

with ω a parameter that can be used to improve the convergence rate.

In this paper we consider explicit preconditioning, which provides an alternative form to (1.2) where (1.1) is multiplied by a matrix Q

$$QAu = Qd \tag{1.4}$$

such that QA is a matrix which has a simple splitting providing a noval iterative method. For instance, the Jacobi form of the explicit preconditioned method is given by the following equations.

Consider the splitting $A = I - B$.

Then we precondition by premultiplication with $Q = (I+B)$ to obtain

$$(I+B)Au = (I+B)d$$

or

$$(I-B^2)u = (I+B)d$$

and in explicit form

$$u = B^2u + (I+B)d \ . \tag{1.5}$$

While the preconditioned Gauss-Seidel method is given by the splitting $A = I-L-U$.

Then the Gauss-Seidel iteration is given by,

$$(I-L)u = Uu + d \ .$$

Again we precondition by premultiplying by $(I+L)$ to obtain

$$u = L^2u + (I+L)(Uu+d) \ . \tag{1.6}$$

We shall consider the systolic implementation of the former and relate this to existing systolic iterative arrays.

1.2 Systolic Iterative Array Formats

There are certain forms which an iterative algorithm must take when it is implemented systolically. An early systolic format was described by Berzins, Buckley and Dew [1] and is illustrated for easy reference purposes in Figure 1, and will be referred to in this paper as the Cascaded Iteration Array (CIA). Essentially, the CIA is a sequence of pipelined linear arrays with each array computing a single iteration, the initial matrix A being split at each array. A cascade of r linear arrays produces r iterations of the method. Fig.2 indicates the structure of the linear array of Fig.1 for the Jacobi iteration and is attributed to Berzins et al, who also considered the Gauss-Seidel methods with successive overrelaxation. They concluded that the iterative schemes could be computed in a time of,

$$T_0 = 2n + 2r(p+1)-1 \ , \tag{1.7}$$

where n is the order of the matrix A, r the number of iterations required for convergence, and p is the number of superdiagonals. The timings are trivial to derive once the operations of the arrays of Kung and Leiserson [5] are understood. Each

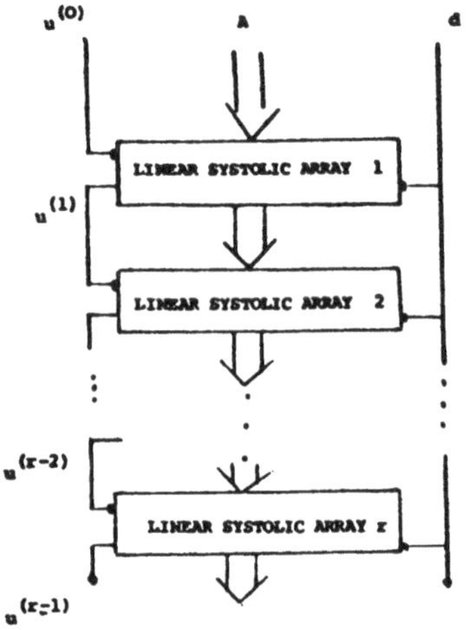

FIGURE 1: Cascaded systolic arrays for matrix iteration

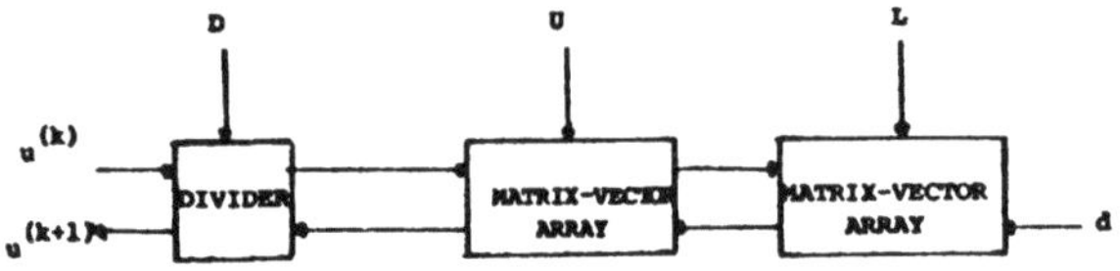

FIGURE 2: Linear systolic array for Jacobi iteration (A=D-U-L) taken from [1]

linear array requires W cells, when W is the bandwidth of the matrix. Although if cells corresponding to null sub(super)-diagonals are replaced by simple delays only W-S cells are required (where S=number of null diagonals).

Thus, the total number of cells is given by r*W or r*(W-S) with amendments for null sub(superdiagonals). With respect to preconditioned arrays we introduce a global format indicated in Fig.3, where the computation is divided into two phases, a pre-processing phase for preconditioning the problem, and an iteration section consisting of a CIA similar to Fig.1. Our designs are compared with those of [1] for a number of cases:

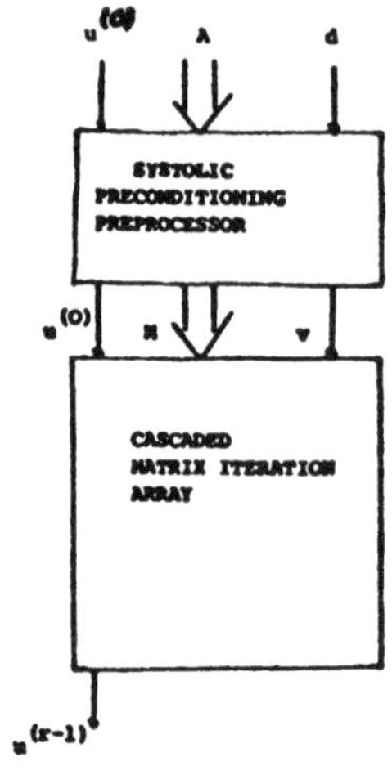

FIGURE 3: Pipelined preconditioned iterative array

case (i) Unlimited amount of hardware: the CIA can have as many iterations as required for convergence.

case (ii) Finite number of iterations: the length of the CIA is bounded.

These cases allow the effectiveness of the preconditioned strategies to be assessed, in relation to existing methods and some restrictions on actual implementation. For instance, applying case (ii) to (1.7) where r_1 is the total number of iterations and r is the finite size of the CIA results in the timings,

$$T_1 = 2\left\lceil\frac{r_1}{r}\right\rceil n + 2\left\lceil\frac{r_1}{r}\right\rceil r(p+1) - \left\lceil\frac{r_1}{r}\right\rceil$$

or

$$T_1 = 2\,\frac{r_1}{r}\,n + 2r_1(p+1) - \frac{r_1}{r}\,, \tag{1.8}$$

when r_1 is divisible by r. This result gives a better assessment of the cost for a true implementation with a finite sized systolic device.

2.0 SYSTOLIC PRE-CONDITIONED ARRAYS

The result given by equation (1.8) illustrates an important concept in systolic design generally and one which has particular consequences for the arrays detailed below as the final implementation of a systolic device ultimately decides how it will perform.

A good systolic array which makes the assumption of unlimited hardware can be seriously flawed when it comes to implementation no matter how intricate the computational arrangement. The same is also true of numerical methods translated to systolic forms. A method which is computationally fast may be slower than an existing systolic scheme based on a slower method, while algorithms suitable for other forms of parallel computation can be useless systolically.

2.1 Explicit Preconditioning

We consider the Jacobi iteration of (1.5) where the global structure of the array is indicated in Fig.4 it consists of the preprocessing section and a modified CIA. The computation itself is easily formulated by the following sequence,

$$\begin{aligned}&\text{STEP 1:}\quad M=B^2,\ z=(I+B)d\\&\text{STEP 2:}\quad u^{(i+1)} = Mu^{(i)}+z\text{: GOTO STEP 2.}\end{aligned} \tag{2.1}$$

This is an especially convenient structure because step (1) forms the preprocessing or preconditioning stage which reduces to a simple matrix-vector computation for each iteration. Hence, the CIA section of the pre-conditioned method consists of linear arrays which are simple matrix-vector arrays.

The preprocessor requires some explanation, it consists of three separate arrays; a matrix-vector array for producing z, a specially modified hexagonally connected array for producing M, and a reformatting array to create the correct input format for the CIA section. Notice that the host inputs only a single matrix to the preprocessor and so the host interface is proportional to the bandwidth of the matrix A. Once input B passes through the first matrix vector starting the preprocessing/preconditioning, as the first array generates the vector z, B is pipelined onto the special hex form. The special hex is different from the traditional matrix product

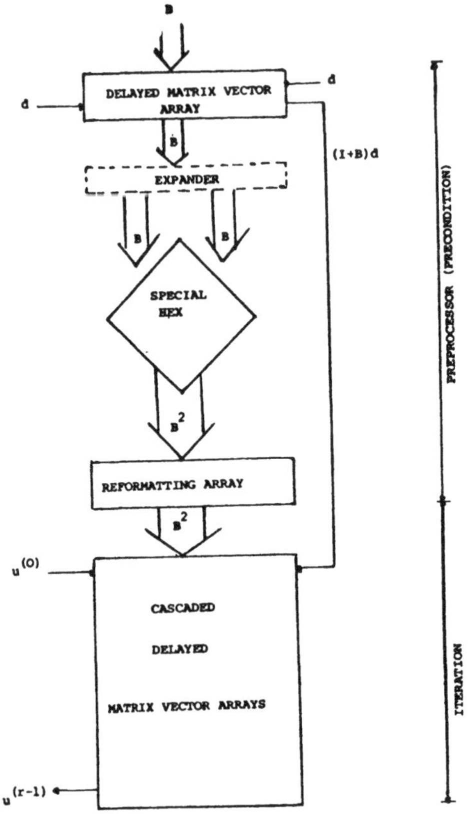

FIGURE 4: Systolic preconditioned Jacobi iteration

hex in [5], because in it all the data is input in the same direction. The explanation of the internal arrangement is beyond the scope of this paper, but such an array can be constructed and is given in [6]. We only note that the delay through the special hex is still proportional to the bandwidth of B, and that the output of B^2 is in the same format as the original hex array of Kung and Leiserson which allows it to be pipelined with other systolic arrays in the literature. The expander as indicated simply expands the input B into two identical streams required by the special hex and this is also explained in [6]; the delays are only a constant number of cycles. This leaves only the reformatting array to discuss, which is essentially a linear array of delay register cells which add additional delays to the hex output so the data is properly synchronised with the vector z and $u^{(0)}$ when it is input to the CIA section of the array. To complete the picture of the preconditioned systolic array we now have to define a linear array for Fig.1, which as stated above is a matrix vector array, but is not the usual type used in [3] and [1]. The matrix B must be input to the preprocessor in a form suitable for the hex to use, but it passes through a matrix vector array before it reaches the hex. Likewise when B^2 leaves the preprocessor it is still in the hex format. A matrix input to a Kung and Leiserson matrix vector array requires 2n cycles with every element separated by a single dummy element for synchronisation, while a hex array inputs a matrix in 3n cycles with two dummy elements between each matrix element on the same path. In short, the inputs to the matrix-vector arrays are not the same as for the hex and our pipelining scheme appears to collapse, because adjusting the number of dummy elements 'on-the-fly' cannot be accomplished. To overcome the synchronisation problem we define a new matrix vector array which accepts the same input format as the hex, such an array is shown in Fig.6. Each cell computes an inner product operation y=y+a*x, and is separated from its neighbours by a single delay register on the y data path. Notice that the leftside of the input matrix is delayed by a single cycle, the special hex will accept this format and modify it for its own input/output. Fig.5 also shows the first few cycles of operation, if the input matrix is of bandwidth W=p+q-1, the first result y_1 is output after (3p-2) cycles allowing p cycles for x_1 to reach the centre cell, this is the latency of the array. Thus the total time for all the y components to be output is

$$T = 3n + 2w-1 .$$

Now allowing a propagation delay of c (>0) cycles for B^2 to emerge from the preconditioner after B started to input, the preconditioned Jacobi scheme has a time

$$T_2 = 3n + r(6p-4) + c , \qquad (2.2)$$

to compute r iterations, with r CIA delayed matrix vector arrays.

Remark: The term (6p-4) is determined as follows; the delay of the modified matrix vector array is (3p-2). The bandwidth of B is W=p+q-1, hence the bandwidth of B^2 is (2W-1). Then it follows that the CIA arrays have (2W-1) cells and a latency of 2(3p-2).

Although the preconditioned Jacobi scheme uses cascaded arrays we still have a number of undesirable features which could degrade the design:

(i) The computation of a matrix vector computation or single iteration has been increased from 2n to 3n cycles.

(ii) We have used twice as much hardware in an iteration for the preconditioned case than for the unpreconditioned case.

(iii) We have a hardware overhead for the preconditioning.

How does this affect the array performance when compared with the ordinary iterative schemes in [1]? To find the speed-up when both methods can use unlimited hardware we use (1.7) and (2.2) to give,

$$S_p = \frac{T_0}{T_1} = \frac{2n+2r_1(p+1)-1}{3n+r_2(6p-4)+c} .$$

Hence for $S_p>1$ we require,

$$2n+2r_1(p+1)-1 > 3n+r_2(6p-4)+c$$

or

$$r_1 > \frac{1}{2(p+1)} [(n+c+1) + r_2(6p-4)] , \qquad (2.3a)$$

where r_1 is the number of unpreconditioned iterations and r_2 is the number of preconditioned iterations. Thus, it appears that where unlimited hardware is concerned the ordinary schemes are always faster than the preconditioned schemes when n is sufficiently large as $r_1>r_2$ due to preconditioning. We may however be able to use less hardware provided that $r_1>2r_2$. Each iteration of the ordinary case requires W ips cells, while each preconditioned case requires 2W-1, giving a saving in cells of

$$S = r_1w-(2w-1)r_2 = r_1w-2wr_2+r_2 = w(r_1-2r_2) + r_2 , \qquad (2.3b)$$

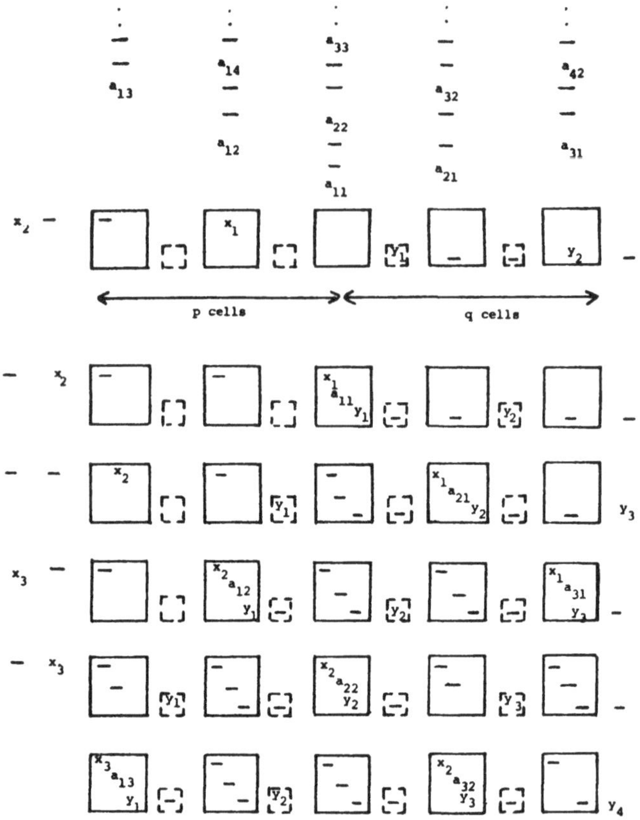

FIGURE 5: Delayed matrix vector array

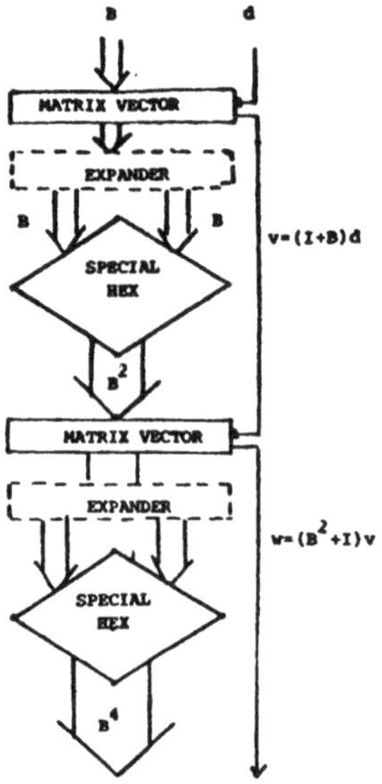

FIGURE 6: Compressed Jacobi preprocessor

and when $r_1=2r_2$ we save $S=r_2$ cells. This relates the convergence rates of the two methods to the saving in cells, and compensates for the loss of speed-up, if r_1 is large.

Next we restrict the CIA's to a fixed number of arrays. Let $\bar{r}_1$ and r_1 be the number of iterations and number of arrays in the ordinary case, $\bar{r}_2$ and r_2 the corresponding numbers for the preconditioned array. We now define the speed-ups as,

$$S_p = \frac{\bar{r}_1\{\frac{2n}{r_1} + 2(p+1) - \frac{1}{r_1}\}}{\bar{r}_2\{\frac{3n}{r_2} + 2(3p-2) + \frac{c}{r_2}\}}$$

and for $S_p>1$, we must have,

$$\frac{\bar{r}_1}{\bar{r}_2} > \frac{\{\frac{3n}{r_2} + 2(3p-2) + \frac{c}{r_2}\}}{\{\frac{2n}{r_1} + 2(p+1) - \frac{1}{r_1}\}}$$

or

$$\frac{\bar{r}_1}{\bar{r}_2} > \frac{3}{r_2}(\frac{r_1}{2}) \text{ for n sufficiently large,}$$

giving,

$$\bar{r}_1 > \frac{3}{2}(\frac{r_1}{r_2}) \cdot \bar{r}_2 \ . \qquad (2.4a)$$

Now suppose $r_1 = \alpha r_2$, $\alpha>1$ then the saving in hardware is given by,

$$S = wr_1-(2w-1)r_2 = w\alpha r_2-2wr_2+r_2 = r_2w(\alpha-2)+r_2 \ . \qquad (2.4b)$$

This result relates the convergence rates to the speed-up of the arrays, and the saving in cells to the relative sizes of the two CIA's. It follows that if we can put bounds on the rates of convergence of the ordinary and preconditioned matrices we can compute a bound on α with,

$$\frac{2\bar{r}_1}{3\bar{r}_2} > \alpha \ , \qquad (2.4c)$$

and hence we can locate the maximum savings for still achieving a speed-up. It follows from (2.4b) that if $\alpha>2$ and $r_2>w$ which is perfectly feasible for sparse systems and good preconditioning then we obtain the saving $S=O(W^2)$. Now the special hex will require W^2 cells and the matrix vector in the preprocessor requires an additional W cells so the saving of cells can be used to compensate for the extra preprocessor cells.

2.3 Compressing Iterations

Given the success in relating the preconditioning strategy, reduced iterations and hardware savings we may further attempt to reduce the hardware or the time by more preprocessing. For instance, the Jacobi scheme of (1.5) can be modified to perform two iterations for every linear array in the CIA Two successive Jacobi iterations are given as follows,

$$u^{(i+1)} = B^2u^{(i)} + (I+B)d \qquad (2.5a)$$

$$u^{(i+2)} = B^2u^{(i+1)} + (I+B)d \ , \tag{2.5b}$$

which after substitution produces the result,

$$u^{(i+2)} = B^4u^{(i)} + B^2(I+B)d + (I+B)d. \tag{2.6}$$

When formulated as an algorithm it is,

STEP (i) compute B^2 and $v=(I+B)d$

STEP (ii) compute $M=B^2*B^2$ and $w=(B^2+I)v$

STEP (iii) $u^{(i+2)} = Mu^{(i)}+w$: GOTO STEP (iii),

which is again a simple matrix-vector problem, with steps (i) and (ii) forming an extended preprocessing or preconditioning task.

The preprocessor for the compressed iteration is shown in Fig.6 and consists of two pipelined special hex arrays separated by matrix-vector arrays and expander arrangements. The delay through the preconditioner is again proportional to the bandwidths of B and B^2 and hence is still a constant, but larger than the uncompressed version. The matrix $M=B^4$ has a bandwidth $W_2=2(W_1-1)=2(2W_0-1)-1=4W_0-3$ with each compressed linear array requiring approximately four times the hardware of an unpreconditioned array. It follows that with $W_0=p+q-1$ the latency of the compressed linear array is 12p-7 yielding,

$$T_3 = 3n + r(12p-7) + c_1 \ , \tag{2.7}$$

where c_1 is the preprocessing delay with unlimited hardware. With $\bar{r}_1, r_1, \bar{r}_2$, and r_2 defined as previously we now express the array speed-up as,

$$S_p = \frac{2\bar{r}_1[\frac{2n}{r_1} + (p+1) - \frac{1}{r_1}]}{\bar{r}_2[\frac{3n}{r_2} + (12p-7) + \frac{c_1}{r_2}]} \ ,$$

which for a speed-up becomes,

$$\frac{2\bar{r}_1}{\bar{r}_2} > \frac{[\frac{3n}{r_2} + (12p-7) + \frac{c_1}{r_2}]}{[\frac{2n}{r_1} + (p+1) - \frac{1}{r_1}]}$$

or

$$\frac{\bar{r}_1}{\bar{r}_2} > \frac{\frac{3}{r_2}}{\frac{4}{r_1}} = \frac{3}{4}(\frac{r_1}{r_2}) \text{ for n sufficiently large.}$$

Similarly as before with $r_1=\alpha r_2$ the saving becomes:

$$\left.\begin{aligned} s &= wr_1-(4w-3)r_2 = w\alpha r_2-4w_2+3r_2 \\ &= r_2w(\alpha-4)+3r_2 \\ \text{with} \quad & \bar{r}_1 > \tfrac{3}{4}\alpha\bar{r}_2 \ , \ \alpha>4 \ . \end{aligned}\right\} \tag{2.8}$$

Thus we can conclude that the preconditioning matrix must improve the convergence rate to reduce the number of iterations by at least a third before hardware can be saved in the CIA. However we have made a considerable addition to the preprocessor hardware and significant savings in the CIA must be made to offset this increase.

4.0 CONCLUSIONS

A global systolic design has been presented for preconditioned iterative procedures. The design consists of two arrays, a preconditioning preprocessor, and a cascaded iterative array (CIA) for pipelined iterations to maximise throughput.

Preprocessors for the preconditioning of the Jacobi preconditioned iterative scheme were discussed and the structure of the CIA reduced to a sequence of delayed matrix-vector computations. The delayed matrix vector array was presented as a linear array which performed matrix vector computations with a systolic input similar to the hexagonal output structure, allowing the preprocessor to be pipelined with the CIA.

REFERENCES

[1] Berzins, M., Buckley, T.F., Dew, P.M., Systolic Matrix Iterative Algorithms, 'Parallel Computing 83', Eds. M. Feilmeier, G. Joubert and U. Schendel, pp.483-488, North Holland, 1984.

[2] Megson, G.M. and Evans, D.J., Soft-Systolic Pipelined Matrix Algorithms, 'Parallel Computing 85', Eds. M. Feilmeier, G. Joubert and U. Schendel, pp.171-180, North Holland, 1986.

[3] Megson, G.M. and Evans, D.J., Compact Systolic Arrays for Incomplete Factorization Methods, Comp.Stud. Rep. 321, L.U.T., 1986.

[4] Evans, D.J., Ed., Preconditioning Methods, Theory and Applications, Gordon & Breach, 1983.

[5] Mead and Conway, Introduction to VLSI Design, Ch.8, Addison-Wesley, 1980.

[6] Megson, G.M. and Evans, D.J., Matrix Power Generation Using an Optically Reduced Hex, Comp.Stud. Rep. 314, L.U.T. 1986.

MULTIPROCESSOR SYSTEMS
FOR LARGE NUMERICAL APPLICATIONS

G. Fritsch and J. Volkert

Institut für Mathematische Maschinen
und Datenverarbeitung (Informatik III)
Universität Erlangen-Nürnberg
Martensstr. 3, D-8520 Erlangen, F.R. Germany

Abstract:

Numerical simulation in physics, chemistry and engineering sciences, as for instance in fluid dynamics can be grouped in two classes: Continuum models and many-body-models. The mathematical approximative methods used are numerical grid methods, molecular dynamics, Monte Carlo methods etc. The more complicate the considered phenomenon and the more refined the model is, the higher is the demand for computational power and storage capacity. Future high performance computers will be parallel machines in order to be able to safisfy the users of large numerical applications. Appropriate parallel architectures in particular of the multiple-instruction-multiple-data type (MIMD) are discussed in view of the mapping requirements and varying subtask structure of the considered numerical applications. Two distributed memory architectures are presented in more detail: SUPRENUM, a German supercomputer project and the Erlangen multiprocessor architecture. The SUPRENUM prototype, based on the message-passing communication principle, will consist of 256 processors with a theoretical overall peak performance of 2 GFLOPS. The Erlangen architectural concept is characterized by interprocessor communication via distributed shared memory (DSM) and a functional hierarchy of 3 levels. This multiprocessor architecture adapts especially well to the mapping requirements of most numerical simulation problems. This is due to the fact that DSM architectures match efficiently the local communication needs of the considered problem classes.

1. Introduction

Most mathematical models of natural phenomena in physics, chemistry and engineering sciences, as for instance in fluid dynamics can be grouped in two classes: Continuum models and many-body-models. Continuum models are typically represented by a set of coupled non linear partial differential equations (PDE). In general, the PDE system can only be solved by approximative methods. Continuous space and time are replaced by a mesh and time steps, respectively. Continuous physical variables are replaced by arrays of values. By numerical grid methods new values of the physical variables on the numerical grid are calculated out of the old values in adjacent neighbors of each grid point.
Many-body-models often use molecular dynamics (MD) methods or Monte-Carlo (MC)-methods. By MD-methods the behavior of an assembly of particles is determined by calculation of the position and velocity of each particle, taking into account an assumed particle interaction potential. Many-body and many-configuration ensembles with a high number of degrees of freedom can be treated by a statistical approach. By using random variables weighted over an assumed distribution function, the physical ensemble is approximated by a number of samples.
The more complicate the considered phenomenon and the more refined the model is, the higher is the demand for computational power and storage capacity. Future high performance computers will be parallel machines in order to be able to satisfy the users of large numerical applications of the before-mentioned type. As we will show in the next chapter parallel architectures of the multiple-instruction-multiple-data (MIMD) type will be most appropriate. Such systems are generally known as multiprocessors or multicomputers.

2. Characterisation of numerical problems in natural and engineering sciences.

2.1 General

Only recently, with the advent of supercomputers numerical simulation of natural phenomena has become a third column in scientific methodology: Beside theory and laboratory experiment, computational science has been established as an effective methodical approach. The main feature of numerical simulation is the point-wise or particle-wise iterative calculation on many points of a numerical grid or on many particles of a particle system, respectively. The numerical models reflect basic

features of natural phenomena as for instance local interaction, i.e. action through an immediate medium. This fundamental property should be taken into account with any parallel architecture for efficient computation (e.g. nearest-neighbor multiprocessor structure with distributed shared memory).
In the next paragraphs (2.2, 2.3, 2.4) we discuss essential features of the main mathematical methods used with numerical simulation:
Matrix operations (dense and sparse matrices), numerical grid methods and many-particle methods (Monte-Carlo- and Molecular Dynamics Methods).

2.2 Matrix Operations

Many problems in numerical mathematics can only be solved after linearization. Therefore vector and matrix operations play an important part in numerical methods. Hardware designers as well as algorithm theorists accommodate to these facts. A lot of special systems (e.g. systolic arrays), architectures rather well suited (e.g. vector processors, array processors) and algorithms for general purpose computers have been developed.
The architectural aspect of that wide field was reported by us in occassion of PARCELLA 84 /19/. Therefore we can summarize the main demands on computers:

- Large memory (several GB)
- High computational power (many GFLOPS)
- Efficient features for manipulating vectors and matrices.

The consequence of the latter issue depend on the fact whether the matrices are dense or sparse. In case of dense matrices the architecture has to support real matrix structure. This means e.g. in context of multiprocessors a nearest neighbor connectivity is sufficient (proximity feature). In contrary to that, sparse matrices demand for global shared memory. But in case of large systems this cannot be fulfilled (hot spot problem /20/). Therefore the trend is to algorithms which do not need a global memory.

2.3 Numerical Grid methods

Physical phenomena are often described by a set of partial differential equations (PDE). For solving a special problem a discretization method is applied to these PDEs. Continuous physical variables are replaced by arrays of values and the set of PDE is transformed into a set of algebraic equations.

The resulting systems of equations were mostly solved by relaxation methods. Presently, multigrid algorithms are used for the sake of much better convergence. This new approach is based on relaxation, interpolation and restriction using several grids. Interpolation and restriction are local operations well-suited to computer systems which support proximity. This is also true for point relaxation especially in red black order. But the smoothing capacity of point relaxation proved to be too bad in comparision to other smoothers like line relaxation, incomplete LU decomposition (ILU) and conjugate gradient method. The disadvantage of these latter techniques is that the proximity feature is lost.
In case of simple relaxation this problem can be neglected since wave front technique can be used. But if a multigrid method is applied, only two or three relaxations in series are performed and therefore a wave front algorithm will cause too much loss.
Therefore, for architectures without global memory additional transports cannot be avoided. But relaxation is only a part of the total algorithm and the loss of the additional transports is not important on the whole (on DIRMU with 25 processors we measured about 10% loss).
Furthermore, the newest trend seems to go back to point relaxation. W. Hackbusch developed an new point smoother for multigrid /21 /. This new technique uses several coarse grids at any level to improve the smoothing property.
No matter as the discussion will issue, the demand for computer power (speed and memory) is enormous in context with PDE. E.g. Dr. Graves from NASA estimated /22/ the needed performance to the equivalence of 1 billion CRAY 1.

2.4 Many-particle methods

Physical systems of many interacting particles can be modelled by a mathematical treatment of a representative sample. "Particles" can mean quite different objects as e.g. electrons, molecules or even galaxies. In general, the computational goal is the calculation of overall system magnitudes. Essentially, there are two methodical approaches:

- Molecular Dynamics (MD): Classical calculation of the interaction of a number of particles (Newtonian equations of motion) which represent the real system.
- Monte Carlo Methods (MC): Stochastic sampling of many-particle systems with many degrees of freedom. System magnitudes (e.g. total energy) are calculated as statistical averages.

By use of MD- and MC-methods "computer experiments" can be performed which allow to study the structure and the dynamic behavior of molecular systems. There are applications in various disciplines as different as fluid mechanics, biochem-

istry, solid state physics, chemical reaction kinetics and others.
Based on MD- and MC-methods, algorithms have been constructed which have high inherent parallelism so that they can be run efficiently on parallel machines. For instance, with the MD-method the kinetic motion of molecules in gases or liquids can be simulated over a period of time subdivided into time steps. Thus for a system of many particles which have known positions and velocities at time zero macroscopic quantities (e.g. energy) can be calculated. In order to obtain sufficiently accurate results, particle ensembles of up to 1,000,000 particles must be calculated. The most compute-intensive part of MD calculations is the interparticle force evaluation. On the other hand, stochastic computer simulation of many-particle systems with many degrees of freedom uses so-called MC-methods. The name is due to the use of random numbers for the calculation of configurational probabilities of the particle ensemble. With each computational step only one particle is moved (or its state is changed) so that the many-particle ensemble changes from one configuration (or state) to another.

3. Mapping problem structures onto multiprocessor structures

3.1 Parallel architectures

Current parallel architectures - built or only designed - can be subdivided in three main classes: Multiprocessors (MIMD/MSIMD), processor arrays (SIMD) and cellular automata. Table 1 resumes the main architectural features and applicability. As to the pipeline principle, it can be realized with SIMD and with MIMD systems, within the interconnection net as well as within the nodes.

Table 1: Classes of parallel architectures.

	Multiprocessors (MIMD/SIMD)	*Processor Arrays (SIMD)*	*Cellular Automata*
Performacve per node	high	small	very small
Memory per node	high	small	very small
Number of nodes	10-1,000	10-10,000	≈1,000,000
Application range	general prurpose	special class	special algorithms
Flexipility	high	low	very low
Efficiency	good to moderate	high for suitable applications	very high very special problems
Granularity	medium to large (10^3-10^9 operations)	small, constant (10^2-10^3 operations)	"atomic" (≈1 operation)

Applications in natural and engineering sciences can vary with regard to the following features:
- -Heterogeneity of the subtask structure (e.g. inner and boundary space of numerical grids, local refinement),
- -granularity of the computational structure,
- -ratio between local and global data exchange rate,
- -number of operations to be executed per data access.

Because of the large variation of computational features between different user problems parallel architectures must be sufficiently flexible in order to match the computational requirements. This implies the need for separate control in each node (MIMD). On the other hand, there is a strong advantage of SIMD machines over MIMD machines for special applications which match well the SIMD architecture, as for instance with low level image processing (preprocessing, segmentation, feature extraction).

3.2 Multiprocessor Architectures

On the premises of equal overall performance, a multiprocessor generally is not preferable to a monoprocessor; an exception may be represented by fault-tolerant requirements. On the contrary, multiprocessor systems can produce additional losses:
- Interprocessor communication overhead,
- load unbalance,
- algorithmic losses, e.g. due to forced parallelisation.

Therefore, the design of multiprocessors is mainly justified by the aim of high performance. During the last years a broad spectrum of multiprocessor systems has been designed. Architectural differences show up in the nodes and in the interconnection system. In the following we give a coarse classification scheme of multiprocessor systems with respect to the interconnection system:

(a) Message oriented multiprocessor systems with distributed local memory (e.g. SUPRENUM /5/, /6/, Cosmic Cube /7/).

(b) Shared memory systems:
- Global shared memory systems: there is a common memory, which can be accessed by all processors e.g. IBM/RP3 /8/, SIMPSON /9/.
- Distributed Shared Memory (DSM) systems: The total memory is partitioned for communication purposes. Each part can be accessed by a subset of processors (EGPA /10/, /11/, DIRMU /12/, /13/, PAX /14/, /15/, HAP /16/).

In the following we discuss the architectures of one example of either class:
SUPRENUM, a message-passing architecture and the Erlangen General Purpose Architecture (EGPA), a distributed shared memory architecture (DSM).

The goal of the SUPRENUM-project /5/, is a prototype system consisting of 256 nodes which is planned to be available by 1989. Thirteen German partner institutions are involved in the project. The contributions of the partners are sponsored by the German Federal Ministry of Research and Technology. The SUPRENUM architecture is depicted in Fig. 1. The CPU of the node is a Motorola MC 68020 microprocessor and a high performance co-processor whose essential part is a Weitek WT 2264/2265 vector unit. Each node will be equipped with a local private memory of 8 MB. The peak performance of each node is expected to be 8 MFLOPS, therefore the theoretical overall peak performance of the system will be more than 2 GFLOPS. Communication between two processes is realized via message passing. The message exchange can occur between nodes which are located within the same cluster (clusterbus 256 MB/s) or which belong to different clusters. Each cluster will consist of 16 computing nodes, a high performance disk, a diagnosis node, a communication node and the SUPRENUM bus link. For I/O, programming and system control a front-end computer system (3 MPR 2300, Krupp Atlas Elektronik) is connected to the 16-cluster high performance system via the SUPRENUM bus.

The concept of a high performance Erlangen General Purpose Architecture (EGPA) /3/ is based on experiences gained with the EGPA-pilot-pyramid /11/, /19/. and the DIRMU-25 system /17/. The hierarchy of the multiprocessor system has 3 levels (see Fig. 2):

A Working-processor level: Regular nearest-neighbor array of processor-memory modules (PMMs), neighboring PMMs being coupled by mutual access to their memories (distributed shared memory system, DSM).

B Administrative level: Operating system functions, global communication, I/O to mass storage. The interconnection system can be realized by DSM (as at level A), or by a global shared memory (e.g. as SIMPSON /9/) or by a bus system.

C Top PMM for overall control and connection to the host, the user and a communication net.

As the nodes can be equipped with powerful components (e.g. co-processor /3/) as in the case of SUPRENUM, the same overall peak performance of more than 2 GFLOPS is attainable with 256 worker PMMs. An important architectural feature of this DSM architecture is (in principle unlimited) expandability. Thus larger systems, as for instance consisting of 1024 worker PMMs with peak performance of more than 8 GFLOPS can be built. DSM communication is very effective due to its strong parallelism. The number of simultaneous data exchanges can be equal the number of PMMs (e.g. all processors access simultaneously the memories of their northern neighbors). Access to the memory of a neighboring PMM takes the same time as access to the "own" memory. As we have shown, compute-intensive numerical applications predominantly require local data exchange. This property allows for direct mapping of the subtask structure onto the DSM processor array whereas mapping onto SUPRENUM needs an interposed virtual nearest-neighbor machine in order to transform logically the cluster structure into a nearest-neighbor structure.

3.3 Mapping of numerical problems

In order to minimize typical losses occurring with multiprocessor systems, the problem structure and the multiprocessor structure must be matched.
Appropriate mapping of the programs and the data structure of a given user problem onto a multiprocessor system is an important task for the programmer. In order to be able to use some suitable mapping technique the programmer must have sufficient knowledge of the interconnection network of the multiprocessor which he is going to use.
As a prerequisite the user problem has to be partitioned in an appropriate manner. Partitioning at the task level mostly is unsuitable for large multiprocessor systems because the number of subtasks is small compared to the number of processors and because the computational work for one single subtask can vary considerably. In comparision with task partitioning, **data partitioning** is much more an appropriate parallelization procedure for computing with large multiprocessors. This is due to the large amount of data to be treated - often given in a regular structure - which allows partitioning down to nearly any granularity. With numerical simulation problems, 2- or 3-dimensional physical space is given as a grid. By an approximation procedure (relaxation methods) the values of physical magnitudes in each grid point are iteratively improved until a given convergence criterion is satisfied. This class of problems allow for natural partitioning (Fig. 3). Each processor handles its portion of the grid and needs only (boundary) values produced by neighboring processors. Partitioning can simply be done in a load balancing manner and only local synchronisation with neighbors is needed. Therefore, speedups near the number of processors can be achieved.
The simulation of many-particle systems, for instance in fluid mechanics, chemical reaction kinetics etc. has been achieved successfully by molecular dynamics (MD) and by Monte Carlo methods. In MD simulations the time evolution of many-particle systems is calculated by integrating numerically the classical equations of motion of the particles. For the calculation the total time lapse has to be subdivided in several thousand time steps. In a MD program the main computational effort is required for the force evaluation of all interacting pairs of N particles (often more than 95% of the CPU time) and the subsequent integration of the equations of motion, for each single time step. As the interaction between molecule i and j is independent of the interaction between molecule i and k, the calculation of the corresponding interaction force f_{ij} and f_{ik} can be executed in parallel. Partitioning of the particle ensemble can be done either by subdividing the particle ensemble in subgroups with an equal number of particles (Lagrange scheme) or by subdividing the physical space in subspaces which contain an equal number of particles (Euler scheme). The particle subgroups or the subspaces can be mapped directly onto the processors of a multiprocessor system. Both mapping schemes were efficiently implemented on nearest-neighbor multiprocessor systems, for instance on the PAX /18/.
Dependent on the many-particle model to be computed, stochastic methods - so called Monte Carlo (MC) methods - can prove more appropriate. For instance MC methods can be used to estimate mean values of macroscopic quantities. Calculated statistical averages are multi-dimensional integrals over all degrees of a large particle ensemble. The number of degrees of freedom is proportional to the number of points in the space-time continuum which must be approximated by a finite lattice. The resulting multidimensional integrals are estimated by stochastic sampling techniques by using only a small portion of all possible configurations of the ensemble.

4. Conclusions

Large numerical applications, for instance from areas as fluid mechanics, condensed matter physics, theoretical chemistry and others, demand high computational power and large memory. Such growing demands cannot be satisfied by conventional monoprocessors. Therefore highly parallel systems are required. Furthermore, the task structure of such applications can vary considerably. This needs enough flexibility of the computing system so that it can match different heterogeneous structures of the user problems. For such problem classes this can be achieved with multiprocessor systems whose nodes have separate control. The considered applications have strong inherent locality since data exchange predominantly occurs between "neighboring" computational subregions. This feature of the user problems favors nearest-neighbor multiprocessor architectures which have strong local communication facilities. Distributed shared memory systems turn out to be efficient especially as they can be designed with many parallel processor-memory "communication channels" represented by shared memories.

5. References

/1/ Händler, W.; Bode, A.; Fritsch, G.; Henning, W.; Volkert, J.: A tightly coupled and hierarchical multiprocessor architecture. Comp. Phys. Comm. 37 (1985), 87-93. North Holland Amsterdam.

/2/ Henning, W.; Volkert, J.: Programming EGPA systems. Proc. 5th Int. Conf. Distributed Computing Systems, Denver/Col., May 13-17, 1985, 552-559.

/3/ Bode, A.; Fritsch, G.; Händler, W.; Hofmann, F.; Volkert, J.: Multi-grid oriented computer architecture. Proc. 1985 Int. Conf. Parallel Processing, St. Charles, 81-95. IEEE Comp. Soc. 1985.

/4/ Volkert, J.; Henning, W.: Multigrid algorithms implemented on EGPA multiprocessor. Proc. 1985 Int. Conf. Parallel Processing, 799-805, IEEE Comp. Soc. Press 1985.

/5/ Trottenberg, U.: The SUPRENUM Projekct: Idea and Current State. SPEEDUP, Vol. 2, No. 1, 1988, 20-24. Universität Bern/Switzerland.

/6/ Behr, P.M.; Giloi, W.K.; Mühlenbein, H.: SUPRENUM: The German Supercomputer architecture - rationale and concepts. Proc. 1986 Int. Conf. Parallel Processing, Aug. 19-22, 1986, 567-575. IEEE Comp. Soc. Press 1986.

/7/ Seitz, C.L.: The cosmic cube. CACM Vol. 28, 22-33 (1985).

/8/ Pfister, G.F.; et al.: The IBM Research Parallel Processor Prototype (RP3). Proc. 1985, Int. Conf. Parallel Processing; IEEE Comp. Soc. Press, Washington D.C. (1985).

/9/ Regenspurg, G.: Hochleistungsrechner - Architekturprinzipien, Kap. 3.6, Mc Graw-Hill Book Comp. GmbH Hamburg (1987).

/10/ Händler, W.; Hofmann, F.; Schneider, H.J.: A General Purpose Array with a Broad Spectrum of Applications. In: Händler, W.: Computer Architecture, Informatik Fachberichte, Springer Verlag Berlin Heidelberg New York, 4, 311-35 (1976).

/11/ Händler, W.; Herzog, U.; Hofmann, F.; Schneider, H.J.: Multiprozessoren für breite Anwendungsgebiete: Erlangen General Purpose Array. GI/NTG-Fachtagung "Architektur und Anwendungsgebiete: Erlangen General Purpose Array. GI/NTG-Fachtagung "Architektur und Betrieb von Rechensystemen", Informatik-Fachberichte, Springer Verlag Berlin Heidelberg New York, 78, 195-208 (1984).

/12/ Händler, W.; Rohrer, H.: Thoughts on a Computer Construction Kit. Elektronische Rechenanlagen 22, 1, 3-13; 1980.

/13/ Händler, W.; Maehle, E.; Wirl, K.: DIRMU Multiprocessor Configurations, Proc. 1985 Int. Conf. on Parallel Processing, St. Charles 1985, 652-656. IEEE Comp. Soc. 1985.

/14/ Hoshino, T., et al.: Highly parallel processor array PAX for wide scientific applications. Proc. 1983 Int. Conf. Parallel Processing, 95-105. IEEE Comp. Soc. Press (1983).

/15/ Hoshino, T.: An invitation to the world of PAX. Computer, May 1986, 68-79.

/16/ Momoi, Sh.; Shimada, Sh.; Kobayashi, M.; Ishikawa, T.: Hierarchical array processor system (HAP). CONPAR 86, Aachen/F.R.Germany, Sept. 17-19 1986.

/17/ Maehle, E. and Wirl, K.: Parallel programs for numerical and signal processing on the Multiprocessor System DIRMU 25; in: Highly Parallel Computers (Ed.: G.L. Reijns, M.H. Barton), Elsevier Science Pub., IFIP 1987.

/18/ Hoshino, T.; Takenouchi, K.: Processing of the molecular dynamics model by the parallel computer PAX. Comput-er Phys. Comm. 31, 287-296 (1984).

/19/ Händler, W.; Fritsch, G.; Volkert, J.: Applications implemented on the Erlangen General Purpose Array. Proc. Parcella 84. Math. Forschung, Bd. 25. Akademie Verlag Berlin 1985.

/20/ Pfister, G.F.; Norton, V.A.: "Hot Spot" Contention and Combining in Multistage Interconnection Networks. IEEE Trans. Comp., Vol. C-34, 10, pp. 934-948; (1985).

/21/ Hackbusch, W.: Frequency Decomposition Method. 4. GAMM Workshop on Robust Multigrid Methods, Notes on Fluid Mechanics, Vieweg (1988).

/22/ Graves, R.: Numerical Aerodynamic Simulation-Creating the Digital Wind Tunnel. International Conference on Supercomputers, pp. 181-197,Paris (1984).

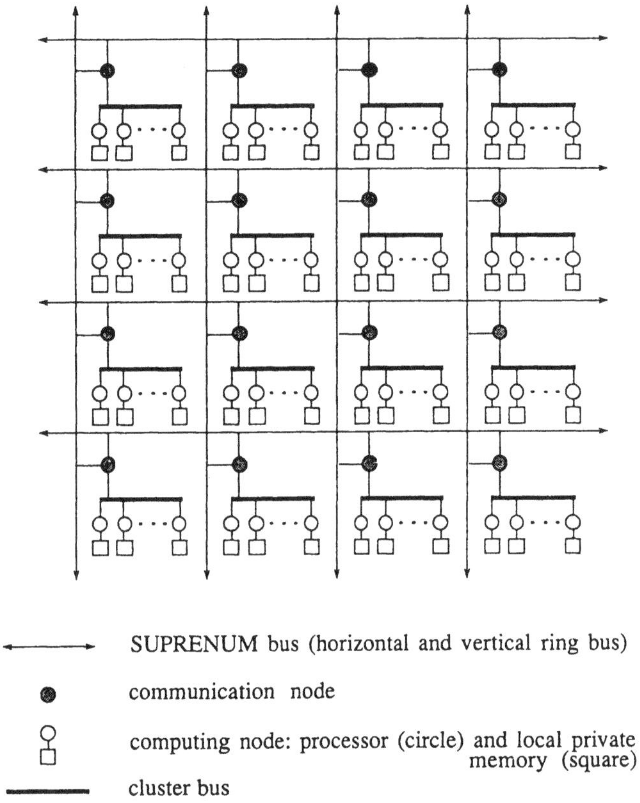

Fig. 1: SUPRENUM Prototype Architecture:
4x4 Clusters connected by 4 horizontal and 4 vertical ring buses. Each cluster consists of 16 computing nodes (8 MFLOPS each), one disk (1 GB), a diagnosis node and a communication node.

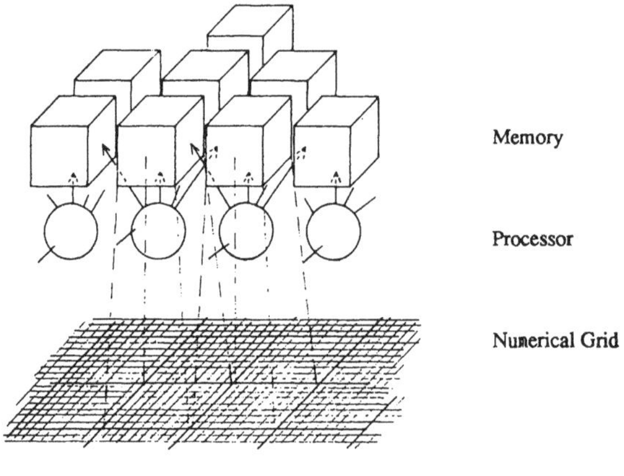

Fig. 3: Mapping a numerical grid onto a DSM processor-memory array

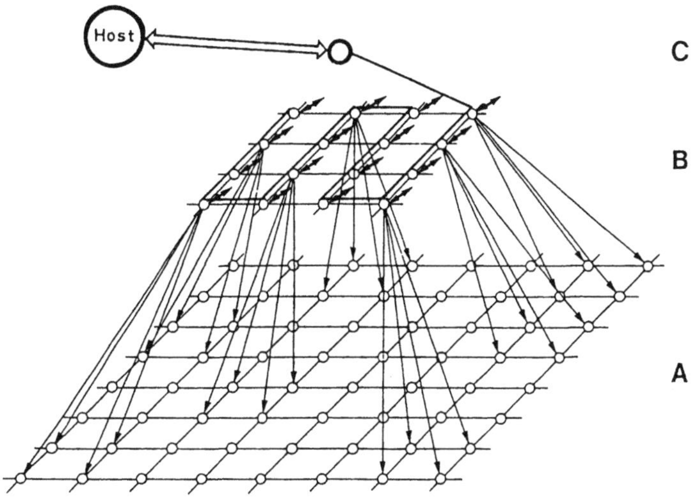

O Processor-Memory-Module (PMM)

——— symmetric multiport memory connection between neighboring PMMs

———→ asymmetric multiport memory connection between PMMs of different hierarchical levels

▬▬▬ communication bus with broadcasting ability

←→ I/O communication channel

Fig. 2: Erlangen General Purpose Architecture (EGPA):
Neighboring processor-memory-modules (PMMs) are tightly coupled through multiport memories (one multiport in each PMM).

Level A: Worker PMMs (256 or 1024 PMMs with theoretical overall peak performance of 2 or 8 GFLOPS resp.).
Level B: Operating system functions, I/0 to mass storage.
Level C: Top PMM for overall control and connection to host.

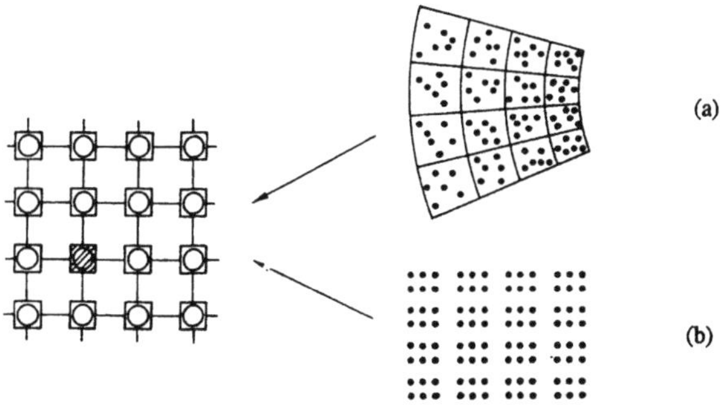

Fig. 4: Mapping a many-particle problem onto a DSM processor-memory array.
Two partitioning schemes:
(a) Subdividing physical space in subspaces with equal number of particles
(b) Subdividing the particle ensemble in equal subgroups.

SYSTOLIC ARRAY FOR EIGENVALUE OF JACOBI MATRIX

M. A. Frumkin *) **)

1.Introduction. Programs for solving eigenvalue problem for symmetric tridiagonal and Jacobi matrices are included in LINPACK and EISPACK [4,1] and occupy an important place in mathematical software. Several systolic arrays were proposed for solving eigenvalue problem for dense and band matrices [2,3]. The general feature of known algorithms for eigenvalues is linear or quadratic (on the order of the matrix) depth. Thus a combination of Newton method and QR-algorithm (program RATQR from LINPACK) finds eigenvalues in sequential order and performs O(log log M/e) iterations costing O(n) that results in total depth $O(n^2 \log \log M/e)$, where M is the spectral radius of the matrix, e is the precision of the eigenvalue computation. A systolic array for realising bisection algorithm (program BISECT from LINPACK) with depth is O(n log M/e) is proposed in [2].

We develop a systolic array realizing a new fast parallel algorithm for eigenvalue problem of Jacobi matrix. The depth of the algorithm is $O(\log^3 n \log M/e)$ and its time complexity is $O(n \log^3 n \log M/e)$. The systolic array has O(n) cells and execution time O(n log n log M/e). Using shuffle exchange network for sorting and a fast algorithm for computation values of the characteristic polynomial of tridiagonal matrix in several points execution time may be reduced to $O(\log^3 n \log M/e)$.

2. Fast parallel algorithms. Fast parallel algorithm for eigenvalue is based on 1. Recursive relation for characteristic polvnomial of Jacobi matrix, 2. Method of localization of

*)Inst. of Problems of Cybernetics of Acad. of Sci. of the USSR
**)The author is obliged to S.P. Tarasov for help in translation of the text

eigenvalues of Jacobi matrix by eigenvalues of its submatrices and 3. Fast parallel algorithm for computation of characteristic polynomial of tridiagonal matrix values in several points.

Let A(t)=J-tI, where J is Jacobi matrix of order n.

$$J = \begin{vmatrix} a_1 & b_1 & & & \\ c_2 & a_2 & b_2 & & \\ & & \ddots & & \\ & & c_{n-1} & a_{n-1} & b_{n-1} \\ & & & c_n & a_n \end{vmatrix} \qquad \gamma_i = b_i * c_{i+1} > 0$$

B_i and C_j are the upper left and the lower right minors of A of the orders i and j correspondingly. Then the recursive relation is as follows.

$$\det A = \det \begin{vmatrix} B_k & \gamma_k B_{k-1} \\ C_{n-k-1} & C_{n-k} \end{vmatrix}$$

The relation implies that eigenvalues of J (i.e. the roots of det A) are localized in consecutive intervals into which the real axis is partitioned by the roots of the polynomials B_k, $B_{k-1}, C_{n-k-1}; C_{n-k}$. More accurate approximations of the eigenvalues may be performed by the following algorithm.

Algorithm REF($\alpha_0, \alpha_\infty, B_k, B_{k-1}, C_{n-k-1}, C_{n-k}$, A, e).

Input. Elements of A, eigenvalues of $B_k, B_{k-1}, C_{n-k-1}, C_{n-k}$.

Output. Approximations with error e of eigenvalues of A.

Step 1. Sort eigenvalues of $B_k, B_{k-1}, C_{n-k-1}, C_{n-k}$ into sequence $\alpha_0 < \alpha_1 \le \ldots < \alpha_{2(n+k-1)} \le \alpha_{2(n+k)-1} < \alpha_\infty$.

Step 2. par i=0 to n-1 do steps 3-6.

Step 3. while $\alpha_{2i+1} - \alpha_{2i} \ge e$ do steps 4-6.

Step 4. set $\beta_i = (\alpha_{2i} + \alpha_{2i+1})/2$.

Step 5. set $z_i = A(\beta_i)$.

Step 6. if i mod 2=0 then (if $z_i>0$ then $\alpha_{2i}=\beta_i$ else $\alpha_{2i+1}=\beta_i$)

if i mod 2=1 then (if $z_i>0$ then $\alpha_{2i+1}=\beta_i$ else $\alpha_{2i}=\beta_i$)

The time complexity of REF is $O(n^2 \log M/e)$ due to $n \log M/e$ executions of Step 5 costing $O(n)$ and depth of REF is $O(c \log M/e)$. These values may be reduced to $O(n \log^3 n \log M/e)$ and $O(\log^3 n \log M/e)$ correspondingly if we use the following fast parallel algorithm for evaluating characteristic polynomial of tridiagonal matrix in several points.

Let
$$d_k(t) = (a_k - t)*d_{k-1}(t) - \gamma_k * d_{k-2}(t), \quad k=2,\dots,n,$$
$$d_1 = a_1 - t, \quad d_0 = 1,$$

be linear recurrency for characteristic polynomial of J. The recurrency may be rewritten in the matrix form

$$\begin{vmatrix} d_n(t) \\ d_{n-1}(t) \end{vmatrix} = \begin{vmatrix} a_n - t & -\gamma_n \\ 1 & 0 \end{vmatrix} \begin{vmatrix} d_{n-1}(t) \\ d_{n-2}(t) \end{vmatrix} = \dots = \prod_{i=n}^{1} Q_i(t) \begin{vmatrix} a_1 - t \\ 1 \end{vmatrix}$$

We shall consider a bit more general problem of fast computation of entries of matrix products

$$\prod_{i=n}^{1} Q_i(t_j), \quad j=1,\dots,m$$

where entries of 2*2 matrices $Q_i(t)$ are linear functions.

Entries of the product of s such matrices are polynomials of degree equal or less than s and are unique defined by the values in s different points, for example, in roots of unity $w_i = \exp(2\pi\sqrt{-1}\, i/s)$.

Let f be a vector of the polynomial values $f(t)$ in points t_j, $j=1,\dots,m$, e be the vector of the polynomial values in the roots of unity, $V(t_1,\dots,t_m)$ be Vandermonde matrix built on points $t_1,\dots,t_m$, $F_s=V(w_0,\dots\dots,w_{s-1})$ be the matrix of s-point Fourier transform. Then $$f = V(t_1,\dots,t_m)\, F_s\, e \qquad (**)$$

and using Fast Fourier Transform and fast algorithm for multiplication Vandermonde matrix by a veotor one can may compute f from e in time $O(\, m \log^2 n)$ $(m \geq n)$.

Let

$$Q^i_j(t) = Q_{(j-1)*2^i}(t)\cdot\ldots\cdot Q_{j*2^i-1}(t)\ ,\ i=1,\ldots,l;\ j=1,\ldots,2^{l-i}.$$

Entries of matrices $Q_j{}^i(t)$ polynomials of degree 2^i or less so they can be evaluated in roots of unity of degree 2^i and then using the relation (**) its values can be computed in the other roots of degree 2^{i+1}. Using the last values one can directly evaluate entries of matrix $Q^{i+1}{}_j(t) = Q^i{}_{2j}(t)*Q^i{}_{2j+1}(t)$ in the roots. The algorithm is as follows.

for i=1 to l do

 par j=1 to 2^{l-1} do

  begin par k=1 to 2^{l-i} do

   par p,q=0 to 1

$$Q^i_j[p,q](w_{k,i}) = Q^{i-1}_{2j-1}[p,0](w_{k,i})*Q^{i-1}_{2j-1}[0,q](w_{k,i}) + Q^{i-1}_{2j-1}[p,1](w_{k,i})*Q^{i-1}_{2j-1}[1,q](w_{k,i});$$

$$(Q^i_j[p,q](w_{1+2^i,i+1}),\ldots,Q^i_j[p,q](w_{2^{i+1}-1,i+1}))^t =$$

$$= \bar{F}_{2^i} * F^{-1}_{2^i}\ (Q^i_j[p,q](w_{0,i}),\ldots,Q^i_j[p,q](w_{2^i-1,i}))^t;$$

 end

where $w_{k,i} = \exp(2\pi\sqrt{-1}\,k/2^i)$, $F_s = V(w_{s,2s},\ldots,w_{2s-1,2s})$.

Let A[i], i =1,...,4 be the minors of A defined in the figure1.

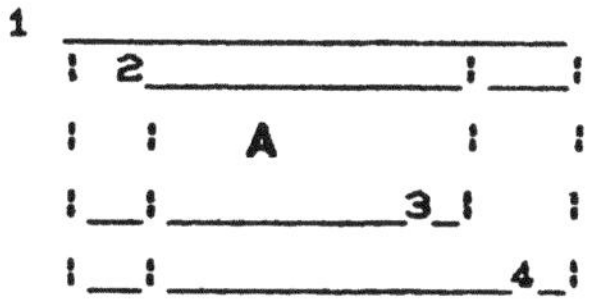

A[1] - (1,3), A[3] - (2,3),
A[2] - (1,4), A[4] - (2,4)

Fig. 1.

Let B[i] and C[i] (similar to A[i]) be te minors of upper left and lower right submatrices B and C of A of order k and n-k correspondingly. It is not hard to see that

$$A[1] = \det \begin{vmatrix} B[2] & \gamma_k & B[1] \\ C[3] & & C[1] \end{vmatrix} \qquad A[2] = \det \begin{vmatrix} B[2] & \gamma_k & B[1] \\ C[4] & & C[2] \end{vmatrix}$$

$$A[3] = \det \begin{vmatrix} B[4] & \gamma_k & B[3] \\ C[3] & & C[1] \end{vmatrix} \qquad A[4] = \det \begin{vmatrix} B[4] & \gamma_k & B[3] \\ C[4] & & C[2] \end{vmatrix} \qquad (*)$$

Let A_j^i be the submatrix of order 2^i of A arranged in rows and columns with indices $j*2^i+1,\dots,(j+1)*2^i$. Then the following algorithm computes eigenvalues of matrix J of order $n=2^l$ (α_0 and α_∞ are apriory bounds of the spectrum).

Algorithm EIGVAL(A,e).

Step 1. for i=1 to l do steps 2-3.

Step 2. par j=0 to $2^{(l-i)}-1$ do step 3.

Step 3. set $k=j*2^i$;

REF($\alpha_0,\alpha_\infty,A_{2*j}^{i-1}[2],A_{2*j+1}^{i-1}[1],A_{2*j}^{i-1}[1],A_{2*j+1}^{i-1}[3],A_j^i[1],e$);

REF($\alpha_0,\alpha_\infty,A_{2*j}^{i-1}[2],A_{2*j+1}^{i-1}[4],A_{2*j}^{i-1}[1],A_{2*j+1}^{i-1}[2],A_j^i[2],e$);

REF($\alpha_0,\alpha_\infty,A_{2*j}^{i-1}[4],A_{2*j+1}^{i-1}[3],A_{2*j}^{i-1}[3],A_{2*j+1}^{i-1}[1],A_j^i[3],e$);

REF($\alpha_0,\alpha_\infty,A_{2*j}^{i-1}[4],A_{2*j+1}^{i-1}[4],A_{2*j}^{i-1}[3],A_{2*j+1}^{i-1}[2],A_j^i[4],e$);

3. <u>A systolic programming language</u>. We shall use a systolic programming language for description of operation of systolic arrays. As far as systolic array carries out computations in time and space systolic algorithm has two special variables t for time and s for space. Time t is an integer variable and space s is a

variable with set S of vertices of graph $G=(S,A)$ of systolic array as domain. Time and space are attached to every data element of systolic algorithm. For variable $X[t,s]$ values of t and s point out when and where X must be computed (or input). Assignment statement of systolic algorithm has the following form

$$X[t,s] = F(x_1[t-1,v_1(s)],\ldots,x_k[t-1,v_k(s)]);$$

where F is a function supported by the cell s of systolic array, $X,x_1,\ldots,x_k$ are variables of systolic algorithm, $v_1(s) \in S$ are neighbours of s. Condition statement of systolic algorithm is as follows

if B[t,s] then OP[t,s];

where B[t,s] is a Boolean expression computed in cell s in time t and OP[t,s] is an assignment statement of systolic algorithm.

Systolic algorithm consists of feeding of initial values, keeping boundary conditions and operation phases. If the systolic array does not execute exchanges with external devices during operation phase then keeping boundary conditions phase may be omitted. General form of systolic algorithm is as follows.

```
Initial values.
  par s∈ S do
       X[O,s] = A[s];
Boundary conditions.
       for t=1 to T do
        par s∈∂ S do
           X[t,s]=B[t-1,v(s)];
Operation.
      for t=1 to T do
        par s∈ S\∂ S do
          par i=1 to l do
            C_i[t,s];
```

Here A and B are input arrays, ∂ S is the set of input vertices of the graph of the systolic array, {(v(s)} is the set of neighbours of s, $C_i[t,s]$ i=1,...,l are conditional statement of systolic algorithm which are supported by the cell s.

4. <u>The systolic array</u>. Using the systolic programming language we shall describe a systolic array for eigenvalues computation. The array consists of two interactive subarrays for merging four sequences and for evaluation of characteristic polynomial in sequence of points.

The first array is a modification of H.T. Kung systolic array for odd even sorting and it executes step 1 of algorithm REF. Initial values.

par s=1 to k do

begin $x_s^0=\alpha_s^1$; $x_{k+s}^0=\alpha_s^2$; $y_s^0=\alpha_s^3$; $y_{k+s}^0=\alpha_s^4$; end

Operation.

for t=1 to 2*k do

par s=1 to 2*k do

if t(mod 2)=0 then

begin $x_s^t= \min(x_s^{t-1},y_s^{t-1})$; $y_s^t= \max(x_s^{t-1},y_s^{t-1})$; end

else

begin $x_s^t= \max(x_s^{t-1},y_{s-1}^{t-1})$; $y_s^t= \min(x_{s+1}^{t-1},y_s^{t-1})$; end

The structure of the array and its cell are shown in figures 2 and 3.

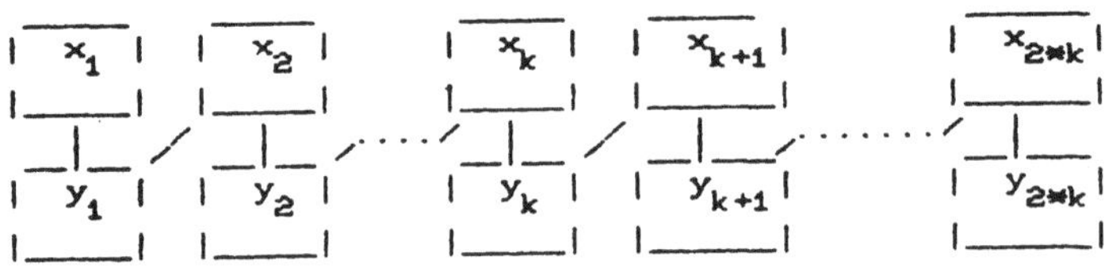

Fig. 2. Systolic array for execution of the step 1 of the algorithm REF.

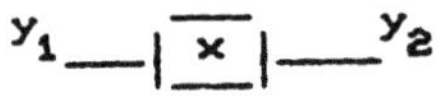

if t mod 2 = 1 then $x' = \min(x, y_2)$ else $x' = \max(x, y_1)$

Fig. 3. Cell 1

Now using the systolic programming language we describe a systolic array for evaluation of characteristic polynomial of a tridiagonal matrix in points $\beta_1, \ldots, \beta_k$.

Initial values.

par s=1 to k do

begin $G_s^0 = \gamma_s$; $A_s^0 = a_s$; end;

Boundary conditions.

for t=1 to k do

begin $z_1^t = 0$; $w_1^t = 1$; $B_1^t = \beta_t$; end

Operation.

for t=1 to 2*k do

par s=1 to k do

begin $w_s^t = (A_s^{t-1} - B_{s-1}^{t-1}) * w_{s-1}^{t-1} - G_s^{t-1} * z_{s-1}^{t-1}$;

$z_s^t = w_{s-1}^{t-1}$; $B_s^t = B_{s-1}^{t-1}$; $A_s^t = A_s^{t-1}$; $G_s^t = G_s^{t-1}$; end

Cell of the array is shown in the figure 4.

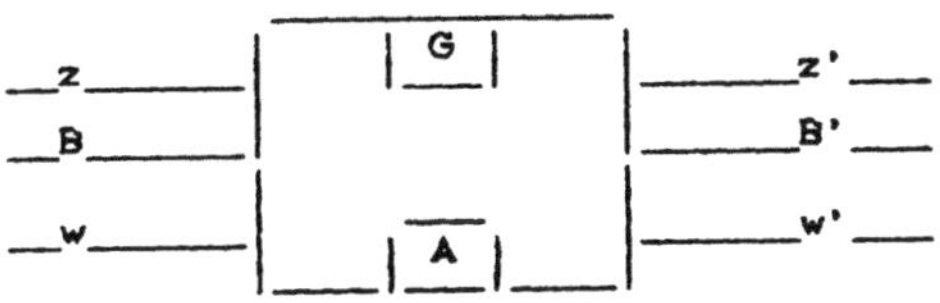

$z' = w$: $B' = B$; $w' = (A - B) * w - G * z$

Fig. 4. Cell 2

The systolic array shown in the Fig. 5. is attached with systolic memory transmitted contents of its cells without changing from right to left. After completion the operation phase cells of systolic memory will contain values of characteristic polynomial of J in points $\beta_1, \ldots, \beta_k$.

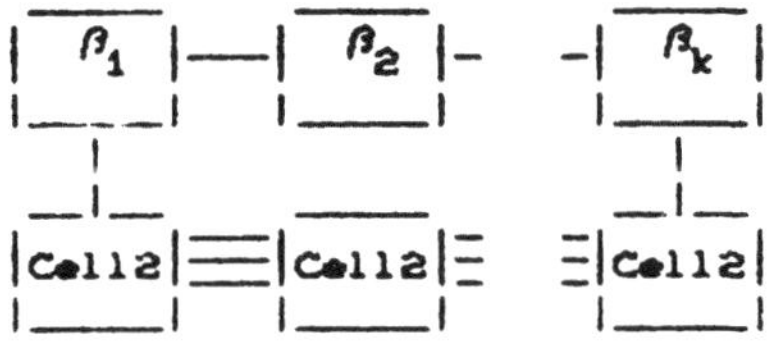

Fig. 5. Systolic array for computing values of characteristic polynomial.

A systolic array for execution of the algorithm REF may be constructed by simple transformation of preceding array. We must only attach additional systolic memory to values of characteristic polynomial computed in medians of given intervals and additional systolic memory for boundaries of the intervals that include eigenvalues. Boundaries are circulate in the systolic memory and are updated in the first cell of the array which keeps the following boundary condition.

Boundary condition.

for $t=1$ **to** $k*\log M/e$ **do**

begin $z_1^t=0$; $w_1^t=1$; $B_1^t=(\alpha_t+\bar{\alpha}_t)/2$;

  if $\beta_t>0$ **then**

    if $t \bmod 2 = 0$ **then**

      begin $\gamma_2^t=\alpha_{t-1}$; $\bar{\gamma}_2^t=(\alpha_{t-1}+\bar{\alpha}_{t-1})/2$ **end**

    else **begin** $\gamma_2^t=(\alpha_{t-1}+\bar{\alpha}_{t-1})/2$; $\bar{\gamma}_2^t=\alpha_{t-1}$ **end**

  else

    if $t \bmod 2 = 0$ **then**

      begin $\bar{\gamma}_2^t=\alpha_{t-1}$; $\gamma_2^t=(\alpha_{t-1}+\bar{\alpha}_{t-1})/2$ **end**

    else **begin** $\bar{\gamma}_2^t=(\alpha_{t-1}+\bar{\alpha}_{t-1})/2$; $\gamma_2^t=\alpha_{t-1}$ **end**

end

The structure of the array is shown in figure 6.

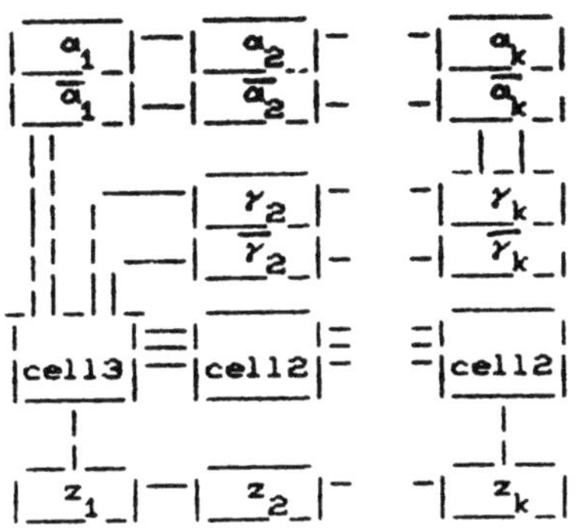

Figure 6. Systolic array REF for computing approximations of Jacobi matrix

In order to construct a systolic array for algorithm EIGVAL we may connect four copies of arrays of Fig. 6. in vertical direction into a block and to connect several blocks in horizontal direction. After this we may add special tags that circulate in the array for marriage blocks after every $2^i*\log M/e$ iterations. The final structure of array and its cross section are shown in Fig. 7.

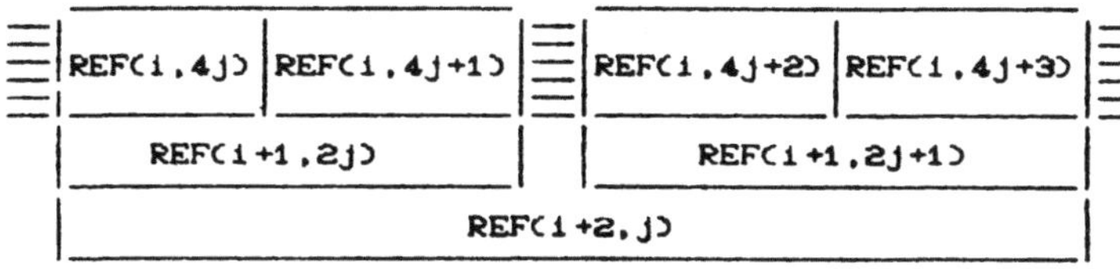

Marriage of blocks

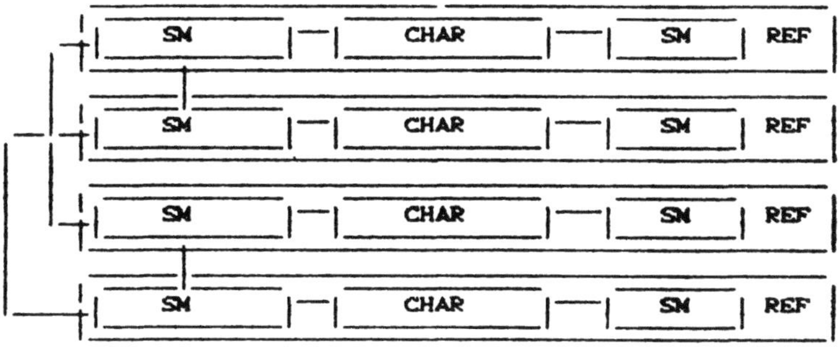

Cross section of a block

Figure 7. Structure of systolic array for eigenvalue problem of Jacobi matrix

On the Fig. 7 REF is the systolic array of Fig. 6, SM is a systolic memory, CHAR is a systolic array for computing values of characteristic polynomial. The systolic array had been modeled by special tools for modelling using Turbo Pascal.

Further transformation of the array may be done to carry out its integration with perfect shuffle for merge and for Fast Fourier Transformation. Such modification of the array will decrease execution time to $O(\log^3 n \log M/e)$.

REFERENCES

1. Garbow B.S., Boyle J.M., Dongarra J.J., Moler C.B. Matrix eigensystem routines - EISPACK guide extension. LNCS, v. 51, 1977.

2. Schreiber R. Systolic arrays for eigenvalues. LNM, v. 1005, 1983, pp. 284-296.

3. Scott D.S., Heath M.T., Ward R.C. Parallel block Jacobi eigenvalue algorithms for using systolic arrays. Lin. Alg. and Appl., v. 77, 1986, pp. 345-356.

4. Wilkinson J.H., Reinsch C. Handbook for automatic computation. Linear Algebra. Heidelberg, Springer-Verlag, 1971.

5. Frumkin M.A. Systolic arrays and VLSI computation. Information material of Scientific Council on Cybernetics, No. 5, M., 1987 (in Russian).

(paper is retyped from the original manuscript of the author partially)

A TRANSITIVE CLOSURE ALGORITHM
FOR A 16-STATE CELLPROCESSOR

Endre Katona[1)]

__Abstract__. Cellprocessors can be considered as microprogrammed Boolean array machines, thus they can process Boolean matrices with very high efficiency. It will be shown that transitive closure of a relation, represented by an nxn Boolean matrix, can be computed in 5n steps using an (n+1)xn array of 16-state cells. If there are several relations, the transitive closure of which should be computed, then a continuous pipeline processing is possible where the processing cost of one matrix is only n steps. The transitive closure algorithm can be partitioned so that arbitrary size relations can be handled with a fixed size cellular array.

1. CELLPROCESSOR ARCHITECTURE

A 16-state cellprocessor hardware has been described in [6], here we give only a simplified "cellular automata model" of it.

Consider a pxq array of orthogonally connected cells. Each cell contains a 4-bit state register S and executes a transition function

$$f: (S, S_n, S_e, S_s, S_w) \mapsto S'$$

in each time-step. (Indices n, e, s, w mean the north, east, south, west neighboring cells, respectively.) Different cells may work with different transition functions, and from step to step different transition functions can be applied for each cell. (There are some limitations concerning this inhomogeneity of transition functions, arising from the microprogramming technique of the cellprocessor, but here we do not go into details.)

Input-output processes are performed by an I/O processor transmitting data between a parallel memory and the border of the cellular array. To give a simplified model for I/O, we suppose input buffer cells around the array (see I-s in Fig.1) that do not execute transition functions, but they can be loaded by the I/O processor in each step.

1) Research Group on Automata Theory
Hungarian Academy of Sciences
H-6720 Szeged, Somogyi u. 7, Hungary

For output we assume that the I/O processor can read out the state of each border cell (see 0-s in Fig.1).

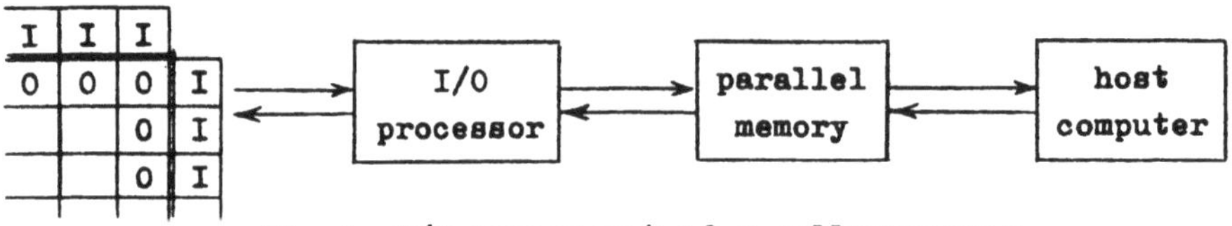

Fig.1. I/O management of a cellprocessor.

2. THE TRANSITIVE CLOSURE PROBLEM

Let A be an nxn Boolean matrix representing a relation $R_A \subset \{r_1,\ldots,r_n\} x \{r_1,\ldots,r_n\}$. Suppose that $a_{i,i}=1$ for any $i=1,\ldots,n$. Matrix A', representing the transitive closure of R_A, can be computed through a sequence of matrices $A=A^{(0)}, A^{(1)},\ldots,A^{(n)}=A'$ where

$$a_{i,j}^{(k)} = a_{i,j}^{(k-1)} \vee (a_{i,k}^{(k-1)} \wedge a_{k,j}^{(k-1)}) \ . \qquad (1)$$

(This algorithm is discussed for instance in [1].) It can be seen that during the transformation $A^{(k-1)} \rightarrow A^{(k)}$ the k-th row and k-th column of the matrix does not change.

In the next section we give a cellular algorithm - originally presented in [3] - based on the computation strategy above. Our solution requires a full time 5n and a pipeline processing time n (see Section 5). Note that the systolic array of [5] applies a similar method for the algebraic path problem with a full time 5n and pipeline processing time 2n. The systolic array of [2] computes transitive closure in a very different way during 6n steps and without pipeline processing possibility.

3. THE CELLULAR SOLUTION

Our cellular algorithm is illustrated in Figures 2,3,4,5. Each square 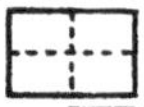 represents the 4 state bits of a cell identified by the numbers 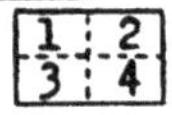

. The cellular algorithm needs a 2n x n array (Fig.2) where only (n+1) x n cells are utilized (Fig.3). Input matrix A is written step by step into the right side input buffer cells, and the result A' leaves the array at the left side border cells.

Rightmost column of the array performs the transformation $A^{(0)} \rightarrow A^{(1)}$ so that first row is written after the last one and first column after the last one (Fig.5). Transition function f_1 (Fig.4) puts the elements of the first row of A into the 4th state bit where they are shifted

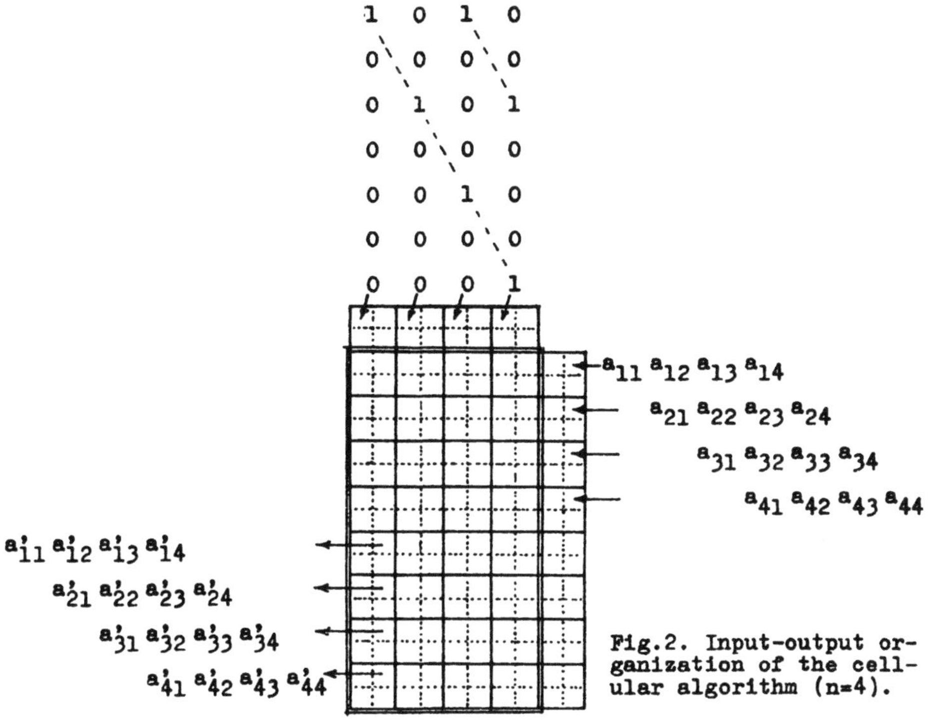

Fig.2. Input-output organization of the cellular algorithm (n=4).

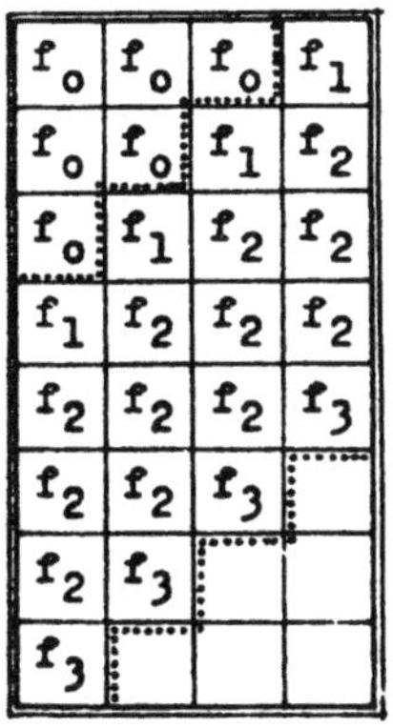

Fig.3. Arrangement of transition functions in the cellular array. Empty cells are not utilized and cells with f_o perform only shift function. (n=4)

down by function f_2, and function f_3 rewrites them into the 2nd state bit (Fig.4). Elements of the first column of A are stored into the 3rd bits of cells. This process is controlled by special signals coming from above (Fig.2) and moving down on the 1st state bits. Each cell gets a control signal 1 exactly when the first column of A is processed. After the last column of A, the stored elements are rewritten into the 2nd bits of cells, this process is controlled by a second wave of signals (Fig.2). In the case of a control signal 0, function f_2 performs the computation (1).

Each column of the array performs a transformation shown in Fig.5,

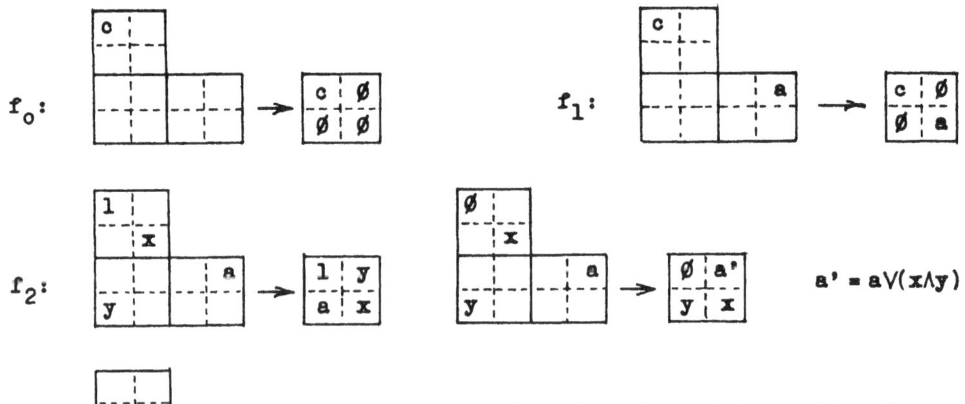

Fig.4. Definition of transition functions. Only upper and right-hand neighboring cell are displayed (the other two neighbors are indifferent).

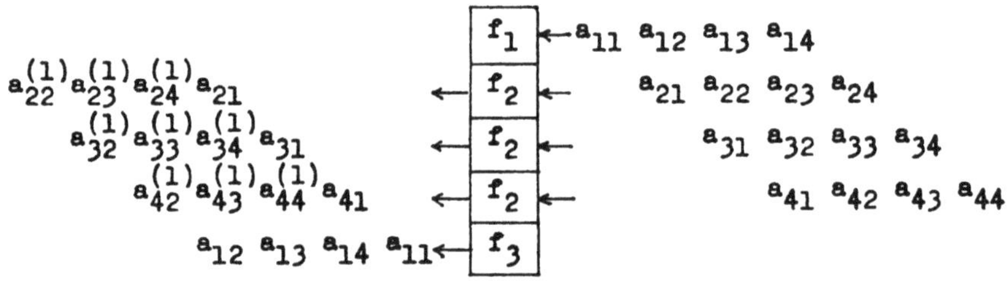

Fig.5. Transformation performed by the rightmost column of the array (n=4).

therefore the whole array computes the transitive closure of the input matrix.

Each column of the array produces 3 steps delay, therefore a'_{11} appears after 3n steps at the left border. Further 2n steps are needed to obtain the whole result, that is, total computation time is 5n steps.

4. IMPLEMENTATION TRICKS

(i) It is clear that only $(n+1)\times n$ cells are working effectively in the $2n\times n$ array (see cells with transition functions f_1, f_2, f_3 in Fig. 3). To eliminate this redundancy, we can use the switching network of the cellprocessor architecture [6] which makes it possible to connect blocks of 8x8 cells according to a nearly arbitrary topology. Using this ability, our algorithm needs only $(n+z)\times n$ cells where $8\leq z<16$.

(ii) Transition function f_0 can be replaced by f_1, hereby the inhomogeneity of the array decreases.

(iii) Control signals can be generated inside the cellular array by the help of special transition functions. In this case no input is needed at the upper border of the array.

5. PIPELINE PROCESSING

The cellular array described previously has the nice property that an arbitrary number of matrices can be processed in a continuous pipeline manner (Fig.6). Transition function f_2 ensures the change between two consecutive matrices if the corresponding stream of control signals is ensured. For m matrices a total computation time (m+4)n is needed, that is, processing of one matrix costs only n steps!

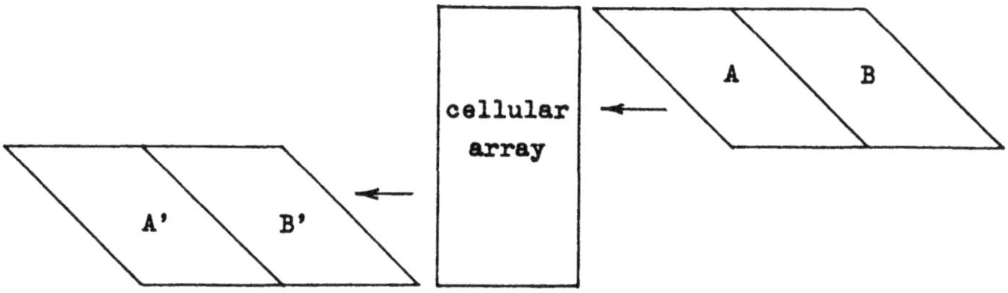

Fig.6. Pipeline processing scheme.

6. PARTITIONING

Suppose that there is an nxn array of cells and an NxN matrix, with $N>n$, the transitive closure of which should be computed. In this case the general partitioning method, discussed in [4], can be applied.

Consider a virtual cellular array of size 2N x N and divide it into partitions of size n x n (Fig.7). Cells of the virtual array communicate only from right to left and from up to down, therefore partitions can be computed in the sequence of numbers of Fig.7, with an n x n array, as follows. First, partition 1 is computed with the input submatrix A_1 and the partial results, leaving the n x n array on the left-hand and lower border, are stored into the parallel memory (see Fig.1). After that, partition 2 is computed with the input submatrix A_2 and with an additional input from above, stored previously into the parallel memory, etc.

If two consecutive partitions have different transition function arrangement, then the cellular array may need some reconfiguration between the computation of these partitions. Applying a microprogrammable cellprocessor, this reconfiguration needs no time overhead.

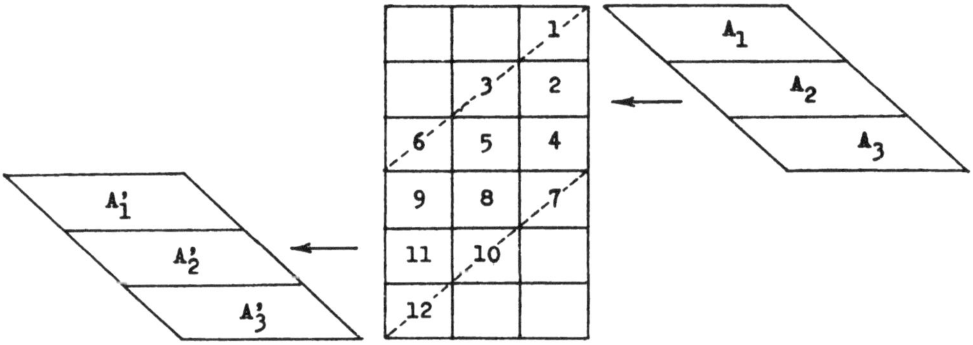

Fig.7. Partitioning of a 2N x N virtual array into n x n blocks (N=3n).

REFERENCES

[1] Aho, A., Hopcroft, J.E. and Ullman, J.D.: The design and analysis of computer algorithms. Addison-Wesley, Reading, Massachusetts, 1975.

[2] Guibas, L.J., Kung, H.T. and Thompson, C.D.: Direct VLSI implementation of combinatorial algorithms. Proc. Caltech Conf. on VLSI, California Inst. Technology, Pasadema 1979, 509-525.

[3] Katona, E.: Examples of cellular algorithms for a 16-state cell-processor architecture. Chapter of a study made on the commission of the Hungarian Government Program on Microelectronics, 1984, in Hungarian.

[4] Katona, E.: A general partitioning method for cellular algorithms. Proc. of the 4th Cellular Meeting, T.U. Braunschweig, 1988.

[5] Robert, Y. and Trystram, D.: Parallel implementation of the algebraic path problem. Proc. of CONPAR 86, Lecture Notes in Computer Science 237, 1986, pp. 149-156.

[6] Zsótér, A.: A cellprocessor based on 16-state cells. Proc. of PARCELLA'86, Akademie-Verlag Berlin, 1986, pp. 66-69.

CONTROL OF SENSORY PROCESSING - A HYPOTHESIS ON AND SIMULATION OF THE ARCHITECTURE OF AN ELEMENTARY CORTICAL PROCESSOR

E. Koerner[+], M. Gross[+], A. Richter[+] and H. Shimizu[++]

1. The Problem

The cortex with its high flexibility of processing consists of a regular columnar structure, where the minicolumn as a firmware structure of about 110 Neurons can be considered to be the elementary processing element. There is an interesting model concerning this columnar structure based on localized groups of homogeneous formal elements with probabilistic features (2). However, those minicolumns are not a pool of randomly connected neurons but have a characteristic layered structure and are composed of several distinct neuron types with specific processing characteristics. There is evidence, that these layers cannot be explained by a coding hierarchy (3) and only some part of that may be due to mapping processes between different phase spaces (4).What then is it for? In putting this problem into the framework of a definitive job in early visual processing, we submitted evidence that this layered structure represents a kind of flexible control hierarchy which enables the manipulation of the thalamic interface such that the highly parallel sensory inputs to the cortex can be picked up as a sequence of lower dimensional parallel bytes, which are reassembled towards a completly parallel representation ,in a way to ensure a rapid and smooth convergence of the interpretation process (1). We argue, that such a more complex structure of a single node in a network may be crucial for getting more flexibility in the network's behavior.

2. The model

In Brain computing interpretation means the formation of an activity distribution in the cortex which sufficiently matches the activity distribution of sensory inputs at the interface to the cortex. For a couple of reasons (1), the thalamus can be regarded to be such an interface.

+ The Ilmenau Institute of Technology, Ilmenau, 6300, GDR
++ Tokyo University, Pharm. Faculty, Dep. Biophysics, Tokyo 113, Hongo 3-chome, Japan

Results in psychophysics suggest, that the retinal input does never enter completely in parallel the pathways to the cortex but that there is an internal scanning process even between the fixation saccades of the eye (6). (For more details see (1).)

Our model framework submits a hypothesis in which way this internal scanning could be controled by cortical feedback as to get a random access grouping such that the parallel visual byte at the interface is decomposed into a sequence of smaller dimensional bytes representing definite known parts of the image which are subsequently reassembled via synchronization towards complete and consistent interpretation of the input. This temporary partial sequencing of the parallel input may prevent a combinatorical explosion of the interpretaion process since the cortical control guides the associative search towards the most probable decision.

2.1. The model thalamic interface

Sensory inputs enter the cortex via thalamic relay neurons (Th) passing the reticular formation, the neurons of which (Re) form a mutually locally inhibiting network. There is a recurrent feedback from pyramidal neurons of layer 6 (Py6) to the Re and Th by the entrained cortical activity. A local inhibition (Li) produces a raising inhibitory level with entrained cortical activity that tends to close all channels except those which get support by cortical feedback, the Re of which carving this channel out of the inhibitory block by inhibiting the respective Li.

$$Th(i,j,k)=Schw\left\{ (1+W\_ThI*I(i,j,k-1)+W\_ThP6*Py6(i,j,k-1) +lam11*Th(i,j,k-1))/(1+w4*\ Li(i,j,k-1))-1 \right\}$$

$$Re(i,j,k)=Schw\left\{ (1+W\_ReP6*Py6(i,j,k-1)+\ W\_ReTh*Th(i,j,k-1) +lam12*Re(i,j,k-1))/(1+a03*\sum_{u,v\in sur2} Re(u,v,k-1)-1 \right\}$$

$$Li(i,j,k)=Schw\left\{ (1+a04*\sum_{u,v\in sur1} Py6(u,v,k-1)\ +\ a05*\sum_{u,v\in sur3} Th(u,v,k-1) + a06*\sum_{u,v\in sur3} I\ (u,v,k-1)\ +\ lam13*\ Li(i,j,k-1)/ (1+W\_LiRe*Re(i,j,k-1))-1 \right\}$$

$$\text{where } Schw(a) = \begin{cases} (0 & \text{if } a < 0) \\ (a & \text{if } a \in (0,20)) \\ (20 & \text{if } a > 20) \end{cases}$$

Hence, a limited part of the parallel input is only to be decided on by the cortex. Then these related channels are purged from the input by a cortical erase command and the next strongest set of inputs can enter the pathway to the cortex.

2.2. The model macrocolumn

In which way is the cortico-thalamic control organized to start this decomposition of the parallel input into a sequence of flashing groups of input channels which contain the information most appropriate for a rapid convergence of the interpretation and, second, how to link these subsets of the input image back to synchronism while creating a semantic structure?

Based on the principle of modular organization of the neocortex including the available sound knowledge on the cortical hardware we propose a model of a neocortical minicolumn as an elementary cortical processor, which can support such a content dependent selforganization within a large scale system composed of such elements /1/,/2/. According to our computational hypothesis on early vision the architecture of the 6-layered neocortical columns fits best into a framework of a dynamic control hierarchy for pattern formation. A model minicolumn consists of

i) a syntactic detector which limits the visual byte (parallel visual input) to a drastically smaller dimensional byte containing only the input channels with the highest local and global syntactic complexity, (R0)

ii) a semantic classificator which modifies this grouping towards the largest possible semantic structure and generates a repetitive sequence of a limited number of such puls-like flashing "variable bytes" (sets of input channels representing a semantic concept at the retinal image) (R1) and

iii) a semantic linker, (R2) which guides this time sequence of variable bytes back to synchronism by means of consensus formation and its feedforward to the semantic classification.

R0 consists of an associative memory (Py6) resembling the pyramidal neurons of layer 6 which is continually communicating with an adaptive filter made up by a two layered structure of excitatory spiny stellate cells (SSO) and inhibitory nonspiny stellate of layer 4 (NSSO).

$$\text{Py6\_1}(i, j, k)=\text{Schw}\left\{ \text{lam61}* \text{Py6}(i, j, k-1)+\text{W\_P6Th} *\text{Th}(i, j, k-1) +\text{w\_P6P6}*\text{sumPy6}(i, j, k-1)+\text{W\_P6Ss}*\text{sumSs}(i, j, k-1) +\text{W\_P6P3}*\text{sumPy3}(i, j, k-1)-\text{m61} * \text{mglob6} \right\}$$

$$\text{Py6}(i, j, k)=\text{Schw}\left\{ \text{Py6\_1}(i, j, k) - \text{SBc6}(i, j, k-1)\right\}$$

$$\text{SBC6}(i, j, k)=\text{SchwBa}\left\{ \text{WBa60}*\text{Py6}(i, j, k-1)+\text{WBa61}*\text{SBC6}(i, j, k-1) \right\}$$

$$\text{Ss0}(i, j, k)=\text{Schw}\left\{ \text{lam41} * \text{Ss1}(i, j, k-1)+ \text{W\_SsTh} * \text{Th}(i, j, k-1) + \text{W\_SsP6} * \text{sumPy6}(i, j, k-1) - \text{m41} * \text{mglob4} - \text{NSs}(i, j, k) \right\}$$

$$\text{NSs0}(i, j, k)=\text{Schw}\left\{ \text{va} \Big/ (1+\text{b43} * \sum_{u, v=-r}^{r} \text{NSs}(i+u, j+v, k-1)+\text{v45}*\text{Ss}(i, j, k-2) -1 \right\}$$

with

$$\text{sum\_Source}(i, j, k-1)=\text{Schw}\left\{\sum_{u, v} \text{W\_Target\_Source}(i, j, u, v)*\text{Source}(u, v, k-1)\right\}$$

$$\text{SchwBa}(a) = \begin{cases} (\ 0 & \text{if } a < \text{Schw\_Ba}) \\ (\ a & \text{if } a <= 20\ ) \\ (20 & \text{if } a > 20) \end{cases}$$

This first decision on the input is a local one, since Py6 is only connected to the next nearest neighbour minicolumn. SS0 feeds this decision to R1, an autoassociative memory of the HASP-type (7), while Py6 gives the feedback to Th, Re trying to support and keep the input active. The range of autoassociative mapping at R1 exceeds all next nearest neighbour macrocolumns, furthermore by sending and receiving the selected decision to and from all other macrocolumns (LCC), the local decission is turned towards a global one.

$$\text{Py3}(i, j, k)=\text{Schw}\left\{ \text{lam31}*\text{Py3}(i, j, k-1)+\text{W\_P3Ss}*\text{Ss}(i, j, k-1) +\text{W\_P3Th}*\text{Th}(i, j, k-1) - \text{a31}*\text{sumPy3}(i, j, k-1) -\text{m31} * \text{mglob3}\right\}$$

$$\text{sumPy3}(i, j, k-1)=\text{Schw}\left\{\sum_{u, v} \text{WP3P3}(i, j, u, v)*\text{Py3}(u, v, k-1)\right\}$$

R2 was not included into this model minicolumn because of its tremendous complexity and the shortage of available working memory. To emulate in a primitive but instructive way the R2 we simply added a system Py2

Py2(i, j, k)=Schw{ lam21*Py2(i, j, k-1)+lam22* Schw{Py3(i, j, k-1)-MinPy3} }

which keeps strong R1 decisions and gives a feedforword to R1, R0 to support the synchronization of noncompetitive parts of the image.
The thalamic inhibition Li strongly depends on "cortical" activity. Since while starting the process only R0 is active, any Py6 has the chance to control its thalamic input channel via Re. With entraining R1, R2 then Py6 activity is not sufficient to suppress LI locally via Re except it gets additional support by R1, R2 feedback.
An inhibitory neuron type sbc6 (small basket cell of layer 6) acts with its nonlinear switching characteristics to delete the support for those thalamic channels which belong to a stable entrained (and therefore recognized) pattern. Any subsystem of the module has its normalization procedure (mglob 3, 4, 6) to keep the full dynamic range of neural activity ready for processing.

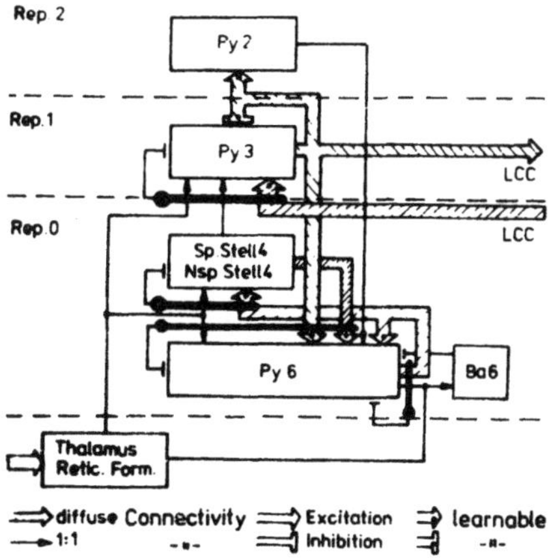

Fig.1
Schematic structure of an elementary cortical processor modul; most important subsystems and signal flow paths are market (see text)

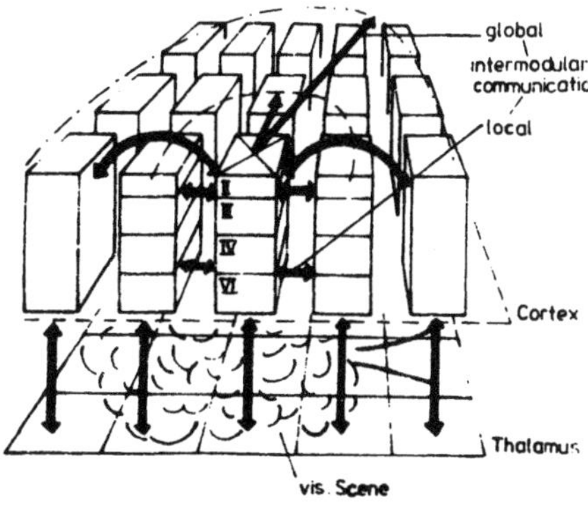

Fig.2
5 x 5 macrocolumnar array each of which consisting of 3 x 3 minicolumns. The intramodular connectivity is heavy between all subsystems vertically, the intermodular connectivity is horizontally local in layer 6 and golbal in 3.

2.3. The model columnar array

Limited by the memoryspace of the PC used for simulation, only 3 x 3 matrix dimensions for the subsystems of minicolumns in each macrocolumn was accepted. The array is consisted of 5 x 5 macrocolumns each of which is autonomous to some degree but can slave other ones or can be slaved via the connectivity LCC in R1. A minicolumn in this array corresponds to a set of elementary feature detectors (not pixels!) (cf. Fig. 2).

3. Simulation results

In the case of a single column the emphasis in simulation was given to the dynamics of the decompositon parallel to sequence and the variable byte formation. Fig. 3 shows the sequential ranking of 3 texture elements according to its syntactic complexity (lower part of the fig.) while another texture cannot enter the input to the cortex (Thal 42). Related R0, R1 activity is shown (middle part) and the upper traces show the Li-control for both a selected channel and a nonrelevant channel.

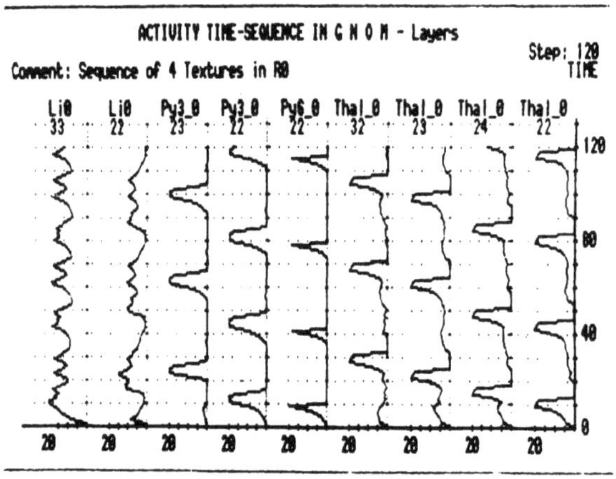

Fig. 3
Turning a parallel thalamic scene into a sequence of known texture elements by R0 control in a macrocolumn. Any symbolic texture element is a pool of 3 line detectors, coded in the subsequent process of learning.

In the case of the columnar array, a scene covers the 5 x 5 matrix, to be seen in Fig. 4. Two of the modular subsystems of the array, the thalamic interface and R1, are shown 5 time steps after presentation af a scene composed of 6 texture elements. The known ones are instantly synchronized to a parallel recall, the unknown part having been ranked in the sequence according to the completeness of texture groups.

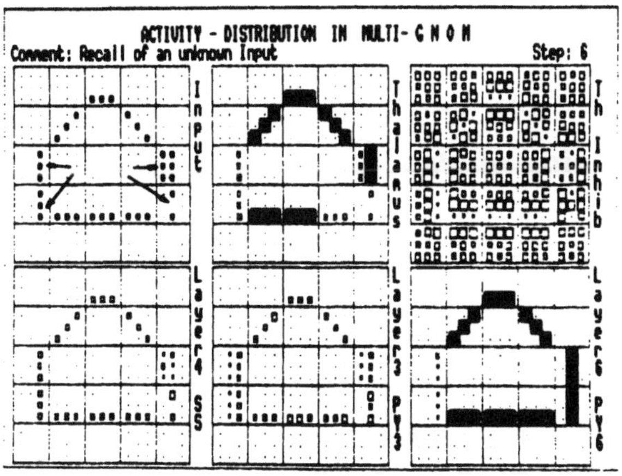

Fig. 4
Processing of a "scene" by the columnar array (see text). The number of texture elements that could be synchronized define the position of this grouping within the sequence.

4. Conclusion

The results demonstrate the potential ability of a network composed of such type complex processing nodes for flexible scene interpretation. A simulation in a more realistic scale is required to prove this hypothesis on early visual processing.

5. References

/1/ E. Koerner, I. Tsuda and H. Shimizu: "Take-grant control, variable byte formation and processing parallel in sequence-characteristics of a new type of holonic processor" in: "Parallel Algorithms and Architectures," A. Albrecht, H. Jung and K. Mehlhorn, Akademie-Verlag Berlin 1987

/2/ G. L. Shaw, D. J. Silverman and J. C. Pearson: "Trion Model of Cortical Organisation: Toward a Theory of Information Processing and Memory". in: "Brain Theory," G. Palm and A. Aertsen (eds.) p. 177 - 92 Springer Verlag Berlin, Hdbg., NY, Tokyo 1986

/3/ G. A. Orban: "Neuronal operations in the visual cortex". Springer Verlag Berlin, Hdbg., NY, Tokyo 1984

/4/ P. M. Churchland: "Cognitive neurobiology: a computational hypothesis for laminar cortex". Biology and Philosophy 1, 1986, 25 - 51

/5/ T. Winograd and F. Flores: "Understandig Computer and Cognition: A New Foundation for Design". Ablex, Norwood, NY, 1986

/6/ F. Crick: "The function of the thalamic reticular complex: the searchlight hypothesis". Proc. Natl. Acad. Sci. USA, 81, 1984, 4586 - 90

/7/ Y. Hirai: "A model of human associative processor (HASP)" IEEE Trans. Syst., Man and Cyb. SMC-13, 1983, 851 - 7

Bounds for l-Selection and Related Problems on Grids of Processors

Manfred Kunde *
Institut für Informatik
Technische Universität
Arcisstr. 21
D-8000 München 2

Abstract

The problem of l-selection and sorting on one- and two-dimensional grids of processors is studied. It is shown that in contrast to sequential computation median search can be as hard as sorting in many cases. For sorting on $n \times n$ grids a new lower bound of 2.25 n steps is presented which is valid for arbitrary index schemes. Moreover, it is demonstrated that $3n$ steps are necessary for sorting with respect to almost all index functions. For median search and sorting on an $n \times n$ torus of processors a lower bound of 1.5 n is given which is independent of the chosen index function.

1. Introduction and notation

In this paper we study the problem of l-selection and sorting on certain grids of processors or mesh-connected computers [KH, NS, TK] which has turned out to be a suitable model for $VLSI$-architectures. It is well-known that data movement is a significant factor in the performance of parallel computation. We will give lower and upper bounds for the number of data transmissions for the above mentioned problems and discuss the question whether finding the median is easier than sorting or not. We will consider two types of architectures: mesh-connected arrays without wrap-around connections and arrays with wrap-around connections. An r-dimensional mesh-connected array is a set mesh$(n_1, \ldots, n_r)$ of $N = \Pi_{i=1}^{r} n_i$ identical processors $P = (p_1, \ldots, p_r), 0 \leq p_i \leq n_i - 1$, each one directly interconnected only to all its nearest neighbours $Q = (q_1, \ldots, q_r)$ with $d(P,Q) = \sum_{i=1}^{r} \mid p_i - q_i \mid = 1$. If wrap-around connections are allowed, then a nearest neighbour has to fulfill $d_{wrap}(P,Q) = \sum_{i=1}^{r} \mid (p_i - q_i) mod\ n_i \mid = 1$, where for $a_i\ mod\ n_i$ is assumed that $-n_i/2 \leq a_i\ mod n_i \leq +n_i/2$. We assume that N elements from a linearly ordered set are loaded in the N processors, each one receiving exactly one element. The processors are thought to be indexed by a one-to-one mapping f from $\{1, \ldots, n_1\} \times \ldots \times \{1, \ldots, n_r\}$ onto $\{1, \ldots, N\}$.

Let A be any nonempty subset of [1, N]. With respect to index function f the problem of A-selection is to move the i-th smallest element to the processor indexed by i for all $i \in A$. If $A = \{l\}$, then the problem is called l-selection. Special cases are the problem of finding the minimum ($l = 1$), maximum ($l = N$) and median ($l = \lceil N/2 \rceil$). If $A = [1, N]$ then the sorting problem is to be solved.

The problem of A-selection can be solved by sequences of parallel comparisons and data movements. In order to get lower and upper bounds the restrictions of the model of computation must carefully be given. The model of computation we use is as follows. At each time step a processor is allowed to interchange its contents with one of its nearest neighbours. This interchange may be caused by a comparison or not. Without comparison a

* This work was supported by the Siemens AG, München

processor is allowed to send its contents to a directly neighboured processors while it is receiving the contents from another nearest neighbour. That is, shifting the data on cycles of more than 2 directly interconnected processors also is possible. (Compare Figure 1)

Figure 1 mesh-connected arrays

a) index function

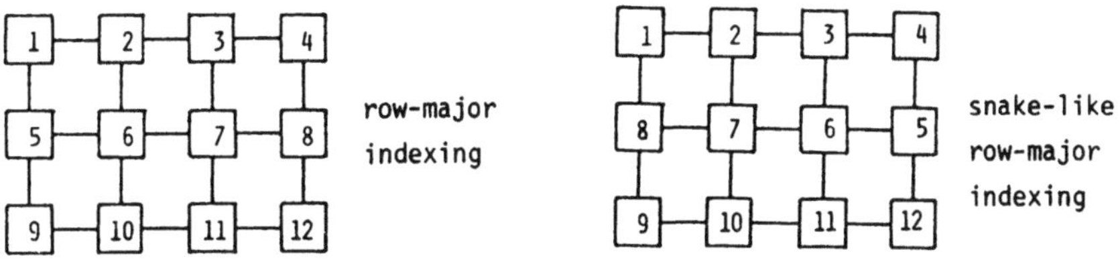

b) model of computation

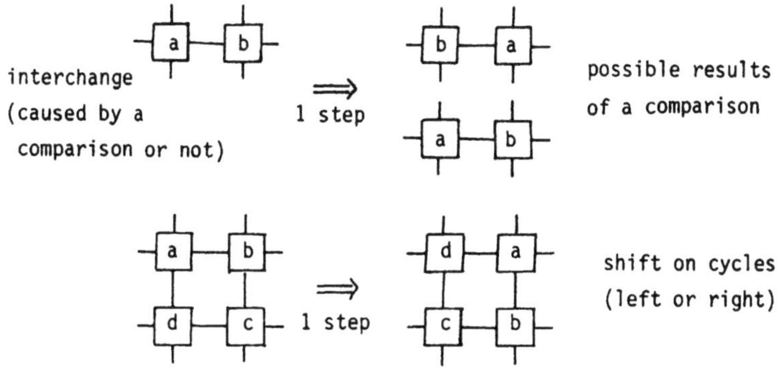

A trivial bound for A−selection is the so-called distance bound given by $max\{d(P;Q) \mid P,Q \in mesh(n_1,\ldots,n_r),\quad f(Q) \in A\}$. It is easily seen that the distance bound is at most $n_1 + \ldots + n_r - r$ for meshes without wrap-around connections and half of that sum in the wrap-around case. In this paper we will demonstrate that the distance bound cannot be reached in nearly all cases of the A−selection problem.

In the next section we present a general formulation of a technique to get lower bounds for A−selection. The technique, called joker-argument, was firstly presented in [Ku1,SS]. In the first section we show that in many cases the easier looking median search is as hard as the sorting problem for one-dimensional chains of processors. Furthermore we give upper and lower bounds for arbitrary l−selection problems. For a ring of n processors a lower bound of $3n/4$ steps is stated for median search, merging and sorting. Even in the case of median search it is still open whether this bound is tight.

In the fourth section we discuss bounds for A−selection on two-dimensional meshes. For $n \times n$ meshes without wrap-around connection we show that for every $l \geq 7$ there are index functions f such that l−selection with respect to f need more than $2n$ steps. But for arbitrary indexing l−selection can be solved by approximately $7n/2$ steps. Furthermore it is shown that there are index schemes such that sorting needs about $4n$ steps. The so far best sorting algorithms use snake-like indexing [TK,SS] or block-wise snake-like indexing [MSS] and take asymptotically $3n$ steps which has been shown to be optimal for the used type of indexing [Ku1, SS]. It is still an open question whether there exist indexings for which faster sorting algorithms are possible. We show that for all index functions sorting needs at least 2.25 n steps and that for almost all indexings $3n$ steps is a lower bound. On an $n \times n$ torus of processors sorting with respect to blockwise snake-like indexing can be performed by asymptotically $2n$ steps [Ku3, MSS]. We show that for all index functions $3n/2$ steps are necessary not only for sorting but for median search, too. At the end of the fourth section bounds for A–selection problems on 2–dimensional grids with arbitrary sidelengths are discussed.

2. The joker-argument

In this section we generalize a method for obtaining lower bounds for sorting and l-selection on meshes. The method is called joker-argument [Ku1] and a similar approach was also used in [SS].

For an r-dimensional mesh let f be the given index function and let ALG be an arbitrary, but fixed algorithm for solving an A-selection problem for a given index set $A \neq \emptyset$. Let us define three nonempty subsets of processors: the target-zone TZ with $f(TZ) = A$, the joker-zone JZ and the observation-zone OZ, which is disjoint to both the other sets and will normally contain only one processor. Note that in the case of l-selection the target-zone TZ only consists of that processor Q indexed by $f(Q) = l$. For two nonempty subsets of processors A and B let the distance be defined by
$d(A,B) = min\{d(P,Q)/P \in A, Q \in B\}$.

Note that at any time $t \geq 0$ the contents of any processor in A cannot reach any processor in B during the time period from t to $d(A,B)-1$ (Compare Figure 2). Let the set mesh$(n_1,...,n_r)$ - JZ contain as an initial loading the integers $1,...,N-|JZ|$ and the contents of JZ consists of zeroes and N's only. That means, if JZ contains exactly x zeroes, then the number k, $1 \leq k \leq N-|JZ|$ becomes the $(k+x)$-th smallest element. A processor in the observation-zone OZ has no information about the contents of the joker-zone for the first $d(OZ,JZ)-1$ steps and therefore its computation cannot be influenced by the joker-loading during that period. In a certain sense we decide at the end of that period which joker contents we have to choose to win the game.

Figure 2 Illustration to the joker-argument

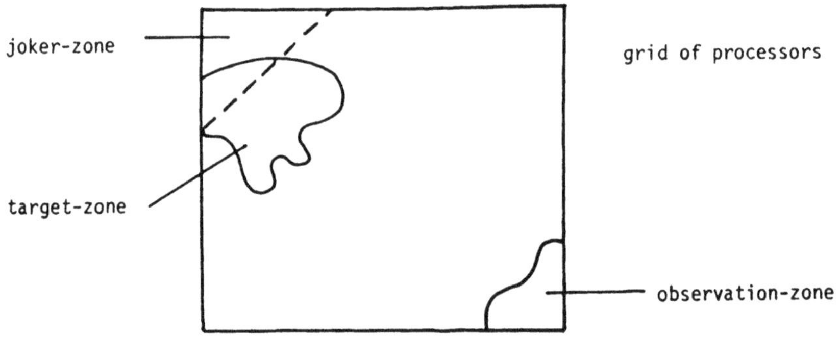

Lemma 1 (joker-argument)

If after t steps of algorithm ALG, $t \leq d(OZ,JZ)-1$, any processor of OZ contains a k with $k \leq f(Q) \leq k+|JZ|$ for any Q in the target-zone, then ALG needs at least $t + d(OZ,TZ)$ steps.

Proof: After $t \leq d(OZ,JZ)-1$ steps all processors in the observation–zone only contain elements initially loaded in the zone mesh$(n_1, ..., n_r) - JZ$ and the elements are chosen by the algorithm ALG independently of the contents of the joker-zone. If there is a k in a processor $P \in OZ$ with $k \leq f(Q) \leq k + \mid JZ \mid$ for a Q in the target-zone TZ, then let the joker-zone initially contain exactly $f(Q) - k$ zeroes. Hence k is the $f(Q)$-th smallest element with respect to the total loading and therefore must be transported to processor Q. This will at least cost additional $d(OZ, TZ)$ steps.

We will use this argument in the following sections several times. It should be pointed out that this argumentation can be generalized to arbitrary communication networks.

3. One–dimensional meshes

For the whole section let $n = n_1$ be the number of processors in a one–dimensional array. We will first discuss algorithms and lower bounds for meshes without wrap-arounds, called chains of processors.

3.1 Chains of processors

For the index functions *inc*, defined by $inc(x) = x + 1$ for $x = 0, ..., n - 1$, and *dec*, given by $dec(x) = n - x$, the problem of sorting is already solved in a satisfactorial way by the well-known odd-even-transposition sort (abbreviated: oets–algorithm) [Kn] which needs n parallel compare and interchange steps. The oets–algorithm will be a basic tool for nearly all algorithms presented in this section. For l-selection we assume that $1 \leq l \leq \lceil n/2 \rceil$ and that the processor i with index $f(i) = l$ is on the left side of the chain that is $0 \leq i \leq \lceil n/2 \rceil - 1$. All other cases can be handled in a similar way.

Algorithm SELECT$_1(l, i)$

1. oets–algorithm with respect to index function *inc*.
2. Transport l–th smallest element to processor i.

Note that after the first stage the l–th smallest element is in processor l–1. Hence the number of steps is $n + \mid l - i - 1 \mid$. An improvement of the algorithm can be obtained as follows:

Algorithm SELECT$_2(l, i)$

1. if $3l \geq 2(i + 1)$ then SELECT$_1(l, i)$ else in parallel
   oets-algorithm on subarray: $0, \ldots, i$ with indexing $g_1(j) = i - j + 1,\ 0 \leq j \leq i$.
   oets-algorithm on subarray $i + 1, \ldots, n - 1$ with indexing $g_2(j) = j - i,\ i + 1 \leq j \leq n - 1$
2. oets algorithm on subarray $i - l + 1, \ldots, i + l$ with indexing $h(j) = j + l - i$,
   $i - l + 1 \leq j \leq i + l$

Note that in the case $3l < 2(i + 1)$ we get immediately $l < i$. Then after the first stage the $l - th$ smallest element must be in one of the $2l$ processors $i - l + 1, \ldots, i + l$. After the second stage the $l - th$ smallest element is sorted into processor i. In this case the number of steps is $n - i - 1$ for the first stage and $2l$ for the second one. Hence in total $n - i + 2l - 1$ steps are needed. We will now demonstrate that for $i \leq l - 1$ the algorithms are optimal up to one single step.

Theorem 3.1

For arbitrary l,1 $\leq l \leq n/2$, and index function f with $f(i) = l$, l-selection needs at least $n - i + l - 2$ steps.

Proof Let $JZ = [0, n - l - 1], TZ = \{i\}$ and $OZ = \{n - 1\}$. At the beginning let the processors $n - l$ to $n - 1$ be loaded by the integers $1, ..., l$. Then after $l - 1$ steps an integer $j, 1 \leq j \leq l$ is placed in observation processor $n - 1$. Since $l - 1 \leq d(JZ, OZ) - 1$ and $j \leq l = f(i) \leq j + (n - l) = j + \mid JZ \mid$ we can apply the joker-argument (lemma 1).

Let us first make some remarks on the results.

1. Note that for median search the worst-case of 3n/2 - 2 is reached if the median has to be placed in border processor $i = 0$ (or $i = n - 1$). This case is especiallly interesting when data input and output is only allowed at the border processors.
2. Since the ordering of the initial loading of the joker-zone does not influence the lower bound generation, one may assume that the contents of the joker-zone and the other zone is already sorted. Hence we have shown that merging of two files of length n/2 is at least as hard as median search. In the case where the index function is *inc* or *dec* then sorting, merging and median search all are equally hard.

Of course the lower bounds for l-selection are lower bounds for sorting and merging with respect to an index function f with $f(i) = l$. The question arises whether there are cases in which sorting is provable worse then any l-selection problem.

First of all note that any sorting problem with arbitrary function f can be solved by two applications of the oets–algorithm.

SORT(n,f)

1. oets–algorithm with index function *inc*
2. data transport according to data movement of the oets-algorithm with index function *inc* and $f^{-1}(i)$ as the initial loading of processor $i - 1, 1 \leq i \leq n$.

For correctness of the algorithm note that after the first step processor $i-1, 1 \leq i \leq n$, contains the $i-th$ smallest element which has to be transported to processor $f^{-1}(i)$. Thus the following proposition holds

Proposition 1.1

Sorting on a linear array of length n with arbitrary index function can be solved within $2n$ steps.

A little bit surprising is that this simple sorting approach is optimal for certain index functions.

Proposition 1.2

There are index functions such that sorting needs at least $2n - 2\sqrt{n} - 1$ steps.

Proof For simplicity assume that n is a square number. Take $JZ = TZ = \{0, ..., \sqrt{n} - 1\}$ and $OZ = \{n - 1\}$. Consider the following index function f with $f(i) = (i + 1)\sqrt{n}$ for $i = 0, \ldots \sqrt{n} - 1$ .For $i \geq \sqrt{n}$ let f be defined in any reasonable manner. Let the number $1, \ldots, n - \sqrt{n}$ be initially loaded into processors $\sqrt{n}, \ldots, n - 1$. After $n - \sqrt{n} - 1$ steps an element k, $1 \leq k \leq n - \sqrt{n}$ is at processor $n - 1$. Of course there is a j, $j = (i + 1)\sqrt{n}$ with $k \leq j \leq k + \sqrt{n} = k + \mid JZ \mid$. Hence by the joker argument at least $n - \sqrt{n} - 1 + n - \sqrt{n} = 2n - 2\sqrt{n} - 1$ steps are necessary to sort the array with respect to indexing f.

By the proof of proposition 1.2 we have not only shown that bad indexings for sorting exist but that these indexings are also bad for $\{\sqrt{n}, 2\sqrt{n}, \ldots, n\}$ - selection.

3.2 Ring of processors

If we consider a linear array with wrap-around connections or a ring the situation changes a little bit. The maximal distance between two processors is now only $n/2$. For brevity suppose that in this section n is an even integer.

An obvious algorithm for l-selection ($l \leq n/2$) is to make an oets on the ring interpreted as an array without wrap-arounds. If i is the processor for the l-th smallest element, then let $i - l + 1$ mod n be the first processor of the array with increasing index function.

If $l \leq n/4$, then another algorithm similar to SELECT_2 is a little bit better. As before let i be that processor the l-th smallest element has to be transported to. Sort the subarray

$(i-n/2+1) \bmod n, \ldots, i$ in decreasing order and the subarray $(i+1) \bmod n, \ldots, (i+n/2) mod n$ in increasing order. Then the l-th-smallest element is in subarray $(i-l+1) \bmod n, \ldots, (i+l)$ mod n, which is to be sorted by additional 2l steps. The algorithm needs in total $n/2+l$ steps.

A lower bound for l-selection can be obtained as follows. Let $OZ = \{(i+n/2) mod\ n\}$, $TZ = \{i\}$ and $JZ = \{(i-l/2) mod\ n, \ldots, (i+l/2) mod\ n\}$. At the beginning let the integers $1, \ldots, l$ be loaded into the processors $(i+n/2-l/2+1) mod\ n, \ldots, (i+n/2+l/2) mod\ n$. After $l/2-1$ steps there is a k, $1 \leq k \leq l$, in the observation processor. Then by the joker-argument (lemma 1) we obtain at once the first part of the following theorem.

Theorem 3.2

For all l, $1 \leq l \leq n/2$, l-selection on a ring of n processors needs at least $n/2 + l/2 - 2$ steps and at most min $\{n, n/2 + 2l\}$ steps.

Note that the upper bound differs from the asymptotic lower bound $(n+l)/2$ by a factor of at most 8/5. Furthermore, in difference to the arrays without wrap-arounds the bounds of the above theorem are valid for all index functions. Hence we can state the following corollary.

Corollary 3.3

On a ring of n processors sorting, merging and median search need at least $3/4\ n - 2$ steps.

Proof: Take the bound for median search in theorem 3.2. For merging observe that both the loading of the joker-zone and the remaining zone can be chosen as sorted subfiles.

The bound given in the corollary is so far the best for sorting and merging with arbitrary index function. But from the first part of this section we know that there are index fuctions such that asymptotically n steps are necessary for sorting. Until now the best algorithms for sorting on ring are more or less the same as those on a chain of processors.

4. Bounds for two-dimensional meshes

In this section we will present upper and lower bounds for l-selection and sorting on 2-dimensional meshes. At the beginning we will only consider $n \times n$ meshes.

4.1 Meshes without wrap-around connections

As in the last section we assume that for l-selection the integer l is restricted to the first half of the indices, that is $1 \leq l \leq n^2/2$. (For $k \geq n^2/2+1$ we can obtain the same results as for $l = n^2+1-k$). For a given index function f let $dmax_f(l) = max\{d(P,Q) \mid f(P) = l,\ Q = (i,j),\ i,j \in \{0, n-1\}\}$ be the maximal distance of the processor P, indexed by l, to any of the four corner processors. Then the following lower bound can be stated.

Theorem 4.1

On an $n \times n$ mesh l-selection, $1 \leq l \leq n^2/2$, with respect to indexing f needs at least $dmax_f(l) + \lfloor\sqrt{2l} - 1/2\rfloor - 1$ steps.

Proof: Let the observation processor Q be one of that corner processors which fulfills $d(P,Q) = dmax_f(l)$ for processor P with $f(P) = l$. Let the target-zone $TZ = \{P\}$ and $JZ = \{R \mid d(R,Q) \geq n-1\}$. Let $A(l) = \{R \mid d(R,Q) \leq \lfloor\sqrt{2l} - 1/2\rfloor\}$. Then $\mid A(l) \mid \leq l$. Initially load the integers $1, \ldots, \mid A(l) \mid$ into the processors in A(l). Then for an arbitrary l-selection algorithm after $\lfloor\sqrt{2l} - 1/2\rfloor - 1$ steps there is a j in Q with $1 \leq j \leq l$. Since $\mid JZ \mid \geq n^2/2$ and $dmax_f(l) = d(TZ, OZ)$ the theorem can be proved by the joker-argument (lemma 1).

Corollary 4.2

a) For every l, $1 \leq l \leq n^2/2$, there are indexings such that l-selection needs at least $2n + \lfloor\sqrt{2l} - 1/2\rfloor - 3$ steps.

b) There are indexings such that median search needs at least $3n - 4$ steps.

Proof: a) Take an indexfunction f with $f(P) = l$, P one of the corner processors. b) is obvious.

Theorem 4.3

For arbitrary indexing f l-selection, $1 \leq l \leq n^2/2$, on an $n \times n$ mesh can be done with at most $3n + max\{n/2 + 1 - l/n, l/n\} + 0(n^{2/3})$ steps.

The too lengthy proof is omitted here. Theorem 4.3 demonstrates that l-selection can be solved by at most $7n/2 + 0(n^{3/4})$ steps. The next theorem demonstrates that for some indexfunctions sorting is provable harder than l-selection problem.

Theorem 4.4

There are indexings f such that sorting needs at least $4n - 2\lceil\sqrt{2n}\rceil - 4$ steps.

Proof Let $OZ = \{(n-1,\ n-1)\}$and$JZ = \{P \mid d(P,\ (0,0)) \leq \lceil\sqrt{2n}\rceil - 1\}$. Then $\mid JZ \mid = \geq n$.Let TZ be any subset of JZ with $\mid TZ \mid = n$ and let f be any index function with $f(TZ) = \{in \mid i = 1, \ldots, n\}$. In the beginning let the integers $1, \ldots, n\sqrt{2} - \mid JZ \mid$ be loaded in the processors of mesh-JZ. Then, after $2n - \lceil\sqrt{2n}\rceil - 2$ steps, there is a k in $(n-1,\quad n-1)$ with $(i-1)n \leq k \leq i\,n$ for an i, $1 \leq i \leq n$. Hence by the joker argument we get the theorem.

In corollary 4.2 and theorem 4.4 we have constructed index functions which seem to be bad for l-selection or sorting. In the following we will discuss the question which lower bounds can be obtained by the help of the joker-argument in the case of an arbitrarily given index function.

Theorem 4.5

Let f be an arbitrary index function for an $n \times n$ mesh. Then

a) there is an $l, 1/3n^2 \leq l \leq 2/3n^2$, such that l-selection needs at least $(1 + \sqrt{3/2})n - 4 \geq 2.224\, n - 4$ steps.

b) sorting needs at least $2.224\, n$ steps.

Proof b) is obvious by a). For a) let $C_1 = (0,0), C_2 = (0, n-1), C_3 = (n-1, n-1)$ and $C_4 = (n-1, 0)$ denote the processors placed in the corners of the mesh. For $i = 1,2,3,4$ let $A_i = \{P/d(P, C_i) \leq \lceil(1 - \sqrt{1/6})n\rceil - 1\}$ and $A = \bigcup_{i=1}^4 A_i$. Then number of processors in the center $B = mesh - A$ is bounded by $\mid B \mid \leq 1/3n^2$. (Compare Fig. 3). Hence the set of indices $\{n^2/3, \ldots, 2n^2/3\}$ cannot be contained in $f(B)$. Therefore an $l, 1/3n^2 \leq l \leq 2/3n^2$, and a processor $P \notin B$ exist such that $f(P) = l$. Note that $P \notin B$ implies $P \in A_i$ for an $i, 1 \leq i \leq 4$. Thus $dmax_f(l) \geq n - 1 + n - \lceil(1 - \sqrt{1/6})n\rceil$. By theorem 4.1 we obtain that for this l l-selection needs at least

$dmax_f(l) + \lfloor\sqrt{2l} - 1/2\rfloor - 1 \leq 2n - 1 - \lceil(1 - \sqrt{1/6})n\rceil + \lfloor\sqrt{2/3}n - 1/2\rfloor - 1$
$\leq 2n - 4 - (1 - \sqrt{1/6})n + \sqrt{2/3}n = n - 4 + \sqrt{3/2}n = n + \frac{\sqrt{6}}{2}n - 4$

For sorting a further improvement of the lower bound is possible. This bound is also valid for A-selection problem with A consisting of two indices. As in the proof of theorem 4.5 let C_i, $i = 1, \ldots, 4$, denote the corner processors. Let $A_i = \{P/d(P, C_i) \leq \frac{n}{2} - 1\}$ and $B_i = \{P/d(P, C_i) \leq \frac{3}{4}n - 1\}$. Then the following lemma holds.

Figure 3 Illustration to theorem 4.5

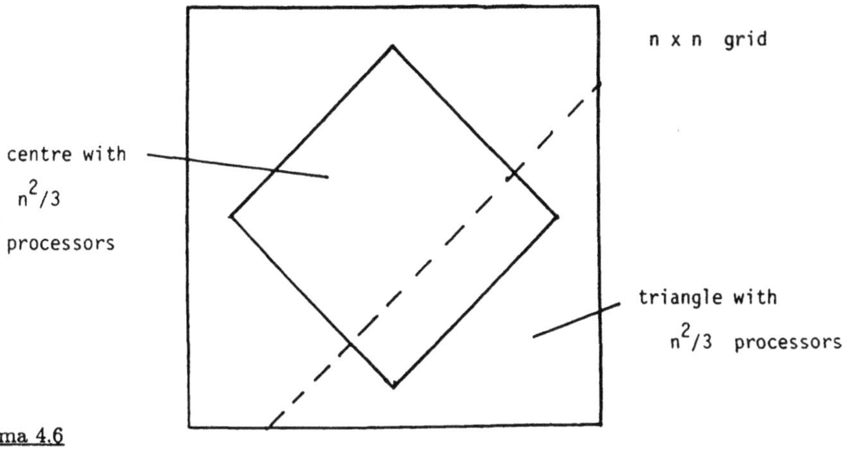

Lemma 4.6

Let f be an arbitrary index function for an $n \times n$ mesh. Then there is an i, $1 \leq i \leq 4$, such that at least one of following claims is valid:

i) $f(A_i) \cap \{9/32\ n^2 + 1, \ldots, 23/32\ n^2 - 1\} \neq \emptyset$ or

ii) there are integers l, $u \in f(B_i)$ with $l \leq n^2/2$, $u \geq n^2/2 + 1$ and $u - l \leq n^2/2$.

The lenghty proof is omitted here and can be found in the appendix of a full paper.

Theorem 4.7

Sorting on a $n \times n$ mesh with arbitrary index function needs at least 2.25 n steps.

Proof Suppose that claim i) of lemma 4.6 is true. Then there is a processor $P \in A_i$ with $f(P) = l$, $9/32n^2 + 1 \leq l \leq 23/32n^2 - 1$. Hence $dmax_f(l) \geq \frac{3}{2}n - 2$. By theorem 4.1 we immediately obtain that at least $\frac{3}{2}n - 2 + \lfloor\sqrt{9/16n^2} - 1/2\rfloor - 1 \geq 2\,1/4\,n - 5$ steps are necessary. If claim i) is not true then ii) must hold. Let B_i be the set of processors containing processors P and Q with $f(P) = l$ and $f(Q) = n$. In this case let $TZ = B_i$, $JZ = \{P \mid d(P, C_i) \leq n-1\}$. Let the observation zone OZ consist of that corner processor C_j with $j = (i+2) mod\ 4$. That is the processor just opposite of TZ and JZ. Let the zone (mesh $-JZ$) be initially loaded by integers $1, \ldots, n^2 - \mid JZ \mid = n^2/2 - n$. Then after $n - 2$ steps there is a k, $1 \leq k \leq n^2/2$, in the observation processor. Since either $1 \leq k \leq l \leq \mid JZ \mid$ or $l \leq k \leq u \leq l + \mid JZ \mid$ we are allowed to use the joker-argument (lemma 1) and therefore at least $n - 2 + n + 1/4\,n - 2 = 2\,1/4\,n - 4$ steps are necessary for sorting.

It is not clear if the bound of 2.25 n for sorting on an $n \times n$ mesh is a good lower bound. But it seems that the joker-argument comes here to its limits. But by the same technique one can get an impression that almost all index functions are worse than the snake-like indexing.

Theorem 4.8

For an arbitrary integer $j, n^2/2 \leq j < n^2$ let $c = j/n^2$ and k be an arbitrary integer with $-2\ log\ n/log\ c \leq k \leq n^2/2$. Then sorting on an $n \times n$ mesh needs at least $4n - \lceil n\sqrt{2(1-c)}\rceil - \lceil\sqrt{2k}\rceil - 4$ steps for at least $(1 - (n^2 - k + 1) \cdot c^k) \cdot (n^2)!$ index functions.

The proof is omitted here and can be found in a full version of this paper.

Corollary 4.9

Sorting on a n $n \times n$ mesh needs at least $3n - \lceil\sqrt{2n + 4\ log\ n}\rceil - 4$ steps for at least a portion of $(1 - \frac{1}{2^n})$ of all index functions.

Proof Let $k = n + 2\ log\ n$ and $j = n^2/2$, that is $c = 1/2$. Apply theorem 4.8.

The corollary shows that for almost all index function an asymptotic lower bound of $3n$ steps for sorting can be shown.

4.2 Torus of processors

For an $n \times n$ mesh with wrap-around connections or a torus of processors all the lower bounds of the last section can be divided by 2 and are then valid. But we can derive better bounds for nearly all index functions, since we have no side-effects like corner processors on a torus.

Theorem 4.10

For arbitrary indexing f and for arbitrary l, $1 \leq l \leq n^2/2$, l-selection on an $n \times n$ torus needs at least $n + \lfloor\sqrt{l/2}\rfloor - 2$ steps.

Proof Let $TZ = \{P\}$ with $f(P) = l$. Let the observation processor be any Q with $d_{wrap}(Q, P) = n - 1$ and define a zone $A(l) = \{R \mid d_{wrap}(Q, R) \leq \sqrt{l/2} - 1\}$. Let $JZ = mesh - A(l)$. Note that $\mid A(l) \mid \leq l$ and $\mid JZ \mid \geq n^2/2$. If the numbers $1, \ldots, \mid A(l) \mid$ are initially loaded into the processors of $A(l)$, then after $\lfloor\sqrt{l/2} - 1\rfloor$ steps there is a k, $1 \leq k \leq l$, in Q. Since $k \leq l \leq k+ \mid JZ \mid$ we can apply the joker-argument.

Corollary 4.11

For arbitrary index function f median search and sorting on an $n \times n$ torus need at least $3n/2 - 2$ steps.

In $[MSS, Ku3]$ a sorting algorithm for an index function bsrm (block-wise snake-like row-major) is proposed sorting a torus by only $2n + 0(n^{2/3})$ steps. Let f be an arbitrary indexing for the torus. Then one can shift the bsrm-indexing in such a way that the processor P with $f(P) = l$ gets the index l with respect to shifted bsrm-indexing. Hence for arbitrary l l-selection can be performed by about $2n$ steps. For sorting with respect to arbitrary indexing f then $4n$ steps are asymptotically sufficient. Note that as for theorem 4.4 we can immediately give indexings such that about $2n$ steps are at least necessary for sorting.

4.3 Rectangles of processors and multidimensional meshes

In this section we briefly discuss bounds for sorting and l-selection on rectangles of processors that are $a \times b$ meshes with ab. Let us assume that we have always $a < b$. Let $C_1 = (0, 0)$, $C_2 = (0, b-1)$, $C_3 = (a-1, b-1)$, and $C_4 = (a-1, 0)$ denote the corner processors and for meshes without wrap-arounds define $dmax_f(l) = max\{d(P, C_i) \mid f(P) = l,\ i = 1, \ldots, 4\}$. As before we only consider those indices l with $l \leq ab/2$.

Theorem 4.12

On an $a \times b$ mesh, $a < b$, l-selection with respect to arbitrary indexing f needs at least

a) $dmax_f(l) + \lfloor\sqrt{2l} - 1/2\rfloor - 1$ steps for $l \leq a(a+1)/2$ and

b) $dmax_f(l) + \lceil l/a + (a-1)/2\rceil - 1$ steps for $a(a+1)/2 < l \leq ab/2$.

The proof of this theorem and a more detailed discussion on rectangles of processors can be found in a full version of this paper. Moreover the case of r-dimensional meshes, $r \geq 3$, is presented there.

Conclusion

In this paper we presented lower and upper bounds for l–selection and sorting on one– and two–dimensional grids of processors. It was shown that in contrast to sequential computing median search is as hard as sorting on grids of processors in many cases . For two–dimensional meshes we proved that for arbitrary index schemes there are l–selection problems needing more steps than the simple distance bound for their solution.

For $n \times n$ grids without wrap–around connections we were able to prove a lower bound of 2.25 n steps for sorting with respect to arbitrary indexing. It remains an open question, whether there are index schemes for which sorting algorithms exist needing less than 3 n steps. However, we demonstrated that this bound is valid for almost all index functions.

For tori of processors we could prove a lower bound for median search and sorting which is 50 per cent bigger than the simple distance bound. For some index functions (e.g. snake–like indexing) this bound is optimal within a factor of 4/3. However, even in the case of median search it is open whether this bound can be matched or not.

References:

[KH] Kumar, M., Hirschberg, D.S.: An efficient implementation of Batcher's odd-even merge algorithm and its application in parallel sorting schemes. IEEE Trans. Comput. C-**32**, 254-264 (1983)

[Ku1] Kunde, M.: Lower bounds for sorting on mesh-connected architectures. Acta Informatica 24, 121-130 (1987).

[Ku2] Kunde, M.: Optimal sorting on multi-dimensionally mesh-connected computers. Proceedings of STACS 87. In: Brandenburg, F.J., Vidal-Naquet, G., Wirsing, M. (eds.) Lect. Notes Comp. Sci., vol. 247, pp. 408-419. Berlin-Heidelberg-New York-Tokyo: Springer 1987

[Ku3] Kunde, M.: Routing and Sorting on mesh-connected arrays. Proceedings of AWOC 88. Lect. Notes Comp. Sci., Berlin-Heidelberg-New York-Tokyo: Springer 1988

[KL] Kung, H.T., Leiserson, C.E.: Systolic arrays for VLSI. Symposium on Sparse Matrix Computation 1978, Proceeding, Duff, I.S., Stewart, C.G. (eds.) 1978

[Kn] Knuth, D.E.: The art of computer programming , vol. 3: Sorting and Searching, Addison Wesley, Reading, 1973, pp. 224-225.

[LSSS] Lang, H.-W., Schimmler, M., Schmeck, H., Schröder, H.: Systolic sorting on mesh-connected network. IEEE Trans. Comput. C-**34**, 652-658 (1985)

[MSS] Ma, Y., Sen, S., Scherson, I.D.: The distance bound for sorting on mesh-connected processor arrays is tight. Proceedings FOCS 86, pp. 255-263

[NS] Nassimi, D., Sahni, S.: Bitonic sort on a mesh-connected parallel computer. IEEE Trans. Comput. C-**28**, 2-7 (1979)

[SS] Schnorr, C.P., Shamir, A.: An optimal sorting algorithm for mesh-connected computers, Proceedings STOC 1986. Berkley 1986, pp. 255-263.

[TK] Thompson, C.D., Kung, H.T.: Sorting on a mesh-connected parallel computer. CACM **20**, 263-271 (1977)

RECURSIVE DESIGN OF COMMUNICATION SCHEMES FOR PARALLEL COMPUTATION WITH R E L A C S®

Christoph Meinel
Karl-Weierstraß-Institut für Mathematik
Akademie der Wissenschaften der DDR
Mohrenstr.39 ,PF 1304
DDR-1086 Berlin

and

Peter Zienicke
Sektion Mathematik
Humboldt-Universität
Unter den Linden 6, PF 1297
DDR-1086 Berlin

Extended Abstract

One of the most successful paradigms for designing algorithms is the recursive design paradigma. Its power becomes obvious regarding efficient algorithms. Most of them are recursive ones. The recursive design paradigma consists of breaking a problem of size N into smaller problems in such a way that the solutions of the smaller problems can easily be combined to a solution of the entire problem. With the smaller subproblems we proceed in the same way up to that moment trivial subproblems occur.

If we replace the notions "problem" and "solution" by the notions "pattern" and "design", respectively, we obtain a paradigm for designing circuit structures recursively. Having in mind the common VLSI design methodologies it becomes obvious that the recursive design paradigma suites well for the design of VLSI circuits. It provides highly regular structures on the basis of careful designed recursive generation schemes. Although it is not trivial and sometimes rather difficult to discover a recursive design solution for a given problem the design task complexity is reduced: The recursive design approach allows one to look for solutions on a very small scale. Hence sophisticated solutions for small scale instances will be transformed by the recursive iteration schemes to sophisticated solutions for large scale instances where it would be much more difficult to discover satisfying design solutions. Finally, the recursive design approach allows a mathematical analysis of the complexity of the design which provides a solid basis for comparing different design proposals.

The recursive layout computing system **RELACS** implements the recursive design approach. It provides a powerful tool for designing certain VLSI structures. **RELACS** is developed in Berlin under the leadership of L.Budach (FB Mathematik/Informatik der Akademie der Wissenschaften der DDR) by E.G.Giessmann, H.Grassmann, P.Zienicke (Humboldt Universität Berlin) and B.Graw, Ch.Meinel, B.Molzan (Institut für Mathematik der Akademie der Wissenschaften der DDR).

The **RELACS**-design process is described by **RELACS**-programs which consists of different blocks. One block f.e. contains the initial patterns from which the circuit is constructed. Other blocks contain **RELACS**-polynomials and simplified MODULA-2 programs which describe the design process of certain pattern by means of certain **RELACS**-operations which are to be applied to initial and to already designed pattern. Such **RELACS**-operations are **Be** (juxtapose a list of equal-length patterns along the x-axis), **Ov** (juxtapose a list of equal-width patterns along the y-axis), **T1**, ..., **T4** (rotate the pattern clock-wise by 90°, 180°, 270°, 360°, respec.), **Rx**, **Ry** (reflect the pattern on the x- or the y-axis, respec.). In order to support the input of the generation schemes there is a further operation **Mo** which transforms a pictural representation of a pattern, showing it built from other pattern, into a sequence of geometrical operations).

Now the **RELACS**-system works as follows: The initial pattern given in the **RELACS**-program and the pattern which have been already generated are listed in a catalog. All pattern are handled during the computation by their catalog numbers. The polynomials of the given **RELACS**-program describe sequences of operations applied to the catalog which change that content. In order to obtain the desired recursive effects these sequences are designed in such a way that they can be applied several times to the catalog.

One of the most interesting fields, we applied **RELACS**, is the design of communication schemes for highly parallel computations. So we have designed f.e. different layouts for the Cube Connected Cycles and the Mesh of Trees,two communication schemes which have proved to be very important in the field of parallel computation. Discussing these **RELACS**-designs we obtain new insights into the recursive design approach and its importance for implementing highly parallel computing structures.

REFERENCES:

/Bu83/ L.Budach: Mathematische Probleme beim Entwurf von VLSI-Schaltkreisen. Mitteilungen der Math. Gesellschaft der DDR, Heft 2, 1983, pp. 5-23

/BBMZZ87/ F.Balfanz, L.Budach, Ch.Meinel, S.Zahn, P.Zienicke: Entwurfserfahrungen mit dem rekursiven Layoutentwurfs-system RELACS. Seminarber. Nr.88, Sekt. Mathematik der Humboldt-Univ., Mai 1987

/Me87/ Ch.Meinel: The recursive design paradigma and its application in the layout computing system **RELACS**-. Proc. SOFSEM'87, ČSSR, 1987

SOLUTION OF DENSE SYSTEMS OF LINEAR EQUATIONS USING CELLULAR PROCESSORS

Kálmán Palágyi[1/]

A cellular processor is a totally reconfigurable universal purpose device for highly parallel processing, where computations are performed by a homogeneous array of microprogrammable Boolean processors [6].

In this paper three cellular algorithms are proposed for solving dense systems of linear equations. For simplicity these algorithms are given as systolic arrays, but our attention is focussed on their implementation with cellular processors.

1. Introduction

Solution of linear systems of equations are needed in many important scientific and engineering application areas. Recently, several algorithms have been constructed for solving the above task on parallel computers, see for instance [1],[2],[5],[7].

In this paper three further parallel algorithms are presented for solving the equation A·X=B, where A is an nxn dense matrix, X and B are nxm matrices. /This problem is equivalent to linear systems of equations $A\cdot\underline{x}_1=\underline{b}_1,\dots,A\cdot\underline{x}_m=\underline{b}_m$, where vector $\underline{x}_i$ is the i-th column of matrix X and $\underline{b}_i$ denotes the i-th column of matrix B /i=1,2,...,m/./

The first algorithm is based on the Gauss-Jordan elimination without pivoting. The Gaussian elimination without pivoting can be executed by the second solution. /If the matrix A is not special /e.g. symmetric positive definite or an irreducible diagonally dominant/ then pivoting is generally necessary to guarantee numerical stability. To avoid the pivoting problem we propose a widely known method in section 5./ The orthogonal factorization is applied by the third algorithm.

For simplicity these algorithms are presented as systolic arrays in sections 2,3,4. /They are suitable for special purpose hardware realization./ All of these algorithms require O(n) steps with $O(n^2)$ processors. Their implementation with cellular processors is described in section 6. The proposed algorithms can be partitioned efficiently thus arbitrary size of linear systems of equations can be solved by a given size cellular space.

1/ Attila József University, Computer Science Department, Somogyi u. 7. H-6720 Szeged, Hungary

2. A systolic array for Gauss-Jordan elimination

The solution shown in Fig.1 requires 5n+m-2 steps with n(n+1) PEs. /If A^{-1} is not needed as a result then it requires only 4n+m-2 steps. On the other hand, if more equations should be solved and the inputs come successively then solution of an equation $A_i \cdot X_i = B_i$ requires only n+m steps in average /i=1,2,..././

Detailed description of the above solution can be found in [8]. We remark that a similar systolic array is given for algebraic path problem in [9].

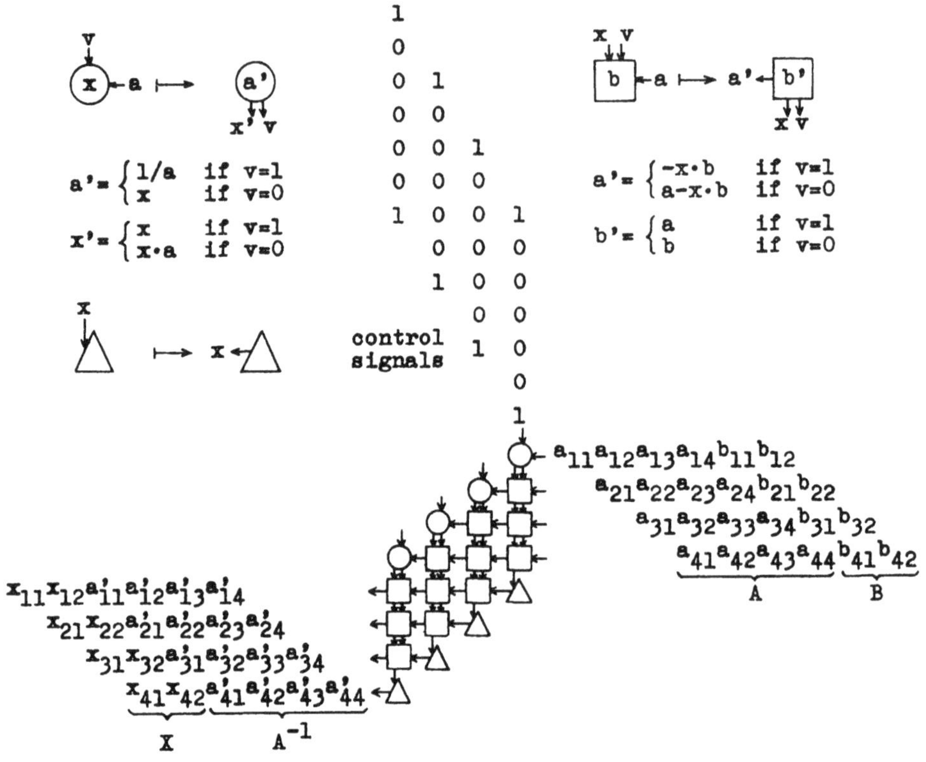

Fig.1. Sketch of a systolic array for solving the equation A·X=B in the case n=4,m=2.

3. A systolic array for Gaussian elimination

The systolic array shown in Fig.2 can transform the equation A·X=B into the equation U·X=B', where matrix U is upper triangular. Once the matrices U and B' are known, it is relatively easy to solve the equation U·X = B' . A back substitution process should be applied to the triangular systems. A systolic array for back substitution is shown in Fig.3.

The solution shown in Fig.2 requires 3n+m-2 steps with n(n+2m+1)/2 PEs.

Detailed description of the systolic array shown in Fig.2 can be found in [8]. Note that LU decomposition without pivoting can be executed by a similar systolic array described in [8].

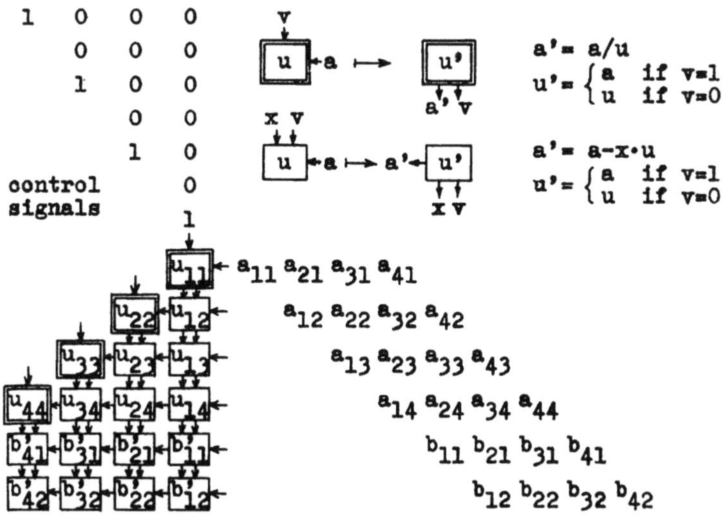

Fig.2. Sketch of a systolic array for Gaussian elimination in the case n=4,m=2. The output is found in the processor array.

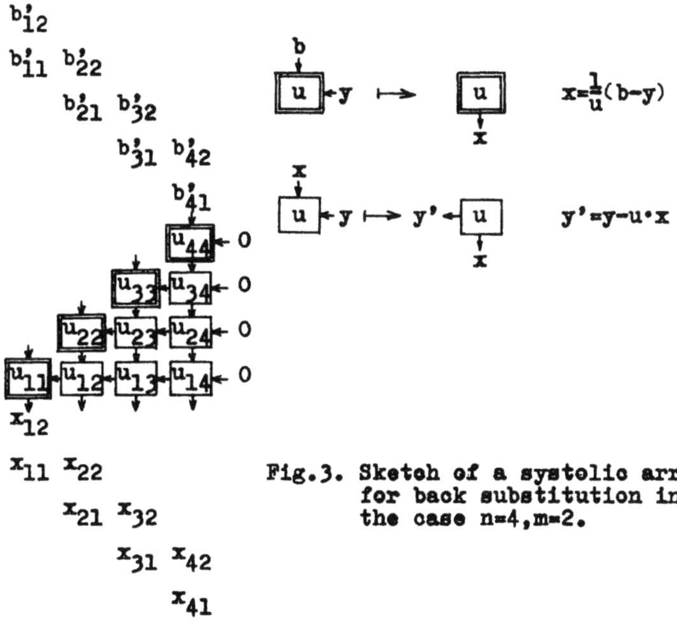

Fig.3. Sketch of a systolic array for back substitution in the case n=4,m=2.

4. A systolic array for orthogonal factorization

The systolic array shown in Fig.4 can transform the equation A·X=B into the equation U·X=B', where matrix U is upper triangular. The matrices A and B are reduced to matrices U and B' by Givens' rotations. The equation U·X=B' can be solved by a back substitution process.

The solution shown in Fig.4 requires 4n+m-3 steps with (n-1)(n+m) PEs. /If more equations should be solved and the inputs come successively , then transformation of an equation $A_i \cdot X_i = B_i$ requires only n steps in average /i=1,2,..././

We mention that a homogeneous systolic array has been constructed in [1] for orthogonal factorization requiring O(n) steps with O(n^2) PEs too, but square root extraction and division are performed by each PE. In our solution PEs have less complexity.

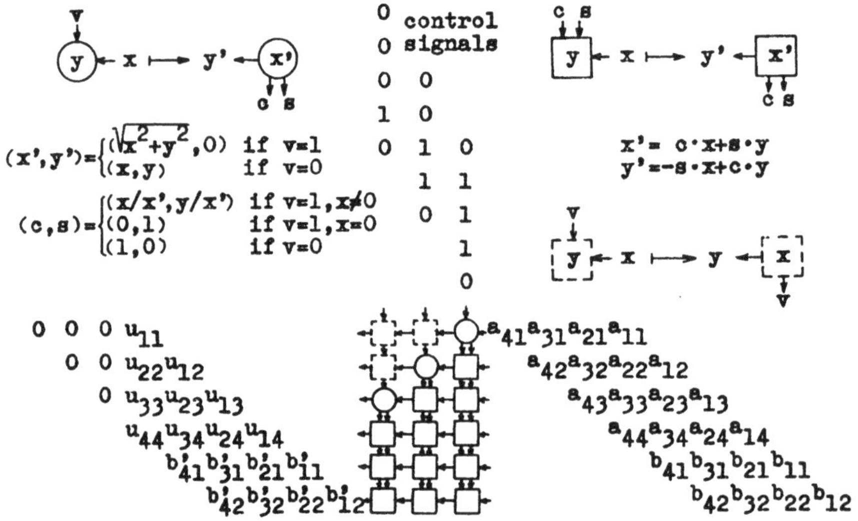

Fig.4. Sketch of a systolic array for orthogonal factorization in the case n=4,m=2.

5. Numerical stability

The solutions sketched in sections 2,3 are problematical because pivoting is generally necessary to guarantee numerical stability. To avoid the pivoting problem we propose a widely known method. This method is based on the following fact: If a quadratic matrix A is not singular then $A^T \cdot A$ is a symmetric positive definite matrix. $A^T \cdot A$ has the property that its inversion and LU decomposition can be done by Gauss-Jordan elimination and Gaussian elimination without pivoting. In this case the following procedure is proposed:

step 1. Compute the matrices $A^T \cdot A$ and $A^T \cdot B$.
step 2. Solve the equation $(A^T \cdot A) \cdot X = A^T \cdot B$ /which is equivalent to the original task/.

The solution in section 4 is numerically stable thus it can be applied for any non-singular matrix.

6. Cellular algorithms for solving the equation A·X=B

The programming of cellular processors is described in [3]. Although the cellular space consists of Boolean processors /cells/, groups of cells may form any kind of fixed-point or floating-point arithmetic processing elements /cellular PEs/ and these PEs can be interconnected by data channels. If each PE of the systolic arrays in sections 2,3,4 is replaced by the corresponding cellular PE, regular arrays of cells are gained resulting cellular algorithms for solving the given task.

The planned cellular processors contain 4000 to 1 million cells. If the given cellular array is too small to solve the equation A·X=B, then cellular algorithms should be partitioned. Algorithms sketched in sections 2,3,4 can be partitioned by a general method described in [4]. /We make use of the data channels free from any circle./

For instance, a partitioned cellular algorithm will be sketched for solving Gauss-Jordan elimination. The systolic array of section 2 is divided into 20 partitions /Fig.5/ supposing that the actual cellular array is great enough to simulate each of these partitions.

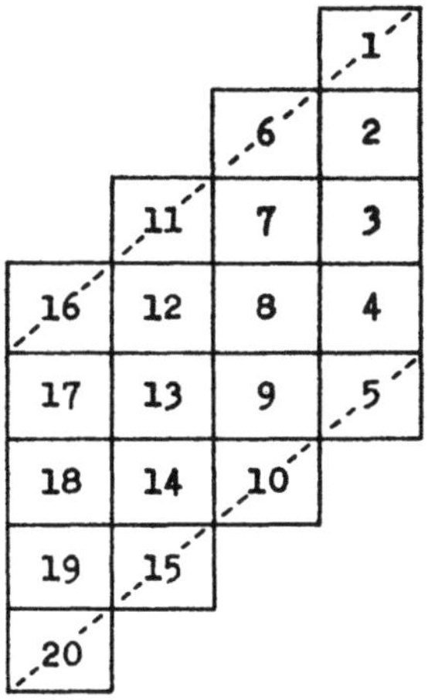

Fig.5. Partitioning structure of the cellular array for solving Gauss-Jordan elimination. Numbers denote the computation sequence of partitions.

The partitioned computation is sketched in Fig.6. The further algorithms described in sections 3,4 can be partitioned in a similar way. We should remark that a cellular divider and a cellular square root extractor are slower than a multiplier, thus the partitioned cellular algorithms contain $O(n^2)$ "fast" and $O(n)$ "slower" processes.

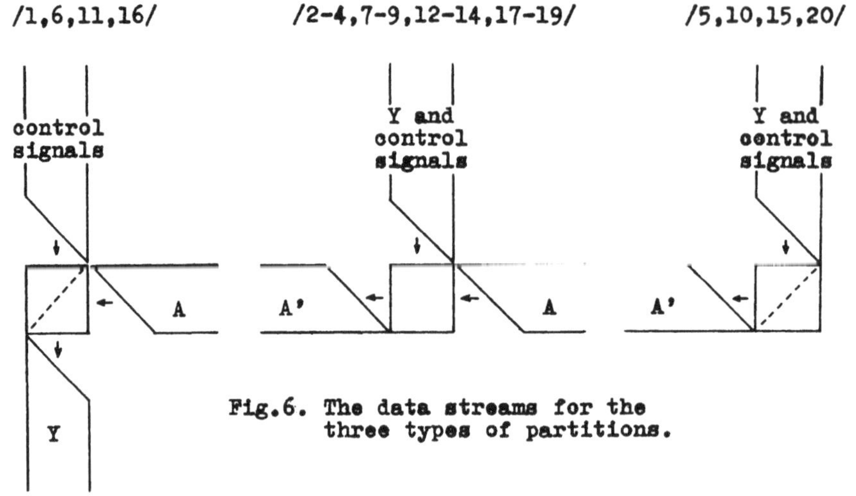

Fig.6. The data streams for the three types of partitions.

References

[1] Boyanczyk, A.- Brent, R.P.- Kung, H.T.: Numerically Stable Solution of Dense Systems of Linear Equations Using Mesh-connected Processors, Carnegie-Mellon Univ. /1981/ 21.

[2] Hwang, K.- Cheng, Y.H.: Partitioned Matrix Algorithms for VLSI Arithmetic Systems, IEEE Trans. on Comp., Vol. C-31. No. 12 /1982/ 1215-24.

[3] Katona, E.: A Programming Language for Cellular Processors, Proc. of Conf. "Parallel Computing'85", W-Berlin /1986/ North-Holland.

[4] Katona, E.: A General Partitioning Method for Cellular Algorithms, Proc. of the 4th Cellular Meeting, T.U. Braunschweig /1988/.

[5] Kung, H.T.- Leierson, C.E.: Systolic Arrays /for VLSI/, Carnegie-Mellon Univ. /1978/ 32.

[6] Legendi, T.: Cellprocessors in Computer Architecture, Computational Linguistics and Computer Languages 11 /1977/ 147-167.

[7] Miklosko, J.: Four Specialized VLSI Computers for the Fast Gauss-Jordan-Rutishauer Elimination Algorithm with Partial Pivoting, Computers and Artificial Intelligence, 4 /1985/, No. 2, 163-186.

[8] Palágyi, K.: Computing Matrix Problems on Cellular Processors, Thesis, József A. Univ., Szeged /1984/, in Hungarian.

[9] Robert, Y.- Trystram, D.: Parallel Implementation of the Algebraic Path Problem, Proc. of the Conf. "Conpar'86", Aachen /1986/ 149-56.

RUNNING ORDER STATISTICS ON A BIT-LEVEL SYSTOLIC ARRAY

N. Petkov[1)]

Abstract - A two-dimensional bit-level systolic array for running order statistics is presented. Both word-level and bit-level parallelism are employed. The array is extremely easy to implement in VLSI, because its cells are very small and simple. Since extensive pipelining is used at both word and bit level, the array can be operated at very high clock frequencies achieving very high throughputs. The algorithm delivers full running order statistics in time $\theta(n)$ and area $\theta[n(w+\log n)]$ where n is the cardinality of the processed set and w is the word width of its elements.

Index terms - running order statistics, bit-level systolic arrays, VLSI

1. Introduction

Running order statistics is a fundamental computational problem [1,2] having many important applications in signal and image processing [4,5,6,21] and data base management (see e.g. [7]). It is closely related to and can be used for sorting [1,2]. A number of algorithms have been proposed for running order statistics and we refer to [1,2] for more information and further references.

In the following, we are concerned with parallel algorithms for running order statistics which are suitable for VLSI implementation. Systolic arrays have been shown to perfectly match the restrictions of VLSI design due to their homogeneous cellular structure, local and regular interconnections, absence of broadcasting and rippling etc. Other merits of systolic algorithms with respect to parallel processing are their high efficiency, pipelined processing and transfer of data, overlapping of data transfer and processing, minimized communication between a systolic array and host computer etc. [8,9,10].

The original motivation for putting forward the systolic concept was its high potential for VLSI implementation. However, up to now, ten years after this concept was explicitely formulated, only few systolic arrays have been implemented as single chips. The reason is that a systolic array can benefit from its cellular homogeneous structure and regular local interconnection pattern for VLSI implementation only if the array cells are quite small and simple. We refer to [9,11-16,22-24] for some representative examples of systolic arrays which make use of simple cells requiring only small area. Since these cells operate on single-bit data flows, we refer to the corresponding arrays as bit-level systolic arrays.

In this paper, a new systolic algorithm for running order statistics is presented. In section 2, a systolic array for word-level parallelism is given. Bit-level parallelism is introduced in the array in section 3. Our objective is to use both word- and bit-level parallelism and extensive pipelining at both the word and the bit level, and to obtain a design which is well suited for VLSI implementation. Comparison with alternative algorithms is made in section 4, and results are summarized in section 5.

1) Dr.sc.techn. N. Petkov, Int'l Lab. Image Processing & Computer Graphics, Central Institute of Cybernetics and Information Processes Kurstr. 33, P.O. Box 1298, Berlin, DDR-1086

2. Word-level systolic algorithm

Usually, running order statistics on a set S of real numbers is introduced by sorting the set and considering its elements with respect to their running order in the sorted set. We rather use another (equivalent) definition here[1).
Given a set $S = \{a_i | i = 1, 2, \dots, n\}$ of n numbers, for each element a_i of S, two integers x_i and y_i, to be called in the following lower and upper rank boundaries, respectively, are defined as follows:

$$x_i = 1 + card\{a | a \in S,\ a_i > a\}, \tag{1}$$

$$y_i = card\{a | a \in S,\ a_i \geq a\}, \qquad i = 1, 2, \dots, n. \tag{2}$$

An element a_i of S is called element of running order (rank) r, if

$$x_i \leq r \leq y_i \qquad (r \in \{1, 2, \dots, n\}) \tag{3}$$

Notice that, according to (3), some elements of the set can have more than one single rank. For instance, the element 5 has ranks 2 and 3 in the set $S = \{6, 5, 1, 7, 5, 9\}$.

Figure 1 shows a linear systolic array for gathering running order statistics by means of computing the lower and upper rank boundaries x_i and y_i, $i = 1, 2, \dots, n$, according to eq. (1) and (2), respectively. More precisely, this array is a linear pipeline, a special case of a linear systolic array in which all data flows in one direction at the same velocity. (The small black boxes in Figure 1 denote delay elements which are controlled by a common clock.) This array qualifies as a word-level array, because the operations executed by its cells are word-level operations.

The array function is described shortly in the following. The elements of a set S are preloaded in the array, one element in each cell. A second copy of each element of S is input at the left side of the array and moved to the right at a velocity of one array cell per clock period. On its way through the array,

1) In fact, this is the precise definition of running order statistics as mentioned in the first footnote of ch.3.6 in [1].

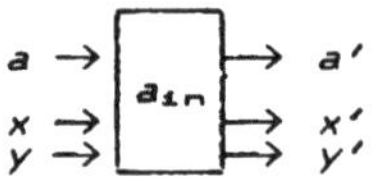


```
procedure cell (a,a',a_in: real;
     x,y,x',y': integer)
begin
   a':= a;
   if a > a_in then x':= x + 1 (*increment*)
   else x':= x;
   if a ≥ a_in then y':= y + 1 (*increment*)
   else y':= y
end
```

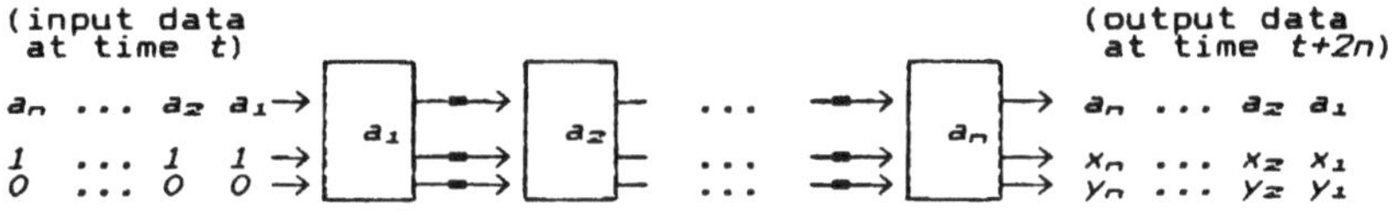

Fig.1 – Systolic array for running order statistics.

an element a_i $(i = 1, 2, \ldots, n)$ of S meets all elements of S which are stored in the array cells. In the j-th cell, the element a_i which is input from the left is compared with the element a_j which is stored in the cell. If $a_i > a_j$, the lower rank boundary x_i which is moved together with a_i through the array is incremented by 1. If $a_i \geq a_j$, the upper rank boundary y_i which is also moved together with a_i through the array is incremented by 1. The ultimate values of the lower and upper rank boundaries x_i and y_i, respectively, $i = 1, 2 \ldots n$, leave the array at its right side together with the element a_i n clock periods after a_i was input in the array.

In Figure 2, the array is extended for the preloading of the cells concurrently with the input of the elements of the set S in the leftmost array cell. The loading is performed by broadcasting of an element to all cells. (The broadcasting is due to the fact that no delay elements are arranged in the corresonding interconnections). In each clock period, only one of the cells is activated to load by a control bit c valued 1 which is moved from left to the right at a velocity of one cell per clock period. The elements of a second set S' can be input in the array immediately after the the elements of the first one and other sets can follow. In this mode, the array is able to process one set of n numbers every n clock periods. (In a single-set processing mode, the overall processing time is $2n$ clock periods.)

3. Bit-level array

We now consider the case in which the elements of S are fixed-point real numbers represented by w-bit words. The bits of an element a shall be denoted by $a^0, a^1 \ldots a^{w-1}$, with a^0 being the least significant bit (LSB) and a^{w-1} the most significant bit (MSB), respectively.

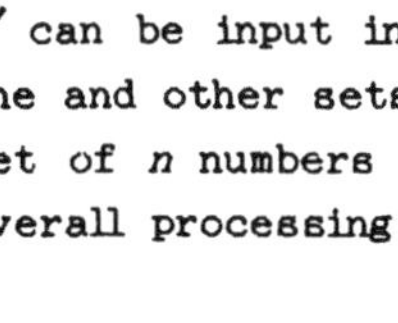


```
procedure cell (s,s': boolean; a,a',
  b, b',a_in: real; x,y,x',y': integer)
begin
  a':= a;  b':= b; s':= s;
  if s then a_in:= b;                  (*load*)
  if a > a_in then x':= x + 1 ;        (*increment*)
  else x':= x;
  if a ≥ a_in then y':= y + 1          (*increment*)
  else y':= y
end
```

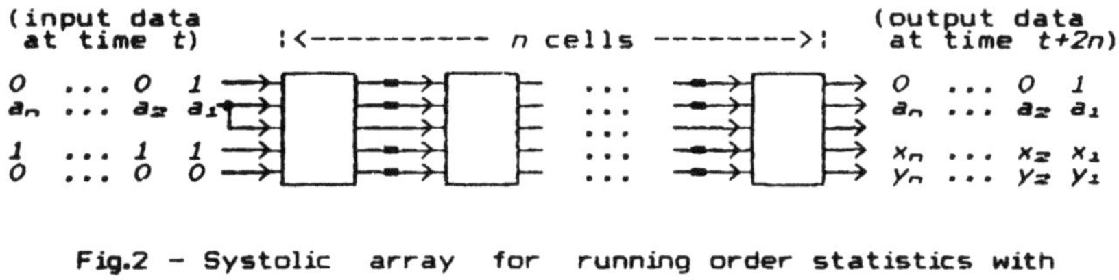

Fig.2 - Systolic array for running order statistics with concurrent preloading of the set elements.

Figure 3 shows a linear bit-level systolic array which realises the word-level cell function given in Fig.2a. This array qualifies as a bit-level array, because its cells operate on single-bit data flows. The upper part of the array consists of w ($w = 4$ in Fig.3) bit-level comparator cells. The function of one comparator cell is specified in Fig.3b. The g'-output of the bottommost comparator cell of the array outputs a binary *1*, if $a > a_{in}$, and a binary *0* else. The ge'-output of the same cell outputs a binary *1*, if $a \geq a_{in}$, and a binary *0* else. These signals are input in the lower part of the array which realises the incrementation of the rank boundaries x and y. This lower part consists of $w_{xy}-1$ bit-level incrementer cells. (w_{xy} denotes the word width of x and y which will be generally determined by the relation $w_{xy} \geq \lceil \log_2 n \rceil$.) Each incrementer cell consists of two independent half adders (Fig. 3c): one for the incrementation of the lower rank boundary x and the other for the incrementation of the upper rank boundary y. Notice that

(a)

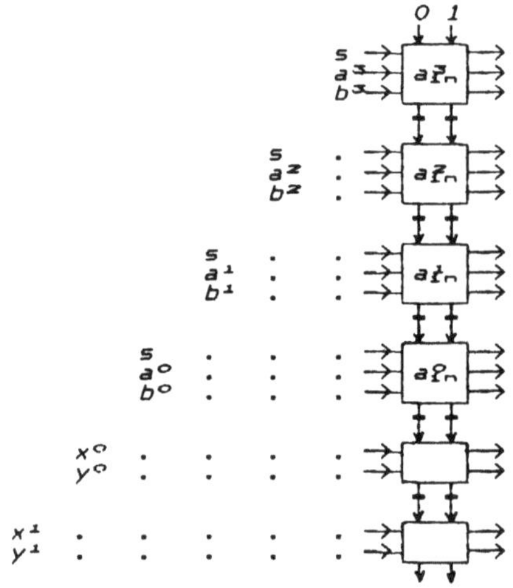

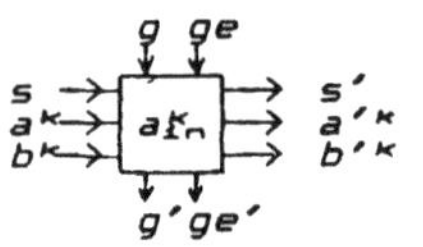

(b)

```
procedure comparator cell
(all variables: boolean)
begin
  if s then ain := bk;        (*load*)
  a'k:= ak;  b'k:= bk;  s':= s;
  g':= g or ge and (ak > ain);
  ge':= g or ge and (ak ≥ ain)
end
```

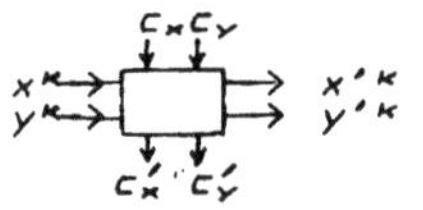

(c)

```
procedure incrementer cell
(all variables: boolean)
begin
  x'k  := xk exor cx;         (*sum*)
  c'x  := xk and cx;          (*carry*)
  y'k  := yk exor cy;         (*sum*)
  c'y  := yk and cy           (*carry*)
end
```

Fig.3 - Linear bit-level systolic array for primitive word-level operations.

delay elements are arranged between the cells and that neighbouring bits of the input elements *a* and *b* and the rank boundaries *x* and *y* (related to *a*) are scewed by one clock period. By means of this pipelining on the bit level, the time period can be reduced to the delay of a single bit-level cell. This leads to a high clock frequency and high throughput of the array.

We now combine the results presented so far to obtain the two-dimensional bit-level systolic array shown in Fig.4. More precisely, the array shown in Fig.4 consists of two different bit-level systolic arrays: a semi-systolic comparator array and a full-systolic incrementer array. The comparator array qualifies as a semisystolic array, because of the partial broadcasting in horizontal direction for the loading of the comparator cells via their *b*-inputs (no delay elements are arranged in the corresponding interconnections). Both word-level and bit-level parallelism are employed in the array and all processing, down to the bit level, is pipelined. It is extremely easy to implement this array in VLSI, because its cells are very small and simple - roughly, about 10 gates per cell are required to implement the Boolean cell functions. Only two cell types have to be designed, varified, simulated and tested, and the overall array design is obtained by replication of these two cell types. The delay elements can be realised at a very low area cost as two-phase dynamic registers.

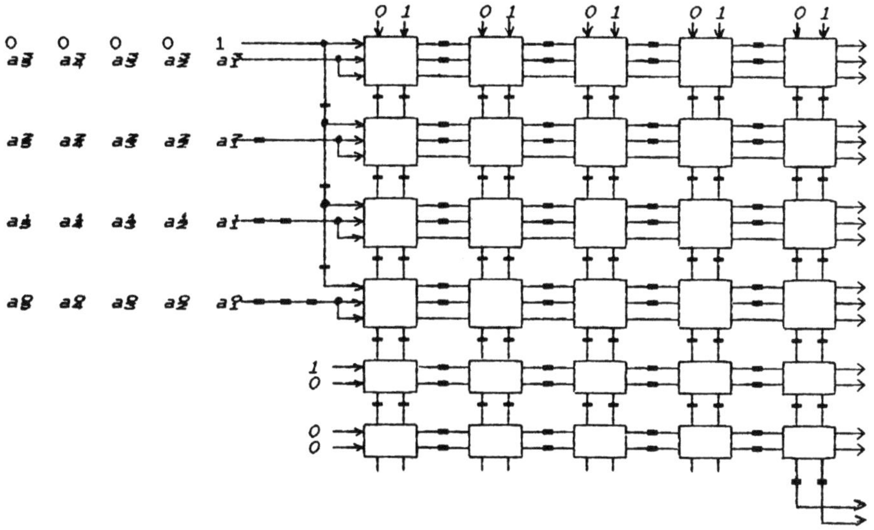

Fig.4 - Two-dimensional bit-level systolic array for running order statistics (n = 5, w = 4, w_{xy} = $\lceil \log_2 n \rceil$ = 3).

4. Performance evaluation and comparison

The array given in the previous section consists of $n(w+\lceil \log_2 n \rceil -1)$ bit-level cells, so that it requires area $\Theta[n(w+\log n)]$. One set of n elements is processed every n clock periods and the clock period does not depend on the number n of elements in the set and on their word width w. Hence, one set is processed in time $\Theta(n)$. (Complexity denotions after [3].)

An algorithm, refered to as parallel enumeration sorting, has been proposed for VLSI implementation in [7]. It is closely related to the word-level systolic algorithm presented in section 2 above. A linear array of (word-level) cells is used; the elements of the set are loaded in the cells by broadcasting and moved from cell to cell exactly as in the algorithm given in section 2 (Fig.2). The rank boundaries x_i, i = 1, 2, ... , n, (denoted by c_i and slightly modified in [7]) are, however, computed by accumulation "in place", x_i in the i-th cell. These integers are sent to the host computer by means of an additional broadcasting bus. Hence, this algorithm makes use of two broadcasting busses opposite to just one for the algorithm presented in section 2. The control structure is also more complex requiring more than one control signals. Since no pipelining has been introduced for data processing at the bit level, the array proposed in [7] is supposed to exhibit clock frequency and throughput which are w times smaller than the clock frequency and througput, respectively, of the bit-level systolic array presented in this paper.

A lot of other running order statistics algorithms for rank filtering have been proposed elsewhere, but we refer here for a comparison only to those of them which are well suited for VLSI implementation and which are capable of providing complete running order statistics, i.e. the rank boundaries of all elements. We refer to Table 1 for performance comparison of these algorithms.

Table 1 - Performance of different running order statistics algorithms for signal and image processing. (n - number of pixels in a window, w - word width of a pixel value, d - image dimensionality)

Criteria / Algorithm	Area	Time (per pixel)
Bit-level systolic algorithm (this paper)	$\Theta[n(w+\log n)]$	$\Theta(n)$
Enumeration sort [7]	$\Theta[n(w+\log n)]$	$\Theta(wn)$
Bit-refinement method [20,21]	$\Theta(2^n)$	$\Theta(w)$
Fisher's 1-D algorithm [18]	$\Theta(nw)$	$\Theta(\log w)$
Priority queue generalization [19]	$\Theta[n(w+\frac{1}{d}\log n)]$	$\Theta[\log(\frac{1}{d}\log n)+n^{(d-1)/d}\log w]$
Fisher's 2-D algorithm [18]	$\Theta[n(w+\log n)]$	$\Theta[n(\log w+\log\log n)]$
Bubble-sorting[22]	$\Theta(wn)$	$\Theta(n)$

A-bit refinement method has been proposed by *Rösler et al.* [21] for rank filtering and mask operators. (The well-known algorithm of *Ataman et al.* [20] is a special case of this algorithm for median filtering.) In this algorithm, the separate bits of an element of S which has a given rank are computed one after another, MSB first, LSB last. Hence, the algorithm requires time $\theta(w)$ and is, in this way, the only algorithm to exhibit time which does not depend on n. However, a look-up-table is used which requires area $\theta(2^n)$. This is obviously not acceptable for large n. It should also be noted that only one rank position is obtained by this algorithm . For more complex applications as range filtering or filtering by linear combinations of more than one rank positions [5,6], the complete running order statistics has to be computed. In this case, either the area or the time complexity given for this algorithm in Table 1 should be multiplied with an additional factor n.

Fisher [18] has generalized *Leiserson's* systolic priority queue array [17] for running order statistics on a window of n samples which is slided over a one-dimensional signal. This algorithm, refered to in Table 1 as Fisher's 1-D algorithm, delivers running order statistics for one position of the window in time which does not depend on n. Leiserson's systolic priority queue array has been generalized for multidimensional images achieving sublinear dependence on n oposite to the the linear dependence on n of the algorithm presented above [19]. Both priority queue generalization systolic algorithms have, however, an additional multiplicative factor $\log w$ in their time complexity. The reason for this factor is that these algorithms make use of word-level cells which can not be effectively pipelined at the bit level; one word-level (comparison) operation should be completed before the next one is started. The algorithm presented in the previous section makes use of word-level cells which can be effectively pipelined at the bit level. Many word-level operations can be run concurrently in one (word-level) cell and the clock period does not depend on the word width w of the elements. It can be shown that, for typical applications (e.g. $d = 1,\ n < 7$ or $d = 2,\ n < 25$), the factor $\log w$ "overhelms" the n-dependence resulting in better time performance of the bit-level systolic algorithm presented in this paper. The algorithm given by Fisher [18] for 2-D (image) processing exhibits $\theta(\log w + \log\log n)$ time performance when used for computing just one rank position, but requires time $\theta[n(\log w + \log\log n)]$ when applied to the complete running order statistics problem.

The bubble-sorting algorithm have been effectively pipelined on bit and word level to achieve time performance $\theta(n)$ on area $\theta(wn)$ [22]. Both the bubble-sort algorithm and the running order statistics algorithm presented above show the same time complexity $\theta(n)$, but the running order statistics algorithm exhibits an area overhead which is due to the incrementer part and is characterized by an additional logarithmic factor ($n\log n$). These statements hold not only for the complexity performance. Since both arrays use bit level (comparator) cells which are comparable with respect to area and time delay, the statements made are true not only in the asymptotic case, but also for small values of the parameter n. At this place, a natural question should arise whether the bit-level bubble-sort algorithm should not be used instead of the running order statistics algorithm presented above. We, however, give preference to the running order statistics algorithm for the following reason:

The rank boundaries x_i and y_i, i = 1, 2, ... , n, can be directly used to compute a histogramm over S. Consider the diference $d = y-x+1$; it gives how often a value a appears in the set S. Furthermore, the algorithm given above can easily be generalized to realise mask operators, another kind of local, non-linear filtering operators which are widely used in image processing. Since our purpose was to implement as many functions as possible by a single VLSI algorithm, we are ready to sacrifice the additional area mentioned above. It should be also noticed that for typical applications it holds $\log n < w$ and the area of the incrementer part is small in comparison to the area of the comparator part.

An alternative running order statistics algorithm which is based on computing the rank boundaries (1-2) and is closely related with the algorithm presented in this paper has been proposed elsewhere especially for image and signal processing [22,24]. It makes use of window overlapping in a fashion similar to the one used in fast sorting algorithms for signal and image processing [18,19]. The area and time complexities of this algorithm are $\theta(n^{(d-1)/d}(w+\log n))$ and $\theta(n)$, respectively, the sublinear area complexity being obviously superiour to the linear area complexity of the bubble-sort algorithm and the other algorithms mentioned above. (In [19,22,24] it is supposed that the image is d-dimensional and is processed with a window in form of a d-dimensional hypercube.) Such an area reduction is not possible for the bubble-sorting algorithm, since it can not utilize window overlapping.

5. Summary and conclusions

A two-dimensional bit-level systolic array for running order statistics was presented in this paper. This array can easily be extended to perform histogramm computations and mask operators covering in this way a large field of signal and image processing by local non-linear operators. Both word- and bit-level parallelism are employed in the array and the data processing is pipelined at both the word and bit level. The array is highly regular and extremely easy to implement in VLSI, because its cells are quite simple. Since the clock period is determined by the delay of a single bit-level cell, the array can be operated at very high clock frequencies achieving very high throughputs.

The systolic algorithm presented requires area $\theta[n(w+\log n)]$ and time $\theta(n)$. The detailed analysis made elsewhere has shown that for typical signal and image processing applications this algorithm is superior to fast rank filtering methods. Bit-level bubble-sort systolic arrays yield comparable time performance and area results which are only slightly better for typical applications. Bubble-sorting can, however, not be used directly for histogram computation.

References:

[1] A. V. Aho, J. E. Hopcroft, and J. D. Ullman: "*The Design and Analysis of Computer Algorithms*" (Reading, Massachusetts: Addison-Wesley, 1974)

[2] D. E. Knuth: "*The Art of Computer Programming, Volume 3: Sorting and Searching*" (Don Mills, Ontario: Addison-Wesley, 1973)

[3] D. E. Knuth: "Big omicron, big omega, and big theta", SIGACT News **8** (1976) 2, pp.18-24

[4] R. M. Hodgson, D. G. Bailey, M. J. Naylor, A. L. M. Ng, and S. J. McNeill: "Properties, implementations, and applications of rank filters". Image and Vision Computing 3 (1985) 1, pp.3-14

[5] J. B. Bednar and T. L. Watt:"Alpha trimmed means and their relationship to median filters". IEEE Trans.Acoust.,Speech, Signal Process. **32** (1984) pp. 145-153

[6] A. C. Bovik, T. S. Huang, and D. C. Munson: "A generalization of median filtering using linear combinations of order statistics". IEEE Trans. Acoust., Speech, Signal Process. **31** (1983) pp. 1342-1349

[7] H. Yasuura, N. Tagaki, and S. Yajima: "The parallel enumeration sorting scheme for VLSI", IEEE Trans. Computers **C-31** (1982), pp. 1192-1201

[8] H. T. Kung and C. E. Leiserson: "Systolic arrays (for VLSI)", Sparse Matrix Proc. 1978, Society for Industrial and Applied Mathematics, 1979, pp.256-282. or "Algorithms for VLSI processor arrays", in C. Mead and L. Conway: "*Introduction to VLSI Systems*" (Readinn MA: Addison-Wesley, 1980) sect. 8.3

[9] M.J.Foster and H.T.Kung:" The design of special purpose VLSI chips", Computer **13** (1980) 1, pp.26-40.

[10] H. T. Kung: "Why systolic architectures", Computer **15** (1982) 1, pp. 37-46.

[11] R. A. Evans, J. V. McCanny, J. G. McWhirter, A. McCabe, D. Wood, and K. W. Wood: "A CMOS Implementation of a systolic multibit convolver chip", Proc. VLSI 83 (Trondheim, Norway), pp.227-235, 1983.

[12] F. Jutand, N. Demassieux, D. Vicard, and G. Chollet: "VLSI architectures for dynamic time warping using systolic arrays," IEEE ICASSP 1984, pp. 34.A.5.1-34.A.5.4.

[13] T. Noll:"Semi-systolic maximum rate transversal filters with programmable coefficients", in W.Moore, A.McCabe, and R.Urquhart (eds.): "Systolic Arrays" (Bristol: Adam Hilger, 1987), pp.103-112.

[14] N. Petkov-Turkedjiev: "Bit-organised systolic convolution algorithm", Int'l Workshop on Systolic Arrays, Oxford, 1986, pp.I.2.1-I.2.10

[15] N. Petkov-Turkedjiev: "Bit-organisierte systolische Schaltungsanordnung für FIR-Filter", 19. Fachkolloquium Informationstechnik, Jan. 1986, TU Dresden, Teil II, S.227-232

[16] N. Petkov: "Bit-organised systolic FIR filter", Proc. 1st Hungarian Custom Circuit Conference 1987, pp.161-168.

[17] C. E. Leiserson: "Systolic priority queues". Technical report CMU-CS-79-115, Carnegie-Mellon Univ., Computer Science Dept., April 1979

[18] A.L.Fisher: "Systolic algorithms for running order statistics in signal and image processing". In "VLSI Systems and Computations", eds. H.T.Kung et al. (Comp.Sci. Press, 1981), pp.265-272

[19] N. Petkov: "Systolic array for fast multidimensional rank filtering", Preprint Basic Laboratory for Image Processing and Computer Graphics, Central Institute of Cybernetics and Information Processes, Berlin, 1988

[20] E. Ataman, V. K. Aatre, and K. M. Wong: "A fast method for real time median filtering". IEEE Trans. Acoust., Speech, Signal Process. **28** (1980), pp.415-420

[21] U. Rösler, G. Schwarze, und T. L. Chung: Lokale Bildoperatoren zur Manipulation von Grauwertobjekten und ihre Implementierung durch den Prozessor GIPP. Elektron. Inf.verarb.Kybern. EIK 21 (1985) 7/8, S.343-354.

[22] S. G. Akl and H. Schmeck: "Systolic sorting in a sequential input/ output environment", Parallel Computing 3 (1986) 1, pp.11-23

[23] N. Petkov: "Bit-level systolic array for running order statistics", Preprint Basic Laboratory for Image Processing and Computer Graphics, Central Institute of Cybernetics and Information Processes, Berlin, 1988

[24] N. Petkov: "*Systolische Algorithmen und Arrays*" (Berlin: Akademie-Verlag, to appear by the end of 1988)

Realization of Sets of Permutations
by Permutation Networks

R.Pöschel [1]), F.Wächter [2]), F.Börner [1])

1. Introduction

Permutation networks as special interconnection networks are essential parts of parallel computers and have extensive applications in multiprocessor systems. Permutation networks can serve for the memory-processor data transfer and for the processor-processor communication (described e.g. in [6], cf. [4]). Important objectives for designing such networks are low hardware costs and simple control of the network.

In the last years many different types of permutation networks have been described. Surveys can be found e.g. in [5],[10]. This wide variety of networks results from the large number of $N!$ possible permutations of N inputs and from the great hardware costs and difficult control of rearrangeable networks which can realize all $N!$ permutations. The best solution of rearrangeable networks (known to the authors) is given in [11] with $N \cdot \lceil \mathrm{ld}\, N \rceil - 2^{\lceil \mathrm{ld}\, N \rceil} + 1$ control signals and the same number of 2x2-switching cells (if N is a power of two, see also [17]).
Other types of rearrangable networks have higher demand of switching elements and control signals, as for example 3n-4 shuffle-exchange stages with $(3n-4) \cdot 2^{n-1}$ control signals and switching elements in case $N = 2^n \geq 8$ ([15]). Networks with lower hardware and control demands can be used in order to realize special sets of permutations.

In this paper we are dealing with permutation networks the general structure of which is given in Fig. 1. It consists of a serial connection of layers. Each layer i, $i = 1, \dots, m$, has N inputs and N outputs $0, 1, \dots, N-1$ and realizes (in dependence of its control input c_i) a permutation from a set L_i of permutations.* As shown in [4; Prop. 1.3] one can assume without lost of generality that each L_i contains the identical permutation e, i.e., $L_i = \{e, p_i\}$ with $p_i \in S_N$, where S_N denotes the full symmetric group of all permutations. The network given in Fig. 1 will be denoted by $(L_1, L_2, \dots, L_m)$.

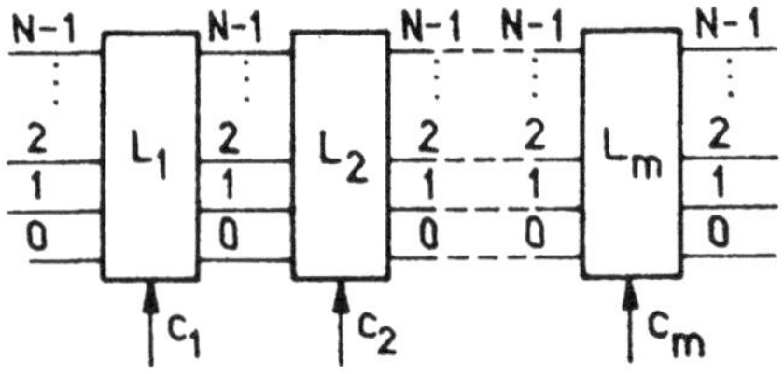

* We are mainly interested in binary control inputs c_i, therefore each set L_i contains no more than two permutations.

Fig. 1

For special sets of permutations this structure gives a better solution than the networks mentioned above. Especially, as shown in §§ 3, 4 below, this structure can be used for the realization of cyclic or abelian groups of permutations.
Special examples of such permutation networks are implemented in the STARAN computer [2],[3], the Burroughs Scientific Processor [1],[8] and in the parallel memory described in [13],[12]; the realized permutations are of the form $x \mapsto x \oplus i$ in case of the STARAN computer (where $\oplus$ denotes the component-wise addition modulo 2) or of the form $x \mapsto (x \cdot F + S) \bmod N$ with prime N in the last two cases. Thus the realized sets of

----

1) AdW der DDR, Karl-Weierstraß-Instiut für Mathematik, Mohrenstr. 39 Berlin, DDR-1086

2) AdW der DDR, Zentralinstitut für Kybernetik und Informationsprozesse, IT Dresden, Haeckelstr. 20, Dresden, DDR-8027

permutations form abelian and cyclic groups, respectively, and fit in the general theory developed in [4] and sketched in §§ 3, 4; the number of control signals is minimal. Methods for the optimization of networks of the second type are given in [16].

A systematical treatment of permutation networks of the form shown in Fig. 1 realizing special sets of permutations as well as the full symmetric group can be found in [4]. In the present paper we present results for more concrete cases. Note that (in difference to many other papers) N can be an arbitrary natural number.

2. Preliminaries

Let S_N be the full symmetric group of all permutations on the set $\{0,1,\dots,N-1\}$ $(N = 1)$, e denotes the identity. We say, a set $K \subseteq S_N$ is realized by the permutation network $(L_1,\dots,L_m)$ (cf. Fig. 1) if

$$K \subseteq L_1 \cdot \dots \cdot L_m = \{a_1 \dots a_m \mid a_1 \in L_1, \dots, a_m \in L_m\} .$$

(The product (superposition) of permutations is denoted by juxtaposition.) We assume $e \in K$. Let $\lambda(K)$ be the least m such that K can be realized by some $(L_1,\dots,L_m)$ with $L_i = \{e,p_i\}$, $p_i \in S_N$, $i = 1,\dots,m$.

Thus $\lambda(K)$ is the least number of binary control signals neccessary for the realization of K.

Since $(L_1,\dots,L_m)$ can realize at most 2^m permutations we get the lower bound

$$\lceil \mathrm{ld}\,|K| \rceil \leq \lambda(K) \tag{1}$$

for every $K \subseteq S_N$. ($\lceil x \rceil$ denotes the least natural number greater than or equal to x.)

3. Realization of cyclic permutation groups

3.1 Theorem (cf. [4]). Let $K = \{e,a,a^2,\dots,a^{r-1}\}$ be a cyclic subgroup of S_N of order r generated by $a \in S_N$. Then

$$\lambda(K) = \lceil \mathrm{ld}\,|K| \rceil = \lceil \mathrm{ld}\ r \rceil$$

and K is realized e.g. by the following permutation network

$(L_1,\dots,L_\lambda)$: $\quad L_i = \{e, a^{2^{i-1}}\}$, $i = 1,2,\dots,\lambda$, $\lambda = \lceil \mathrm{ld}\ r \rceil$.

Remark. Because of (1), the number of binary control inputs is minimal. Of course there are other minimal realizations, e.g. for $r \leq 5$ the sets L_i $(i \leq 3)$ can be chosen as $\{e,a\}$ or $\{e,a^2\}$ in such a way that again $K = L_1 \cdot L_2 \cdot L_3$.

3.2 Example.

Let $a_i \in S_{i+1}$ be the cyclic shift permutation $x \longmapsto x + 1 \pmod{i+1}$ and $U_i = \{e,a_i,a_i^2,\dots,a_i^i\}$ the cyclic group of order $i+1$ generated by a_i. Then U_1,U_2,U_3,U_4, resp., can be realized e.g. (according to the above remark) by the permutation networks

$$(L_1) = (\{e,a_1\}), \quad (L_1,L_2) = (\{e,a_2\},\{e,a_2\}),$$
$$(L_1,L_2) = (\{e,a_3\},\{e,a_3^2\}),$$
$$(L_1,L_2,L_3) = (\{e,a_4\},\{e,a_4\},\{e,a_4^2\}), \text{ respectively.}$$

Fig. 2 shows a concrete realization of these permutation networks. Each layer consists of a number of switches S with one input and two outputs (called the 0-output and 1-output). In dependence of the control input $c = 0$ or $c = 1$ of the j-th layer, every switch of the layer connects its input with its 0-output or 1-output, respectively.

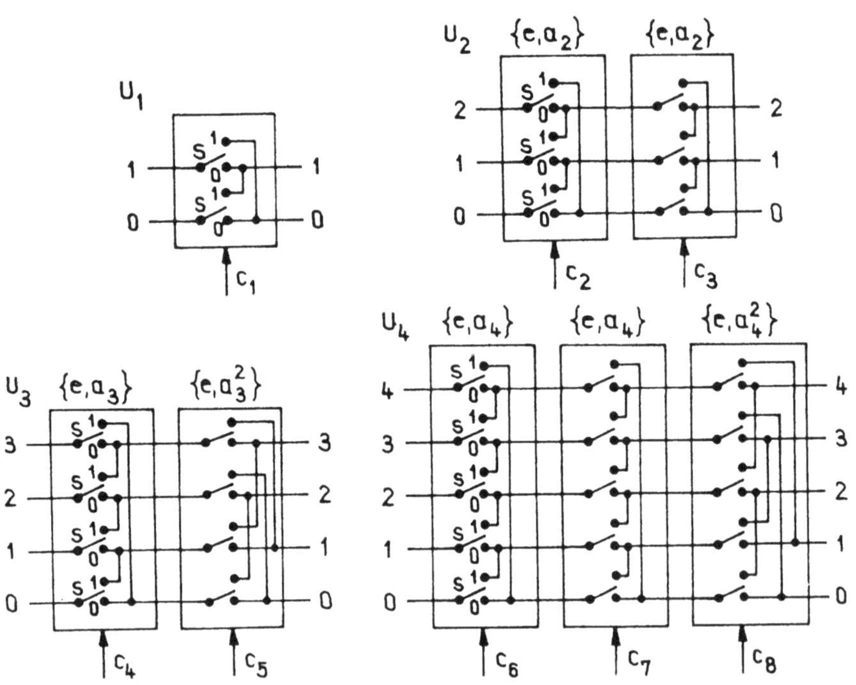

Fig. 2

4. Realization of abelian permutation groups

If a subgroup $G \leq S_N$ is the direct product (cf., e.g., [7; 1.7.2]) of subgroups $G_1, G_2 \leq S_N$, then, in particular, $G = G_1 \cdot G_2$ and we have $\lambda(G) \leq \lambda(G_1) + \lambda(G_2)$. Consequently, if G is the direct product of cyclic permutation groups of order $r_1, \dots, r_s$, then according to 3.1 we have

$$\lambda(G) \leq \sum_{i=1}^{s} \lceil \mathrm{ld}\ r_i \rceil .$$

It is well-known (see e.g. [9; p. 113]) that every abelian group G with m elements is the direct product of cyclic groups of the following form: Let $m = p_1^{k_1} \cdot \dots \cdot p_r^{k_r}$ be the prime number decomposition of m. For every k_i $(i = 1, \dots, r)$ choose a partition $k_i = a_1 + \dots + a_s$ $(a_1 \geq a_2 \geq \dots \geq a_s)$, and let G_i be the direct product of s cyclic groups of order $p_i^{a_1}, \dots, p_i^{a_s}$, resp. Finally, let G be the direct product of $G_1, \dots, G_r$.

4.1 Theorem (cf. [4]). Let G be an abelian group in the form described above. Then

$$\lambda(G) \leq \sum_{i=1}^{r} \lambda(G_i)$$

and

$$\lambda(G_i) \leq \lceil \mathrm{ld}\ p_i^{a_1} \rceil + \lceil \mathrm{ld}\ p_i^{a_2} \rceil + \dots + \lceil \mathrm{ld}\ p_i^{a_s} \rceil .$$

A permutation network which realizes G is, e.g., the serial composition of permutation networks realizing the G_i's, which in turn are serial compositions of permutation networks of the form described in 3.1 realizing the cyclic groups appearing in the direct decomposition of G_i.

4.2 Example.

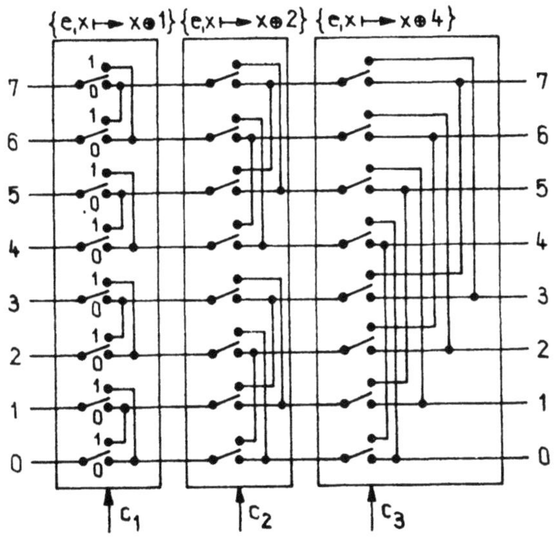

Let $N = 8$ and let $G \leq S_8$ be the abelian group consisting of all permutations

$$x \longmapsto x \oplus i$$

(componentwise addition modulo 2 of x and i in its binary representation), $i = 0, 1, \dots, 7$.
G is the direct product of three cyclic groups of order 2 (generated e.g. by $x \longmapsto x \oplus 1$, $x \longmapsto x \oplus 2$ and $x \longmapsto x \oplus 4$, respectively). According to 4.1, G can be realized by the permutation network shown in Fig. 3 (which corresponds to the STARAN computer network, cf. introduction).

Fig. 3

If one collects several factors in the direct product representation of an abelian group G, one can improve the upper bound for $\lambda(G)$ given in 4.1.

4.3 Example. Let $G = Z_3 \times Z_5 \times Z_7$ be the direct product of cyclic groups of order 3,5,7. With 4.1 we get

$$\lambda(G) \leq \lceil \mathrm{ld}\ 3 \rceil + \lceil \mathrm{ld}\ 5 \rceil + \lceil \mathrm{ld}\ 7 \rceil = 2 + 3 + 3 = 8.$$

But $Z_3 \times Z_5 \cong Z_{15}$, thus $G \cong Z_{15} \times Z_7$ gives

$$\lambda(G) \leq \lceil \mathrm{ld}\ 15 \rceil + \lceil \mathrm{ld}\ 7 \rceil = 4 + 3 = 7.$$

On the other hand, by (1) we have

$$\lambda(G) \geq \lceil \mathrm{ld}\, |G| \rceil = \lceil \mathrm{ld}\ 105 \rceil = 7,$$

i.e., $\lambda(G) = 7$, and the decomposition $G = Z_{15} \times Z_7$ gives a realization by a permutation network with a minimal (=7) number of control signals.

5. Realization of the full symmetric group

The full symmetric group S_N can easily be decomposed into a product of smaller subgroups (a method was developed and successfully used by C.C. Sims, see e.g. [14]).
Let G_i be the subgroup of S_N consisting of all permutations which fix the elements $i, i+1, \dots, N-1$. Now, let $U_i \subseteq G_{i+1}$ be a system of representatives of the right cosets of G_i in G_{i+1}, i.e. $G_{i+1} = \dot{\bigcup}_{u \in U_i} G_i u$ (disjoint union).

Then every $g \in S_N$ has a unique representation of the form

$$g = u_1 u_2 \dots u_{N-1}$$

with $u_i \in U_i$ $(i = 1, \dots, N-1)$; therefore

$$S_N = U_1 \cdot U_2 \cdot \dots \cdot U_{N-1}$$

and we get

$$\lambda(S_N) \leq \sum_{i=1}^{N-1} \lambda(U_i).$$

One can choose the following special systems U_i $(i = 1, \dots, N-1)$:

$$U_i = \{e, a_i, a_i^2, \dots, a_i^i\}$$

where a is the cyclic permutation $0 \mapsto 1 \mapsto 2 \mapsto \dots \mapsto i \mapsto 0$ fixing the remaining elements $i+1, \dots, N-1$. Obviously, U_i is a cyclic group of order $i+1$, which can be realized with minimal number of control inputs (see §3), $\lambda(U_i) = \lceil ld(i+1) \rceil$, and S_N can be realized as a permutation network which is the serial connection of permutation networks realizing the U_i's.

<u>5.1</u> Theorem (cf. [4]). For $N \geq 2$ we have

$$\lceil ld(N!) \rceil \leq \lambda(S_N) \leq \sum_{i=2}^{N} \lceil ld\ i \rceil = 1 + N \cdot \lceil ld\ N \rceil - 2^{\lceil ld\ N \rceil}.$$

In [17] is argued that $\sum_{i=2}^{N} \lceil ld\ i \rceil$ equals $\lambda(S_N)$ but no proof is known to the authors (moreover, the formula mentioned in the abstract of [17] is not correct for arbitrary N).
The following table shows the difference between the lower bound LB (which is definitely not sharp, cf. [4; 1.4c]) and the upper bound UB for $\lambda(S_N)$ given in 5.1.

N	2	3	4	5	6	7	8	9	10	11	12	13	14	15	16	17	18	19	20	30	31	32
LB	1	3	5	7	10	13	16	19	22	26	29	33	37	41	45	49	53	57	62	108	113	118
UB	1	3	5	8	11	14	17	21	25	29	33	37	41	45	49	54	59	64	69	119	124	129

<u>5.2</u> Example.
The full symmetric group S_5 can be realized by the permutation network shown in Fig. 4, where the U_i are defined as above. The realization of U_i $(i = 1, \dots, 4)$ was already given in 3.2. By 5.1 (cf. the above table) we have $7 \leq \lambda(S_5) \leq 8$. We conjecture $\lambda(S_5) = 8$.

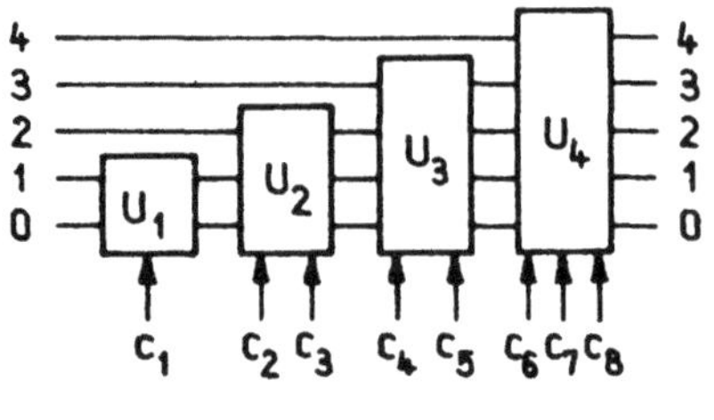

Fig. 4

References

[1] BARNES, G., Ausrichtnetzwerk für parallelen Zugriff. Patent DE OS 2843471, (1978).

[2] BATCHER, K.E., The multidimensional access memory in STARAN. IEEE Trans. Comput. C-26 (1977), 174-177.

[3] BATCHER, K.E., Permutation network. Patent US PS 3812467, (1974).

[4] BÖRNER, F., R. PÖSCHEL, M. GÖSSEL, Sets of permutations and their realization by permutation networks. EIK 21 (1985), 331-342.

[5] FENG, T., A survey of interconnection networks. Computer 14 (1981), 12-27.

[6] GÖSSEL, M., B. REBEL, Parallel memory with recursive address computation. In: Parallel Computing 83; Eds.: M. Feilmeier et al., Elsevier Science Publ., 1984; pp. 515-520.

[7] KLIN, M.Ch., R. PÖSCHEL, K. ROSENBAUM, Angewandte Algebra. DVW, Berlin 1988, and Vieweg, Braunschweig/Wiesbaden 1988.

[8] LAWRIE, D.H., C.R. VORA, The prime memory system for array access. IEEE Trans. Comput. C-31 (1982), 435-442.

[9] LIDL, R., G. PILZ, Angewandte abstrakte Algebra. I.B.I., Mannheim-Wien-Zürich 1982.

[10] McMILLEN, R., A survey of interconnection networks. Proc. IEEE Global Telecommunication Conf., Alabama, Georgia Nov. 26-29, 1984.

[11] OPFERMAN, D.C., N.T. TSAO-WU, On a class of rearrangable networks. BSTJ 50 (1971), 1579-1618.

[12] PÖSCHEL, R., M. GÖSSEL, B. REBEL, Ein dekomponiertes Permutationsnetzwerk für einen parallelen Bildspeicher. In: INFO 84, Dresden, February 1984, Vol. 5, pp. 40-44.

[13] REBEL, B., M. GÖSSEL, Ein paralleler Speicher. Forschungsbericht ZKI AdW d. DDR, Berlin 1982.

[14] SIMS, Ch.C., Computational methods in the study of permutation groups. In: Comput. Problems in Abstract Algebra; Pergamon Press, Oxford 1970; pp. 169-184.

[15] VARMA, A., C.S. RAGHAVENDRA, Rearrangeability of multistage shuffle/exchange networks. Proc. 14th Annual Int. Symp. on Comp. Architecture 1987, pp. 154-162.

[16] WÄCHTER, F., Zur Strukturierung spezieller Permutationsnetzwerke. AdW d. DDR, ZKI-Inf. 2/85.

[17] WAKSMAN, A., Apermutation network. Journal of the ACM 15 (1968), 159-163.

SIMULATION OF LEARNING NETWORKS

Thorsten Pöschel, Werner Ebeling, Thorsten Boseniuk[1)]

1. Introduction

With the progress of semiconductor engineering the costs of computer hardware are halving each 12-20 months. On the other hand the costs for software increase more and more. For this reason in several disciplines researchers try to develop the principles of learning systems which design at least a part of their software themselves. Under the term "learning" we want to understand here the adaptive variation of the internal structure or programme by error correction.
The general schema is the following: An external "teacher" presents several problems to the machine and the machine treats first these problems by its present structure or programme. Usually a machine, which has not taught yet does not solve the problem in the desired way. The teacher determines the error by comparing the machine-result with the requested one and gives an information about the error to the machine. Then the machine changes its structure or programme in such a way that the error will reduce /3,4/.

One way for the construction of such a learning machine is the design of a computer programme on a seriel computer with learning abilities. Another way is the design of special hardware.

In our paper we want to discuss a special type of learning systems called network machines and to demonstrate some of their capabilities by computer simulation.

2. General Features of Information Processing Networks

A nonlinear network as we will consider in this paper consists of a large number of processing elements connected by directed or undirected links. Each of these elements is characterized by its internal state. The links transfer the information about this state from one element to the other.

Some of these elements (input and output) serve as interface to the environment. The information which should be processed (the problem) expressed in binary digits is clamped onto the input elements of the net. Then the other elements get an activation transferred by the links. According to this activation the elements modify their states due to the activation rule. In this way all non-input elements (including out-

[1)] Humboldt-Universität zu Berlin, Sektion Physik PB 04, Invalidenstr. 42, Berlin 1040

put elements) vary their states until some kind of equilibrium is achieved. Now the network-solution for the problem can be obtained as the states of the output elements.

In the following we want to describe two examples of networks:

2.1. The Error Propagation Network (EPN)

The EPN consists of simple elements arranged in successive layers whereby each element gets its activation from all elements of the preceding layer /4,5/ (Fig. 1).

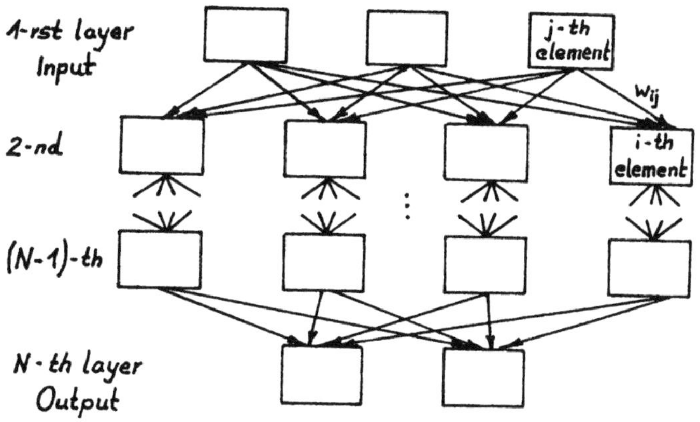

Fig. 1 EPN

The states of the elements are designated by a real number out of the interval 0...1. The activation a_i of an element i of the (n + 1)-layer is given by:

$$a_i = \sum_j w_{ij} s_j - \theta_i \qquad (1)$$

where s_j is the state of element j of layer n. w_{ij} is the strength of the link from j to i; θ_i is the threshold of element i. The state of element j (s_j) is determined by the following activation rule:

$$s_j = f(s_j) \qquad (2)$$

with $f(x) = 1/(1+\exp(-x))$.

The EPN acts in the following way: The elements of the first layer are fixed to the given input values. Then the activation and the state for the elements of the second layer can be determined according (1) and (2); afterwards those for the third layer and so on. The states of the elements of the last layer are the output values of the EPN. In this way the EPN is a strictly deterministic network; i.e. for a given input always the same output will be obtained./1,5/

2.2. The Boltzmann Machine Network (BMN)

In opposition the BMN works stochastically. Here the states of the elements are designated by 0 or 1. The elements are not arranged in layers, but there are three groups: input, output and hidden elements. Again each element gets an activation due to (1); but the weights are symmetrically ($w_{ij} = w_{ji}$). Now the state is not an deterministic function of the activation but it is determined stochastically. With the probability:

$$p(a_i) = 1/(1+\exp(-a_i/T)) \qquad (3)$$

the state of element i is set to 1 otherwise it becomes 0. This algorithm is called Metropolis Algorithm /1/ and it is mostly used in statistical physics to approximate partition functions. T is a parameter which has some similarity to the thermodynamic temperature. With clamped to the environment input elements the other states of the elements flip stochastically. These flips are not without any order. One can show that the probability to find the hidden and output elements in states $\{s_i\}$ ($\{s_i\}$ means $s_1, \ldots, s_{max}$) for long times converges to :

$$P(\{s_i\}) = const * \exp(-E(\{s_i\})/T$$

$$\text{with} \quad E(\{s_i\}) = -1/2\sum_{i\neq j} w_{ij}s_is_j + \sum_i \Theta_i . \qquad (4)$$

This formula is known from statistical physics; where E would be the internal energy of the network. It should be noted here that convergence can be increased by simulated annealing; i.e. slowly lowering the temperature T. As a result of the stochastic flip dynamics one obtains a probability distribution for the states of the output elements $\{s_i\}_o$. Like in the EPN this is the answer of the system to the given input.

One might ask whether a probability distribution can be interpreted as an answer. Therefore the distribution must be almost zero for all $\{s_i\}_o$ with exception of the desired combination $\{s_i\}_T$. /1/

3. Learning Rules

Until now we described the information processing in networks which have already captured the regularities of the problem. Below we will discuss learning rules for the EPN and the BMN. In both cases learning means to change the weights in such a way that the deviation from the desired output (ERROR) is reduced.

3.1. The Error Propagation Learning Rule

In the case of EPN the ERROR is defined as:

$$\text{ERROR} = 1/2 \sum_i (s_i - s_i^T)^2 \tag{5}$$

where the summation goes over all output elements; s_i^T is the desired output. To improve the performance one has to vary the weight w_{ij} due to:

$$w_{ij} := w_{ij} - \varepsilon * \partial \text{ERROR} / \partial w_{ij} . \tag{6}$$

The derivations can be obtained by the Delta-Rule:

$$\frac{\partial \text{ ERROR}}{\partial w_{ji}} = \frac{\partial \text{ERROR}}{\partial s_j} * \frac{\partial s_j}{\partial a_j} * \frac{\partial a_j}{\partial w_{ji}} \tag{7}$$

$$= \Delta_j * f'(a_j) * s_i$$

with $\Delta_j = (s_j - s_j^T)$ if $n+1 = N$

or $\Delta_j = \sum_k \Delta_k * \dfrac{\partial s_k}{\partial a_k} * \dfrac{\partial a_k}{\partial s_j}$

$$= \sum_k \Delta_k * f'(a_k) * w_{jk} \quad \text{if } n+1 \neq N .$$

3.2. The Boltzmann Machine Learning Rule

The learning rule for the BMN is closely related to basic principles of statistical mechanics. Following /1/ we define the so called Information Gain G as follows:

$$G = \sum_{\{s_i\}_o} P(\{s_i\}_o) \ln \frac{P(\{s_i\}_o)}{P'(\{s_i\}_o)} \quad (8)$$

where P is the probability that the configuration $\{s_i\}_o$ of the output elements occurs due to formula (4); and P' is the desired probability for this configuration. That means P is obtained by running the system according to the Metropolis algorithm (3) where the input elements are clamped to environmental input and all others are freely running. Corresponding P' is the probability which the BMN should learn; i.e. which should be achieved by freely running the system after learning.

For an unlearned network the two probabilities are unequal ($P \neq P'$) and hence G is positive. Only for a learned network one finds $P = P'$ and $G = 0$. Similar like in the EPN case one has to change the weights in such a way that G will decrease. After some calculations /1/ one finds for the derivations:

$$\partial G / \partial w_{ij} = (p_{ij} - p'_{ij}) \cdot \frac{1}{T} . \quad (9)$$

Here p_{ij} is the probability that s_i as well as s_j is 1 for free outputs; while p'_{ij} is the same probability for clamped outputs. The p_{ij} can easily be determined by Monte Carlo simulation.

Now one has to change w_{ij} in the same way like in the EPN case (6).

4. Examples

In the following section we will describe and discuss some results we got by means of the BMN and the EPN. We want to point out here, that every of our example problems can be solved much better by other specific algorithms. The goal of the learning networks is, that we can treat different tasks by means of the same network-structure. This means, that network machines possess certain degree of universality in comparization to special task programmes. Our examples were carried out on the same simulated networks (EPN and BMN); only the number of the elements varied according to the complexity of the task. The second benefit of learning nets is, that the programmer has not to spend time to find out, how to encode a given input into the wished output. Especially the last problem becomes more and more difficult with the complexity of the task.

4.1. Error Propagation Network

The most simple problem we have investigated was the XOR-problem with insignificant inputs. Fig. 2 shows the truth table for the two significant elements.

XOR	1-rst bit		
2-nd bit		T	F
	T	F	T
	F	T	F

Fig. 2 XOR

These elements were hidden within an input string of length 15. The other 13 input elements have got no influence to the output. They were chosen randomly each run anew. After about 100 learning cycles the problem was captured by the machine and the system has reached 100% reliability.

The next problem we will present here is a pattern recognition problem. For this the input consists of 150 elements arranged in a 10 by 15 matrix. The machine was trained with 12 alphabets written by different authors (see Fig. 3).

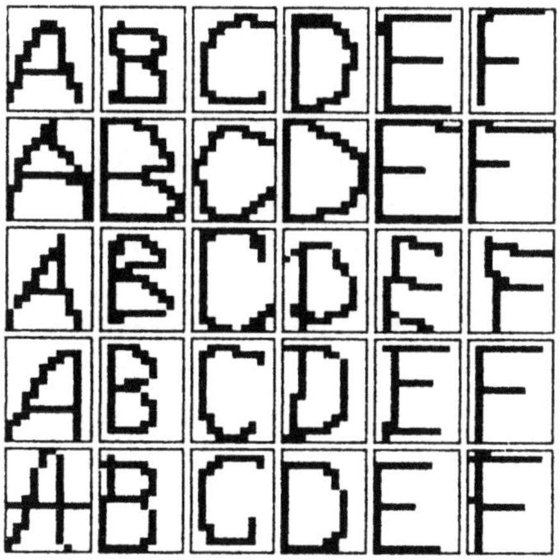

Fig. 3 Examples for Letters

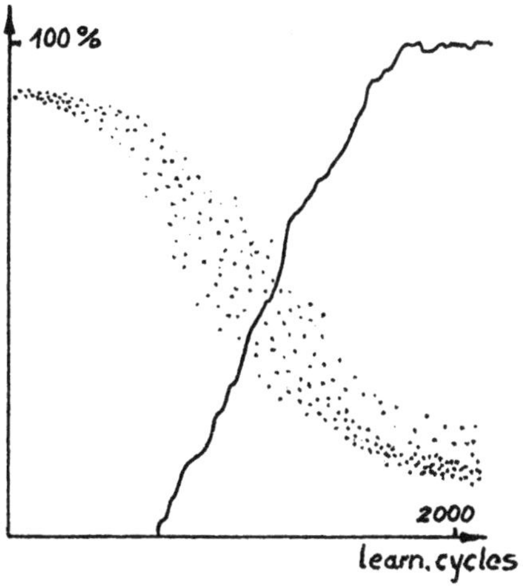

Fig. 4 Time Development of Total Error and Reliability

Fig. 4 shows the time development of the total ERROR and the reliability during learning. After learning the network was able to recognize the learned patterns with about 99% reliability. Unknown patterns were recognized with about 70%.

4.2. The Boltzmann Machine Network

For the BMN we only want to discuss a simple problem of pattern recognition. Therefore we taught the machine to recognize 20 3 3 patterns independent of their location within a 5*5 matrix. Examples are shown in fig. 5.

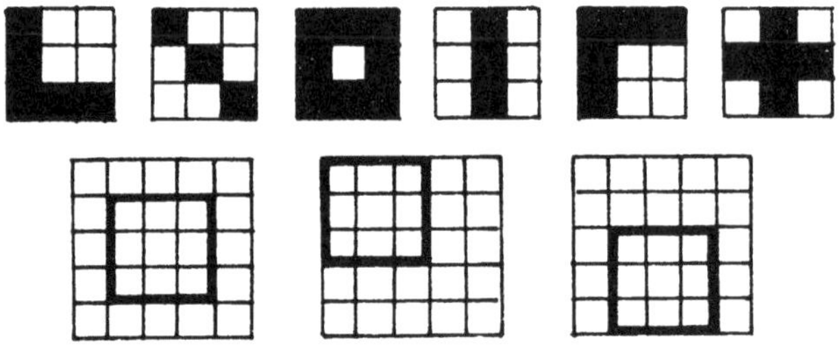

Fiq. 5 Examples for 5 * 5 Patterns

Again the machine was able to recognize the different patterns.

5. Conclusions

We have seen that networks with the same structure are able to solve different problems only by presenting them learning examples. One of the unsolved but very important problems for all kinds of networks is the question: how complex must be a machine to solve a problem of given complexity? In other words: how many layers and elements are necessary to solve a certain problem?

Comparing EPN and BMN one finds that the EPN is much more faster in learning performance. This is due to the fact that the determination of the probability distribution (4) takes a lot of computing time. But both algorithms are well suited for parallel processing with simple computing elements. This is a great advantage of the networks we have investigated.

A possible direction of further investigations is the exploration of evolutionary algorithms like mutation, selection and other biological approaches /2/.

References:

/1/ Ackley, D.H., G.E. Hinton, T.J. Sejnowski: A Learning Rule for Boltzmann Machines. Cognitive Sc. 9(1985)

/2/ Ebeling, W., R. Feistel: Physik der Selbstorganisation und Evolution. Akademie-Verlag Berlin (1987)

/3/ Ebeling, W.: Physik komplexer nichtlinearer Netzwerke und neue Wege der Informationsverarbeitung. Sitzungsberichte der Akademie der Wissenschaften der DDR 4N Akademie-Verlag Berlin (1987)

/4/ Rumelhart, D.E., J.L. McClelland eds.: Parallel Distributed Processing: Explorations in the Microstructure of Cognition. Vol. 1 and 2 (Cambridge: MIT Press, 1986)

/5/ Sejnowski, T.J., C.D. Rosenberg: Parallel Networks that Learn to Pronounce English Text. Complex Systems 1 (1987)

GIVEN'S ROTATION ON AN INSTRUCTION SYSTOLIC ARRAY

Andreas Dittrich, Hartmut Schmeck[1]

Abstract

In this paper we show that the concept of instruction systolic arrays allows to implement efficiently a transformation scheme for triangularizing rectangular m×n-matrices using Given's rotations. Based on a careful choice of an appropriate set of instructions, a program for the instruction systolic array can be designed having a time complexity of O(min(n,m-1)). Although the instruction systolic array allows for much greater flexibility, the time complexity is of the same order as that of the special purpose triangular systolic array designed by Gentleman and Kung.

1 Introduction

The instruction systolic array (ISA) has been suggested as a new type of parallel computer architecture based on a two-dimensional mesh-connected array of processors [5], which combines the advantages of special-purpose systolic arrays with the flexible programmability of general purpose machines. The feasability of the ISA-concept has been demonstrated in a comparative study of different control structures for mesh-connected arrays [4]. Furthermore, efficient ISA-programs have been designed for comparison-based algorithms (especially for sorting) [7, 9, 11] and for graph problems [6, 10].

In this paper we illustrate how an instruction systolic array can be designed and programmed to triangularize an m×n-matrix using Given's rotation, thereby showing the ISA-concept to allow for the efficient solution of numerical problems, too. Matrix triangularization is an important operation used e.g. in the solution of systems of linear equations. Compared with the simpler Gaussian elimination, Given's rotation has the advantage of greater numerical stability (see e.g. [3]). Gentleman and Kung (see [2] and also [8]) designed a special-purpose (triangular) systolic array for the triangularisation of matrices using Gaussian elimination or Given's rotation. Our design of the ISA-program for Given's rotation is based on their ideas.

The paper is organized as follows: The ISA-concept and Given's rotation are briefly described in Sections 2 and 3. This is followed by an outline of the design of an ISA-program for Given's rotation in Section 4. Finally, the results of this paper are summarized and discussed.

2 The ISA-Concept

As described in detail in [4] and [5], an *instruction systolic array* or $ISA_{m,n}$ consists of a mesh-connected m×n-array of processors. The array is synchronized by a global clock assuming that all the possible instructions take the same time. It is programmed by a sequence $p^1, \ldots, p^r$ of n-tuples of instructions and a sequence $s^1, \ldots, s^r$ of m-tuples of selectors ("0" or "1") which are sent through the array row by row and column by column, respectively (see Figure 1). Instructions are executed whenever they meet a selector "1". Otherwise, a NOOP instruction is executed. An *ISA-program* is a pair (p,s), consisting of the sequences of instructions and selectors. The *time* of an ISA-program is the length of its program, i.e. program execution stops after the input of the last instructions or selectors. Every processor has a

1 Institut für Informatik u.P.M., Universität Kiel, D-2300 Kiel 1, Federal Republic of Germany

communication register K which is accessible to all its four direct neighbors. K_N, K_E, K_S, and K_W denote the K-registers of a processor's neighbors to the north, east, south or west. The strict seperation of the read and write phases during the execution of an instruction and the fact that a processor can write only into its own communication register guarantees that no read/write conflicts can occur.

Observe that while a selector bit moves through a row of the array, it is combined with all the instructions on a diagonal of the instruction part of a program and - analogously - that while an instruction moves through a column of the array, it is combined with all the selector bits on a diagonal of the selector part of the program. Therefore, very often programs for the

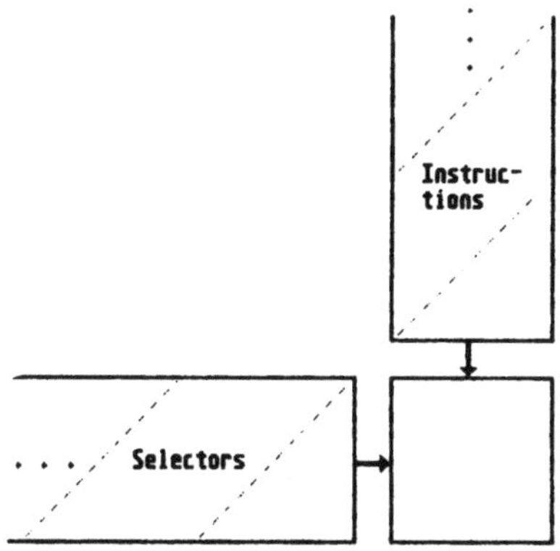

Fig. 1: The instruction systolic array.

ISA are "diamond shaped" (cf. Figure 1). This motivates the definition of the *period* of an ISA-program which is the minimal time from the first input of an instruction of this program to the first input of an instruction of the next program. Obviously, the period of diamond-shaped $ISA_{m,n}$-programs is equal to the number of their diagonals, which is n-1 time-units less than their time, if n=m.

Input and output occurs at the boundary of the array using the "open-ended" data links of the processors, which might be interpreted as I/O-pads of a chip. In particular, a data item is input whenever a processor on the boundary of the array executes an instruction that attempts to read from the communication register of a nonexistent neighbor. Simple programs for initializing an array and for unloading it may be found in [11].

An essential feature of the instruction systolic array is its programmability. But, in order to keep the array as simple (and as close to conventional systolic arrays) as possible, it is not a general purpose array, i.e. the processors of the array are designed to "understand" a set of instructions tuned to a specific problem or class of problems (cf. [6, 11]). Therefore, the design of ISA-programs has to include the design and choice of an appropriate, small set of instructions.

3 Given's Rotation

Given's rotations can be used to transform a given m×n matrix $A=(a_{i,j})$ into (upper) triangular form, i.e. $a_{i,j}=0$ whenever i>j. The transformation can be represented as the execution of the following piece of program:

$$\textit{for } i := 1 \textit{ to } \min(n, m-1) \textit{ do}$$
$$\textit{for } j := i+1 \textit{ to } m \textit{ do}$$
$$A := T_{i,j} \cdot A$$

where $T_{i,j} \in \mathbb{R}^{m \times m}$ is the Given's rotation with respect to rows and columns i and j which is the identity matrix except for elements $c=\cos(\alpha)$ and $s=\sin(\alpha)$ for some $\alpha \in \mathbb{R}$ in rows and columns i and j, i.e. all the $T_{i,j}$ are orthogonal (see Figure 2).

$$T_{i,j} = \begin{pmatrix} 1 & & & & & & \\ & \ddots & & & & & \\ & & 1 & & & & \\ & & & c & & s & & \\ & & & -s & & c & & \\ & & & & & & 1 & \\ & & & & & & & \ddots \\ & & & & & & & & 1 \end{pmatrix} \begin{matrix} \\ \\ \\ \leftarrow i \\ \leftarrow j \\ \\ \\ \\ \end{matrix}$$
$$\qquad\qquad \uparrow \qquad \uparrow$$
$$\qquad\qquad i \qquad\; j$$

Fig. 2: The shape of the matrix $T_{i,j}$ for Given's rotation.

A multiplication of $T_{i,j}$ with a vector $x \in \mathbb{R}^n$ only changes the coefficients at positions i and j, i.e. if $y=T_{i,j}x$ then

$$y_i = cx_i + sx_j$$
$$y_j = -sx_i + cx_j$$
$$y_k = x_k \qquad \text{for } k \neq i \text{ or } j.$$

c and s have to be chosen such that $y_j=0$. Thus, premultiplication of A with $T_{i,j}$ zeroes the element at position (j,i) of $T_{i,j}A$ and the transformation scheme above yields a triangular matrix. The appropriate values of c and s can be computed by a call *generate(* a_{ii}, a_{ji}, c, s*)* of the

procedure generate (x, y, c, s)
if y = 0
then c := 1, s := 0
else if |y| ≥ |x|
then $t := \frac{x}{y}$, $s := \frac{1}{\sqrt{1+t^2}}$, $c := st$
else $t := \frac{y}{x}$, $c := \frac{1}{\sqrt{1+t^2}}$, $s := ct$

By inserting the statement $b := T_{i,j}b$ into the inner loop of the triangulation scheme, we can use it to solve the linear system Ax = b. A thorough treatment of methods for triangularizing matrices may be found in [3].

4 Implementation on the ISA

Besides the communication register K every processor of the mesh-connected m×n-array contains the four internal registers C, S, A, and B.

Initially, register K of processor (i, j) contains the element $a_{i,j}$ of the matrix to be triangularized. As outlined below, at the end of the computation the element $a_{i,j}$ of the resulting upper triangular matrix is stored in register K of processor (m-i+1, j) (see Figure 3). During the

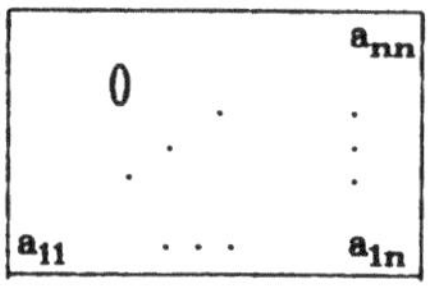

Fig. 3: The final contents of the registers K for the case m=n.

calculation, the K-registers are needed for communication with neighboring processors.

The registers C and S are used to store the values of c and s of the Given's rotations to be applied to the matrix A. The registers A and B are needed for intermediate storage of values computed during the computation.

Fig. 4: Global structure of the ISA-program.

Only the registers K have to be initialized and contain valid data at the end of the computation. The programs for initializing and for unloading the array (see [11]) are not considered to be part of the ISA-program designed below, since the triangularization can be just one part within a larger computation.

The ISA-program is divided into min(n, m-1) diamond shaped blocks, starting with a block $G_{m,n}$ and ending with block $G_{o,p}$, where o=2 or p=1 (see Figure 4). Every block $G_{i,j}$ only operates on rows 1 to i and columns n-j+1 to n of the array (see Figure 5).

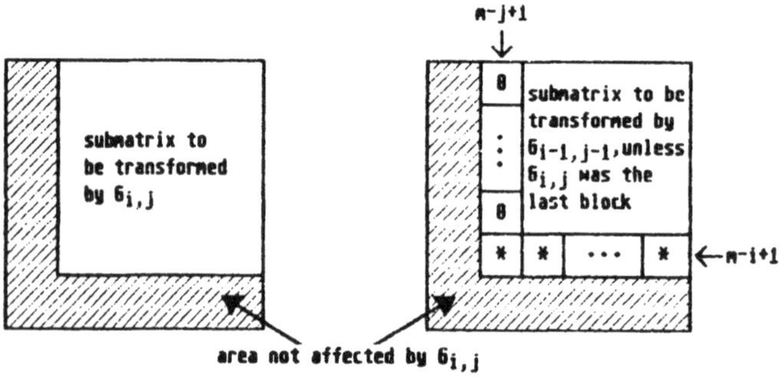

Fig. 5: Effect of $G_{i,j}$ on the array.

The program uses the following instructions :

Some only copy data from one register into another, e.g. AK is A := K. (KC, KS, KA, KB and BK are defined analoguously).

—C executes the operation K := C := K_W, while —S executes K := S :=K_W. They are used to propagate the values c and s of a rotation.

$\overset{|}{a}$ and $\underset{|}{a}$ apply a rotation with the values c and s given in the C and S registers of the processor. $\overset{|}{a}$ executes B := K := C * K_N + S * A and $\underset{|}{a}$ executes K := - S * B + C * K_S.

Instructions $\overset{|}{g}$ and $\underset{|}{g}$ compute the c and s-values of a rotation and apply it. $\overset{|}{g}$ executes *generate(* K_N, K, C, S *)* (or an equivalent procedure) and applies the rotation using the just com-

puted values in the C and S registers : A := K, B := K := C * K_N + S * K. q executes *generate(B, K_S, C, S)* and sets K := C , A := 0, which is short for A := - S * B + C * K_S, because in this case C and S have been chosen to give zero.

Besides these, some read instructions are needed for initializing and unloading the array (see [11]).

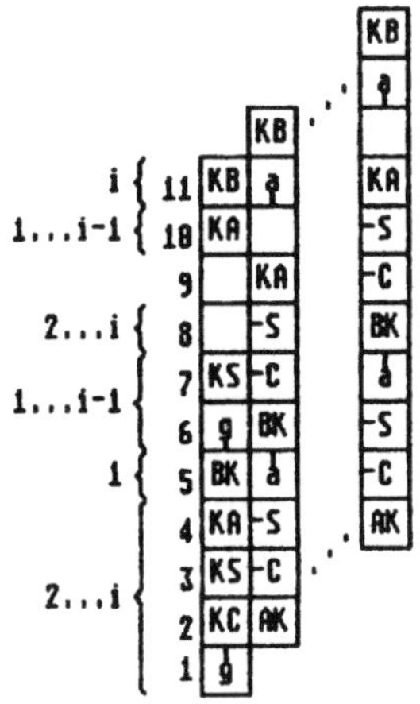

Fig. 6: Structure of block $G_{i,j}$.

As depicted in Fig. 6, every block $G_{i,j}$ has j columns of two different types:

(i) The leftmost column generates the rotations and applies them to this column.

(ii) The other j-1 columns propagate data to the right and apply the rotations generated in the leftmost column.

Instead of showing the selector part of the program, the numbers on the lefthand side of Fig. 6 indicate the rows where the diagonals are to be exectuted, e.g. diagonals 6, 7, and 10 are executed in rows 1 through i-1 only. The diagonals perform the following computations:

The instruction g of diagonal 1 reads a matrix value from its upper neighbor, which is always possible since it is not executed in row 1, calculates the values c and s for the rotation and applies it. The instructions AK save the matrix values into the A-registers.

The diagonals 2 and 3 send the values of the rotation to the right and the first part of the rotation is applied by diagonal 4. After this the matrix values of the first row are saved into the B-registers.

In diagonals 6 and 7, the processor executing instruction g reads a matrix value from its lower neighbor and generates and applies a rotation zeroing register A. This rotation is the same as created by g of diagonal 1 which was executed at its lower neighbor. The other instructions send the values c and s to the right.

In rows 2 to i of the array the matrix values which have been saved into the A-registers by diagonal 1, are copied back into the K-registers by diagonal 8.

The a instructions of diagonal 10 must be delayed by the NOOP-instructions of diagonal 9 since they have to wait until diagonal 8 has restored the matrix values to the K-register of their lower neighbors. Diagonal 10 then applies the second part of the rotation.

The last diagonal of $G_{i,j}$ stores the new row of the final triangularized matrix into the K-registers of the i-th row of the array. The following blocks will not change this row again.

Observe that the execution of $G_{i,j}$ in the array corresponds to the execution of the inner loop of the triangularization scheme given in Section 3. The program has 11 diagonals per block and min(n,m-1) blocks. Therefore, the program has a period of 11·min(n,m-1).

5 Conclusion

In this paper we have described the design of a program for the triangularization of m×n-matrices on an instruction systolic array using Given's rotations. After a careful choice of an appropriate set of instructions, the ISA-program could be designed systematically in close correspondance with the standard triangularization scheme. The period of our program has to be compared with the period of the systolic algorithm of [2] which is just min(n, m-1). The constant factor increase of the period of the ISA-program is mainly due to the fact that the processors have only one communication register. If they were allowed to read the contents of two arbitrary registers of their neighbors, the blocks $G_{i,j}$ could be reduced to only two diagonals which would apply the two parts of the rotation. Thus, the constant of the period could be reduced to 2. Most of the instructions used by the program are simple, except for the instructions $\overset{\downarrow}{g}$ and $\underset{\downarrow}{g}$ to generate the rotation values c and s. Since the final value computed during their execution in a processor (i,j) is needed at the begin of their execution in processor (i+1,j), it is not possible to break the g-instructions into a sequence of simpler ones without significantly increasing the time complexity of the program. The operations executed by the processors of the triangular systolic array of Gentleman and Kung [2] are as complex as the g-instructions. In [1] programs are designed for executing various matrix operations on an instruction systolic array, including multiplication and inversion of matrices and the solution of linear systems of equations. This shows that instruction systolic arrays may be used efficiently for the solution of numeric problems.

References

[1] Dittrich, A.: Matrixoperationen auf dem befehlssystolischen Feld. Diplomarbeit, Institut für Informatik und Praktische Mathematik, Universität Kiel, 1988.

[2] Gentleman, W.M., and H.T. Kung: Matrix Triangularisation by Systolic Arrays. In: Proc. SPIE Symp., vol. 298, Real-Time Signal Processing IV (1981), 19-26.

[3] Golub, G.H., and C.F. Van Loan: Matrix Computations. The John Hopkins University Press, Baltimore, 1985.

[4] Kunde, M., H.-W. Lang, M. Schimmler, H. Schmeck, and H. Schröder: The Instruction Systolic Array and Its Relation to Other Models of Parallel Computers. In: M. Feilmeier, G. Joubert, and U. Schendel (eds.): Parallel Computing '85, North-Holland (1986), 408-419.

[5] Lang, H.-W.: The Instruction Systolic Array, a Parallel Architecture for VLSI. Integration, the VLSI Journal 4 (1986), 65-74.

[6] Lang, H.-W.: Transitive Closure on an Instruction Systolic Array. Bericht 8718, Informatik und Praktische Mathematik, Universität Kiel, 1987.

[7] Makait, J.: Sortieren auf dem befehlssystolischen Feld. Diplomarbeit, Institut für Informatik und Praktische Mathematik, Universität Kiel, 1987.

[8] Robert, Y.: Systolic Algorithms and Architectures. RR 621-I, CNRS, Lab. TIM3, Institut National Polytechnique de Grenoble, 1986.

[9] Schimmler, M.: Fast Sorting on the Instruction Systolic Array. Bericht 8709, Informatik und Praktische Mathematik, Universität Kiel, 1987.

[10] Schimmler, M., Schröder, H.: Finding All Cut-Points on the Instruction Systolic Array. Bericht 8717, Institut für Informatik und Praktische Mathematik, Universität Kiel, 1987.

[11] Schmeck, H.: A Comparison-Based Instruction Systolic Array. In: M. Cosnard, Y. Robert, P. Quinton, M. Tchuente (eds.): Parallel Algorithms and Architectures, North-Holland, Amsterdam (1986), 281-292.

Worst Case Analysis for Reducing Algorithms on Instruction Systolic Arrays with Simple Instruction Sets

Thomas Tensi *

Abstract

In this paper we investigate a technique to transform algorithms for Instruction Systolic Arrays (ISA's) to ones with very simple instruction sets. ISA's are a systolic mesh-connected architecture where besides data also instructions and binary selectors are shifted through the array. Many algorithms for different applications using complex instructions sets have been proposed for the ISA. To allow the combination and composition of algorithms on a single generic ISA they have to be reduced to ones with simple instructions. This paper shows that in the worst case on a m×n-Array a slowdown of factor m has to be accepted.

1 Introduction

In [KUN85] the *instruction systolic array* (ISA) has been proposed as a new architecture for VLSI which meets the requirements of [KNG82] very well. Many algorithms for different applications have been designed for the ISA (e.g. [LAN85], [SCHR87]).

ISA's are a systolic mesh-connected architecture where besides data also instructions and binary selectors are shifted through the array. This main difference between conventional systolic arrays and ISA's allows to gain a higher flexibility by being able to use processors with some variations in the instructions they perform at a given moment contrasting to the fixed design and purpose of a systolic array.

m×n-ISA's have been shown to be functionally equivalent (with a slowdown of $min(m,n)$) to m×n-processor arrays which are mesh-connected architectures where each processor has its own program and data memory and communicates with its four neighbours [KUN85]. This fact is especially interesting, as ISA's don't have any program memory except for a memory cell for the current instruction and the current selector.

* Author's address: Thomas Tensi, Institut für Informatik, Technische Universität München, Arcisstr. 21, D-8000 München 2, Federal Republic of Germany

This work was partially supported by SIEMENS AG, München.

The algorithms for ISA's often suffer from using complex instructions. That is unrealistic for a VLSI processor especially when considering an ISA as a generic array for diverse systolic algorithms. This paper focusses on the slowdown induced by substitution of complex instructions by sequences of simple instructions.

2 Description of ISA's and PA's

A processor array is a mesh-connected array of identical processors. Every processor has its own program and data memory and a special *communication register*. It is used to allow communication with the four direct neighbours. Every neighbour can read the communication register but only the processor itself can write to it.

The execution of instructions in the program memory is done linearly and synchronous with the other processors. Each cycle can be divided into two substeps: In step one every processor can read all or part of the communication registers of its neighbours into its own memory; in step two the current instruction in its program memory is executed.

Thus more formally a program on a m×n-PA is a sequence $p_1, \ldots, p_r$ of m×n matrices of instructions (from some set I). The processor (i,j) executes instruction $(p_t)_{ij}$ at time t (with $1 \leq t \leq r$, $1 \leq i \leq m$, $1 \leq j \leq n$). Each instruction may contain references to the contents of the c.r. of the processors with offsets $(-1,0)$, $(0,-1)$, $(0,1)$ and $(1,0)$. The program p consumes time $T(p) = r$ as the PA stops after r instruction cycles.

A instruction systolic array is a mesh-connected array of identical processors. Every processor has its own data memory, a communication register (for communication identical to PA's) and two program registers: one for an instruction and one for a binary selector. Similarly to the processor array the instruction cycle is divided into two steps with the same communication interaction possible between the processors.

The instruction to execute is given by the contents of the instruction register. If the selector register is 1, the instruction is really executed, otherwise it is ignored. After one cycle the contents of the all instruction registers are shifted down by one row, the selector registers are shifted right by one column.

More formally a program on a m×n-ISA is a sequence $tp_1, \ldots, tp_r$ of n-tuples of instructions from some set I (the so-called *top program*) and a sequence $lp_1, \ldots, lp_r$ of m-tuples from $\{0,1\}$ (the so-called *left program*). The processor (i,j) executes instruction $(tp_{t-i+1})_j$ at time t, if $(lp_{t-j+1})_i = 1$ (with $max(i,j) \leq t \leq r$, $1 \leq i \leq m$, $1 \leq j \leq n$). Otherwise the processor performs a NOOP. Each instruction may contain references to the contents of the c.r. of the processors with offsets $(-1,0)$, $(0,-1)$, $(0,1)$ and $(1,0)$. The program (tp,lp) consumes time $T(tp, lp) = r$ as the ISA stops after r instruction cycles.

The result in both architectures is given by the final contents of the communication registers. Input is done by loading all communication registers prior to executing the first instruction. Normally access to nonexistent communication registers (done by boundary processors) can also be interpreted as an input request. For the sake of brevity we don't consider that, but above definition is sufficient for our purposes.

3 Equivalence of ISA's and PA's

The notion of equivalence can be defined as follows: Two programs on ISA or PA are called equivalent if for every interpretation of their instructions and every set of data supplied to them they produce the same result [SCHR86].

It's easy to see that a PA can simulate an ISA if they both have the same instruction set in their processors [KUN85]. The sequence of program matrices on the PA simply reflects the way the instructions are shifted through the ISA and masked by 0 selectors. Hence

Theorem 3.1 [KUN85]:

Any program on an $ISA_{m \times n}$ can be simulated on a $PA_{m \times n}$ with equivalent instruction set with $T_{PA} = T_{ISA}$.

The simulation of a PA on an ISA is also simple. The program matrices are sheared and concatenated as the top program; the selectors are r repetitions of (m-1) 0-vectors and one 1-vector, the total sequence being terminated by (n-1) 0-vectors (see figure 1). The problem that the contents of communication register (i,j-1) reflect the value <u>after</u> step t when processor (i,j) performs step t can easily be handled by doubling the c.r. wordlength, storing the old c.r. value in one half and modifying the instructions which access to the left neighbour's c.r. slightly (the idea with minor technical errors can be found in [SCHR86]).

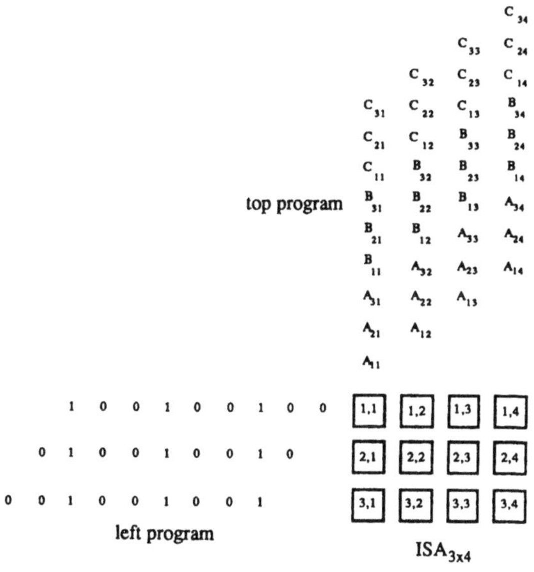

Figure 1: Simulation of a PA on an ISA

Thus we have

Theorem 3.2:

Any program on a $PA_{m\times n}$ can be simulated on a $ISA_{m\times n}$ with slighly modified instruction set with $T_{ISA} = m \cdot T_{PA} + n - 1$.

Of course in both cases there are programs which can be simulated faster. The techniques in the theorems are just worst case simulations.

4 Substitution of complex ISA instructions by simpler ones

In section 2 and 3 the necessary formal background for the retiming of ISA programs was introduced. Algorithms for instruction systolic arrays generally contain very complex instructions which aren't realistic for VLSI processors. Those complex instructions can of course be substituted by sequences of very elementary instructions. This substitution also allows to run diverse algorithms on the same ISA thereby making the ISA a generic systolic array.
Every instruction $s \in I$ on the ISA is substituted by a sequence $(s_1, \dots, s_{k(s)})$ of elementary instructions. Let $k(X) = max_{s \in X} k(s)$ be the maximum sequence length for a set of instructions. We now substitute the complex ISA instructions by a three-step process: first the ISA program is transformed into an equivalent one for a PA, secondly the complex instruction matrices for the PA are substituted by a sequence of matrices for the PA and third the resulting PA program is transformed into an equivalent ISA program.
(Assume in the following an m×n-ISA and an m×n-PA, and start with a r-step ISA program.)

Transformation step 1 (ISA → PA): We transform the r-step ISA program into a PA program with r steps. The PA program consists of r m×n-matrices with complex instructions.

Transformation step 2 (instruction substitution): $\forall t \in \{1, \dots, r\}$: Let $X = \{s \mid s = (p_r)_{ij}\}$, $k = k(X)$; substitute p_r by the sequence $(p_{r,1}, \dots, p_{r,k})$ of simple instructions (straightforward; padding with NOOP's if necessary).

Transformation step 3 (PA → ISA): The resulting PA program (with $\sum_{t=1}^{t=r} k_t$ steps) is transformed into an equivalent ISA program using $m \cdot \sum_{t=1}^{t=r} k_t + n - 1$ steps.

This means that possibly the throughput through the ISA is reduced by a factor of m. But this reduction can be reached by specific programs.

Theorem 4.1:

There are ISA programs and substitution sequences which cause a throughput reduction by m and a slowdown of m.

Proof (Outline):

Consider a PA instruction matrix p_f as in figure 2. Assume a substitution of a by $(a_1, \dots, a_k)$ and b by $(b_1, \dots, b_k)$. As all the rows are "linearly independent" the ISA must shift out the matrix $tp_{f,c}$ completely before working on $tp_{f,c+1}$ in a fashion similarly to simulation of arbitrary PA programs. (In fact, those matrices are the worst case ones for which bound 3.2 applies; that means also that the slowdown is not caused by our method but by principal communication requirements of the algorithm).

EndProof

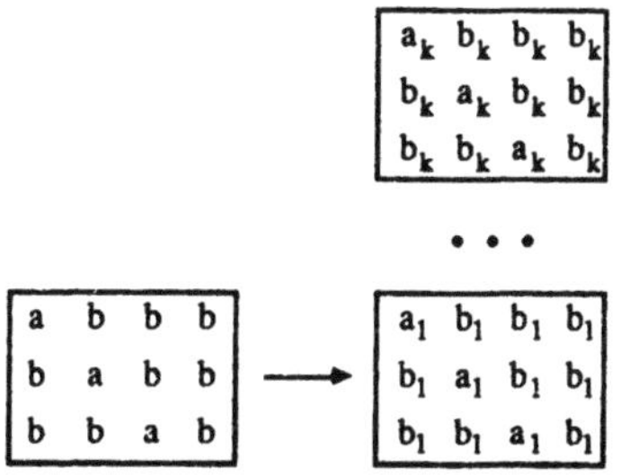

Figure 2: Throughput reduction in the worst case

There are algorithms and sibstitutions for which this bound is hopelessly pessimistic. But nearly all ISA programs I currently know of (e.g. [LAN87]) show this behaviour when substituting the instructions given by simple instruction sequences.

5 Conclusion

The paper discusses a way to substitute ISA's with complex instruction sets by ISA's with simple ones. This technique should establish the ISA as a generic systolic array being able to run systolic algorithms from a wide spectrum of applications without hardware modification. This hope is somewhat diminished by the fact that in worst cases a large number of processors is idle and the slowdown is proportional to the height of the array.

6 References

[KNG82] Kung, H.T.:
Why Systolic Architectures?
IEEE Computer **15** 1982, 1, pp. 37-46

[KUN85] Kunde, M.; Lang, H.W.; Schimmler, M.; Schmeck, J.; Schröder, H.:
The Instruction Systolic Array and its Relation to Other Models of Parallel Computers
Feilmeier, M.; Joubert, G.; Schendels, U. (eds.): Parallel Computing '85, North Holland, pp. 491-497, 1986

[LAN85] Lang, H.W.:
The Instruction Systolic Array, a parallel Architecture for VLSI
Bericht 8502, Institut für Informatik und Praktische Mathematik, Universität Kiel, 1985

[LAN87] Lang, H.W.:
Transititve Closure on the Instruction Systolic Array
Technischer Bericht, Institut für Informatik und Praktische Mathematik, Universität Kiel, 1987

[SCHR86] Schröder, H.:
Systolic Arrays Versus Instruction Systolic Arrays
Technical Report TR-CS-86-08, Australian National University, Canberra Computer Science Laboratory, 1986

[SCHR87] Schröder, H.; Krishnamurthy, E.V.:
Generalized Matrix Inversion Using Instruction Systolic Arrays
Technical Report, Australian National University, Canberra, Computer Science Laboratory, 1987

SELF-CHECKING PROCESSING ELEMENTS IN CELLULAR ARRAYS

Nandor Toth[1)]

1. INTRODUCTION

In cellular processors, in addition to achieving high performance, high reliability is also important to ensure that the results of computations are valid. System reliability can be improved by the use of existing fault-tolerant techniques. Fault tolerance could be obtained either by masking the errors caused by physical failures or by detecting them, locating the faulty cells and reconfiguring the system. Error masking is usually done by replicating the hardware and voting on the outputs of the replicated modules. The price which has to be paid for this is, unfortunately, high so we consider the other method. One of the most common approaches to detect errors is to run test programs on the system. We discuss an other alternative; error detection in cellular arrays by using self-checking processing elements. This technique is not generally applicable, however, in the specific cases where it is useful, fault-tolerance can be achieved with a surprisingly low overhead. We do not concern ourselves with fault recovery or reconfiguration strategies in this paper. Assuming that all the faulty cells are detected and located in the cellular array, a fault-tolerant programming method for reconfiguration is proposed in [4].

The paper is organised as follows. Section 2 discusses the methodology of cellular programming and the basic idea of self-checking processing elements. After a short overview of low-cost arithmetic codes, self-checking PEs are presented for arithmetic operations in section 3. Self-checking PEs for non-arithmetic operations is the topic of section 4 where an associative storage PE with parity checking is detailed. Concluding remarks are made in section 5.

2. CELLULAR PROGRAMMING, SELF-CHECKING PROCESSING ELEMENTS

The cellular processor architecture and main principles of cellular programming were suggested by T. Legendi [3].
Three levels of languages has been developed as programming tools for cellprocessors:

---

1) Research Group on Automata Theory Hungarian Academy of Sciences
H-6720 Szeged, Somogyi u. 7., HUNGARY

- microassembly language
- cellular assembly language
- cellular graph language

In the high-level language (CELLGRAPH, see [1]) algorithms are expressed in a concise and machine independent form. Cellular programs are considered as a directed graph (so-called CP-graph), where the nodes represent PEs and the edges represent interconnections between the PEs.

The PEs are functional units of cells performing certain elementary computation and interconnections are implemented as data channels in the cellular array. The translation from graph-level to assembly level involves the placement of PEs and data channels into the cellular array. This placement is realized by loading a suitable internal state configuration. The compilation process requires a set of PEs containing basic arithmetic operations, Boolean operations, etc., which seems to be sufficient to construct CP-graph to any kind of computational problem. In most cases several versions with different parameters are available to a given operation.

Our approach to detect errors in the cellular array provides an extended set of building blocks which includes the set of elementary PEs and their modified self-checking version.

The idea of self-checking PEs is derived from the standard hardware approaches to reliability such as error detection and error correction codes. A processing element is said to be self-checking PE if it has some checking mechanism to signal error if any of its cells becomes faulty. The construction of such a PE consists of three main steps

- encoding data
- modification of the algorithm performed by the PE
- decoding and checking procedures

The modification of the algorithm in most cases needs its redesigning to operate on encoded data. Besides the additional cells, the modified algorithm takes more time, compared with the original one, but this time overhead is not excessive.

In the following section we show simple examples for self-checking PEs performing arithmetic operations and encoding, decoding algorithms for arithmetic codes.

3. ARITHMETIC OPERATIONS

In [5] we can find many applications of error detection and error correction codes. Here, we consider the arithmetic codes which can serve as a basis for self-checking PEs performing arithmetic operations.

Arithmetic codes are classified into separate and nonseparate codes. Both classes possess many common properties, but differ significantly in their implementation.

For separate codes the codewords are partitioned into two groups of bits, one for the information bits (data) and one for redundant check bits. Separate codes are the residue codes in this paper. Encoding of a data item, x is a mapping

$x \rightarrow \langle c(x), x \rangle$, where the checking symbol $c(x)$ is the modulo A residue of x and A is the generator of the code.

For nonseparate codes the codeword $f(x)$ is a function of x. Here, nonseparate codes are so-called AN codes, where

$f(x) = A \cdot x$, A is the generator of the code.

We present the encoding and decoding algorithms for the codes mentioned above.

Since division is a complex cellular algorithm the encoding in separate codes for most A requires relatively high cost. The case of $A = 2^a-1$ ($a > 1$ arbitrary integer) is an exception because for such a generator we have an encoding algorithm well suited for cellular implementation.

The algorithm is based on the following identity:

$$u \equiv u \cdot (2^a)^i \text{ modulo } 2^a-1 , \quad i \geq 0 \text{ integer}$$

If $X = \sum_{0 \leq i \leq n-1} x_i \cdot (2^a)^i$, $0 \leq x_i \leq 2^a-1$, the a-bit bytes of X

then $(X \text{ modulo } 2^a-1) = \sum_{0 \leq i \leq n-1} x_i \text{ modulo } 2^a-1$. From which it follows that $c(X) = X \text{ modulo } 2^a-1$ can be computed by addition of the a-bit bytes of X. Thus the encoder is a modulo 2^a-1 binary adder PE which gets the a-bit bytes as input in every a-th step. In figure 1. the addition steps are shown.

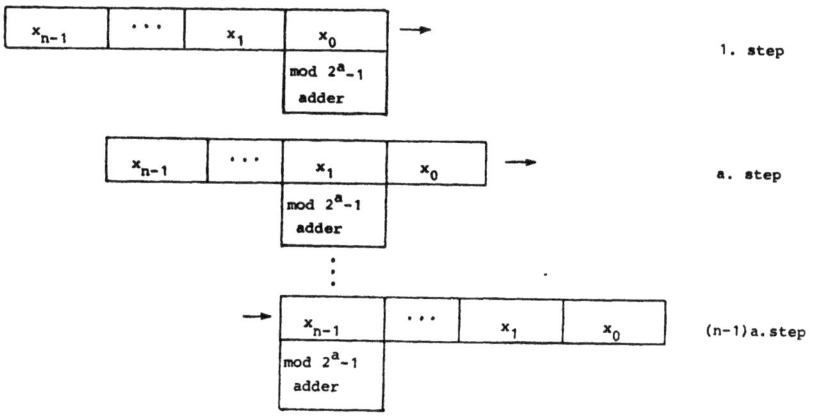

Fig. 1. Encoding in modulo 2^a-1 residue code

One of the advantages of separate codes is that they require no extra decoder. Cutting off the checking symbols we can get the decoded data. It would be ideal in the sense of space and time overhead required if we could perform the encoding and decoding algorithms just one time and a sequence of modified PEs could operate on encoded data in cellular programs.

In particular, it would be advantageous for AN code where the encoder is a multiplier and the decoder is a divider. In the case of $A = 2^a-1$ the checking procedure can be done by a residue encoder, a modulo 2^a-1 adder without division.

Now we give rough sketches of self-checking PEs for arithmetic operations such as addition and multiplication using residue and AN codes.

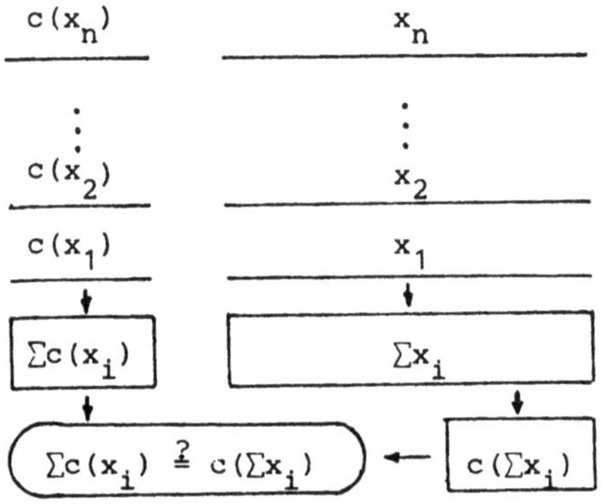

Fig. 2. Addition in residue code

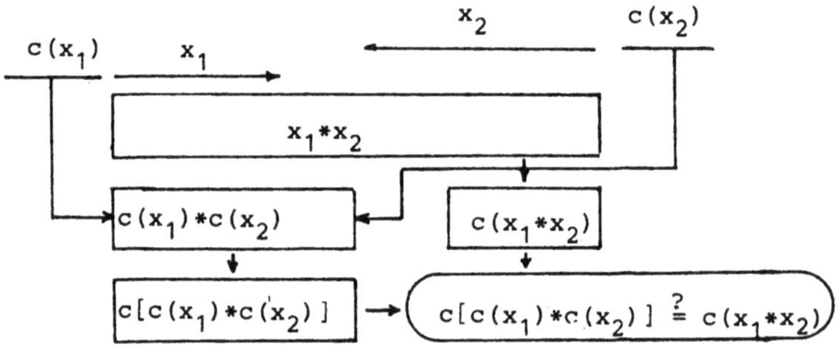

Fig. 3. Multiplication in residue code

From the properties of residue arithmetic it follows:

$$(x+y) \bmod q = (x \bmod q + y \bmod q) \bmod q \quad \text{and}$$
$$(x*y) \bmod q = (x \bmod q * y \bmod q) \bmod q.$$

This means that $\Sigma C(x_i) = C(\Sigma x_i)$ holds for addition and $C[C(x_1)*C(x_2)] = C(x_1*x_2)$ for multiplication if no error occured in the PEs.

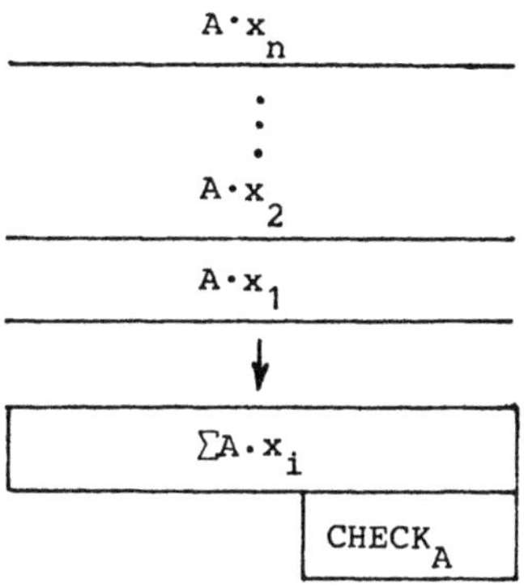

Fig. 4. Addition in AN code

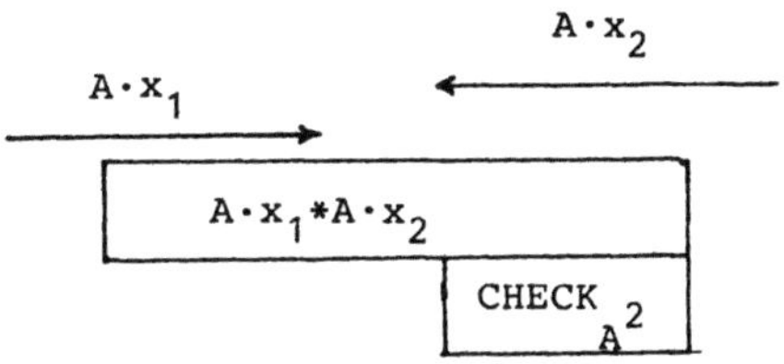

Fig. 5. Multiplication in AN code

We can choose a modulo A adder as $CHECK_A$ PE if $A = 2^a-1$ but, unfortunately, the checking in multiplication must be performed by a divider.

4. NON-ARITHMETIC OPERATIONS

The method of error detection may be generalized for non-arithmetic operations in the following manner. There are several cellular PEs in which some data are moved without change. For example image processing algorithms such as rotation, histogram computation, etc., have the property mentioned above. For these PEs the basic idea of error detection is to generate the checking symbol of data two or more times at different places in the PE and then compare these symbols.

In this way we can construct many self-checking PEs applying different kinds of error detection codes such as parity check code, Berger code, etc.

Here, we present a self-checking PE for the associative storage cellular algorithm with parity checking which is a well known example of error detection codes.

Associative storage is considered as a special cellular PE having a stored word in each of its rows. Every stored word consists of two vectors: the cue vector and the data vector. Input bitvectors and cue vectors have the same length. Input vectors, entering in slanting format into the storage, are compared with each cue vector and if they are the same then the appropriate data vector are read out as output. The comparison is made as follows. From the leftmost cells a control signal of value 1 starts and moves to the right comparing the bits one by one. If a cue vector is equal to the input vector a control signal 1 appeares at the rightmost bit of the cue vector, otherwise it changes into Ø. Then the control signal 1, moving through the parity channel, reads out the appropriate data vector in the right side of the PE. The output leaves the PE in slanting form, too. The detailed discription of the PE and its applications are discussed in [2].

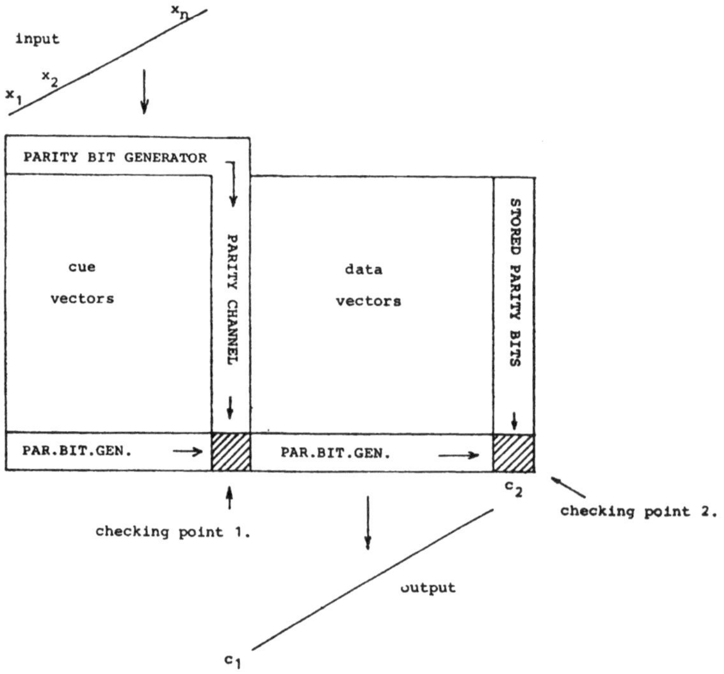

Fig. 6. Associative storage with parity checking

Before entering the associative storage, one parity check bit p_1 is appended to the input vector so that the value of p_1 is the sum of $x_1 \oplus x_2 \oplus \ldots \oplus x_n$. This parity check bit moves from up to down in the parity channel. The parity check bit p_2 of the same input vector is generated when leaving the associative storage and at the checking point 1 p_2 is compared to p_1. If the two values differ then the control bit c_1 gets value 1 showing that there is something wrong in the left side of the PE. If, on the other hand, the two values are equal then $c_1 = \emptyset$ and it is assumed that no error occured. Using this code, a change of the value of any single bit will be detected but, unfortunately, a change of several bits will only sometimes be detected. On the right side of the associative storage we store data vectors with their parity check bit p_1. If a data vector is read out its parity check bit p_2 generated when leaving the PE and p_1 is compared to p_2 at the checking point 2. The control bit

$$c_2 = \begin{cases} \emptyset & \text{if } p_1 = p_2 \\ 1 & \text{otherwise} \end{cases} .$$

c_1 and c_2, as additional parts of the output, signal the errors in the PE.

5. CONCLUSIONS

In this paper we have presented a method to detect errors in cellular arrays. Space limitation of cellular processors forced us to look at the approaches whose overhead is as little as possible. Therefore, we have shown some simple examples for self-checking processing elements where we managed to get reasonable results in additional space and time. Cellular programs using self-checking PEs as building blocks ensure higher reliability of cellprocessors. We hope that this concept will lead to new results in cost-effective fault-tolerance procedures for various applications.

REFERENCES

[1] Katona E.: A programming language for cellular processors. Proceedings of "Parallel Computing'85", Berlin (West), 1986.

[2] Katona E.: A software realization of an associative storage in a cellprocessor and its applications. Proceedings of Second Braunschweig Cellular Meeting, Informatik-Skripten 2, 1982.

[3] Legendi T.: Cellprocessor in computer architecture. Computational Linguistics and Computer Languages, 11 (1977), 147-167.

[4] Tóth N.: Fault tolerant programming of a two-layer cellular array. Proceedings of PARCELLA'86, North-Holland, 1987, 101-108.

[5] J. Wakerly: Error detecting codes, self-checking circuits and applications, Alsevier North-Holland, 1978.

CELLULAR DIAGNOSTIC IN PARALLEL SYSTEMS

Roman Trobec
University of Ljubljana
Institute Jozef Stefan
Jamova 39, 61000 Ljubljana
Yugoslavia

ABSTRACT -- In this work a new, cellular, local diagnostic procedure for a class of massively parallel systems with a regular topology is reported. The fault model is proposed to be suited for a given realistic system therefore production and run-time failures are assumed. Appropriate cluster and random faults are possible; additionally, permanent and/or intermittent faults are permitted. The system architecture is proposed to be a regular network with low network connectivity, a high number of intelligent nodes, and with no passive hardware redundancy. The diagnostic procedure is organized in parallel communication rounds, and is the same for all system units.

I. INTRODUCTION

Advancing semiconductor technology enables an interconnection of a large number of computational units on a single wafer element. However, with increasing dimension and density the probability of faults becomes essentially high. A real WSI implementation is tightly dependent on a well suited fault-tolerante procedure which must increase production yield and run-time reliability. A natural solution proposed by many researchers is an additional redundancy with an appropriate reconfiguration policy in the presence of faults.

We propose a diagnostic procedure for a class of massively parallel systems with an initial regular interconnection network with low network connectivity (2-8), high number (N > 100) of intelligent units, and no specialized passive hardware redundancy (redundant switches). In the fault model, production and run-time failures are expected. Production testing evaluates a permanent failure distribution in the whole system. The failure distribution and application demands are the main factors for "passing" the initial production test. An upper bound of production (link or unit) failures with a specific distribution are present on any wafer. The resulting system is called a system with a quasiregular interconnection topology. The redundancy is implicitly covered by regular system units. Appropriate detection and isolation procedures are the main issues in the proposed local diagnostic procedure. Knowledge about the actual diagnostic state in a neighborhood, acquired with the local diagnostic procedure, is a basis for further unit actions.

In related papers /4/,/6/ an assumption has been commonly made that each fault-free unit is capable of determining the diagnostic state of all other units in the system. The resulting algorithm is unacceptable complex for a massively parallel system. Additionally, the upper bound for a number of simultaneous faults in the system depends on a system connectivity; if the actual number of faults is greater than the upper bound, false diagnostic results are obtained. These facts introduce serious drawbacks for earlier developed methods implementation, especially in regular parallel systems which are a topic of this paper. Many authors propose for this class of systems a hardware /4/,/8/

redundancy. In several works /4/,/3/,/1/ it was shown that local procedure will find potential use in WSI systems. Some authors /7/ proposed the internal coding of computational data. This method may be used for a reliability improvement since it covers intermittent faults well during primary system functions. In combination with a self-test procedure (detected errors are interpreted as self-test inputs), it is possible to achieve an appropriate intermittent faults coverage.

In the following section a system architecture, and a system model is presented. Next, an assumed fault model, and a cellular diagnostic procedure is described. In conclusion, a discussion on the described method, and some main topics for further research are given.

II. SYSTEM AND FAULT MODEL

We suppose a parallel system with a two-dimensional regular array topology. According to the proposed taxonomy in /4/, the system is represented with a 5-tuple $\langle P, S=\emptyset, E_p, E_s=E_{p-s}=\emptyset \rangle$ which implies that only processing elements P and communication links E_p are present. All communication links are bi-directional and support an asynchronous message passing communication protocol.

The following is true for faulty units and faulty communication links:

i) faulty unit is incapable for communication and computation;
ii) fault-free unit possess a computation and communication ability. It may directly communicate with all adjacent neighbors and may perform unit actions. Consequently, a system function is a set of unit actions performed on a subset of all fault-free units;
iii) faulty link is unable to transmit a correct message;
iv) fault-free link on the other hand, always transmits a message correctly with no delay.

A message structure is represented in the following way:

send/rec.<initiator IDentification, Action, Data> = s/r<ID,A,D>.

All system units may be partitioned into three sets:

- set of faulty units which do not "know" this fact (*F*),
- set of faulty units which "know" this fact (*P*),
- set of fault-free units which "know" this fact (*V*).

In assumed parallel systems the subsequent relation is true (n is the number of all units in the system):

$$0 \le |F| < |P| < |V| \le n.$$

All three sets represent the whole system, hence:

$$|F| + |P| + |V| = n.$$

Units from *P* may drastically simplify diagnostic procedure by declaring themselves as faulty, and announcing this to all its neighbors.

A **basic diagnostic cell** (BDC) is defined as a small number of neighboring units which often coordinate in system functions. We constructed **BDC** from all units and corresponding links which are directly connected with a diagnostic initiator. A fault-detection procedure is the main goal in a single **BDC**, however, a diagnostic procedure involves more neighboring **BDCs** in mutual action.

Unit's **degree (d)** is the number of directly connected neighboring units.

The **shortest path** between two units, composed of **m** system units and **m**-1 communication links is called **distance (D)**, and is equal to **m-1**.

A **fault-cluster** is a subset of faulty units or links which may be surrounded with a path of fault-free units and communication links.

Diagnostic diameter (Dd) is the shortest path which enables a diagnostic initiator to properly diagnose all units and their communication links in a fault-cluster.

If a diagnostic procedure serves diagnostic information from units with distance **D≤k**, then this diagnostic procedure has level **k**.

Assume that the diagnostic initiator on the surrounding path of a given fault-cluster is chosen then the level of diagnostic procedure **k** has to be:

$$k \geq Dd+1,$$

to achieve the diagnosibility of this fault-cluster.

For proper diagnostic procedure it is necessary to test all communication links on the edge of the fault-cluster. **Dd** is the longest possible distance on the surrounding path. However, each unit has to test also its own connection with the fault-cluster. Consequently, the worst case diagnostic procedure level is **Dp+1**.

In Figure 1. an example of the parallel system **(d=4)** and some of the defined expressions are shown.

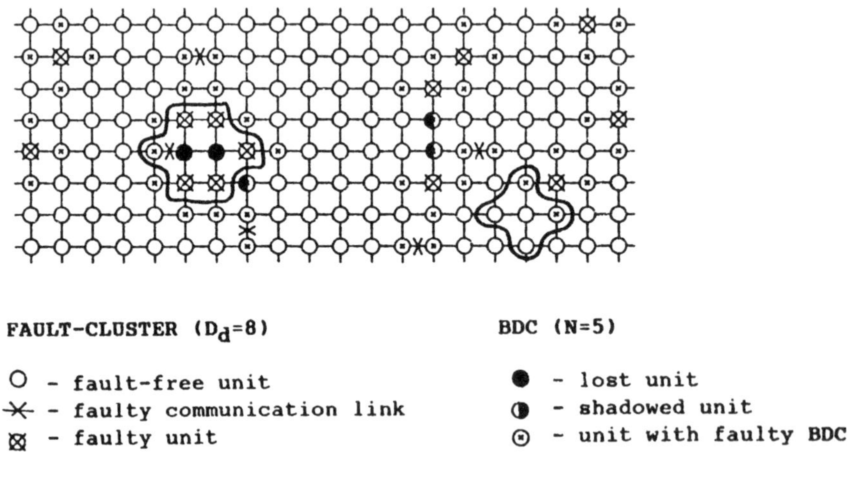

Figure 1. The two-dimensional parallel system **(d=4)**.

In the fault model, production failures which are described with cluster-fault distribution /4/, and run-time failures covered by random-fault distribution are assumed. Production failures represent 10%-20% of all system units. Run-time failures are some order of magnitude less frequent. The majority of system units are fault-free. Faults may be permanent, transient or intermittent. In this work we assumed that faults are permanent at least for the period necessary for diagnostic procedure. The diagnostic procedure may be implemented periodically in order to cover non-permanent faults also.

III. CELLULAR DIAGNOSTIC PROCEDURE

A local diagnostic procedure in parallel systems would be especially important if all system units performed the same diagnostic actions. The question is: "How complex is this procedure in regard to failure distribution?" It is possible to estimate this complexity, which was shown in /2/. In this paper only the procedure necessary to perform the local diagnosis is described.

Each non-faulty unit is assumed to possess an ability for self-testing (ST), communicating self-test results (STR) to neighbors, evaluating neighbors' self-test results, and performing a local diagnostic algorithm.

Cellular diagnostic procedure (CDA) may be implemented in four consecutive steps.

In the **first diagnostic step** all units start the self-test procedure **(ST)**. One has to be aware that a faulty unit form *(F)* is not able to diagnose itself reliably. On the other hand, all units from *(P)*, which on the basis of **(STR)** correctly estimate their own state, send an appropriate message to all neighbors. After that it may disconnect itself which significantly simplifies the rest of the algorithm. At the end of the first step all units constructed "self-diagnosis". This is, of course, not enough because there exist unidentified faulty units. Consequently, the main goal of the second step is the **BDC** diagnosis construction.

In **second diagnostic step** all units from *(F)* or *(V)* send their (STR) to all neighbors. The analysis of these results leads to the diagnosis of the neighborhood. Edge units represent a special case, hence we assume that all nonexistent neighbors are from set *(P)*.

After the second diagnostic step different cases for diagnostic initiator's stand point are possible:

i) if the diagnostic initiator is from *(P)*,all results are unreliable because the unit is faulty;

ii) if the diagnostic initiator is from *(V)*,it always diagnoses its neighborhood correctly except in the case when it is not able to distinguish between unit or link fault;

iii) if the diagnostic initiator is from *(F)*, several cases are possible.

First, an unit from **(F)** is surrounded with units from *(V)*. All neighbors detect the fault in the diagnostic initiator and in this way isolate it from further work. Consequently, all units from *(F)* and *(P)* are always surrounded with the units from *(V)*. Second, a unit from (V) is totally surrounded with units from *(F)* or *(P)*. Such a unit is **lost** for application, because it is not connected with the edge of the system. If there is more than one connected lost units they do not even "know" their status. (**Shadowed** units are not accessible over straight paths from edge units.)

The procedures performed in the first two steps are shown in Figure 2.

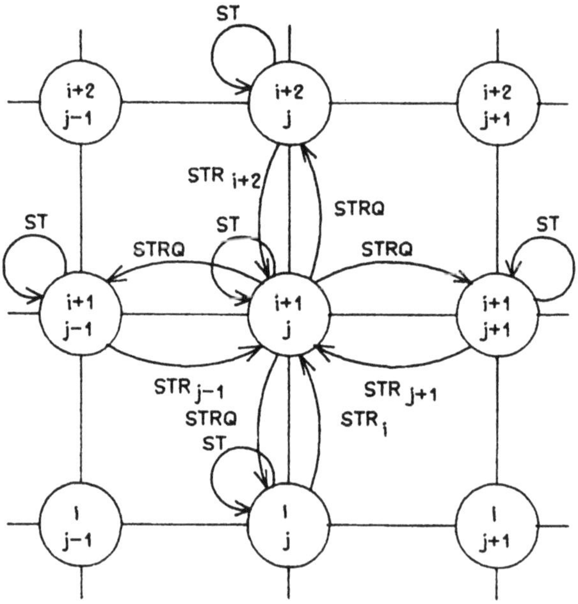

Figure 2. First and second diagnostic steps (**CDA**) in the parallel system.

After the second diagnostic step, without analysis of indirect diagnostic results, it is not possible to distinguish between unit or link fault. Because of the mentioned problems the **third diagnostic step** is necessary. In this step **k-level** diagnosis is performed which means that the diagnostic neighborhood is composed now from many **BDCs**. The diagnostic level depends on the maximal fault-cluster diagnostic diameter, and, of course, also on the fault distribution /2/.

Finally, the situation which appears when lost units are present has to be solved . Therefore, in the **last diagnostic step**, all non-faulty units search the access to an edge unit. All units which succeeded in this attempt are classified as **useful** system units.

Final results of the described cellular diagnostic procedure are collected as follows:

- all units from **(*P*)** are identified and disconnected in the first diagnostic step,
- all other faults are discovered in the second diagnostic step,
- all faulty communication lines and all faulty units from **(*F*)** are diagnosed in the third diagnostic step,
- after the last diagnostic step all lost units from **(*V*)** "know" that they are totally surrounded with units from **(*P*)** or **(*F*)**. All useful units from **(*V*)** are mutually connected, and have already diagnosed all neighbors within distance **D≤k-1**.

IV. CONCLUSIONS

A simple diagnostic procedure which promises several advantages has been proposed. The greater part of the described procedures are carried out in parallel, no specialized redundant switching and control circuitry are needed, dynamic reconfiguration during normal work is possible, and no restrictive upper bound on the number of faults is required.

However, the described cellular diagnostic procedure has several disadvantages: a communication overhead is added, and for now, a relatively poor environment for practical applications is developed.

Advancing technology will lower the amount of production failures which will make the proposed method even more actual.

In the future work we will try to generalize the local diagnostic procedure, simulate different failure types and distributions, and study application areas of the local knowledge which is gained with the described diagnostic procedure.

V. REFERENCES

/1/ D.Fussel, P.Varman, "Fault-Tolerant Wafer-Scale Architecture for VLSI," Proc. 9th Annu. Symp. on Computer Architecture, April 1982, pp. 190-198.

/2/ R.Trobec, "A Local Distributed Diagnosis," Tehnical Report Jozef Stefan Institute, IJS-1432, December 1986.

/3/ R.C.Russell, I.Catt, "Wafer-Scale Integration - A Fault-Tolerant Procedure," IEEE Journal of Solid-State Circuits, Vol.SC-13, No.3, June 1978, pp. 339-344.

/4/ I.Koren, D.K.Pradhan, "Yield and Performance Enhancement Through Redundancy in VLSI and WSI Multiprocessor Systems," Proceeding of the IEEE, Vol.74, No.5, May 1986, pp. 699-711.

/5/ J.G.Kuhl, S.M.Reddy, "Distributed Fault-Tolerance for Large Multiprocessor System," Proc. 7th Annu. Symp. Comput. Arch., May 1980, pp. 23-30.

/6/ F.J.Meyer, D.K.Pradhan, "Dynamic Testing Strategy for Distributed System," Proc. of the 15th Inter. Symp. on Fault-Tolerant Computing Systems, June 1985, pp. 84-90.

/7/ P.Banerjee, J.A.Abraham, "Fault-Secure Algorithms for Multiple-Processors Systems," Proc. of the Inter. Conf. on Computer Architecture, June 1984, pp. 147-154.

/8/ F.R.K.Chung, F.T.Leighton, A.L.Rosenberg, "Diogenes: A Methodology for Designing Fault-Tolerant VLSI Processor Array," Proc. 13th Inter. Symp. on Fault-Tolerant Computing,1983, pp. 26-32.

RELIABLE NETWORKS FOR BOOLEAN FUNCTIONS WITH SMALL COMPLEXITY

Dietmar Uhlig[1)]

A B S T R A C T . We show that there are Boolean functions with linear (combinatorial) complexity for which there are reliable networks 1) having almost the same small complexity as the unreliable networks and 2) having, nethertheles, a very small error probability.

1. Introduction

The study of networks with small error probability was inaugurated by J. v. Neumann in [1] in 1952. One of the central results of this study is the following. A function computed (realized) by a unreliable network of N gates can be computed by a reliable network (having very small error probability about that of the elements) of O(NlogN) gates. A very important and interesting result in this field was obtained by N. Pippenger in [2] in 1985: "Almost all" Boolean functions (functions with very great complexity) can be realized by a reliable network containing only the multiple number of elements from the minimal unreliable network. (The author of this article improved this result in [6,7] in 1986/87.)

On the other hand, the minimal unreliable realization of function $x_1 \oplus \dots \oplus x_n$ has a linear complexity O(n), but it can be shown that the minimal reliable realization of this function has a nonlinear complexity O(nlogn) [5].

We show that there are Boolean functions having unreliable realizations with linear complexity and such that the reliable realizations are only a little greater (the $(1+\gamma)$-multiple, where $\gamma \to 0$).

2. Definitions

Let us consider combinatorial networks. Precise definitions are given in [3,4]. For the reader's convinience we consider the set consisting of 2-input AND, 2-input OR and the NOT-function. Let us assume that each gate has an error probability ε ($\varepsilon < 0.5$), i.e. the probability of the event "the gate realizes the function according to it" is $1-\varepsilon$, and the probability of the event "the gate does not realize the function according to it" is ε. Let $\tilde{a}=(a_1,\dots,a_n)$ be any input vector of a network A. We define the error probability $p_{\tilde{a}}(A)$ according to vector

1) Ingenieurhochschule Mittweida, Platz der DSF 17, Mittweida, 9250, DDR

$\tilde{a}$ and network A as the probability that network A for input vector $\tilde{a}$ does not put out the signal which it puts out in case that no gate has failed. The error probability p(A) of a network A is defined as $\max p_{\tilde{a}}(A)$ where $\tilde{a}$ ranges over all input vectors of network A. We denote the number of elements of A by C(A). Number C(A) is called the complexity of A. Furthermore, we define C(f)=minC(A), where A ranges over all networks realizing Boolean function f assuming no gate has failed and define $C_\delta(f)=\min C(A)$, where A ranges over all networks realizing f and having an error probability p(A) not greater than δ.

3. Results

To understand our main result (Theorem 2) we point out that the error probabilities of networks tend to 1 if their number of elements tends to infinity and if they are not constructed in a special modified way. For instance, if for each gate and each input vector $\tilde{a}$ the probability of the event "the gate for input vector $\tilde{a}$ puts out a false output signal" is not smaller than ε', where $\varepsilon' > 0$ (but of course $\varepsilon' \leq \varepsilon$), then the following theorem can be proved in a very simple way.

T h e o r e m 1. The network B_n represented in figure 1 has the property

$$p(B_n) \to 1 \quad \text{if } n \to \infty .$$

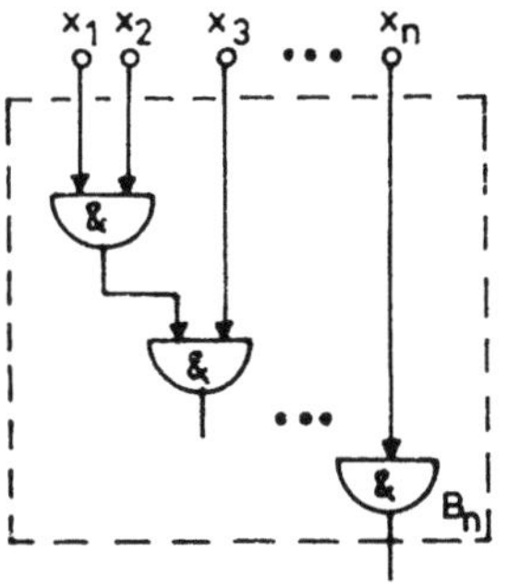

Fig. 1

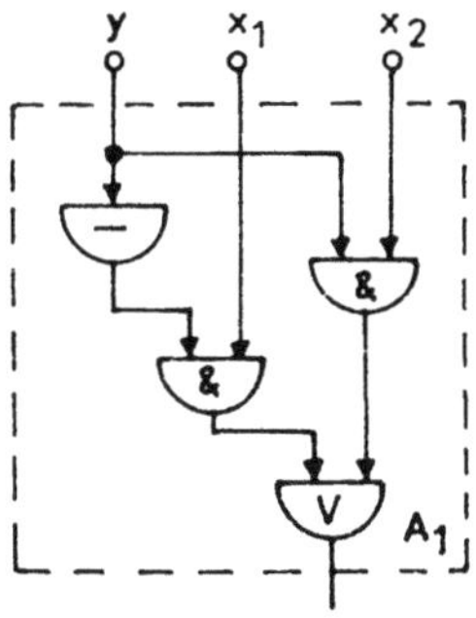

Fig. 2

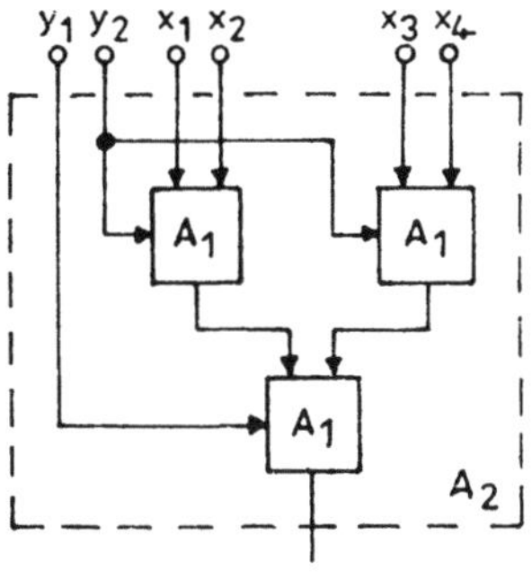

Fig. 3

T h e o r e m 2. For sufficiently small ε there are Boolean functions f_n, n=1,2,..., with the following properties:
Function f_n depends on n variables.
For every positive number c_1 there is a constant $K=K(c_1)$ such that if $\delta \geq K\varepsilon$ (i.e. δ depends only on c_1 and ε) then

$$n \leq C_\delta(f_n) \leq (1 + c_1)n. \qquad (1)$$

Note that from this follows that Boolean functions f_n can be realized by networks having very small error probabilities, more precisely, having an arbitrarily small error probability δ, if ε is sufficiently small, and this error probability does not depend on the number of elements.

4. Proof of Theorem 2

For the reader's convinience we do not consider the general case, but take $n=k'+l2^{k'}$, where $l=l(k',c_1)$ and k' is even. In order to describe Boolean function f_n we need the function $g_k=g(y_1,\dots,y_k,x_1,\dots,x_{2^k})$, defined by $g(a_1,\dots,a_k,x_1,\dots,x_{2^k}) = x_i$ where $i=a_1+a_2 2+\dots a_k 2^{k-1}+1$. The last function can be realized by induction in the following way: The network A_1 represented in figure 2 realizes $g(y_1,x_1,x_2)$. If k=2, then network A_2 from figure 3 realizes g_2. Let $k=k_0$ and let us assume that network A_{k_0} realizing g_{k_0} is constructed. Then the network represented in figure 4 realizes g_{k_0+1}. Consequently, for every k network A_k realizing g_k is constructed.

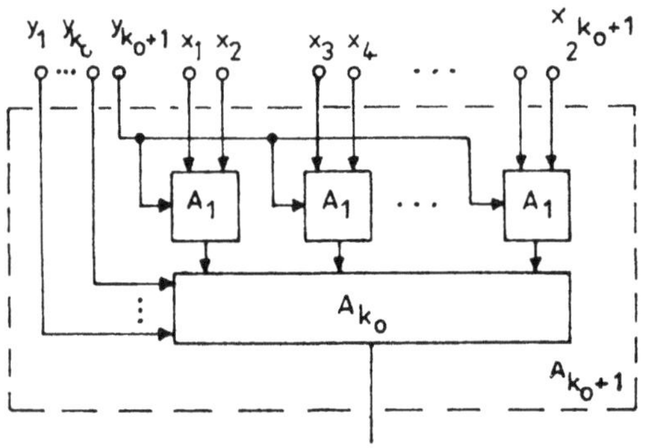

Fig. 4

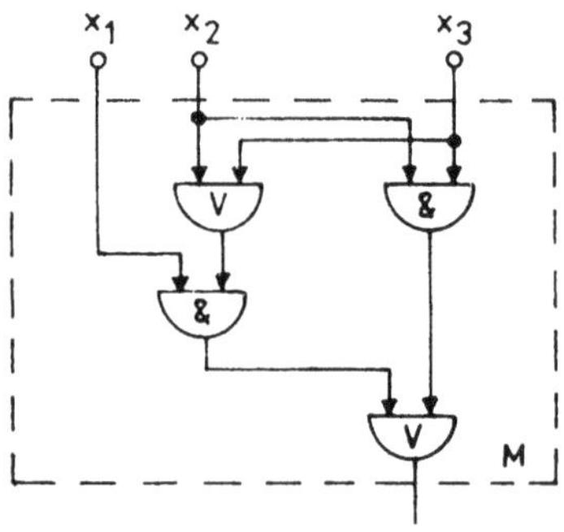

Fig. 5

Later instead of A_k we construct networks $A^*_{k'}$ with smaller error probability, but we do it only in case that k' is even.

Now let us construct these reliable networks A^*_k for $g_{k'+2k'}$, where k' is even. We take a network M realizing the 3-argument majority function $x_1x_2 \vee x_1x_3 \vee x_2x_3$. Network M is represented in figure 5, and we have

$$C(M) \leq 4. \tag{2}$$

Let B be an arbitrary network. Then by B^* we denote the network containing network M and 3 copies of network A which are connected as shown in figure 6. Network B^* realizes the same function as network B assuming no gate has failed, but the error probability of B^* is smaller than that of B (if $C(B) \geq 5$).

By induction we define network A^*_{2k}. For k=1 network A^*_{2k} is represented in figure 7. Let us assume that network $A^*_{2k_0}$ is constructed. Then we obtain $A^{*}_{2(k_o+1)}$ from network A_{2k_o+2} represented in figure 8. Thus, A^{*}_{2k} is defined for all k.

Now we show that

$$C(A^{*}_{2k}) \leq c_2 2^{2k}. \qquad (3)$$

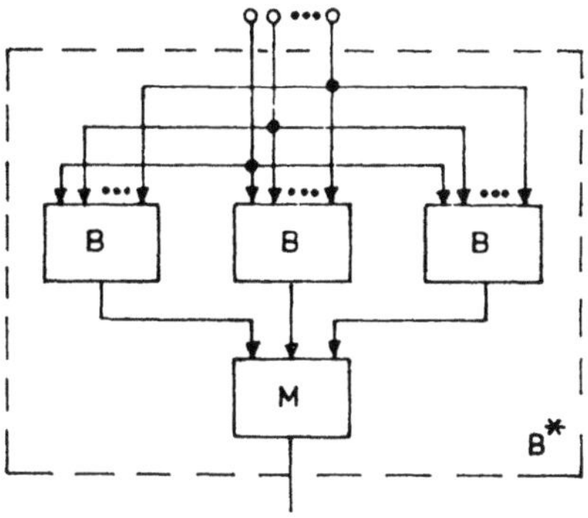

Fig. 6

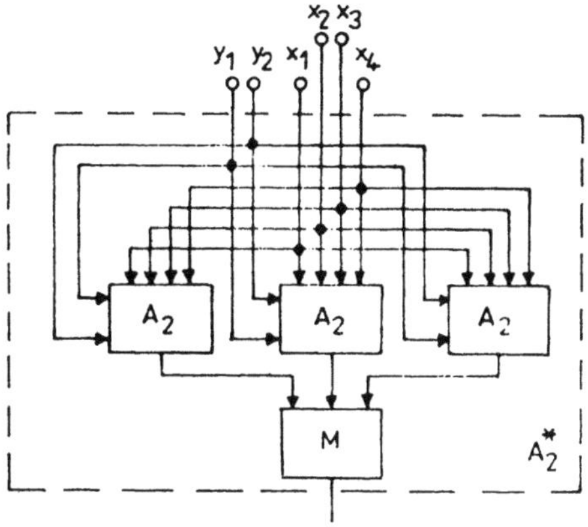

Fig. 7

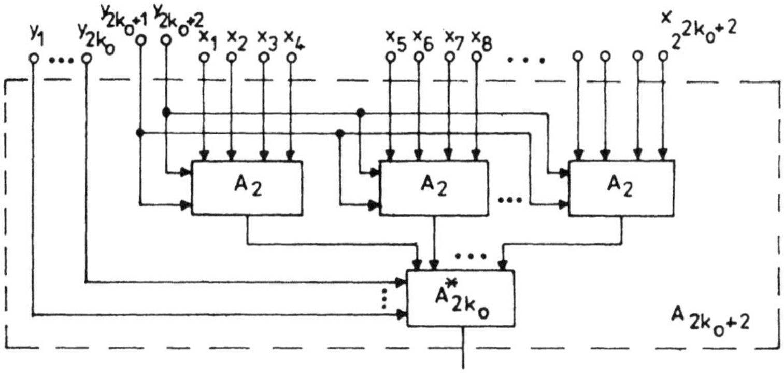

Fig. 8

where $c_2 = 3C(A_2) + 1$.

As shown in figures 2,3,7 we have

$$C(A^{*}_{2\cdot 1}) = 3C(A_2) + C(M) \leq c_2 2^{2\cdot 1}.$$

Assume that $C(A^{*}_{2k_o}) \leq c_2 2^{2k_o}$, then

$$\begin{aligned} C(A^{*}_{2k_o+2}) &\leq 3C(A_{2k_o+2}) + C(M) \\ &\leq 3(C(A_{2k_o}) + C(A_2)2^{2k_o}) + C(M) \\ &\leq 3(c_2 + C(A_2))2^{2k_o} + C(M) \\ &= c_2 2^{2k_o+2} + (3C(A_2) - c_2)2^{2k_o} + C(M) \end{aligned}$$

$\leq c_2 2^{2k_0+2}$ (see (2)), which completes the proof of (3).

Now we show by induction that

$$p(A_{2k}) \leq \gamma \qquad (4)$$

where γ is an arbitrary number satisfying expressions $4\varepsilon+12\gamma^2 < \gamma$ and $p(A_2) \leq \gamma$ (where $\gamma \leq 5\varepsilon$ if ε is sufficiently small).

If k=1, then (4) is obviously satisfied.

Let us consider network A_{2k_0+2}. Note that if its subnetwork $A^*_{2k_0}$ computes correctly, then for an arbitrary input vector $(a_1,\dots,a_{2k_0})$ of inputs $y_1,\dots,y_{2k_0}$ the output signal of $A^*_{2k_0}$ (i.e. the output signal of A_{2k_0+2} depends only on the input x_i where $i=a_1+a_2 2+\dots+a_{2k_0}2^{2k_0}+1$. Therefore

$$p(A_{2k_0+2}) \leq p(A^*_{2k_0}) + p(A_2).$$

Assume that $p(A^*_{2k_0}) \leq \gamma$. Then

$$\begin{aligned} p(A^*_{2k_0+2}) &\leq p(M) + (1-p(M))(3p^2(A_{2k_0+2}) - 2p^3(A_{2k_0+2})) \\ &\leq 4\varepsilon + 3p^2(A_{2k_0+2}) \\ &\leq 4\varepsilon + 3(\gamma + p(A^*_{2k_0}))^2 \\ &\leq 4\varepsilon + 12\gamma^2 < \gamma \end{aligned}$$

which completes the proof of (4).

In order to define and realize function f_n we take Boolean functions of l variables

$$h_1 = z_1 z_2 \dots z_l,\ h_2 = z_{l+1} z_{l+2} \dots z_{2l}, \dots,$$
$$h_{2^{k'}} = z_{l2^{k'}-l+1} z_{l2^{k'}-l+2} \dots z_{l2^{k'}}$$

and minimal networks $T_1, T_2, \dots, T_{2^{k'}}$ realizing them. Obviously, we have

$$p(K_i) \leq l\varepsilon\ ,\ i=1,\dots,2^{k'}.$$

Let us assume k' is even. We set

$$f_n(y_1,\dots,y_{k'}, z_1,\dots,z_{l2^{k'}}) = g_{k'}(y_1,\dots,y_{k'}, h_1,\dots,h_{2^{k'}})$$

for $n=k'+l2^{k'}$. Connecting the inputs $x_1,\dots,x_{2^{k'}}$ of $A^*_{k'}$ with the outputs of $T_1,\dots,T_{2^{k'}}$, we obtain a network D_n which realizes f_n and, as follows from (4), has an error probability

$$p(D_n) \leq \gamma + l\varepsilon \leq K\varepsilon = \delta' \ (K=l+5) \qquad (5)$$

where $\delta' \to 0$ if $\varepsilon \to 0$. By (3) we obtain for even k'

$$C(D_n) \leq c_2 2^{k'} + (l-1)2^{k'} \leq (\frac{c_2}{l} + 1)l2^{k'} < (1 + c_1)l2^{k'},$$

where must be taken $l > \frac{c_2}{c_1}$. Therefore by (5) and $l2^{k'} < n$ we obtain

$$C_\delta(f_n) \leq (1 + c_1)n \quad \text{if } \delta > \delta'. \qquad (6)$$

Function f_n depends on all of its variables, from which follows

$$C_\delta(f_n) \geq n,$$

which together with (6) completes the proof of (1), i.e. the proof of Theorem 2.

References

[1] Neumann von, J.: Probabilistic logic of reliable organism from unreliable components. In: C. E. Shannon and J. Mc Carthy (Eds.), Automata studies, Princeton University Press (1956) 43-98.

[2] Pippenger, N.: On networks of noisy gates. 26. Symposium on Foundation on Computer science, 21. - 23.10.1985, Portland, 30-38.

[3] Lupanov, O.B.: On a method of synthesis of networks. Izv. Vyss. Ucebn. Zaved. Radiofizika 1 (1958) 1, 120-140. (Russian)

[4] Savage, J.E.: The complexity of computing. Wiley-Interscience, New York, 1976.

[5] Dobrushin, R.L. and S.I. Ortyukov: On the lower bound for redundancy of self-correcting networks of unreliable functional elements. Prob. Peredaci Informacii 13 (1977) 1, 82-89. (Russ.)

[6] Uhlig, D.: On reliable networks from unreliable gates. In: Lect. Notes in Comp. Science 269, Springer Verlag (1987).

[7] Uhlig, D.: On reliable networks from unreliable gates with almost minimal complexity. In: Lect. Notes in Comp. Science, Springer Verlag, to appear.

Pipeline-Automata - A Model for Acyclic Systolic Systems

Karl-Heinz Zimmermann

Abstract

In this paper semisystolic systems with acyclic interconnection structures are investigated. Their underlying acyclic graphs represent partially ordered set diagrams of specific partially ordered sets. To understand the nature of such systems a new kind of polyautomata is introduced which we call pipeline-automata. The dynamical behavior of a pipeline-automaton resembles that of a pipeline. After providing the necessary order theoretic concepts the abilities of pipeline-automata with respect to equivalence, isomorphy and simulation are discussed. Because of their outstanding practical relevancy pipeline-automata with grid like interconnection structures are studied. To demonstrate the power of the formalism introduced, important results about semisystolic systems are transferred into the concept of pipeline-automata. This provides also a new proof of the "Retiming Lemma", which is shorter and even more comprehensible than the original one from Leiserson and Saxe.

1 Introduction

Semisystolic systems [2] are networks of synchronised processors, also called cells, which process data in parallel. Data are passed from one cell to the neighboring ones in a regular rythmical pattern. Our aim is to study the nature of semisystolic systems with unidirectional data flow. Such systems are working in a pipelined fashion. Their underlying interconnection structures are acyclic graphs, which can be regarded as partially ordered set diagrams of specific partially ordered sets. This leads us to the notion of pipeline-automata [8]. In a pipeline-automaton the flow of information is determined by an ordering relation on the cells. Before introducing the concept of pipeline-automata some order-theoretic notes are required (see [1] and [9] for details).

2 Order-Theoretic Preliminaries

Let V be any set and let R be a binary relation on V. Sequences $K = (v_i | i \in \mathcal{N}_0)$ and $K' = (v_0, \ldots, v_n)$, $n \in \mathcal{N}_0$, are called *R-chains* of V if $v_i R v_{i+1}$ for all $i \in \mathcal{N}_0$ and $i \in \{0, \ldots, n-1\}$, respectively; the *length* of the R-chains K and K' is denoted by $lg(K) = \infty$ and $lg(K') = n$, respectively. An R-chain K is called *finite* if $lg(K) \in \mathcal{N}_0$; a finite R-chain $K = (v_0, \ldots, v_n)$ is called a $v_0 - v_n - R - chain$; v_0 is the starting point and v_n the ending point of K.
Now let $(V, \leq)$ be a *partially ordered set* or, briefly, a *poset*. We abbreviate $(V, \leq)$ to V if no ambiguities arise. Let us say that in the poset V, u *is covered by* v (in notation, $u \prec v$) if $u < v$ and for no $x \in V$ $u < x < v$ holds. A poset V is called *chained* if there is a finite $u - v - \prec$-chain for every two elements u and v of V with $u < v$. The covering relation $\prec$ of a chained poset V uniquely determines the partial ordering relation $\leq$ of V.

We stipulate that all posets under consideration are to be chained.

A poset V is called *well-founded* if every $>$-chain of V is finite. For a well-founded poset V, the set $Min(U)$ of minimal elements of each non-empty subset U of V is not empty.
Let us denote by $\succ$ the inverse relation of $\prec$.
A function $b : \succ \longrightarrow \mathcal{N}_0$ is called a *valuation* of V. b is called *positive* if the image of b is a subset of $\mathcal{N}$. A poset V endowed with a valuation is called a *valued poset* and is denoted by $(V, \leq, b)$ - instead of $(V, \leq, b)$ we write V if no confusion arises. The valuation b on V can be extended to $\succ$-chains of V. This extension is denoted by b^*. The valuation of $K = (v_i | i \in \mathcal{N}_0)$ and $K' = (v_0, \ldots, v_n)$, $n \in \mathcal{N}_0$, is defined by

$$b^*(K) = \sum_{i=0}^{\infty} b(v_i, v_{i+1}) \text{ and } b^*(K') = \sum_{i=0}^{n-1} b(v_i, v_{i+1}),$$

respectively. In the same fashion the valuation of $\prec$-chains is defined.
A well-founded and valued poset V is called *graded* if the valuations of every two $\succ$-chains K and K' of V with the same starting and ending point are equal, i.e. $b^*(K) = b^*(K')$.

*Mathematical Institute, University of Bayreuth, 8580 Bayreuth, FRG.

We stipulate that all posets in question are to be well-founded, graded and valued.

For the concept of pipeline-automata the notion of stage plays a central role. Let V be a poset. The sequence $\{W_i \mid i \in \mathcal{N}_0\}$ of subsets of V with the property

$$v \in W_i \quad :\Longleftrightarrow \quad \exists u \in Min(V)\ \exists v - u - \succ - \text{chain } K : \ b^*(K) = i$$

for all $v \in V$, $i \in \mathcal{N}_0$, is called the *sequence of stages* of V. W_i is called the *i-th stage* of V.

For subsequent use, we define $SW_i = \cup_{j=0}^{i} W_j$ for all $i \in \mathcal{N}_0$. SW_i is denoted as the *ith S-stage* of V.

Moreover let $T \in \mathcal{N}$, for all $i \in \mathcal{N}_0$ we declare $BSW_i^T = \cup_{j=i-T+1}^{i} W_j$, if $i - T \geq 0$, and $BSW_i^T = \cup_{j=0}^{i} W_j$ otherwise.

It can be proved that the set $\{W_i \mid i \in \mathcal{N}_0 \ \wedge \ W_i \neq \emptyset\}$ of non-empty stages of a poset V is a partition of V.

Therefore the function $St : V \to \mathcal{N}_0$ with the property

$$St(v) = i \quad :\Longleftrightarrow \quad v \in W_i \quad \text{for all } v \in V$$

is well-defined and is called the *staging function* of V. $St(v)$ is called the *stage* of $v \in V$.

It can be shown that every non-empty stage of a poset V, endowed with a positive valuation, is an anti-chain of V.

Example 1 *Let $n \in \mathcal{N}$ and $k_1, \ldots, k_n \in \mathcal{N}_0$. The set $S(k_1, \ldots, k_n)$ consisting of all n-tuples $(a_1, \ldots, a_n)$ of non-negative integers with the property $0 \leq a_i \leq k_i$, for $i = 1, \ldots, n$, is partially ordered by*

$$(a_1, \ldots, a_n) \ \leq \ (b_1, \ldots, b_n) \quad :\Longleftrightarrow \quad \forall\, i \in \{1, \ldots, n\} \ : \ a_i \leq b_i\,;$$

n is called the dimension *of $S(k_1, \ldots, k_n)$. It can be shown that $S(k_1, \ldots, k_n)$ is a modular lattice. Endowing $S(k_1, \ldots, k_n)$ with the trivial valuation b, i.e. $b^* = lg$, the stage of an element $(a_1, \ldots, a_n)$ of $S(k_1, \ldots, k_n)$ is $\sum_{i=1}^{n} a_i$. Especially in the two-dimensional case the poset diagram of $S(k_1, k_2)$ represents the interconnection structure of a two-dimensional systolic array. This order theoretic structures are perfectly obeying the constraints posed on the VLSI-layout and, consequently, are well suited as abstract views of VLSI chips [7].* □

3 Equivalence, Isomorphy and Simulation of Pipeline-Automata

Our approach to study semisystolic systems with unidirectional data flow is purely automata-theoretic oriented. First we introduce the notion of pipeline-automata.

Definition 1 *An (autonomous)* **generalised pipeline-automaton (GPA)** *is a tuple $A = (V, \leq, b, Q, nb, f)$ such that*

V is a non-empty denumerable set of **cells**,

$(V, \leq, b)$ is a well-founded and graded poset,

Q is a non-empty set of **states**,

$nb : V \to V^*$ is a mapping, denoted as **neighborhood function**, *and*

$f : V \to \bigcup\{Q^{(Q^i)} \mid i \in \mathcal{N}_0\}$ is a function with $f(v) \in Q^{(Q^{|nb(v)|})}$ for all $v \in V$; $f(v)$ is called the **local transition function** *of cell v.*

The neighborhood function nb maps each cell $v \in V$ onto a repetition free word $nb(v)$ which is called the **neighborhood** *of v. $nb(v)$ consists of v and all elements covered by v; without loss of generality we write $nb(v) = v_0 \ldots v_n$ with $v = v_0$.*

For each neighboring cells u and v the value $b(v, u)$ is denoted as the **delay** *from u to v.*

If the extension b^* of the valuation b is identical to the length function lg, then A is called a **pipeline-automaton (PA)** *and is denoted by $A = (V, \leq, Q, nb, f)$.*

A pipeline-automaton can be regarded as an abstraction of a VLSI chip. Thus the host is - in contrary to [6] - not integrated into the automaton. To avoid large-scale terminology we restrict our attention to automous pipeline-automata, although pipeline-automata with input and output of data have also been studied ([8], [9]) and all theorems stated can also be proved for pipeline-automata with input/output behavior.

The state of a GPA $A = (V, \leq, b, Q, nb, f)$ will be formalized with the notion of configuration.

A **configuration** a of A is a mapping $a : V \to Q$. $a(v)$ is called the *state* of cell $v \in V$ in the configuration a.

Let $Id(V)$ be the identity relation on V. For a given valuation $b : \succ \to \mathcal{N}_0$ of a poset V the function $d : \succ \cup Id(V) \to \mathcal{N}_0$ denotes the extension of b onto $\succ \cup Id(V)$ with $d(v, v) = 1$ for all $v \in V$.

Now we can precisely describe the dynamical behavior of GPA.

Definition 2 *Let $A = (V, \leq, b, Q, nb, f)$ be a GPA. A sequence $(a_i \mid i \in \mathcal{N}_0)$ of configurations of A is called a* **computation** *of A if*

$$a_i(v) = \begin{cases} f(v)(a_{i-d(v,v_0)}(v_0), \ldots, a_{i-d(v,v_n)}(v_n)) & \text{if } v \in SW_{i-1} \\ a_{i-1}(v) & \text{otherwise} \end{cases} \quad (1)$$

holds for all $i \in \mathcal{N}$ and each $v \in V$ with $nb(v) = v_0 \ldots v_n$ $(n \in \mathcal{N}_0)$.
The configuration a_0 is called the **initial configuration** *of the computation $(a_i \mid i \in \mathcal{N}_0)$. A computation $(a_i \mid i \in \mathcal{N}_0)$ with initial configuration a_0 is denoted by $\underline{a}_0$.*

To illustrate the concepts introduced above we give a small example.

Example 2 *Let $A = (\mathcal{N}_0, \leq, \mathcal{N}_0, nb, f)$ be a PA equipped with the natural ordering relation "less or equal than" on $\mathcal{N}_0$. Thus, the neighborhood function of A is given by $nb(0) = 0$ and $nb(i+1) = (i+1)i$ for all $i \in \mathcal{N}_0$. Suppose, the local transition functions of A are defined by $f(0)(x) = 1$ and $f(v)(x, y) = x + y$ for all $v \in \mathcal{N}$, $x, y \in \mathcal{N}_0$, and suppose, that $\underline{a}_0$ is the computation of A with $a_0(v) = 0$ for all cells v of A. Then the states of the cells $0, \ldots, j-1$ of configuration a_j contain the j-th row of the pascal triangle (see the following Table).*

	configuration								
cell	a_0	a_1	a_2	a_3	a_4	a_5	a_6	a_7	a_8
7	0	0	0	0	0	0	0	0	1
6	0	0	0	0	0	0	0	1	7
5	0	0	0	0	0	0	1	6	21
4	0	0	0	0	0	1	5	15	35
3	0	0	0	0	1	4	10	20	35
2	0	0	0	1	3	6	10	15	21
1	0	0	1	2	3	4	5	6	7
0	1	1	1	1	1	1	1	1	1

A comparison between pipeline-automata and the notion of pipelining, prevailing in computer architecture, can be found in [9].

To compare the behavior of GPA we introduce the notion of simulation. To gain maximal flexibility we use the concept of index transformation. An **index transformation** of a GPA $A = (V, \leq, b, Q, nb, f)$ is a mapping $ind : \mathcal{N}_0 \times V \to \mathcal{Z}$ with the property

$$\forall i, j \in \mathcal{N}_0 \ \forall v \in V \ : \ j = i + 1 \implies ind(j, v) = ind(i, v) + 1.$$

Notation: If the correspondence between a GPA A and its components does not follow from the context we write, for example, $\leq_A$ instead of $\leq$.

Definition 3 *Let A and B be GPA. We say that B* **simulates** *A if there is*

- *a relation $Sim \subseteq Q_A \times Q_B$, such that $\forall q \in Q_A \ \exists q' \in Q_B \ : \ q \ Sim \ q'$,*
- *an order preserving mapping $g : V_A \to V_B$, i.e. $u \leq v$ in V_A implies $g(u) \leq g(v)$ in V_B and*
- *two index transformations ind_1 and ind_2 of A,*

such that for each computation $\underline{a}_0$ of A there is a computation $\underline{b}_0$ of B with the property

$$\forall i \in \mathcal{N}_0 \ \forall v \in V_A \ : \ ind_1(i, v) \geq 0 \wedge ind_2(i, v) \geq 0 \implies a_{ind_1(i,v)}(v) \ Sim \ b_{ind_2(i,v)}(g(v)). \quad (2)$$

Two GPA A and B are called **equivalent** if A simulates B and, vice versa, B simulates A.

Definition 4 *Two GPA A and B are called* **≤-isomorphic** *$(A \sim B)$ if there is*

- *a bijective mapping $Sim : Q_A \to Q_B$ and*
- *an order isomorphism, i.e. an order preserving bijective mapping $g : V_A \to V_B$,*

such that for all cells v of A with neighborhood size $|nb(v)| = n + 1$ the following holds:

1. *g is neighborhood preserving, i.e. $nb_A(v) = v_0 \ldots v_n \implies nb_B(g(v)) = g(v_0) \ldots g(v_n)$,*
2. *Sim preserves the local behavior of A and B, i.e. for all $q_0, \ldots, q_n \in Q_A$:*
   $Sim(f_A(v)(q_0, \ldots, q_n)) = f_B(g(v))(Sim(q_0), \ldots, Sim(q_n))$.

Now let $(SW_i^A \mid i \in \mathcal{N}_0)$ and $(SW_i^B \mid i \in \mathcal{N}_0)$ denote the sequence of S-stages of GPA A and B, respectively. If A and B are $\leq$-isomorphic, then the following can easily be proved [9]:

$$\forall k \in \mathcal{N}_0 \ \forall v \in V \ : \ v \in SW_k^A \iff g(v) \in SW^B_{k+St_B(g(v))-St_A(v)} \tag{3}$$

$$\forall (v,u) \in \succ \cup Id(V_A) \ : \ St_A(v) - St_A(u) - d_A(v,u) = St_B(g(v)) - St_B(g(u)) - d_B(g(v), g(u)) \tag{4}$$

Theorem 1 *If GPA A and B are $\leq$-isomorphic, then A and B are equivalent.*

Proof: Let A and B be $\leq$-isomorphic GPA. Hence, there is a bijection $Sim : Q_A \to Q_B$ and an order isomorphism $g : V_A \to V_B$ such that the properties specified in Definition 4 hold. From (3) it follows that a cell v of A performs a local transition at time t if and only if cell $g(v)$ performs a local transition at time $t + St_B(g(v)) - St_A(v)$. Therefore, the index transformations ind_1 and ind_2 are defined by

$$ind_1(i,v) = i \ \text{ and } \ ind_2(i,v) = i + St_B(g(v)) - St_A(v) \ \text{ for all } i \in \mathcal{N}_0,\ v \in V_A.$$

Suppose that $\underline{a}_0$ is a computation of A. We define a computation $\underline{b}_0$ of B such that (2) is satisfied.
Let $b_0(g(v)) := Sim(a_0(v))$ for all v of A. Then (2) is true for $i = 0$. To see this, suppose $ind_2(0,v) \geq 0$. Then from (1) it follows that

$$b_{St_B(g(v))-St_A(v)}(g(v)) = b_{St_B(g(v))}(g(v)) = b_0(g(v)).$$

Now let (2) be proved for all $i \leq k$, $k \in \mathcal{N}_0$, as well as for each $u \in V_A$ with $u < v$ in the case of $i = k+1$. Moreover, let $ind_B(k+1, v) \geq 0$. Then we distinguish two cases:

(a) If $v \notin SW_k^A$, then $Sim(a_{k+1}(v)) = Sim(a_0(v)) = b_0(g(v)) = b_{k+1+St_B(g(v))-St_A(v)}(g(v))$.

(b) If $v \in SW_k^A$ with $nb_A(v) = v_0 \dots v_n$, then

$$\begin{aligned}
Sim(a_{k+1}(v)) &= Sim(f_A(v)(a_{k+1-d_A(v,v_0)}(v_0), \dots, a_{k+1-d_A(v,v_n)}(v_n))) \text{ from (1)}\\
&= f_B(g(v))(Sim(a_{k+1-d_A(v,v_0)}(v_0)), \dots, Sim(a_{k+1-d_A(v,v_n)}(v_n))) \text{ from 4.2}\\
&= f_B(g(v))(b_{k+1+St_B(g(v_0))-St_A(v_0)-d_A(v,v_0)}(g(v_0)), \dots, b_{k+1+St_B(g(v_n))-St_A(v_n)-d_A(v,v_n)}(g(v_n))) \text{ induction}\\
&= f_B(g(v))(b_{k+1+St_B(g(v))-St_A(v)-d_B(g(v),g(v_0))}(g(v_0)), \dots, b_{k+1+St_B(g(v))-St_A(v)-d_B(g(v),g(v_n))}(g(v_n))) \text{ fr. (4)}\\
&= b_{k+1+St_B(g(v))-St_A(v)}(g(v)) \text{ from (1) and (3).}
\end{aligned}$$

Thus A is simulated by B; interchanging the roles of A and B yields their equivalence. □

Corollary 1 *Let A be a GPA. Then there is a PA B which is equivalent to A.*

4 Pipeline-Automata with a Grid-like Topology

Most systolic algorithms share the property that all cells perform exactly the same number of local transitions. This observation leads to a new definition of the notion of computation. Moreover, Corollary 1 suggests to restrict our attention onto the class of ordinary pipeline-automata.

Definition 5 *Let A be a PA and $T \in \mathcal{N}$.*
A sequence $(a_i \mid i \in \mathcal{N}_0)$ of configurations of A is called a **T-computation** *of A if*

$$a_i(v) = \begin{cases} f(v)(a_{i-d(v,v_0)}(v_0), \dots, a_{i-d(v,v_n)}(v_n)) & \text{if } v \in BSW^T_{i-1} \\ a_{i-1}(v) & \text{otherwise} \end{cases} \tag{5}$$

holds for all $i \in \mathcal{N}$ and each $v \in V$ with $nb(v) = v_0 \dots v_n$ $(n \in \mathcal{N}_0)$. A T-computation with initial configuration a_0 is also denoted by $\underline{a}_0$.

A T-computation is thus a sequence of T consecutive computational wavefronts [4]. In a T-computation $\underline{a}_0$ each cell v performs local transitions only at time-points $St(v), \dots, St(v) + T - 1$. Consequently, the state $a_{St(v)+T}(v)$ of cell v never changes in $\underline{a}_0$ at subsequent time-points and therefore it is called the **result** of v in $\underline{a}_0$. This special behavior of T-computuations suggests a simplyfication of the notion of simulation.

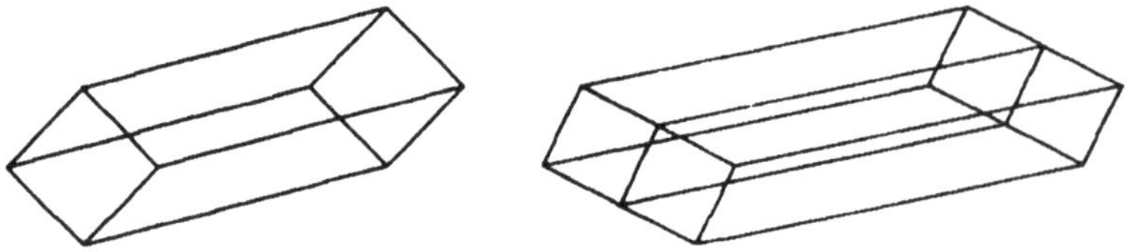

Figure 1: Poset Diagrams of $S(1,1,1)$ and $S(1,1,2)$

Definition 6 *Let A and B be GPA and T, $T' \in \mathcal{N}$. We say that A is* **(T,T')-simulated** *by B if there is*

- *a relation $Sim \subseteq Q_A \times Q_B$, such that $\forall q \in Q_A \; \exists q' \in Q_B \; : \; q \; Sim \; q'$,*
- *an order preserving mapping $g : V_A \to V_B$ and*
- *a function $zf : V_A \to \mathcal{N}_0$,*

such that for each T-computation $\underline{a}_0$ of A there is a T'-computation $\underline{b}_0$ of B with the property

$$\forall v \in V_A \; : \; a_{St(v)+T}(v) \; Sim \; b_{zf(v)}(g(v)). \tag{6}$$

Formula (6) states that the result of cell v in $\underline{a}_0$ corresponds to the state of cell $g(v)$ in $\underline{b}_0$ at time-point $zf(v)$. At first we present - without proof - a special kind of *Speedup* Theorem [9].

Theorem 2 *Let A be a PA and $T \in \mathcal{N}$. Then there is a PA B such that A is (T,1)-simulated by B.*

Now we investigate PA with n-dimensional grid-like interconnection structures. For that purpose, we consider PA with a special neighborhood structure.
The neighborhood function nb of A is called **dotted** if the neighborhood $nb(v)$ of each cell v consists of all elements covered by v, but without v itself. In this case, we say that A has a **dotted neighborhood.** The following theorem was proven in [5] for the most trivial case $T = 1$ and $n = 2$.

Theorem 3 *Let $T \in \mathcal{N}$, $n \in \mathcal{N}$, $k_1, \ldots, k_n \in \mathcal{N}_0$ and $i \in \{1, \ldots, n\}$. If A is a PA with a dotted neighborhood and interconnection structure $V_A = S(k_1, \ldots, k_i, \ldots, k_n)$, then there is a PA B with interconnection structure $V_B = S(k_1, \ldots, k_{i-1}, T-1, k_{i+1}, \ldots, k_n)$ such that A is $(T, k_i + 1)$-simulated by B.*

Sketch of Proof: The proof is based upon the observation that it is possible to perform the local transition function of cell $v = (j_1, \ldots, j_n)$ of A successively in the following cells of B:

$$(j_1, \ldots, j_{i-1}, 0, j_{i+1}, \ldots, j_n), (j_1, \ldots, j_{i-1}, 1, j_{i+1}, \ldots, j_n), \ldots, (j_1, \ldots, j_{i-1}, T-1, j_{i+1}, \ldots, j_n).$$

Therefore, it is necessary to prove that the information, which is available in the neighborhood of cell v at time $t = St(v) + l$, is also available to the simulating cell $v' = (j_1, \ldots, j_{i-1}, l, j_{i+1}, \ldots, j_n)$, $0 \le l < T$, at time $t' = St(v') + j_i$. Details can be found in [8],[9]. □

Example 3 *A PA A with interconnection structure $S(1,1,1)$ is (3,2)-simulated by a PA B with interconnection structure $S(1,1,2)$ (see Figure 1). An overview about the progress of the simulation is given in the following table - the cells of A are represented in the first, the cells of B in the remaining rows.*

time	cells of A							
point	(0,0,0)	(0,0,1)	(0,1,0)	(0,1,1)	(1,0,0)	(1,0,1)	(1,1,0)	(1,1,1)
0	*(0,0,0)*							
1	*(0,0,1)*	*(0,0,0)*	*(0,1,0)*		*(1,0,0)*			
2	*(0,0,2)*	*(0,0,1)*	*(0,1,1)*	*(0,1,0)*	*(1,0,1)*	*(1,0,0)*	*(1,1,0)*	
3		*(0,0,2)*	*(0,1,2)*	*(0,1,1)*	*(1,0,2)*	*(1,0,1)*	*(1,1,1)*	*(1,1,0)*
4				*(0,1,2)*		*(1,0,2)*	*(1,1,2)*	*(1,1,1)*
5								*(1,1,2)*

For example, at time-point $t = 0$ cell $(0,0,0)$ of A is simulated by cell $(0,0,0)$ of B, at time-point $t = 1$ cell $(0,0,0)$ is simulated by cell $(0,0,1)$ and at time-point $t = 2$ cell $(0,0,0)$ is simulated by cell $(0,0,2)$ of B. □

5 Retiming of Pipeline-Automata

In a sufficiently large semisystolic system the clock period depends on the time signals are rippling down the system. In general, this period is longer than in a systolic system of the same size, because in a systolic system it depends only on the time information is transferred between neighboring cells. Consequently, systolic systems are more time-efficient than semisystolic ones. Leiserson and Saxe [6] have proposed a theoretical framework to convert semisystolic systems into purely systolic systems. This framework is very useful for practical applications. Because semisystolic systems can be designed conveniently, however, systolic systems can be implemented efficiently in VLSI. The conversion of semisystolic into systolic systems is based upon the notion of "retiming". The mathematical access to the concept of "retiming" results from the concept of "restaging" of posets.

In order to introduce this concept, we say that posets $(V, \leq, b)$ and $(\hat{V}, \hat{\leq}, \hat{b})$ are **isometric** if there is an order isomorphism $g : (V, \leq) \rightarrow (\hat{V}, \hat{\leq})$ such that $b(v,u) = \hat{b}(g(v), g(u))$ holds for all $u, v \in V$ with $u \prec v$.

Definition 7 *Let $(V, \leq, b)$ be a well-founded, not necessarily graded poset and let $Rst : V \rightarrow Z$ be a mapping.*

1. *The mapping Rst is called a* **restaging function** *of V if $Rst(v) = 0$ for all $v \in Min(V)$ and*

$$b(u,v) + Rst(v) - Rst(u) \geq 0 \quad \text{for all } u, v \in V \text{ with } u \prec v.$$

2. *A restaging function Rst is called* **positive** *if*

$$b(u,v) + Rst(v) - Rst(u) > 0 \quad \text{for all } u, v \in V \text{ with } u \prec v.$$

3. *Let $(\hat{V}, \hat{\leq}, \hat{b})$ be any poset. $(V, \leq, b)$ is called* **restagable** *into $(\hat{V}, \hat{\leq}, \hat{b})$ if there is a restaging function $Rst : V \rightarrow Z$ such that the poset $(V, \leq, b')$ with the following valuation is isometric to $(\hat{V}, \hat{\leq}, \hat{b})$:*

$$b'(u,v) = b(u,v) + Rst(v) - Rst(u) \quad \text{for all } u, v \in V \text{ with } u \prec v.$$

Lemma 1 *Let $(V, \leq, b)$ be a well-founded, graded poset with staging function St and let $(\hat{V}, \hat{\leq}, \hat{b})$ be any valued, not necessarily graded poset isomorphic to $(V, \leq, b)$, i.e. $g : V \rightarrow \hat{V}$ is an order isomorphism. Then the following holds:*

1. *If $(\hat{V}, \hat{\leq}, \hat{b})$ is graded, then $(V, \leq, b)$ is restagable into $(\hat{V}, \hat{\leq}, \hat{b})$.*
2. *If $(V, \leq, b)$ is restagable into $(\hat{V}, \hat{\leq}, \hat{b})$ by restaging function $Rst : V \rightarrow Z$, then $(\hat{V}, \hat{\leq}, \hat{b})$ is, plainly, well-founded as well as graded and the staging function $\hat{St}$ of $(\hat{V}, \hat{\leq}, \hat{b})$ has the property*

$$\hat{St}(g(v)) = St(v) + Rst(v) \text{ for all } v \in V.$$

For the proof of the Lemma see [8].

Before extending the concept of restaging to GPA, it should be pointed out that a GPA specifies an *autonomous* acyclic systolic system. In contrary to [6] the host is not integrated into the GPA. Nevertheless the concept of "retiming" works also for autonomous GPA and can plainly be applied to GPA with input/output[9].

Definition 8 *Let A and B be GPA. A is called* **restagable** *into B ($A \sim_r B$) if A and B are $\leq$-isomorphic and V_A is restagable into V_B.*

Obviously, the relation $\sim_r$ is an equivalence relation. From Lemma 1 we conclude the following

Theorem 4 *Let A and B be arbitrary GPA. Then*

$$A \sim B \iff A \sim_r B$$

This result is very remarkable, because the direction left to right does not hold in the context of arbitrary semisystolic systems [9]. Now we can state the so called *Retiming Lemma*. Our proof of this statement follows easily from Theorem 1 and 4 and is thus more comprehensible and even shorter than the original one from [6].

Theorem 5 *Let A and B be arbitrary GPA. Then the following holds:*

$$A \sim_r B \implies A \text{ and } B \text{ are equivalent.}$$

The following well known *Systolic Conversion Theorem* [6] states that for every GPA A there is "retimed" GPA B with a reduced period of the system clock.

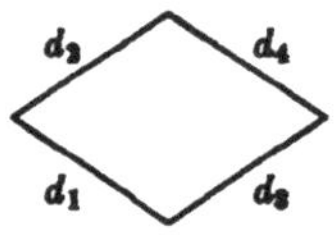

Figure 2: The Local Correctness Criterion: $d_1 + d_2 = d_3 + d_4$

Theorem 6 *Let A be any GPA. Then there is a systolic GPA B, i.e. a GPA with a positive valuation, such that A and B are equivalent.*

Proof: The mapping $Rst : V_A \rightarrow Z$ with the property

$$Rst(v) = \begin{cases} 0 & v \in Min(V_A) \\ max\{ Rst(u) \mid u \in V_A \wedge u \prec v \} + 1 & \text{otherwise} \end{cases}$$

for all $v \in V_A$, is a positive restaging function of V_A. Thus, V_A is restagable (via Rst) into a poset V_B with a positive valuation. By replacing V_A with V_B a GPA B results, which is $\leq$-isomorphic and, consequently, equivalent to A. □

In [3] the problem of determining the equivalence of systolic systems with a grid-like interconnetion structure is reduced to a smaller problem, which only takes into account local properties. These local features are comprised by the so called *Local Correctness Criterion*, which states that

for each square of adjacent cells in the grid, the number of delays on each of the two paths joining the two diagonally opposite corners is the same (see Figure 2).

To formulate the Theorem of Kung and Lam [3] in the context of GPA with n-dimensional grid-like interconnection structures we observe the following proposition [8].

Lemma 2 *Let $n \in \mathcal{N}$ and $k_1, \ldots, k_n \in \mathcal{N}_0$.*
Then $(S(k_1, \ldots, k_n), \leq, b)$ is graded if and only if it satisfies the Local Correctness Criterion.

Thus, the following statement is equivalent to the Theorem of Kung and Lam [3] (p. 43).

Theorem 7 *Let $n \in \mathcal{N}$ and $k_1, \ldots, k_n \in \mathcal{N}_0$. Moreover, let A be a PA with interconnection structure $S(k_1, \ldots, k_n)$ and let B be a GPA $\leq$-isomorphic to A, which satisfies the Local Correctness Criterion. Then A and B are equivalent.*

Another important statement of the theory of pipeline-automata, the so called *Cut Theorem* [3], has also been transferred into the context of GPA. See [9] for details.

It should be pointed out that all theorems states within this section - including the Cut Theorem mentioned above - are inferences of Theorem 1 and some order theoretic propositions.

6 Conclusion

The theory of acyclic systolic systems, as presented by the notion of pipeline-automata, can be developed on the basis of well-founded posets as their underlying interconnection structure. This provides a rather strong mathematical proof principle, namely, transfinite induction, even for the proof of simulation results concerning pipeline-automata. It should be noted that all theorems discussed so far are also valid for pipeline-automata with input/output [9]. This kind of automata can be integrated into a comprehensive computational process. But this requires the knowledge of its behavior as seen by an external observer or a host, respectively. The problem to infer the global behavior of a pipeline-automaton A with input/output from its internal properties, as stated by its definition, is called the *verification problem* (of A). In [8] a mathematical framework for the verification of pipeline-automata, using the notion of invariant, is presented.

References

[1] Abbott, J.C.: *Sets, Lattices and Boolean Algebras*, Allyn & Bacon Inc., Boston, 1969.

[2] Kung, H.T.: *Why Systolic Architectures?*, Computer Magazine 15 (1982), 37-46.

[3] Kung, H.T.; Lam,M.S.: *Wafer-Scale Integration and Two-Level Pipelined Implementations of Systolic Arrays*, Journal of Parallel and Distributed Computing 1 (1984), 32-63.

[4] Kung, S.-Y.; Arun, K.S.: *Wavefront Array Processor: Language, Architecture and Applications*, IEEE Transactions on Computers $C-31$ (1982), 1054-1065.

[5] Lee, R.C.T.; Yang, C.B: *The Mapping of 2-D Array Processors to 1-D Array Processors*, Parallel Computing 3 (1986), 217-229.

[6] Leiserson, C.E.; Saxe, J.B.: *Optimizing Synchronous Systems*, Journal of VLSI and Computer Systems 1 (1983), 41-68.

[7] Seitz, C.S.: *Concurrent VLSI Architectures*, IEEE Transactions on Computers $C-33$ (1984), 1247-1265.

[8] Zimmermann, K.-H.: *Acyclic Systolic Systems and Their Verification*, Preprint, submitted to Journal of Parallel and Distributed Computing, 1988.

[9] Zimmermann, K.-H.: *Pipeline-Automaten*, Arbeitsberichte des Instituts für Mathematische Maschinen und Datenverarbeitung der Universität Erlangen-Nürnberg 20, Erlangen, 1987.

A U T H O R S I N D E X

INFORMATIK · KYBERNETIK · RECHENTECHNIK

Herausgegeben von der Akademie der Wissenschaften der DDR | Zentralinstitut für Kybernetik und Informationsprozesse

Die Schriftenreihe INFORMATIK · KYBERNETIK · RECHENTECHNIK umfaßt alle Fachgebiete, die in der Hauptforschungsrichtung Kybernetik und Rechentechnik der Akademie der Wissenschaften der DDR integriert und Gegenstand der Vorlesungen und Forschungsauftäge an Universitäten und Technischen Hochschulen sind.

Folgende Themenkomplexe werden behandelt:

Automaten- und Algorithmentheorie

Informationstheorie und Automatisierung

Programmiersprachen und Rechentechnik

Datenerkennung und Datenverarbeitung

Dieter Bochmann/Christian Posthoff

1 Binäre dynamische Systeme

Siegfried Unger/Fritz Wysotzki

2 Lernfähige Klassifizierungssysteme

Horst Völz

3 Information I

Studie zur Vielfalt und Einheit der Information. Theorie und Anwendung vor allem in der Technik

Horst Völz

4 Information II

Ergänzungsband zur Vielfalt und Einheit der Information. Theorie und Anwendung vor allem in der Biologie, Medizin und Semiotik

5 Programmsysteme

Anwendung — Entwicklung — Fundierung

Herausgegeben von Peter Bachmann

Günter Riedewald/Jan Małuszyński/Piotr Dembiński

6 Formale Beschreibung von Programmiersprachen

Eine Einführung in die Semantik

Norbert Ahlbehrendt/Volker Kempe

7 Analyse stochastischer Systeme

Nichtlineare dynamische Systeme

Henning Schoch

8 Programmieren in PL 1

9 Handbuch der Systemtheorie

Herausgegeben von Gerhard Wunsch

Helmut Löffler

10 **Rechnerverbundsysteme**

Klaus Mätzel/Klaus Nehrkorn

11 **Formelmanipulation mit dem Computer**
Systeme und Algorithmen

Gerhard Paulin/Hans Schiemangk

12 **Programmieren mit PASCAL**

Klaus Fritzsch

13 **Visuelle Sensoren**
Algorithmen, Systeme, Anwendungen

Fritz Bulla

14 **Digitalgrafik**
Zugang zur rechnergestützten Modellierung

Steffen Graf/Michael Gössel

15 **Fehlererkennungsschaltungen**

Wolf-Joachim Fischer/René Schüffny

16 **MOS-VLSI-Technik**
Eine Einführung in Technologie — Entwurf — CAD-Systeme — Schaltkreise

Hans Loeper/Hans-Jörg Jäkel/Wolfgang Otter

17 **Compiler und Interpreter für höhere Programmiersprachen**

Helmut Löffler

18 **Lokale Netze**

FRIEDBERTH RIEDEL

19 **MOS – Analogtechnik**

Lutz Voelkel/Jürgen Pliquett

20 **Signaturanalyse**
Theoretische Grundlagen und Probleme — Ausblick auf Anwendungen

Ulrich Geske

21 **Programmieren mit PROLOG**

Gerhard Bergholz

22 **Leistungsmodellierung von Rechnersystemen**

Klaus Voss

23 **Theoretische Grundlagen der digitalen Bildverarbeitung**

Winfried Kalfa

24 **Betriebssysteme**

Wolfgang Meiling/Ruprecht Fülle

25 **Mikroprozessoren und Mikrorechner**

Band 1

Inverse and Improperly Posed Problems in Differential Equations

Proceedings of the Conference on Mathematical and Numerical Methods, held in Halle/Saale (GDR) from May 29 to June 2, 1979

Edited by Gottfried Anger

296 Seiten, 1979 (vergriffen)

Band 2

Fundamentals of Computation Theory FCT '79

Proceedings of the Conference on Algebraic, Arithmetic and Categorial Methods in Computation Theory, held in Berlin/Wendisch-Rietz (GDR) September 17–21, 1979

Edited by Lothar Budach

576 Seiten, 1979

Band 3

Decidability and Generalized Quantifiers

By Andreas Baudisch, Detlef Seese, Hans-Peter Tuschik, and Martin Weese

XII, 235 Seiten, 1980

Band 4

Zur Elastizitäts- und Thermoelastizitätstheorie

Potentialtheoretische Methoden in Anwendung auf verschiedene Modelle

Von Lothar Jentsch und Johannes Maul

157 Seiten, 1980

Band 5

Systems Analysis and Simulation 1980

Proceedings of the International Symposium held at Berlin (GDR) September 1–5, 1980

Edited by Achim Sydow

496 Seiten, 1980 (vergriffen)

Band 6

Nichtlineare diskrete Optimierung

von Eberhard Girlich und Michail M. Kowaljow

218 Seiten, 1981

Band 7

Completeness Problems in the Structural Theory of Automata

By Jürgen Dassow

148 Seiten, 1981

Band 8

Darstellung von Lösungen linearer elliptischer Differentialgleichungen

Von Günther Wildenhain

92 Seiten, 1981

Band 9

Introduction to the Spectral Theory of Operators in Spaces with an Indefinite Metric

By I. S. Iohvidov, M. G. Krein, and H. Langer

120 Seiten, 1982 (vergriffen)

Band 10

Nonlinear Time-discrete Systems

A General Approach by Nonlinear Superposition

By Michael Gössel

115 Seiten, 1982 (vergriffen)

Band 11

Preprimal Algebras

By Klaus Denecke

162 Seiten, 1982

Band 12

Ergodic Theory and Related Topics

Proceedings of the Conference held in Vitte/Hiddensee (GDR) October 19–23, 1981

Edited by Horst Michel

232 Seiten, 1982

Band 13

Singularly Perturbed Differential Equations

By H. Goering, A. Felgenhauer, G. Lube, H.-G. Roos, and L. Tobiska

176 Seiten, 1983

Band 14

Leben wir in einer Volterra-Welt?

Ein ökologischer Zugang zur angewandten Systemanalyse

Von Manfred Peschel und Werner Mende

233 Seiten, 1983

Band 15

Markov Decision Problems with Countable State Spaces

Optimality Criteria – Algorithms – Clustering

By Hans Michael Dietz and Volker Nollau

174 Seiten, 1983

Band 16

Stochastische Verfahren zur Suche nach dem Minimum einer Funktion

Von Ryszard Zieliński und Peter Neumann

133 Seiten, 1983

Band 17

Invertibility and Asymptotics of Toeplitz Matrices

By Albrecht Böttcher and Bernd Silbermann

200 Seiten, 1983

Band 18

Structural Induction on Partial Algebras

Introduction to Theory and Application of Partial Algebras – **Part II**

By Horst Reichel

205 pages, 1984

Band 19

Algebraic Methods for Toeplitz-like Matrices and Operators

By Georg Heinig and Karla Rost

212 pages, 1984

Band 20

Frege Conference 1984

Proceedings of the International Conference held at Schwerin (GDR), September 10–14, 1984

Edited by Gerd Wechsung

408 pages, 1984

Band 21

Numerical Analysis of Selected Semilinear Differential Equations

Edited by Christian Großmann, Thomas Riedrich, and Hartmut Schönheinz

203 pages, 1984

Band 22

Singular Ordinary Differential Operators and Pseudodifferential Equations

By Johannes Elschner

200 pages, 1985

Band 23

Lotka-Volterra-Approach to Cooperation and Competition in Dynamic Systems

Proceedings of the 5th Meeting of UNESCO's Working Group on Systems Theory held on the Wartburg, Eisenach (GDR) at March 5–9, 1984

Edited by Werner Ebeling and Manfred Peschel

271 pages, 1985

Band 24

Convergence Structures 1984

Proceedings of the Conference on Convergence held in Bechyně (Czechoslovakia), September 24–28, 1984

Edited by Josef Novák, Werner Gähler, Horst Herrlich, and Jan Mikusiński

254 pages, 1985

Band 25

Parcella '84

Proceedings of the II. International Workshop on Parallel Processing by Cellular Automata and Arrays held in Berlin (GDR), September 25–27, 1984

Edited by Wolfgang Händler, Tamás Legendi, and Gottfried Wolf

239 pages, 1985 (vergriffen)

Band 26

Multiobjective and Stochastic Optimization Based on Parametric Optimization

By Jürgen Guddat, Francisco Guerra Vasquez, Klaus Tammer, and Klaus Wendler

175 pages, 1985

Band 27/28

Systems Analysis and Simulation 1985
I: Theory and Foundations
II: Applications

Proceedings of the International Symposium held in Berlin (GDR), August 26–31, 1985

Edited by Achim Sydow, Manfred Thoma, and Robert Vichnevetsky

per volume 495 pages, 1985

Band 29

Parcella '86

Proceedings of the III. International Workshop on Parallel Processing by Cellular Automata and Arrays held in Berlin (GDR), September 9–11, 1986

Edited by Tamás Legendi, Dennis Parkinson, Roland Vollmar, and Gottfried Wolf

279 pages, 1986

Band 30

Fuzzy Sets Applications, Methodological Approaches, and Results

Proceedings of the International Workshop on Fuzzy Sets Applications cosponsored by IIASA and convened in cooperation with IAEA held on the Wartburg, Eisenach (GDR), at March 3–8, 1985

Edited by Steffen Bocklisch, Sergei Orlovski, Manfred Peschel, and Yasushi Nishiwaki

233 pages, 1986

Band 31

Mathematical Methods of Specification and Synthesis of Software Systems '85

Proceedings of the International Spring School, held in Wendisch-Rietz (GDR), April 22–26, 1985

Edited by Wolfgang Bibel and Klaus P. Jantke

245 pages, 1986 (vergriffen)

Band 32

A Model Theoretic Oriented Approach to Partial Algebras

Introduction to Theory and Application of Partial Algebras – Part I

By Peter Burmeister

319 pages, 1986

Band 33

Finite Difference Method on Irregular Networks

A Generalized Approach to Elliptic Problems of Second Order

By Bernd Heinrich

206 pages, 1986

Band 34

Modern Algorithms for Large Sparse Eigenvalue Problems

By Arnd Meyer

125 pages, 1987

Band 35

Parametric Optimization and Related Topics

Edited by Jürgen Guddat, Hubertus Th. Jongen, Bernd Kummer, and František Nožička

407 pages, 1987

Band 36

Discretization in Differential Equations and Enclosures

Edited by Ernst Adams, Rainer Ansorge, Christian Großmann, and Hans-Görg Roos

250 pages, 1987

Band 37

Factorization of Measurable Matrix Functions

By Georgi Semenovich Litvinchuk and
Ilya Matveyevich Spitkovskiĭ

372 pages, 1987

Band 38

Parallel Algorithms and Architectures

Proceedings of the International Workshop on Parallel Algorithms and Architectures held in Suhl (GDR), May 25–30, 1987

Edited by Andreas Albrecht, Hermann Jung, and Kurt Mehlhorn

205 pages, 1987

Band 39

Parametric Integer Optimization

By Bernd Bank and Reinhard Mandel

138 pages, 1988

Band 40

Computer Analysis of Images and Patterns 1987

Proceedings of the II. International Conference CAIP '87 on Automatic Image Processing, held in Wismar (GDR), September 2–4, 1987

Edited by Leonid P. Jaroslavskii, Azriel Rosenfeld, and Wolfgang Wilhelmi

282 pages, 1987

Band 41

Multivariable Control

A Graph-theoretic Approach

By Kurt J. Reinschke

274 pages, 1988

Band 42

Equilibrium Distributions of Branching Processes

By Alfred Liemant, Klaus Matthes, and Anton Wakolbinger

240 pages, 1988

Band 43

Andreotti-Grauert Theory by Integral Formulas

By Gennadi Markovich Henkin and Jürgen Leiterer

270 pages, 1988

Band 44

Continual Means and Boundary Value Problems in Function Spaces

By Efim Mikhailovich Polishchuk

164 pages, 1988

Band 45

Advances in Mathematical Optimization

Invited papers dedicated to Prof. Dr. Dr. h. c. F. Nožička on occasion of his 70th birthday

Edited by Jürgen Guddat et al.

332 pages, 1988

Band 46/47

Systems Analysis and Simulation 1988

Proceedings of the International Symposium held in Berlin (GDR),
September 12–16, 1988

I: Theory and Foundations
II: Applications

Edited by Achim Sydow, Spyros G. Tzafestas, and Robert Vichnevetsky

426/425 pages, 1988

Band 48

Parcella '88

Proceedings of the IV. International Workshop on Parallel Processing by Cellular Automata and Arrays, held in Berlin (GDR),
October 17–21, 1988

Edited by Gottfried Wolf, Tamás Legendi, and Udo Schendel

379 pages, 1988

Band 49

Algebraic and Logic Programming

Proceedings of an International Workshop held in Gaussig (GDR), November 14–18, 1988
Edited by Jan Grabowski, Pierre Lescanne, and Wolfgang Wechler

256 pages, 1988

The profile of the PARCELLA-workshop series – the first of this type in the socialist countries – is focused on problems of parallel processing by regular structures, i. e. on their "flexibilization" or their adapting to "irregular" algorithms and, closely related to this, on the "regularization" of algorithms for their embedding into regular structures. It seems that these problems will have an increasing priority within the list of central problems in research for parallel processing.
The workshop PARCELLA 88 gathered, as its predecessors, many scientists engaged and interested in this field. This volume contains the selected papers of it, surveying general trends as well as informing on solutions of detailed problems.

Das Profil der Workshop-Reihe PARCELLA – der ersten dieses Fachgebiets in den sozialistischen Ländern – ist auf die Probleme der Parallelverarbeitung durch regelmäßige Strukturen ausgerichtet, d. h. auf deren „Flexibilisierung" oder deren Anpassung an „unregelmäßige" Algorithmen und eng damit zusammenhängend auf die „Verregelmäßigung" von Algorithmen im Hinnblick auf ihre Einbettung in regelmäßige Strukturen. Es ist zu erkennen, daß diese Probleme in der Reihe der zentralen Probleme der Forschung auf dem Gebiet der Parallelverarbeitung in ihrer Bedeutung zunehmen.
Der Workshop PARCELLA 88 hat, wie seine Vorgänger, viele Wissenschaftler zusammengeführt, die auf diesem Gebiet arbeiten bzw. daran interessiert sind. Der vorliegende Band enthält ausgewählte Beiträge dieser Tagung, die sowohl Einblicke in allgemeine Trends als auch in die Lösung von Einzelproblemen geben.

ISBN 3-05-500656-9
ISSN 0138-3019

Bei Fragen zur Produktsicherheit wenden Sie sich bitte an:
If you have any questions regarding product safety,
please contact:

Walter de Gruyter GmbH
Genthiner Straße 13
10785 Berlin
productsafety@degruyterbrill.com